Society, Delinquency,
and Delinquent Behavior

Society, Delinquency, and Delinquent Behavior

Edited by

HARWIN L. VOSS *University of Kentucky*

 Little, Brown and Company *Boston*

To my children,
DIRK, JON, GREG, and LYNN

PREFACE

This volume is designed to provide the student with a selection of articles dealing with sociological aspects of juvenile delinquency. The work in this area is widely scattered throughout a variety of professional journals, books, and reports; thus, it would be difficult for a student to cover this literature.

In this volume articles are included in their entirety without editorial adaptation or deletion of footnotes, and introductory comments precede each selection. These introductions are designed to highlight the authors' work and to place the selections in perspective.

The materials in this volume have been selected and organized to maximize their utility in courses dealing with juvenile delinquency. They may be used with supporting lectures and other materials in a delinquency course, or as supplementary readings with a standard text. The readings may also be useful in courses in social problems, education, and social work that focus upon delinquency.

The goal of the editor is to offer to the student material that will permit him to comprehend the present state of sociological knowledge about delinquency. However, I have not attempted to provide a comprehensive coverage of all aspects of the field. That would require inclusion of factual, speculative, theoretical, and antitheoretical pieces; such a collection would give the student the impression that little is known about delinquency — and more devastating — that little can be known about "so complex an issue." Until quite recently, writers in the field of delinquency pursued such multiple-factor eclecticism; fortunately, recent developments reflect a growing reliance on theory as a guide to research and research as a means of testing theory.

To select articles for inclusion in a reader so that a student can comprehend the current state of knowledge in the area is a challenging task. Although more or less adequate answers are available for a few questions, on many other points not only is consensus lacking but viewpoints are diametrically opposed. Specifically, the field of delinquency currently has an abundance of tantalizing theories, but as yet too little research has focused directly on theory testing. If it were feasible, each article setting forth a theoretical explanation would be followed by another in which a definitive empirical analysis was reported. In this volume I devote particular attention to contemporary theories and controversies. For didactic purposes each important theoretical position is followed by an alternative formulation or critique, as well as some empirical analyses growing out of the theoretical statements. I have also selected articles on controversial topics — the nature and extent of delinquency, the nature of man, the place of theory in the field of delinquency, types of delinquents, the means whereby causal knowledge can be obtained, and appropriate societal responses to delinquency. That diverse answers have been proposed to the key questions in the field is a sign of intellectual vigor in the study of delinquency.

I wish to express my appreciation to the authors whose work appears in this volume for their contribution to our understanding of juvenile delinquency. Above all, I acknowledge the encouragement and assistance given me by my wife, Carol.

Harwin L. Voss

CONTENTS

ix

Section Two
THEORETICAL ISSUES
IN THE STUDY OF DELINQUENCY

Section Three
SOCIOLOGICAL THEORIES AND CONTROVERSIES

Anomie

Section Five
SOCIETAL RESPONSES
TO DELINQUENCY

The Police, Probation, and Court

Issues in Treatment and Prevention

Community Programs and Prospects

Society, Delinquency,
and Delinquent Behavior

INTRODUCTION

The authors of the first selection in this volume appropriately begin their discussion of juvenile delinquency with the assertion that "America's best hope for reducing crime is to reduce juvenile delinquency and youth crime." One of the fundamental difficulties in understanding delinquency, an essential prerequisite to efforts to prevent and control it, is that the terms "juvenile" and "delinquency" are not precisely defined. In most states one is legally a juvenile until the age of eighteen is attained, but in some states one is no longer a juvenile after reaching the age of sixteen, whereas in still other states one remains a juvenile until after the age of twenty-one. Similarly, the acts or conditions included within definitions of "delinquency" vary from state to state; and legal definitions are distinguished primarily by their breadth and vagueness. In the statutes "juvenile delinquency" is a term used to describe (1) violations of the criminal law committed by persons below a certain chronological age, which varies from state to state, and (2) actions forbidden to juveniles but not to adults, for example, truancy and consumption of alcoholic beverages. With such a comprehensive conception of delinquency, one may legitimately inquire, how can investigators achieve an understanding of delinquency, predict its occurrence, or suggest measures to control it?

In Section I the "legal wilderness" that comprises the statutory definitions of "delinquency" is charted; the unanticipated consequences of granting the juvenile court jurisdiction in a wide variety of cases involving juveniles are also discussed in conjunction with the legislative standards for juvenile-court intervention proposed by the President's Commission on Law Enforcement and Administration of Justice. For further study, information on the extent of officially recorded delinquency is also needed. The only national data on juvenile delinquency — the FBI's arrest statistics and the juvenile-court statistics collected by the Children's Bureau — are summarized by Perlman (Section I).

Awareness of the variety of meanings and definitions associated with the concept "delinquency" led the National Probation Association to suggest deletion of the definition of "delinquency" from the statutes, but acceptance of this suggestion would blur essential distinctions. A more promising alternative is to identify the diverse meanings of the term "delinquency."

The first section of this book is devoted to problems and issues in defining and measuring "delinquency" on the premise that an important source of confusion in the field has been the failure to recognize the diverse ways the term "delinquency" has been employed. Careful attention to the manner in which writers conceptualize delinquency will not solve all of the other problems in the field, but it will remove one important source of ambiguity.

At times theorists and investigators use a behavioral conception of delinquency, and for them delinquent *behavior* serves as the unit of analysis. At other times attention is focused on "delinquency" as a quality or attribute of *persons*. It is in this sense that delinquency is described as a status, and recently some sociologists have considered the process whereby a juvenile is labeled a delinquent. In addition to behavior and persons as units of analysis, some theorists describe "delinquent subcultures," and investigators take as their object of inquiry delinquent gangs. Here the unit of analysis is the *group*, and emphasis is placed on delinquency as a group phenomenon or on the group setting of delinquency. Finally, some writers refer to delinquency as a *social problem*. In this usage "delinquency" refers to patterns of behavior and vaguely defined conditions deemed undesirable. This conceptualization of delinquency tends to lead investigators virtually to ignore the nature of delinquent action itself. In any event, four quite distinct usages appear: "delinquency" as (1) behavior, (2) an attribute of persons, (3) a quality of groups, and (4) a social problem.

Awareness of these distinctions is essential, as is recognition of the important task of linking appropriate operational definitions with the different usages of the concept "delinquency." This has been viewed as an innocuous process in the area of delinquency, but it is here that many of the current disputes in the field originate. Despite its obviousness, analysis of a series of cases known to the police will not necessarily produce results comparable to an analysis of juveniles incarcerated in a correctional institution. This simple point is often overlooked.

There is little agreement on the point at which a juvenile's behavior or the juvenile himself becomes, or is to be considered, delinquent for purposes of research. Is a juvenile to be considered a delinquent when he commits an act in violation of the law, whether or not he is apprehended? Is a child a delinquent when he is detected by the police but handled informally? Is a juvenile a delinquent when his behavior or illegal act is formally recorded in the juvenile records of a police department? Is a juvenile a delinquent when he is referred to a juvenile court or only when a judge adjudicates him as a delinquent? Those who adopt a legalistic stance maintain that a juvenile is not a delinquent unless adjudicated in court. Technically this is correct, but acceptance of this view would seriously hamper investigators. It would place them in a position comparable to that which psychiatrists would face if forced to restrict their consideration of mentally ill persons to those so certified in court.

The foregoing questions suggest that a variety of referents have been employed in research in delinquency, and that prominent among these operational definitions are referents emphasizing either the behavior of the individual or his legal status as an offender. On first glance this implication might appear to be less true of analyses directed at delinquent gangs. Yet, the reflections of participant observers and the impressions of gang workers, primary sources of data in these investigations, are often directed largely at the behavior, particularly the delinquent behavior of gang boys.

The referents of the term "delinquency" employed by researchers include the following. The first category, the unrecorded delinquents, includes those juveniles who commit one or more delinquent acts which do not become subject, for one reason or another, to reaction by law-enforcement agents. The act of such a person may be described as an instance of delinquent behavior; it is part of the volume of delinquent acts which remains hidden from public view and escapes official attention. This category includes technical violations, which an officer might ignore, as well as many petty offenses and more serious violations. The second category includes those who commit petty and serious delinquent acts and are apprehended. These individuals constitute delinquents known to the police. Generally speaking, these juveniles either commit delinquent acts more frequently or commit violations viewed socially as more serious, or both, than do those unrecorded delinquents. Although some serious persistent offenders escape apprehension, it may be argued on logical grounds that one's chance of apprehension is a function of the number of offenses perpetrated, as well as the seriousness of those acts. Recently, some empirical evidence has appeared suggesting that both seriousness and the number of offenses committed are related to the probability of apprehension. Juveniles apprehended for behavior proscribed by law are often handled informally by police officers; in the jargon of the police they are "counseled and released." The officer may, of course, believe that the juvenile is in need of additional "help." He may, therefore, refer the juvenile to the court; and the juvenile-court personnel may handle the case informally, or they may file a petition alleging that the juvenile is a delinquent. The court, at its option, may withhold such a judgment and refer the juvenile to a social agency. Not all juveniles known to a social agency are delinquent; many come to the attention of the agency on the basis of family- or school-related problems. Next, there are those alleged delinquents whom the juvenile court adjudicates or finds to be delinquents. Finally, some of the adjudicated delinquents are sent to correctional institutions, rather than being placed on probation.

This perplexing array of definitions of "delinquency" has affected the type of research conducted in this area. Many investigators have accepted the existence of some type of official record or institutionalization as the criterion of delinquency. The general approach in the past has been to select a sample of official delinquents — police cases, juvenile-court cases, or juveniles in a correctional facility — as the delinquent group and a sample of noninstitutionalized adolescents as the control group. Lacking an official record, juveniles in the general population were assumed to be nondelinquent.

This procedure has been questioned on several grounds. A crucial weakness of the dichotomy based on official judgment is that it ignores the unknown, but presumably important effects of treatment as a delinquent. Numerous arrests by police officers, confinement in a jail or detention home, appearance in court, probation, and incarceration may involve a series of traumatic events. Although the effects of this process are not fully known, the result may be an alteration of the juvenile's self-conception, his attitudes toward society, and his interpersonal relations. Because much delinquent behavior is not followed by official processing, studies which use some type of official contact as the criterion of delinquency may reveal spurious differences between delinquents and nondelinquents.

Analysis of delinquent behavior by means of self-reports has been suggested as an alternative to exclusive reliance on analysis of cases known to the police, court referrals, or institutional populations. The techniques and findings of several studies using self-reports are presented in Section I. These studies, in which samples of juveniles are asked about their involvement in delinquent acts, supplement the official picture of delinquency; they reveal that many juveniles have committed at least one act for which they could have been brought to the juvenile court. Many of these acts are relatively trivial, but the statutes define "delinquency" so broadly that almost any child could be declared delinquent by a juvenile court.

In Section II a number of theoretical issues in the study of delinquency are examined. Browning discusses the four distinct usages of the concept "delinquency" already noted, and he concentrates on the theoretical implications of the behavioral dimension of delinquency. The implication of Hirschi and Selvin's discussion of false criteria of causality is that whether one uses official sources of data or relies on self-reports, a basic problem in delinquency research is that of deciding when the observed relationships between delinquent behavior and other variables are, or are not, causal. The need for investigation of homogeneous types of delinquents, rather than analyses of heterogeneous samples, is widely recognized; and Rodman and Grams discuss the possible advantages of distinguishing at least three types of delinquents.

Another question discussed in Section II is an outcome of the attention devoted to theoretical issues. Quinney considers the "nature of human nature" implied by sociological theories. He considers the effects of reliance on structure-functional theory and explores the possibility of viewing man's behavior as voluntary, purposive action. Also included in Section II is an article exemplifying the trend toward formalization in sociology: Turk develops an axiomatic model and offers a limited sociological theory of delinquency.

In Section III attention is focused on four sociological theories and on some of the controversies surrounding these formulations. Two of these are "established" positions — Merton's theory of anomie and Sutherland's theory of differential association. (An understanding of these formulations is a necessary prerequisite for comprehension of the contemporary emphasis on subcultural delinquency, the topic of Section IV.) Whereas Merton focuses on broad social pressures toward deviance, Sutherland emphasizes socialization into delinquent behavior through normal learning processes. The work of Reckless and his associates on socialization and self-concepts is also included, as are selections which present the labeling perspective.

In Sections III and IV, in addition to a statement of an important theoretical position, an alternative formulation or critique is included, as well as some empirical analyses growing out of the theoretical statements. The seminal work of Cohen, the theory of Cloward and Ohlin, and the alternative formulations which emphasize techniques of neutralization, lower-class culture, and commitment to conformity are included in Section IV.

It may be apparent that theoretical explanations occupy a prominent place in this volume; and the reader may inquire why devote so much attention to theories. A common view is that, after all, it is *only* theory. Attention is focused on theoretical explanations of delinquency because those who only want the facts fail to recognize that the "facts" from different studies may be contradictory. The facts are, of course, simple statements of relationship of the form "A is related to B" — for example, birth order is related to delinquency — but the importance of a particular relationship is by no means self-evident. Rather, the meaning of the facts — or their implications for an understanding of the process leading to delinquency — lies in the part a particular relationship plays in the criminogenic process.

For illustrative purposes let us consider the fact of participation or non-participation in playground activities. Lacking the guidance of theory, the researcher will undoubtedly hypothesize that participation in playground activities, a seemingly wholesome endeavor, is negatively related to involvement in delinquent activities. That is to say, boys who participate in playground activities are expected to commit fewer delinquent acts than boys who are not so involved. This certainly seems a logical expectation. In fact, some might chastise an investigator who pursued this hypothesis with the criticism that he was trying to prove the obvious or what everyone already knows. Because most Americans have been socialized in a culture in which it is deemed good to play, it is well to restate our point of departure: Do the facts speak for themselves?

From the perspective of the theory of differential association, participation in playground activities may be related to delinquent behavior in three possible ways: (1) participation in playground activities may have little effect on the participant's attitudes regarding delinquency, but they may at least "keep him from committing delinquencies during some of his waking hours; he cannot play baseball and participate in burglaries at the same time" (Sutherland and Cressey [1966:211]); (2) boys who participate in playground activities may come into contact with delinquent behavior patterns on the playground (if the playground has become the gathering place for the neighborhood's delinquents, then joining in playground activities may serve to promote rather than hinder the participant's involvement in delinquent activities); and (3) the recreation director may present antidelinquent behavior patterns to those who participate in the recreational activities, or the participant may come into contact with others of his age and sex who are best classified, according to their behavior patterns and attitudes, as "antidelinquent." [1] In short, participation in playground activities may be a neutral factor insofar as delinquency is concerned; its only relevance for delinquency may be that it serves as a "time filler." It is also possible that participation is "conducive to either delinquency or non-delinquency, depending upon the nature of the associations experienced" (Sutherland and Cressey [1966:212]).

Do the facts speak for themselves? A negative answer must be given to that query. However, this illustration is not designed to suggest that investigators should ignore participation in playground activities. Rather, an investigator cannot be content merely to note whether a juvenile participates in such activities; he must probe beyond this superficial level to determine the significance of a juvenile's participation or nonparticipation.

Finally, the central issue is not whether Sutherland's formulation — or any other for that matter — is a perfect explanation of delinquency rates and delinquent behavior. By using a theory which attempts to make sense of the available accumulated knowledge about delinquency, one's attention is directed beyond the superficial level to a search for evidence to verify or to falsify a causal linkage of a number of variables, the essence of a theory.

Theories are not, however, all equally useful, and in Section V, Shannon offers criteria whereby an appropriate judgment can be made of the adequacy of competing explanations. Shannon suggests "the ability to predict human behavior" as the first criterion of competence; and Toby examines two efforts to identify and to treat "predelinquents."

One reason why the problem of definition continues to exist in the study of delinquency is the widespread concern over identification of the "delinquency prone" or predelinquent child. The idea is that before the child commits a delinquent act, the state should intervene and institute treatment to prevent delinquency. To accept the concept "predelinquent" is to deny the need for a carefully delimited definition of a "delinquent." Two other issues in the subject of treatment and prevention are tackled by Miller and Warren in Section V. Miller indicates how interinstitutional conflict impedes application of knowledge germane to delinquency prevention, whereas Warren cogently argues the case for differential treatment of delinquents.

Also included in Section V are analyses of societal responses to delinquency as exemplified by the police, probation departments, and juvenile courts. Of particular importance is the United States Supreme Court's recent *Gault* decision. In the final three selections, respectively, Empey and Rabow discuss the Provo Experiment, a community-based program in delinquency rehabilitation, which holds considerable interest because of its re-

---

[1] These distinctions are based on Sutherland and Cressey's (1966:211–212) discussion.

liance on sociological theory. Similarly, Arnold assesses the impact of Mobilization for Youth, another community-based program designed largely to reflect the implications of Cloward and Ohlin's provocative theory of delinquency. And Toby analyzes the prospects for reducing delinquency rates in industrial societies.

REFERENCE

Edwin H. Sutherland and Donald R. Cressey, *Principles of Criminology*, 7th ed. (Philadelphia: J. B. Lippincott Co., 1966).

Section
One

PROBLEMS AND ISSUES IN DEFINING AND MEASURING DELINQUENCY

Nature and Extent
of Official Delinquency

In the summary of *The Challenge of Crime in a Free Society*, a report of the President's Commission on Law Enforcement and Administration of Justice, the Commission (p. v *) remarks that currently one of every six boys in American society is referred to the juvenile court and that approximately "40 percent of all male children now living in the United States will be arrested for a nontraffic offense during their lives." The Commission (p. vi) further states that "young people commit a disproportionate share of crime and the number of young people in our society is growing at a much faster rate than the total population. Although the 15- to 17-year-old age group represents only 5.4 percent of the population, it accounts for 12.8 percent of all arrests. Fifteen and sixteen year olds have the highest arrest rate in the United States. The problem in the years ahead is dramatically foretold by the fact that 23 percent of the population is 10 or under."

In the following selection it is pointed out that the different racial and ethnic groups in our population have widely varying delinquency rates. Further, a higher proportion of juveniles from the lower class are officially defined as "delinquent" than is the case among middle- and upper-class juveniles. On the basis of these and other facts, many of which are summarized in this selection, the President's Commission appropriately begins its discussion of juvenile delinquency and youth crime with the assertion that "America's best hope for reducing crime is to reduce juvenile delinquency and youth crime." Although this conclusion does not suggest a particular program or programs for the prevention and control of delinquency, the Commission (p. v) also states that "No single formula, no single theory, no single generalization can explain the vast range of behavior called crime. Many Americans think controlling crime is solely the task of the police, the courts, and correction agencies. In fact, as the Commission's report makes clear, crime cannot be controlled without the interest and participation of schools, businesses, social agencies, private groups, and individual citizens."

On July 31, 1968, the United States government took a major step toward translating these views into action. On that date the President signed into law the Juvenile Delinquency Prevention and Control Act of 1968 (PL90–445) and thereby created a new federal action program designed to

* The cross-references refer to the source of this selection.

assist states and local communities in developing and implementing comprehensive programs of juvenile delinquency prevention and control. Two definitions provided in the regulations accompanying this act are of interest: " 'Delinquent youth' refers to any youth who has been found to be delinquent by a court" and " 'Youth in danger of becoming delinquent' refers to any youth whose behavioral patterns or environmental or situational influences are likely to bring him to the attention of law enforcement agencies and courts." *

* *Federal Register*, vol. 34, no. 124, June 28, 1969, p. 2.

THE PRESIDENT'S COMMISSION ON
LAW ENFORCEMENT AND ADMINISTRATION OF JUSTICE

Juvenile Delinquency and Youth Crime

America's best hope for reducing crime is to reduce juvenile delinquency and youth crime. In 1965 a majority of all arrests for major crimes against property were of people under 21, as were a substantial minority of arrests for major crimes against the person. The recidivism rates for young offenders are higher than those for any other age group. A substantial change in any of these figures would make a substantial change in the total crime figures for the Nation.

One of the difficulties of discussing the misconduct, criminal or not, of young people is that "juvenile" and "youth" are not precise definitions of categories of people. People are legally juveniles in most States until they pass their 18th birthdays, but in some States they stop being juveniles after they turn 16 or remain juveniles until they turn 21. The problems and behavior patterns of juveniles and youths often are similar.

Facts About Delinquency

To prevent and control delinquency, we must first know something about the nature of delinquency and the dimensions of the

From the President's Commission on Law Enforcement and Administration of Justice, "Juvenile Delinquency and Youth Crime," in *The Challenge of Crime in a Free Society* (Washington, D.C.: U.S. Government Printing Office, 1967), pp. 55–57.

problem. We need to know how serious delinquency is. How much of it is there? How many of our youth are involved? What sorts of illegal acts do they commit? What have the trends in delinquency been in the past, and what can we expect in the future? We also need knowledge about the people who become delinquent — information such as where most delinquents live and under what economic conditions.

But we are severely limited in what we can learn today. The only juvenile statistics regularly gathered over the years on a national scale are the FBI's Uniform Crime Reports, based on arrest statistics, and the juvenile court statistics of the Children's Bureau of the U.S. Department of Health, Education, and Welfare, based on referrals of juveniles from a variety of agencies to a sample of juvenile courts. These reports can tell us nothing about the vast number of unsolved offenses, or about the many cases in which delinquents are dealt with informally instead of being arrested or referred to court. Supplementing this official picture of delinquency are self-report studies, which rely on asking selected individuals about their delinquent acts. While efforts are made to insure the validity of the results by such means as guaranteeing anonymity, and verifying results with official records and unofficial checks, such studies have been conducted only on a local and sporadic basis, and they vary greatly in quality.

Clearly, there is urgent need for more and better information. Nonetheless, enough is available to give some of the rough outlines of juvenile delinquency in the United States.

Seriousness of the Delinquency Problem

Volume. Enormous numbers of young people appear to be involved in delinquent acts. Indeed, self-report studies reveal that perhaps 90 percent of all young people have committed at least one act for which they could have been brought to juvenile court. Many of these offenses are relatively trivial — fighting, truancy, running away from home. Statutes often define juvenile delinquency so broadly as to make virtually all youngsters delinquent.

Even though most of these offenders are never arrested or referred to juvenile court, alarming numbers of young people are. Rough estimates by the Children's Bureau, supported by independent studies, indicate that one in every nine youths — one in every six male youths — will be referred to juvenile court in connection with a delinquent act (excluding traffic offenses) before his 18th birthday.

Youth is apparently responsible for a sub-stantial and disproportionate part of the national crime problem. Arrest statistics can give us only a rough picture — probably somewhat exaggerated since it is likely that juveniles are more easily apprehended than adults. In addition, it may be that juveniles act in groups more often than adults when committing crimes, thus producing numbers of juvenile arrests out of proportion with numbers of crimes committed. But even with these qualifications, the figures are striking. FBI figures reveal that of all persons arrested in 1965 (not counting traffic offenders) about 30 percent were under 21 years of age, and about 20 percent were under 18 years of age. Arrest rates are highest for persons aged 15 through 17, next highest for those aged 18 through 20, dropping off quite directly with increases in age, as Table 1 indicates.

The picture looks even worse if attention is directed to certain relatively serious property crimes — burglary, larceny, and motor vehicle theft. The 11- to 17-year-old age group, representing 13.2 percent of the population, was responsible for half of the arrests for these offenses in 1965 (Table 2). Table 1 shows that the arrest rates for these offenses are much higher for the 15- to 17-year-olds than for any

Table 1
Arrest Rates for Different Age Groups, 1965

(*Rates per 100,000 population*)

Age groups	Arrest rates for all offenses (excluding traffic)	Arrest rates for willful homicide, forcible rape, robbery, aggravated assault	Arrest rates for larceny, burglary, motor vehicle theft
11 to 14	3,064.4	71.0	1,292.3
15 to 17	8,050.0	222.8	2,467.0
18 to 20	7,539.6	299.8	1,452.0
21 to 24	6,547.2	296.6	833.7
25 to 29	5,366.9	233.6	506.7
30 to 34	5,085.8	177.5	354.4
35 to 39	4,987.4	132.5	260.4
40 to 44	4,675.3	94.0	185.4
45 to 49	4,102.0	65.3	131.9
50 and over	1,987.4	24.2	55.2
Overall rate	3,349.9	99.9	461.5

Source: FBI, Uniform Crime Reports Section, unpublished data. Estimates for total U.S. population.

other age group in the population. But not all of the acts included within these categories are equally serious. Larceny includes thefts of less than $50, and most motor vehicle thefts are for the purpose of securing temporary transportation and do not involve permanent loss of the vehicle. Moreover, although juveniles account for more than their share of arrests for many serious crimes, these arrests are a small part of all juvenile arrests. Juveniles are most frequently arrested or referred to court for petty larceny, fighting, disorderly conduct, liquor-related offenses, and conduct not in violation of the criminal law such as curfew violation, truancy, incorrigibility, or running away from home.

It is an older age group — beyond the jurisdiction of almost all juvenile courts — that has the highest arrest rate for crimes of violence. The 18- to 24-year-old group, which represents only 10.2 percent of the population, accounts for 26.4 percent of the arrests for willful homicide, 44.6 percent of the arrests for rape, 39.5 percent of the arrests for robbery, and 26.5 percent of the arrests for aggravated assault (Table 2).

Trends. In recent years the number of delinquency arrests has increased sharply in the United States, as it has in several Western European countries studied by the Commission. Between 1960 and 1965, arrests of persons under 18 years of age jumped 52 percent for willful homicide, rape, robbery, aggravated assault, larceny, burglary and motor vehicle theft. During the same period, arrests of persons 18 and over for these offenses rose only 20 percent. This is explained in large part by the disproportionate increase in the population under 18 and, in particular, the crime-prone part of that population — the 11- to 17-year-old age group.

Official figures may give a somewhat misleading picture of crime trends. Over the years there has been a tendency toward more formal records and actions, particularly in the treatment of juveniles. In addition, police efficiency may well have increased. But, considering other factors together with the official statistics, the Commission is of the opinion that juvenile delinquency has increased significantly in recent years.

The juvenile population has been rising, and at a faster rate than the adult population. And an increasing proportion of our society is liv-

Table 2

Percentage of Arrests Accounted for by Different Age Groups, 1965

(*Percentage of total*)

	Persons 11–17	Persons 18–24	Persons 25 and over
Population	13.2	10.2	53.5
Willful homicide	8.4	26.4	65.1
Forcible rape	19.8	44.6	35.6
Robbery	28.0	39.5	31.4
Aggravated assault	14.2	26.5	58.7
Burglary	47.7	29.0	19.7
Larceny (includes larceny under $50)	49.2	21.9	24.3
Motor vehicle theft	61.4	26.4	11.9
Willful homicide, rape, robbery, aggravated assault	18.3	31.7	49.3
Larceny, burglary, motor vehicle theft	50.5	24.7	21.2

Source: FBI, Uniform Crime Reports Section, unpublished data. Estimates for total U.S. population.

ing in the cities where delinquency rates have always been highest. These trends and the increase in the total volume of crime that they appear to foretell are testimony enough that programs for the prevention and control of delinquency deserve our full attention.

Who the Delinquents Are

Almost all youths commit acts for which they could be arrested and taken to court. But it is a much smaller group that ends up being defined officially as delinquent.

Official delinquents are predominantly male. In 1965 boys under 18 were arrested five times as often as girls. Four times as many boys as girls were referred to juvenile court.

Boys and girls commit quite different kinds of offenses. Children's Bureau statistics based on large-city court reports reveal that more than half of the girls referred to juvenile court in 1965 were referred for conduct that would not be criminal if committed by adults; only one-fifth of the boys were referred for such conduct. Boys were referred to court primarily for larceny, burglary, and motor vehicle theft, in order of frequency; girls for running away, ungovernable behavior, larceny, and sex offenses.

Delinquents are concentrated disproportionately in the cities, and particularly in the larger cities. Arrest rates are next highest in the suburbs, and lowest in rural areas.

Delinquency rates are high among children from broken homes. They are similarly high among children who have numerous siblings.

Delinquents tend to do badly in school. Their grades are below average. Large numbers have dropped one or more classes behind their classmates or dropped out of school entirely.

Delinquents tend to come from backgrounds of social and economic deprivation. Their families tend to have lower than average incomes and social status. But perhaps more important than the individual family's situation is the area in which a youth lives. One study has shown that a lower class youth has little chance of being classified as delinquent if he lives in an upper class neighborhood. Numerous studies have revealed the relationship

between certain deprived areas — particularly the slums of large cities — and delinquency.

It is inescapable that juvenile delinquency is directly related to conditions bred by poverty. If the Fulton County census tracts were divided into five groups on the basis of the economic and educational status of their residents, we would find that 57% of Fulton County's juvenile delinquents during 1964 were residents of the lowest group which consists of the principal poverty areas of the City of Atlanta. Only 24% of the residents of the county lived within these tracts. Report of the Atlanta Commission on Crime and Juvenile Delinquency, *Opportunity for Urban Excellence* (1966), p. 24.

Thus Negroes, who live in disproportionate numbers in slum neighborhoods, account for a disproportionate number of arrests. Numerous studies indicate that what matters is where in the city one is growing up, not religion or nationality or race. The studies by Shaw and McKay . . . followed a number of different national groups — Germans, Irish, Poles, Italians — as they moved from the grim center of the city out to better neighborhoods. They found that for all groups the delinquency rates were highest in the center and lowest on the outskirts of the city.

There is no reason to expect a different story for Negroes. Indeed, McKay found Negro delinquency rates decreasing from the center of the city outward, just as they did for earlier migrant groups. And when delinquency rates of whites and Negroes are compared in areas of similar economic status, the differences between them are markedly reduced. But for Negroes, movement out of the inner city and absorption into America's middle class have been much slower and more difficult than for any other ethnic or racial group. Their attempts to move spatially, socially, and economically have met much stiffer resistance. Rigid barriers of residential segregation have prevented them from moving to better neighborhoods as their desire and capacity to do so have developed, leading to great population density and to stifling overcrowding of housing, schools, recreation areas. Restricted access to jobs and limited upward mobility in those jobs that are available have slowed economic advance.

It is likely that the official picture exaggerates the role played by social and economic conditions, since slum offenders are more likely than suburban offenders to be arrested and referred to juvenile court. In fact, recent self-report studies reveal suburban and middle-class delinquency to be a more significant problem than was once assumed. But there is still no reason to doubt that delinquency, and especially the most serious delinquency, is committed disproportionately by slum and lower-class youth.

A balanced judgment would seem to be that, while there is indeed unreported delinquency and slower resort to official police and court sanctions in middle-class areas than in the central sectors of our cities, there is also an absolute difference in the amount and types of crimes committed in each area. In short, the vast differences represented in official statistics cannot be explained by differential police or court action toward children of varying backgrounds. There are, in fact, real differences leading to more frequent assaults, thefts, and breaking and entering offenses in lower socio-economic areas of our urban centers. Wheeler and Cottrell, *Juvenile Delinquency — Its Prevention and Control* (Russell Sage Foundation 1966), pp. 12–13.

Many writers have recognized the lack of a clear conception of what is meant by the generic term "juvenile delinquency." Consequently, references to delinquency as a "blanket concept" or as an "umbrella term" are made to signify that the term is an all-encompassing one; in these usages "juvenile delinquency" is recognized to be an ambiguous, catchall term. Examination of the statutory definitions reveals that "juvenile delinquency" is a term encompassing (1) violations of the criminal law committed by persons below a certain chronological age, which varies from state to state, and (2) acts or courses of conduct which are forbidden to juveniles but not to adults, as is the case, for example, in truancy, incorrigibility, association with vicious and immoral persons, and growing up in idleness or crime.

Tappan cites more than thirty items of this type which appear in the state laws on delinquency. Because much of what may be labeled "delinquency" goes beyond any definition of crime, it is incorrect to view delinquents as "junior criminals," or the juvenile equivalents of adult offenders. According to Sussmann (1959) a decade ago the state laws averaged eight or nine of these additional prohibitions. Of these, habitual truancy appeared most frequently; in thirty-eight states a juvenile who is habitually truant may be found to be a delinquent. Free public education is not only offered to youth; in most jurisdictions young people are required to accept the offer. In contrast with the specificity of the criminal statutes, in several jurisdictions the precise nature of the offenses constituting delinquency is not stated. The situation differs little in the jurisdictions which provide specific prohibitions, because the referent of "incorrigible" or "beyond the control of parent or guardian" is sufficiently vague that at almost any point parents who feel unequal to the task of controlling and supervising their offspring can call upon the courts for aid. In these cases no "crime," in the usual sense of the term, has been committed.

One may inquire, how can investigators achieve an understanding of delinquency, predict its occurrence, or suggest measures to control it, when the term includes all criminal behavior, as well as an additional diverse set of acts including, but not limited to, smoking, patronizing pool halls, and begging. Quite appropriately, Tappan describes this confused state of affairs as "legal nihilism," and it is not surprising that the National Probation Association recommends deletion of the definition of "delinquency" from juvenile-court statutes. Avoidance of the concept of delinquency is in keeping with modern casework practice (see Tappan [1949:17]). Although discussion of the origin, philosophy, and operation of the juvenile court is deferred to a later section, one must recognize here that in the juvenile court there is a blending of two diverse approaches, the legal and the casework, and the disparate views associated with these approaches are reflected in the statutes.

The legal approach is evident in the age limitations for delinquency. In addition, legal influences, seemingly a necessary part of the operation of the court, may be observed "in the statutory specification of particular conduct deemed to be delinquent, in the preservation of some measure of procedural regularity and of due process rights, and in the very effort itself to provide children with special protection" (Tappan [1949:7]). On the other hand, casework influences may be seen in the view that the child's infractions are merely symptoms of the underlying maladjustment from which he suffers. The function of the court is perceived in large measure in terms of social-casework supervision, in which the task is "to find the underlying social and psychological maladjustments of the child in the court, to see the total problem, and to resolve his difficulties by probation treatment. The specific delinquent act is considered to be relatively unimportant except as a symptom of the real problems" (Tappan [1949:8]). The influence of casework is also revealed in the resistance probation officers, and at times judges, offer "to the legal requirements of proving an offense, excluding hearsay and prejudicial testimony, allowing counsel to the defendant, and permitting appeal. The argument runs that the court exists for the care, protection, and benefit of the child; it is therefore unnecessary to set up safeguards and frustrating limitations on the agency that would help him" (Tappan [1949:9]).

REFERENCES

Frederick B. Sussmann, *Law of Juvenile Delinquency* (New York: Oceana Publications, 1959), p. 19.

Paul W. Tappan, *Juvenile Delinquency* (New York: McGraw-Hill Book Co., Inc., 1949).

PAUL W. TAPPAN

The Meaning of "Juvenile Delinquency"

Juvenile delinquency is a status peculiarly difficult to define as to its behavioral connotations
compared with most other classes of offense
or status that are covered by modern systems
of law. It should be observed that the doctrine
of "justice under law" (*nullum crimen sine
lege*) is among the most basic of the conceptions of due process of law not only in the
Anglo-American system of justice but in numerous other legal systems as well. Under the
state and federal constitutions of the United
States, and quite generally among English-
speaking peoples, the principle has been interpreted to mean that only that conduct is illegal
that is specifically prohibited by statutory definitions and that to be brought properly before
the court the defendant must be charged with
a definite offense proscribed by statute. *Ex
post facto* laws and vague, general substantive
provisions which fail to inform the citizen
clearly of what the State considers wrong are
repugnant to ordinary ideas of sound justice
in the western world.[1]

There are certain types of statutes which
deviate to a greater or less extent from the
general standard of clear and definite substantive norms, exceptions that cause some concern because of the apparent danger of abuse
in their administration. Disorderly conduct,
vagrancy, conspiracy and attempt statutes are
of this character: they are nets loosely woven
of elastic strands that may be stretched as
much or as little as the conscience of police
and prosecution direct. Among substantive
statutes that are vaguely drawn, none is more

so than those defining juvenile delinquency,
particularly in jurisdictions of the United
States.

Several arguments have been employed to
justify the loose definitions of delinquency,
the most common being that, although these
statutes are generally a part of the criminal
law, they exempt the child from criminal responsibility, their purpose being educative and
corrective rather than punitive, and that due-
process considerations are therefore irrelevant.
Moreover, the antecedents of the juvenile
court are commonly traced to the old chancery functions of care and protection for infants along with other incompetents, tasks that
were for a time at least (until equity became
standardized like the common law) more administrative and discretionary than the operations of the ordinary criminal courts. It may
appear that the historical rationale should have
little or no contemporary applicability, since
juvenile jurisdictional powers today are in fact
generally vested in criminal courts that hold
"trials," adjudicate the delinquency status, and
then apply correctional measures that are most
closely comparable to the punishments administered under the ordinary adult penal law.
Practice relates little or not at all to old chancery, and the ancient doctrines relating to responsibility have little real relevance under
modern theory and practice of correction.[2]

[2] "It is not infrequently stated that the court is
a court of equity and that its procedure is of a
chancery or equity nature. This concept is sometimes urged as a justification for a looseness in
procedures permitted neither in law nor equity.
This concept is inaccurate. The founders of the
juvenile court found precedents in chancery cases
but juvenile courts were not actually derived from
courts of chancery. Specialized children's courts
are in fact special statutory courts having jurisdiction over certain causes and as such have their
own procedure adapted to the type of case heard."
*Standards for Specialized Courts Dealing with
Children* (U.S. Children's Bureau, 1954), p. 55
(footnotes omitted).

From *Comparative Survey of Juvenile Delin-
quency, Part 1. North America* (New York:
United Nations, 1958), pp. 1–4, 7–8, and 111–113.
Reprinted by permission.
[1] See Jerome Hall, *Principles of Criminal Law*
(Indianapolis, Bobbs Merrill, 1947), chap. 2, and
L. Radzinowicz and W. C. Turner, *The Modern
Approach to Criminal Law* (New York, Mac-
millan, 1945), chap. V.

Much more pertinent to modern norms and practice is the widening gap between the basic philosophy of justice that has characterized court behavior generally and that which has been evolving in the children's courts. The latter have come to be dominated increasingly by the persuasion of child-welfare and other case-work authorities, who have been strongly administrative and often anti-legal in orientation. Moreover, since prosecutors and defense attorneys are lacking in the children's courts and the judges and referees are themselves often untrained in the law, and appeals to higher courts are very rare, a juridical approach to the delinquent is quite uncommon. The consequence has been that a tribunal which is socio-legal and correctional in function has had virtually no attention in recent years from the legal profession and very little more from social scientists or specialists in correction.

By the indifference and default of others, children's care through courts as well as through social agencies generally has come into the hands of a group that is oriented rather completely to the philosophies of voluntary social work, with emphasis upon individualized diagnosis and therapy for emotionally unadjusted clients. The view has become very common that the nature of the child's delinquent behavior is unimportant except as a symptom of his underlying emotional problems, that jurisdiction should be predicated upon "the child's need for help," a need which itself is commonly inferred simply from his presence in court rather than from an act of delinquency. This implies that the juvenile court comes to be considered by some authorities as a very general tool in the arsenal of child-welfare resources to help those youngsters who are in trouble — whether with their parents, school, neighbors or the police. It should be clearly understood, however, that among case-work and child-welfare authorities who are not associated with the courts it is the generally accepted view that the official and authoritarian agencies should be used only very rarely, when it is essential because of the type of problem presented.

Taking the view that the function of the court is to protect and "save the child" rather than to correct or recondition him, courts have come to direct but little inquiry into what the child has done or whether his behavior is socially dangerous, and have focused instead on what his social and emotional problems may appear to be. This is true even though the child needing "help" is adjudicated delinquent and submitted to correctional facilities such as probation or institutional incarceration in order to receive it.

The de-emphasis upon definition of delinquency that is implicit in the approach we have described is facilitated by the substantive statutes that have developed in the United States. These are represented at the extreme by eight jurisdictions where delinquency is not defined at all in their statutes but only the jurisdictional powers of the court. That this sort of legal nihilism accords with the views of a substantial segment of probation authorities is evidenced by the recommendation of the National Probation and Parole Association of the United States that definitions of delinquency should be deleted from juvenile court statutes. The laws throughout the United States and in the Canadian provinces contain one class of clearly defined delinquency: any act which if committed by an adult would be a crime. Thus the violations of laws and ordinances constitute delinquency in the child. In most jurisdictions the delinquency statute also includes a wide variety of acts or courses of conduct that are not punishable if committed by an adult, generally at least eight or nine supplementary clauses being used to define these more general circumstances.[3] In decreasing order of frequency

[3] The New York statute, which is fairly typical in its substantive coverage, defines a delinquent as a child under sixteen years of age who

(*a*) Violates any law or any municipal ordinance, or

(*b*) Commits any acts which if committed by an adult would be a crime, except a child of fifteen years of age who commits an act which if committed by an adult would be punishable by death or life imprisonment, unless the case has been removed to the children's court pursuant to a specified procedure, or

(*c*) Who is incorrigible or ungovernable or habitually disobedient and beyond the control of

of occurrence in the laws of the United States, these are the conditions included in the statutory description of delinquency:

1. Violates any law or ordinance;
2. Habitually truant;
3. Associates with thieves, vicious or immoral persons;
4. Incorrigible;
5. Beyond control of parent or guardian;
6. Growing up in idleness or crime;
7. So deports self as to injure or endanger self or others;
8. Absents self from home without consent;
9. Immoral or indecent conduct;
10. (Habitually) uses vile, obscene or vulgar language (in public place);
11. (Knowingly) enters, visits policy shop [4] or gaming place;
12. Patronizes, visits policy shop or gaming place;
13. (Habitually) wanders about railroad yards or tracks;
14. Jumps train or enters car or engine without authority;
15. Patronizes saloon or dram house where intoxicating liquor is sold;
16. Wanders streets at night, not on lawful business;
17. Patronizes public poolroom or bucket shop;
18. Immoral conduct around school (or in public place);
19. Engages in illegal occupation;
20. Smokes cigarettes (or uses tobacco in any form);
21. Frequents place the existence of which is in violation of the law;
22. In occupation or situation dangerous or injurious to self or others;
23. Is found in place for permitting which adult may be punished;
24. Addicted to drugs;
25. Disorderly;
26. Begging;
27. Uses intoxicating liquor;
28. Makes indecent proposal;
29. Loiters, sleeps in alleys, vagrant;
30. Runs away from state or charity institution;
31. Found on premises occupied or used for illegal purposes;
32. Operates motor vehicle dangerously while under influence of liquor;
33. Attempts to marry without consent, in violation of law;
34. Given to sexual irregularities.[5]

It may be apparent upon inspection that the types of behavior most frequently appearing in the juvenile court statutes are so imprecise as to invite an unfettered discretion: ineffectual parental control, idleness, endangering self and others, absence from home, immoral conduct, vulgar language; these concepts are so loose indeed that to many they may appear to describe the normal behavior of the little-inhibited and non-neurotic child.

Police arrest-data, as reported by the Federal Bureau of Investigation, make it clear that juveniles and youths commit a large proportion of the serious property offenses in the United States each year. Thus, 53.9 percent of the arrests for burglary in 1956 were of youths below the age of 18, who were also responsible for 66.4 percent of auto-theft arrests, 50.4 percent of ordinary larcenies, and 24.7 percent of robberies. Youths between the ages of 18 and 21 account for a further large incre-

---

his parent, guardian, custodian or other lawful authority, or

(d) Who is habitually truant, or

(e) Who, without just cause and without the consent of his parent, guardian, or other custodian, repeatedly deserts his home or place of abode, or

(f) Who engages in any occupation which is in violation of law, or

(g) Who associates with immoral or vicious persons, or

(h) Who frequents any place the existence of which is in violation of law, or

(i) Who habitually uses obscene or profane language or who begs or solicits alms or money in public places under any pretense, or

(j) Who so deports himself as to wilfully injure or endanger the morals or health of himself or others.

[4] A policy shop is a place where illegal gambling on the terminal digits of certain numbers takes place.

[5] List compiled by Frederick B. Sussmann, *Law of Juvenile Delinquency*, p. 20.

ment in the total of arrests. However, a relatively small proportion of crimes against the person, such as homicide, assault, rape, drug law violations, and offenses against the family, are committed by young people. It is estimated that over one-half million children between 10 and 17 years of age were taken to court in 1955, a figure representing a rise of 70 percent between 1948 and 1955, during which period the total child population increased only 16 percent.[6]. . . Moreover, since it is predicted that the age group from 10 to 17 will increase almost 50 percent between 1954 and 1965, it is reasonable to believe that the juvenile courts may handle a million or more delinquent children by the latter date if present trends continue. Boys' cases outnumbered those of girls in a ratio of five to one, whereas, according to reports of the Federal Bureau of Investigation, there are nine arrests of males for every female arrest in all age groups. Thus, girls are disproportionately represented in children's courts. This may well reflect in considerable measure the trivial grounds of many of the petitions issued in these courts and the relatively high proportion of cases of female delinquency in which parents are the petitioners. According to the last reports dealing with this matter, issued by the Children's Bureau, 41 percent of male delinquency cases and 79 percent of female cases were brought before children's courts for such minor misconduct as carelessness or mischief, truancy, running away, ungovernability, and petty sex offenses.[7] It is clear from researches in the field that a great many of the same sorts of behavior problems that are handled by some juvenile courts are treated elsewhere by private social agencies or by the parents themselves without resort to court authority.[8] The

development of "unofficial handling" in the juvenile courts . . . has contributed further to this trend toward court control in cases that would not be considered delinquent normally or in other countries of the world. There is abundant evidence here of a confusion between "delinquency" and other social, emotional, and behavioral problems of children, and of a related confusion as to the appropriate functions and methods of the children's courts. . . .

Age Limits

Court jurisdiction over juvenile delinquency is defined in terms of age limits as well as by substantive norms of conduct, and a similarly wide diversity of policy is revealed as to the former in the laws of the various states. Customarily, juvenile court legislation establishes some maximum age for original jurisdiction where delinquency is charged, ranging between 16 and 21, and a terminal age of juvenile court control once jurisdiction has been established, ordinarily at 21. In many of the statutes it is not clear whether the age of original jurisdiction relates to the time of the commission of the offense or the commencement of proceedings, but the case law has most frequently held that the age at the time of the proceedings is determinative, so that an offense committed by a child may be prosecuted criminally where action is deferred until the alleged offender has passed the age of juvenile court jurisdiction.

The age of original jurisdiction of the children's courts has most commonly been set at 18 (in twenty-nine states, in parts of two others, and for girls in an additional two), while it has been fixed at 16 in five states and in parts of two others, at 17 in seven states and for boys in two others, and at 21 in three

[6] *Juvenile Court Statistics*, 1955 (U.S. Children's Bureau, 1956).

[7] *Social Statistics* (U.S. Children's Bureau, 1945).

[8] In a study proposed by the Children's Bureau and conducted by Edward E. Schwartz, an effort was made to discover the total volume of delinquency as recorded by the children's court and by all the public agencies of the District of Columbia which have responsibility for dealing with delinquent children. It was found that, save for the more serious types of law violation, the juvenile

court handled only a limited, and in some categories very small, proportion of cases of the kind that might have been taken to court. Non-court agencies rather than the juvenile court had assumed responsibility for 98 percent of the cases of running away, 95 percent of truancy, 76 percent of sex offenses, 46 percent of being ungovernable, 23 percent of acts of carelessness or mischief, 21 percent of assault and injury to the person, and 20 percent of stealing.

states. The situation is complicated, however, by the fact that in twenty-one jurisdictions the criminal courts have exclusive control as to certain crimes or offenses, in some states above a specified age. Moreover, in nearly half of the states either the criminal court has original jurisdiction as to certain crimes or at specified ages, with power to transfer such cases to the juvenile court (twelve states) or it has concurrent jurisdiction with the juvenile court (eleven states). Criminal jurisdiction is most frequently exercised where serious crimes are involved. Thus, the ameliorative objective of juvenile court legislations is commonly overcome by a policy permitting criminal court actions and sanctions in the very cases where the penalties are most onerous. Such policy reflects the view that, even where children are concerned, considerations of public protection should sometimes prevail over the inclination to deal leniently with the young.

The Children's Bureau finds that the majority of children who come before juvenile courts for delinquency are between 15 and 17 years of age.[9] However, approximately 35 percent of those who appear have previously been before the courts on one or more occasions, so that the age of first appearance is somewhat lower.[10]

It should be observed that the general trend is to raise the age limits of juvenile court jurisdiction in the United States, a number of states revising their statutes in recent years to provide broader inclusion. This has undoubtedly reflected both a growing concern for the serious and recidivistic offenses of the young adult population and a sense that ordinary criminal court treatment is not ideally designed to meet their specialized problems. It may well represent, too, an idealized view of the competence of juvenile courts. . . .

[9] "A Few Facts about Juvenile Delinquency," *The Child*, vol. 17, December 1952, p. 63.
[10] The age at which the greatest number are first apprehended or referred to court appears to be between thirteen and fifteen. *Ibid.*

In the previous selection the confused state of affairs characterizing delinquency statutes was attributed to the blending of legal and casework influences. Tappan, the author of that selection, was a sociologist who also had legal training; he suggests that the question of definition is not only one of the most difficult to answer but also is of central importance to the field "because on the interpretation of the term depend all those vital differences which set off the juvenile delinquent from the adult criminal at the one extreme and from the nonoffender at the other. In theory at least and, to a large degree, in fact, the delinquent child is dealt with differently from the criminal: in the conduct involved, the court and its methods employed; the treatment philosophy, purposes, and methods applied; and in the individual's status, reputation, and civil rights in the community after adjudication" (Tappan [1949: 3–4]).

One "solution" to the problem of definition is to ignore it; yet, in recent years concern has been expressed that the judgment against a youth that he is delinquent is a serious reflection upon his character. It may be argued that such a decision should not be made outside a framework in which the juvenile's constitutional rights are scrupulously guarded. Avoidance of the label "delinquency" and substitution of the terms "maladjusted" or "unfortunate" do not remove delinquency proceedings from the legal arena — the juvenile court is not simply another social-work agency. As Tappan has stated, the wedding of the legal and casework approaches has not produced a wholly compatible marriage. Nevertheless, the result has been that almost any form of youthful behavior may be considered part of the "problem" of delinquency.

It is apparent that retention of a "definition" of delinquency so broad that it embraces practically all forms of juvenile behavior will not lead to the discovery of the causes of delinquency, will not benefit efforts at treatment, nor will it lead to the identification and use of successful preventive measures. As a first step toward clarification, the presumed equivalence of "delinquency" and "maladjustment" must be rejected. Acceptance of the view that delinquency is symptomatic of maladjustment commits the student to an explanation of delinquency for which evidence is, at least currently, lacking. Some delinquents may be maladjusted, but a causal relation between maladjustment and delinquency has not been established.

In this selection standards for juvenile-court intervention are discussed. That the President's Commission does not share the optimism of the founders of the juvenile court regarding the potential of the court is apparent. The jurisdiction of the court in cases involving conduct in violation of the criminal code is discussed, including the use of waiver of certain offenders to the criminal court. Also examined is the court's jurisdiction in cases involving conduct illegal only for children or "juvenile misbehavior," as well as in cases of parental neglect or dependency. It is suggested that the meaning of the term "juvenile delinquent" be restricted to those juveniles who have committed offenses which would constitute criminal behavior if perpetrated by an adult. Acts which may be undesirable for youth, but are not criminal offenses, should be excluded from statutory definitions of delinquency. Stated differently, a distinction must be made between juvenile offenders and juveniles who experience problems in living and are therefore in need of help or supervision. Unfortunately, such a distinction is partly only a matter of semantics for some stigma apparently is attached to being labeled "a person in need of supervision."

REFERENCE

Paul W. Tappan, *Juvenile Delinquency* (New York: McGraw-Hill Book Co., Inc., 1949).

THE PRESIDENT'S COMMISSION ON
LAW ENFORCEMENT AND ADMINISTRATION OF JUSTICE

Legislative Standards for Juvenile Court Intervention

A hallmark of the juvenile court has traditionally been the inclusion in its jurisdiction of a very diverse group, sometimes characterized as children in trouble — whether the trouble consists of youthful criminality, truancy or other conduct wrong only for children, or a parent's inadequacy or abusiveness. The fact that serious question is now being directed at that jurisdictional breadth and generality is a measure of the depth of current doubt and dissatisfaction concerning the juvenile court. This section considers the rationales for broad-based jurisdiction and suggests a number of reasons for circumscribing the sorts of conduct in which the court intervenes.

The basic philosophy of the juvenile court was considered antithetical to narrow, restrictively specific jurisdictional requisites, which were discarded in favor of all-encompassing formulations intended to bring within the court's jurisdiction virtually every child in need of help, for whatever reason and however the need was manifested. To the chancery court's traditional clientele of neglected children was added the category of underage criminal lawbreakers, who were, however, not to be designated or considered as such and toward whom, despite their considerably more threatening behavior, the judicial attitude was to be equally solicitous. In accordance with the protective and rehabilitative theories of the juvenile court, the definition of conduct making one eligible for the category of delinquency was not limited to conduct criminal for adults but rather amounted virtually to a manual of undesirable youthful behavior. A precocious tobacco user or a youngster with shady friends or foul speech could be brought into court, adjudicated a delinquent, and sentenced to a plan of treatment, as well as the grade-school housebreaker and the strong-arming teenager.

Besides enforcing the penal law, the commonly accepted standards of conduct for youth, and the basic obligations of parents to children, the juvenile court also undertook to reinforce the duties owed schools and parents by children. Thus truancy was included among the bases for juvenile court jurisdiction and so was a catchall state variously called incorrigibility, ungovernability, uncontrollability, or simply beyond control, which basically means defying parental authority.

The rationale for this comprehensive array of jurisdictional pegs generally emphasized the growth of social as opposed to legalistic justice and the new efforts to bring the law out of isolation and into partnership with the ascending social and behavioral sciences. It was strengthened by precepts of optimism and paternalism. Children, assumed to be malleable, seem eminently salvageable; as the rehabilitative theme crept into the criminal law, it naturally appeared most applicable to children. Thus the juvenile court was to arrest the development of full-fledged criminals by catching them early and uncovering and ameliorating the causes of their disaffection. Symptoms take many shapes, some of them only indirectly related to the disease. The "child savers" saw in youthful cursing and carousing the beginnings of a life of crime, and they feared that the conditions of the neglected were all too likely to breed the behavior of the delinquent.[1] The practicality of a stitch in time combined with an idealistic faith in the social sciences

From the President's Commission on Law Enforcement and Administration of Justice, "Legislative Standards for Juvenile Court Intervention," in *Juvenile Delinquency and Youth Crime* (Washington, D.C.: U.S. Government Printing Office, 1967), pp. 22–28.

[1] See Platt, "The Child Savers: The Emergence of the Juvenile Court in Chicago," 1966 (unpublished thesis, Univ. of Cal., Berkeley, Cal.).

and treatment to give them a zealous desire to extend the juvenile court's helping hand as far as it could reach and a somewhat uncritical conviction that whatever the court did, as long as it meant well, was in the child's best interest.

But the postulates of specialized treatment and resulting reclamation basic to the juvenile court have significantly failed of proof, both in implementation and in consequences. The dispositions available for most youths adjudicated delinquent are indistinguishable from those for adult criminals: Probation with a minimum of contact — much less supervision worthy of the name — with a probation officer who commonly does not have time to uncover underlying problems but can only spot-check the probationer's conformance with such arbitrary rules as early curfew, total abstinence from alcohol and tobacco, isolation from companions deemed undesirable (who may be his best friends); or institutionalization in what is often, as a result of overcrowding and understaffing, a maximum security warehouse for youths. The vaunted intermediate and auxiliary measures — community residential centers, diversified institutions and institutional programs, intensive supervision — with which youth was to be reclaimed have come to pass only sporadically, hampered by lack of money, lack of staff, lack of support, lack of evaluation.

Nor has the juvenile court had the reclaiming and preventing effects its founders anticipated. It has been reported that one-third of all delinquency cases involved repeaters;[2] in the District of Columbia the figure has reached 60 percent, and in one recent year over a quarter of the cases involved juveniles who had been referred to court three or more times before.[3] And the national total of court referrals continues to increase: 503,000 cases (excluding traffic) in 1961, 555,000 in 1962, 601,000 in 1963, 686,000 in 1964 — a 14-percent increase

from 1963 to 1964, while the population of children between 10 and 17 increased 4 percent.[4]

In addition to the ineffectiveness of court-ordered action, there are serious negative implications of a delinquency label. Delinquents are considered bad employment risks. They are excluded from ostensibly ameliorative programs, notably the Office of Economic Opportunity's Job Corps. Private social agencies deem them too difficult to work with and regulate their intake accordingly. Parents object to their presence in recreation and other activities.

A further source of concern about court intervention is based on the assertion of many who have observed adjudicated and unadjudicated delinquents that, with or without intervention, most of them if given time and leeway will simply grow out of their trying ways. They will find a girl or a paying job or just fall prey to the sedateness of adulthood and become bored with adolescent highjinks.[5]

In view of the stigma and the disabilities that accompany being labeled a delinquent and the growing doubt about the need for intervention in many cases, the increasingly accepted theory (or, perhaps, merely recognition) of so-called reinforcement seems no more than logical. According to many sociologists, penologists, and other students of delinquency, the youth who has once been through the process and comes out a delinquent is more likely to act delinquent again. His tendency toward objectionable conduct has been strengthened by his treatment at the hands of the juvenile justice system.[6]

Thus, for reasons stemming from unde-

---

[2] Children's Bureau, U.S. Dep't HEW, stat. ser. no. 83, Juvenile Court Statistics — 1964, at 1.

[3] 1 Stanford Research Institute, *A Description of Active Juvenile Offenders and Convicted Adult Felons in the District of Columbia, Juvenile Offenders* 7 (prepared for Office of Law Enforcement Assistance, U.S. Dep't of Justice 1966).

[4] Children's Bureau, U.S. Dep't HEW, stat. ser. no. 69, Juvenile Court Statistics — 1961, stat. ser. no. 73, Juvenile Court Statistics — 1962, stat. ser. no. 79, Juvenile Court Statistics — 1963, stat. ser. no. 83, Juvenile Court Statistics — 1964.

[5] See Werthman, *The Function of Social Definitions in the Development of Delinquent Careers.* [Published as an Appendix to the source of this selection.]

[6] See McKay, *Report on the Criminal Careers of Male Delinquents in Chicago.* A longer, more detailed version of this paper will be available from the Superintendent of Documents, U.S. Government Printing Office, as a separately published consultant's paper submitted to the Commission.

sired as well as inadequate impact, reconsideration of the juvenile court's jurisdiction is in order.

Conduct in Violation
of the Criminal Code

Within even the relatively clear classification of behavior that is criminal regardless of the offender's age lies a wide range of possibilities, from the apple thievery out of which autobiographies grow through the economically significant but nonviolent and, in many cases, individually short-lived habit of joyriding to the muggings, rapes, and robberies of the hard-core young criminal. All involve specific criminal code violations, however, and situations as to which identity and other matters of proof are vital and contestable. The variety is not necessarily greater than in adult court, nor the possibilities of background and motive simpler. These factors should be explored as they traditionally are in criminal charges. Indeed, the essentials of fair procedure are the more imperative in light of the fact that the juvenile court's broad jurisdiction and indefinite commitment power lead not infrequently to sanctions more severe than those an adult could receive for like behavior — commitment to a State training school for $13 worth of vandalism; incarceration at age 14 to last until the 21st birthday for a misdemeanor violation for which an adult could be fined $50 or jailed for 30 days.[7] The undesirability of putting a youngster through an essentially criminal process for an unimportant misdeed should be dealt with not by diluting procedures for serious offenders but by improving preadjudication screening, expanding services that offer alternatives to court referral, and limiting adjudication to cases of grave or repeated misconduct. . . . The New York Family Court Act attempts to provide the latter sort of control by requiring, for an adjudication of delinquency, not only the commission of a criminal act but also a need for "supervision, treatment, or confinement."[8]

Traffic Violations

One subject of continuing contention is the handling of traffic offenses in the juvenile court. Proponents of removal of this jurisdiction point out that most such violations are committed by older juveniles and are no more complex to determine or significant in indicating the defendant's need for assistance than if they were committed by adults. Those advocating juvenile court treatment argue that a traffic offender may be signaling his need for help in the same way as a runaway or truant, and that social study and counseling services are therefore equally relevant.[9]

In view of their great burden on the juvenile court and the almost routine nature of their occurrence, ordinary traffic violations, such as illegal parking or turning or failing to come to a full stop, appear to be appropriate matters for a traffic court regardless of the violator's age. The suggestion that such conduct is indicative of delinquent tendencies seems implausible, and use of it as a basis for a more severe sanction than an adult could receive is unjustified and unfair. It is, as the Children's Bureau Standards state,[10] the more serious offenses — vehicular homicide, driving while under the influence of alcohol or narcotics — that may indicate the need for juvenile court intervention, and these should be dealt with by the juvenile court when children are involved, just as similar adult cases are frequently handled in criminal rather than traffic court.

Waiver

More difficult problems are created by the serious offense and the recalcitrant offender, especially if the incident has been highly publicized and has aroused widespread indignation. It is in such a situation that it becomes

---

[7] See Paulsen, "The Delinquency, Neglect, and Dependency Jurisdiction of the Juvenile Court," in *Justice for the Child*, 44, 52 (Rosenheim ed. 1962).

[8] N.Y. Family Ct. Act § 731 (1963).

[9] See Kenny & Pursuit, *California Juvenile Traffic Study* (Cal. Youth Authority 1952); Sheridan, "Youth and the Traffic Problem," 25 *The Police Chief* 27 (1958); Middendorf & Wolf, "A Criminology of Traffic Offenses," 27 *Fed. Prob.* 36 (1963); ABA Traffic Ct. Program, "Procedures Governing the Hearing and Disposition of Charges of Traffic Offenses by Juveniles" (unpublished, undated).

[10] Standards for Juvenile and Family Courts 37.

clear that the juvenile court is indeed a court — a tribunal of last resort, applying often severe sanctions where other institutions and agencies have already intervened to no avail, invoking the deterrent effort of sternness as a last barrier to adult criminality, and sometimes simply employing its authority to protect a threatened community.

One explanation of the general failure to admit the court's social protection function is, of course, the traditional view that the juvenile court must and does act always and only in the child's best interest, regardless of any interest society may have. A second and, perhaps, more significant reason lies in the fact that most juvenile courts are legislatively provided with mechanisms for evading the social protection responsibility in its purest and most public posture. The methods include waiver of certain cases or offenders to adult court (the commonest method and currently an embattled issue in the juvenile court arena), concurrent jurisdiction with the adult court in certain cases, and exclusion of some serious crimes from the court's jurisdiction. Each of these achieves the basic goal of providing an adjustment in individual cases for the inevitable arbitrariness of age, but not without importing new disadvantages.

Exclusion of certain crimes, for instance, is in its own way as arbitrary as age. It precludes, for example, noncriminal court treatment for the 15-year-old who shot his stepfather in a blind rage that climaxed years of abusive treatment and that all who knew him agreed was not characteristic either of his past or of their expectations for his future. The serious offenses excepted are, however, the ones most likely to shock the public and arouse its hostility toward the perpetrator and, in turn, toward a court that holds itself out as treating or helping rather than punishing or incapacitating him.

An example of concurrent jurisdiction is the California system, in which the juvenile court has exclusive jurisdiction to the age of 18 and shares jurisdiction from 18 to 21 with the adult court.[11] In practice, most juveniles 18

or older are dealt with by the adult court.[12] If the juvenile court has the choice whether to transfer, it can be expected that at least minimally informed consideration will have been given such matters as the alleged offender's performance as a juvenile and the disposition alternatives available. It is undesirable for the decision to be made by the prosecutor or adult court judge, who is less likely to be familiar with institutions and other treatment resources and less accustomed to concentrating on the individual aspects of a given case. To the extent that the concurrent jurisdiction method of choosing the forum purports to be premised on appraisal of a condition generally called amenability to treatment, however, it partakes of the same disadvantage as waiver.

Waiver is the method used to adjust the age limit in about 40 states. Waiver provisions vary with respect to age and offense, some limiting both, others allowing transfer for any offense but only over a specified age, still others restricting offense but not age, and nearly half including no limitations at all.[13]

Reasons and procedures for waiver have typically been vague, if enunciated at all. The Supreme Court may have substantially altered that situation last year in *Kent v. United States*,[14] its first juvenile court case, holding that in the District of Columbia (and perhaps elsewhere by force of constitutional requirements), waiver requires a hearing at which the juvenile is represented by counsel, access by the juvenile to social investigation reports, and

---

[11] See Cal. Welf. & Inst'ns Code §§ 600, 604 (1961).

[12] Lemert, *The Juvenile Court — Quest and Realities*. [Published as the Appendix to the source of this selection.]

[13] Standards for Juvenile and Family Courts 34–35 recommends that the juvenile court be able to transfer its jurisdiction to a criminal court in the case of a child 16 years of age or older "who has committed an act which would be a felony if committed by an adult" where, after social study and a hearing, "the court finds that the child is not committable to an institution for the mentally deficient or the mentally ill and is not treatable in any institution or facility of the State designed for the care and treatment of children, or where the court finds that the safety of the community clearly requires that the child continue under restraint for a period extending beyond his minority or the facilities of the criminal court provide a more effective setting for disposition."

[14] 383 U.S. 541 (1966).

a statement by the juvenile judge of the reasons for his decision to waive.

Those are substantial improvements in the fairness and rationality of the waiver procedure. The substance behind the procedure, however, remains unrecognized for what it really is: Not a scientific evaluation of whether the youth will respond successfully to a juvenile court disposition but a front for society's insistence on retribution or social protection. While it may remove from the juvenile court youths who are in fact older and tougher, it also sends to the criminal court the one-shot youngster whose offense and its attendant outcry make him too difficult for the juvenile court to handle but who may well respond better to treatment than the habitual petty thief. Determining amenability to treatment involves evaluation of such qualities as criminal sophistication, about which information is difficult to acquire and harder to assess. And to the extent — a substantial one — that adult and juvenile institutions resemble each other, application of the standard makes little difference in the end.[15] Furthermore, waiver does not necessarily achieve the longer term or more severe sentence that is the goal of many of its supporters, for the youth who in juvenile court would have been a recidivist is a first offender in the adult tribunal.

One alternative is to lower the juvenile court age limit to 16, eliminating both waiver and the unchildlike older adolescents who now account for most of the waivers. Although the juvenile court would thereby lose a way out of trouble that can be valuable in the case of a heinous offense by a young child, when an outraged community is likely to view any-thing a children's court does as mollycoddling, those cases are relatively rare and often involve mental disturbance or some other ground for a totally different disposition. The obvious disadvantage would be that the immature as well as the obstreperous 16- and 17-year-olds would be dealt with by the criminal court.

Another suggestion frequently made is that an intermediate court be created to deal with youths from 16 to 18 or, perhaps, 21 (some would say 25) years of age. There is some logic supporting separation of that group from both children and grownups with respect to dispositions and facilities, but it seems unlikely that court procedures or judicial expertness with respect to that segment of the population should or would be so special as to require a specialized tribunal. Indeed, the current trend is toward judicial consolidation, not further splintering and specializing. The Children's Bureau Standards, for instance, advocate establishing a family court with jurisdiction over all juvenile and domestic relations matters, on the grounds of greater efficiency, uniformity of procedures, elimination of conflicting decisions, and improvement of services.[16] And if the inexactness of age as a dividing line among individuals is at the root of the difficulty with which waiver was designed to deal, multiplying the arbitrary age categories would only compound the complications.

On the assumption that juvenile court procedures will become more like model adult court ones, incorporating standard procedural safeguards and factfinding methods to a greater extent than at present, a tendency already marked in practice and recommended later in this report, a third method of eliminating the waiver problem is to maintain the upper age limit of 18 that now obtains in the majority of courts but to allow sentencing of certain juvenile offenders to terms extending beyond their majority. In that way the court confronted with the nearly-18-year-old who

[15] It has been suggested that, where institutional facilities are not truly therapeutic but simply penal institutions, they should not be available to the juvenile court judge as dispositional alternatives; if society's need for security demands confinement, the juvenile's case should be waived to an adult criminal court for trial. *Juvenile Delinquents* 810. It is not clear, however, what *truly therapeutic* is or how its presence can be determined, or what is accomplished for the youth needing confinement by having him sent to an inadequate institution by a criminal rather than a juvenile court judge.

[16] Standards for Juvenile and Family Courts 43–45; see also Goldberg & Sheridan, *Family Courts: An Urgent Need* (Children's Bureau, U.S. Dep't HEW 1960).

has a long record or has committed an outrageous, highly publicized offense would not be limited to a 3-year commitment but could sentence more consistently with the community's demand, the gravity of the offense, and the sentence the offender might receive in adult court. At the same time use could be made of the diagnostic and treatment-planning resources of the juvenile court. But while more formal procedures would obviate the injustice of imposing prolonged terms without protections of a criminal trial, absence of jury trial might raise a serious question. Also, to avoid overly long sentences of very young offenders, it would be necessary to establish either a limit on the overall length of the sentence or a minimum age below which an offender could not be sentenced beyond majority.

Thus waiver may well be a necessary evil, imperfect but not substantially more so than its alternatives. If that is so, the effort should be to make it as fair and frank as possible. The *Kent* case, by instituting procedural regularity, goes far toward eliminating invisible abuse of the waiver prerogative. The danger of using waiver to accommodate community pressure without regard to appropriateness in an individual case, however, can be avoided only by circumscribing the standards so as to include the offenders who are in fact tougher and exclude those who merely seem to be. To be waived, a youth should be over a certain age (perhaps 16); the alleged offense should be relatively grave (the equivalent of a felony, at least); his prior offense record should be of a certain seriousness; his treatment record discouraging. Waived youths would then be dealt with other than cursorily by the criminal court, and the juvenile court's action in transferring them would be based on an honest and open assessment of individual suitability.

Conduct Illegal Only for Children

In addition to behavior that would be criminal on the part of an adult, delinquency includes behavior illegal only for a child: Conduct uniquely children's — truancy, incorrigibility — and conduct tolerated for adults but objectionable for children — smoking, drinking, using vulgar language, violating curfew laws, hanging around in bars or with felons or gamblers.[17]

The provisions on which intervention in this category of cases is based are typically vague and all-encompassing: Growing up in idleness and crime, engaging in immoral conduct, in danger of leading an immoral life. Especially when administered with the informality characteristic of the court's procedures, they establish the judge as arbiter not only of the behavior but also of the morals of every child (and to a certain extent the parents of every child) appearing before him.[18] The situation is ripe for overreaching, for imposition of the judge's own code of youthful conduct. One frequent consequence has been the use of general protective statutes about leading an immoral life and engaging in endangering conduct as a means of enforcing conformity — eliminating long hair, levis, and other transitory adolescent foibles so unsettling to adults. One need not expound the traditional American virtues of individuality and free expression to point out the wrongheadedness of so using the juvenile court; it is enough to reflect that the speed with which such fads come and go is equaled only by the strength of their resistance to outside attack.

On the other hand, the need that led to the creation of that broad and general jurisdiction was and remains a real one. It is not a favor to children to have no authoritative way of attempting to protect them from themselves and, often, from their environments. It would surely be undesirable to make schools more like courts; some parents simply lack the personal and other resources to enforce their will, however wise and well-intentioned. A firm, objective way is needed to apply the truancy laws, fortify flagging parents, and encourage substitution of healthful for self-destructive pursuits before it is too late.[19]

[17] See generally discussion in Paulsen, "The Delinquency, Neglect, and Dependency Jurisdiction of the Juvenile Court" in *Justice for the Child, op. cit. supra* note 7, at 44.

[18] See, *e.g.,* Tappan, "Juridical and Administrative Approaches to Children With Problems" in *Justice for the Child, op. cit. supra* note 7, at 144, 156–57.

[19] See, *e.g.,* Paulsen, *supra* note 7, at 49–51.

Two recently adopted juvenile court acts attempt to solve the problem by retaining juvenile court jurisdiction over the conduct in question but naming it something other than delinquency. The Illinois Juvenile Court Act (1966) creates the category of "minor otherwise in need of supervision" (that is, for reasons other than delinquency, which is defined as violation or attempted violation of a Federal or State law, municipal ordinance, or court order):

Those otherwise in need of supervision include (a) any minor under 18 years of age who is beyond the control of his parents, guardian, or other custodian; and (b) any minor subject to compulsory school attendance who is habitually truant from school.[20]

The category of "neglected minor" includes, besides the usual case of parental inattention or abandonment, "any minor under 18 years of age . . . (b) whose environment is injurious to his welfare or whose behavior is injurious to his own welfare or that of others."[21]

The New York Family Court Act (1963) calls a noncriminal misbehaver a "person in need of supervision" (PINS):

(a) "Juvenile delinquent" means a person over 7 and less than 16 years of age who does any act which, if done by an adult, would constitute a crime.
(b) "Person in need of supervision" means a male less than 16 years of age and a female less than 18 years of age who is an habitual truant or who is incorrigible, ungovernable or habitually disobedient and beyond the lawful control of parent or other lawful authority.[22]

The New York Joint Legislative Committee on Court Reorganization, in the report that it submitted with proposed family court legislation, makes clear the reasons for those categories:

Avoiding stigma. "Juvenile delinquent" is now a term of disapproval. The judges of the Children's Court and the Domestic Relations Court of course are aware of this and also aware that government officials and private employers often learn of an adjudication of delinquency. Some judges are therefore reluctant to make such an adjudication in the absence of conduct violating the Penal Law. In some cases, however, they feel compelled to do so when they conclude that supervision is necessary for the proper development of the child.[23]

The study presents data showing that from 1949 to 1956, 77 percent of the juveniles placed on probation were adjudicated delinquent for a criminal law violation such as auto theft, robbery, burglary; 10 percent for ungovernability; 10 percent for "carelessness or mischief"; and 3 percent for running away. The report continues:

The Committee has been asked to avoid the need for an adjudication of "delinquency" in those circumstances by the expedient of not using that term or any similar name in describing the occasions for the exercise of the court's jurisdiction. The practical result of this proposal, the Committee fears, would be an indiscriminate gouping of all children within the court's jurisdiction as "delinquent." The Committee therefore proposes to retain, but redefine, the category of juvenile delinquency and add the new category of person in need of supervision. Though there is no certainty about these judgments, the Committtee expects that this pattern will reduce the instances of stigma and at the same time permit the court to use appropriate resources in dealing with persons in need of supervision.[24]

The second reason for the new category is to define police and court powers in such cases. While an alleged juvenile delinquent may under certain circumstances be taken into custody without court order, a person said to be in need of supervision may not. An alleged delinquent, but not an alleged PINS, may be detained pending court proceedings and, in the original act, only a delinquent, not a PINS, may be committed.[25]

---

[20] Ill. Juvenile Ct. Act § 702-3 (1966).
[21] *Id.* § 702-4.
[22] N.Y. Family Ct. Act § 712 (1963).

[23] N.Y. Joint Legislative Comm. on Court Reorganization, The Family Court Act pt. 2, at 7 (1962) [hereinafter cited as N.Y. Report].
[24] *Ibid.*
[25] *Id.* at 7-8.

Such a realignment has at least the substantial advantage of recognizing the extent to which the general public equates *delinquent* with *criminal* and of making it immediately clear, without the necessity of inquiring into the specific basis of court action, that the child has not committed a criminal act. Nevertheless — and not surprisingly — there is indication that a new sort of stigma is attaching to being labeled a person or minor in need of supervision. That result is probably unavoidable as long as any sort of official action is taken. And action by a court — however benign — is likely to be the most severely and permanently labeling of all. Therefore, especially in instances of conduct that is delinquent but would not be criminal for an adult, it is of the greatest importance that all alternative measures be employed before recourse is had to court. Truants, incorrigibles, smokers, cursers should be referred by the police, the school authorities, their parents, or some other complaining grownup to the youth services bureau . . . or, in communities where there is no such center, to any available neighborhood or other service agency, in accordance with the procedures outlined above, for more particularized referral or other disposition as seems indicated by the situation.

In addition to efforts to limit in operation the extent and range of the juvenile court's intervention, attempts should be made to redefine its legislative bases for action so as to make clear the intention that coercion be available only where the conduct involved carries a real risk of long-term harm to the child. Experimenting with addictive drugs is an example of such seriously self-destructive behavior that the State's concern for the child's welfare may outweigh doubts about the justification for and effectiveness of intervention. Conduct resulting in repeated unmarried pregnancy is another example. Frequent truancy is a third. Simply staying out late at night without a showing of more, however, or smoking or swearing should not be grounds for the exercise of coercive power. Furthermore, those cases in which the conduct, though noncriminal, is thought sufficiently serious to warrant court intervention and co-ercion should be dealt with separately from criminal cases in treatment and perhaps in court proceedings as well. Except in the unlikely instance of a showing of special appropriateness or utter absence of alternatives, a child committed for truancy or other noncriminal misbehavior should never be sent to an institution for delinquents.[26] Consideration should be given to transferring the proceeding for considering noncriminal but seriously hazardous conduct to an agency other than the juvenile court, with a court hearing required only if the extreme sanction of incarceration ultimately became unavoidable. As one specific limitation on the court's overuse in place of parental control, petitioning the court for action should be unavailable to parents, who too frequently find it a convenient method both of evading their own responsibilities and of venting their hostility toward their offspring.

It must be recognized, however, that the most earnest efforts to narrow broad jurisdictional bases, in language or practice, will not altogether remove the possibility of overextension. Statutory drafting deals necessarily in the general; applying legislation is in the last analysis subject to its administrator's views. Therefore, and in view of the serious stigma and the uncertain gain accompanying official action, serious consideration should be given complete elimination from the court's jurisdiction of conduct illegal only for a child. Abandoning the possibility of coercive power over a child who is acting in a seriously self-destructive way would mean losing the opportunity of reclamation in a few cases. It is hard to contemplate having no way of preventing a teenage girl from damaging her life with an illegitimate child when a sufficiently strong hand might have gotten her through the belligerent years without so permanent a blight. But in declining to relinquish power over her, we must bluntly ask what our present power achieves and must acknowledge in answer that at the most we do not really know, and in at least some cases we suspect it may do as much harm as good.

[26] Sheridan, "Juveniles Who Commit Noncriminal Acts: Why Treat in a Correctional System?" 31 Fed. Prob. 26–30 (1967).

Neglect and Dependency

Besides delinquency, the other major branch of juvenile court jurisdiction deals with cases of neglect (usually including dependency). Neglect cases generally concern children whose parents have abandoned them or are neglecting or refusing to provide proper care (including medical care) or education or a fit environment. A protective function in such situations is conferred by statute on almost all juvenile courts (although legislative language and criteria vary) and is widely exercised (157,000 dependency and neglect cases in 1965).[27] It is estimated that more than half of all neglect proceedings involve children under 6, 90 percent children under 12 years old.[28]

The juvenile court's neglect jurisdiction should not be used to impose a judge's child-rearing preferences any more than its delinquency jurisdiction should be exercised against an adolescent's nonconformity. It is undeniable, however, that numbers of parents are either unfit or dangerously erratic to a degree that actually endangers the physical or emotional well-being of their children, and that in many such instances the State is the only available intervening party. The neglect jurisdiction of the juvenile court should therefore be retained, as an appropriate embodiment of the State's concern and responsibility for the welfare of children.

Although the effort in a case of parental neglect is always to improve the home and leave the child in it, there are instances in which his own interest requires that he be removed. Since in such an order the State is contravening the basic custodial rights of parenthood, the order should be issued by a court as the outcome of judicial proceedings conducted with all the safeguards commonly observed when conflicting custodial rights are adjudicated.

Dependency, where it is defined separately from neglect, usually means either complete absence of a legal custodian or lack of proper care not as a result of willful failure to provide

but because of physical, mental, or financial inability. Thus the new Illinois act provides that a neglected minor is anyone under 18 years of age:

(a) Who is neglected as to proper or necessary support, education as required by law, or as to medical or other remedial care recognized under State law or other care necessary for his well-being, or who is abandoned by his parents, guardian, or custodian. . . .[29]

while a dependent minor is one under 18:

(a) Who is without a parent, guardian, or legal custodian; or
(b) Who is without proper care because of the physical or mental disability of his parent, guardian, or custodian. . . .[30]

Accepting that common distinction, based on willfulness, between neglect and dependency, dependency should be eliminated from the jurisdiction of the juvenile court. The Children's Bureau Standards do not use the term dependent child on the ground that:

No child should be subject to the jurisdiction of the court for economic reasons alone. The term dependent child generally implies a child in need of economic assistance. Such assistance should be provided by a social agency. Unless there is an element of neglect involved, the court's jurisdiction should not be exercised in situations of dependency.[31]

The New York Family Court Act likewise restricts the court's jurisdiction to neglect: Cases in which those responsible for the child, though having or being offered financial means, fail to provide adequate "food, clothing, shelter, education, or medical or surgical care" or "moral supervision" or abandon or desert him.[32] Problems caused by financial inability are to be "dealt with administratively under the Social Welfare law rather than judicially under the Family Court Act."[33] The Illinois act appears to reach the same result by specifying, as set

[27] Children's Bureau, U.S. Dep't HEW, stat. ser. no. 85, Juvenile Court Statistics — 1965, at 6.
[28] N.Y. Report pt. 2, at 15–16.
[29] Ill. Juvenile Ct. Act § 702–4 (1966).
[30] *Id.* § 702–5.
[31] Standards for Juvenile and Family Courts 34.
[32] N.Y. Family Ct. Act § 312 (1963).
[33] N.Y. Report pt. 2, at 13–14.

out above, the sorts of parental incapacity on which a finding of dependency may be based and by excluding, in section 5–7 (Placement; Legal Custody or Guardianship), wards of the court whose guardians fail to provide properly for them for "financial circumstances alone."

The Standards point out in a note that "there are situations where the parent, however willing, is unable to provide the child with proper care because of parental incapacity — mental, physical, or otherwise," and that in such cases protection of the child may require court action even in the absence of neglect.[34] The note states, however, that the drafters believe such action to be provided for by the jurisdiction already given the court, especially in connection with other proceedings such as adoption, termination of the legal relationship between parent and child, and appointment of a guardian.[35] Similarly, the New York Family Court Act appears to deal with dependency cases involving absence of a custodian under provisions for permanent ter-

mination of parental rights, adoption, guardianship, and custody.[36]

Where the child's dependency stems from his guardian's good-faith failure to cope, what is needed is not the force of law but the assistance of a social agency. Courts, even ones as informal and socially oriented as the juvenile court, traditionally deal with willful or at least negligent harmful conduct. Maximum use of social services and facilities to treat the causes of illegal conduct is a most desirable juvenile court goal. Acting as a mere conduit for the referral of well-meaning people overwhelmed by life to a source of assistance for their economic and social ills is a burdensome task for any court, and one there is no need to handle judicially. Especially in view of the inevitably stigmatizing effects of going to court, whatever the court and outcome are called, dependency alone should not be a subject for court consideration. As demonstrated by the Children's Bureau Standards and the New York Family Court Act, the cases in which adjudication of rights and coercion are required raise problems in addition to dependency and can be comprehended by other jurisdictional bases.

---

[34] Standards for Juvenile and Family Courts 34 n. 60; see also Paulsen, *supra* note 7.
[35] Standards for Juvenile and Family Courts 38–40.

[36] N.Y. Family Ct. Act art. 6 (1963).

Utilizing official data based on the legal definition of delinquency, Perlman provides useful information on the number of juveniles arrested annually and the nature of their delinquent acts, as well as the number of children referred to juvenile courts each year, their origin in terms of the rural-urban dimension, and the disposition of their cases. To evaluate the size of the "problem" and trends over time, Perlman defines "delinquency" according to children who come to the attention of law-enforcement agencies and juvenile courts. His assessment is based on two series of data collected on a national basis by the Federal Bureau of Investigation and by the Children's Bureau. The FBI's data on arrests are gathered from police departments on a voluntary basis and consequently may not be completely representative; for example, rural areas are not covered as well as urban areas. Nevertheless, the available data permit useful approximations: it was estimated that in 1962 approximately 1.1 million persons under eighteen years of age were arrested for offenses other than traffic violations. With the cooperation of the Bureau of the Census, the Children's Bureau selected a representative national sample of 502 juvenile courts, and the data on children who appear in these courts serve as the basis for national estimates of the volume of delinquency cases processed annually in juvenile courts. In 1962 some 555,000 juvenile delinquency cases involving an estimated 478,000 different children were handled by these courts. Thus, approximately one-half of the 1.1 million arrests of juveniles result in a court appearance. Perlman indicates that one-third of these arrests were for "juvenile misbehavior" or juvenile-status offenses, rather than "crime"; he also observes that approximately one-half of the cases handled by the juvenile court were processed unofficially, without the filing of a petition, an indication that these cases involved relatively minor offenses. These figures place the "problem" of delinquency in perspective; without denying that juveniles commit serious delinquent acts it is apparent that a considerable portion of this country's delinquency "problem" involves relatively minor deviations.

Perlman also discusses the trends apparent in the arrest and court data and concludes that delinquency is increasing; in this discussion the possibility should be recognized that increases in the recorded delinquency rate may reflect not an increase in delinquency but changes in society's response to delinquent acts. For example, the likelihood that a citizen will respond to the acts of juveniles by calling the police increases with urbanization. Undoubtedly a generation ago farmers were unimpressed with the pranks of youth, but when boys overturned a farmer's outhouse his response commonly was to talk to the boys' fathers, whereas in contrast the urbanite responds to acts of vandalism by calling the police.

The official statistics presented in this selection are "social bookkeeping data" and pertain to the activity of the police and courts; they are not simply descriptive of the behavior of children, for they also involve the response of citizens and the behavior of officials operating within our system of law enforcement. In this sense the records of law-enforcement agencies and courts serve as a useful reflection of the kinds of cases to which the police and judiciary give attention. Whether the official statistics provide an adequate index of the volume of delinquent acts committed by the entire population of juveniles is another question. Not all delinquent acts are officially recorded, and those that are recorded obviously do not constitute a random sample of the delinquent acts committed. It is for this reason that the charge that the official statistical data are biased or unrepresentative is often made. These are, of course, terms pertinent to samples, not populations; and the possibility of misinterpretation arises when the data pertaining to the entire population of juveniles arrested or appearing in court are treated as a sample.

The evidence is not disputed that police arrests and juvenile court cases are increasing; the point is that some argue that changes in the number of children handled by the police and courts adequately indicate changes in the total volume of delinquency. This argument, seductive in its simplicity, is based on the assumption that there is a constant ratio between the recorded delinquency rate and the "true" delinquency rate. This assumption may be questioned because the recorded delinquency rate is a product of the behavior of children, the response of citizens, and the activity of the police.

I. RICHARD PERLMAN

Antisocial Behavior of the Minor in the United States

In the United States, antisocial behavior of the minor is perhaps best understood when related to the laws that define juvenile delinquency. While differing in minor details and in the ages of the child over which they have jurisdiction, most state laws define as a delinquent a juvenile who violates any state or local law or commits any act that would be considered a crime if committed by an adult. In addition, most state statutes in the United States include certain acts which are violations of law only when committed by children, i.e. truancy, running away, incorrigibility, and ungovernable behavior.

A "delinquent" in the United States, then, is any child committing a delinquent act, as defined by the law, whether or not he comes to the attention of the legal authorities. The measurement of delinquency by this definition would require knowledge not only of the number of children handled by social agencies, child guidance clinics, schools, law-enforcement and judicial agencies, and others, but also of the number who do not come to the attention of any agency — those who are not apprehended.

And the number of unapprehended delinquents is substantial. This is suggested by several studies. One study [1] summarized the confessions of some 1,700 law-abiding men and women regarding their "delinquent" and "criminal" acts. Almost all these persons admitted to having committed offenses under existing laws. Two-thirds of them engaged in behavior which were felonies under their state laws. Another study [2] found that college students acknowledged committing a considerable number of offenses similar to those found among youth brought into court. Yet the offenses of these college students rarely appeared in any official statistics. Several other studies confirm that the number of hidden delinquents is large, particularly among the middle or higher income goups — those groups which appear in strikingly small numbers in official statistics.

To measure delinquency by this definition — that is, the number of children committing delinquent acts whether or not they come to the attention of an official agency — is practically impossible. Even its appropriateness is questioned by those who believe a child is delinquent only when so adjudicated by a court.

Statistics for evaluating the size of the delinquency problem and trends over a period of time must of necessity be limited to reports on children coming to the attention of law-enforcement agencies and courts. Such statistics represent a portion of all children whose misconduct could, if detected, be dealt with by the law. Hopefully they reflect trends in the numbers and characteristics of the entire group. The two series of national data most frequently cited are (1) the police arrest data collected by the Federal Bureau of Investigation and (2) the juvenile court delinquency data collected by the Children's Bureau. These data shed light not only on the volume and trend of delinquency, but also on the types of offenses committed and on the characteristics of the juvenile offenders by sex, age, and residence.

From *Federal Probation*, 28 (December 1964), 23–30. Reprinted by permission.

Note: Much of the information in this article was provided by the Office of Juvenile Delinquency and Youth Development of the Welfare Administration and Office of Education (U.S. Department of Health, Education, and Welfare); U.S. Department of Labor; Bureau of the Census; and the President's Committee on Juvenile Delinquency and Youth Crime. Of exceptional help were the Department of Labor's Manpower Research Bulletins.

[1] James S. Wallerstein and Clement J. Wyle, "Our Law-Abiding Law-Breakers," *Probation*, March–April 1947.

[2] Austin L. Porterfield, *Youth in Trouble*. Fort Worth: Leo Potishman Foundation, 1946.

Police Arrest of Juveniles

The only source of federally collected statistics on police arrests of juveniles is the uniform crime-reporting plan of the Federal Bureau of Investigation. Established in 1930, this plan has steadily increased in coverage. By 1962, some 3,975 city and county law-enforcement agencies serving 123.5 million persons (67 percent of the U.S. population) were reporting arrest data. Arrest information, primarily a measure of law-enforcement activity, provides useful data on persons arrested for criminal acts. Estimated on the basis of arrest rates reported by the Federal Bureau of Investigation, roughly 1.1 million youngsters under 18 years of age were arrested in 1962. Traffic violations, except driving while intoxicated, are excluded from this estimate.

Of all offenses charged in the juvenile arrest data reported by the Federal Bureau of Investigation for 1962, the most frequent single offense was larceny, followed by burglary (see Table 1). Property offenses [3] constituted 42 percent of all arrests of juveniles; offenses against persons [4] only 4 percent.

Disorderly conduct accounted for 9 percent and liquor law violations and drunkenness for 6 percent of the arrests of persons under 18 years of age. Sex offenses accounted for less than 2 percent of the arrests and narcotic drug violations for less than ½ of 1 percent.

The Federal Bureau of Investigation uniform reporting system, designed primarily for adult offenses, does not specifically identify such offenses as running away, truancy, violation of curfew. It is noteworthy that 33 percent of juvenile arrests are included in the "all other offense" category where most of such offenses (characterized as juvenile misbehavior rather than crime) are likely to be classified. Nearly half of the arrests of girls are categorized in "all other offenses" compared to less than one-third of the arrests of boys. Younger

[3] Robbery, burglary, larceny, auto theft, embezzlement and fraud, stolen property (buying, receiving, possessing), and forgery and counterfeiting.
[4] Murder (negligent and manslaughter), forcible rape, aggravated assault, and other assaults (non-aggravated).

children are also more likely to be classified in this category.

Over one-fourth of the girls, but more than two-fifths of the boys were arrested for property offenses. For both boys and girls the most frequent single offense was larceny, but boys were arrested far more often than girls for burglary and auto theft. Arrests for murder and manslaughter by negligence were rare for both sexes, but less frequent for girls. Sex offenses other than forcible rape accounted for nearly 4 percent of the girls arrested compared to 1.5 percent of the boys arrested. Liquor law violations, drunkenness, driving while intoxicated, disorderly conduct, vagrancy, and gambling accounted for 15 percent of the girls arrested and 18 percent of the boys.

By age groups, offenses against persons (murder, manslaughter by negligence, forcible rape, and assaults), while comprising a small proportion of total offenses, increased in frequency with age, in both urban and rural areas. Certain property offenses (robbery, fraud, and forgery or counterfeiting) increased slightly but progressively with age whereas arrests for burglary sharply decreased with age and more strikingly for boys than for girls. Larceny arrests also decreased progressively with age, particularly in the cities. Arrests for auto theft peaked at 15 years of age.

Burglary and property offenses in general, as well as liquor law violations, drunkenness, and driving while intoxicated, represented greater proportions of arrests in rural areas than in the cities. However, city youngsters were more likely to be arrested for disorderly conduct and for offenses against persons than their rural peers.

Juvenile Court Delinquency Cases

The national source of juvenile court statistics is the Children's Bureau. Since 1926 when a plan was first worked out for the uniform reporting of a few essential statistics by juvenile courts, reporting procedures and content have been modified several times. Currently, the Children's Bureau is collecting data from a national representative sample of 502 juvenile courts to provide a basis for national estimates that have a known degree of reliability. The

Table 1
Police Arrest of Juveniles Under 18 Years of Age, 1962 ᵃ

Type of offenses	Number			Percentage ᵇ								
	Total	Urban	Rural	All	Under 15	15	16	17	Male	Female	Urban	Rural
Total	729,890	693,151	36,739	100.0	100.0	100.0	100.0	100.0	100.0	100.0	100.0	100.0
Criminal homicideᶜ	622	543	79	.1	e	.1	.1	.2	.1	e	.1	.2
Forcible rape	1,744	1,636	108	.2	.1	.2	.3	.4	.3	—	.3	.3
Aggravated assault	9,028	8,758	270	1.3	1.0	1.3	1.4	1.6	1.3	1.0	1.3	.8
Other assault	20,110	19,583	527	2.8	2.6	2.7	3.0	3.3	2.8	3.1	3.0	1.5
Robbery	10,016	9,799	217	1.4	1.3	1.3	1.5	1.7	1.6	.4	1.5	.6
Burglary	80,360	73,615	6,745	11.4	13.6	11.0	9.8	8.8	13.0	2.5	10.9	18.8
Larceny-theft	147,282	141,663	5,619	20.7	27.1	19.0	16.6	14.0	20.6	22.1	21.1	15.6
Auto theft	48,666	45,670	2,996	7.0	4.5	10.5	8.8	6.3	7.8	1.9	6.8	8.3
Embezzlement & fraud	1,128	997	131	.2	.1	.1	.2	.3	.2	.2	.1	.4
Stolen property offenses	4,069	3,835	234	.6	.6	.6	.6	.6	.6	.3	.6	.7
Forgery & counterfeiting	2,077	1,799	278	.3	.1	.3	.4	.5	.3	.4	.3	.8
Prostitutionᵈ	539	512	27	.1	e	e	.1	.2	e	.4	.1	e
Other sex offenses	12,901	12,453	448	1.8	1.7	2.0	1.9	1.9	1.5	3.7	1.9	1.3
Narcotic drug laws	2,535	2,462	73	.4	.2	.4	.4	.6	.4	.4	.4	.2
Weapons (carrying, possessing)	8,810	8,620	190	1.3	1.0	1.3	1.5	1.6	1.4	.3	1.3	.5
Offenses against family and children	962	843	119	.1	.1	.1	.1	.2	.1	.3	.1	.3
Liquor laws	24,817	22,048	2,769	3.5	.6	2.5	5.2	8.9	3.6	3.0	3.3	7.7
Driving while intoxicated	1,520	1,345	175	.2	e	e	.3	.8	.3	e	.2	.5
Disorderly conduct	65,556	63,960	1,596	9.3	8.0	8.4	9.7	12.6	9.3	9.0	9.5	4.4
Drunkenness	18,366	17,275	1,091	2.6	.8	1.8	3.5	6.4	2.8	1.8	2.6	3.0
Vagrancy	11,190	10,837	353	1.6	.7	1.2	1.8	3.6	1.6	1.3	1.6	1.0
Gambling	1,983	1,972	11	.3	.1	.3	.4	.6	.3	e	.2	e
All other offenses	231,755	219,844	11,911	32.8	35.8	34.9	32.4	24.9	30.1	47.9	32.8	33.1
Suspicionᵇ	23,854	23,082	772									

Source: Federal Bureau of Investigation, *Uniform Crime Reports, 1962,* and unpublished sources.

ᵃ These reported data cover an aggregate population of 123.6 million or 67 percent of the total U.S. population — 94.0 million in 2,936 cities of over 2,500 population, 13.2 million in 118 agencies in metropolitan counties and 16.4 million in 921 agencies in rural counties.

ᵇ In computing percentages, arrests for suspicion were omitted.

ᶜ Includes both manslaughter by negligence and murder and nonnegligent manslaughter.

ᵈ Includes commercialized vice.

ᵉ Less than 0.1 of 1 percent.

Table 2

Delinquency Cases (Excluding Traffic) Disposed of by Juvenile Courts in the United States, 1962

Type of court	Total		Boys		Girls	
	Number	Percentage	Number	Percentage	Number	Percentage
Total	555,000	100	450,500	100	104,500	100
Urban	383,000	69	306,700	68	76,300	73
Semi-urban	132,500	24	110,500	25	22,000	21
Rural	39,500	7	33,300	7	6,200	6

delinquency data collected are limited to a simple count of cases by sex of the child. Traffic cases are also reported, but separately from other delinquency cases.

Although juvenile court statistics are not perfect measures of delinquency, they do include children whose delinquencies were considered important enough to refer to a court. They approximate more closely than do other series of data the definition of those who consider a child delinquent only when the courts have so adjudicated. These statistics exclude children whose behavior is handled by the police without referral to court — nationally these exclusions account for almost one-half of the police arrests and are primarily for minor offenses.

The juvenile courts in the United States processed roughly 555,000 juvenile delinquency cases (excluding traffic cases) in 1962. The estimated number of different children involved in these cases was somewhat lower (478,000) since the same child may have been referred more than once during the year. These children represent 1.8 percent of all children aged 10 through 17 in the country.

Juvenile court delinquency cases in 1962 continued to be primarily a problem for boys — they were referred to court more than four times as often as girls.

Cases handled unofficially by the court — without filing a petition — comprised almost half of the court delinquency cases in 1962.

Delinquency in the United States is concentrated in urban areas both in numbers and in rates. The rate of delinquency court cases (the number of cases per 1,000 child population aged 10 through 17) was about three times

higher in predominantly urban areas than in predominantly rural areas. Courts in predominantly urban areas handled more than two-thirds (69 percent) of all the delinquency cases in the country, as shown in Table 2.

Boys were referred to courts for considerably different reasons than girls. Based on reports from courts serving very large cities, more than half of the offenses committed by girls were for violations of laws applicable to juveniles only — runaway, truancy, violation of curfew, ungovernable behavior, etc. One-fifth of the boys were involved in offenses of this nature. On the other hand, over half of the offenses for which boys were referred were for offenses against property — larceny, auto theft (including unauthorized use of auto), vandalism, robbery and burglary; less than a fifth of the girls were involved in such cases. This was also characteristic of arrest data. Boys were referred to court for the following offenses in their order of frequency: larceny, burglary, and auto theft. Girls were most frequently referred for running away, ungovernable behavior, larceny, and sex offenses.[5]

More than two-fifths of the delinquency cases referred to courts serving large cities were dismissed with warning or adjustment. This high proportion of dismissals does not mean that the children were not involved in delinquent acts. (In only about 7 percent of the cases either the children were not so involved or the complaints were not substantiated). Rather the stability of the child's family

[5] For a more detailed listing of reasons for referral to juvenile court in delinquency cases, see *Juvenile Court Statistics, 1962*, Children's Bureau, Statistical Series No. 73.

and his potential for receiving proper parental supervision appeared to warrant this type of disposition. There is no significant difference in the disposition of boys' and girls' cases. However, the types of dispositions vary significantly when the cases are handled "with petition" or "without petition." This is to be expected, since certain actions taken by the court that curtail or deny the freedom of the child or the rights of the parents to the child's care, custody, and control usually are handled in an official manner with full hearing.

In about half of the delinquency cases handled "with petition" the child is placed on probation; in almost one-fifth of the cases, the child is committed to care and custody of an agency or institution. More than half of the cases handled "without petition" are adjusted, indicating either that the offense is relatively minor or that the child has had no serious delinquency record.

In addition to the 555,000 delinquency cases (including some multiple referrals), the juvenile courts in 1962 disposed of about 312,000 traffic cases involving some 269,000 children or 1 percent of the child population. These traffic cases did not represent all traffic cases of juveniles, since many juvenile courts lack jurisdiction of such cases.

Trends in Police Arrest and Juvenile Court Data

Police arrests of juveniles and juvenile court delinquency data, while differing in definitions, extent of coverage, geographic representation, and other factors, nevertheless show a remarkable similarity in their trends (see Chart 1).

Following a sharp increase during World War II, both arrests and court cases dropped abruptly until 1948. From then on until 1960 there was a steady increase in both series of data.

Police arrests continued to climb in 1961 but delinquency cases heard by juvenile courts decreased slightly in that year for the first time since 1948. In 1962, however, both police arrests and delinquency court cases again increased over the previous year — 9 percent and 10 percent, respectively.

The striking similarity between the trends in these two series of data suggests that they are each influenced by some common determining factor, perhaps "delinquency," however defined.

Why Juvenile Delinquency Continues to Rise

While many theories have been advanced to explain juvenile delinquency in general, the baffling question is why delinquency continues to rise in so prosperous a country as the United States. Among the factors cited as possible explanations are:

1. Postwar prosperity with "success" being increasingly emphasized in material terms. This emphasis, coupled with the lack of opportunities for achieving success by legitimate means, brings increasing pressure toward deviant behavior.

2. Poor housing conditions, primarily in central cities, where recent waves of in-migration have caused overcrowding.

3. Increasing breakdown of traditional controls in families and neighborhoods and transfer of the control to the formal law-enforcement agencies.

4. Growing numbers of employed mothers.

5. Expanding influence of mass media with strong emphases on violence, toughness, glitter, and false values.

6. Impending threats of war and annihilation producing attitudes of irresponsibility and normlessness.

None of these factors, alone, is sufficient to explain the increase in delinquency nor has the degree of causal influence always been proved. The theories are often based on logic rather than facts. It is, however, universally recognized that juvenile delinquency is an enormously complicated, many-faceted problem and that many factors interact to produce it.

More and more, though, it is realized that the rising tide of delinquency cannot be understood in isolation fom other youth problems. Whether these problems, like the ones mentioned above, are causal or merely con-

Chart 1

*Police Arrests of Juveniles, Juvenile Court Delinquency Cases,
and Child Population, U.S., 1940–1962*

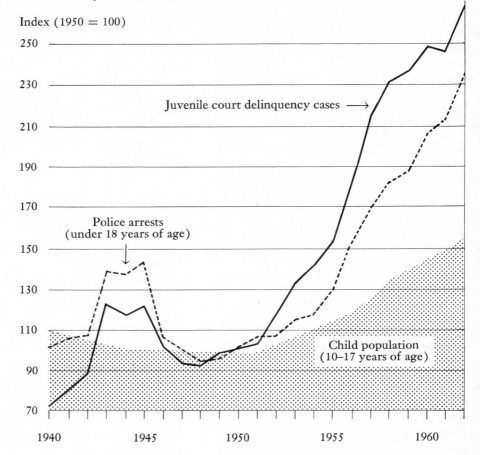

Index (1950 = 100)

Juvenile court delinquency cases ⟶

Police arrests
(under 18 years of age)

Child population
(10–17 years of age)

Source: Children's Bureau, Federal Bureau of Investigation, and Bureau of the Census

comitant, there is too frequently an unhappy connection between high rates of delinquency and conditions of social and economic deprivation. Most disturbing to us in the United States are the forecasts of social and economic trends which will make it increasingly difficult for young people, especially those living in slum areas, to achieve their goals of success. Some of the trends — population growth, increasing urbanization, youth unemployment, and school dropouts — exert their heaviest pressures against youth at the bottom of the social

and economic ladder who, when caught in a web of problems, will be the most likely candidates for the police blotter. Each of these trends constitutes a problem of major dimensions and statistics regarding them are important to the future outlook regarding antisocial behavior of minors.

Population Growth

The greatest increase in our population during the 1960's will be in the age group most vulnerable to delinquency and youth crime.

This is shown in the following table of projected population increases for various age groups:

Age group	Percentage increase 1960–1970
All ages	+19%
10–14	+20
15–19	+41
20–44	+12
45 and over	+18

Juveniles born in the late 1940's when birth rates were high, are now swelling the ranks of the 15- and 16-year-olds. These are the peak ages for juvenile delinquency. They coincide with the critical time when compulsory school attendance ends in many states, when many young persons are making the difficult transition from school to work without too much special attention from program planners and when all young persons experience the pressures of trying to bridge the gap between childhood and adulthood status.

Delinquency in the past decade increased twice as fast as the child population (see Chart 1). Will we see a repeat performance of this in the coming decade? Not necessarily so, but the predicted growth of the youth population in the 1960's, together with other concomitant problems occurring during that time, do not paint an optimistic picture.

Increasing Urbanization

More and more of our youth are living in urban areas. The decade from 1950 to 1960 witnessed the continuing trend toward urbanization in this country, and this affected youth particularly. For example, between 1950 and 1960 the number of youth (aged 10 through 17) living in urban areas increased by 72 percent, whereas those living in rural areas increased only 11 percent. Much of the increase in urban areas was due to the migration from rural into urban areas. The increase was even more pronounced when nonwhites are compared with whites. For nonwhite youth, the increase in urban areas was 78 percent; for whites, 71 percent.

In 1950, about 1 of every 2 youths was living in urban areas; in 1960, 2 of every 3; by 1970 it is estimated that 3 out of 4 will be living in such areas.

There are many positive influences associated with urban living — more abundant educational opportunities, more health and welfare services, more exposure to cultural activities, more diverse job opportunities, etc. But for some individuals, urbanization brings with it a host of problems.

Delinquency, as we have seen from our juvenile court data, concentrates in urban areas where rates are about three times higher than in rural areas. Within the boundaries of most urban cities are certain sectors which are plagued with a host of social, economic, and health problems. Such sectors are characterized by high percentages of economically deprived breadwinners, poorly assimilated in-migrants, poor housing, etc. Such neighborhoods usually are centers for crime and delinquency and the inhabitants are culturally isolated fom people living more productive lives. Will the increasing trend toward urbanization compound the unfavorable conditions that already exist in many parts of urban areas and spawn further delinquency?

Youth Unemployment and School Dropouts

The most dramatic change in the labor force in the 1960's will be the influx of youngsters. During that period, some 26 million youngsters will enter the job market. Of these, 7.5 million will not have completed high school; 2.5 million will not even have a grade school diploma.

This comes at a time when automation will be creating some drastic changes in our total economy. Fewer workers will be needed; there will be less room for unskilled workers; more and more jobs will require special knowledge and skills. The situation will affect all participants in the labor market, but its effect on young people will be especially harsh. Young workers already have the highest unemployment rates — about twice that of adults.

Those who drop out of school before completing high school are even worse off. In the United States, despite the steady improvement in the amount of schooling completed by our population, an average of about 3 in every 10 children who enter high school drop out before graduation. Studies indicate that they are the last to be employed and the first to be fired. They change jobs more frequently, earn less, and are out of work for longer periods of time than those who complete high school. Those who dropped out of school in 1960 had a rate of unemployment in October 1962 about twice as high as that for the high school graduates of 1960. Altogether a total of 430,000 dropouts 16 to 24 years old were unemployed in October 1962, accounting for about one-half of all persons in these ages who were unemployed and out of school. They accounted for about 13 percent of all unemployed persons.

Nonwhite youth face greater unemployment problems than other young workers. In 1962, about one out of four nonwhite teenagers in the labor force was unemployed compared with about one out of eight white teenagers. Even when the nonwhites have high school diplomas, their unemployment rate is about double that for white graduates. Nonwhite youth, whether graduates of high school or school dropouts, are primarily employed in low-paying service occupations and in farm labor jobs.

Certainly not all children who drop out of school or who are unemployed or who live in slum areas become delinquent. Nor do those who have studied the situation carefully claim that providing full employment for youth in the large cities would automatically banish juvenile delinquency. Research in this interrelationship among these factors [is] not abundant nor consistent. Nevertheless, we do know that slum areas produce disproportionately high rates of delinquency and that the problems of school dropouts and youth unemployment are particularly acute in such areas. We know, too, that a high proportion of delinquents have had a history of school retardation and truancy — characteristics which describe many school dropouts. So even in the absence of reliable research, it seems almost axiomatic that a youth out of school and out of work is a potential candidate for getting into trouble.

The impact of these social and economic trends — population growth, increasing urbanization, youth unemployment, and school dropouts — on our society as a whole is already being felt. Their direct influence on the delinquency problem in the future remains in the area of speculation, although the signs are ominous. In the face of some of these signs, the Federal Government, as well as many state and local governments, agencies, and organizations have undertaken action programs to forestall some of the consequences. These include "back-to-school" drives, urban renewal programs, slum clearance, youth employment training programs, research and demonstration projects directed at the prevention and control of delinquency, particularly in depressed areas of large cities, etc. The ultimate purpose of these programs is to provide for every child, whether potentially delinquent or not, every opportunity to utilize his fullest capacities.

In Conclusion

In brief summary, the best statistical indicators of antisocial behavior of minors in the United States — police arrests of juveniles and juvenile court delinquency cases — show a general upward trend beginning in 1949. Even after a decade or more of these annual increases, however, only about 4 percent (1.1 million) of the juveniles aged 10 through 17 were arrested by the police in 1962, only 1.8 percent (478,000) were referred to juvenile courts for delinquent behavior, and only 0.2 percent (65,000) were committed to institutions for delinquent children.

Such is the U.S. picture of antisocial behavior of minors. At international conferences there seems always to be a tendency to compare the nature and extent of juvenile delinquency in one country with that in another. This presumably has some significance in evaluating the quality of the social and political organization and structure of the countries. But delinquency comparisons among nations are difficult, if not impossible. The following statement concerning data from various countries that appeared in a report prepared for the Second United Nations Congress on the Prevention of Crime and the Treatment of

Offenders held in London in August 1960 makes the point very tersely:

> The statistical data presented in this report are, in many instances, incomplete and at times fragmentary. . . . They should be treated with caution and should not be used for purposes of comparison since they are subject to many varying factors. Even within a country, changing conditions over a period of time affect the statistics and make comparisons precarious. The data submitted have been prepared by different methods and come from different agencies. Some emanate from judicial and others from police sources. In different countries, the meaning of the term "juvenile delinquency" varies, the relevant age levels are not uniform and legislation is dissimilar. The passage of new legislation or modification of existing legislation may also greatly affect the data.[6]

In interpreting the delinquency data of the United States, particular emphasis should be placed on its concept of juvenile delinquency. In this country, juvenile delinquency is not considered to be synonymous with adult crime. Public concern in the case of a juvenile offender is directed toward the welfare of the child rather than his punishment. The specific offense committed by the child is not so important as the type of care needed and his potential for rehabilitation. Because of this protective aspect, most statutes defining juvenile delinquency list acts or patterns of behavior which are violations of law only when committed by juveniles. They include ungovernable behavior, running away, truancy, and curfew violations. More than one-fourth of juvenile court delinquency cases involve such behavior.

Because of the concept of juvenile delinquency and the types of behavior included in the statutes, rarely is there a lower age limit for juvenile delinquency in the United States. This accounts for the fact that almost one-fourth of the juvenile court delinquency cases involve juveniles under 14 years of age.

While other countries may also hold the concept of protecting the welfare of the child, they often handle the younger children and even some older children through "educational" measures rather than through law-enforcement agencies. Many countries, consequently, limit their delinquency data to those offenses which would be crimes if committed by an adult and exclude completely the lower age groups. Sometimes only the very serious crimes are included.

These factors emphasize some of the difficulties of intercountry comparison of delinquency data.[7]

---

[6] *New Forms of Juvenile Delinquency: Their Origin, Prevention and Treatment.* Report prepared by the Secretariat, United Nations, New York, 1960, p. 3.

[7] For a further discussion, see Peter J. Lejins, "American Data on Juvenile Delinquency in an International Forum," *Federal Probation*, June 1961.

An Alternative Approach: Self-Reports

The previous selections indicate the breadth of the legal definition of delinquency, the number of juveniles arrested annually by the police, and the volume of juvenile court referrals. For years criminologists have recognized that statistics on crime and delinquency are among the most unsatisfactory of all social statistics (Cressey [1966:141–143]). Dissatisfaction with the adequacy of official statistics led Short and Nye to suggest the use of behavioral reports as an alternative to reliance on official statistics. The use of subjects' reports of their involvement in delinquency is a dramatic departure from the usual research design in which official discretion serves as the criterion of delinquency.

The general approach in the past had been to select a sample of official delinquents — police cases, juvenile-court cases, detention-home residents, or juveniles in state training schools — as the delinquent group and a sample of noninstitutionalized adolescents as the control group. In the absence of an official record the latter group, juveniles in the general population, were assumed to be nondelinquent. This approach implies that there are only two kinds of children, delinquent and nondelinquent. A crucial weakness in the dichotomy based on official judgment is that it ignores the effects of numerous arrests, confinement in the detention home or jail, appearance in the juvenile court, probation, and institutionalization. Juveniles who have undergone some or all of these experiences may indeed exhibit greater hostility toward law-enforcement officers or the larger society than those who have not. In methodological terms the observed differences may simply reflect the influence of the criterion variable upon the independent variables. A more critical objection is that research of this type is quite likely to treat the outcome of involvement in the legal process as having causal significance. A brief example may clarify this point. If judges believe that juveniles from one-parent homes are more likely to become involved in serious types of delinquency than those from unbroken homes, they may order institutionalization, rather than probation or outright release, for children from broken homes. An investigator may then find that a higher proportion of children in institutions than in the general population come from broken homes. In this case the investigator has "discovered" not the cause of delinquency but the effect of the judges' views.

The use of data on reported behavior does not eradicate this hazard in empirical research, but "self-reports" allow the possibility of investigating the effect of the process in which a juvenile is labeled a delinquent. In addition to their discussion of the theoretical and practical advantages of the use of data on reported behavior, Short and Nye indicate that this approach also raises certain methodological issues, prominent among which are the problems of reliability and validity. Aware of these problems, Short and Nye attempted to build into their questionnaire items designed to reveal those who respond randomly, as well as the "over-conformist," and those who exaggerate their participation in delinquent activities. Since their questions referred to the entire period since the subject entered grade school, problems of memory are also involved in this approach, although the time period specified could be shortened.

Further efforts to ensure the collection of reliable and valid information through this approach are essential, as Short and Nye suggest. However, it is germane that sociologists frequently rely on responses to paper and pencil tests, questionnaires, or the verbal responses obtained in interviews as sources of data. All sociologists, not simply those interested in self-reports of delinquent behavior, must pay greater attention to the basic issues of the reliability and validity of their data. Finally, Short and Nye do not propose the gathering of behavioral reports as a replacement for the collection of official data; nevertheless, research utilizing their approach can serve as a useful supplement to studies based on official data.

REFERENCE

Donald R. Cressey, "Crime," *Contemporary Social Problems*, 2nd ed., eds. Robert K. Merton and Robert A. Nisbet (New York: Harcourt, Brace and World, Inc., 1966).

JAMES F. SHORT, JR.

F. IVAN NYE

Reported Behavior as a Criterion of Deviant Behavior

Sociologists have long felt hampered by the limitations of official statistics on the one hand and by the lack of precision and statistical

From *Social Problems*, Vol. 5, no. 3 (Winter, 1957–58), pp. 207–213. Reprinted by permission of the Society for the Study of Social Problems.

Revision of a paper read before the Pacific Sociological Society, Eugene, Oregon, April 19–20, 1957. This paper is part of a larger study made possible by grants from the Social Science Research Council and the College Committee on Research of the State College of Washington.

amenability of clinical data on the other. That is, we have recognized the weaknesses of such official dichotomies as the institutionalized vs. the non-institutionalized (in the study of delinquency and crime) and the divorced vs. the non-divorced (in the study of the "broken home"), but we have failed to do much about the problem of refinement of such data in our research. Official statistics provide false dichotomies which do violence to the continuity, distribution, and antecedents of human behavior, while clinical data are often beclouded with doctrinal dogmatism or circular reasoning which casts doubt on their validity.

The literature on social deviance is replete with caution and foreboding on the subject of official statistics. We are warned that such problems cannot be measured in terms of dollars and cents (3), that reporting systems are only recently and imperfectly developed, and that varying referral practices (16, 18) and jurisdictional procedures (19) distort the accuracy of data for index purposes. Yet most research proceeds to utilize official statistics without regard for these cautions, perhaps because of the apparent lack of alternatives. It is true that much current research utilizes data collected directly from persons defined as criminal, alcoholic, divorced, neurotic, etc. But such data as are collected rarely treat the *basic* dependent variables under consideration, i.e., crime, alcoholism, broken homes, or emotional stability. Rather, they are concerned with etiological variables and processes, having accepted the definitions of subjects as criminal, alcoholic, from broken homes, or neurotic. The continuous distribution of the deviant behavior is ignored.

There *are* exceptions. A few studies of crime treat criminality as a continuous variable to the extent of recognizing differences in offenses for which people have been officially adjudged criminal. Notable, also, are such studies as Lindesmith's (6) on drug addiction and Cressey's (4) on the violation of financial trust, which carefully delineate the phenomena to be studied and proceed to construct meaningful hypotheses on the basis of cases so selected.

But these are exceptions and not the subject of primary interest in the present paper. The alternative to the present confusion in measurement of social deviation which we suggest is the utilization of data on reported behavior. That is, we suggest going *directly* to the segments of the population in which the researcher is interested and studying such groups by asking questions relative to the behavior under consideration. This can be done by systematic sampling techniques, as Locke (7) has demonstrated in the study of certain family problems, or by studying entire groups, as the authors of this paper have done in the study of juvenile delinquency (10, 14, 20, 21) and family relations. (9, 11)

Studies of juvenile delinquency by reported behavior, whether by the children themselves or by agencies concerned with the problem, have attracted much attention since Sophia Robison's query as to whether delinquency can be measured. (16) Until recently, however, little in the way of systematic research has been done in this area. (8, 15, 25) Cohen has recently called for expansion of such studies (1, 2) and prospects seem good for extensive studies in several areas of the United States.[1]

Certain theoretical and immediately practical advantages to this type of study are apparent. In the study of juvenile delinquency, for example, the extent and nature of various types of delinquent conduct and its variability can be investigated. This is in contrast to the usual procedure of assuming that a group of institutionalized children are "delinquent" and comparing them with a group of non-institutionalized children who are defined as "non-delinquent." Further, such investigation *can* be made in all *segments* of the population, rather than in the socio-economically biased institutionalized or officially apprehended group. For purposes of etiological inquiry, such data have the advantage that they can recognize the existence of *institutionalization* and in fact study its influence as an etiological process. That is, a frequent criticism of past studies has been that some of the processes studied, e.g., emotional instability, strained family relations, and school maladjustment, may *result from* institutional experiences, or the *fact* of institutionalization, rather than being a cause of the delinquency being studied.[2] Such confusion of cause and effect relationships is not entirely eliminated by the use of data on reported be-

[1] The authors are aware of studies currently under way in Indiana, Chicago, Kansas City, and in the state of Washington.

[2] *Evidence* on this matter is not clear. The point we are making is that many studies have assumed causality in the personal pathology of their subjects *without* knowledge of whether or not personal pathology was a prior condition to delinquency.

Table 1

Delinquency by Socio-Economic Status: Institutionalization as the Criterion of Delinquency

Socio-economic status	Training school boys		High school boys	
	no.	%	no.	%
I (Lowest)	73	50.0	112	13.3
II	48	32.9	333	39.6
III	19	13.0	282	33.5
IV (Highest)	6	4.1	114	13.6
Total	146	100.0	841	100.0

$X^2 = 117.0$ P is less than .001   C = .45

Table 2

Delinquency by Socio-Economic Status: Reported Behavior as the Criterion of Delinquency

Socio-economic status	Most delinquent (scale types 8–15)		Least delinquent (scale types 1–7)	
	no.	%	no.	%
I (Lowest)	42	16.0	69	12.0
II	101	38.4	233	40.4
III	91	34.6	191	33.1
IV (Highest)	29	11.0	84	14.5
Total	263	100.0	577	100.0

$X^2 = 4.2$ P is less than .30   C = .10

havior, but the technique allows greater control over the variables by the investigator toward this end.

Recent empirical investigations by the writers suggest a further weakness of official delinquency statistics, viz., that such data are *uneven* in their biases. For example, a comparison of the reported delinquent behavior of boys and girls in different socio-economic categories finds few statistically significant differences in the *incidence* of such behavior.[3] (13) The traditional assumption of a higher incidence of delinquent behavior among members of the lower socio-economic groups, based upon official statistics, is *not* substantiated.

Tables 1 and 2 show the extent of socio-economic bias in the institutionalized population as revealed by data obtained from high

[3] Information on delinquent involvement in this study was obtained from a delinquency check list which was "buried" in a larger questionnaire. The introduction to these items explained: "Recent research has found that everyone breaks some laws, rules, and regulations during his lifetime. Some break them regularly, others less often. Below are some frequently broken. Check those that you have broken since beginning grade school." The list of delinquencies ranged from "Driven a car without a driver's license or permit," "Skipped school without a legitimate excuse," and other less serious forms of delinquency, through very serious items such as "Taken things of large value (over $50) that did not belong to you" and "Used or sold narcotic drugs." For a more complete description, see 12, 20, 21.

school students in three contiguous western cities (ranging in size between 10,000 and 25,000) compared with students in this state's training schools for committed delinquents. Table 2 shows that there is little if any difference in delinquent behavior by socio-economic level, while Table 1 shows that a full 50 percent of all institutionalized boys come from the lowest socio-economic category which comprises only 13 percent of the high school population. This raises serious questions not only for the study of socio-economic status and delinquency but for any variables correlated with socio-economic status.

Tables 3 and 4 indicate extent of broken-home bias in institutionalized populations. Table 4 shows that only 24 percent of "most delinquent" boys by reported behavior come from broken homes, but they make up 48 percent of the institutionalized population. The inference must be made that children from broken homes as well as from the lower socio-economic strata are more likely, as the result of the same delinquent behavior, to be committed to institutions.

These comparisons treat quantitative aspects of delinquency only, and the possibility of qualitative differences remains. But, this also can be and is being studied by reported behavior.

On the other hand, a comparison of the incidence of delinquent behavior of boys and girls

Table 3

Delinquency by Family State:
Institutionalization as the Criterion
of Delinquency

State of family	Training school boys		High school boys	
	no.	%	no.	%
Unbroken	81	51.9	934	80.5
Broken	75	48.1	226	19.5
Total	156	100.0	1160	100.0

$X^2 = 63.7$ P is less than .001 $C = .34$

confirms findings based upon official data, i.e., boys commit more offenses in virtually every category, and girls are highest in such offenses as ungovernability, running away, and sex offenses. The unanswered problem with regard to official statistics, then, is: what areas and to what degree are such data biased? These are crucial questions in the search for generalization regarding the extent and nature of social deviance and its etiology.

In addition to these problems, the comparability of official juvenile delinquency statistics from one jurisdiction to another suffers from a weakness inherent in the very concept of juvenile delinquency. This concept embodies a rehabilitative, clinical approach to the child which demands that each child be dealt with in a manner calculated to serve his best interests — regardless of the legal classification of his behavior. This means that the way in which a child enters into the juvenile delinquency statistics, or whether he enters at all, will vary according to his personality, family and neighborhood relations, etc. — and according to the philosophy, personnel, facilities, and skills available in each court. "Perfectly comparable statistics necessarily imply identical handling of legally identical cases and therefore the negation of the juvenile court (and police) philosophy."[4] Thus, so long as statistics are tied to legal categories, as it appears they must be, this conflict in legal classification and court philosophy will continue to exist.

[4] We are indebted to Albert Cohen for this suggestion. The quotation is from a personal communication.

Table 4

Delinquency by Family State:
Reported Behavior as the Criterion

State of family	Most delinquent (scale types 8–15)		Least delinquent (scale types 1–7)	
	no.	%	no.	%
Unbroken	281	76.4	653	82.4
Broken	87	23.6	139	17.6
Total	368	100.0	792	100.0

$X^2 = 5.9$ P is less than .02 $C = .11$

Finally, the problem of rapport with respondents is likely to be less formidable with the general population than with institutionalized groups. The adolescent who has been branded as a "delinquent" by repeated arrests, probation, and institutionalization, may find it difficult fully and frankly to reveal feelings toward parents, siblings, teachers, and peers. He may rebel against revealing behavior or companionship which might conceivably be related to his deviant behavior. Because of these problems it seems likely that institutionalized delinquents will more often attempt to manipulate the interview situation.

Every social investigator must guard against these problems, regardless of the population he is studying. Such problems are especially important in the study of institutional groups, however, because of the possibility sensed by respondents that the investigator may be used to the advantage of the respondent, or, in cases where confidence and friendship have been established, that the investigator may simply be told what the respondents think the investigator wants to hear. The use of anonymous questionnaires, particularly in the non-institutionalized population, enables the research situation to be so handled that the respondent has nothing to gain either by withholding or distorting information.

The Study of Broken Homes

Students of family problems have cautioned against too much reliance upon measures of the physically broken home as an index of family instability. The "psychologically broken home" is urged upon us as a better indication of instability, yet our chief research concern has remained with divorce and separation. Goode's (5) recent study demonstrates the fallibility of assuming that divorce inevitably indexes greater problems in terms of parent-child relationships and in terms of the happiness of family members. Nye's (9) recent study, from reports by adolescent children, of the relative happiness of broken and unbroken homes demonstrates the fruitful application of our techniques of reported behavior study for this area. Here it was found that children from unhappy unbroken homes reported a *higher* incidence of delinquent behavior and of psychosomatic symptoms, and greater parent-child adjustment problems, than did children from homes broken by divorce.

Emotional Stability

The case for objective and easily administered questionnaires designed to measure emotional stability requires little comment. The lack of objective criteria in clinical diagnosis renders statistical treatment of such data difficult and even with limitations, they are often not available to the researcher. By following careful validating procedures such as those employed by the Neuropsychiatric Branch of the Army in designing and testing the psychosomatic complaint inventory (23), the study of emotional stability by reported behavior becomes feasible. Unless carefully designed validating studies are carried out, however, results are certain to be inconclusive and confusing, as for example, when one attempts to reach a conclusion regarding the relation between personality characteristics and crime. (17)

Methodological Problems

The study of deviant behavior by reported behavior raises a number of methodological problems, some of which have been investigated by the writers of this paper, and all of which require further investigation. Regarding the question of the bias introduced by reliance upon volunteers, our findings support suggestions by Wallin (26) and Locke (7) that such bias is not substantial, though certain variations in response have been noted. (22) We have also been much concerned with problems of response reliability and validity and have "built in" to our questionnaires items designed to catch the random respondent, the over-conformist, and the individual who is out to impress the researcher with his devilishness, the truth notwithstanding.[5] Investigations by the writers on these points have thus far been encouraging. It has been necessary to throw out only a few questionnaires. These results, however, are contingent on good rapport with students and school officials, and upon adequate safeguards for the anonymity of the respondents. Comparisons of questionnaire data with data elicited by interviews based on the questionnaires have also been encouraging.

The latter type of study, carried out on a more thorough basis, is suggested as an important tool in further evaluating data on reported behavior which have been collected by survey methods. Such evaluation might be carried out by first administering questionnaires and then following up the questionnaires by detailed interviews after the investigator has had an opportunity to establish a relationship of confidence with the respondents. Such a program would be time-consuming, but extremely worthwhile in terms of problems of data interpretation and planning for future studies by survey and/or detailed interview techniques.

One final word — it is not the suggestion of this paper that the study of deviant behavior by reported behavior replace the collection of official data. No other system of data collection seems practicable on a continuing basis. Much etiological research must remain in the manipulation of officially defined problems and statistics. Data on reported behavior can, how-

---

[5] Methods employed toward this end include internal consistency in answers to questions and such devices as including "trap" questions. Thus, if a respondent indicated he had never told a lie and had never disobeyed his parents, it seemed likely that he was presenting an altogether too "pure" picture of himself to the researchers. On the other hand, if a high school respondent checked the maximum category for all offenses on the check list, his questionnaire was not used on the theory that such a person would not be at large. These criteria are discussed more fully in (10) and (12).

ever, serve to evaluate official data and suggest improvements in their collection. Nor are we especially concerned at this point with the efficacy of legal norms as a criterion for criminological investigation. (24) We are inclined to accept Tappan's point regarding the validity of legal norms as a unit of study in preference to nebulous extra-legal concepts. But we do not accept the view that the "hidden criminal" must necessarily remain hidden to investigation. This point applies equally well to other problems of deviancy. The dimensions of the problem remain largely unexplored, though the references in this paper shed some light in this area.

We wish to urge the refinement of legal classifications of criminal behavior toward the goal of more behaviorally meaningful categories. Reported behavior studies are also needed, however, to supplement studies conducted with official data in order to refine the tests of hypotheses, old and new. Indeed, it appears that sophisticated social science hypotheses generally require data of a sort not readily available in official form. Alternatives seem to be (a) the refinement of officially defined cases by some such method as selected by Cressey (4); (b) the use of small scale interview or clinical studies; or (c) the use of reported behavior data which enable the researcher to get a larger and less biased sampling of the phenomena under study. More extensive experience and research is needed to demonstrate the optimum choice among these alternatives for the study of particular research problems.

Summary

It is our experience that major categories of deviant behavior can be studied in a general population provided proper attention is given to public relations and provided the anonymity of the individual is protected. It is our contention that this eliminates biases related to the differential classification of deviants, particularly of delinquents. It likewise minimizes the influence of the criterion variable upon the independent variables.

We do not believe that in all etiological research reported behavior should be substituted for official records, but we do contend that a feasible alternate now exists to official records and clinical categories and that future research planning should give this alternative serious consideration.

REFERENCES

1. Cohen, Albert K., *Delinquent Boys* (Glencoe: The Free Press, 1955), pp. 170 ff.

2. ———, "Sociological Research in Juvenile Delinquency," paper delivered at the meetings of the American Orthopsychiatric Association, 1956.

3. Conrad, Frederick A., "Statistics in the Analysis of Social Problems," *Sociology and Social Research*, 26 (July–August 1942), 538–549.

4. Cressey, Donald R., *Other People's Money* (Glencoe: The Free Press, 1953).

5. Goode, William J., *After Divorce* (Glencoe: The Free Press, 1956).

6. Lindesmith, Alfred R., *Opiate Addiction* (Bloomington: Principia Press, 1947).

7. Locke, Harvey J., "Are Volunteer Interviewees Representative," *Social Problems* (April 1954), 143–146.

8. Murphy, Fred J., Mary M. Shirley, and Helen L. Witmer, "The Incidence of Hidden Delinquency," *American Journal of Orthopsychiatry* (October 1946), 686–696.

9. Nye, F. Ivan, "Child Adjustment in Broken and in Unhappy Unbroken Homes," *Marriage and Family Living*, 19 (November 1957), 356–361.

10. ———, "Parent-Adolescent Relationships and Delinquent Behavior," *Research Studies of the State College of Washington*, 24 (June 1956), 160–169.

11. ———, "The Rejected Parent and Delinquency," *Marriage and Family Living*, 18 (November 1956), 291–300.

12. ———, and James F. Short, Jr., "Scaling Delinquent Behavior," *American Sociological Review*, 22 (June 1956), 326–331.

13. ———, James F. Short, Jr., and Virgil J. Olson, "Socio-Economic Status and Delinquent Behavior," *The American Journal of Sociology*, 63 (January 1958), 381–389.

14. Pfuhl, Erdwin H., Jr., "Relationship of Crime and Horror Comics to Juvenile Delinquency," *Research Studies of the State College of Washington*, 24 (June 1956), 170–177.

15. Porterfield, Austin L., *Youth in Trouble* (Fort Worth: Leo Potishman Foundation, 1946), Chapter 2.

16. Robison, Sophia, *Can Delinquency Be Measured* (New York: Columbia University Press, 1936).

17. Schuessler, Karl F. and Donald R. Cressey, "Personality Characteristics of Criminals," *The American Journal of Sociology*, 55 (March 1950), 476–484.

18. Schwartz, Edward E., "A Community Experiment in the Measurement of Juvenile Delinquency," reprinted from *National Probation Association Yearbook*, 1945 (Washington: U.S.G.P.O., 1947).

19. Sellin, Thorsten, *Research Memorandum on Crime in The Depression* (New York: Social Science Research Council, 1937), Chapter 4.

20. Short, James F., Jr., "Differential Association and Delinquency," *Social Problems* (January 1957), 233–239.

21. ——, "Psychosomatic Complaints, Institutionalization, and Delinquency," *Research Studies of the State College of Washington*, 24 (June 1956), 150–159.

22. ——, "The Study of Juvenile Delinquency by Reported Behavior — An Experiment in Method

and Preliminary Findings," paper read at annual meetings of the American Sociological Society, 1955 (mimeographed).

23. Stouffer, Samuel A., et al., *Measurement and Prediction*, Vol. 4 of *Studies in Social Psychology in World War II* (Princeton, N.J.: Princeton University Press, 1950).

24. Tappan, Paul W., "Who Is the Criminal," *American Sociological Review*, 12 (February 1947), 96–102.

25. Wallerstein, James S. and Clement Wyle, "Our Law-Abiding Lawbreakers," *Probation* (April 1947), 107–112.

26. Wallin, Paul, "Volunteer Subjects as a Source of Sampling Bias," *The American Journal of Sociology*, 54 (May 1949), 539–544.

Recognizing the limitations of official statistics on delinquency and the biases inherent in official records, Short and Nye attempted to ascertain the extent of involvement in delinquent behavior in the population of youth. They gathered data from three sources: (1) a sample of 2,350 high school students in three cities of 10,000 to 30,000 population in a western state, (2) a sample of 320 boys and girls in that state's training schools, and (3) a sample — technically, three subsamples — of 596 high school students in a midwestern state. The midwestern students were selected from a rural district ($N = 171$), a rural-urban fringe district ($N = 158$), and a suburban town ($N = 267$) (see Nye and Short [1957]). These respondents were overwhelmingly native Caucasians; that juveniles residing in metropolitan areas and non-Caucasian populations were not included in this study must be recognized before one generalizes on the basis of this research.

To measure involvement in delinquent behavior, Short and Nye included a "delinquency checklist" in the questionnaires, which were administered anonymously. The items in this inventory have "face validity" because they are either violations of law or offenses for which adolescents are adjudicated; however, the more serious offenses, such as murder, rape, and armed robbery are not included because the investigators did not anticipate positive responses to inquiries about these offenses. Responses to the items pertaining to delinquent behavior were dichotomized on the basis of whether or not the respondent admitted having ever committed the act in question at any time since entering grade school.

In this paper the authors show for each of twenty-four specific delinquent acts the proportion of respondents in each sample who reported having committed the offense at least once. It is readily apparent that some, but not all, of these acts would be viewed as "serious" infractions by citizens and law-enforcement officers; however, it is also essential to recognize that the proportions of respondents who admit involvement in the various types of delinquent behavior do not indicate the frequency with which these acts occurred. If these points are recognized, then the conclusion is warranted that Nye and Short's research indicates that involvement in certain types of delinquent behavior is more evenly spread throughout the adolescent population than official records might lead one to believe. In any event, one outcome of using self-reports is to show that a great volume of undetected and unreported delinquent behavior does not become part of the official record.

Another outcome of using unofficial measures is to obtain some measure of the extent to which official data reflect the behavior of law-enforcement personnel rather than simply the behavior of offenders (see the following selection by Voss). In analyzing the data the researchers combined the several items pertaining to delinquent behavior by a procedure known as Guttman scale analysis, and they found quite different distributions of scale scores for incarcerated delinquents and high school students, groups "known to be different." For example, at the "break" between scale types 9 and 10, 86 percent of the high school boys and 14 percent of the institutionalized males were at the low end of the delinquency scale. Although there is some overlapping, use of composite measures of delinquent activities indicates that in comparison with high school students, incarcerated delinquents, both male and female, rank significantly higher in involvement in delinquent behavior.

REFERENCE

F. Ivan Nye and James F. Short, Jr., "Scaling Delinquent Behavior," *American Sociological Review*, 22 (June 1957), pp. 326–331.

JAMES F. SHORT, JR.

F. IVAN NYE

Extent of Unrecorded Juvenile Delinquency: Tentative Conclusions

The frequency and nature of delinquent behavior committed by adolescents never arrested or committed to institutions has been

Reprinted by special permission of the *Journal of Criminal Law, Criminology and Police Science* (Northwestern University School of Law), Copyright © 1958, Volume 49, Number 4.

From two larger studies of adolescent delinquency and adjustment supported in part by grants from the Social Science Research Council and the College Committee on Research of the State College of Washington.

regarded by criminologists as an important but unknown dimension of delinquent behavior. The informed layman also is aware that only a portion of delinquent behavior is followed by arrest and conviction; further, that conviction and committal to a "training school" is much more likely to follow delinquent behavior if the adolescent is from the "wrong side of the tracks." The picture of delinquent behavior obtained from official records only, and particularly the punitive action of the courts, is known to be incomplete and seriously biased.

That concern with unrecorded delinquency is high is indicated by the great interest shown in the pioneer studies of Robison,[1] Schwartz,[2] Porterfield,[3] and the Cambridge-Somerville Youth Study,[4] in texts and in recent papers by the writers.[5] Cohen has called for an extension of such studies,[6] and a number of other investigators are pursuing research projects dealing with unrecorded delinquency.[7]

The methodology of the investigations which form the basis for this paper have been described elsewhere and will not be repeated here.[8] The present paper deals with (1) types and frequency of delinquent behavior as indicated by 23 specific delinquent acts ranging from driving without a license to grand larceny and drug use, and by the use of delinquency scales derived from these items; (2) comparison of delinquent behavior in western and mid-western high school students; and (3) comparison of unrecorded delinquency with official records of delinquency.

The data were gathered by anonymous questionnaire in the classroom under the supervision of the writers. A 75 percent sample was taken from the three western high schools (cities of 10,000 to 30,000 population) and a 100 percent sample in three smaller mid-western communities. Approximately 99 percent of the questionnaires were usable.[9] In addition to being considered generally suitable for present research purposes, these particular communities possessed the positive advantage that active and informed lay people were ready to sponsor the project and interpret it to the community.

The measures of delinquent behavior used in this paper are based upon a list of behavior items commonly referred to in the laws relating to delinquent and criminal behavior. Delinquency has been defined in descriptive terms rather than in terms of legalistic categories. For example, we refer to stealing things of a certain value, rather than to descriptions of property offenses, e.g., robbery, burglary, larceny, etc.

High School Populations

Because they seem likely to be more representative of the general population than are college or training school populations, we have concentrated our research on high school populations. Table 1 presents the percentage of boys in our two high school samples, western and mid-western, and in the western training school group, who report committing each of 21 delinquency items, and the percentage who admit committing these offenses more than once or twice. Table 2 presents these data for the high school and training school girls.

[1] Sophia Robison, *Can Delinquency Be Measured* (New York: Columbia University Press, 1936).

[2] Edward E. Schwartz, "A Community Experiment in the Measurement of Juvenile Delinquency," reprinted from *Nat. Prob. Assoc. Yearbook, 1945* (Washington: U.S.G.P.O., 1947).

[3] Austin L. Porterfield, *Youth in Trouble* (Fort Worth: Leo Potishman Foundation, 1946), Chapter 2.

[4] Fred J. Murphy, Mary M. Shirley, and Helen L. Witmer, "The Incidence of Hidden Delinquency," *Am. Jour. of Orthopsychiatry*, 16 (October 1946), 686–696.

[5] Albert K. Cohen, *Delinquent Boys: The Culture of the Gang* (Glencoe, Illinois: The Free Press, 1955), 37–41. For the authors' statement as to the importance of such data, see James F. Short, Jr. and F. Ivan Nye, "Reported Behavior as a Criterion of Deviant Behavior," *Soc. Problems*, Winter 1957–1958.

[6] Albert K. Cohen, "Sociological Research in Juvenile Delinquency," paper read before American Orthopsychiatric Association, March 1956.

[7] The authors are aware of studies under way in Chicago, Kansas City, Indiana, Tennessee, Columbus, Ohio, New York City, and in the State of Washington.

[8] F. Ivan Nye and James F. Short, Jr., "Scaling Delinquent Behavior," *Amer. Sociol. Rev.*, 22 (June 1957); F. Ivan Nye, *Family Relationships and Delinquent Behavior* (New York: John Wiley and Sons, Inc., 1958), Chapter 1. James F. Short, Jr., "The Study of Juvenile Delinquency by Reported Behavior – An Experiment in Method and Preliminary Findings," paper read at the annual meetings of the American Sociological Society, Washington, D.C., 1955 (dittoed).

[9] Questionnaires were administered by one or both writers, assisted by other staff members or graduate students of the Department of Sociology of the State College of Washington. For further methodological details, see references cited in footnote 8.

Table 1

Reported Delinquent Behavior Among Boys in Three Samples

Type of offense	Percentage admitting commission of offense			Percentage admitting commission of offense more than once or twice		
	M.W.	West	Tr.S.	M.W.	West	Tr.S.
Driven a car without a driver's license or permit	81.1	75.3	91.1	61.2	49.0	73.4
Skipped school	54.4	53.0	95.3	24.4	23.8	85.9
Had fist fight with one person	86.7	80.7	95.3	32.6	31.9	75.0
"Run away" from home	12.9	13.0	68.1	2.8	2.4	37.7
School probation or expulsion	15.3	11.3	67.8	2.1	2.9	31.3
Defied parents' authority	22.2	33.1	52.4	1.4	6.3	23.6
Driven too fast or recklessly	49.7	46.0	76.3	22.7	19.1	51.6
Taken little things (worth less than $2) that did not belong to you	62.7	60.6	91.8	18.5	12.9	65.1
Taken things of medium value ($2–$50)	17.1	15.8	91.0	3.8	3.8	61.4
Taken things of large value ($50)	3.5	5.0	90.8	1.1	2.1	47.7
Used force (strong-arm methods) to get money from another person	6.3	—	67.7	2.4	—	35.5
Taken part in "gang fights"	24.3	22.5	67.4	6.7	5.2	47.4
Taken a car for a ride without the owner's knowledge	11.2	14.8	75.2	4.5	4.0	53.4
Bought or drank beer, wine, or liquor (include drinking at home)	67.7	57.2	89.7	35.8	29.5	79.4
Bought or drank beer, wine, or liquor (outside your home)	43.0	—	87.0	21.1	—	75.0
Drank beer, wine, or liquor in your own home	57.0	—	62.8	24.1	—	31.9
Deliberate property damage	60.7	44.8	84.3	17.5	8.2	49.7
Used or sold narcotic drugs	1.4	2.2	23.1	0.7	1.6	12.6
Had sex relations with another person of the same sex (not masturbation)	12.0	8.8	10.9	3.9	2.9	3.1
Had sex relations with a person of the opposite sex	38.8	40.4	87.5	20.3	19.9	73.4
Gone hunting or fishing without a license (or violated other game laws)	74.0	62.7	66.7	39.6	23.5	44.8
Taken things you didn't want	15.7	22.5	56.8	1.4	3.1	26.8
"Beat up" on kids who hadn't done anything to you	15.7	13.9	48.7	3.1	2.8	26.2
Hurt someone to see them squirm	22.7	15.8	33.4	2.8	3.2	17.5

From these tables it is apparent that the types of delinquent behavior studied are extensive and variable in the populations studied. We have compared students in the western and mid-western samples in order to secure an estimate of the stability of responses in two non-institutionalized populations. Populations in these two regional samples differ in such respects as city size and population mobility. The mid-western sample is comprised of three small communities: a suburb of a large city, a rural town, and a consolidated rural school district. The western sample comprises three small contiguous cities. The population of the mid-western communities has been fairly stable since 1940, in contrast to the rapid population growth experienced by the western cities. These samples are alike in important respects, however. Ethnic composition is similar, both populations being overwhelmingly

Table 2

Reported Delinquent Behavior Among Girls in Three Samples

Type of offense	Percentage admitting commission of offense			Percentage admitting commission of offense more than once or twice		
	M.W.	West	Tr.S.	M.W.	West	Tr.S.
Driven a car without a driver's license or permit	60.1	58.2	68.3	33.6	29.9	54.4
Skipped school	40.3	41.0	94.0	10.1	12.2	66.3
Had fist fight with one person	32.7	28.2	72.3	7.4	5.7	44.6
"Run away" from home	9.8	11.3	85.5	1.0	1.0	51.8
School probation or expulsion	2.7	3.7	63.4	0.3	0.2	29.3
Defied parents' authority	33.0	30.6	68.3	3.7	5.0	39.0
Driven too fast or recklessly	20.9	16.3	47.5	5.7	5.4	35.0
Taken little things (worth less than $2) that did not belong to you	36.0	30.0	77.8	5.7	3.5	48.1
Taken things of medium value ($2–50)	3.4	3.9	58.0	1.0	0.6	29.6
Taken things of large value ($50)	2.0	1.3	30.4	1.7	0.9	10.1
Used force (strong-arm methods) to get money from another person	1.3	—	36.7	0.3	—	21.5
Taken part in "gang fights"	9.7	6.5	59.0	1.7	1.1	27.7
Taken a car for a ride without the owner's knowledge	5.4	4.5	36.6	1.0	0.6	20.7
Bought or drank beer, wine, or liquor (including drinking at home)	62.7	44.5	90.2	23.1	17.6	80.5
Bought or drank beer, wine, or liquor (outside your home)	28.7	—	83.9	10.8	—	75.3
Drank beer, wine, or liquor in your own home	54.2	—	71.1	16.4	—	42.2
Deliberate property damage	21.7	13.6	65.4	5.7	1.6	32.1
Used or sold narcotic drugs	1.3	0.5	36.9	0.3	0.3	23.8
Had sex relations with another person of the same sex (not masturbation)	5.4	3.6	25.0	1.7	0.5	12.5
Had sex relations with a person of the opposite sex	12.5	14.1	95.1	4.1	4.8	81.5
Gone hunting or fishing without a license (or violated other game laws)	20.6	20.3	27.5	5.7	3.9	21.3
Taken things you didn't want	6.4	3.6	43.0	0.7	0.6	13.9
"Beat up" on kids who hadn't done anything to you	5.7	3.1	37.8	1.0	0.9	18.3
Hurt someone to see them squirm	10.4	9.3	35.4	1.0	1.1	20.7

native Caucasian, and age and sex are controlled. Perhaps of greater importance, both populations are non-institutionalized.

Few statistically significant differences between our two non-institutionalized groups are found in Tables 1 and 2.[10] This may be

taken as an indication of stability and reliability of the responses obtained from the two samples. Comparison of sixteen and seventeen year old high school boys on a seven-item delinquency scale, based upon these same data,

[10] Samples from both finite and hypothetical universes are treated. The western state samples represent 25 percent regular-interval samples of the high school population. Mid-western and training school samples represent 100 percent samples

of the individuals in those selected grades in the mid-western high schools and 100 percent samples of the training schools.

Nine of 21 possible comparisons of the percentage of western and mid-western boys who admit committing these offenses are significant at

indicates agreement between the two groups of boys in 90.7 percent of the scale responses.[11] We note that such differences as are found in Tables 1 and 2 indicate that delinquent behavior is somewhat more widespread in the smaller, older, more structured mid-western sample than in the larger, newer, growing western communities.

The most common offenses reported "more than once or twice" by high school boys and girls in Tables 1 and 2 are traffic offenses, truancy, and drinking. Boys also report considerable fighting, stealing (of small things), heterosexual relations, and game violations.

Comparisons of western institutionalized and non-institutionalized boys and girls on the delinquency items in Tables 1 and 2 indicates that significantly higher proportions of the "official" delinquents commit virtually all of the offenses, and commit them more often, than do the high school students.[12] Exceptions to this pattern are found only in the case of homosexual relations among the boys, driving a car without a license among girls, and game violations among both boys and girls. In spite of the statistical significance of these comparisons, however, it is apparent that there is a good deal of "overlapping" between institutionalized and non-institutionalized boys and girls in the frequency of commission of our delinquency items.

In order to specify more precisely the amount of such overlapping, indexes of delinquent behavior in the form of Guttman-type scales have been constructed. Scales for 16 and 17 year old boys, consisting of seven and eleven delinquency items, have been described elsewhere.[13] These scales proved to be nearly equal in their ability to differentiate between institutionalized and non-institutionalized boys. On the seven-item scale, a cutting point is found which maximizes the difference in delinquency involvement between the two groups of boys at 71 percent (see Table 3). At this cutting point, 86 percent of the non-institutionalized boys had been accounted for, as compared with only 14 percent of the training school boys. This difference on the eleven-item scale was maximized at 67 percent.[14] The amount of overlapping between institutionalized and non-institutionalized boys is here specified more closely than has been done in previous research. We have cited only the

_____

least at the .05 level. Eight of these 9 offenses are committed by a higher percentage of mid-western boys. When percentage of boys admitting commission of these offenses more than once or twice is compared, only 6 significant differences (at .05 level) are found, 5 of these being higher for the mid-western boys. When mid-western and western girls are compared as to commission of these offenses, 5 significant differences are found, all being committed by a higher percentage of mid-western girls. Only 1 significant difference between these groups of non-institutionalized girls is found when percentages admitting commission of the 21 offenses more than once or twice are compared.

[11] These data are described and graphically presented in F. Ivan Nye and James F. Short, Jr., "Scaling Delinquent Behavior," *Amer. Sociol. Rev.*, *op. cit.*

[12] This conclusion is based upon statistical comparison of figures presented in Tables 1 and 2, for our institutionalized and non-institutionalized western state boys and girls.

[13] F. Ivan Nye and James F. Short, Jr., *op. cit.* The seven-item scale included the following delinquency items: driving a car without a license or permit, taking little things (worth less than $2) that did not belong to you, buying or drinking beer, wine, or liquor (include drinking at home), skipping school without a legitimate excuse, purposely damaging or destroying public or private property, sex relations with a person of the opposite sex, and defying parents' authority to their faces. Offenses added for the eleven-item scale were: taking things of medium value, taking things of large value, running away from home, and narcotics violations. These data were rescored following the Israel "Gamma" technique in order to remove "idiosyncratic" elements, prior to scaling. For the procedure, and an exposition of its rationale, see M. W. Riley, J. W. Riley, and Jackson Toby, *Scale Analysis* (New Brunswick: Rutgers University Press, 1954), Chapter 18.

[14] It is interesting to compare these findings with results of the delinquency scale of the California Psychological Inventory, as obtained by Gough. Comparing a broad cross section of delinquents (as indicated by their being institutionalized or classed as "high school disciplinary problems") and non-delinquents on this scale, he found a cutting point above which 70 percent of his male delinquents fell, as compared to 20 percent of his male non-delinquents. See Harrison Gough, "Systematic Validation of a Test for Delinquency," paper delivered at the annual meeting of the American Psychological Association, 1954 (mimeographed).

Table 3

Delinquent Behavior Scores of High School and Training School Boys Aged 16 and 17 [a]

Scale type	Delin-quent behavior score	High school		Training school	
		Fre-quency	Cumula-tive per-centage	Fre-quency	Cumula-tive per-centage
1	00	0	0	0	0
2	01	128	22	0	0
3	02	40	29	0	0
4	03	60	40	0	0
5	04	105	58	3	2
6	05	28	63	2	4
7	06	26	68	3	6
8	07	25	72	2	8
9	08	80	86	7	14
10	09	31	92	24	32
11	10	27	96	8	39
12	11	6	97	11	48
13	12	6	98	15	60
14	13	5	99	16	72
15	14	3	100	34	100
		570		125	

[a] No scores were obtained for one training school boy and eight high school boys.

Table 4

Delinquent Behavior Scores of High School and Training School Girls Aged 16 and 17 [a]

Scale type	Delin-quent behavior score	High school		Training school	
		Fre-quency	Cumula-tive per-centage	Fre-quency	Cumula-tive per-centage
1	00	135	26	1	2
2	01	72	40	0	2
3	02	21	44	1	4
4	03	74	59	1	6
5	04	61	71	0	6
6	05	52	81	0	6
7	06	15	84	1	8
8	07	11	86	1	10
9	08	22	90	0	10
10	09	10	92	1	12
11	10	23	97	6	25
12	11	9	99	4	33
13	12	2	99	7	48
14	13	5	100	25	100
		512		48	

[a] No scores were obtained for two training school girls and one high school girl.

maximum differences between the two groups. Thus, if we were to study "delinquent" and "non-delinquent" boys by comparing our institutionalized and non-institutionalized groups, on the basis of the seven-item scale we would in fact be studying a group of delinquent boys, 14 percent of whom are less delinquent than are 14 percent of the "non-delinquent" boys. Comparisons can, of course, be obtained at any point along the scale.

A nine-item scale for the sixteen and seventeen year old western high school and training school girls differentiates somewhat more clearly between the two groups.[15] On this scale a maximum difference of 80 percent is found at scale type 09 (See Table 4). At this point on the scale 90.4 percent of the high school girls and only 10.4 percent of the train-

ing school girls are accounted for. That is, only about 10 percent of the high school girls are more delinquent than is indicated by scale type 08, while nearly 90 percent of the training school girls fall into this more delinquent category.

Sex Differences

Comparison of boys and girls within the high school sample indicates a higher proportion of boys committing nearly all offenses. With few exceptions such differences are statistically significant (at .01 level). This finding is similar to that revealed by official data, though the 5 to 1 ratio of boys to girls reported by the Children's Bureau [16] is not found in many cases, suggesting a bias in under-reporting female delinquency on the part of official data. Offenses for which significant dif-

[15] The girls' scale consisted of the offenses included in the eleven-item boys' scale, with the exception of taking things of large value and narcotics violations.

[16] U.S. Department of Health, Education and Welfare, Social Security Administration, Children's Bureau, *Juvenile Court Statistics*, 1955, Children's Bureau Statistical Series, No. 37.

ferences between the sexes are not found are generally those offenses for which girls are most often apprehended, e.g., running away from home, defying parents' authority (incorrigibility), and drinking. The fact that significantly higher proportions of boys in both samples report engaging in heterosexual relations and the fact that girls are most often referred to court for such activities presumably reflects society's greater concern for the unsupervised activities of girls.

Fewer statistically significant differences are found between training school boys and girls than was the case in our samples of high school students. Significantly greater percentages of the boys report committing 11 of the 24 offenses studied, and 13 of these offenses "more than once or twice." For nine of these offenses the recorded differences are not significant. Four of the offenses are reported by larger percentages of training school girls. These include running away from home, defying parents' authority, narcotics violations, and homosexual relations. A higher percentage of girls also report heterosexual relations, though this difference is not statistically significant. With the exception of narcotics violations, these are offenses for which girls are most often apprehended. The offenses reported by the highest percentage of training school boys, with the exception of fighting, which is a part of "growing up," are also those for which boys are most often apprehended, viz., stealing and traffic offenses.

Arrest Rates

Arrest rates for the high school and training school samples described above are not available. Data from the first phase of our research program, comparing college and training school students, indicate that non-institutionalized (college) students experience arrest in a far smaller proportion of offenses which they report committing than do training school students.[17] This is especially true of girls, for col-

lege girls report arrests only for traffic offenses. These arrest data bear a close relationship to officially available data. For both training school boys and girls arrest rates are highest for offenses against the person exclusive of sex offenses. Arrest rates for property offenses are more than twice as high among boys as among girls in the training school populations, while the reverse is true of sex offenses among these groups. Arrests among college men are reported in only a small percentage of property offenses (.3 percent as compared to 13.7 percent for training school boys), behavior problem offenses (2.3 percent compared to 15.1 percent for training school boys), and "casual" offenses (1.9 percent compared to 5.2 percent).

Socio-Economic Distribution

Finally, the socio-economic characteristics associated with delinquent behavior among our high school and training school populations have been studied.[18] For this purpose analysis of delinquent behavior by individual behavior items and by scale type was made, holding constant sex categories and two age groups in the western and midwestern states. Similar analysis was made for adolescents 16 and older in the "training schools" of the western state. Few significant differences were found between socio-economic strata. Such differences as were found indicated greater delinquent involvement within the highest socio-economic category as often as in the lowest.

Conclusions

While recognizing the limitations of our definition of delinquent behavior, in terms of the behavior categories studied, and the limitations of the samples employed, it appears that the following tentative conclusions regarding the extent of juvenile delinquency in the non-institutionalized population are warranted:

1. Delinquent conduct in the non-institutionalized population is extensive and variable;
2. Delinquent conduct as we have measured it is similar in extent and nature among non-

---

[17] James F. Short, Jr., "A Report on the Incidence of Criminal Behavior, Arrests, and Convictions in Selected Groups," *Proc. of the Pacific Sociol. Soc.*, 1954, published as Vol. 22, No. 2 of *Research Studies of the State College of Washington* (June 1954), 110–118, see Table 3, p. 117.

[18] F. Ivan Nye, James F. Short, Jr., and V. J. Olson, "Socio-Economic Status and Delinquent Behavior," *The Amer. Jour. of Sociol.*, LXIII, January 1958.

institutionalized high school students in widely separated sections of the country;

3. Delinquent conduct *reported* by institutionalized and non-institutionalized students is similar to delinquency and crime as treated officially in the following respects:

(1) sex ratio — non-institutionalized boys admit committing virtually all delinquencies more frequently than do non-institutionalized girls, "once or twice" and "more than once or twice"; fewer differences exist, and these differences are smaller, between institutionalized boys and girls;

(2) the offenses for which boys are most often arrested are generally those which they most often admit committing, e.g., property offenses, traffic violations, truancy, destruction of property, drinking; a few offenses are reported by large proportions of boys which are not often recorded in official statistics, e.g., game violations and fist fights;

(3) the offenses for which girls are most often arrested are, with the exception of sex offenses among high school girls, generally the offenses which girls most often admit committing, e.g., sex offenses, incorrigibility, running away. A few offenses are reported by high proportions of girls which do not find their way into official statistics;

(4) significantly greater proportions of training school boys and girls admit committing virtually all delinquencies, and admit committing them more frequently, than do high school boys and girls;

(5) when training school students are compared with high school students on a composite scale of delinquency activities there is considerable overlapping between groups of both boys and girls, but training school students as a group rank significantly higher, in terms of seriousness of involvement in delinquent behavior, than do high school students;

(6) differences on the delinquency scales, and in the commission of individual delinquencies, are greater between high school and training school girls than between high school and training school boys;

(7) variation in the proportion of reported delinquencies which result in arrest are similar to variations in the "cleared by arrest" figures collected by the Federal Bureau of Investigation.

4. Delinquent conduct reported by non-institutionalized students differs from official data in the following ways:

(1) arrests — comparison of college and training school students indicates that training school students are arrested in higher proportions of all classes of delinquencies which they admit committing than college students;

(2) socio-economic status — delinquency within the non-institutionalized populations studied is distributed more evenly throughout the socio-economic structure of society than are official cases, which are found disproportionately in the lower socio-economic strata.

Further research of this nature may be expected to provide additional clues as to the extent and nature of delinquent behavior in various segments of the population. By such means the structural correlates of delinquency, together with other important etiological considerations, may be better understood. Reported delinquent behavior as a method warrants and requires further investigation.[19] The present status of research by reported behavior is regarded as still in a pioneer stage. It provides an alternative to the use of institutionalized populations and court records, with new opportunities for research in delinquent behavior and comprehension of it.

[19] For a discussion of advantages, as well as methodological problems of this approach, see Short and Nye, "Reported Behavior as a Criterion of Deviant Behavior," *op. cit.*

Perhaps the most controversial finding in the study of delinquency is that reported by Nye, Short, and Olson (1958:388): "there is no significant difference in delinquent behavior of boys and girls in different socioeconomic strata." Although replication of a study has been relatively uncommon in sociology, Nye and Short's retention of the null hypothesis stimulated several investigations. (In fact, Hardt and Bodine [1965] list two dozen publications under the heading, "Selected References on Self-Report Studies.") Like Nye and Short, most of these researchers found little or no association between socioeconomic status and self-reports of delinquent behavior. For this reason, the presumed inverse relationship between social class and delinquency has been seriously questioned (see Empey's article in Section IV).

Yet, it is important to reiterate that "delinquency" is an extremely broad term and that it may include a wide variety of behavior. Some investigators view "delinquency" according to deviation from societal norms; others restrict the term to behavior deemed sufficient to lead to adjudication or at least sufficiently serious to warrant action by the police. The former may be operationalized according to a juvenile's verbal reports of deviations from societal norms, whether serious or not, but the latter presumably requires more serious or frequent misbehavior as well as judgment about the evaluation policemen or judges would make of such behavior. If "delinquency" is conceived broadly without differentiation of types, whether on the basis of seriousness, frequency, or other relevant criteria, then it probably is almost universally distributed throughout the class structure. Clearly, this does not mean that those who perpetrate acts viewed as serious by the community or its representatives, the police, are randomly distributed. Those who argue that there is a class differential in delinquency use one definition, whereas those who maintain that it is rather evenly spread in the class structure use another.

In an earlier paper presenting results of the study described in this selection, Voss (1963) reported that the rank order of the major ethnic groups in Hawaii according to the official delinquency rate was in general agreement with the ordering on the basis of self-reports. One explanation for the minor discrepancies observed consisted of differences in the frequency or seriousness of delinquent activities. The essential point is that in studies using self-reports greater attention has been devoted to differentiating those who, on the basis of the information they provide, are more or less delinquent, whereas the frequency of their violations, as well as the seriousness of their acts, has been given less attention. Finally, notice the unique ethnic composition of the sample analyzed in this selection, although the results are similar to those of comparable investigations conducted in other locales.

REFERENCES

Robert H. Hardt and George E. Bodine, *Development of Self-Report Instruments in Delinquency Research* (Syracuse, N.Y.: Syracuse University Youth Development Center, 1965), pp. 32–33.

F. Ivan Nye, James F. Short, Jr., and Virgil J. Olson, "Socioeconomic Status and Delinquent Behavior," *American Journal of Sociology*, 63 (January 1958), pp. 381–389.

Harwin L. Voss, "Ethnic Differentials in Delinquency in Honolulu," *Journal of Criminal Law, Criminology and Police Science*, 54 (September 1963), pp. 322–327.

HARWIN L. VOSS

Socio-Economic Status and Reported Delinquent Behavior

Nearly all writers who deal with juvenile delinquency in American society conclude that it is primarily concentrated in the lower socioeconomic strata, but few would deny the existence of delinquency among middle class youth.[1] Many undoubtedly would agree that middle class delinquency is increasing, though the evidence for such a view is impressionistic and non-statistical.[2]

Social class is treated as a critically important variable in a number of the current theories of delinquency. These explanations have extended the hypothesis proposed by Merton that "aberrant behavior may be regarded sociologically as a symptom of dissociation between culturally prescribed aspirations and socially structured avenues for realizing these aspirations."[3] The effect of these theories has been to focus attention almost exclusively on lower class delinquency, particularly gang delinquency. For example, Cohen and Cloward and Ohlin have directed their efforts toward explaining gang delinquency, though presumably it accounts for a small, but highly important proportion of all delinquency.[4]

In a study of self reported delinquent behavior among junior high school students in Honolulu, it was found that boys in the two higher social strata reported more extensive involvement in delinquent activities than did the other respondents. As a result, this paper deals with the neglected problem of middle class delinquency. Since most of the current theories of delinquency attempt to account for this phenomenon in the lower class, it is intriguing to consider whether status deprivation may also explain middle class delinquency. The observation of a higher incidence of admitted delinquency among middle class boys conflicts with the findings of previous investigators.

This is, in effect, the fifth in a "series" of investigations in which self reports rather than official contact or adjudication were used as the criterion of delinquency. With one exception, the earlier investigators did not find any significant difference in the overall incidence of delinquent behavior by occupational status levels in the fourteen communities studied. In an extensive study of self reported delinquent behavior in three western cities and in three smaller midwestern communities, Nye and Short found some significant differences for specific delinquent acts, but these did not consistently "favor" one status level. Consequently, they did not reject the null hypothesis, "there is no significant difference in delinquent behavior of boys and girls in different

From *Social Problems*, Vol. 13, no. 3 (Winter, 1966), pp. 314–324. Reprinted by permission of the Society for the Study of Social Problems.

[1] Ernest W. Burgess, "The Economic Factor in Juvenile Delinquency," *Journal of Criminal Law, Criminology and Police Science*, 43 (May–June 1952), pp. 29–42; Albert K. Cohen, *Delinquent Boys: The Culture of the Gang*, Glencoe, Ill.: The Free Press, 1955, p. 37; Bernard Lander, *Towards An Understanding of Juvenile Delinquency*, New York: Columbia University Press, 1954; Clifford R. Shaw and Henry D. McKay, *Juvenile Delinquency and Urban Areas*, Chicago: University of Chicago Press, 1942; William W. Wattenberg and James J. Balistrieri, "Gang Membership and Juvenile Misconduct," *American Sociological Review*, 15 (December 1950), pp. 746–752.

[2] Ralph W. England, Jr., "A Theory of Middle Class Juvenile Delinquency," *Journal of Criminal Law, Criminology and Police Science*, 50 (March–April 1960), p. 535; Albert K. Cohen, "Middle-class Delinquency and the Social Structure," paper read at the annual meeting of the American Sociological Society, 1957.

[3] Robert K. Merton, *Social Theory and Social Structure*, rev. ed., Glencoe, Ill.: The Free Press, 1957, p. 134.

[4] Cohen, *Delinquent Boys, op. cit.*; Richard A. Cloward and Lloyd E. Ohlin, *Delinquency and Opportunity: A Theory of Delinquent Gangs*, Glencoe, Ill.: The Free Press, 1960.

socioeconomic strata." [5] In another investigation, Dentler and Monroe studied seventh and eighth grade students in three small Kansas communities. Like Nye and Short, they found no association between socio-economic status and a specific type of delinquent behavior, theft.[6] Clark and Wenninger investigated the overall rates of admitted illegal behavior and rates for specific offenses among students in the school systems of four communities in northern Illinois, three of which were distinctly lower class. Only in a relatively autonomous industrial city of about 35,000 population were significant inter-class differences observed. Inter-community comparisons revealed no differences in the incidence of nuisance offenses, although significant differences between the diverse areas were observed in the more serious offenses.[7] In another study of inter-class differences within a school system, Akers retested the null hypothesis of the Nye-Short investigation among junior high school students in a large northeastern Ohio community. His results showed a lack of correlation between admitted delinquency and the occupational status of the respondents' fathers.[8]

[5] F. Ivan Nye, James F. Short, Jr., and Virgil J. Olson, "Socio-economic Status and Delinquent Behavior," *American Journal of Sociology*, 63 (January 1958), pp. 381–389.
[6] Robert A. Dentler and Lawrence J. Monroe, "Social Correlates of Early Adolescent Theft," *American Sociological Review*, 26 (October 1961), pp. 733–743.
[7] John P. Clark and Eugene P. Wenninger, "Socio-Economic Class and Area as Correlates of Illegal Behavior among Juveniles," *American Sociological Review*, 27 (December 1962), pp. 826–834.
[8] Ronald L. Akers, "Socio-Economic Status and Delinquent Behavior: A Retest," *Journal of Research in Crime and Delinquency*, 1 (January 1964), pp. 38–46. Omission of the recent study by Reiss and Rhodes is not an oversight. While self reports were obtained from 158 boys, Reiss and Rhodes' study is not comparable to this or the earlier investigations, for they used a composite definition of delinquency. A boy was classified as a delinquent if his self reported acts met the criteria of delinquency used by the juvenile court, or if he had been classified as a delinquent by the court. Cf. Albert J. Reiss, Jr. and Albert L. Rhodes, "The Distribution of Juvenile Delinquency in the Social Class Structure," *American Sociological Review,* 26 (October 1961), pp. 720–732.

These studies reveal that there is not an inverse relationship between the father's occupational status and admitted delinquency *within* rural, small town, or metropolitan districts, but that there is a marked inverse relationship between rates of delinquency and the mean occupational status of the family when comparisons are made *between* school districts or areas. Apparently the school district defines a relatively homogeneous socio-cultural system for youth, since it largely structures their peer contacts.

Methodology

The instruments and techniques used in this study were similar to those employed by Nye and Short. The data were gathered in Honolulu, a metropolitan center in which the majority of the population is non-Caucasian, by administering anonymous questionnaires to a 15.5 percent simple random sample (N = 620) of seventh grade students in the public Intermediate Schools. Attention is focused primarily on the information provided by the 284 male respondents.

Two measures of delinquency are utilized in this study. Guttman-type scale measures of self reported delinquent behavior similar to the scales developed by Nye and Short constitute the first of these. The derivation of these delinquency scales for boys and girls from sixteen items in the Nye-Short delinquency check list has been described elsewhere; the scale scores were dichotomized and the resulting categories were treated as most and least delinquent.[9] With this criterion, 99 of the seventh grade boys are defined as delinquent. Some might criticize this use of self reported delinquent behavior. The check list includes some acts which might never be considered delin-

[9] The items in the boys' scale were: "Ever skipped school without an excuse? Ever had a fist fight with another person? Ever taken little things (worth less than $2) that did not belong to you? Ever take part in 'gang fights'? Ever purposely damaged or destroyed public or private property that did not belong to you? Ever driven a car without a driver's license or permit?" Cf. Harwin L. Voss, "Ethnic Differentials in Delinquency in Honolulu," *Journal of Criminal Law, Criminology and Police Science*, 54 (September 1963), pp. 322–327.

Table 1

Delinquent Acts and Frequency of Reporting Required for Definition as Serious

Delinquent act	*Minimum frequency required*
Skipped school without an excuse	very often
Had a fist fight with another person	very often
"Run away" from home	twice
Placed on school probation or expelled from school	once
Taken little things (worth less than $2) that did not belong to you	once
Taken things of medium value (between $2 and $50)	once
Taken things of large value (over $50)	once
Taken part in "gang fights"	three times
Bought or drank beer, wine, or liquor without your parents' consent	very often
Purposely damaged or destroyed public or private property	several times
Had sex relations with a person of the opposite sex	once

quent behavior by officials, and others would not warrant official attention unless committed with considerable frequency. Since some of the nuisance offenses of a minor, petty nature are included in the scale,[10] an additive measure of seriousness of reported behavior was developed. Table 1 shows the acts and the frequency required for inclusion as a serious act. According to this self reported criterion, a respondent is defined as a delinquent if he reports with the required frequency three or more of the acts defined as serious; 31 boys are defined as delinquent on the basis of this measure. With the exception of the behavioral deviation item pertaining to school probation and expulsion, each of these acts constitutes a law violation, and involvement in three of these would be generally accepted as sufficient basis for adjudication by the juvenile court. These delinquent acts are not heinous, but they are more serious than those included in the scale and this measure helps to overcome

the criticism that the self-report approach does not treat "real crime."[11]

As in the Nye-Short investigation, occupation of the father was utilized as an index of socio-economic level. Empey's occupational prestige scale was used to classify occupations, and the ten categories in the scale were combined into four status groupings, which include the following types of occupations: (1) unskilled and semiskilled labor, (2) skilled labor and craftsmen, (3) white collar and small business, and (4) professional and large business.[12]

Occupation as a measure of socio-economic status has several advantages, but a potential source of bias is introduced when those respondents who do not provide adequate information on paternal occupation are excluded. One procedural difference was introduced in an effort to reduce the number of "non-classified" respondents. The questionnaires were picked up from the students upon completion and the information on father's occupation was checked; if it was not codeable, an in-

[10] The requirement that one eliminate items that do not fall within the 80–20 percent range of marginal frequencies restricts the utility of Guttman scaling in the analysis of reported delinquent behavior. For many of the serious types of delinquent behavior more than 80 percent of the respondents consistently fall in the "did not commit" category, and these items are eliminated to meet this requirement. The result is that delinquency scales, at least for young noninstitutional populations, are weighted with nuisance-type offenses.

[11] It may be noted that the more serious types of delinquency are not included, such as burglary, armed robbery, assault, and rape. This measure does include some of the most common types of juvenile offenses, such as theft, vandalism, and truancy.

[12] LaMar T. Empey, "Social Class and Occupational Aspiration: A Comparison of Absolute and Relative Measurement," *American Sociological Review*, 21 (December 1956), pp. 703–709.

Table 2
*Reported Delinquent Behavior and
Socio-Economic Status for Males*

Socio-economic level		Reported delinquent behavior			
		Most delinquent		Least delinquent	
		No.[a]	%	No.	%
(High)	IV	8	40.0	12	60.0
	III	22	52.4	20	47.6
	II	35	29.9	82	70.1
(Low)	I	26	29.2	63	70.8
	Total	91	34.0	177	66.0

Kendall's $\text{tau}_c = .13$ $P < .001$ gamma $= .21$

[a] The difference between the number in this column and the figure reported in the text is a result of excluding "non-classified" boys.

quiry was made. As a result, information concerning paternal occupation was inadequate for only 11 respondents. No attempt was made to classify adolescents who live with families in which no adult male is present; this eliminated 24 respondents. Of the 35 respondents who were not classified in terms of socio-economic status, there were 16 boys and 19 girls, or approximately 6 percent of the sample.

Findings

The data were subjected to three tests in an attempt to locate significant differences in the incidence of delinquent behavior by socio-economic status. First, the distribution of most and least delinquent groups of boys and girls by socio-economic status was tested for significant differences. The girls in the various status levels do not differ significantly in the reporting of delinquent behavior. However, for the boys, socio-economic status is significantly related to the incidence of delinquent behavior reported, as measured by the dichotomized delinquency scale. Boys in the two higher social strata report more extensive involvement in delinquent activities than do the other respondents. The difference is greater among the lower-middle class boys in category III, the sons of white collar workers and small businessmen, than among the upper-middle class boys in category IV. These data are presented in Table 2.

In seeking the possible reason for the sex differential, the modal age of the respondents, thirteen, must be considered. It may be that at this age girls in all socio-economic levels are more closely supervised by their parents than are boys. Since Japanese adolescents comprise approximately half of the respondents, it is noteworthy that Japanese boys are permitted greater latitude in their behavior than are girls. According to Sutherland, "the female crime rate shows some tendency to approach closest to the male in countries in which females have the greatest freedom and equality with males, such as Western Europe, Australia, and the United States, and to vary most from the male rate in countries in which females are closely supervised, such as Japan and Algiers."[13] The common explanation of the low delinquency rate among the Japanese emphasizes their closely knit family system, characterized by strong parental controls.[14] Japanese girls are more closely supervised than boys, and it appears that in the early teens they rarely break away from this parental control, regardless of social class.

The findings in Table 2 are divergent from those of the four previous studies of admitted delinquency. In only one of the fourteen com-

[13] Edwin H. Sutherland and Donald R. Cressey, *Principles of Criminology,* 6th ed., Philadelphia: J. B. Lippincott, 1960, p. 112.

[14] Milton L. Barron, *The Juvenile in Delinquent Society,* New York: Knopf, 1956, p. 57.

munities studied were there significant inter-class differences in the overall incidence of delinquent behavior, and these "favored" the lower status levels. One possible explanation of this difference in results has been suggested. The substantive importance of the difference in delinquent behavior by socio-economic status for boys may be vitiated by the inadequacy of the delinquency scales as measuring devices. Therefore, a second test was made; the socio-economic status distribution of boys who reported at least three serious delinquent acts and those who did not was tested. The results are given in Table 3. A slightly larger percentage of the boys in the two higher status levels reported at least three serious delinquent acts, but the differences were not significant. A less stringent measure which required the reporting of only two serious delinquent acts was then used, and the differences again were not significant. Thus, the difference between the findings in Table 2 and those of previous investigations of admitted illegal behavior may be the result of including nuisance offenses in the scale measure of delinquency.

In addition to these overall tests, differences in specific delinquent acts were tested under the presumption that the types of delinquent behavior reported might differ by status level. Four-by-two tables were constructed using the four status groupings based on paternal occupation and a simple dichotomy of "commit-ted" and "did not commit" the delinquent act. Acts for which there was insufficient positive response were not tested; eighteen analyses were conducted, eleven for males and seven for females. At the .05 level, only one significant relationship was observed.[15] "Purposely damaged or destroyed property" was reported most frequently by boys in the two higher strata, as may be seen in Table 4.

The findings of this study are restricted to the type of population utilized and in this respect are rather unique. While Clark and Wenninger studied a Negro community, this is the only investigation of self reported delinquent behavior in a predominantly Oriental population. In two ways the findings are comparable to those of Nye and Short and other investigators — in Honolulu one does not find a higher incidence of self reported delinquent behavior in the lower social strata. In addition, the finding that the incidence of admitted il-

[15] Two of the items in the check list were treated as nondelinquency and were not included in the tests of specific delinquent acts. These were: "Ever disobeyed your parents?" and "Ever told a lie?" Significant inter-class differences in response to the former question were found for males and for females. Only 4 of the boys in the two upper strata but 38 of the boys in the lower strata responded negatively. In another socio-cultural setting one might question the veracity of these respondents, but in Honolulu such an interpretation is probably incorrect. To the investigator it suggested the existence of interclass differences in the kind of parental control exercised.

Table 3

Serious Reported Delinquent Behavior and
Socio-Economic Status for Males

		Number of serious acts reported			
Socio-economic status		3 or more		0–2	
		Number [a]	%	Number	%
(High)	IV	3	15.0	17	85.0
	III	6	14.3	36	85.7
	II	9	7.7	108	92.3
(Low)	I	11	12.4	78	87.6
	Total	29	10.8	239	89.2

Kendall's tau_c = .01   P:N.S.   gamma = .03

[a] Two of the 16 non-classified boys reported at least three serious acts.

Table 4

Socio-Economic Status and Property Destruction for Males

| | | Property destruction | | | |
| | | Committed | | Did not commit | |
Socio-economic level		Number	%	Number	%
(High)	IV	9	45.0	11	55.0
	III	22	52.4	20	47.6
	II	33	28.2	84	71.8
(Low)	I	28	31.5	61	68.5
	Total	92	34.3	176	65.7

Kendall's $tau_c = .12$ $\qquad$ $P < .001$ $\qquad$ gamma $= .19$

legal behavior, when defined in terms of seriousness, does not differ significantly by paternal occupational level is comparable to the results of previous studies. Nevertheless, the findings are different.

The incidence of reported delinquent behavior, as measured by the dichotomized delinquency scale, and the admission of a specific type of delinquent behavior, property destruction, are significantly greater among boys in the higher social strata. In contrast, Nye and Short found more significant differences but, in the 33 delinquent acts for which significant differences by socio-economic status obtained, the pattern was not consistent: 16 were reported most frequently by those in the lower socio-economic category, 4 by those in the middle level, and 13 were reported most frequently by the respondents in the upper stratum.[16]

Ethnicity is a complicating variable in the relationship between socio-economic status and delinquency in Honolulu. The significant associations in Tables 2 and 4 result primarily from variations in status levels III and IV. There are 62 boys in these strata; 34 are Japanese and 18 are Caucasian. In addition, there are 3 Hawaiian and 3 Chinese boys and 4 boys from the smaller ethnic groups. In the following interpretation of the findings, attention is focused on the Japanese respondents, who are numerically predominant.

The finding that property destruction is

[16] Nye, Short, and Olson, *op. cit.*, p. 383, p. 387.

significantly related to socio-economic position for boys, but not for girls, parallels experience in Great Britain. Mannheim comments on the contrast in the number of boys and girls brought to the magistrates' court for malicious damage.[17] In Honolulu vandalism, to the extent that the questionnaire item measures it, is apparently concentrated in the lower- and upper-middle levels of the social structure. Shulman speculates that the offenses of lower class boys generally involve some form of theft, and that malicious mischief is more characteristic of middle class adolescents.[18]

The available empirical evidence concerning the relationship of vandalism to socio-economic status is conflicting. Nye reports that the act, purposely damaging or destroying property, was admitted most frequently by girls in the highest socio-economic level.[19] Research conducted in Kansas City indicates that vandalism occurs most frequently among juveniles from middle class residential areas, but a study of vandalism in Denver suggests that it is concentrated in low income sections, while in a survey of twenty-five cities vandalism was found to be as frequent in the poorer

[17] Hermann Mannheim, "The Problem of Vandalism in Great Britain," *Federal Probation*, 18 (March 1954), pp. 14–15.

[18] Harry M. Shulman, "The Family and Juvenile Delinquency," *The Annals*, 261 (January 1949), pp. 30–31.

[19] F. Ivan Nye, *Family Relationships and Delinquent Behavior*, New York: John Wiley and Sons, 1958, p. 27.

sections as in the higher socio-economic districts.[20]

The fact that boys in the two higher strata report significantly more property destruction than the boys in the lower strata conflicts with Cohen's position. In describing the delinquent subculture, he suggests that of the "antisocial" activities of the delinquent gang, stealing looms largest, but it tends to go hand-in-hand with vandalism. He further observes that vandalism "has been for many years part and parcel, indeed the very spirit, of the delinquent subculture." [21] The findings in Table 4, then, are precisely the opposite of Cohen's prediction.

Cohen hypothesizes that the development of a delinquent subculture is a solution to the typical status anxiety experienced and shared by working class boys, while delinquent behavior among middle class boys is their way of coping with ambivalence and anxiety concerning the achievement of male identity.[22] This interpretation of middle class delinquency is rejected, for it does not satisfactorily fit the facts regarding the Japanese family where males hold a superordinate position.[23] The father is accorded considerable respect by the mother, and presumably serves as a role-model for his sons, whether or not the requirements of his occupation are time-consuming.

It is, nevertheless, important to consider whether Cohen's theory of status anxiety explains the involvement in delinquency of the middle class boys. At first glance, an extension of Cohen's argument appears to offer a plausible explanation of the findings. It was hypothesized, *ex post facto*, that middle class Japanese youth may face difficulties of status achievement as a result of social mobility. Their fathers were able to make enormous advances over their parents, who were migrants to the city, either from the plantation areas or from a foreign country, Japan. They may expect their sons to advance in status as rapidly as they themselves did. However, it undoubtedly is more difficult for a boy to rise above his father's middle class position than it was for the father to surpass the lower class position attained by his foreign-born parents. A boy could easily feel inferior in competition with a successful father.[24] As a result, he might seek status in a delinquent peer group which denies the validity of his father's value system. Whether in a group setting or individually, a destructive attack on property would be particularly meaningful to the boy because respect for property is emphasized in Japanese culture and in middle class American society.[25]

The available data permit only a crude test of this hypothesis. The questionnaire included items pertaining to occupational aspirations and expectations.[26] From these items, a measure of status deprivation was derived. This is a discrepancy measure; boys who aspired to high status positions but did not have expectations of a high status occupation were defined as experiencing status deprivation. All others were defined as not experiencing status deprivation. The relationship between the dichotomized delinquency scale and socio-economic

[20] Marshall B. Clinard and Andrew L. Wade, "Toward the Delineation of Vandalism as a Sub-Type in Juvenile Delinquency," *Journal of Criminal Law, Criminology and Police Science*, 48 (January–February 1958), pp. 493–499.

[21] Cohen, *Delinquent Boys, op. cit.*, p. 185, p. 29.

[22] *Ibid.*, pp. 157–169.

[23] Jitsuichi Masuoka, "Changing Moral Bases of the Japanese Family in Hawaii," *Sociology and Social Research*, 21 (November–December 1936), pp. 158–169; Jitsuichi Masuoka, "The Japanese Patriarch in Hawaii," *Social Forces*, 17 (December 1938), pp. 240–248; Jitsuichi Masuoka, "The Life Cycle of an Immigrant Institution in Hawaii: The Family," *Social Forces*, 23 (October 1944), pp. 60–64. Wilensky and Lebeaux reject this interpretation and suggest that anxiety about male identity is a greater problem for the working class boy because femininity would produce ridicule in the family. Cf. Harold L. Wilensky and Charles N. Lebeaux, *Industrial Society and Social Welfare*, New York: Russell Sage Foundation, 1958, pp. 199–200; Cloward and Ohlin, *op. cit.*, pp. 48–54; Walter B. Miller, "Lower Class Culture as a Generating Milieu of Gang Delinquency," *The Journal of Social Issues*, 14, no. 3 (1958), pp. 5–19.

[24] Jessie Bernard, *Social Problems at Midcentury*, New York: The Dryden Press, 1957, pp. 408–445.

[25] *Ibid.*; Cohen, *Delinquent Boys, op. cit.*, pp. 91–93, 134.

[26] These items were: "If you had your choice, what occupation would you like as your life's work?" and "What occupation do you actually expect to be your life's work?"

status was examined among those who were and were not status deprived, with the Japanese and non-Japanese differentiated. None of the Japanese boys with high status who are status deprived are delinquent. On the other hand, almost one-half of the Japanese boys with high status who are not status deprived are delinquent. Among the non-Japanese boys with high status, the percentage of status deprived and non-status deprived who are delinquent is identical. This measure appears, however, to tap an important dimension among the non-Japanese boys whose fathers occupy lower status positions. Of those who are status deprived, all are delinquent. There are, however, only 11 such boys. As an important qualifier to this finding, it should be noted that the occupational aspirations and expectations reported by junior high school students are often unrealistic.[27] It nevertheless appears that the Japanese males are not enmeshed in problems of upward social mobility. The obvious, though tentative, conclusion is that one cannot extend Cohen's theory of status anxiety to account for middle class delinquency.

Rejection of this interpretation led to the development of an alternative explanation of the difference by paternal occupational level in self reported delinquent behavior. The limited participation of the Japanese in delinquency has often been attributed to their closely knit family system, characterized by strong parental controls. In view of the findings, one might speculate that parental control loses something of its effectiveness among those who have achieved high social status in the community. Those who are vertically mobile may be less prone to follow the traditional Japanese patterns. Thus, one might plausibly argue that the demands of positions in the lower- and upper-middle occupational levels interfere with the continuation of a family-centered life. In commenting on the contradictory evidence regarding differences in child-rearing practices between middle class and working class mothers, Kahl suggests that the longer people have been in the middle class, "the less they show some of the competitive values that got them there, and the more they train their children to enjoy life and to broaden their perspective beyond business."[28] Non-systematic observation of Japanese families in Honolulu suggests that the traditional pattern of child-rearing has undergone change, and the Japanese equivalent of the deferred gratification pattern appears to be disintegrating. The data currently available do not permit adequate assessment of the crucial question: Do the Japanese, who have achieved middle class standing according to objective criteria such as occupation, income, or education, adhere to traditional Japanese patterns, or has middle class American culture been accepted, as a concomitant of occupational mobility? To answer this question, one needs scales that measure class-related attitudes, values, and goals.[29] The foregoing explanation implies that among the Japanese there are significant inter-class differences in delinquency. One might also expect that the Japa-

[28] Joseph A. Kahl, *The American Class Structure*, New York: Rinehart, 1957, p. 297.

[29] One of the limitations of this and earlier studies of socio-economic status and delinquency stems from concentrating on occupation and disregarding normative systems and value orientations. The development of reliable and valid instruments to measure the degree to which a given family approximates lower class or middle class culture also is necessary to test the views of Cohen and Miller. This requires the operationalization of what we refer to as the "middle class measuring rod" and the focal concerns of lower class culture. Such an effort would be relevant to the recurrent question that arises regarding the theories of cultural strain — why is it that the proportion of delinquents in the lower class is so small? Part of the answer may be that families which are lower class in economic terms or live in lower class neighborhoods may accept the norms of middle class culture and may attempt to inculcate them in their children. Cf. Robert H. Bohlke, "Social Mobility, Stratification Inconsistency and Middle Class Delinquency," *Social Problems*, 8 (Spring 1961), pp. 351–363; David Matza and Gresham M. Sykes, "Juvenile Delinquency and Subterranean Values," *American Sociological Review*, 26 (October 1961), pp. 712–719, esp. pp. 715–716.

[27] William H. Sewell and Alan M. Orenstein, "Community of Residence and Occupational Choice," *American Journal of Sociology*, 70 (March 1965), p. 552.

Table 5

Differential Association and Reported Delinquent Behavior by Socio-Economic Status for Japanese Males

	Socio-economic status			
	Higher strata III–IV		Lower strata I–II	
Differential association	Most delinquent	Least delinquent	Most delinquent	Least delinquent
Most associative	10	4	12	34
Least associative	4	16	6	46
Total	14	20	18	80

Kendall's $tau_c = .50$ Kendall's $tau_c = .14$
$P < .001$ $P < .05$
$Q = .82$ $Q = .47$

nese in the higher strata would be similar to the non-Japanese in the reporting of delinquent behavior.

At this point the relationships in the preceding tables were stratified by introducing the variable of ethnicity to test the interpretation of the findings in terms of Japanese family structure and mobility. If this interpretation is tenable, the relationships should be stronger in the Japanese half than in the non-Japanese half of the sample. This is the case; the association between socio-economic status and property destruction is higher among the Japanese boys than in the remainder of the sample. Japanese males in the two upper strata, in comparison with those in the two lower strata, report more property destruction. The results are similar in the partials of Tables 2 and 3. With the scale measure, significant differences between the Japanese males in the upper and lower strata were observed, though the differences between strata in the other ethnic groups were not significant. Next, socio-economic status categories I and II were combined, as were levels III and IV, to test for ethnic differences in delinquency *within* social strata. For males and for females there are significant differences in reported delinquent behavior between the Japanese and other respondents in the lower strata, but not in the higher strata.

One of the possible consequences of the presumed weakening of parental controls could be that middle class Japanese boys may commit delinquent acts in response to association with delinquent peers. An important gap in current knowledge concerns the extent to which middle class boys are isolated from the influence of lower class varieties of the delinquent subculture; isolation implies that residential areas and schools are homogeneous in terms of social class.[30] The status structure of each intermediate school in Honolulu was determined by aggregating the ascribed status positions of the respondents. These schools serve a heterogeneous population, for the lower class is well-represented in each school. Thus, the middle class boys are not isolated ecologically from the influence of lower class patterns of delinquency. The multivariate relationship between differential association, as measured by a scale,[31] reported delinquent behavior, and socio-economic status among the Japanese boys is shown in Table 5. According to the measure of differential association employed, the proportion of Japanese boys who

[30] The social class composition of residential areas in the United States varies considerably; some are quite homogeneous in class while others are not. Consequently, residential areas and the schools adolescents attend vary in opportunities for cross-class contacts.

[31] Harwin L. Voss, "Differential Association and Reported Delinquent Behavior: A Replication," *Social Problems*, 12 (Summer 1964), pp. 78–85.

associate extensively with delinquent peers, i.e., are "most associative," is higher among those with low status than those with high status. Because of the more extensive reporting of delinquency by boys with high status, the socio-economic status variable specifies the "original relationship" between differential association and admitted delinquency ($Q = .58$). The association between these variables is higher among the boys with high status than among the boys with low status. Cross-sectional data do not permit determination of the time-order relation between differential association and delinquent behavior. If one assumes that differential association precedes delinquency, it is evident that Japanese boys in the higher and lower strata respond differentially to the presentation of delinquent patterns of behavior.

Section
Two

THEORETICAL ISSUES
IN THE STUDY OF
DELINQUENCY

In this selection Browning poses a number of the key issues in the study of delinquency, and in many respects this paper serves as the keynote to the collection of readings in this volume. First, the author convincingly portrays several reasons why there is a lack of conceptual clarity regarding delinquency. The first section of this paper might well be read in conjunction with the papers in Section I because one source of conceptual confusion Browning does not emphasize is the "legal wilderness" of juvenile-court statutes which Tappan examines.

Browning then turns to theoretical issues. Although each of the meanings and dimensions of "delinquency" has theoretical implications, Browning's discussion deals particularly with those related to the behavioral dimension of delinquency because in his view "it is delinquency as deviant behavior that seems to be the hard, tough core of the total problem." Browning rejects the pessimistic view regarding the possibility of developing adequate explanations of delinquency. He recognizes the need for detailed information regarding delinquent behavior; "valid descriptive knowledge" would provide the base for the development of typologies and classificatory schemes which "fit" the data and the variations in the data on delinquent behavior. (The development of such baseline data may require further development of the "self-report" technique described by Short and Nye in Section I.) Along the same line Browning argues for investigations of homogeneous types of delinquents, rather than analysis of heterogeneous samples (see the selection by Rodman and Grams in this section). He also rejects use of an eclectic, multiple-factor approach, for Browning correctly asserts that we need hypotheses of limited range which, collectively, will permit the development of "special theories."

Browning points out another question examined in this volume: the attention devoted to theoretical issues in delinquency has forced us to consider the view of the "nature of human nature" implied by our theories (see Quinney's article in this section). Another set of issues depends upon the kind of answer one gives to the question of the nature of delinquency as human behavior. Although these views are not necessarily contradictory or inconsistent and may be complementary, delinquency may be viewed as a result of weak or inadequate personal or social controls or as a positive product of particular kinds of socialization. Finally, though he remarks that the fields dealing with man's behavior are interdependent, Browning rejects the notion that advances in any one discipline are dependent upon the development of the others. Thus, Browning suggests that valid generalizations or principles regarding delinquency can be developed. He thereby sounds a positive note and suggests that sociologists get on with the business of charting the dimensions of delinquency in all its variability as well as with the task of testing the rich body of theory currently available.

CHARLES J. BROWNING

Toward a Science of Delinquency Analysis

A common thread running through the critical literature on juvenile delinquency is the conclusion that the accumulating researches are inadequate. Periodically, inventories and evaluations of both old and new studies are undertaken, indicating that little advance has been made in the scientific understanding and control of delinquency.[1] It is now represented as a "baffling problem" of overwhelming complexity.[2] Some suggest that a science of delinquency analysis may not be possible because of the unyielding difficulties encountered when trying to discover and develop a body of causal and etiological theory.[3]

This paper proposes that (1) research in delinquency need not continue indefinitely to be impotent, (2) certain necessary conditions for the development of a science have not yet been met in delinquency analysis, (3) there are a number of unresolved theoretical issues that retard the development of bodies of integrated theory, and (4) elementary analysis of the term "juvenile delinquency" indicates that the various parts of it are not equally difficult to explain and understand. In order to support these propositions, the following problems have been selected for examination: (a) the lack of a clear conception of what juvenile delinquency means and includes, or the neglect of what has been called qualitative analysis in some sciences; (b) the prolonged lack of consensus as to what constitutes the theoretical foundations of a science of delinquency analysis; and (c) the argument that delinquency analysis like criminology is a dependent science.

What Is Juvenile Delinquency?

Social and behavioral scientists have frequently found a pressing social problem — or the phenomenon giving rise to the social problem — to be the subject of their research. The burden of the researcher's task in this setting tends to bear upon etiological and causal analysis, especially when the research is sponsored by an agency primarily concerned with checking and controlling the problem. Matters of definition, conceptualization, and classification of delinquency itself, *the dependent variable*, are quickly passed over in order to identify possible causes, such as slum housing,

From *Sociology and Social Research*, 46 (1961–1962), pp. 61–74. Reprinted by permission.

[1] Jerome Michael and Mortimer Adler, *Crime, Law, and Social Science* (New York: Harcourt-Brace, 1933); Barbara Wootton, *Social Science and Social Pathology* (New York: The Macmillan Company, 1959); Helen L. Witmer and Ruth Kotinsky, "New Perspectives for Research on Juvenile Delinquency" (Washington, D.C.: U.S. Children's Bureau, 1956); Sophia Robison, *Juvenile Delinquency* (New York: Holt, Rinehart and Winston, 1960); and others.

[2] Negley Teeters in the Foreword to Clyde B. Vedder, *The Juvenile Offender* (New York: Random House, 1954), v, vi.

[3] See Peter Lejins, "Pragmatic Etiology of Delinquent Behavior," *Social Forces*, 29 (March 1951), 317–20.

broken homes, and gang membership, *the independent variables*. Research in delinquency has been handicapped by the lack of careful descriptive analysis of what juvenile delinquency includes and means.

The term "juvenile delinquency" was coined in the community, probably by reporters, social workers, humanitarians, or educators; and it was intended to designate a phenomenon which they continuously observed and knew could not be easily explained. As it came to be generally used, an implication that the phenomenon was somewhat unitary if not homogeneous developed. Cohen has observed that delinquency, like measles, seems to have been regarded as a homogeneous something which people have or have not, and that it is thought sufficient, therefore, to simply note that a person is or is not a "delinquent." [4] But, today, the phenomenon has become so complex in character that it subsumes a variety of meanings, dimensions, and definitions. Identified as a "blanket concept" [5] and an "umbrella term," [6] its present content hardly allows for unitary theoretical explication. One is tempted to abandon such an ambiguous, catchall term, but that might only result in the admission of another term just as indiscriminate. A more promising alternative is to identify the distinct, if overlapping or related, meanings or dimensions of the generic term or the multiple phenomena that the term may now subsume, and then go on to deal with each of them definitively.

A survey of the scholarly literature on juvenile delinquency reveals at least four distinct uses of the term. These are: (1) delinquency as deviant behavior, (2) delinquency as distinct legal and/or social status, (3) delinquency as a subculture trait, and (4) delinquency as a social problem. Deviant behavior occurs as individual acts of behavior, but often these acts combine to form behavior patterns,

deviant personality organizations, and finally careers in a deviant way of life. Delinquency as a distinct legal and social status may include predelinquency, protodelinquency (unofficial), real delinquency (adjudicated), and confirmed delinquency (recidivistic). Delinquency as a form of subculture generally refers to juvenile "gangland," but "teen-age" subculture in general now seems to be generating some middle and upper class delinquency not directly associated with "gangland." Delinquency as a social problem has its social class and local, regional, and national characteristics and dimensions. All of these appear to be elemental and must be reckoned with. Generalizations about delinquency may be confusing, misleading, or false unless the usage or meaning for which they hold is specified.

Nye and others have called attention to the critical methodological and theoretical problems that arise when studies confuse or equate delinquent behavior with official delinquency.[7] Legally adjudicated delinquency is held to be unrepresentative of delinquent behavior in general. In addition, delinquency depends in many cases on other things than delinquent behavior, such as community practices, court standards, and concentration of preventive efforts on predelinquency; and in other cases it is largely independent of delinquent behavior, e.g., adjudication on the basis of attitude or social situation. Tappan has identified the difficulties inherent in trying to define delinquency in terms of behavior, has developed a strong case for proving delinquency in court, and has definitively analyzed delinquency as a distinct legal and social status.[8]

Cohen has questioned whether all juvenile delinquent behavior can be fitted to a single descriptive theoretical concept or frame of reference, has emphasized the danger of as-

[4] Albert K. Cohen, *Delinquent Boys: The Culture of the Gang* (Glencoe, Ill.: The Free Press, 1955), 172.

[5] Robert K. Merton in Witmer and Kotinsky, *op. cit.*, 27.

[6] Earl Raab and Gertrude Selznick, *Major Social Problems* (Evanston, Ill.: Row, Peterson and Co., 1959), 60.

[7] F. Ivan Nye, *Family Relationships and Delinquent Behavior* (New York: John Wiley and Sons, 1958), 24; Cohen, *op. cit.*, 170–71; Merton in Witmer and Kotinsky, *op. cit.*, 27–28. Nye actually demonstrated in a field study that this problem has a basis in experience, that findings are different when official and unofficial delinquent populations are compared.

[8] Paul W. Tappan, *Juvenile Delinquency* (New York: McGraw-Hill Book Company, 1949), 4–30.

suming that delinquent and criminal behavior represent different degrees of development of a common dimension, and has presented a strong case for equating some juvenile delinquency with a delinquency subculture rather than with adjudicable behavior as such. "The delinquent's conduct is right, by the standards of his subculture, precisely *because* it is wrong by the norms of the larger culture." [9]

Little attention seems to have been given to the difficulties that arise when delinquency as a social problem is equated with the generic term or when it is not specifically differentiated from other uses or meanings included in the generic term. Textbooks which affirm that delinquency is a social problem tend to focus their analysis on problems of determining what delinquency is and who delinquents are legally and behaviorally. Analysis of the nature of delinquency consistently ends with admittedly indefinite and unsatisfying definitions of delinquency. Delinquency as a social problem is confused with delinquency as a legal, behavioral, or methodological problem. These problems may be related, but they are not the same problem. Fuller and Myers conceive of social problems as behavior patterns or conditions that are considered undesirable and in need of correction by many members of a society. [10] The use of the concept in this paper is intended to be consistent with theirs. A behavioral problem may or may not be a social problem. And the analysis of delinquency as a social problem does not necessarily give rise to the same theoretical or empirical points of dispute that analysis of delinquency as a legal term or behavioral concept does.

Examination of the following descriptive statements indicates some of the difficulties which arise when generalizations are attempted without considering adequately the specific dimensions and meanings of the generic term:

It [juvenile delinquency] is distinctly a phenomenon of the modern world. [11]

Delinquency is a world wide phenomenon and is not peculiar to any one nation. [12]

Such a phenomenon [juvenile delinquency] is unknown among primitives and has been relatively unknown among most of the great cultural systems of the world. Asiatic countries, the Middle East, and Africa are only beginning to experience it in a serious way. [13]

Juvenile delinquency is an urban and/or industrial phenomenon. [14]

For delinquency is not . . . a property of individuals or even of subsubcultures; it is a property of the social systems in which these individuals and groups are enmeshed. [15]

Generally speaking, delinquency is a function of social marginality. [16]

In the first place, delinquency *in general* is mostly male delinquency. [17]

When each of the four usages is substituted for the generic term in these statements, it becomes evident that the accuracy of the statements is affected. Delinquency as deviant behavior is not distinctly a phenomenon of the modern world. Delinquency as a distinct legal and social status and delinquency as a subculture are not yet world-wide phenomena. Delinquency as antisocial deviant behavior did not begin in, nor is it limited to, urban and/or industrial societies; it has and does exist among preliterates. Delinquency as deviant behavior is a property of social systems but also of individuals — at least, individuals-as-group-members. Delinquency as legal status (official rates) may suggest that delinquency in general has

[9] Cohen, *op. cit.*, 28.

[10] Richard C. Fuller and R. C. Myers, "The Natural History of Social Problems," *American Sociological Review*, 6 (June 1941), 320–29.

[11] Henry M. Shulman, *Juvenile Delinquency in American Society* (New York: Harper and Brothers, 1961), 1.

[12] Martin H. Neumeyer, *Juvenile Delinquency* (New York: D. Van Nostrand Company, Inc., 1961), v.

[13] Paul H. Landis, *Social Problems* (Chicago: Lippincott, 1959), 345.

[14] Shulman, *op. cit.*, 158–60; Frank Tannenbaum, "Social Forces in the Development of Crime," in Clyde B. Vedder, Samuel Koenig, and Robert E. Clark, *Criminology: A Book of Readings* (New York: Dryden Press, 1953), 220–23.

[15] Richard A. Cloward and Lloyd E. Ohlin, *Delinquency and Opportunity: A Theory of Delinquent Gangs* (Glencoe, Ill.: The Free Press, 1960), 211.

[16] Herbert A. Bloch and Frank Flynn, *Delinquency: The Juvenile Offender in America Today* (New York: Random House, 1956), 44.

[17] Cohen, *op. cit.*, 44.

its locus in marginal groups, but it is doubtful whether the same can be said for antisocial behavior in general. The same predicament arises when generalizations on the basis of sex are attempted. Only some of the more gross instances of equivocation or ambiguity can be presented here; there are many others of lesser degree in the learned as well as the popular literature on the subject.

The above statements are obviously presented out of context, but examination of the context will reveal that the issue in point cannot be explained away on that basis. It also amounts to more than a semantic problem, or oversights on the part of those who write about delinquency. And, changing from one umbrella or blanket term to another hardly resolves the issue. It is no longer defensible to simply list and decry the variety of ways in which the term has been used throughout the community, or to simply catalogue the obstacles confronted when trying to define it, or even to conclude that the only alternative is "to define the reference that it shall carry within the framework of a given discussion." [18] Nothing short of careful and systematic identification, conceptualization, and delineation of the several valid meanings of delinquency (the dependent variable in most studies) and their several dimensions will be sufficient. The failure of students of delinquency to do this kind of sound exploratory and "qualitative" analysis is substantially responsible for the slow development of a science of delinquency. Superficial analysis at this level frustrates the identification and formulation of the most significant etiological and causal hypotheses in the beginning, and ends by impeding the communication lines on which social workers, public officials, and citizens depend for reliable knowledge about delinquency.

Theoretical Foundations for a Science of Delinquency

There is increasing agreement among social scientists that research must be guided by the most rigorous available theory if it is to be fruitful. But this continuing emphasis on theory is generating fundamental questions about the nature of theory and how bodies of theory are developed in an emerging science. It is also focusing attention on a number of unsettled issues whose resolution might well stimulate the development of theoretical foundations for a science of delinquency. There is rather complete agreement that neither a single-factor nor a unitary theory that is capable of explaining all delinquency in space and time is likely to be discovered; but beyond that, researchers and writers are saying a variety of things about what is required if a science of delinquency analysis is to be forthcoming.

Of the several meanings and dimensions of delinquency which have been identified, it is delinquency as deviant behavior that seems to be the hard, tough core of the total problem. There are theoretical implications for each of the other meanings also, but the discussion that follows bears upon the behavioral meaning and dimensions for the most part.

One of the most subtle of the theoretical issues involved in the development of a science of delinquency analysis is whether or not descriptive knowledge is scientific knowledge. Robison seems to agree with Michael and Adler that it is not.[19] Tappan declares that the study of delinquency "must go beyond a merely descriptive level of conduct and personality analysis to discover the inter-relationships and dynamics of elements that determine conduct." [20] But, what science is without its descriptive knowledge — its "qualitative" as well as its "quantitative" analysis? And, what rigorous and fruitful hypotheses of etiological and causal inter-relationships in any science do not depend upon painstaking descriptive analysis? While there is some validity to this general position, it is premature and overdone. Valid descriptive knowledge is a property of a science, and students of delinquency would be better advised to systematically analyze delinquent action itself; the central concepts of the subject matter; variations of delinquency in individual, group, and collective situations; and the social and cultural context of specific patterns of delinquency. Critics have been prone

[18] L. J. Carr, *Delinquency Control* (New York: Harper & Brothers, 1950), 90.

[19] Robison, *op. cit.*, 191, 192. Interpreting Michael and Adler, *op. cit.*
[20] *Op. cit.*, 56.

to assume that, because the allegedly vast number of studies which have been done have not produced reliable and valid etiological and causal theories, they have *ipso facto* exhaustively and satisfactorily dealt with all matters short of etiological and causal analysis. The assumption is not sound, but its continued use by implication may have contributed to the widespread pessimism that an etiological and causal science of delinquency is not possible.

Growing partly out of these circumstances has been the resistance or reluctance of researchers to study limited and more homogeneous categories of delinquents — a procedure that might have given us some rigorous special theories of delinquency, if not an all-embracing unitary, general theory. It is special or limited theories at this stage of development that seem to offer the greatest hope for the accumulation of a body of integrated theory, but there is yet substantial difference of opinion among mature scholars on this point. The Gluecks, for example, in their most recent major research effort, state:

. . . in the present volume we view delinquents as well as non-delinquents as a unitary class. This does not mean that we fail to recognize that there may be clearly definable subgroups among both delinquents and non-delinquents. However, *the first and basic step is to discover similarities and differences in the mass*, in order to arrive eventually at factors in the background and make-up of the delinquents which most markedly differentiate them from non-delinquents, and to construct prognostic tables based on such differentiation by means of which the probability of delinquency in certain children may be early and meaningfully determined without waiting for the actual appearance of delinquent behavior.[21]

Most research studies and theoretical writings, like theirs, while directed toward representative cross-sections of delinquents in the mass and general theories of delinquency, have not turned out to be exhaustively or convincingly general. Students are urged to embrace the eclectic, multiple-factor, interdisciplinary approaches — presumably to arrive at a causal

formula which accommodates all levels of analysis, channels of influence, and their dynamic interplay. The heterogeneous samples (however well matched or representative) sought for studies of this kind have not given us a verifiable all-embracing causal or etiological theory, and emphasis on this methodology has probably diverted or held up research based on reliable subcategories of delinquents which are capable of giving us testable hypotheses of limited range.

It hardly seems necessary that issues of this kind should continue retarding the development of a science of delinquency analysis. Sciences approaching the complexity of human behavior in their subject matter develop bodies of theory. "General theory" and "special theory" are relative terms and both appear to be common to the development of bodies of theory. Sometimes the discovery of special theories has led to the discovery of more general unifying theories, and sometimes general theories have been able to predict special theories yet undiscovered or unconceived. What Merton has said so well for sociology as a whole is applicable to the emerging science of delinquency analysis:

. . . sociology will advance in the degree that its major concern is with developing theories of the middle range and will be frustrated if attention centers on theory in the large. I believe that our major task *today* is to develop special theories applicable to limited ranges of data — theories, for example, of class dynamics, of conflicting group pressures, of the flow of power and the exercise of interpersonal influence — rather than to seek at once the "integrated" conceptual structure adequate to derive these and all other theories. . . . To say that both general and special theories are needed is to be correct and banal: the problem is one of allocating our scant resources. I am suggesting that the road to effective conceptual schemes in sociology will be the more effectively built through work on special theories, and that it will remain a largely unfulfilled plan, if one seeks to build it directly at this time.[22]

Applied specifically to the problem of developing an adequate body of delinquency

---

[21] Sheldon and Eleanor Glueck, *Unraveling Juvenile Delinquency* (Cambridge: Harvard University Press, 1950), 15.

[22] Robert K. Merton, *Social Theory and Social Structure* (Glencoe, Ill.: The Free Press, 1957), 9.

theory, this is a suggestion that theories be tested first which are designed to relate empirical uniformities and segregated hypotheses in relatively limited areas, e.g., the subcultural theory advanced by Cohen that explains at the same time why most delinquency committed by juvenile gangs is male delinquency and is located in the working class (two of the most persistent findings in delinquency studies), or the formulation of a theory that will explain simultaneously the unlawful sexual behavior of male and female juveniles in upper, lower, and middle social classes.

Another set of detracting issues revolves around the nature of delinquency as human behavior. Is it normal or abnormal? Is it necessary to create a pathology to explain it? Is delinquent behavior symptom or syndrome, sickness or disease? Is it a positive thing that can be explained as one of the products of socialization or a negative thing that comes with the failure of social controls to restrain it? Does delinquent behavior constitute a single or more than one dimension? These are only a part of a perplexing array of points of dispute that confront those who seek to understand delinquent behavior.

The work of Porterfield, Robison, Short, and Nye with general populations of juveniles, adolescents, or college students has demonstrated that most young people commit delinquencies of one kind or another even though they vary in frequency according to sex, social class, and other criteria.[23] That is to say, a normal child engages in some delinquent behavior sometime during the process of becoming an adult. Tappan, Merrill, and others also regard delinquent behavior as normal when viewed etiologically.[24] They see it as the expected response to disorganized family life, for example, just as socially approved and nondelin-

quent behavior is the expected response to organized and supervised family life. If, also, it is assumed that every child has a delinquency potential, that no child is born with built-in adjustments to the standards imposed by an adult external world, and that socially acceptable, alternative behavior patterns are not always live options, then this provides additional support for interpreting delinquent behavior as normal behavior. And, of course, delinquent behavior which can be equated with a subculture that is delinquent is normal to that culture. Delinquent behavior is abnormal when it violates the limits of established conduct norms and is committed or practiced by a minority of the members of a community; it becomes statistically, if not substantively, normal when committed or practiced by the majority. It is also abnormal when it is not prescribed by one's own reference groups and when it is neurotic or psychotic — i.e., when it is the type of behavior with which practicing psychiatrists are ordinarily concerned.[25] But, in the latter case, if it can be substantially demonstrated that the mental illness or handicap preceded the delinquent act(s), even the courts are now inclined to regard those acts as normal functions of an abnormal x factor that gives rise to deviant behavior. Present knowledge, therefore, seems to indicate that a pathology is not necessary to explain most delinquent behavior; and that a minority of persons and acts that seem to require it appears to be as reliably accounted for as other categories of deviants and deviant behavior by theories currently used by psychologists and psychiatrists studying abnormal behavior.

The conception of delinquency as a disease has been generally discounted for some time, but "symptomology" still persists. Truancy, possession of alcoholic beverages, and forcible rape are all held to be only or merely symptomatic of "complex interrelated causes,"[26] "the essential elements,"[27] or "maladjustment"[28] —

[23] Austin L. Porterfield, *Youth in Trouble* (Austin: Leo Potishman Foundation, 1946); Robison, *op. cit.*, Chap. 4; Nye, *op. cit.*; James F. Short, Jr., and F. Ivan Nye, "Extent of Unrecorded Juvenile Delinquency: Tentative Conclusions," *Journal of Criminal Law, Criminology, and Police Science*, 29 (November–December 1958), 296–302.

[24] Tappan, *op. cit.*, 65; Maud A. Merrill, *Problems of Child Delinquency* (Boston: Houghton-Mifflin Company, 1947), Chap. 1; Hertha Tarrasch, *Focus*, 29 (July 1950), 97–101.

[25] Alfred R. Lindesmith and Anselm L. Strauss, *Social Psychology* (New York: Dryden Press, 1956), 663–67.

[26] William C. Kvaraceus, *Juvenile Delinquency and the School* (Yonkers-on-Hudson: World Book Company, 1945), 53.

[27] Tappan, *op. cit.*, 56.

[28] Merrill, *op. cit.*, 19.

presumably some basic, underlying x factor. Delinquencies, in the plural, refers to a variety of acts in violation of the juvenile code; in the singular, the term connotes an x factor that gives rise to full range of symptomatic acts. It is probable that legal persons have tended to make too much of behavioral acts and that clinically oriented persons have tended to regard them too lightly. Cohen has observed that the analogy of delinquency to a symptom meriting little investigation in its own right has been overworked;[29] but, allowing that it may still have some validity, this x factor must be regarded as a hypothesis — not as a postulate or as a verified theoretical fact — until it is identified and substantiated.

Whether delinquent behavior is a negative thing resulting from a failure of controls or a positive thing that can be explained as a product of socialization, depends in part upon what assumptions are made about the nature of human beings. Is it conformity to the regulations of society which must be learned, or deviations from those regulations? Is delinquency caused or prevented? Does a juvenile learn to become a delinquent, or is he a delinquent until he has learned to observe the regulations of his society? The alternatives suggested in these questions are not necessarily inconsistent and may even be complementary. Reiss and Nye have conducted studies using failure of controls as a frame of reference. They allow for the successful operation of controls in delinquent gangs or subcultures at the same time they propose that most delinquency can be explained as a failure of controls in the larger society and the dominant culture.[30] It is probable, taken case by case, that delinquents vary from those whose deviant behavior is natural or normal (least learned) and controls have been most adequate to those where controls have failed and delinquency has been most learned. The identification of distinct types and dimensions of delinquent behavior should resolve

most of the disagreements associated with this issue.

Does delinquent behavior constitute a single or more than one dimension? Nye and Short observe that delinquency has generally been treated as an attribute — not as a variable. Their research showed that as many as eleven different acts occur along a single dimension.[31] Scott, however, obtained some evidence for at least two dimensions: (1) acts affecting anonymous persons or impersonal property and (2) acts that introduce conflict and injury into interpersonal relations.[32] These dimensions derive from the dichotomous character of the *objects* of delinquents' behavior. Other possibilities for multiple dimensions inhere in the primary sources of the behavior itself (e.g., individual, group, institutional, collective) and the levels of organization of behavior (e.g., isolated acts, patterns of acts, deviant personality organization, and careers in a deviant way of life). While this point is not so controversial and depends more upon further research, it illustrates the kind of fundamental descriptive analysis which remains to be done in order to test theories of the middle range.

Is Criminology a Dependent Science?

A number of writers who maintain that criminology may become a science propose that it is a highly synthetic and/or a dependent science. "It receives its contributions from experts in such disciplines as biology, anthropology, physiology, medicine, psychiatry, psychology, social administration, sociology, economics, law, political science, and penology and corrections."[33] "An empirical science of criminology is not at present possible because no empirical sciences of psychology and sociology now exist."[34] "Criminology is a dependent discipline. When the sciences on which criminology depends have progressed further,

[29] Cohen, *op. cit.*, 172.
[30] Albert J. Reiss, "Delinquency as the Failure of Personal and Social Controls," *American Sociological Review,* 16 (April 1951), 196–208; Nye, *op. cit.*

[31] F. Ivan Nye and James F. Short, Jr., "Scaling Delinquent Behavior," *op. cit.,* 22 (June 1957), 326–31.
[32] John Finley Scott, "Two Dimensions of Delinquent Behavior," *American Sociological Review,* 24 (April 1959), 240–43.
[33] Walter C. Reckless, *The Crime Problem* (New York: Appleton-Century-Crofts, 1955), 7.
[34] Michael and Adler, *op. cit.,* 85.

solutions of the problems of 'character disease' will become more likely." [35] "It is not to be expected that criminological theory will develop wholly adequate and acceptable explanations of behavior until the whole group of 'the behavior sciences' reaches a corresponding adequacy of theoretical explanation of human behavior in general." [36] "The point has been well taken that a science of normal behavior is prerequisite to the scientific analysis of problem conduct . . . man does not yet possess a well-systematized science of human behavior." [37]

This argument loses part of its force when it fails to distinguish between criminology and the applied disciplines of penology and corrections. It leads to the same kind of disorder which earlier grew out of the failure to distinguish between sociology as a basic social science and social work as an art or applied science. And, in the main, medicine (including psychiatry) and social administration are not disciplines given over to the pursuit of scientific knowledge; they generally gather it from the basic sciences. Sellin has recommended that the term "criminology" be used to designate only the body of scientific knowledge about crime and the pursuit of such knowledge. [38]

Sellin goes on to observe, however, that ". . . the 'criminologist' . . . actually remains a psychologist, a sociologist, a psychiatrist, a jurist, or a political scientist, with a specialized concern in a question which impinges on his broader interests. The 'criminologist' does not exist who is an expert in all the disciplines which converge in the study of crime." [39] Robison, interpreting Sellin in her textbook on delinquency (1960), concludes from this remark that ". . . lacking these prerequisites one cannot arrive at valid generalizations, principles, or laws which have predictive values." [40] The

conclusion, as interpreted, is untenable. It may become necessary to use terms like "sociological criminologist" or "psychological criminologist," but it is difficult to see why any science must stand or fall on the condition of any one person (or any group of persons trained in a common discipline) being able to master all the disciplines converging upon it. The theoretical model implied in this conclusion is not a body of special and more general theories consistent with one another yet capable of standing alone; but an all-embracing, unitary theory that includes the concepts and contributions of all relevant disciplines and which stands or falls as a whole. A sociology of crime and delinquency is possible apart from equivalent developments in related disciplines, and it is capable of developing valid special theories (if not some of the more general ones) that are necessary to an integrated body of theory. Sociological analysis cannot explain all the data of delinquency and it shares with other disciplines in the emerging body of theory; but this relationship does not constitute dependency to the extent that the theories of any one discipline are invalid or inadequate because they do not embrace and reconcile the contributions of every other relevant discipline.

This reduces the issue to the relation of the behavioral sciences to one another, and, more particularly, to the relation of the general sciences like sociology, psychology, and anthropology to special sciences like criminology and delinquency. The existence of disciplines like social psychology and social anthropology bears witness to the overlapping subject matter of the general behavioral sciences. To say that they are dependent upon one another is not so accurate as to say that they are interdependent. Few scholars would hold that any given social or behavioral discipline could not become a science until some or all of the others did. The case appears to be somewhat the same for general as related to special disciplines or sciences. They, too, are interdependent, and it is not easy to demonstrate that the dependency is great from special to general and small from general to special. A sociologist specializing in the study of a particular range of human behavior,

[35] Gluecks, *op. cit.*, 4, 289.

[36] George B. Vold, *Theoretical Criminology* (New York: Oxford, 1958), 314.

[37] Tappan, *op. cit.*, 56.

[38] Thorsten Sellin, *Culture Conflict and Crime* (New York: Social Science Research Council, Bulletin 41, 1938).

[39] *Ibid.*, 3, 4.

[40] Robison, *op. cit.*, 192.

i.e., deviant behavior which violates the delinquency or criminal code, may be just as able to contribute to the total body of theory on human behavior as the psychologist who starts by constructing a general theory of human behavior and then proceeds to test it exhaustively in selected ranges or dimensions of that behavior. The position that criminology is necessarily dependent upon any one or all of the general behavioral sciences; (a) can be reduced to a division-of-labor judgment, (b) assumes that the organization of knowledge has been accomplished and that the boundaries have been rather permanently established, (c) assumes that the phenomenon, crime, consists essentially or exhaustively of the deviant behavior of individual criminals, and (d) ignores the fact that bodies of theory which have become established in the mature sciences have accumulated piece-meal, i.e., from delimited or special problems or ranges of subject matter, until more general theories capable of organizing them consistently and parsimoniously were discovered.

In what way is a science of normal conduct prerequisite to the scientific analysis of problem conduct? Obviously, this question is irrelevant if one accepts the proposition that problem conduct is normal conduct. It is also irrelevant in a multicultural setting where conduct is problematic primarily because one culture does not accept the normal behavior of another culture or subculture. It probably has its greatest force where the problem conduct is pathological and severe, e.g., psychotic conduct.

Conclusions

Each of the basic sciences involved in delinquency analysis can proceed to work on theory that comes within the segment of human experience for which it is ordinarily responsible in the academic division of labor. A reasonable goal for a science of delinquency analysis is a body of theory built up from the smaller bodies or ranges of theory contributed by the interdependent basic sciences. Theoretical issues that have become stumbling blocks in delinquency analysis stand to be substantially resolved if both theorists and empiricists will give the necessary attention to systematic and definitive qualitative or descriptive analysis. And the several phenomena that have been identified as constituent parts of the generic concept, juvenile delinquency, call for individual assessment with regard to their complexity, resistance to understanding and explanation, and susceptibility to intelligent control. In addition, the possible dimensions of each one deserve to be explored. If these tasks are undertaken with reasonable rigor, delinquency research will not continue to be unconvincing, and a science of delinquency analysis will at least have moved beyond some of the necessary conditions for its establishment.

The implication of this selection by Hirschi and Selvin is that whether an investigator uses official data, depends on self-reports, or employs a combination of these approaches to establish a criterion of delinquency, adequate causal analysis is essential. According to these authors, many investigators, upon observing a statistical association between an independent variable and the dependent variable, delinquency (however it is defined), do not recognize that they have thereby made the first step in inferring causality, but rather proceed to argue that the observed relation is not causal. Hirschi and Selvin write that at times assertions of noncausality are based on the misuse of statistical tools or misinterpretation of findings, and that investigators frequently invoke one or more false criteria of causality in dismissing the importance of a statistical association of some independent variable with delinquency. Hirschi and Selvin argue that in an adequate causal analysis the investigator must show that (1) there is a statistical association between the independent and the dependent variable, (2) the independent variable is causally prior to the dependent variable, that is, a causal variable must occur prior to its presumed effect, and (3) the original association does not disappear when the influence of other variables which are causally prior to both of the original variables are removed, that is, the relation must be tested to show that it is not spurious.

Hirschi and Selvin discuss six illegitimate or false criteria. The first of these, the criterion of perfect association, implies that there is a single cause of delinquency; the principle of multiple causation is thereby rejected. The second and third of the false criteria are variants of the first. In discussing the third criterion the authors elaborate on a simple point, namely, if one wishes to determine the importance of a variable such as "the external situation" then elements in this variable must vary. The authors indicate that one cannot determine the importance of the external situation by considering only a boy's response to police, neighbors, and strangers on his doorstep, because "the group at the doorstep" is a constant, not a variable; hence, its effect cannot be measured. One would also have to inquire what the boy's response would be if elements in the situation were changed — if his mother were waiting alone on the doorstep, if his best friend were waiting for him, if a salesman were standing on the porch, or if there were no one present as he approached his home. Differentiation or the "method of difference" is fundamental in the quest for scientific explanation; to determine the importance of a variable the investigator must compare the outcomes according to at least two different values of the variable.

The fifth false criterion also deserves comment. In this case the problem arises largely because investigators cannot directly measure abstract variables such as anomie or status frustration. They therefore use indicators of these abstract variables. For example, to test the hypothesis that a negative attitude toward school leads to delinquency, one might construct a series of questionnaire items to measure attitude toward school. Responses to these items would be combined by some means such as scaling, and the association of the resulting scores with some measure of delinquency would be calculated. The investigator would not argue that the responses to the questionnaire items cause delinquency, but he could argue, given appropriate checks on reliability and validity, that these responses were indicators of the respondents' attitude toward school. If an association between attitude and delinquency were observed, the investigator would have to demonstrate that a negative attitude toward school preceded involvement in delinquency as well as that the relation was not spurious, in order to argue that a negative attitude toward school is causally related to delinquency.

TRAVIS HIRSCHI
HANAN C. SELVIN

False Criteria of Causality in Delinquency Research

Smoking per se is not a cause of lung cancer. Evidence for this statement comes from the thousands of people who smoke and yet live normal, healthy lives. Lung cancer is simply unknown to the vast majority of smokers, even among those who smoke two or more packs a day. Whether smoking is a cause of lung cancer, then, depends upon the reaction of the lung tissues to the smoke inhaled. The important thing is not whether a person smokes, but how his lungs react to the smoke inhaled. These facts point to the danger of imputing causal significance to superficial variables. In essence, it is not smoking as such, but the carcinogenic elements in tobacco smoke that are the real causes of lung cancer.[1]

The task of determining whether such variables as broken homes, gang membership, or anomie are "causes" of delinquency benefits from a comparison with the more familiar problem of deciding whether cigarette smoking "causes" cancer. In both fields many statistical studies have shown strong relations between these presumed causes and the observed effects, but the critics of these studies often attack them as "merely statistical." This phrase has two meanings. To some critics it stands for the belief that only with experimental ma-

nipulation of the independent variables is a satisfactory causal inference possible. To others it is a brief way of saying that observing a statistical association between two phenomena is only the first step in plausibly inferring causality. Since no one proposes trying to give people cancer or to make them delinquent, the fruitful way toward better causal analyses in these two fields is to concentrate on improving the statistical approach.

In setting this task for ourselves we can begin with one area of agreement: all statistical analyses of causal relations in delinquency rest on observed associations between the independent and dependent variables. Beyond this there is less agreement. Following Hyman's reasoning,[2] we believe that these two additional criteria are the minimum requirements for an adequate causal analysis: (1) the independent variable is causally prior to the dependent variable (we shall refer to this as the criterion of "causal order"), and (2) the original association does not disappear when the influences of other variables causally prior to both of the original variables are removed ("lack of spuriousness").[3]

The investigator who tries to meet these criteria does not have an easy time of it.[4] Our examination of statistical research on the causes of delinquency shows, however, that many in-

From *Social Problems* (Winter 1966), Vol. 13, no. 3, pp. 254–268. Reprinted by permission of the Society for the Study of Social Problems.

This is publication A-56 of the Survey Research Center, University of California, Berkeley. We are grateful to the Ford Foundation for financial support of the larger study from which this paper is drawn. An early account of this study, which does not include the present paper, is *The Methodological Adequacy of Delinquency Research*, Berkeley: Survey Research Center, 1962. Ian Currie, John Lofland, Alan B. Wilson, and Herbert L. Costner made useful criticisms of previous versions of this paper.

[1] This is a manufactured "quotation"; its source will become obvious shortly.

[2] Herbert H. Hyman, *Survey Design and Analysis*. Glencoe, Illinois: The Free Press, 1955, chs. 5–7.

[3] Hyman appears to advocate another criterion as well: that a chain of intervening variables must link the independent and dependent variables of the original relation. We regard this as psychologically or theoretically desirable but not as part of the minimum methodological requirements for demonstrating causality in nonexperimental research.

[4] Hirschi and Selvin, *op. cit.*

vestigators do not try to meet these criteria but instead invent one or another new criterion of causality — or, more often, of noncausality, perhaps because noncausality is easier to demonstrate. To establish causality one must forge a chain of three links (association, causal order, and lack of spuriousness), and the possibility that an antecedent variable not yet considered may account for the observed relation makes the third link inherently weak. To establish noncausality, one has only to break any one of these links.[5]

Despite the greater ease with which noncausality may be demonstrated, many assertions of noncausality in the delinquency literature turn out to be invalid. Some are invalid because the authors misuse statistical tools or misinterpret their findings. But many more are invalid because the authors invoke one or another false criterion of noncausality. Perhaps because assertions of noncausality are so easy to demonstrate, these invalid assertions have received a great deal of attention.

A clear assertion that certain variables long considered causes of delinquency are not really causes comes from a 1960 *Report to The Congress:*

Many factors frequently cited as causes of delinquency are really only concomitants. They are not causes in the sense that if they were removed delinquency would decline. Among these factors are:
Broken homes.
Poverty.
Poor housing.
Lack of recreational facilities.
Poor physical health.

Race.
Working mothers.[6]

According to this report, all of these variables are statistically associated with delinquency, i.e., they are all "concomitants." To prove that they are not causes of delinquency it is necessary either to show that their relations with delinquency are spurious or that they are effects of delinquency rather than causes. Since all of these presumptive causes appear to precede delinquency, the only legitimate way to prove noncausality is to find an antecedent variable that accounts for the observed relations. None of the studies cited in the *Report* does this.[7] Instead, the assertion that broken homes, poverty, lack of recreational facilities, race, and working mothers are not causes of delinquency appears to be based on one or more of the following false "criteria": [8]

1. Insofar as a relation between two variables is not *perfect*, the relation is not causal.

---

[5] Popper calls this the asymmetry of verifiability and falsifiability. Karl R. Popper, *The Logic of Scientific Discovery*, New York: Basic Books, 1959, esp. pp. 27–48. For a fresh view of the verification-falsification controversy, see Thomas S. Kuhn, *The Structure of Scientific Revolutions*, Chicago: University of Chicago Press, 1962. Kuhn discusses Popper's views on pp. 145–146. Actually, it is harder to establish noncausality than our statement suggests, because of the possibility of "spurious independence." This problem is discussed in Hirschi and Selvin, *op. cit.*, pp. 38–45, as "elaboration of a zero relation."

[6] U.S. Department of Health, Education and Welfare, *Report to The Congress on Juvenile Delinquency*, United States Government Printing Office, 1960, p. 21. The conclusion that "poor housing" is not a cause of delinquency is based on Mildred Hartsough, *The Relation Between Housing and Delinquency*, Federal Emergency Administration of Public Works, Housing Division, 1936. The conclusion that "poor physical health" is not a cause is based on Edward Piper's "unpublished Children's Bureau manuscript summarizing the findings of numerous investigators on this subject." Since we have not examined these two works, the following conclusions do not apply to them.

[7] The works cited are: broken homes, Negly K. Teeters and John Otto Reinemann, *The Challenge of Delinquency*, New York: Prentice-Hall, 1950, pp. 149–154; poverty, Bernard Lander, *Towards an Understanding of Juvenile Delinquency*, New York: Columbia University Press, 1954; recreational facilities, Ethel Shanas and Catherine E. Dunning, *Recreation and Delinquency*, Chicago: Chicago Recreation Commission, 1942; race, Lander, *op. cit.*; working mothers, Eleanor E. Maccoby, "Children and Working Mothers," *Children*, 5 (May–June 1958), pp. 83–89.

[8] It is not clear in every case that the researcher himself reached the conclusion of noncausality or, if he did, that this conclusion was based on the

    a. Insofar as a factor is not a *necessary condition* for delinquency, it is not a cause of delinquency.

    b. Insofar as a factor is not a *sufficient condition* for delinquency, it is not a cause of delinquency.

2. Insofar as a factor is not "*characteristic*" of delinquents, it is not a cause of delinquency.

3. If a relation between an independent variable and delinquency is found for a *single value of a situational or contextual factor,* then the situational or contextual factor cannot be a cause of delinquency.[9]

4. If a relation is observed between an independent variable and delinquency and if a psychological variable is suggested as *intervening* between these two variables, then the original relation is not causal.

5. *Measurable* variables are not causes.

6. If a relation between an independent variable and delinquency is *conditional* upon the value of other variables, the independent variable is not a cause of delinquency.

In our opinion, all of these criteria of noncausality are illegitimate. If they were systematically applied to any field of research, no relation would survive the test. Some of them, however, have a superficial plausibility, both

as stated or implied in the original works and as reformulated here. It will therefore be useful to consider in some detail just why these criteria are illegitimate and to see how they appear in delinquency research.

False Criterion 1. Insofar as a relation between two variables is not perfect, the relation is not causal.

Despite the preponderance of Negro delinquency, one must beware of imputing any causal significance to race per se. There is no *necessary* concomitance between the presence of Negroes and delinquency. In Census Tracts 9–1 and 20–2, with populations of 124 and 75 Negro juveniles, there were no recorded cases of delinquency during the study period. The rates of Negro delinquency also vary as widely as do the white rates indicating large differences in behavior patterns that are not a function or effect of race per se. It is also of interest to note that in at least 10% of the districts with substantial Negro juvenile populations, the Negro delinquency rate is lower than the corresponding white rate.[10]

There are three facts here: (1) not all Negroes are delinquents; (2) the rates of Negro delinquency vary from place to place; (3) in some circumstances, Negroes are less likely than whites to be delinquent. These facts lead Lander to conclude that race has no causal significance in delinquency.

In each case the reasoning is the same: each fact is another way of saying that the statistical relation between race and delinquency is not perfect, and this apparently is enough to disqualify race as a cause. To see why this reasoning is invalid one has only to ask for the conditions under which race *could be* a cause of delinquency if this criterion were accepted. Suppose that the contrary of the first fact above were true, that *all* Negroes are delinquent. It would then follow necessarily that Negro delinquency rates would not vary from place to place (fact 2) and that the

---

false criteria discussed below. Maccoby's article, for example, contains a "conjectural explanation" of the relation between mother's employment and delinquency (i.e., without presenting any statistical evidence she suggests that the original relation came about through some antecedent variable), but it appears that the conclusion of noncausality in the *Report* is based on other statements in her work.

[9] All of the foregoing criteria are related to the "perfect relation" criterion in that they all require variation in delinquency that is unexplained by the "noncausal" variable. A more general statement of criterion 3 would be: "if variable X is related to delinquency when there is no variation in variable T, then variable T is not a cause of delinquency." In order for this criterion to be applicable, there must be some residual variation in delinquency after T has had its effect.

Although both forms of this criterion fairly represent the reasoning involved in some claims of noncausality, and although both are false, the less explicit version in the text is superficially more plausible. This inverse relation between explicitness and plausibility is one reason for the kind of methodological explication presented here.

[10] Bernard Lander, *Towards an Understanding of Juvenile Delinquency*, New York: Columbia University Press, 1954, p. 32. Italics in original. An alternative interpretation of the assumptions implicit in this quotation is presented in the discussion of criterion 6, below.

white rate would never be greater than the Negro rate (fact 3). Thus in order for race to have "any" causal significance, all Negroes must be delinquents (or all whites nondelinquents). In short, race must be perfectly related to delinquency.[11]

Now if an independent variable and a dependent variable are perfectly associated,[12] no other independent variable is needed: that is, perfect association implies single causation, and less-than-perfect association implies multiple causation. Rejecting as causes of delinquency those variables whose association with delinquency is less than perfect thus implies rejecting the principle of multiple causation. Although there is nothing sacred about this principle, at least at the level of empirical research it is more viable than the principle of single causation. All studies show that more than one independent variable is needed to account for delinquency. In this field, as in others, perfect

relations are virtually unknown. The researcher who finds a less-than-perfect relation between variable X and delinquency should not conclude that X is not a cause of delinquency, but merely that it is not the *only* cause.[13]

For example, suppose that tables like the following have been found for variables A, B, C, and D as well as for X:

Table 1

Delinquency by X, Where X Is Neither a Necessary Nor a Sufficient Condition for Delinquency, But May Be One of Several Causes

	X	Not X
Delinquent	40	20
Nondelinquent	60	80

The researcher using the perfect relation criterion would have to conclude that none of the causes of delinquency has yet been discovered. Indeed, this criterion would force him to conclude that there are *no causes* of delinquency except *the* cause. The far-from-perfect relation between variable X and delinquency in the table above leads him to reject variable X as a cause of delinquency. Since variables A, B, C, and D are also far from perfectly related to delinquency, he must likewise reject them. Since it is unlikely that *the* cause of delinquency will ever be discovered by quantitative research, the researcher who accepts the perfect relation criterion should come to believe that such research is useless: all it can show is that there are *no* causes of delinquency.

False Criterion 1-a. Insofar as a factor is not a necessary condition for delinquency, it is not a cause of delinquency.

The "not necessary" (and of course the "not sufficient") argument against causation is a variant of the "perfect relation" criterion. A factor is a necessary condition for delinquency if it must be present for delinquency to occur — e.g., knowledge of the operation of an auto-

---

[11] Strictly speaking, in this quotation Lander does not demand that race be perfectly related to delinquency, but only that all Negroes be delinquents (the sufficient conditions of criterion 1-b). Precedent for the "perfect relation" criterion of causality appears in a generally excellent critique of crime and delinquency research by Jerome Michael and Mortimer J. Adler published in 1933: "There is still another way of saying that none of the statistical findings derived from the quantitative data yields answers to etiological questions. The findings themselves show that every factor which can be seen to be in some way associated with criminality is also associated with non-criminality, and also that criminality is found in the absence of every factor with which it is also seen to be associated. In other words, what has been found is merely additional evidence of what we either knew or could have suspected, namely, that there is a plurality of related factors in this field." *Crime, Law and Social Science*, New York: Harcourt, Brace, p. 53.

[12] "Perfect association" here means that all of the cases fall into the main diagonal of the table, that (in the 2×2 table) the independent variable is both a necessary and a sufficient cause of the dependent variable. Less stringent definitions of perfect association are considered in the following paragraphs. Since Lander deals with ecological correlations, he could reject race as a cause of delinquency even if it were perfectly related to delinquency at the census tract level, since the ecological and the individual correlations are not identical.

[13] We are assuming that the causal order and lack of spuriousness criteria are satisfied.

mobile is a necessary condition for auto theft (although all individuals charged with auto theft need not know how to drive a car). In Table 2 the independent variable X is a necessary (but not sufficient [14]) condition for delinquency.

Table 2
Delinquency by X, Where X Is a Necessary But Not Sufficient Condition for Delinquency

	X	Not X
Delinquent	67	0
Nondelinquent	33	100

The strongest statement we can find in the work cited by the Children's Bureau in support of the contention that the broken home is not a cause of delinquency is the following:

We can leave this phase of the subject by stating that the phenomenon of the physically broken home is a cause of delinquent behavior is, in itself, not so important as was once believed. In essence, it is not that the home is broken, but rather that the home is inadequate, that really matters.[15]

This statement suggests that the broken home is not a necessary condition for delinquency (delinquents may come from intact but "inadequate" homes). The variable with which the broken home is compared, inadequacy, has all the attributes of a necessary condition for delinquency: a home that is "adequate" with respect to the prevention of delinquency will obviously produce no delinquent children. If, as appears to be the case, the relation between inadequacy and delinquency is a matter of definition, the comparison of this relation with

the relation between the broken home and delinquency is simply an application of the illegitimate "necessary conditions" criterion. Compared to a necessary condition, the broken home is "not so important." Compared to some (or some *other*) *measure* of inadequacy, however, the broken home may be very important. For that matter, once "inadequacy" is empirically defined, the broken home may turn out to be one of its important causes. Thus the fact that the broken home is not a necessary condition for delinquency does not justify the statement that the broken home is "not [a cause of delinquency] in the sense that if [it] were removed delinquency would decline."[16]

False Criterion 1-b. Insofar as a factor is not a sufficient condition for delinquency, it is not a cause of delinquency.

A factor is a sufficient condition for delinquency if its presence is invariably followed by delinquency. Examples of sufficient conditions are hard to find in empirical research.[17] The nearest one comes to such conditions in delinquency research is in the use of predictive devices in which several factors taken together are virtually sufficient for delinquency.[18] (The

---

[14] To say that X is a necessary condition for delinquency means that all delinquents are X (i.e., that the cell in the upper right of this table is zero); to say that X is a sufficient condition for delinquency implies that all X's are delinquent (i.e., that the cell in the lower left is zero); to say that X is a necessary and sufficient condition for delinquency means that all X's and no other persons are delinquent (i.e., that both cells in the minor diagonal of this table are zero).

[15] Teeters and Reinemann, *op. cit.*, p. 154.

[16] *Report to The Congress*, p. 21. Two additional illegitimate criteria of causality listed above are implicit in the quotation from Teeters and Reinemann. "Inadequacy of the home" could be treated as an intervening variable which interprets the relation between the broken home and delinquency (criterion 4) or as a theoretical variable of which the broken home is an indicator (criterion 5). These criteria are discussed below.

[17] In his *Theory of Collective Behavior* (New York: The Free Press of Glencoe, 1963), Neil J. Smelser suggests sets of necessary conditions for riots, panics, and other forms of collective behavior; in this theory the entire set of necessary conditions for any one form of behavior is a sufficient condition for that form to occur.

[18] In the Gluecks' prediction table, those with scores of 400 or more have a 98.1% chance of delinquency. However, as Reiss has pointed out, the Gluecks *start* with a sample that is 50% delinquent. Had they started with a sample in which only 10% were delinquent, it would obviously have been more difficult to approach sufficiency. Sheldon Glueck and Eleanor Glueck, *Unraveling Juvenile Delinquency*, Cambridge: Harvard University Press, 1950, pp. 260–262; Albert J. Reiss, Jr., "Unraveling Juvenile Delinquency. II. An Ap-

fact that several variables are required even to approach sufficiency is of course one of the strongest arguments in favor of multiple causation.) Since sufficient conditions are rare, this unrealistic standard can be used against almost any imputation of causality.

First, however, let us make our position clear on the question. Poverty per se is not a cause of delinquency or criminal behavior; this statement is evidenced by the courage, fortitude, honesty, and moral stamina of thousands of parents who would rather starve than steal and who inculcate this attitude in their children. Even in the blighted neighborhoods of poverty and wretched housing conditions, crime and delinquency are simply nonexistent among most residents.[19]

Many mothers, and some fathers, who have lost their mates through separation, divorce, or death, are doing a splendid job of rearing their children.[20]

Our point of view is that the structure of the family *itself* does not cause delinquency. For example, the fact that a home is broken does not cause delinquency, but it is more difficult for a single parent to provide material needs, direct controls, and other important elements of family life.[21]

The error here lies in equating "not sufficient" with "not *a* cause." Even if every delinquent child were from an impoverished (or broken) home — that is, even if this factor were a necessary condition for delinquency — it would still be possible to show that poverty is not a sufficient condition for delinquency.

In order for the researcher to conclude that poverty is a cause of delinquency, it is not necessary that all or most of those who are poor become delinquent.[22] If it were, causal variables would be virtually impossible to find.

From the standpoint of social action, this criterion can be particularly unfortunate. Suppose that poverty were a necessary but not sufficient condition for delinquency, as in Table 2. Advocates of the "not sufficient" criterion would be forced to conclude that, if poverty were removed, delinquency would not decline. As the table clearly shows, however, removal of poverty under these hypothetical conditions would *eliminate* delinquency!

To take another example, Wootton reports Carr-Saunders as finding that 28% of his delinquents and 16% of his controls came from broken homes and that this difference held in both London and the provinces. She quotes Carr-Saunders' "cautious" conclusion:

We can only point out that the broken home may have some influence on delinquency, though since we get control cases coming from broken homes, we cannot assert that there is a direct link between this factor and delinquency.[23]

Carr-Saunders' caution apparently stems from the "not sufficient" criterion, for unless the broken home is a sufficient condition for delinquency, there must be control cases (nondelinquents) from broken homes.

In each of these examples the attack on causality rests on the numbers in a single table. Since all of these tables show a non-zero relation, it seems to us that these researchers have misinterpreted the platitude "correlation is not causation." To us, this platitude means that one must go beyond the observed fact of association in order to demonstrate causality. To those who employ one or another variant of the perfect relation criterion, it appears to mean that there is something suspect in any numerical demonstration of association. Instead of being the first evidence for causality, an observed association becomes evidence against causality.

False Criterion 2. Insofar as a factor is not "characteristic" of delinquents, it is not a cause of delinquency.

Many correlation studies in delinquency may conquer all these hurdles and still fail to sat-

praisal of the Research Methods," *American Journal of Sociology*, 57:2, 1951, pp. 115–120.

[19] Teeters and Reinemann, *op. cit.*, p. 127.

[20] *Ibid.*, p. 154.

[21] F. Ivan Nye, *Family Relationships and Delinquent Behavior*, New York: John Wiley, 1958, p. 34. Italics in original.

[22] We are of course assuming throughout this discussion that the variables in question meet what we consider to be legitimate criteria of causality.

[23] Barbara Wootton, *Social Science and Social Pathology*, New York: Macmillan, 1959, p. 118.

isfy the vigorous demands of scientific causation. Frequently a group of delinquents is
found to differ in a statistically significant way
from a nondelinquent control group with
which it is compared. Nevertheless, the differentiating trait may not be at all characteristic
of the delinquent group. Suppose, for example,
that a researcher compares 100 delinquent girls
with 100 nondelinquent girls with respect to
broken homes. He finds, let us say, that 10%
of the nondelinquents come from broken
homes, whereas this is true of 30% of the delinquent girls. Although the difference between the two groups is significant, the researcher has not demonstrated that the broken
home is characteristic of delinquents. The fact
is that 70% of them come from unbroken
homes. Again, ecological studies showing a
high correlation between residence in interstitial areas and delinquency, as compared with
lower rates of delinquency in other areas,
overlook the fact that even in the most marked
interstitial area nine tenths of the children do
not become delinquent.[24]

This argument is superficially plausible. If a
factor is not characteristic, then it is apparently not important. But does "characteristic"
mean "important"? No. Importance refers to
the variation accounted for, to the size of the
association, while "being characteristic" refers
to only one of the conditional distributions
(rows or columns) (in the table on page 88
X is characteristic of delinquents because more
than half of the delinquents are X). This is not
enough to infer association, any more than the
statement that 95% of the Negroes in some
sample are illiterate can be taken to say anything about the association between race and
illiteracy in that sample without a corresponding statement about the whites. Although Negroes are predominantly ("characteristically")
illiterate, race has no effect on literacy, for the
whites are equally likely to be illiterate.

	Race	
	Negro	White
Literate	5	5
Illiterate	95	95

[24] Milton L. Barron, *The Juvenile in Delinquent Society*, New York: Knopf, 1954, pp. 86–87.

More generally, even if a trait characterizes
a large proportion of delinquents and also
characterizes a large proportion of nondelinquents, it may be less important as a cause of
delinquency than a trait that characterizes a
much smaller proportion of delinquents. The
strength of the relation is what matters — that
is, the *difference* between delinquents and
nondelinquents in the proportion having the
trait (in other words, the difference between
the conditional distributions of the dependent
variable). In the quotation from Barron at the
beginning of this section, would it make any
difference for the imputation of causality if
the proportions coming from broken homes
had been 40% for the nondelinquents and 60%
for the delinquents, instead of 10 and 30%?
Although broken homes would now be "characteristic" of delinquents, the percentage difference is the same as before. And the percentage difference would still be the same if the
figures were 60 and 80%, but now broken
homes would be characteristic of *both* nondelinquents and delinquents!

The "characteristic" criterion is thus statistically irrelevant to the task of assessing causality. It also appears to be inconsistent with
the principle of multiple causation, to which
Barron elsewhere subscribes.[25] If delinquency
is really traceable to a plurality of causes,
then some of these causes may well "characterize" a minority of delinquents. Furthermore,
this "inconsistency" is empirical as well as
logical: in survey data taken from ordinary
populations it is rare to find that any group
defined by more than three traits includes a
majority of the cases.[26]

[25] *Ibid.*, pp. 81–83.
[26] There are two reasons for this: the less-than-
perfect association between individual traits and
the fact that few traits are simple dichotomies. Of
course, it is always possible to take the logical
complement of a set of traits describing a minority
and thus arrive at a set of traits that does "characterize" a group, but such artificial combinations
have too much internal heterogeneity to be meaningful. What, for example, can one say of the
delinquents who share the following set of traits:
not Catholic, not middle class, not of average intelligence?

The problem of "characteristic" traits arises only

False Criterion 3. If a relation between an independent variable and delinquency is found for a single value of a situational or contextual factor, that situational or contextual factor cannot be a cause of delinquency.

No investigation can establish the causal importance of variables that do not vary. This obvious fact should be even more obvious when the design of the study restricts it to single values of certain variables. Thus the researcher who restricts his sample to white Mormon boys cannot use his data to determine the importance of race, religious affiliation, or sex as causes of delinquency. Nevertheless, students of delinquency who discover either from research or logical analysis that an independent variable is related to delinquency in certain situations or contexts often conclude that these situational or contextual variables are not important causes of delinquency. Since personality or perceptual variables are related to delinquency in most kinds of social situations, social variables have suffered most from the application of this criterion:

Let the reader assume that a boy is returning home from school and sees an unexpected group of people at his doorstep, including a policeman, several neighbors, and some strangers. He may suppose that they have gathered to welcome him and congratulate him as the winner of a nationwide contest he entered several months ago. On the other hand, his supposition may be that they have discovered that he was one of several boys who broke some windows in the neighborhood on Halloween. If his interpretation is that they are a welcoming group he will respond one way; but if he feels that they have come to "get" him, his response is likely to be quite different. In either case he may be entirely wrong in his interpretation. *The important point, however, is that the external situation is relatively unimportant.*

Rather, what the boy himself thinks of them [it] and how he interprets them [it] is the crucial factor in his response.[27]

There are at least three independent "variables" in this illustration: (1) the external situation — the group at the doorstep; (2) the boy's past behavior — entering a contest, breaking windows, etc.; (3) the boy's interpretation of the group's purpose. As Barron notes, variable (3) is obviously important in determining the boy's response. It does not follow from this, however, that variables (1) and (2) are unimportant. As a matter of fact, it is easy to see how variable (2), the boy's past behavior, could influence his interpretation of the group's purpose and thus affect his response. If he had not broken any windows in the neighborhood, for example, it is less likely that he would think that the group had come to "get" him, and it is therefore less likely that his response would be one of fear. Since Barron does not examine the relation between this situational variable and the response, he cannot make a legitimate statement about its causal importance.

Within the context of this illustration it is impossible to relate variable (1), the group at the doorstep, to the response. The reason for this is simple: this "variable" does not vary — it is fixed, given, constant. In order to assess the influence of a group at the doorstep (the external situation) on the response, it would be necessary to compare the effects of groups varying in size or composition. Suppose that there was no group at the doorstep. Presumably, if this were the case, the boy would feel neither fear nor joy. Barron restricts his examination of the relation between interpretation and response to a single situation, and on this basis concludes that what appears to be a necessary condition for the response is *relatively unimportant!*

In our opinion, it is sometimes better to say nothing about the effects of a variable whose range is restricted than to attempt to reach some idea of its importance with inadequate

---

when the dependent variable is inherently categorical (Democratic; member of a gang, an athletic club, or neither) or is treated as one (performs none, a few, or many delinquent acts). In other words, this criterion arises only in tabular analysis, not where some summary measure is used to describe the association between variables.

[27] Barron, *op. cit.*, pp. 87–88. Italics added.

data. The first paragraph of the following statement suggests that its authors are completely aware of this problem. Nevertheless, the concluding paragraphs are misleading:

We recognized that the Cambridge-Somerville area represented a fairly restricted socioeconomic region. Although the bitter wave of the depression had passed, it had left in its wake large numbers of unemployed. Ten years after its onset, Cambridge and Somerville still showed the effects of the depression. Even the best neighborhoods in this study were lower middle class. Consequently, our results represent only a section of the class structure.

In our sample, however [*therefore*], there is not a *highly* significant relation between "delinquency areas," or subcultures, and crime. If we had predicted that every child who lived in the poorer Cambridge-Somerville areas would have committed a crime, we would have been more often wrong than right. Thus, current sociological theory, by itself, cannot explain why the majority of children, even those from the "worst" areas, never became delinquent.

Social factors, in our sample, were not strongly related to criminality. The fact that a child's neighborhood did not, by itself, exert an independently important influence may [*should not*] surprise social scientists. Undeniably, a slum neighborhood can mold a child's personality — but apparently only if other factors in his background make him susceptible to the sub-culture that surrounds him.[28]

False Criterion 4. If a relation is observed between an independent variable and delinquency and if a psychological variable is sug- gested as intervening between these two variables, then the original relation is not causal.

There appear to be two elements in this causal reasoning. One is the procedure of *conjectural interpretation*.[29] The other is the confusion between *explanation*, in which an antecedent variable "explains away" an observed relation, and *interpretation*, in which an intervening variable links more tightly the two variables of the original relation. In short, the vanishing of the partial relations is assumed, not demonstrated, and this assumed statistical configuration is misconstrued.

This criterion is often encountered in a subtle form suggestive of social psychological theory:

The appropriate inference from the available data, on the basis of our present understanding of the nature of cause, is that whether poverty, broken homes, or working mothers are factors which cause delinquency depends upon the meaning the situation has for the child.[30]

It now appears that neither of these factors [the broken home and parental discipline] is so important in itself as is the child's reaction to them.[31]

A factor, whether personal or situational, does not become a cause unless and until it first becomes a motive.[32]

The appropriate inference about whether some factor is a cause of delinquency depends on the relation between that factor and delinquency (and possibly on other factors causally

---

[28] William McCord and Joan McCord, *Origins of Crime*, New York: Columbia University Press, 1959, pp. 71 and 167.
In a study restricted to "known *offenders*" in which the dependent variable is the *seriousness* of the *first offense* Richard S. Sterne concludes: "Delinquency cannot be fruitfully controlled through broad programs to prevent divorce or other breaks in family life. The prevention of these would certainly decrease unhappiness, but it would not help to relieve the problem of delinquency." Since the range of the dependent variable, delinquency, is seriously reduced in a study restricted to *offenders*, such conclusions can not follow from the data. *Delinquent Conduct and Broken Homes*, New Haven: College and University Press, 1964, p. 96.

[29] Like conjectural explanation, this is an argument, unsupported by statistical data, that the relation between two variables would vanish if the effects of a third variable were removed; here, however, the third variable "intervenes" causally between the original independent and dependent variables.
[30] Sophia Robison, *Juvenile Delinquency*, New York: Holt, Rinehart and Winston, 1961, p. 116.
[31] Paul W. Tappan, *Juvenile Delinquency*, New York: McGraw-Hill, 1949, p. 135.
[32] Sheldon and Eleanor Glueck, *Family Environment and Delinquency*, Boston: Houghton-Mifflin, 1962, p. 153. This statement is attributed to Bernard Glueck. No specific reference is provided.

prior to both of these). All that can be determined about meanings, motives, or reactions that *follow from* the factor and *precede* delinquency can only strengthen the conclusion that the factor is a cause of delinquency, not weaken it.

A different example may make our argument clearer. *Given* the bombing of Pearl Harbor, the crucial factor in America's response to this situation was its interpretation of the meaning of this event. Is one to conclude, therefore, that the bombing of Pearl Harbor was relatively unimportant as a cause of America's entry into World War II? Intervening variables of this type are no less important than variables further removed from the dependent variable, but to limit analysis to them, to deny the importance of objective conditions, is to distort reality as much as do those who ignore intervening subjective states.[33]

This kind of mistaken causal inference can occur long after the original analysis of the data. A case in point is the inference in the *Report to The Congress* [34] that irregular employment of the mother does not cause delinquency. This inference appears to come from misreading Maccoby's reanalysis of the Gluecks' results.

Maccoby begins by noting that "the association between irregular employment and delinquency suggests at the outset that it may not be the mother's absence from home per se which creates adjustment problems for the children. Rather, the cause may be found in the conditions of the mother's employment or the family characteristics leading a mother to undertake outside employment." [35] She then lists several characteristics of the sporadically working mothers that might account for the greater likelihood of their children becoming delinquent. For example, many had a history of delinquency themselves. In our opinion, such conjectural "explanations" are legitimate guides to further study but, as Maccoby says, they leave the causal problem unsettled:

It is a moot question, therefore, whether it is the mother's sporadic employment as such which conduced to delinquency in the sons; equally tenable is the interpretation that the emotionally disturbed and antisocial characteristics of the parents produced both a sporadic work pattern on the part of the mother and delinquent tendencies in the son.[36]

Maccoby's final step, and the one of greatest interest here, is to examine simultaneously the effects of mother's employment and mother's supervision on delinquency. From this examination she concludes:

It can be seen that, whether the mother is working or not, the quality of the supervision her child receives is paramount. If the mother remains at home but does not keep track of where her child is and what he is doing, he is far more likely to become a delinquent (within this highly selected sample), than if he is closely watched. Furthermore, if a mother who works does arrange adequate care for the child in her absence, he is no more likely to be delinquent . . . than the adequately supervised child of a mother who does not work. But there is one more lesson to be learned from the data: among the working mothers, a majority did not in fact arrange adequate supervision for their children in their absence.[37]

It is clear, then, that regardless of the mother's employment status, supervision is related to delinquency. According to criterion 3, employment status is therefore not a cause of delinquency. It is also clear that when supervision is held relatively constant, the relation

[33] "Write your own life history, showing the factors *really* operative in your coming to college, contrasted with the external social and cultural factors of your situation." Barron, *op. cit.*, p. 89.

[34] *Op. cit.*, p. 21.

[35] Eleanor E. Maccoby, "Effects upon Children of Their Mothers' Outside Employment," in Norman W. Bell and Ezra F. Vogel (eds.), *A Modern Introduction to The Family*, Glencoe, Illinois: The Free Press, 1960, p. 523. In fairness to the Children's Bureau report, it should be mentioned that Maccoby's argument against the causality of the relation between mother's employment and

delinquency has a stronger tone in the article cited there (see footnote 7) than in the version we have used as a source of quotations.

[36] *Ibid.*

[37] *Ibid.*, p. 524.

between employment status and delinquency disappears. According to criterion 4, employment status is therefore *not* a cause of delinquency. This appears to be the reasoning by which the authors of the *Report to The Congress* reject mother's employment as a cause of delinquency. But criterion 3 ignores the association between employment status and delinquency and is thus irrelevant. And criterion 4 treats what is probably best seen as an intervening variable as an antecedent variable and is thus a misconstruction of a legitimate criterion. Actually, the evidence that allows the user of criterion 4 to reach a conclusion of noncausality is, at least psychologically, evidence of *causality*. The disappearance of the relation between mother's employment and delinquency when supervision is held relatively constant makes the "How?" of the original relation clear: working mothers are less likely to provide adequate supervision for their children, and inadequately supervised children are more likely to become delinquent.

False Criterion 5. Measurable variables are not causes.

In tract 11–1, and to a lesser extent in tract 11–2, the actual rate [of delinquency] is lower than the predicted rate. We suggest that these deviations [of the actual delinquency rate from the rate predicted from home ownership] point up the danger of imputing a causal significance to an index, per se, despite its statistical significance in a prediction formula. It is fallacious to impute causal significance to home ownership as such. In the present study, the author hypothesizes that the extent of home-ownership is probably highly correlated with, and hence constitutes a measure of community anomie.[38]

As a preventive, "keeping youth busy," whether through compulsory education, drafting for service in the armed forces, providing fun through recreation, or early employment, can, at best, only temporarily postpone behavior that is symptomatic of more deep-seated or culturally oriented factors. . . . Merely "keeping idle hands occupied" touches only surface symptoms and overlooks underlying factors

known to generate norm-violating behavior patterns.[39]

The criterion of causation that, in effect, denies causal status to measurable variables occurs frequently in delinquency research. In the passages above, home ownership, compulsory education, military service, recreation, and early employment are all called into question as causes of delinquency. In their stead one finds as causes anomie and "deepseated or culturally oriented factors." The appeal to abstract as opposed to more directly measurable variables appears to be especially persuasive. Broad general concepts embrace such a variety of directly measurable variables that their causal efficacy becomes almost self evident. The broken home, for example, is no match for the "inadequate" home:

[T]he physically broken home as a cause of delinquent behavior is, in itself, not so important as was once believed. In essence, it is not that the home is broken, but rather that the home is inadequate, that really matters.[40]

The persuasiveness of these arguments against the causal efficacy of measurable variables has two additional sources: (1) their logical form resembles that of the legitimate criterion "lack of spuriousness"; (2) they are based on the seemingly obvious fact that "operational indices" (measures) do not *cause* the variations in other operational indices. Both of the following arguments can thus be brought against the assertion that, for example, home ownership causes delinquency.

Anomie causes delinquency. Home ownership is a measure of anomie. Anomie is thus the "source of variation" in both home ownership and delinquency. If the effects of anomie were removed, the observed relation between home ownership and delinquency would disappear. This observed relation is thus causally spurious.

Home ownership is used as an indicator of

---

[38] Lander, *op. cit.*, p. 71.

[39] William C. Kvaraceus and Walter B. Miller, *Delinquent Behavior: Culture and the Individual*, National Education Association, 1959, p. 39.
[40] Teeters and Reinemann, *op. cit.*, p. 154.

anomie, just as responses to questionnaire items are used as indicators of such things as "authoritarianism," "achievement motivation," and "religiosity." No one will argue that the responses to items on a questionnaire *cause* race hatred, long years of self-denial, or attendance at religious services. For the same reason, it is erroneous to think that home ownership "causes" delinquency.

Both of these arguments beg the question. As mentioned earlier, conjectural explanations, although legitimate guides to further study, leave the causal problem unsettled. The proposed "antecedent variable" may or *may not* actually account for the observed relation.

Our argument assumes that the proposed antecedent variable is directly measurable. In the cases cited here it is not. If the antecedent variable logic is accepted as appropriate in these cases, all relations between measurable variables and delinquency may be said to be causally spurious. If anomie can "explain away" the relation between *one* of its indicators and delinquency, it can explain away the relations between *all* of its indicators and delinquency.[41] No matter how closely a given indicator measures anomie, the indicator is not anomie, and thus not a cause of delinquency. The difficulty with these conjectural explanations is thus not that they may be false, but that they are *non-falsifiable*.[42]

The second argument against the causality of measurable variables overlooks the following point: it is one thing to use a measurable variable as an indicator of another, not directly measurable, variable; it is something else

again to assume that the measurable variable is *only* an indicator. Not owning one's home may indeed be a useful indicator of anomie; it may, at the same time, be a potent cause of delinquency in its own right.

The user of the "measurable variables are not causes" criterion treats measurable variables as epiphenomena. He strips these variables of all their causal efficacy (and of all their meaning) by treating them merely as indexes, and by using such words as *per se, as such*, and *in itself*.[43] In so doing, he begs rather than answers the important question: Are these measurable variables causes of delinquency?

False Criterion 6. If the relation between an independent variable and delinquency is conditional upon the value of other variables, the independent variable is not a cause of delinquency.

The rates of Negro delinquency also vary as widely as do the white rates indicating large differences in behavior patterns that are not a function or effect of race per se. It is also of interest to note that in at least 10 percent of the districts with substantial Negro juvenile populations, the Negro delinquency rate is lower than the corresponding white rate.[44]

The appropriate inference from the available data, on the basis of our present understanding of the nature of cause, is that whether poverty, broken homes, or working mothers are factors which cause delinquency depends upon the meaning the situation has for the child.[45]

Both of these quotations make the same point: the association between an independent variable and delinquency depends on the value of a third variable. The original two-variable relation thus becomes a three-variable conditional relation. In the first quotation, the relation between race and delinquency is shown

---

[41] As would be expected, Lander succeeds in disposing of all the variables in his study as causes of delinquency — even those he says at some points are *"fundamentally* related to delinquency."

[42] While Lander throws out his measurable independent variables in favor of anomie, Kvaraceus and Miller throw out their measurable dependent variable in favor of "something else." "Series of norm-violating behaviors, which run counter to legal codes and which are engaged in by youngsters [delinquency], are [is] only symptomatic of something else in the personal make-up of the individual, in his home and family, or in his cultural milieu." *Op. cit.*, p. 34. The result is the same, as the quotations suggest.

[43] The appearance of these terms in the literature on delinquency almost invariably signals a logical difficulty.

[44] Lander, *op. cit.*, p. 32. This statement is quoted more fully above (see footnote 10).

[45] See footnote 30.

to depend on some (unspecified) property of census tracts. In the second quotation, each of three variables is said to "interact" with "the meaning of the situation" to cause delinquency.

One consequence of showing that certain variables are only conditionally related to delinquency is to invalidate what Albert K. Cohen has aptly named "the assumption of intrinsic pathogenic qualities" — the assumption that the causal efficacy of a variable is, or can be, independent of the value of other causal variables.[46] Invalidating this assumption, which Cohen shows to be widespread in the literature on delinquency, is a step in the right direction. As many of the quotations in this paper suggest, however, the discovery that a variable has no *intrinsic* pathogenic qualities has often led to the conclusion that it has no pathogenic qualities at all. The consequences of accepting this conclusion can be shown for delinquency research and theory.

Cloward and Ohlin's theory that delinquency is the product of lack of access to legitimate means *and* the availability of illegitimate means assumes, as Palmore and Hammond have shown,[47] that each of these states is a necessary condition for the other — i.e., that lack of access to legitimate and access to illegitimate means "interact" to produce delinquency. Now, if "conditional relations" are non-causal, neither lack of access to legitimate nor the availability of illegitimate means is a cause of delinquency, and one could manipulate either without affecting the delinquency rate.

Similarly absurd conclusions could be drawn from the results of empirical research in delinquency, since all relations between independent variables and delinquency are at least conceivably conditional (the paucity of empirical generalizations produced by delinquency research as a whole shows that most of these relations have already actually been found to be conditional).[48]

Although conditional relations may be conceptually or statistically complicated and therefore psychologically unsatisfying, their discovery does not justify the conclusion that the variables involved are not causes of delinquency. In fact, the researcher who would grant causal status only to unconditional relations will end by granting it to none.

Any one of the criteria of causality discussed in this paper makes it possible to question the causality of most of the relations that have been or could be revealed by quantitative research. Some of these criteria stem from perfectionistic interpretations of legitimate criteria, others from misapplication of these legitimate criteria. Still others, especially the argument that a cause must be "characteristic" of delinquents, appear to result from practical considerations. (It would indeed be valuable to the practitioner if he could point to some easily identifiable trait as the "hallmark" of the delinquent.) Finally, one of these criteria is based on a mistaken notion of the relation between abstract concepts and measurable variables — a notion that only the former can be the causes of anything.

The implications of these standards of causality for practical efforts to reduce delinquency are devastating. Since nothing that can be pointed to in the practical world is a cause of delinquency (e.g., poverty, broken homes, lack of recreational facilities, working mothers), the practitioner is left with the task of combatting a nebulous "anomie" or an unmeasured "inadequacy of the home"; or else he must change the adolescent's interpretation of the "meaning" of events without at the same time changing the events themselves or the context in which they occur.

[46] "Multiple Factor Approaches," in Marvin E. Wolfgang *et al.* (eds.), *The Sociology of Crime and Delinquency*, New York: John Wiley, 1962, pp. 78–79.

[47] Erdman B. Palmore and Phillip E. Hammond, "Interacting Factors in Juvenile Delinquency," *American Sociological Review*, 29 (December 1964), pp. 848–854.

[48] After reviewing the findings of twenty-one studies as they bear on the relations between twelve commonly used independent variables and delinquency, Barbara Wootton concludes: "All in all, therefore, this collection of studies, although chosen for its comparative methodological merit, produces only the most meager, and dubiously supported generalizations." *Op. cit.*, p. 134.

Mills has suggested that accepting the principle of multiple causation implies denying the possibility of radical change in the social structure.[49] Our analysis suggests that rejecting the principle of multiple causation implies denying the possibility of *any* change in the social structure — since, in this view, nothing causes anything.

[49] C. Wright Mills, "The Professional Ideology of Social Pathologists," *American Journal of Sociology*, 44 (September 1942), pp. 165–180, esp. pp. 171–172.

As a number of the previous selections indicate, "delinquency" is a catchall term encompassing a wide variety of behavior; consequently, the need for an adequate typology of delinquents is widely recognized. The current view is simply that examination either of homogeneous types of offenders or of those who engage in a particular class of behavior would be more productive than investigation of a miscellaneous grab bag of "delinquents." In this view the development of theory requires, as a preliminary step, the development of classifications and typologies (see Clinard and Quinney [1967:1–14]).

Recognizing that efforts to define homogeneous units of behavior are preferable to efforts to account for delinquency as a unitary category of behavior, Rodman and Grams propose a typology of delinquents in this selection. They point out that there are striking similarities in the personal characteristics and family backgrounds of the delinquent types identified theoretically or empirically by sociologists, psychologists, and psychiatrists, an indication of convergence in theory and findings in apparently diverse fields. One of the issues involved in generating a typology is the old one of the definition of "delinquency" to be employed. Rodman and Grams develop their typology on the basis of an implicit definition of "delinquency" in terms of "official discretion," in that their largest subgroup includes one-time offenders who experience police contact. In contrast, in his typological work, Gibbons (1962, 1965) rejects the definition of "delinquency" as behavior likely to be treated as delinquent if known to law-enforcement agencies. Gibbons (1962:238) defines "delinquency" in a way not unlike those who employ the technique of self-reports; he generates his typology on the basis of juvenile behavior "ranging from repetitive, felony-like acts to occasional, minor acts of technically-illegal misbehavior."

In this selection Rodman and Grams discuss three general types — the occasional delinquent, the gang delinquent, and the maladjusted delinquent. Delinquents can be distinguished along at least three dimensions, and these are involved in the types discussed by the authors. Each dimension involves an implicit continuum. Hence, delinquency may range from an occasional to an habitual type of activity; it may involve a single offender, a small clique, or a gang; and it reflects various degrees of adjustment or maladjustment. Rodman and Grams use these three dimensions to generate eight logical types of delinquents. Research is needed to discover the differences in social class, family background, peer-group association, and experience with law-enforcement agencies of these types. Indicating some of the limitations involved in the typological approach, the authors suggest that the potential value of delineating types can be overemphasized.

REFERENCES

Marshall B. Clinard and Richard Quinney, *Criminal Behavior Systems: A Typology* (New York: Holt, Rinehart and Winston, Inc., 1967).

Don C. Gibbons, *Changing the Lawbreaker: The Treatment of Delinquents and Criminals* (Englewood Cliffs, N.J.: Prentice-Hall, Inc., 1965).

——, "Prospects and Problems of Delinquent Typology," *Sociological Inquiry*, 32 (Spring 1962), pp. 235–244.

HYMAN RODMAN
PAUL GRAMS

Types of Delinquents

Many studies of juvenile delinquents and their families and peers have pointed to the fact that there seem to be several fairly well-defined types of delinquents. These various groups can be differentiated in many ways — by type of offense, family background, residence, peer-group relations, personality characteristics, and psychiatric measures such as the development of the ego and superego. Some of the subculture theorists, Cloward and Ohlin (1960) especially, have given much attention to the formation of gangs composed of similar delinquent types. Other writers have pointed to the importance of different treatments for different types of delinquents (Jenkins and Hewitt, 1944). A recent statement by Gibbons (1965) makes a strong case for both the etiological and treatment importance of a typology of delinquency.

Another reason for focusing on delinquent types is to be able to put studies which have dealt solely with one type of delinquent into correct perspective. Any comparison of the

findings of the Gluecks (1950) and Nye (1958), for instance, must take into account the fact that the Gluecks studied lower class incarcerated delinquents while Nye studied a sample of schoolchildren who were rated "most" or "least" delinquent from their responses to a self-report questionnaire.

The number of types delineated by theorists varies. Some make two divisions: gang boys and nongang boys (Wattenberg and Balistrieri, 1950); property offenders and personal offenders (Ferdinand, 1964; Scott, 1959); boys and girls (Wattenberg and Saunders, 1954). Most studies, however, have pointed to three types of juvenile delinquents and three general types will be discussed here.

One important point must be kept in mind. This discussion of delinquent types will be largely a comparison of various findings and theories of sociologists, psychologists, and psychiatrists. The basis for comparing these studies is the striking similarities in personal characteristics and family backgrounds which they assign to the different delinquent types. The seriousness of criminal participation by the delinquents varies greatly from study to study. It seems that this variation is largely a result of community differences; perhaps the seriousness of the delinquent behavior is more

From "Juvenile Delinquency and the Family: A Review and Discussion," in *Juvenile Delinquency and Youth Crime* (Washington, D.C.: U.S. Government Printing Office, 1967), pp. 203–205. Reprinted by permission of the authors.

strongly influenced by the community environment while the extent of participation in delinquency is more strongly influenced by the adolescent's family experiences and his personality. Community variations might be ascribed to the "toleration level" of the neighborhoods, i.e., some delinquent acts may be considered serious in some communities and not so serious in others.

The Occasional Delinquent

Probably the largest subgroup among delinquents appearing before juvenile court or having police contact is one-time offenders charged with minor violations. Usually these delinquents have participated in acts of vandalism or petty theft, generally in a group. These "normal" or casual delinquents have been discussed by several commentators. Reiss (1952), for instance, in one of the earliest sociological studies of delinquent types, found 730 of 1,110 delinquent probationers examined by Cook County court psychiatrists to be "relatively integrated." John W. Kinch (1962), in a more recent study of Washington, D.C., delinquents, called his group of casual delinquents "prosocial." The similarities in the family backgrounds of these delinquents are noticeable. Reiss' "integrated" delinquents came from unbroken homes in which there was little family tension, had average school records and adjustments, and had short, recent court records. Kinch's "prosocial" delinquents came from unbroken, harmonious homes and described themselves as "friendly," "warmhearted," "courteous," and so on. Moreover, Wattenberg and Balistrieri (1952), in a Detroit study of juvenile auto theft (a "middle class delinquency"), found that these delinquents usually came from intact homes and had strong peer-group ties with a gang dedicated to having fun.

Several writers have pointed to types of delinquents in many ways analogous to this description of the occasional delinquent. Cloward and Ohlin (1960), for instance, explain how adolescents in a slum where racketeering or organized gambling flourishes often become assimilated into the existing adult criminal subculture, a process which usually involves normal boys from intact homes. These boys, although delinquent in a legal sense, are not considered as such by the norms of the neighborhood. Spergel (1964) found several of these "organized" slums in New York, and Drake and Cayton (1962) have vividly described the slum rackets and "policy" games of Chicago. Another picture of the occasional delinquent is given by William F. Whyte in "Street Corner Society" (1943), a study of a lower class Italian slum. Whyte's "corner boys" were well socialized to the society they lived in, and although they engaged in occasional "binges" and minor delinquencies, they were usually nondelinquent.

The Gang Delinquent

Most studies of the different types of delinquency have concentrated on the habitual rather than the occasional delinquent. This is the delinquent who generally commits the most serious infractions, is most often sent to a correctional institution, and most often continues in a pattern of semiprofessional criminal behavior as an adult. Once again, the studies by Kinch and Reiss give the best picture of this general type. Reiss (1952) describes the habitual offender as one with a "weak superego." They are loyal gang members from poor residential areas; their families more often are large and broken and contain other delinquent members; they do poorly in school; they have the highest rate of recidivism of the three types Reiss studied. Kinch (1962) termed these delinquents "antisocial" and also found them to be urban gang members coming from large families with lax discipline techniques. Their siblings were often delinquent. The "antisocial" delinquents had records of poor achievement and truancy in school. On a self-description inventory, they described themselves as "smart," "excitable," "stubborn," and not "warmhearted." Kinch indicates the similarity of these self-descriptions to Miller's description (1958) of the "focal concerns" of the lower class — excitement, smartness, toughness and autonomy — and, indeed, probably the best way to describe the habitual delinquent is as a "lower class gang delinquent." Also in keeping with Miller's position is Reiss' (1952,

p. 717) description of this delinquent type: "The defective superego type does not internalize the norms of conventional society, and experiences little sense of guilt over his delinquent acts. Rather, he accepts the content of, and membership in, a delinquent peer culture."

The habitual delinquent has also been identified by other theorists and researchers, although generally in different terms. Lees and Newson (1954), studying the effect of ordinal position in the family on a child's delinquency, discovered a great many intermediates in the delinquent group, most of them gang members. Scott (1959) reported that in his study of delinquency he found two unrelated scales, one of which involved offenses against "anonymous persons or impersonal property," a form which Scott suggested resulted from "normal" socialization to a deviant peer-group.

The property offense-personal offense difference has led some commentators to delineate two kinds of habitual delinquents. Cloward and Ohlin (1960), for example, distinguish between a conflict-oriented and a criminal subculture. Spergel (1964) found two kinds of serious delinquent gangs in New York City slums — a conflict-oriented gang and a theft-oriented gang. Short and Strodtbeck (1965) reported similar kinds in Chicago. Jenkins and Hewitt (1944), in an early psychiatric study of Michigan child guidance clinic patients, divided the serious delinquents into three groups, two of which were the "pseudosocial" gang offender and the "unsocialized" aggressive offender. Both groups suffered from superego defects, but the "pseudosocial" group refrained from conflicts within the gang, and were only aggressive toward outsiders, while the "unsocialized" group had no such inhibitions. And finally, Yablonsky (1962) made a similar distinction when he discussed the "delinquent" (theft-oriented) gang and the "violent" (conflict-oriented) gang.

The Maladjusted Delinquent

The third type of delinquent usually identified is a maladjusted one. His criminal activity stems from personality disturbance rather than gang activity or slum residence. Reiss (1952) called this type the "weak ego" delinquent and

reported the most significant characteristics of this type to be high-tension homes, small families, much school retardation, and "lone" delinquencies. Kinch (1962), naming his maladjusted group "asocial," found its major characteristic to be "early and severe parental rejection." These delinquents also had very poor peer relations and suffered general social isolation. On the self-description inventory that Kinch administered, the "asocial" group saw themselves as "disorderly," "nervous," "confused," and "not dependable," adjectives highly suggestive of pathological disturbance. Other studies have found similar patterns of maladjustment among delinquents. Jenkins and Hewitt (1944) labeled their third group of delinquents "neurotic" and found much parental repression and lack of warmth in the background of the boys of this group. Scott's second dimension of delinquent behavior included offenses against persons who were known to the delinquent, and his explanation of this dimension of delinquency was that it was due to the "abnormal" socialization of children in disturbed families (Scott, 1959). The study by Lees and Newson (1954) found a large number of eldest and only children in the group of serious, lone offenders, and Reiss' study (1952) also found that many of the "weak ego" delinquents were eldest children from small families. An explanation for this finding may be found in Reiss' suggestion that these eldest delinquents are the scapegoats for parental anxieties or marital tensions.

Furthermore, theoretical and observational work done by several "subculture" writers has indicated that there may be a form of delinquent subculture analogous to the maladjusted, individual delinquent. Both Cohen and Short (1958) and Cloward and Ohlin (1960) identify a "retreatist" or drug-using subculture which they suggest arises when adolescents, out of frustration or lack of opportunity, seek to escape reality. Although Spergel (1964) was unable to find a "retreatist" gang in his New York City survey, Short and Strodtbeck (1965) did find one in Chicago.

Understanding that several general types of delinquents exist makes it easier to understand the differences in the various theories that

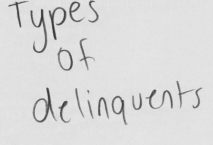

have been ⟨…⟩
chiatric the ⟨…⟩
relevant to ⟨…⟩
justed delin ⟨…⟩
ply primari ⟨…⟩
Some idea ⟨…⟩
can be fou ⟨…⟩
were 730 ' ⟨…⟩
superego," ⟨…⟩
a group of ⟨…⟩
County Ju ⟨…⟩
likely from ⟨…⟩
the 135 "w ⟨…⟩
most seriou ⟨…⟩
the relative ⟨…⟩
types of del ⟨…⟩
related antecedent variables, however, it is extremely difficult to say which group presents the most serious problem to a community interested in reducing delinquency. Further research is needed dealing with delinquency types as variables in order to sift out the varying etiological factors that are involved in different kinds of delinquency.

Dimensions of Delinquency

The three types of delinquents discussed above — the occasional delinquent, the gang delinquent, and the maladjusted delinquent — are not based upon a single dimension. There are, rather, three different dimensions involved, and it is worth spelling these out in order to demonstrate that there are some very rough edges to any classification of delinquent types. Delinquents can be distinguished along at least the following three dimensions: (1) Occasional delinquency-habitual delinquency; (2) gang delinquency-lone delinquency; (3) maladjusted delinquency-adjusted delinquency. The simple classification into occasional, gang, and maladjusted delinquent types makes a number of assumptions about the interrelationships of the three dimensions — for example, that the occasional delinquent is relatively adjusted or that the gang delinquent is a habitual and a relatively adjusted delinquent. But some of the data published about delinquency suggest that matters are not quite so simple. The Yablonsky (1962) material suggests that some gang delinquents may be maladjusted; some

gangs, such as those by Thrasher ⟨…⟩ Whyte (1943), suggest that some ⟨…⟩ency is occasional. If we there⟨…⟩o use the three dimensions to gen⟨…⟩ent types, we come up with eight ⟨…⟩practically no research has been ⟨…⟩he etiology of delinquency that ⟨…⟩ese types, we will do little more ⟨…⟩m. Further, it should be under⟨…⟩ese are merely logical types and ⟨…⟩ed from empirical data.

⟨…⟩djusted-Occasional-Gang Delin⟨…⟩ang consists of members showing ⟨…⟩d personality adjustment, and the ⟨…⟩es of the gang are nondelinquent. Nevertheless, their activities are occasionally delinquent. William F. Whyte (1943) has described a gang of this type.

Type 2. Adjusted-Habitual-Gang Delinquent: The members of the gang show relatively good personality adjustment; their behavior is frequently or habitually delinquent. The accounts by Miller (1958) and Cloward and Ohlin (1960) of gangs manifesting lower class "focal concerns" or oriented to a "criminal subculture" are closely related to this type.

Type 3. Adjusted-Occasional-Lone Delinquent: This type refers to the relatively adjusted adolescent who occasionally engages in delinquency on his own. Many of the delinquents that are turned up on a self-report questionnaire are probably of this type (see Nye, 1958).

Type 4. Adjusted-Habitual-Lone Delinquent: The delinquent is relatively well adjusted and engages in delinquent behavior largely on his own. The "precocious delinquent" who has taken over a "rational" criminal career would fall into this type.

Type 5. Maladjusted-Occasional-Gang Delinquent: This delinquent, as an individual, may have difficulty remaining a member within a delinquent gang of relatively well adjusted boys; delinquent behavior therefore takes place only occasionally. His maladjustment would show up in other areas of behavior more than it does in delinquent behavior.

Type 6. Maladjusted-Habitual-Gang Delinquent: The members of the gang show relatively poor personality adjustment; their behavior is habitually delinquent. The "retreatist subculture" described by Cloward and Ohlin (1960) or the gang as a near-group described by Yablonsky (1962) would fit this pattern.

Type 7. Maladjusted-Occasional-Lone Delinquent: The personality disturbance ordinarily manifests itself in nondelinquent ways and occasionally in lone delinquent acts.

Type 8. Maladjusted-Habitual-Lone Delinquent: Personality maladjustment habitually manifests itself in some type of lone delinquent behavior.

Since relatively little research has been done on the etiology of different types of delinquency, it is easy to be optimistic about the possible gains from further research which does focus upon delinquency types. There are several reasons for tempering such optimism, however. First of all, some of the research done in the past, while it may not have dealt deliberately with delinquent types as a variable, actually did study delinquents of a particular type because of the manner in which the samples were selected. It therefore remains to be seen whether a more deliberate treatment of delinquency types as a variable will lead to a substantial increase in our knowledge of delinquency causation. Secondly, there are many other dimensions of delinquency in addition to the 3 we have elaborated here; adding a fourth dimension would permit us to generate 16 types of delinquency; adding a fifth would lead to 32 types. This would undoubtedly lead to an interesting exercise in classification and naming, but it might not contribute very much to our ability to predict and control delinquency. Thirdly, each of the dimensions represents a continuum, and the typology therefore involves sacrificing the variability in the various dimensions of delinquency. Finally, several research studies cited by Quay (1965, pp. 162–165) suggest that it is necessary to deal with personality dimensions that are related to delinquency rather than with delinquency types. This is because the studies could not place an appreciable number of delinquents into clearly delineated types. In short, focusing upon the existence of delin-

quency types might add some clarity to past and future research on delinquency, but it remains to be seen whether it will also add to our ability to predict and control delinquency.

REFERENCES

Cloward, Richard A., and Lloyd E. Ohlin (1960), *Delinquency and Opportunity*, Glencoe, Ill.: Free Press.

Cohen, Albert K., and James F. Short, Jr. (1958), "Research in Delinquent Subcultures," *Journal of Social Issues*, 14:20–36.

Drake, St. Clair, and Horace R. Cayton (1962), *Black Metropolis*, rev. and enl. ed., New York: Harper & Row.

Ferdinand, Theodore N. (1964), "The Offense Patterns and Family Structures of Urban, Village and Rural Delinquents," *Journal of Criminal Law, Criminology, and Police Science*, 55:86–93.

Gibbons, Don C. (1965), *Changing the Lawbreaker*, Englewood Cliffs, N.J.: Prentice-Hall.

Glueck, Sheldon, and Eleanor Glueck (1950), *Unraveling Juvenile Delinquency*, New York: Commonwealth Fund.

Jenkins, R. L., and Lester Hewitt (1944), "Types of Personality Structure Encountered in Child Guidance Clinics," *American Journal of Orthopsychiatry*, 14:84–94.

Kinch, John W. (1962), "Self-Conceptions of Types of Delinquents," *Sociological Inquiry*, 32:228–234.

Lees, J. P., and L. J. Newson (1954), "Family or Sibship Position and Some Aspects of Juvenile Delinquency," *British Journal of Delinquency*, 5:46–65.

Miller, Walter B. (1958), "Lower Class Culture as a Generating Milieu of Gang Delinquency," *Journal of Social Issues*, 14:5–19.

Nye, F. Ivan (1958), *Family Relationships and Delinquent Behavior*, New York: Wiley.

Quay, Herbert C. (1965), "Personality and Delinquency," chapter in Quay, Herbert C., ed., *Juvenile Delinquency: Research and Theory*, Princeton, N.J.: D. Van Nostrand, pp. 139–166.

Reiss, Albert J., Jr. (1952), "Social Correlates of Psychological Types of Delinquency," *American Sociological Review*, 17:710–718.

Scott, John Finley (1959), "Two Dimensions of Delinquent Behavior," *American Sociological Review*, 24:240–243.

Short, James F., Jr., and Fred L. Strodtbeck (1965), *Group Process and Gang Delinquency*, Chicago: University of Chicago Press.

Spergel, Irving (1964), *Racketville, Slumtown, Haulburg*, Chicago: University of Chicago Press.

Thrasher, Frederic M. (1927), *The Gang*, Chicago: University of Chicago Press.

Wattenberg, William W., and James Balistrieri (1952), "Automobile Theft: A 'Favored-Group'

Delinquency," *American Journal of Sociology*, 57: 575–579.

———, and Frank Saunders (1954), "Sex Differences Among Juvenile Offenders," *Sociology and Social Research*, 39:24–31.

Whyte, William Foote (1943), *Street Corner Society*, Chicago: University of Chicago Press.

Yablonsky, Lewis (1962), *The Violent Gang*, New York: Macmillan.

This article is one example of what the first author in this section, Browning, meant when he wrote that attention to theoretical issues almost inevitably leads to consideration of the conception of human nature underlying our theories. Yet, questions about the nature of man, the nature of society, and the relationship between the individual and the group have concerned writers throughout recorded history. Although a variety of answers have been proposed, the two contrasting sets of ideas in Quinney's article, involving quite different conceptions of the nature of man and society, are important today. Quinney's rationalistic frame of reference is a contemporary statement of the classical position; it is a modification of the orientation of classical thought in religion, politics, philosophy, economics, law, and criminology (see Vold [1958]). In its classical form this perspective holds that a person calculates potential pleasures and pains in advance of action and regulates his behavior in accordance with his calculations; criminal acts result from the deliberate, calculated choice of the individual. The key assumptions in the rationalistic viewpoint are that the criminal is no different from anyone else; he is a free agent who has in the exercise of this freedom chosen to violate the law; and he is personally responsible for the offenses he commits. An Italian scholar, Cesare Bonesana, Marchese de Beccaria, made the principal application of this doctrine to penology in 1764 (Vold [1958:18]; see Monachesi [1955]). It soon became evident that modifications were required, and the doctrine of responsibility was modified to provide mitigation of punishment where limited age, insanity, imbecility, or other conditions which could affect "knowledge and intent" in "criminal" actions existed (Vold [1958:26]). Although these changes might be viewed as comparable to allowing the camel to put his head in the tent, the basic doctrine of the neoclassical school "continued to be that man is a creature guided by reason whose will is free and who therefore is responsible for his acts and who can be controlled by his fear of punishment" (Vold [1958:25]).

Rejection of the rationalistic perspective did not result from continued erosion of the doctrine of responsibility; rather, in the century after Beccaria, a dramatic shift occurred in man's thinking about himself. According to Vold (1958:27), this shift was "of such magnitude that it can well be considered an intellectual revolution. During this century the logic and basic methodology of objective, empirical, and experimental science became well established." Answers to the age-old question regarding the nature of man were phrased in terms of scientific views. Developments in biology, such as the appearance of Darwin's *Descent of Man* in 1871, led to the identification of man with the rest of the animal kingdom. Although man was viewed as more highly evolved than simpler forms of life, he was seen as the same kind of creature as other animal forms. Also, some men were viewed as more highly evolved than others (Vold [1958:27]). These ideas provided the intellectual climate in which Lombroso and his students, particularly Ferri, established what is sometimes called the "positive school of criminology."

In 1876 Cesare Lombroso theorized in *L'uomo delinquente* [The Criminal Man] that criminals are an atavistic phenomenon; that is, he proposed that the physical traits of the criminal are those of primitive man. This hypothesis of physical type was examined in 1913 in *The English Convict* in which Charles Goring reports his monumental analysis of anthropometric measures of more than 3,000 prisoners and various nonrandom segments of the noncriminal population of England and Scotland. Goring's conclusion that the evidence does not support the existence of a physical criminal type was widely accepted.

Matza (1964:3) suggests that in establishing positivistic criminology, Lombroso and Ferri "laid the basic assumptions of criminological thought, and these assumptions persist to this day. Like Ferri, most of us are positivists in that we share the same conceptions of the nature of criminological inquiry and the character of the subject we explore — the criminal actor." Matza's point is that although criminologists rejected Lombroso's theory, they did not reject his positivistic approach and thereby tacitly accepted some of his key assumptions. One of these is important in this discussion. Matza (1964:5) suggests that in seeking scientific status, "positive criminology fashioned an image of man to suit a study of criminal behavior based on scientific determinism. It rejected the view that man exercised freedom, was possessed of reason, and was thus capable of choice." Continuing, Matza distinguishes between determinism as a heuristic principle or guide to the researcher and as a conception of human nature. Although he expresses reservations, Matza allows that the first usage may be appropriate, but as an image of man he rejects the deterministic view as clearly inadequate. This is a useful distinction to keep in mind since Quinney questions whether the positivistic approach limits our understanding of human behavior.

With regard to sociological theory Quinney observes that reliance on structure-functional theory leads to an emphasis on consensus; accompanying the overintegrated conception of society is the overintegrated conception of man. He explores the possibility of viewing man's behavior as voluntary, purposive action, rather than as analogous to chemical particles acted upon rather than acting and, by implication, not responsible for their movements (see Hartung [1965] for a similar perspective). Taking a moderate view, Quinney does not argue for rejection of determinism but offers a conception of man and society which deserves attention.

REFERENCES

Frank E. Hartung, *Crime, Law and Society* (Detroit: Wayne State University Press, 1965).

David Matza, *Delinquency and Drift* (New York: John Wiley and Sons, Inc., 1964).

Elio D. Monachesi, "Pioneers in Criminology: Cesare Beccaria (1738–94)," *Journal of Criminal Law, Criminology and Police Science*, 46 (November–December 1955), pp. 439–449.

George B. Vold, *Theoretical Criminology* (New York: Oxford University Press, 1958).

RICHARD QUINNEY

A Conception of Man and Society for Criminology

It is not unusual, in fact, it is commonplace, that in the development of a body of knowledge a particular mode of thought, while responsible for the discovery and ordering of important facts, is at the same time responsible for the obstruction of equally important truths. This appears especially to be the case in the sociological study of criminal behavior. There has been the overwhelming conception of criminal behavior (and deviant behavior in general) as behavior that is produced by a variety of impersonal, deterministic forces rather than by voluntaristic, purposive action. The former perspective found in much of criminology today results from a particular conception of man and society. The object of this paper is to explore the possibility of an alternative conception of man and society for criminology.

It must be noted that several writers have already made observations that are pertinent to a new conception of crime. The failure to pursue these lines of thought by others can be accounted for in part by the lack of emphasis and sustained argument by the writers. The absence of concrete studies that would demonstrate the utility of these ideas also has impeded new lines of thought. In addition, the uncritical acceptance of current theoretical frames of reference has prevented the development of other perspectives. One recent notable exception — and basic to the arguments presented here — is found in a distinction made by Merton between "nonconforming" and "aberrant" behavior.[1] The nonconformist in contrast to the aberrant (1) announces his dissent publicly, (2) challenges the legitimacy of the norms and laws he violates, (3) aims to change the norms he is denying in practice, (4) is acknowledged by conventional members of the society to depart from prevailing norms for disinterested purposes and not for what he personally can get out of it, and (5) lays claim to a higher morality and to ultimate values rather than to the particular norms of the society. In this sense, sociologists have concentrated attention on aberrant behavior to the almost total neglect of nonconforming behavior.

While my purpose is to offer suggestions for an alternative perspective of man and society in the study of criminal behavior, I do not mean to imply that all criminal behavior can be profitably analyzed within this framework. A commitment to the belief that the study of criminal behavior advances with the delineation and analysis of homogeneous units of behavior prevents me from generalizing about all behavior that is defined as criminal. The suggestions offered here perhaps best apply to a set of crimes that may be variously called

From *Sociological Quarterly*, Spring 1965, pp. 119–127. Reprinted by permission.

[1] Robert K. Merton, "Social Problems and Sociological Theory," in Robert K. Merton and Robert A. Nisbet (eds.), *Contemporary Social Problems* (New York: Harcourt, Brace, 1961), pp. 725–28.

political crime, ideological crime, crime of protest and dissent, philosophical crime, value-laden crime, religious or moral crime, or crime of conscience.[2] It is likely, however, that many of the criminal behaviors already studied in terms of more traditional frameworks may be analyzed to advantage within the perspective provided here.

It is becoming clear that the emphasis in sociological theory in general has been almost solely on one dominant conception of man and society. A pervasive reliance on structural-functional theory has resulted in the tendency to stress consensus of values in a "boundary-maintaining system." As recently noted by Wrong, the consequence has been for the most part a conception of man as a thoroughly conforming creature — the oversocialized conception of man.[3] Accompanying this model of man has been the overintegrated conception of society — a society characterized by stability, harmony, and consensus rather than by change, conflict, and constraint.[4]

The overwhelming use of the oversocialized model of man and the integrated conception of society seems especially obvious in the socio-

logical study of crime. Much of the difficulty in explaining criminal behavior, and deviant behavior in general, can be attributed to the failure to use alternative conceptions of man and society. Because man has been so thoroughly viewed as a creature who is constantly attempting to conform to the norms and values of his society, deviation from these norms and values has become a theoretical problem of gravest concern. The behavior of the criminal is thus usually seen as a result of integrative problems of the society or problems in the socialization of the individual. The criminal as thus portrayed has been driven either by forces and conditions outside of himself (such as structured role conflict) or by aspects of his own irrationality. If, on the other hand, an individualistic and rational conception of man has been used, the criminal has been one who has failed to willfully choose the moral standards of the observer.

This is not to argue, however, that these previous theoretical orientations to man and society are to be abandoned in future studies of crime and that the view presented here — a more rationalistic model of man (with man capable of more than conformity) and a coercion, conflict, change conception of society — is to replace these theories. Rather, a strategy better than the choice of one perspective over the other is one, suggested in a larger context by Bendix and Berger, with an intellectual tradition of its own which views man and society in terms of forces that are linked and opposite at the same time.[5] The use of "paired concepts," as they suggest, which point in opposite directions but are at the same time inextricably linked, should be developed and considered together in any analysis.

Thus, something other than the oversocialized conception of man and the stable conception of society must be given consideration in future theories of criminal behavior. The autonomous nature of man and the nonintegrative aspect of society are necessary compo-

[2] These crimes have been mentioned by Donald J. Newman, "Legal Norms and Criminological Definitions," in Joseph S. Roucek (ed.), *Sociology of Crime* (New York: Philosophical Library, 1961), pp. 71–75; George B. Vold, *Theoretical Criminology* (New York: Oxford University Press, 1958), pp. 299–300; Paul B. Horton and Gerald R. Leslie, *The Sociology of Social Problems* (New York: Appleton-Century-Crofts, 1960), pp. 126–28, and chap. 19; and Mabel A. Elliott, *Crime in Modern Society* (New York: Harper & Brothers, 1952), pp. 179–97.

[3] Dennis H. Wrong, "The Oversocialized Conception of Man in Modern Sociology," *American Sociological Review*, 26:183–93 (Apr. 1961).

[4] Ralf Dahrendorf, "Out of Utopia: Toward a Reorientation of Sociological Analysis," *American Journal of Sociology*, 67:115–27 (Sept. 1958); also see David Lockwood, "Some Remarks on 'The Social System,'" *British Journal of Sociology*, 7:134–46 (June 1956); Barrington Moore, Jr., *Political Power and Social Theory* (Cambridge: Harvard University Press, 1958); Richard A. Schermerhorn, *Society and Power* (New York: Random House, 1961); and Pierre L. Van Den Berghe, "Dialectic and Functionalism: Toward a Theoretical Synthesis," *American Sociological Review*, 28:695–705 (Oct. 1963).

[5] Reinhard Bendix and Bennet Berger, "Images of Society and Problems of Concept Formation in Sociology," in Llewellyn Gross (ed.), *Symposium on Sociological Theory* (Evanston: Row, Peterson, 1959), pp. 92–118.

nents of a balanced perspective in the study of criminal behavior.

A conception of man which views man as a being who is constantly attempting to find rewards, trying to avoid punishment, and desiring to win the approval of his fellows omits an important dimension of man. Man after all, is a reflective being; man alone is capable of considering alternative actions, of breaking from the established social order.[6] Once the individual has an awareness of self, acquired as a member of society, he is able to choose his actions. A purposive, voluntaristic conception of man and his behavior is thus essential to the study of human behavior.[7]

The conception that basic to human social behavior is the attempt to find meaning has an established tradition in sociology. The individual defines himself and gains identity through his relations with others. It also follows that the extent to which a person does conform depends in large measure upon his own self-control.[8] And it is also true that violation of the criminal law may actually be part of the process of finding self-identity. It is thus

against something that the self can emerge.[9]

The ability of the individual to break with the established order is perhaps nowhere better illustrated than in some forms of deviant and criminal behavior. Protest on a large scale can be interpreted as a desire by persons to find meaning, identity, or a "reality world." [10] Dissatisfaction with present values and norms can produce a response by entire groups of people. Much juvenile delinquency can be seen as a reaction of individuals and groups to situations defined as difficult or undesirable.[11] "Political extremism," some of which may be defined as criminal or may result in criminal offenses, appears to be a conscious attempt by individuals to improve particular situations. Violation of the law may be carried out as a protest against policies and conditions that are regarded by some persons as unjust.[12] Behavior that is defined as criminal may at times be the only appropriate means for achieving desired ends.

It is also the case that the pursual of criminal behavior may represent the following of an "ideal" or "utopian" norm, a norm held by many people but rarely realized in actual behavior.[13] The conscientious objector, for ex-

[6] For essentially this conception of man see Peter Berger, *Invitation to Sociology: A Humanistic Perspective* (New York: Doubleday, 1963), chap. 6; and Max Mark, "What Image of Man for Political Science?" *Western Political Quarterly*, 15:593–604 (Dec. 1962).

[7] The "social action" orientation in sociology provides a purposive, voluntaristic conception of behavior that is yet to be seriously considered in the study of criminal behavior: Talcott Parsons, *The Structure of Social Action* (Glencoe: The Free Press, 1949); Florian Znaniecki, *Social Actions* (New York: Farrar and Rinehart, 1936); Robert M. MacIver, *Social Causation* (Boston: Ginn, 1942); and Howard Becker, *Through Values to Social Interpretation* (Durham: Duke University Press, 1950).

[8] Tamotsu Shibutani, *Society and Personality: An Interactionist Approach to Social Psychology* (Englewood Cliffs, N.J.: Prentice-Hall, 1961), especially pp. 60, 91–94, 276–78; Albert J. Reiss, Jr., "Delinquency as the Failure of Personal and Social Controls," *American Sociological Review*, 16:196–206 (Apr. 1951); and Simon Dinitz, Frank R. Scarpitti, and Walter C. Reckless, "Delinquency Vulnerability: A Cross Group and Longitudinal Analysis," *American Sociological Review*, 27:515–17 (Aug. 1962). Also see S. F. Nadel, "Social Control and Self-Regulation," *Social Forces*, 31:265–73 (Mar. 1953).

[9] Erving Goffman, *Asylums* (New York: Doubleday, 1961), pp. 318–20.

[10] Hadley Cantril, *The Psychology of Social Movements* (New York: John Wiley & Sons, 1941); and his *The Politics of Despair* (New York: Basic Books, 1958), especially chap. 1.

[11] Harold W. Pfautz, "Near-Group Theory and Collective Behavior: A Critical Reformulation," *Social Problems*, 9:167–94 (Fall 1961); and Albert K. Cohen, *Delinquent Boys* (Glencoe, Ill.: The Free Press, 1955).

[12] The best recent example of this in the United States is the Negro protest. See Louis Lomax, *The Negro Revolt* (New York: Harper, 1962); also Merrill Proudfoot, *Diary of a Sit-In* (Chapel Hill: University of North Carolina Press, 1962); James W. Vander Zanden, "The Non-Violent Resistance Movement Against Segregation," *American Journal of Sociology*, 68:544–50 (May 1963); Essien Udosen Ession-Udom, *Black Nationalism: A Search for an Identity in America* (Chicago: University of Chicago Press, 1962); and Charles E. Lincoln, *The Black Muslims in America* (Boston: Beacon Press, 1961).

[13] Robin M. Williams, *American Society* (New York: Alfred A. Knopf, 1960), pp. 379–80. Regarding selective law obedience, see Marshall B.

ample, refuses to qualify the moral injunction against killing.[14] The person who is disloyal to his country is nevertheless being true to higher loyalties. The traitor is not disloyal in his own eyes but is loyal to something he regards as more worthy of allegiance.[15] Such criminals are conscientiously following a set of values which differs from that of the political majority.

A conception of man based upon man's ability to reason and choose courses of action allows us to view man himself as changing and becoming rather than merely being.[16] It is only man that builds a culture. The kind of culture he develops shapes to a considerable degree the ability of the human being to be creative. Man may develop the capacity through his culture to have greater freedom of action.[17] He not only is shaped by his physical, social, and cultural experiences, but is able to select what he is to experience and develop. Emerging in contemporary culture is the belief in human possibilities and potential, that man can be realized to a far greater extent.[18] Can a theory of human behavior fail to incorporate that which man now is beginning to think and act in practice?

The deterministic, oversocialized conception of man must be balanced by the facts of man's reason, creativity, freedom of action, autonomy, consciousness, and potential — facts which

require an alternative, not necessarily mutually exclusive, but complementary, conception of man. The criminal, the deviant, may not be produced by impersonal forces so much as he is the mover of events. May not some of our criminals be among the "great men" of history in that they are not only shaped by history but, more so, are the makers of it. "In every age men ask in some form the questions: Who am I? Where do I belong?" [19] The degree of awareness and the emphasis of the questions vary at different periods of time, but may not the questions at some times be answered most effectively through deviant and criminal behavior?

There is need for an alternative conception of society, in relation to criminal behavior, that is consistent with the important dimensions of the nature of the human beings that constitute the society. The oversocialized model of man has usually had associated with it this integrated and stable conception of society. We would suggest that the conflict, change, and constraint conception of society would provide a valuable perspective in combination with the humanistic model of man in the study of criminal behavior. It is suggested that, particularly for the study of criminal behavior, society has another side of reality which has not been considered seriously enough in the sociological study of crime.

The basic assumptions of this conception of society have been outlined by Dahrendorf as follows: (1) Every society is at every point subject to the processes of change — social change is ubiquitous; (2) Every society displays at every point dissensus and conflict — social conflict is ubiquitous; (3) Every element in a society renders a contribution to its change; (4) Every society is based on the coercion of some of its members by others.[20] In this view societies are held together not by consensus only, but by consensus and con-

Clinard, *Sociology of Deviant Behavior* (New York: Holt, Rinehart, and Winston, 1963), pp. 172–74.

[14] Mulford Q. Sibley and Philip E. Jacob, *Conscription of Conscience* (Ithaca, N.Y.: Cornell University Press, 1952); and Alfred Hassler, *The Diary of a Self-Made Convict* (Chicago: Regnery, 1954).

[15] Morton Grodzins, *The Loyal and Disloyal: Social Boundaries of Patriotism and Treason* (Chicago: University of Chicago Press, 1956).

[16] Richard A. Schermerhorn, "Man the Unfinished," *Sociological Quarterly*, 4:5–17 (Winter 1963); and Gordon W. Allport, *Becoming: Basic Considerations for a Psychology of Personality* (New Haven: Yale University Press, 1955).

[17] Herbert J. Muller, *The Uses of the Past* (New York: Oxford University Press, 1952), especially pp. 40–42.

[18] Julian Huxley, *New Bottles for New Wine* (New York: Harper, 1957).

[19] Helen M. Lynd, *On Shame and the Search for Identity* (New York: Harcourt, Brace, 1958), p. 13.

[20] Ralf Dahrendorf, *Class and Class Conflict in Industrial Society* (Stanford, Calif.: Stanford University Press, 1959), p. 162.

straint. Furthermore, values are not only accepted, but are enforced as well. And in the process of coercion and constraint, conflict is generated which, in turn, results in continuous change.

We may submit that this conception of society not only complements the more traditional one but is superior in that it best fits the facts of the phenomena that are associated with crime. In the first place, criminal law must be regarded as an instrument of formal social control whereby an organized effort is made to regulate certain areas of behavior. As such, criminal law is political in that (1) specific rules of conduct are created by a recognized authority, (2) designated officials interpret and enforce the rules, and (3) the code is binding on all persons within a given political unit.[21] The content of the criminal law, in turn, including the kind of conduct prohibited and the nature of the sanctions attached, depends upon the values of those in the society that are in the positions of power to influence legislation, court decisions, and administrative rulings. Furthermore, the realities of the political process operate not only in the formulation of the criminal law but in the interpretation and enforcement of the law as well. The values of those individuals and groups that have the ability to coerce others can enter at any point in establishing the criminality of any individual.[22]

The coercion and change model of society is imperative for understanding the criminal behavior of individuals. The correspondence between what some segments of society define as appropriate and other segments define as deviant and criminal is always tenuous in a changing society. There is no reason to assume widespread agreement throughout a population on what behaviors are defined as appropriate, deviant, or criminal. Such an assumption cannot pass the test of empirical inspection.

Furthermore, criminology, and most of sociology for that matter, has rested on the faith that norms do in fact exist for nearly every conceivable area of human behavior and that these norms provide little flexibility of interpretation.[23] Sociology and criminology, if the purpose is to understand behavior as it actually exists, cannot operate on the assumption that norms exist to regulate all situations, that norms are stable and unchanging, that norms are known to all members of the society, and that norms are interpreted in the same way by all individuals. When the opposite of each of these conditions is recognized, the most difficult task becomes that of explaining conformity, not deviation. Deviation in this conception of society is normal, to be expected, and the most prevalent kind of behavior in society. The problem becomes one of explaining how at certain times in history norms develop and persist with any amount of consensus for a period of time. The astonishing fact is that some persons are *not* deviants and criminals, which calls into question the very use of the term deviant. If norms are problematic, as we suggest, what is usually termed deviant is actually normal or regular and that which the observer tries to label as conforming behavior is really the deviant behavior. Should the sociologist allow the few, the "moral entrepreneurs," [24] to define for him what behavior is deviant and what is not? The answer, of course, is both yes and no, depending upon the purpose of the inquiry and the conception of man and society that is being used in the analysis.

In conclusion, crime and deviation should be viewed as normal and expected phenomena. From a time perspective, crime and deviation

21 See Edwin H. Sutherland and Donald R. Cressey, *Principles of Criminology* (Philadelphia: J. B. Lippincott, 1960), chap. 1; and F. James Davis, "Law as a Type of Social Control," in F. James Davis, Henry F. Foster, Jr., C. Ray Jeffery, and E. Eugene Davis (eds.), *Society and the Law* (New York: The Free Press of Glencoe, 1962), chap. 2.
22 This view is elaborated upon in my article, "Crime in Political Perspective," *American Behavioral Scientist*, 8:19–22 (Dec. 1964).

23 Irving Louis Horowitz, "Consensus, Conflict, and Cooperation: A Sociological Inventory," *Social Forces*, 41:177–88 (Dec. 1962); and Williams, *op. cit.*, pp. 33, 219–24.
24 Howard S. Becker, *Outsiders: Studies in the Sociology of Deviance* (New York: The Free Press of Glencoe, 1963), chap. 8.

are crucial in producing important social changes in a society. A type of behavior which is criminal or deviant at one time may be respected behavior of another time.[25] Thus, the apparent indicators of conflict, deviancy, and instability may be the ingredients of a new social order. Much of a society's criminal behavior initiates, as well as represents, important social changes, changes without which a society might otherwise cease to have any semblance of order.

Finally, any future attempts to explain criminal behavior must be pursued with Mills' warning that man has to be viewed in his particular time and place setting.[26] The meaning of crime can only be understood when the criminal and his behavior are studied in the proper historical context. To divorce crime from its historical context is to deny that crime has any meaning. At every point in the study of crime, a more general perspective has to be retained. A larger social and historical

perspective should be basic strategy in the study of crime. This is not to argue, however, that explanations of criminal behavior can only account for crime in particular historical settings. The formulation of theories that transcend unique time and place settings is a commitment of the criminologist. Yet an interplay of the particular and the general is necessary. Suggested is the strategy as noted by Wrong: "A subtle interplay between trans-historical problems and their embodiment in the structure of the historical individuals we directly confront is the hallmark of the work of the great theorists of the recent past."[27]

The conception of man and society presented here should be given consideration in future studies in criminology. If our search for an understanding of crime is preoccupied with old models of observation and interpretation, we will miss the new, that is, fail to understand crime as it actually exists. Much of criminal behavior is the attempt of modern man to define his existence. In the final analysis, the ability of man to break with the established order may not only be a change in the observer's conception of man but may be change in man himself. To expose the conditions of contemporary man should be the ultimate task in the study of crime.

[25] Lewis A. Coser, "Some Functions of Deviant Behavior," *American Journal of Sociology*, 68: 172–81 (Sept. 1962); Lewis A. Coser, "Social Conflict and the Theory of Social Change," *British Journal of Sociology*, 8:197–207 (Sept. 1957); Herbert Menzel, "Innovation, Integration, and Marginality," *American Sociological Review*, 25:704–13 (Oct. 1960); and Roger Nett, "Conformity-Deviation and the Social Control Concept," *Ethics*, 64: 38–45 (Oct. 1953).

[26] C. Wright Mills, *The Sociological Imagination* (New York: Oxford University Press, 1959), especially chaps. 7 and 8.

[27] Dennis H. Wrong, "Human Nature and the Perspective of Sociology," *Social Research*, 30:318 (Autumn 1963).

Those interested in delinquency and criminality have produced a variety of theoretical formulations, but theoretical explanations in this substantive area, as in sociology in general, are essentially premathematical in form. That is, the preferred mode of stating theoretical explanations is in words or verbal symbols. This selection is part of the trend toward "formalization" in sociology; Turk develops an "axiomatic model" and offers a limited sociological theory of delinquency as a sociolegal phenomenon. This is an intergenerational conflict theory of delinquency.

In developing his theory Turk carefully defines each of his terms and then states six postulates and nine implications of the postulates. Of equal importance is his discussion of the alternative assumptions according to which research regarding culture and social conflict can proceed, for too frequently important assumptions are left unstated.

Turk proceeds according to the assumption that there is a direct correspondence between culture conflict and social conflict. Although his results are encouraging, they are inconclusive with respect to his theoretical model. Nevertheless, Turk illustrates the essential ingredients in an effort to verify a theory, and he makes the important point that theoretical deficiencies in the area of delinquency can be remedied by efforts to locate logical and empirical inadequacies in one's theory. Also important is his suggestion of the potential value of translating theorizing into testable theories as well as his recognition of the need for more research designed specifically to test theories.

AUSTIN T. TURK

Toward Construction of a Theory of Delinquency

Among sociologists, Zetterberg [1] and Gross [2] have argued effectively for the view that the significance of a statement is problematic until its precise relation to an "axiomatic" theory is known. Though one may have reservations about such formalization,[3] the writer believes

that it will be of strategic value in the study of delinquency to assume not only that the view is correct but also to insist that the word "theory" properly refers *only* to explicit propositional systems. Though precision and clarity are generally understood to be among the hallmarks of scientific theories, by far the greater part of criminological thought cannot be characterized as either precise or clear from a strict theoretical viewpoint. Without in any sense minimizing the value of sustained theoretically relevant discussion of delinquency,[4] it does now seem time to extend the concept of "research economy" to the presentation of theoretical alternatives. The rich prose of theorizing — though to some extent necessary, enjoyable, and inevitable — tends to obscure possibilities and issues possibly as often as it defines them, and to slow the verification process — especially when it is mistakenly assumed that such relatively lavish verbal displays, however ingenious and promising, actually constitute theories. The processes of scientific thinking

Reprinted by special permission of the *Journal of Criminal Law, Criminology and Police Science* (Northwestern University School of Law), Copyright © 1964, Volume 55, Number 2.

Most of this study in both its theoretical and empirical aspects was carried out during the tenure of a Predoctoral Research Fellowship from the National Institute of Mental Health, United States Public Health Service. The verification research is reported in detail in the author's unpublished Ph.D. thesis, "Adolescence and Delinquency in Urban Society: A Study in Criminological Theory" (University of Wisconsin, 1962). In addition, empirical studies utilizing the same data on delinquency and providing further details of a descriptive and procedural nature are reported in the following unpublished masters theses: Robert M. Terry, "Criteria Utilized by the Police in the Screening of Juvenile Offenders" (Wisconsin, 1962), and Charles M. McCaghy, "Social Areas and Distribution of Juvenile Delinquency in Racine, Wisconsin, 1950–1960" (Wisconsin, 1962).

[1] Zetterberg, *On Theory and Verification in Sociology*, 9–28 (1954).

[2] Gross, "Theory Construction in Sociology: A Methodological Inquiry," in *Symposium on Sociological Theory*, 531–64 (Gross ed. 1959).

[3] *Id.* at 535–38.

[4] The author completely agrees with David Bordua's conclusion that theorizing about delinquency "has led to some of the most exciting and provocative intellectual interchange in all of sociology in recent years." "Delinquent Subcultures: Sociological Interpretations of Gang Delinquency," 338 *Annals*, 119 (1961).

should, of course, be as public as possible, since scientists are concerned with implicit leads found in preliminary discussions as well as with finished products. Nevertheless, at some time in the development of a science emphasis must shift from the pursuit of unexplored subtleties to the rigorous formulation and testing of theories. Though criminologists have been greatly concerned with stating and examining explanatory hypotheses — very often, as Riemer [5] once said, "fished out of the mudhole of common sense" and "vaguely connected with other half-truths about society and the adjustment problems of its members" — the problems of systematic theory-construction have scarcely been recognized. There have been tendencies to confuse theorizing with theory and hypothesis-testing with theory-testing, while the undefined processes by which "orientations" come into being have rarely been supplemented by explicit, logically defensible procedures for constructing deductive chains. The sociology of crime and delinquency has advanced to the point where, in this writer's opinion, emphasis may profitably be placed upon the construction of systems, so that the interrelations and implications of ideas can be efficiently considered as criminologists apply "the criterion of testability . . . to comprehensive systems of hypotheses rather than to single statements." [6]

Scope of the Theory

The traditional assumption that a theory of delinquency must necessarily be a theory of delinquent behavior has aggravated the debate between the more legalistic and those more concerned with problem behavior. Writers such as Wilber and Vold,[7] Cressey,[8] and Jef-

fery [9] have worked toward a resolution of the resultant theoretical and research difficulties by asserting the importance of value conflict, of conditions affecting the definition and recording of crime, and of *legal* social and cultural patterns in the study of crime. Since virtually any person under, generally, 18 years of age could be legally defined as a delinquent in the United States,[10] such considerations may be even more pertinent to a study of delinquency as distinguished from adult crime. It seems apparent that *delinquency* is, from an operational standpoint, not actually a class or combination of classes of behavior, but rather a definition of pre-adults by those in a position to apply legal definitions. This is *not* to say that no relation exists between law and juvenile behavior.[11] While problem behavior is

[9] Jeffery, notably the following: "The Structure of American Criminological Thinking," 46 *J. Crim. L., C. & P.S.*, 658 (1956); "Crime, Law and Social Structure," 47 *id*. 423 (1956); "An Integrated Theory of Crime and Criminal Behavior," 49 *id*. 533 (1959).

[10] Cohen & Short, "Juvenile Delinquency," in *Contemporary Social Problems*, 77–126, 81 (Merton & Nisbet eds. 1961).

[11] Jerome Hall has, in his own efforts to clarify the distinction between legal and behavioristic concepts of crime, on many occasions, pointed out that not only have the "classicists" often failed to recognize the difficulties to which a strict legalism leads, but the students of behavior have tended to minimize the significance of laws and legal processes for any study of "criminality." His view is that law and human behavior are interrelated; laws result from experience. *Studies in Jurisprudence and Criminal Theory, passim* and esp. 200–14 (1958). The work of Paul Tappan has been another important correction factor for students of criminal and delinquent behavior in that he has, rightly, insisted upon the relevance of legal definitions and procedures — without, however, solving the problems of carrying out behavioral research from a legalistic position. In *Juvenile Delinquency*, at 30 (1949), he defines a *delinquent* as "a person who has been adjudicated as such," but proceeds to discuss the general, psychological, biological, and social causes and conditions of *delinquency* defined as "any act, course of conduct, or situation which might be brought before a court and adjudicated." *Ibid*. Thus, legal distinctions, though the criteria are vague, arbitrarily define the distinctions which will be allowed for the purposes of behavioral research. One might well ask, why should biological and other differences between delinquents and

[5] Riemer, "Theory and Quantitative Analysis in Criminological Research," 48 *Am. J. Sociology*, 188 (1942).

[6] Hempel, *Fundamentals of Concept Formation in Empirical Science*, 43 (1952).

[7] Wilber, "The Scientific Adequacy of Criminology Concepts," 28 *Social Forces*, 165 (1949); Vold, *Theoretical Criminology*, esp. 203–19, 279–81 (1958).

[8] Cressey, "Foreword" to Sutherland, *White Collar Crime*, xii (5th ed. 1961).

variously defined and variously handled, the fact remains that it is something about the behavior of pre-adults that provokes age-specific enactment, interpretation, and enforcement of laws. The point is that the *interaction* of behavior and legally supported expectations is the stuff of which records are made, and not merely the *action* of underage "deviants." Moreover, this is interaction over relatively long periods involving thousands of juveniles and adults, and presupposes nothing about the behavior of any particular individual who happens to be labelled a delinquent in one moment of a very complex history of relations between adults and pre-adults. In the absence of reliable *behavioral* data, the sociological problem for now hardly seems that of explaining specific offensive behavior, but rather that of explaining variations in the reactions of official representatives of the adult political community to provocative juvenile actions and attributes, whatever these may be and however vague may be the legal criteria. The problem of delinquency — as conceptualized in this study — is *illegitimation*, the assignment of an individual to the status of offender,[12] and not behavior assumed to characterize the offender. Consequently, the theory which is being developed is a limited sociological theory of delinquency as a socio-legal phenomenon.[13]

Definition of Terms

Concepts of *illegitimation, social position, dominance* and *disadvantage, social* and *cultural conflict*, and *urbanism* represent lines of theoretical development which may be usefully brought together in a sociological theory of delinquency. A survey of the history of thought and research represented by each concept and a discussion of the issues with respect to each are beyond the limits of this paper. At great risk of seeming to ignore problems of fundamental concern, terms will be briefly defined in relation to the purposes at hand, with no special effort to conform to one or another traditional view regarding the use of particular words.[14] The meanings of words will be restricted to the following definitions, which are developed cumulatively as part of the attempt to organize and communicate a number of ideas in an axiomatic form.

Illegitimation is the process by which an individual or category of persons is assigned the status of criminal, i.e., "adjudged to be punishable (or 'treatable') by the authorities in continuous political control over the territory in which he is" because of "an act or omission" ascribed to the person or persons.[15] No assumptions are made as to the actual behavior of illegitimated persons.

Social position refers to the location of one or more individuals in a social structure, a network of interrelated and in part interdependent activities. Expected patterns of activity, or roles, are associated with social positions, which are differentially valued largely according to the significance placed upon the behavior expected from individuals in different locations. Of special importance is the fact that generation, or age, is a universal criterion for locating individuals in a social structure. Although other criteria will enter in as well, the distinction between an *adult* and a *pre-adult* is fundamental.[16]

Social disadvantage and *dominance* are concepts recognizing that difference in social position implies, to a greater or lesser extent, differences in access to resources and opportuni-

---

non-delinquents be expected when we know that the only completely reliable criterion is the fact of identification itself, which is a legal and not a scientific behavioral determination?

[12] Korn & McCorkle, *Criminology and Penology*, 42–48 (1959).

[13] That is, a "macro" theory in the Moles-Lippitt-Withey framework. Moles, Lippitt & Withey, *A Selective Review of Research and Theories Concerning the Dynamics of Delinquency*, 127 (1959).

[14] Perhaps it should be stressed that the words refer not to specific variables but to theoretical constructs, which can never be completely defined by some grouping of terms in a direct empirical equation or sufficiently validated by observed empirical regularities. MacCorquodale & Meehl, "Hypothetical Constructs and Intervening Variables," in *Readings in the Philosophy of Science*, 596–611, esp. 605–06 (Feigle & Brodbeck eds. 1953).

[15] Korn & McCorkle, *op. cit. supra* note 12, at 45–46.

[16] Eisenstadt, *From Generation to Generation: Age Groups and Social Structure* (1956).

ties, i.e., differences in power — the ability to realize goals even against opposition. At the same time, differential exposure to given kinds of experiences and vulnerability to given kinds of pressures and hazards are implied.[17] The essential element in the relations between adult and pre-adult social positions is the relative dominance of adults and disadvantage of pre-adults; a strict chronological distinction is inadequate even though age is a relevant variable. Reciprocal expectations, patterns of activity, and the emphasis placed upon the values of leisure[18] also serve to distinguish full-fledged from apprentice members of a society.

Culture conflict is a conflict of attitudes or meanings to be assigned to objects and situations — which assumes that the concept *culture* refers to the ideational, as distinguished from the associational and behavioral, aspects of human living. The actions of agents of differing cultures tend to some degree to be at odds, since men act on the basis of their interpretations of what is going on around them. Nevertheless, it is crucial to distinguish between the conflict implicit in different views and feelings and the conflict expressed in some direct or indirect manipulation of the environment — which is the difference between *culture conflict* and *social conflict*. While they correlate to a significant degree if human behavior has rhyme or reason, the specific ways in which culture conflict may come to be expressed in social conflict will vary with the tools and perceived opportunities available to the actors and with their involvement in particular cultural patterns. The universality of *some* culture con-

flict between pre-adults and adults is well attested.[19] Increasing barriers between pre-adult and adult social positions is a major theme in much contemporary discussion of crime and delinquency, with attention being devoted to the emergence of fairly autonomous "adolescent societies and cultures" that are "the principal training institution of the adolescent period"[20] and "focus teen-age interests and attitudes on things far removed from adult responsibilities, and which may develop standards that lead away from those goals established by the larger society."[21] To postulate relatively independent social and cultural patterns among pre-adults is not to ignore the fact that such patterns are found within larger social and cultural settings,[22] but simply represents an effort to specify more precisely the patterned influences upon youth of most immediate significance in understanding their behavior in relation to adult interpretations and responses. As Davis noted, "to understand how our society brings to expression the potentiality for conflict, indeed to deal realistically with the relation between the generations, we must do so not in generalized terms but in terms of the specific 'power situation.' "[23]

Cultural diversity and conflict, mobility,

[17] Robert Merton and Robert Nisbet list differential exposure and vulnerability as a major premise of the sociological orientation. *Contemporary Social Problems*, at ix (Merton & Nisbet eds. 1961).

[18] Matza & Sykes, "Juvenile Delinquency and Subterranean Values," 26 *Am. Soc. Rev.*, 712 (1961). Bennett Berger's discussion appears to drive in the opposite direction to the same general conclusion: that "youthful" values are not bound chronologically but are found in the cultures both of the young and the old. Berger, "On the Youthfulness of Youth Cultures," 30 *Social Research*, 319 (1963).

[19] Davis, "The Sociology of Parent-Youth Conflict," 5 *Am. Soc. Rev.*, 523 (1940); Bloch & Niederhoffer, *The Gang: A Study in Adolescent Behavior* (1958).

[20] Ausubel, *Theory and Problems of Adolescent Development*, 341 (1954).

[21] Coleman, *The Adolescent Society*, 9 (1961).

[22] The differences in opportunities to learn and commit both legal and illegal patterns as such differences are determined by the larger social structure have been emphasized in Cloward & Ohlin, *Delinquency and Opportunity: A Theory of Delinquent Gangs* (1960). Albert Cohen stresses clashes between larger class cultures as basic sources of delinquent gang patterns. Cohen, *Delinquent Boys: The Culture of the Gang* (1955). To avoid the tendency to exaggerate cultural variants which the concept of delinquent subcultures appears to encourage, the concept of "contraculture" is suggested as a more valid alternative. For a discussion of subculture and contraculture as supplementary concepts, see Yinger, "Contraculture and Subculture," 25 *Am. Soc. Rev.*, 625 (1960).

[23] Davis, *supra* note 19, at 529.

shifting patterns of social relations, individualism, secularism, materialism, and de-emphasis of personal commitment in primary relations in favor of segmental, impersonal contact in secondary relations — all have been suggested as characteristics of *urbanism*.[24] The concept refers to more rather than less of the indicated attributes of social and cultural patterns, assuming a continuum instead of an urban-rural dichotomy.[25] Derived in large part from the Shevky-Bell formulation,[26] the components of *urbanism* as the concept is presently used are (1) considerable — the minimum being unknown — population size and density, (2) functional specialization of a high order, (3) individualization and structural flexibility in living patterns, and (4) cultural diversity. These components appear to be synonymous with the conditions under which relatively independent social and cultural patterns are elaborated among pre-adults.[27] A distinctive pre-adult "society" requires, in the first place, that juveniles be relatively free of informal social control techniques. A positive association between urbanization and the decline of such controls is now well established. Population size and density beyond a certain point prohibits the degree of extended family-based interaction required for the development and maintenance of effective informal controls. Secondly, occupational specialization and functional interdependence — especially in conjunction with a scientific technology — implies differentiation of the trained from the untrained, as well as job performance by individuals in relatively segregated, highly technical work contexts. Juveniles are, of course, un-

trained for participation in any but the least demanding occupations, and are thereby barred from interaction with adults in what is perhaps the major sector of adult life. Thirdly, individualization means the emancipation of juveniles as well as adults from the dictates of primary groups such as the family; highly structured living patterns tend to be replaced by relatively flexible living patterns that are more conformable to individual inclinations and activities than to "home group" interests.[28] Finally, cultural heterogeneity implies the absence of common standards to which pre-adults might be held; thus, the standards which one individual or group might try to impose are unsupported or even contradicted by other individuals or groups. *Urbanism*, then, refers to the matrix within which conflict between adults and pre-adults develops as the gap between their experiences widens.[29] Given an often inconsistent variety of cultural expectations, a great deal of personal liberty for both pre-adults and adults, little real knowledge of or significant contact with the adult world on the part of pre-adults, the anonymity found in large populations and the presence of large numbers of individuals in similar unstructured, unsupervised, segregated, and subordinate social positions, the accentuation of pre-adult social organizations and contracultures is to be expected.

A preliminary or "working" intergenerational conflict theory of delinquency is now advanced, using the concepts defined in the preceding discussion.

[24] Clinard, *Sociology of Deviant Behavior*, 65–76 (1963).

[25] *Id.* at 67–68, 76–77.

[26] Shevky & Bell, *Social Area Analysis* (1955).

[27] Eisenstadt, *op. cit. supra* note 16, states that in "universalistic" modern societies industrialism (pp. 170, 178), limited scope of the family (170), social mobility (177), preparatory education for specialized occupational roles (160 ff., 228), and other characteristics of these societies are associated with "a great plethora of youth groups, youth agencies and general consciousness of youth as a problem" (178), as well as with the more intense "scope and vitality" of such groups (170).

[28] Research indicates that family controls are largely supplanted by peer controls rather soon in highly urbanized areas. Toby, "The Differential Impact of Family Disorganization," 22 *Am. Soc. Rev.*, 505 (1957); Short, "Differential Association with Delinquent Friends," 1 *Pac. Soc. Rev.*, 20 (1958); Bowerman & Kinch, "Changes in Family and Peer Orientation of Children Between the Fourth and Tenth Grades," 37 *Social Forces*, 206 (1959).

[29] Two thoughtful writers on the subject of delinquent behavior have concluded that "the contemporary youth-adult conflict, although in essence the same as in the past, is much sharper, more acute, and much more in evidence." Kvaraceus & Miller, *Delinquent Behavior: Culture and the Individual*, 25 (1959).

A Theory of Delinquency

Informally and briefly, it is suggested that variations in the incidence of pre-adult illegitimation are mainly accounted for by variations in the extent to which pre-adults are free to elaborate cultural and social patterns conflicting with the expectations of adults, in particular those adults who are dominant in the larger social structure, i.e., whose attitudes are most likely to be reflected in legal definitions and actions. Presentation of a theory consisting of six postulates and nine implications of the postulates does not imply that the theory is completely satisfactory, that all possible implications have been made explicit, or that the writer considers it to be an actual *system*.[30] It is offered not only as a contribution toward a "macro" explanation of delinquency, but also as a stimulus to empirical research directly concerned with the testing of explicit theory and as a stimulus to theoretical efforts directly concerned with the concise statement of systematically related ideas.

Postulates

1. Difference in *social position* implies difference in *culture*.
2. Difference in *culture* implies some degree of *culture conflict*.
3. To the extent that *culture conflict* is expressed in *social conflict, illegitimation* of the relatively *disadvantaged* by the *dominant* will result.
4. The *social position* of *pre-adults* is universally *disadvantaged* relative to *adults* in the same society.
5. The *social position* of *pre-adults* is to some extent different from and independent of the *social position* of local *adults*, i.e., those with whom *pre-adults* live.
6. The relative independence of *pre-adult* so-

cial and cultural patterns increases with *urbanism*.

Implications [31]

1. A difference in social position implies a degree of culture conflict. (from Postulates 1, 2)
2. There is always some culture conflict between pre-adults and adults. (from Postulates 1, 2, 4)
3. To the extent that culture conflict between pre-adults and adults is expressed in social conflict and that the adults are dominant in the larger social structure, illegitimation of the pre-adult will result. (from Postulates 1, 2, 3, 4)
4. To the extent that culture conflict is expressed in social conflict, illegitimation of pre-adults will be positively associated with the difference between the social positions of pre-adults and of adults dominant in the larger social structure. (from Postulates 1, 2, 3, 4)
5. Culture conflict between pre-adults and between pre-adults and non-local adults is to some extent independent of culture conflict between adults and between adults and non-local pre-adults. (from Postulates 1, 2, 3, 4, 5)
6. Illegitimation of pre-adults will vary to some extent independently of the illegitimation of local adults. (from Postulates 1, 2, 3, 4, 5)
7. To the extent that culture conflict is expressed in social conflict, the extent of independent variation in the illegitimation of pre-adults and of adults will be positively associated with the cultural difference between them. (from Postulates 1, 2, 3, 4, 5)
8. Culture conflict between pre-adults and adults, especially adults dominant in the

---

[30] Any efforts to develop systems of propositions constituting criminological theories must be with full understanding that (1) there are always assumptions beyond explicit postulates, (2) the use of words rather than completely neutral symbols inevitably means compromising the rigor of the would-be system, and (3) there is no such thing as a finished theory. *Cf.* Gross, *supra* note 2, at 540–41.

[31] These represent primary inferences drawn from combinations of postulates, a possible 57, and are statements that appear to make "the most sense" in regard to verbal communication. In addition, some coalescence of relatively trivial separate implications seemed desirable. Secondary and higher-order inferences on the basis of combinations of postulates with theorems, theorems with theorems, and so on are not of pressing concern at the present stage in theory construction.

larger social structure, increases with urbanism. (from Postulates 1, 2, 4, 5, 6)

9. To the extent that culture conflict is expressed in social conflict, illegitimation of pre-adults will be positively associated with urbanism. (from Postulates 1, 2, 3, 4, 5, 6)

Research Assumptions

In the process of translating the theoretical propositions into testable operational hypotheses either of two contradictory assumptions must be accepted under the conditions limiting most empirical research. Theoretical advance is most likely to result when results are available from studies carried out under each assumption. The assumptions are as follows:

1. *There is a direct positive association between culture conflict and social conflict, i.e., between measurable difference in culture* [32] *and measurable difference in behavior.* Therefore measurable difference in behavior expressing a measurable difference in orientation toward the same values, beliefs, and normative expectations implies a measurable degree of conflicting behavior, resulting in the illegitimation of those with relatively less influence upon the enactment, interpretation, and application of laws.

2. *There is* no *direct positive association between culture conflict and social conflict, i.e., between measurable difference in culture and measurable difference in behavior.* Therefore, a measurable difference in behavior expressing a measurable difference in orientation toward the same values, beliefs, and normative expectations does *not* necessarily imply a measurable degree of conflicting behavior resulting in the illegitimation of those with relatively less influence upon the enactment, interpretation, and application of laws.

If the first assumption is accepted, measurement of orientation, attitudes, will be sufficient to infer a degree of conflicting behavior. Correlations between attitude scores and illegitimation rates will be determined, along with

other correlations between illegitimation rates and measures of social position — with inferences about dominance and social disadvantage — and urbanism. If the second assumption is accepted, a measure of social conflict can be obtained only in the observation of actual conflicting behavior. Measures of attitudes will be obtained only in order to test for possible associations with social conflict. Correlations between social conflict scores and illegitimation rates will be determined, along with other correlations between illegitimation rates and measures of social position — again with inferences about dominance and social disadvantage — and urbanism. This is, of course, the old problem of attempting to predict behavior from attitude or personality measures. Theoretical and technique preferences determine how it is temporarily resolved for the purpose of getting on with research. Research economy, a disinclination to invest so much of life and to "get dirty" directly observing human behavior in natural settings, and the great obstacles to participant observation have apparently forced most students of human behavior to settle for measurement of orientation and for "interview, or laboratory behaviors." The popularity of psychological measurement suggests that the majority of behavior scientists expect one day to demonstrate direct relations between their measures and variations in human behavior. In any event, many considerations adding up to research economy led to acceptance of the *first* research assumption in the following study, which was an effort to test some of the implications of the theory presented above.

A Verification Study

A hypothesis constitutes a prediction regarding the relations among *classes* of variables, since it is classes of phenomena as defined in a theory which are of concern and not any particular event or any particular observation.[33] In any given verification study the specific variables in each class will depend upon the quality and availability of information. Part of the controversy between "theorists" and "empiricists" has been due to the

[32] Measurement of cultural difference assumes *more* or *less* of the same thing can be determined. There must be a comparable base, since the unique is not within the province of science.

[33] Other than theoretical objectives may demand the use of particular variables.

neglect by both of the problems of relating variables to theoretical constructs in valid and reliable ways. The flat assertion that a particular variable does or does not represent what some theorist is talking about simply reinforces mutual disdain and ignorance of the opponent's domain of competence. At present, the most *reliable* techniques for classifying and selecting variables in terms of theoretical relevance may be those of factor analysis.[34] Consequently, factor analysis was utilized as a classifying and selecting device in the manner described below. The problems in verification research are (1) to obtain presumed indicators of urbanism, illegitimation, social position, and culture conflict, (2) to establish the reliability and validity of the variables as indicators, and (3) to formulate hypotheses in regard to the best available indicators, and test the hypotheses.

Data Collection

Data on delinquency rates, socio-economic characteristics of residential areas, and the attitudes of high school students were obtained for a highly urbanized Midwestern city of 100,000. Thus, urbanism was, for practical research possibilities, a constant, prohibiting tests of predicted relationships between urbanism and intergenerational culture conflict and between urbanism and illegitimation. Moreover, direct measures of the attitudes of adults and of illegitimation of adults were beyond the scope of the research.

The delinquency data were from a 20 percent sample of the master cards contained in the file of the police juvenile bureau. For 94 percent of the 3,148 offenses recorded from the beginning of 1950 to the end of 1960, guilt had been ascertained by confession, by the use of a lie detector with parental permission, or by incontrovertible evidence. The remaining

instances were termed "contacts," [35] and were also classed as offenses, since (1) contacts are considered part of an individual's police record, (2) limited police resources often result in classification of relatively minor cases as contacts for future reference without their having been formally closed, and (3) the imprecise wording of state and local delinquency statutes means that almost any juvenile, especially one having contact with the police, could be charged with some offense, and (4) contacts are subject to the same types of dispositions as formal offenders, since they may be regarded as needing rehabilitative attention.[36] Delinquency rates were, then, calculated on the basis of the most nearly direct yet reliable evidence of the extent of pre-adult illegitimation in the city.

Information from the 1960 U.S. Census,[37] the local school census, city planning commission materials on land-use,[38] and a questionnaire administered to a student sample representing grades 9–12 in all high schools in the city gave presumed measures of social position. Fifteen residential areas were defined in terms of the elementary school districts, since (1) census tracts are not delineated for the city, (2) the school census data were tabulated according to these districts, thus providing intra-city juvenile populations for which delinquency rates could be calculated, (3) the district is the most reliable unit for the demarcation of relatively homogeneous residential areas in the city, and (4) students from the same district generally attend the same high school — which suggests that the home situation may reinforce the social and cultural patterns of youth so strongly encouraged by the internal and external environments of the high schools.[39] Social posi-

---

[34] Raymond Cattell asserts that, "with factor analysis we can experiment with [hypotheses] that extend to statements about the *number* of factors at work in a situation, the *nature of the factors*, their degree of *interaction*, and the *magnitude* of their influence." Cattell, *Factor Analysis: An Introduction and Manual for the Psychologist and Social Scientist*, 20–21 (1952).

[35] All official contacts of whatever nature between police officers and juveniles have been reported in writing on an official form as a matter of policy since 1958.
[36] Terry, "Criteria Utilized by the Police in the Screening of Juvenile Offenders," p. 43 (unpublished thesis, University of Wisconsin, 1962).
[37] 3 U.S. Census of Housing: 1960 (City Blocks; Series HC(3), Number 418).
[38] City Plan Comm'n, Racine, Wis., *Land Use and Community Facilities Plan for the City of Racine and the Racine Area* (1959).
[39] Coleman, *op. cit. supra* note 21, esp. 279–329.

tion measures were, therefore, derived from several sources and with respect to the residential district rather than individuals or groups.

The nearest approximation to indicators of culture conflict which were feasible within the limits of the study were the responses of the 935 high school students to 45 attitude items presumably relevant to areas of special significance in regard to contacts between adults and pre-adults. The five items from Srole's *anomia* scale were included,[40] as were nine items, most in revised form, from the Purdue Opinion Panel.[41] Apart from general alienation, or *anomia*, the items were designed to elicit the attitudes of high school students toward parents, education, work, police, social stratification, and self. It was necessarily assumed that for each of these areas a distinction could be made between *favorable* and *unfavorable* responses. Favorable responses were those indicating acceptance of what were taken to be adult cultural expectations concerning deference to parents, recognition of the values of education and of work, respect for legal authorities, belief in the virtual absence of limits upon opportunities for individual advancement, and self-acceptance and approval.

Classification and Selection of Variables

There were three stages in the classification and selection process, (1) the assignment of attitude items to groups for scaling, (2) the grouping of all variables into social position, culture conflict, and illegitimation categories, and (3) the selection of representative variables for correlation analysis.

Attitude responses were subjected to R-technique factor analysis, using standard computer procedures, by a trained CDC 1604 operator. Extraction of factors was limited to eight, accounting for 80 percent of the total variance, since the limited objective was to select items

constituting tests for certain predetermined attitudes. Inspection of the factor loadings showed that although there were no really pure tests of any one factor, the factors did approximate the expected content areas.[42] For each content area scales were derived from items with loading of at least .30 on the appropriate factor and correlating with each other item with coefficients of at least .20.[43] In view of the small item intercorrelations, the wisest course was to make the fewest possible assumptions regarding scalability by simply summing item scores, weighted by proportion of respondents making each choice, to arrive at a summated scale score for each residential district high school sub-sample. While there was no attempt to order items, the use of correlated items appears, as Peak has said, to be appropriate "to the selection of items of a test to be used chiefly for prediction to a specific external criterion." [44] As the items thus selected were previously selected on the basis of relatively high loadings on factors that reflected the content areas that determined the inclusion of items in the initial pool, the evidence is even stronger for the internal consistency of the final scales. In regard to items appearing in more than one scale, there is no reason to doubt that items designed to measure

[40] Srole, "Social Integration and Certain Corollaries: An Exploratory Study," 21 *Am. Soc. Rev.*, 709, 712–13 (1956).

[41] From numbers 45, 48, 49, 53, and 54. A description of the continuing Purdue Opinion Panel project and a summarization of results to 1957 is found in Remmers & Radler, *The American Teenager* (1957).

[42] Some exceptions which may prove of interest in future research were that all of the Srole *anomia* items loaded highest in the factor dominated by the attitude-toward-parents items, and that the attitude-toward-self items split, one set appearing in a factor whose item composition suggests that self-appraisal in terms of leadership and dating potential, social skills, and personal appearance and talents constitute one object, while the other set appeared dominant in a factor more analogous to the fundamental notion of self-concept. The first exception may mean that general alienation among teenagers is closely linked with their family experiences. The second suggests a distinction between self-appraisal and self-concept; in this study, the first provided scalable items by our criteria, while the second unfortunately did not. Consequently, no attempt was made to deal with the presumably "deeper" level of pre-adults' attitudes-toward-self.

[43] These are, of necessity, arbitrarily chosen but relatively high limiting values.

[44] Peak, "Problems of Objective Observation," in *Research Methods in the Behavioral Sciences*, 255 (Festinger & Katz eds. 1953).

culture conflict might be relevant to more than one issue involved in the conflict. Moreover, there is consistency as well as compartmentalization in human mental processes, so that the same experiences can be involved in the development of attitudes toward a variety of objects. For example, alienation among pre-adults seems to be tied in with their relations with their parents, and items having to do with attitudes toward parents and toward the police show up again in a measure of the extent to which teenagers see themselves as "delinquent." It is concluded that the scales used in the study did satisfy the limited purpose of ordering *aggregates* of pre-adults in terms of the varying degrees to which they accepted or rejected certain adult cultural expectations considered to have particular significance in intergenerational relations.[45] There were, finally, measures for a pre-adult sample from each residential district of alienation from parents, rejection of traditional ideology regarding social status, negative self-appraisal, devaluation of education, "delinquent" self-image, rejection of adult restrictions upon teenage marriage, hostility toward police, and *anomia;* in addition, total scores both including and excluding the *anomia* score were used.

Table 1 identifies the 22 variables derived from the available information for each of the 15 districts, including ten attitude scores, a land-use pattern score, four ratios using data from the housing census, five indicators of ethnicity, social status, and mobility of the student sample, and total and serious[46] delinquency rates. All factors were then extracted from the product-moment intercorrelation matrix, which provided not only a check on the assumed correspondences between theoretical constructs and variables, but also a means for determining which variables were the most representative of their class and therefore the empirical indicators most pertinent to the concept associated with each class.

Table 2 indicates the resulting factors and includes those variables with loadings of at least .70. To insure the best possible tests, only those variables were used in the subsequent analysis that had loadings of at least .80. Where two or more variables are found with high loadings on the same factor, it can be assumed that these variables are measuring essentially the same thing, i.e., that they are duplications from a theoretical standpoint. For this reason only the variables with the highest loadings need be considered in further analytical work. In the case of the first factor, variables 13 (owners/renters), 16 (ethnicity), and 17 (family status) had sufficiently high loadings; but since no variable could be considered a nearly pure test for the factor and since these three variables had approximately the same loadings, all three were retained. Factor I was interpreted as the "social position" factor. Variables 1 (*anomia*), 5 (education), 9 (total including *anomia*) and 10 (total without *anomia*) were high enough on factor II, interpreted as the "culture conflict" factor;

---

[45] Obviously, individuals with quite different response patterns could attain the same total scores — which could be taken to mean that different attitudes were being elicited in different people. While this might have been true, the possibility also exists that different patterns of experience may produce equivalent reactions. "We do not know as yet that independent measures of the same unidimensional processes in different people furnish the best means to the prediction of behavior." *Id.* at 260. In any case, Warren Torgerson has argued that derivation of a Guttman scale does not necessarily mean that the universe of content is scalable. *Theory and Methods of Scaling*, 333 (1958). In other words, even unidimensionality of a set of items does not automatically imply that the same thing is actually being tapped in different individuals.

[46] The adjective *serious* refers to the extent of deviation from the normative expectations of dominant adult culture, i.e., the seriousness of an offense is defined by the severity of the modal or potential official reaction to it, with respect to the curtailment of personal freedom through warning, arrest, probation and institutionalization — which can for most purposes be considered to approximate degrees of severity. In the present study "serious offenses" was an *a priori* category including those offenses with presumably high potential for relatively severe reactions: robbery, burglary, theft (auto and other), assault, sex offenses, forgery, weapons offenses, fraud, escape, and violent property damage. See McGaghy, "Social Areas and Distribution of Juvenile Delinquency in Racine, Wisconsin, 1950–1960," p. 66 (unpublished thesis, University of Wisconsin, 1962).

Table 1
Identification of Variables

Number	Description	Number	Description
1	Srole *anomia* scale score[a]	16	Proportion of district student sub-sample classed as "other than native white"[a, b]
2	Alienation from parents score		
3	Rejection of status ideology score[a]		
4	Negative self-appraisal score	17	Modal family occupational status of district student sub-sample[a, c]
5	Devaluation of education score[a]		
6	"Delinquent" self-image score	18	Proportion of district student sub-sample resident in Racine less than five years[a]
7	Rejection of adult restrictions upon teenage marriage score[a]		
8	Hostility toward police score	19	Proportion of district student sub-sample born outside Wisconsin
9	Total including Srole score[a]		
10	Total excluding Srole score	20	Proportion of district student sub-sample who moved to Racine from outside Wisconsin
11	Land-use pattern score		
12	Ratio of sound to deteriorating and dilapidated housing units		
13	Ratio of owner-occupied units to renter-occupied units[a]	21	District total delinquency rate: no. of offenders/population from 4 through 17 years of age $\times$ 1000 $\times$ 5[a]
14	Proportion of units occupied by non-whites		
15	Proportion of units with 1.01 persons or more per room	22	District serious offense rate: no. of serious offenses/population from 4 through 17 years of age $\times$ 5[a]

[a] Variables subsequently used in correlation analysis.

[b] Self-identification was accepted at face value. In addition, those respondents identifying themselves as "white" were included in the "other than native white" class if one or both parents were born outside the United States.

[c] Both fathers' and mothers' occupations were scored in terms of the Minnesota Scale for Parental Occupations. Where both parents were employed outside the home, a family occupational status score was determined in this fashion: (1) the separate category for farmers was eliminated by random assignment of the scant half-dozen farmers to the adjacent categories; (2) assuming the father's occupation to be the better indicator of the family's social position, the scale value of his occupation was raised one if the mother's occupation ranked two or more categories above his and lowered one if the mother's occupation ranked two or more categories below his. The resulting score would appear to be a more realistic indicator of the social position of the family than the father's occupational score alone.

variable 9, in fact, was virtually a pure test for the factor. Since 9 and 10 are identical except for the *anomia* score, 10 was omitted from further consideration. The third, "illegitimation" factor produced variables 21 (total delinquency) and 22 (serious delinquency); variable 18 (residence less than five years) also appeared, with a loading of .86 — which suggested that short-term residence might be more closely related to illegitimation than any of the other variables, and that "residential mobility" was to some extent independent of the "social position" class of variables.[47] There-

fore, variable 18 (short-term residence) was treated statistically as a representative of an analytically separate class. That variable 3 (status ideology) should appear alone in factor IV and 7 (teenage marriage) should also show up in a separate factor were unexpected, and

loadings on factor I ("social position") almost as high as on factor III ("illegitimation"): — .57 and .57 compared with .66 and .64, respectively. Some connection between mobility and social position would certainly be expected, since much of the immigrant population of the city in recent years has been American-Mexican and Negro, who have generally entered the social structure in relatively disadvantaged positions. McCaghy, *supra* note 46, at 28.

[47] It should be noted that the other "residential mobility" variables, numbers 19 and 20, did have

Table 2
Variables Selected by Factor Analysis [a]

	Factor loadings					
Variables [b]	*I*	*II*	*III*	*IV*	*V*	*VI*
11	−.71	.16	.29	−.34	.40	.17
13	.82	.18	−.27	−.08	.27	−.16
14	−.73	.39	.38	.25	−.01	−.10
16	−.81	.41	.16	−.15	.01	.05
17	−.82	−.26	.16	−.18	−.19	−.07
1	−.02	.87	.11	−.04	.23	.13
2	.08	.72	−.02	−.51	−.16	−.27
5	−.04	.82	−.14	−.24	.24	−.07
6	−.36	.72	.01	−.21	−.24	−.40
8	−.15	.77	.14	.41	−.08	.23
9	.02	.98	−.03	.02	−.08	−.11
10	.04	.91	−.12	.05	−.26	−.25
18	−.07	−.14	.86	.11	−.29	.12
21	−.29	.09	.90	−.08	−.07	.09
22	−.29	.01	.89	−.28	.12	−.03
3	.18	−.20	−.27	.87	−.00	.02
12	.45	−.04	−.02	−.05	.76	.07
7	.14	.15	−.16	−.04	.03	−.93

[a] Variables with high loadings on Factor I are listed first, those with high loadings on Factor II next, and so on.
[b] See Table 1 for identification of variables.

indicated the possibility that these attitude measures were getting at something in each case distinct from the common focus of the other attitude measures. Nevertheless, as attitude scores the variables were treated as additional indicators of the degree of "culture conflict." The final result of the factor analyses was to provide the best available data reliably grouped and of demonstrated, as far as possible, relevance to the testing of theoretically significant hypotheses.

Statement and Tests of Hypotheses

As Blalock [48] has demonstrated, the analysis of correlations does not reveal the causal linkages among a number of variables and is therefore less than adequate as a method by which

to evaluate the causal significance of independent variables. Nevertheless, as a *part* of an attempt to investigate the causal implications of a theory, correlation techniques offer the eminent advantages of precision and reliability of results. Since the empirical objective of this research was to determine the predictive efficiency of a particular theory, the relevant test was the ability of appropriate sets of variables to account for the variance in illegitimation, i.e., delinquency rates. The primary statistical problem was, then, to determine the multiple correlations of various *combinations* of the variables representing the classes of phenomena conceptualized in the theory, the highest value indicating the predictive power of the theory in this particular test. The secondary statistical problem was to estimate the contribution of each class of variables to the overall predictive power of the theory, it being useful to know not only that a theory can predict, but also how it predicts in terms of hypothesized relationships among variables. By partialling it is possible to learn, within the context of a theory, which type of information called for by the theory is of the greatest immediate predictive value. At this point it may be well to stress that prediction and scientific explanation are *not* the same thing. Obviously a theory that cannot lead to prediction is useless, but just as certainly a variable that "associates" without any specific theoretical position is of little value in the development of explanatory systems as well as in scientific, as distinguished from actuarial, prediction. Unless there is a rationale for the recurrence of associations, prediction is a matter of faith and mechanics rather than of science. [49]

Within the limits of the study it was possible to formulate and test only hypotheses suggested by implications 1, 3, and 4. Each theoretical implication will be stated; the operational translations — hypotheses — will be indicated, and the results of the tests reported. Finally, the predictive power of the theory in

[48] Blalock, "Evaluating the Relative Importance of Variables," 26 *Am. Soc. Rev.*, 866 (1961).

[49] For a spirited *de-emphasis* of formal theory in favor of the less selective collection and analysis of much more and better data, see Borgatta, "Toward a Methodological Codification: The Shotgun and the Saltshaker," 24 *Sociometry*, 432 (1961).

this study will be summarized as the greatest amount of variance in delinquency rates which was attributable to a theoretically meaningful combination of variables.

Implication 1. A difference in social position implies a degree of culture conflict.

Since three variables were reliably selected as indicators of "social position" and five as indicators of "culture conflict," positive associations between any of the three and any of the five were predicted. Thus, there were 15 hypotheses relating social position to culture conflict by predicting positive linear correlations. Table 3 indicates that the data did not support the hypotheses in most instances, as 12 of the 15 gross correlations were negative. In particular, none of the three positive correlations was statistically significant, while one at least of the negative coefficients was significant at the .10 level. Controlling for the effects of the short-term residence variable did not significantly alter the relations between the two classes of "social position" and "culture conflict" variables.

As in all efforts to test theoretical implications, the problem was whether to reject the theory or to question the methodology, or to consider both possibilities. Though the implication remains entirely open to question — especially to the findings of verification research — the decision was to let the theory stand for the present. There were three reasons for such a decision; emotional commitment to the theory was definitely not one of them. (1) The factor loadings of the three "social position" variables indicated that none of them approximated a pure test for the factor. The loadings for 13 (owner/renters), 16 (ethnicity), and 17 (family status) were, respectively, .82, −.81, and −.82 on factor I. The possibility exists that the "best available" measures of social position were not good enough for a conclusive test. (2) The presumed social position data were with reference to the larger social structure. Before such data can be used decisively to reject the theory it should be demonstrated that they are directly relevant to the location of *pre-adults*, as well as adults, in the social structure. That is, to what extent can the same criteria be used to dis-

Table 3

Culture Conflict and Social Position

Social position [a]

Culture conflict	Owners/ renters		Ethnicity		Family occupational status	
Anomia	−.15	−.15	.37	.38	−.15	−.15
Status ideology	−.09	−.02	−.45[b]	−.43	−.35	−.31
Education	−.21	−.10	.31	.39	−.25	−.16
Teenage marriage	−.39	−.33	−.14	−.10	−.03	.06
Total score	−.18	−.13	.35	.38	−.23	−.30

[a] For each variable the first column is the gross correlation, the second is the partial correlation coefficient with variable 18 (short-term residence) controlled. In all cases see Table 1 for specific identification of variables; scores are for the elementary school districts. (N = 15)

[b] Significant at .10 level, t = 1.80; with 13 df the value of t with a probability of .90 is 1.77. None of the partial correlations were significant; with 12 df t is 1.78 with p = .90.

tinguish the social positions of pre-adults and of adults? The argument in this paper has been that the same criteria do *not* necessarily apply; the research problem, accordingly, may be to find indicators of more direct relevance in the social positioning of pre-adults *as pre-adults*, rather than to continue with the working assumption that pre-adult social position is merely a function of adult social position. (3) The measurement of attitudes as indicators of culture conflict was limited in the study to the use of summated scores for aggregates of pre-adults determined solely by common residence in a given elementary school district. More refined attitude measures with respect to groups of high schoolers identified sociometrically would clearly provide more valid indicators for the analysis of culture conflict. There is, of course, no guarantee that results would be different if methodological improvements were effected. In essence, the theory is to be given more of a "fair chance."

Table 4

Culture Conflict and Total Delinquency, Controlling Social Position

Social position [b]

Culture conflict	Total delinquency [a]	Owners/ renters	Eth- nic- ity	Family occupa- tional status
Anomia	.21	.34	.04	.30
Status ideology	−.40	−.42	−.23	−.30
Education	−.05	.07	−.24	.06
Teenage marriage	−.25	−.06	−.21	−.26
Total score	.06	.18	−.13	.17

[a] Gross correlations, none significant at the .10 level.

[b] Partial correlations with the indicated social position variables controlled, none significant at the .10 level. See Table 1 for specific identification of variables.

Table 5

Culture Conflict and Serious Delinquency, Controlling Social Position

Social position [b]

Culture conflict	Serious delinquency [a]	Owners/ renters	Eth- ity nic-	Family occupa- tional status
Anomia	.17	.28	.03	.25
Status ideology	−.51[d]	−.53[e]	−.41	−.44
Education	.01	.13	−.13	.12
Teenage marriage	−.15	.04	−.10	−.15
Total score	−.02	.07	−.18	.08

[a] Gross correlations.

[b] Partial correlations with the indicated social disadvantage variables controlled. See Table 1 for specific identification of variables.

[e] Significant at .05 level. With 12 df and p = .95, t = 2.18; the value of t for $r_{12.3} = -.53$ is 2.21.

[d] Significant at .10 level. With 13 df and p = .90, t = 1.77; for p = .95, t = 2.16. For r = −.51, t = 2.13.

Implication 3. To the extent that culture conflict between pre-adults and adults is expressed in social conflict and that the adults are dominant in the larger social structure, illegitimation of the pre-adults will result.

On the assumption that culture conflict was expressed in social conflict, positive associations between "culture conflict" variables and delinquency rates were predicted. With five attitude scores as measures of "culture conflict" and two delinquency rates as indicators of "illegitimation," there were ten hypotheses on the basis of gross correlations. When the effects of each of the three "social position" variables were controlled, another 30 hypotheses were tested. Table 4 reports the results in regard to the total delinquency rates, and Table 5 the results for the serious delinquency rates. For total delinquency rates, neither the gross nor the partial coefficients were statistically significant at the .10 level, although positive sign changes were effected in the relation between delinquency rate and variable 5 (devaluation of education) when variables 13 (owners/renters) and 17 (modal family occupational status) were controlled. Controlling variable 16 (ethnicity) changed the sign from positive to negative for the relation between delinquency and variable 9 (total attitude score). Since the best tests for the "culture conflict" factor — variables 1 (*anomia*), 5 (education), and 9 (total score) [50] — did in general show a positive association with total delinquency when the "social position" variables were controlled, the implication was not rejected at this point. For serious delinquency rates, controlling variable 16 (ethnicity) reinforced the generally negative, though low, correlations with the "culture conflict" variables. However, the fact that seven of the nine partial correlations between serious delinquency and the best "culture conflict" variables were positive — though not significant at the .10 level — again raised the possibility that improved measurement *might* produce stronger support for the proposition and would, in any event, provide more conclusive evidence. Consequently, the implication was not rejected on the basis of present evidence.

[50] With factor II loadings of, respectively, .87, .82, and .98.

Implication 4. To the extent that culture conflict is expressed in social conflict, illegitimation of pre-adults will be positively associated with the difference between the social positions of pre-adults and of adults dominant in the larger social structure.

Positive associations between the "social position" variables and delinquency rates were predicted. Three "social position" variables, 13 (owners/renters), 16 (ethnicity), and 17 (family status), in relation to two delinquency rates constituted six hypotheses, plus an additional 30 when the effects of each of the five "culture conflict" variables were controlled. For total delinquency, Table 6 reveals uniformly positive and fairly high coefficients, particularly in the case of the owners/renters ratio. For serious delinquency, Table 7 shows that every coefficient was positive, though only the owners/renters ratio was significantly related. Subject to more and better research evidence, the implication was accepted.

The relatively independent status of variable 18 (short-term residence) presented additional analytical problems. Sixty-four percent of the variance in total delinquency rates was accounted for by this variable, a proportion which was not significantly affected by controlling for the effects of each of the other independent variables, as shown in Table 8. In every case the relation was highly significant. Short-term residence was also significantly correlated with serious delinquency, accounting for about 48 percent of the variance. Table 9 indicates that partialling the other independent variables did not significantly alter the relation. Tables 10 and 11 show that the second-order partials were significant when both the "social position" and the "culture conflict" variables were controlled. The statistical importance of short-term residence having been established, the correlations between this variable and the total delinquency and serious delinquency rates were used in the computation of multiple correlation coefficients.

Table 12 shows that the variables used in the study were more successful in accounting for variation in total delinquency rates than for variation in rates of serious delinquency. For total delinquency, the most successful combination of variables included 18 (short-term residence), 13 (owners/renters), and 1 (*anomia*), to which 79 percent of the variance was attributable. For serious delinquency, about 68 percent of the variance was accounted for by a combination of 18 (short-term residence), 13 (owners/renters), and 3 (rejection of status ideology).

Conclusion

The results of the verification study must obviously be regarded as at most encouraging rather than as definitive one way or the other. From the theorist's viewpoint, a theory with a predictive power of almost 80 percent is not lightly to be dismissed; from the methodologist's viewpoint, formal theory may appear speculative and pretentious, with the benefit of the doubt to be given the data in terms of which hypotheses were formulated and tested. As has been made apparent, the writer's position is that criminology has now advanced to the point where the systematic construction and verification of axiomatic theories should become increasingly characteristic of the field. Deficiencies in theory can best be remedied by a continuing effort to pinpoint the logical and empirical inadequacies of the theory. This can be done by the improved research designs which greater resources allow, but not by dogged exaggeration of the empirical aspects of research at the expense of the theoretical aspects. Theory *construction* represents the often tedious, unspectacular task of spelling out the linkages among the ideas that flow from theorizing, with full awareness of the problems involved in the execution of relevant verification studies.

Summary

Criminology has advanced to the point where it appears that the systematic construction of axiomatic theories and the design of verification studies need emphasis for the further development of the field as a scientific discipline. The wealth of empirical and theoretical materials with reference to the sociology of delinquency indicates that this is an especially promising area in which to begin. Accordingly, a working "macro" theory of delin-

Table 6
Social Position and Total Delinquency, Controlling Culture Conflict

		Culture conflict [b]				
Social position	Total delinquency [a]	Anomia	Status ideology	Education	Teenage marriage	Total score
Owners/renters	.52[d]	.57[c]	.53[c]	.52[d]	.47[d]	.54[c]
Ethnicity	.48[d]	.44	.37	.52[d]	.46	.49[d]
Family occupational status	.41	.46	.31	.41	.41	.44

[a] Gross correlations.
[b] Partial correlations with the indicated culture conflict variables controlled. See Table 1 for specific identification of variables.
[c] Significant at .05 level. With 12 df and p = .95, t = 2.18; the value of t for $r_{12.3} = .53$ is 2.21.
[d] Significant at .10 level. With 12 df and p = .90, t = 1.78; the values of t for $r_{12.3} = .52$ and for $r_{12.3} = .46$ are, respectively, 2.08 and 1.77. With 13 df and p = .90, t = 1.77; the values of t for r = .52 and r = .41 are, respectively, 2.17 and 1.64. For r = .48, t is 2.00.

Table 7
Social Position and Serious Delinquency, Controlling Culture Conflict

		Culture conflict [b]				
Social position	Serious delinquency [a]	Anomia	Status ideology	Education	Teenage marriage	Total score
Owners/renters	.47[c]	.51[c]	.49[c]	.48[c]	.45	.48[c]
Ethnicity	.39	.36	.21	.41	.38	.42
Family occupational status	.38	.41	.25	.39	.38	.39

[a] Gross correlations.
[b] Partial correlations with the indicated culture conflict variables controlled. See Table 1 for specific identification of variables.
[c] Significant at .10 level. With 13 df and p = .90, t = 1.77; for 12 df, t = 1.78. For p = .95, these values are, respectively, 2.16 and 2.18. For r = .47, t = 1.96; since t for r = .41 is 1.64 (footnote d, Table 6), r = .39 is not significant. For $r_{12.3} = .51$, t = 2.04; since t for $r_{12.3} = .46$ is 1.77 (footnote d, Table 6), $r_{12.3} = .45$ is not significant.

Table 8
Short-Term Residence and Total Delinquency, Controlling Social Position and Culture Conflict [a]

Social position [b]			Culture conflict [b]				
Owners/renters	Ethnicity	Family occupational status	Anomia	Status ideology	Education	Teenage marriage	Total score
.78	.83	.77	.82	.80	.83	.78	.82

[a] Partial correlations with the indicated variables controlled, all significant at the .01 level. With 12 df and p = .99, t = 3.06. Since t for $r_{12.3} = .69$ is 3.29 (footnote c, Table 9), all values are significant. The gross correlation coefficient is .80, t = 4.71, with p. 99.
[b] See Table 1 for specific identification of variables.

Table 9
Short-Term Residence and Serious Delinquency,
Controlling Social Position and Culture Conflict [a]

Social position [b]				Culture conflict [b]			
Owners/renters	Ethnicity	Family occupational status	Anomia	Status ideology	Education	Teenage marriage	Total score
.64[d]	.69[d]	.65[d]	.70[c]	.70[c]	.74[c]	.69[c]	.69[c]

[a] Partial correlations with the indicated variables controlled.
[b] See Table 1 for specific identification of variables.
[c] Significant at .01 level. For $r_{12.3} = .69$, $t = 3.29$.
[d] With 12 df and $p = .95$, $t = 2.18$. The t values for $r_{12.3} = .65$ and $= .64$ are, respectively, 2.95 and 2.88; these coefficients are then significant at the .05 level.

Table 10
Short-Term Residence and Total Delinquency, Controlling Both Social
Position and Culture Conflict [a]

	Culture conflict [b]				
Social position [b]	Anomia	Status ideology	Education	Teenage marriage	Total score
Owners/renters	.82	.79	.83	.78	.82
Ethnicity	.83	.83	.82	.82	.83
Family occupational status	.80	.79	.82	.75	.79

[a] Second-order partial correlations, with the indicated pairs of variables controlled, all significant at the .01 level. With 11 df and $p = .99$, $t = 3.11$. For $r_{12.34} = .75$, $t = 3.75$.
[b] See Table 1 for specific identification of variables.

Table 11
Short-Term Residence and Serious Delinquency, Controlling Both Social
Position and Culture Conflict [a]

	Culture conflict [b]				
Social position [b]	Anomia	Status ideology	Education	Teenage marriage	Total score
Owners/renters	.66[b]	.65[d]	.71[c]	.65[d]	.65[b]
Ethnicity	.69[c]	.70[c]	.70[c]	.69[c]	.68[d]
Family occupational status	.68[d]	.68[d]	.72[c]	.64[d]	.66[d]

[a] Second-order partial correlations with the indicated pairs of variables controlled.
[b] See Table 1 for specific identification of variables.
[c] Significant at .01 level. For $r_{12.34} = .69$, $t = 3.14$.
[d] Significant at .05 level. With 11 df and $p = .95$, $t = 2.20$. The t values for $r_{12.34} = .68$ and $= .64$ are, respectively, 3.09 and 2.78.

Table 12
Accounted-for Squared Variability:
Total Delinquency and Serious Delinquency [a]

| | Anomia | | | Short-term residence | | | | | | | | | | | |
| | | | | Status ideology | | | Education | | | Teenage marriage | | | Total score | | |
	Owners/ renters	Eth- nicity	Family status	O/r	E	Fs	O/r	E	Fs	O/r	E	Fs	O/r	E	Fs
Total delin- quency R^2	.789	.760	.729	.773	.775	.715	.774	.762	.728	.714	.758	.659	.769	.764	.698
Serious delin- quency R^2	.595	.557	.567	.675	.639	.627	.618	.576	.592	.550	.562	.506	.556	.557	.522

[a] Combinations of variables as indicated. All coefficients with a value of .639 or better are significant at or beyond the .01 level. All others are significant at the .05 level. In this case, with p = .99 and p = .95, the values of F are 6.22 and 3.59, respectively. For $R^2 = .639$ and $= .627$, F = 6.45 and 6.15. For $R^2 = .506$, F = 3.76.

quency viewed as a socio-legal phenomenon has been offered, largely as a stimulus to more and better systematic theory development. The two main features of the theory are (1) a definition of delinquency as "illegitimation" of pre-adults without any assumptions regarding the actual behavior of individuals who become classed as delinquents and (2) the attempt to develop the idea of intergenerational conflict as a systematic explanation of pre-adult illegitimation. After noting the alternative empirical assumptions under which research might proceed, an initial verification study was reported in which it was assumed that there was a direct correspondence between culture conflict and social conflict. The results of the study were inconclusive. The primary value of the report has been to illustrate the considerations entering into a verification study, particularly (1) the need to establish the reliability and validity of variables in relation to theoretical constructs, and (2) the fact, sometimes neglected in practice, that "failures" in verification studies may be attributable to methodological deficiencies as much as, or even more than, theoretical shortcomings. The essential point is not the rise or fall of the delinquency theory dealt with in this paper, but the transformation of more theorizing into theories and the design of more research relevant to the testing of theories.

Section
Three

SOCIOLOGICAL THEORIES
AND CONTROVERSIES

Anomie

Although published more than thirty years ago, this selection is perhaps the most widely quoted paper in sociology. One need not search for the reason for this popularity — Merton attempts to locate sociocultural sources of deviance. He offers an explanation of deviant behavior, not simply an explanation of delinquency or crime or suicide, within the context of the social structure, rather than as a product of biological forces, personality deficiencies, or psychiatric complexes within the individual who deviates. Recognizing that elements of the social and cultural structure "merge imperceptibly in concrete situations," Merton distinguishes analytically between the ends, "the culturally defined goals, purposes, and interests," and the approved means of achieving these desired ends, "the acceptable modes of achieving these goals." Noting that emphasis upon certain goals may vary independently of emphasis upon institutional means, Merton suggests that in an integrated society there is balanced emphasis on cultural goals and legitimate means to achieve them. As polar types of cultural malintegration there may be a disproportionate stress upon the value of certain goals or a similar almost exclusive emphasis on means. The occurrence of aberrant behavior, Merton suggests, is a symptom or indication of differential emphasis on goals and means. Various forms of deviant behavior occur with increasing frequency when certain goals are stressed without a corresponding emphasis on the importance of reaching these goals by legitimate means. In American society the overarching goal, Merton argues, is success, particularly the accumulation of wealth as a symbol of success.

Merton also described five logically possible modes of adaptation or possible role adjustments of individuals in specific situations. According to Merton, conformity is the most common response, while retreatism, involving rejection of the goals and means, is least common. However, Merton's primary interest is in the innovative mode in which proscribed, yet often effective, means are used to attain the culturally defined goal of success. Merton argues that a high rate of deviance is not generated simply by lack of opportunity or by an exaggerated emphasis on monetary success; rather, he states: "It is only when a system of cultural values extols, virtually above all else, certain *common* symbols of success *for the population at large* while its social structure rigorously restricts or completely eliminates access to approved modes of acquiring these symbols *for a considerable part of the same population*, that antisocial behavior ensues on a considerable scale." In other words, the pressures toward deviant behavior in general and delinquent behavior in particular are more severe at different points in the social structure. Although the same success symbols are held to be desirable for all, the limited formal education and economic resources of lower socio-economic groups effectively restrict their access to the desired symbols of success.

ROBERT K. MERTON

Social Structure and Anomie

There persists a notable tendency in sociological theory to attribute the malfunctioning of social structure primarily to those of man's imperious biological drives which are not adequately restrained by social control. In this view, the social order is solely a device for "impulse management" and the "social processing" of tensions. These impulses which break through social control, be it noted, are held to be biologically derived. Nonconformity is assumed to be rooted in original nature.[1] Conformity is by implication the result of an utilitarian calculus or unreasoned conditioning. This point of view, whatever its other deficiencies, clearly begs one question. It provides no basis for determining the nonbiological conditions which induce deviations from prescribed patterns of conduct. In this paper, it will be suggested that certain phases of social structure generate the circumstances in which infringement of social codes constitutes a "normal" response.[2]

From *American Sociological Review*, October 1938, pp. 672–682. Reprinted by permission of the American Sociological Association.

[1] E.g., Ernest Jones, *Social Aspects of Psychoanalysis*, 28, London, 1924. If the Freudian notion is a variety of the "original sin" dogma, then the interpretation advanced in this paper may be called the doctrine of "socially derived sin."

[2] "Normal" in the sense of a culturally oriented, if not approved, response. This statement does not deny the relevance of biological and personality differences which may be significantly involved in the *incidence* of deviate conduct. Our focus of in-

The conceptual scheme to be outlined is designed to provide a coherent, systematic approach to the study of socio-cultural sources of deviate behavior. Our primary aim lies in discovering how some social structures *exert a definite pressure* upon certain persons in the society to engage in nonconformist rather than conformist conduct. The many ramifications of the scheme cannot all be discussed; the problems mentioned outnumber those explicitly treated.

Among the elements of social and cultural structure, two are important for our purposes. These are analytically separable although they merge imperceptibly in concrete situations. The first consists of culturally defined goals, purposes, and interests. It comprises a frame of aspirational reference. These goals are more or less integrated and involve varying degrees of prestige and sentiment. They constitute a basic, but not the exclusive, component of what Linton aptly has called "designs for group living." Some of these cultural aspirations are related to the original drives of man, but they are not determined by them. The second phase of the social structure defines, regulates, and controls the acceptable modes of

terest is the social and cultural matrix; hence we abstract from other factors. It is in this sense, I take it, that James S. Plant speaks of the "normal reaction of normal people to abnormal conditions." See his *Personality and the Cultural Pattern*, 248, New York, 1937.

achieving these goals. Every social group invariably couples its scale of desired ends with moral or institutional regulation of permissible and required procedures for attaining these ends. These regulatory norms and moral imperatives do not necessarily coincide with technical or efficiency norms. Many procedures which from the standpoint of *particular individuals* would be most efficient in securing desired values, e.g., illicit oil-stock schemes, theft, fraud, are ruled out of the institutional area of permitted conduct. The choice of expedients is limited by the institutional norms.

To say that these two elements, culture goals and institutional norms, operate jointly is not to say that the ranges of alternative behaviors and aims bear some constant relation to one another. The emphasis upon certain goals may vary independently of the degree of emphasis upon institutional means. There may develop a disproportionate, at times, a virtually exclusive, stress upon the value of specific goals, involving relatively slight concern with the institutionally appropriate modes of attaining these goals. The limiting case in this direction is reached when the range of alternative procedures is limited only by technical rather than institutional considerations. Any and all devices which promise attainment of the all important goal would be permitted in this hypothetical polar case.[3] This constitutes one

type of cultural malintegration. A second polar type is found in groups where activities originally conceived as instrumental are transmuted into ends in themselves. The original purposes are forgotten and ritualistic adherence to institutionally prescribed conduct becomes virtually obsessive.[4] Stability is largely ensured while change is flouted. The range of alternative behaviors is severely limited. There develops a tradition-bound, sacred society characterized by neophobia. The occupational psychosis of the bureaucrat may be cited as a case in point. Finally, there are the intermediate types of groups where a balance between culture goals and institutional means is maintained. These are the significantly integrated and relatively stable, though changing, groups.

An effective equilibrium between the two phases of the social structure is maintained as long as satisfactions accrue to individuals who conform to both constraints, viz., satisfactions from the achievement of the goals and satisfactions emerging directly from the institutionally canalized modes of striving to attain these ends. Success, in such equilibrated cases, is twofold. Success is reckoned in terms of the product and in terms of the process, in terms of the outcome and in terms of activities. Continuing satisfactions must derive from sheer *participation* in a competitive order as well as from eclipsing one's competitors if the order itself is to be sustained. The occasional sacrifices involved in institutionalized conduct must be compensated by socialized rewards. The distribution of statuses and roles through competition must be so organized that positive incentives for conformity to roles and adherence to status obligations are provided *for every position* within the distributive order. Aberrant conduct, therefore, may be viewed as a symptom of dissociation between culturally defined aspirations and socially structured means.

[3] Contemporary American culture has been said to tend in this direction. See André Siegfried, *America Comes of Age*, 26–37, New York, 1927. The alleged extreme (?) emphasis on the goals of monetary success and material prosperity leads to dominant concern with technological and social instruments designed to produce the desired result, inasmuch as institutional controls become of secondary importance. In such a situation, innovation flourishes as the *range of means* employed is broadened. In a sense, then, there occurs the paradoxical emergence of "materialists" from an "idealistic" orientation. Cf. Durkheim's analysis of the cultural conditions which predispose toward crime and innovation, both of which are aimed toward efficiency, not moral norms. Durkheim was one of the first to see that "contrairement aux idées courantes le criminel n'apparait plus comme un être radicalement insociable, comme une sorte d'élément parasitaire, de corps étranger et inassimilable, introduit au sein de la société; c'est un agent régulier de la vie sociale." See *Les Règles de la Méthode Sociologique*, 86–89, Paris, 1927.

[4] Such ritualism may be associated with a mythology which rationalizes these actions so that they appear to retain their status as means, but the dominant pressure is in the direction of strict ritualistic conformity, irrespective of such rationalizations. In this sense, ritual has proceeded farthest when such rationalizations are not even called forth.

Of the types of groups which result from the independent variation of the two phases of the social structure, we shall be primarily concerned with the first, namely, that involving a disproportionate accent on goals. This statement must be recast in a proper perspective. In no group is there an absence of regulatory codes governing conduct, yet groups do vary in the degree to which these folkways, mores, and institutional controls are effectively integrated with the more diffuse goals which are part of the culture matrix. Emotional convictions may cluster about the complex of socially acclaimed ends, meanwhile shifting their support from the culturally defined implementation of these ends. As we shall see, certain aspects of the social structure may generate countermores and antisocial behavior precisely because of differential emphases on goals and regulations. In the extreme case, the latter may be so vitiated by the goal-emphasis that the range of behavior is limited only by considerations of technical expediency. The sole significant question then becomes, which available means is most efficient in netting the socially approved value? [5] The technically most feasible procedure, whether legitimate or not, is preferred to the institutionally prescribed conduct. As this process continues, the integration of the society becomes tenuous and anomie ensues.

Thus, in competitive athletics, when the aim of victory is shorn of its institutional trappings and success in contests becomes construed as "winning the game" rather than "winning through circumscribed modes of activity," a premium is implicitly set upon the use of il-

legitimate but technically efficient means. The star of the opposing football team is surreptitiously slugged; the wrestler furtively incapacitates his opponent through ingenious but illicit techniques; university alumni covertly subsidize "students" whose talents are largely confined to the athletic field. The emphasis on the goal has so attenuated the satisfactions deriving from sheer participation in the competitive activity that these satisfactions are virtually confined to a successful outcome. Through the same process, tension generated by the desire to win in a poker game is relieved by successfully dealing oneself four aces, or, when the cult of success has become completely dominant, by sagaciously shuffling the cards in a game of solitaire. The faint twinge of uneasiness in the last instance and the surreptitious nature of public delicts indicate clearly that the institutional rules of the game *are known* to those who evade them, but that the emotional supports of these rules are largely vitiated by cultural exaggeration of the success-goal.[6] They are microcosmic images of the social macrocosm.

Of course, this process is not restricted to the realm of sport. The process whereby exaltation of the end generates a *literal demoralization*, i.e., a deinstitutionalization, of the means is one which characterizes many [7] groups in which the two phases of the social structure are not highly integrated. The extreme emphasis upon the accumulation of

---

[5] In this connection, one may see the relevance of Elton Mayo's paraphrase of the title of Tawney's well known book. "Actually the problem *is not that of the sickness of an acquisitive society; it is that of the acquisitiveness of a sick society.*" *Human Problems of an Industrial Civilization*, 153, New York, 1933. Mayo deals with the process through which wealth comes to be a symbol of social achievement. He sees this as arising from a state of anomie. We are considering the unintegrated monetary-success goal as an element in producing anomie. A complete analysis would involve both phases of this system of interdependent variables.

[6] It is unlikely that interiorized norms are completely eliminated. Whatever residuum persists will induce personality tensions and conflict. The process involves a certain degree of ambivalence. A manifest rejection of the institutional norms is coupled with some latent retention of their emotional correlates. "Guilt feelings," "sense of sin," "pangs of conscience" are obvious manifestations of this unrelieved tension; symbolic adherence to the nominally repudiated values or rationalizations constitute a more subtle variety of tensional release.

[7] "Many," and not all, unintegrated groups, for the reason already mentioned. In groups where the primary emphasis shifts to institutional means, i.e., when the range of alternatives is very limited, the outcome is a type of ritualism rather than anomie.

wealth as a symbol of success[8] in our own society militates against the completely effective control of institutionally regulated modes of acquiring a fortune.[9] Fraud, corruption, vice, crime, in short, the entire catalogue of proscribed behavior, becomes increasingly common when the emphasis on the *culturally induced* success-goal becomes divorced from a coordinated institutional emphasis. This observation is of crucial theoretical importance in examining the doctrine that antisocial behavior most frequently derives from biological drives breaking through the restraints imposed by society. The difference is one between a strictly utilitarian interpretation which conceives man's ends as random and an analysis which finds these ends deriving from the basic values of the culture.[10]

Our analysis can scarcely stop at this juncture. We must turn to other aspects of the social structure if we are to deal with the social genesis of the varying rates and types of deviate behavior characteristic of different societies. Thus far, we have sketched three ideal types of social orders constituted by distinctive patterns of relations between culture ends and means. Turning from these types of *culture patterning*, we find five logically possible,

alternative modes of adjustment or adaptation *by individuals* within the culture-bearing society or group.[11] These are schematically presented in the following table, where (+) signifies "acceptance," (−) signifies "elimination" and (±) signifies "rejection and substitution of new goals and standards."

	Culture goals	Institutionalized means
I. Conformity	+	+
II. Innovation	+	−
III. Ritualism	−	+
IV. Retreatism	−	−
V. Rebellion[12]	±	±

Our discussion of the relation between these alternative responses and other phases of the social structure must be prefaced by the observation that persons may shift from one alternative to another as they engage in different social activities. These categories refer to role adjustments in specific situations, not to personality *in toto*. To treat the development of this process in various spheres of conduct would introduce a complexity unmanageable within the confines of this paper. For this reason, we shall be concerned primarily with economic activity in the broad sense, "the production, exchange, distribution and consumption of goods and services" in our competitive society, wherein wealth has taken on a highly symbolic cast. Our task is to search out some of the factors which exert pressure upon indi-

[8] Money has several peculiarities which render it particularly apt to become a symbol of prestige divorced from institutional controls. As Simmel emphasized, money is highly abstract and impersonal. However acquired, through fraud or institutionally, it can be used to purchase the same goods and services. The anonymity of metropolitan culture, in conjunction with this peculiarity of money, permits wealth, the sources of which may be unknown to the community in which the plutocrat lives, to serve as a symbol of status.

[9] The emphasis upon wealth as a success-symbol is possibly reflected in the use of the term "fortune" to refer to a stock of accumulated wealth. This meaning becomes common in the late sixteenth century (Spenser and Shakespeare). A similar usage of the Latin *fortuna* comes into prominence during the first century B.C. Both these periods were marked by the rise to prestige and power of the "bourgeoisie."

[10] See Kingsley Davis, "Mental Hygiene and the Class Structure," *Psychiatry*, 1928, I, esp. 62–63; Talcott Parsons, *The Structure of Social Action*, 59–60, New York, 1937.

[11] This is a level intermediate between the two planes distinguished by Edward Sapir; namely, culture patterns and personal habit systems. See his "Contribution of Psychiatry to an Understanding of Behavior in Society," *Amer. J. Sociol.*, 1937, 42:862–70.

[12] This fifth alternative is on a plane clearly different from that of the others. It represents a *transitional* response which seeks to *institutionalize* new procedures oriented toward revamped cultural goals shared by the members of the society. It thus involves efforts to *change* the existing structure rather than to perform accommodative actions *within* this structure, and introduces additional problems with which we are not at the moment concerned.

viduals to engage in certain of these logically possible alternative responses. This choice, as we shall see, is far from random.

In every society, Adaptation I (conformity to both culture goals and means) is the most common and widely diffused. Were this not so, the stability and continuity of the society could not be maintained. The mesh of expectancies which constitutes every social order is sustained by the modal behavior of its members falling within the first category. Conventional role behavior oriented toward the basic values of the group is the rule rather than the exception. It is this fact alone which permits us to speak of a human aggregate as comprising a group or society.

Conversely, Adaptation IV (rejection of goals and means) is the least common. Persons who "adjust" (or maladjust) in this fashion are, strictly speaking, *in* the society but not *of* it. Sociologically, these constitute the true "aliens." Not sharing the common frame of orientation, they can be included within the societal population merely in a fictional sense. In this category are *some* of the activities of psychotics, psychoneurotics, chronic autists, pariahs, outcasts, vagrants, vagabonds, tramps, chronic drunkards and drug addicts.[13] These have relinquished, in certain spheres of activity, the culturally defined goals, involving complete aim-inhibition in the polar case, and their adjustments are not in accord with institutional norms. This is not to say that in some cases the source of their behavioral adjustments is not in part the very social structure which they have in effect repudiated nor that their very existence within a social area does not constitute a problem for the socialized population.

This mode of "adjustment" occurs, as far as

[13] Obviously, this is an elliptical statement. These individuals may maintain some orientation to the values of their particular differentiated groupings within the larger society or, in part, of the conventional society itself. Insofar as they do so, their conduct cannot be classified in the "passive rejection" category (IV). Nels Anderson's description of the behavior and attitudes of the bum, for example, can readily be recast in terms of our analytical scheme. See *The Hobo*, 93–98, *et passim*, Chicago, 1923.

structural sources are concerned, when both the culture goals and institutionalized procedures have been assimilated thoroughly by the individual and imbued with affect and high positive value, but where those institutionalized procedures which promise a measure of successful attainment of the goals are not available to the individual. In such instances, there results a twofold mental conflict insofar as the moral obligation for adopting institutional means conflicts with the pressure to resort to illegitimate means (which may attain the goal) and inasmuch as the individual is shut off from means which are both legitimate *and* effective. The competitive order is maintained, but the frustrated and handicapped individual who cannot cope with this order drops out. Defeatism, quietism and resignation are manifested in escape mechanisms which ultimately lead the individual to "escape" from the requirements of the society. It is an expedient which arises from continued failure to attain the goal by legitimate measures and from an inability to adopt the illegitimate route because of internalized prohibitions and institutionalized compulsives, *during which process the supreme value of the success-goal has as yet not been renounced.* The conflict is resolved by eliminating *both* precipitating elements, the goals and means. The escape is complete, the conflict is eliminated and the individual is a socialized.

Be it noted that where frustration derives from the inaccessibility of effective institutional means for attaining economic or any other type of highly valued "success," that Adaptations II, III and V (innovation, ritualism and rebellion) are also possible. The result will be determined by the particular personality, and thus, the *particular* cultural background, involved. Inadequate socialization will result in the innovation response whereby the conflict and frustration are eliminated by relinquishing the institutional means and retaining the success-aspiration; an extreme assimilation of institutional demands will lead to ritualism wherein the goal is dropped as beyond one's reach but conformity to the mores persists; and rebellion occurs when emancipation from the reigning standards, due to frustration or to marginalist perspectives, leads to the attempt to introduce a "new social order."

Our major concern is with the illegitimacy adjustment. This involves the use of conventionally proscribed but frequently effective means of attaining at least the simulacrum of culturally defined success — wealth, power, and the like. As we have seen, this adjustment occurs when the individual has assimilated the cultural emphasis on success without equally internalizing the morally prescribed norms governing means for its attainment. The question arises, Which phases of our social structure predispose toward this mode of adjustment? We may examine a concrete instance, effectively analyzed by Lohman,[14] which provides a clue to the answer. Lohman has shown that specialized areas of vice in the near north side of Chicago constitute a "normal" response to a situation where the cultural emphasis upon pecuniary success has been absorbed, but where there is little access to conventional and legitimate means for attaining such success. The conventional occupational opportunities of persons in this area are almost completely limited to manual labor. Given our cultural stigmatization of manual labor, and its correlate, the prestige of white collar work, it is clear that the result is a strain toward innovational practices. The limitation of opportunity to unskilled labor and the resultant low income can not compete *in terms of conventional standards of achievement* with the high income from organized vice.

For our purposes, this situation involves two important features. First, such antisocial behavior is in a sense "called forth" by certain conventional values of the culture *and* by the class structure involving differential access to the approved opportunities for legitimate, prestige-bearing pursuit of the culture goals. The lack of high integration between the means-and-end elements of the cultural pattern and the particular class structure combine to favor a heightened frequency of antisocial conduct in such groups. The second consideration is of equal significance. Recourse to the

first of the alternative responses, legitimate effort, is limited by the fact that actual advance toward desired success-symbols through conventional channels is, despite our persisting open-class ideology,[15] relatively rare and difficult for those handicapped by little formal education and few economic resources. The dominant pressure of group standards of success is, therefore, on the gradual attenuation of legitimate, but by and large ineffective, strivings and the increasing use of illegitimate, but more or less effective, expedients of vice and crime. The cultural demands made on persons in this situation are incompatible. On the one hand, they are asked to orient their conduct toward the prospect of accumulating wealth and on the other, they are largely denied effective opportunities to do so institutionally. The consequences of such structural inconsistency are psychopathological personality, and/or antisocial conduct, and/or revolutionary activities. The equilibrium between culturally designated means and ends becomes highly unstable with the progressive emphasis on attaining the prestige-laden ends by any means whatsoever. Within this context, Capone represents the triumph of amoral intelligence over morally prescribed "failure," when the channels of vertical mobility are closed or narrowed [16] *in a society which places a high*

---

[14] Joseph D. Lohman, "The Participant Observer in Community Studies," *Amer. Sociol. Rev.*, 1937, 2:890–98.

[15] The shifting historical role of this ideology is a profitable subject for exploration. The "office-boy-to-president" stereotype was once in approximate accord with the facts. Such vertical mobility was probably more common then than now, when the class structure is more rigid. (See the following note.) The ideology largely persists, however, possibly because it still performs a useful function for maintaining the *status quo*. For insofar as it is accepted by the "masses," it constitutes a useful sop for those who might rebel against the entire structure, were this consoling hope removed. This ideology now serves to lessen the probability of Adaptation V. In short, the role of this notion has changed from that of an approximately valid empirical theorem to that of an ideology, in Mannheim's sense.

[16] There is a growing body of evidence, though none of it is clearly conclusive, to the effect that our class structure is becoming rigidified and that vertical mobility is declining. Taussig and Joslyn found that American business leaders are being *increasingly* recruited from the upper ranks of our

premium on economic affluence and social ascent for all *its members.*[17]

This last qualification is of primary importance. It suggests that other phases of the social structure besides the extreme emphasis on pecuniary success, must be considered if we are to understand the social sources of antisocial behavior. A high frequency of deviate behavior is not generated simply by "lack of opportunity" or by this exaggerated pecuniary emphasis. A comparatively rigidified class structure, a feudalistic or caste order, may limit such opportunities far beyond the point which obtains in our society today. It is only when a system of cultural values extols, virtually above all else, certain *common* symbols of success *for the population at large* while its social structure rigorously restricts or completely eliminates access to approved modes of acquiring these symbols *for a considerable part of the same population,* that antisocial behavior ensues on a considerable scale. In other words,

our egalitarian ideology denies by implication the existence of noncompeting groups and individuals in the pursuit of pecuniary success. The same body of success-symbols is held to be desirable for all. These goals are held to *transcend class lines,* not to be bounded by them, yet the actual social organization is such that there exist class differentials in the accessibility of these *common* success-symbols. Frustration and thwarted aspiration lead to the search for avenues of escape from a culturally induced intolerable situation; or unrelieved ambition may eventuate in illicit attempts to acquire the dominant values.[18] The American stress on pecuniary success and ambitiousness for all thus invites exaggerated anxieties, hostilities, neuroses and antisocial behavior.

This theoretical analysis may go far toward explaining the varying correlations between crime and poverty.[19] Poverty is not an isolated variable. It is one in a complex of interdependent social and cultural variables. When viewed in such a context, it represents quite different states of affairs. Poverty as such, and consequent limitation of opportunity, are not sufficient to induce a conspicuously high rate of criminal behavior. Even the often mentioned "poverty in the midst of plenty" will not necessarily lead to this result. Only insofar

---

society. The Lynds have also found a "diminished chance to get ahead" for the working classes in Middletown. Manifestly, these objective changes are not alone significant; the individual's subjective evaluation of the situation is a major determinant of the response. The extent to which this change in opportunity for social mobility has been recognized by the least advantaged classes is still conjectural, although the Lynds present some suggestive materials. The writer suggests that a case in point is the increasing frequency of cartoons which observe in a tragi-comic vein that "my old man says everybody can't be President. He says if ya can get three days a week steady on W.P.A. work ya ain't doin' so bad either." See F. W. Taussig and C. S. Joslyn, *American Business Leaders,* New York, 1932; R. S. and H. M. Lynd, *Middletown in Transition,* 67 ff., chap. 12, New York, 1937.

[17] The role of the Negro in this respect is of considerable theoretical interest. Certain elements of the Negro population have assimilated the dominant caste's values of pecuniary success and social advancement, but they also recognize that social ascent is at present restricted to their own caste almost exclusively. The pressures upon the Negro which would otherwise derive from the structural inconsistencies we have noticed are hence not identical with those upon lower class whites. See Kingsley Davis, *op. cit.,* 63; John Dollard, *Caste and Class in a Southern Town,* 66 ff., New Haven, 1936; Donald Young, *American Minority Peoples,* 581, New York, 1932.

[18] The psychical coordinates of these processes have been partly established by the experimental evidence concerning *Anspruchsniveaus* and levels of performance. See Kurt Lewin, *Vorsatz, Wille und Bedurfnis,* Berlin, 1926; N. F. Hoppe, "Erfolg und Misserfolg," *Psychol. Forschung,* 1930, 14:1–63; Jerome D. Frank, "Individual Differences in Certain Aspects of the Level of Aspiration," *Amer. J. Psychol.,* 1935, 47:119–28.

[19] Standard criminology texts summarize the data in this field. Our scheme of analysis may serve to resolve some of the theoretical contradictions which P. A. Sorokin indicates. For example, "not everywhere nor always do the poor show a greater proportion of crime . . . many poorer countries have had less crime than the richer countries. . . . The [economic] improvement in the second half of the nineteenth century, and the beginning of the twentieth, has not been followed by a decrease of crime." See his *Contemporary Sociological Theories,* 560–61, New York, 1928. The crucial point is, however, that poverty has varying social significance in different social structures, as we shall see. Hence, one would not expect a linear correlation between crime and poverty.

as poverty and associated disadvantages in competition for the culture values approved for *all* members of the society is linked with the assimilation of a cultural emphasis on monetary accumulation as a symbol of success is antisocial conduct a "normal" outcome. Thus, poverty is less highly correlated with crime in southeastern Europe than in the United States. The possibilities of vertical mobility in these European areas would seem to be fewer than in this country, so that neither poverty *per se* nor its association with limited opportunity is sufficient to account for the varying correlations. It is only when the full configuration is considered, poverty, limited opportunity and a commonly shared system of success symbols, that we can explain the higher association between poverty and crime in our society than in others where rigidified class structure is coupled with *differential class symbols of achievement*.

In societies such as our own, then, the pressure of prestige-bearing success tends to eliminate the effective social constraint over means employed to this end. "The-end-justifies-the-means" doctrine becomes a guiding tenet for action when the cultural structure unduly exalts the end and the social organization unduly limits possible recourse to approved means. Otherwise put, this notion and associated behavior reflect a lack of cultural coordination. In international relations, the effects of this lack of integration are notoriously apparent. An emphasis upon national power is not readily coordinated with an inept organization of legitimate, i.e., internationally defined and accepted, means for attaining this goal. The result is a tendency toward the abrogation of international law, treaties become scraps of paper, "undeclared warfare" serves as a technical evasion, the bombing of civilian populations is rationalized,[20] just as the same societal situation induces the same sway of illegitimacy among individuals.

The social order we have described necessarily produces this "strain toward dissolution." The pressure of such an order is upon

outdoing one's competitors. The choice of means within the ambit of institutional control will persist as long as the sentiments supporting a competitive system, i.e., deriving from the possibility of outranking competitors and hence enjoying the favorable response of others, are distributed throughout the entire system of activities and are not confined merely to the final result. A stable social structure demands a balanced distribution of affect among its various segments. When there occurs a shift of emphasis from the satisfactions deriving from competition itself to almost exclusive concern with successful competition, the resultant stress leads to the breakdown of the regulatory structure.[21] With the resulting attenuation of the institutional imperatives, there occurs an approximation of the situation erroneously held by utilitarians to be typical of society generally wherein calculations of advantage and fear of punishment are the sole regulating agencies. In such situations, as Hobbes observed, force and fraud come to constitute the sole virtues in view of their relative efficiency in attaining goals — which were for him, of course, not culturally derived.

It should be apparent that the foregoing discussion is not pitched on a moralistic plane. Whatever the sentiments of the writer or reader concerning the ethical desirability of coordinating the means-and-goals phases of the social structure, one must agree that lack of such coordination leads to anomie. Insofar as one of the most general functions of social organization is to provide a basis for calculability and regularity of behavior, it is increasingly limited in effectiveness as these elements of the structure become dissociated. At the extreme, predictability virtually disappears and what may be properly termed cultural chaos or anomie intervenes.

This statement, being brief, is also incomplete. It has not included an exhaustive treatment of the various structural elements which

[20] See M. W. Royse, *Aerial Bombardment and the International Regulation of War*, New York, 1928.

[21] Since our primary concern is with the sociocultural aspects of this problem, the psychological correlates have been only implicitly considered. See Karen Horney, *The Neurotic Personality of Our Time*, New York, 1937, for a psychological discussion of this process.

predispose toward one rather than another of the alternative responses open to individuals; it has neglected, but not denied the relevance of, the factors determining the specific incidence of these responses; it has not enumerated the various concrete responses which are constituted by combinations of specific values of the analytical variables; it has omitted, or included only by implication, any consideration of the social functions performed by illicit responses; it has not tested the full explanatory power of the analytical scheme by examining a large number of group variations in the frequency of deviate and conformist behavior; it has not adequately dealt with rebellious conduct which seeks to refashion the social framework radically; it has not examined the relevance of cultural conflict for an analysis of culture-goal and institutional-means malintegration. It is suggested that these and related problems may be profitably analyzed by this scheme.

To understand Merton's argument is important because his conception of anomie has served as the fountainhead for several contemporary theories regarding gang delinquency. Specifically, Cohen (1955) and Cloward and Ohlin (1960), whose theories are presented in the following section, draw extensively upon Merton. This selection offers not only a valuable dissection of Merton's position but also makes a substantive theoretical contribution. Cohen begins by pointing out imperfections and gaps in the theory of anomie; he observes, for example, that the disjunction between goals and means is only one source of strain and that Merton was primarily concerned with structural factors that account for variations in strain. In Merton's original formulation each individual seemingly develops his own solution to strain, while Cloward and Ohlin take the actions of others into account; they do so by integrating anomie with the "cultural transmission-differential association" tradition and the general theory of subcultures developed by Cohen (1955). Notice that this paper appeared a decade after Cohen's *Delinquent Boys* and elaborates and integrates ideas in that volume with Merton's theoretical contribution. Cohen suggests that Merton's theory suffers from "the assumption of discontinuity"; that is, there appears to be an abrupt shift from "a state of strain or anomie to a state of deviance." Cohen observes that human behavior, whether deviant or not, "typically develops and grows in a tentative, groping, advancing, backtracking, sounding-out process." He suggests, therefore, that rather than concentrating on initial states and outcomes, investigators should focus attention on processes. In the final section of his paper Cohen emphasizes the importance of integrating anomie and self-role theory. Utilizing the perspective of symbolic interaction, Cohen shifts his focus to the process whereby one becomes tentatively involved in and progressively committed to social roles. It is suggested that deviant behavior may be expressive of one's role(s) and deviant acts may serve to affirm that "one is a certain kind of person." The implication is that not all deviance involves structural strain; acts may express and confirm an identity. The student may find it helpful to refer to

Cohen's ideas after reading the following selections dealing with differential association and self-conception. For those interested in additional discussion and criticism of Merton's theoretical contribution, the volume edited by Clinard, *Anomie and Deviant Behavior* (1964), is recommended.

REFERENCES

Marshall B. Clinard (ed.), *Anomie and Deviant Behavior* (New York: The Free Press of Glencoe, 1964).

Richard A. Cloward and Lloyd E. Ohlin, *Delinquency and Opportunity: A Theory of Delinquent Gangs* (Glencoe, Ill.: The Free Press, 1960).

Albert K. Cohen, *Delinquent Boys: The Culture of the Gang* (Glencoe, Ill.: The Free Press, 1955).

ALBERT K. COHEN

The Sociology of the Deviant Act: Anomie Theory and Beyond

My concern in this paper is to move toward a general theory of deviant behavior. Taking "Social Structure and Anomie" [1] as a point of departure, I shall note some of the imperfections and gaps in the theory as originally stated, how some of these have been rectified, some theoretical openings for further exploration, and some problems of relating anomie theory to other traditions in the sociology of deviance. It is not important, for my purposes, how broadly or narrowly Merton himself conceived the range of applicability of his anomie theory. Whatever the intention or vision of the author of a theory, it is the task of a discipline to explore the implications of a theoretical insight, in all directions. Many of the points I shall make are, indeed, to be found in Merton's work. In many instances, however, they either appear as leads, suggestions, or *obiter dicta*, and are left undeveloped, or they appear in some other context and no effort is made systematically to link them with anomie theory.[2]

The Anomie Theory of Deviant Behavior

Merton's theory has the reputation of being the pre-eminently *sociological* theory of deviant behavior. Its concern is to account for the distribution of deviant behavior among the positions in a social system and for differences in the distribution and rates of deviant behavior among systems. It tries to account for

From *American Sociological Review*, February 1965, pp. 5–14. Reprinted by permission of the American Sociological Association.

[1] Robert K. Merton, "Social Structure and Anomie," *American Sociological Review*, 3 (October 1938), pp. 672–682, *Social Theory and Social Structure*, Glencoe, Ill.: The Free Press, 1957, Chs. 4 and 5, and "Conformity, Deviation, and Opportunity-Structures," *American Sociological Review*, 24 (April 1959), pp. 177–189; Richard A. Cloward, "Illegitimate Means, Anomie, and Deviant Behavior," *American Sociological Review*, 24 (April 1959), pp. 164–176; and Robert Dubin, "Deviant Behavior and Social Structure: Continuities in Social Theory," *American Sociological Review*, 24 (April 1959), pp. 147–164.

[2] I am not here concerned with empirical applications and tests of anomie theory, on which there is now a large literature. In view of the sustained interest in anomie theory, its enormous influence, and its numerous applications, however, it is worth noting and wondering at the relatively slow and fitful growth of the substantive theory itself. It is of some interest also that, with respect to both substantive theory and its applications, there has been little follow-up of Merton's own leads relative to the implications of anomie theory for intersocietal differences in deviant behavior. Almost all of the work has been on variations in deviance within American society.

these things as functions of system properties — *i.e.*, the ways in which cultural goals and opportunities for realizing them within the limits of the institutional norms are distributed. The emphasis, in short, is on certain aspects of the culture (goals and norms) and of the social structure (opportunities, or access to means). The theory *is*, then, radically sociological. And yet, as far as the formal and explicit structure of Merton's first formulation is concerned, it is, in certain respects, atomistic and individualistic. Within the framework of goals, norms, and opportunities, the process of deviance was conceptualized as though each individual — or better, role incumbent — were in a box by himself. He has internalized goals and normative, regulatory rules; he assesses the opportunity structure; he experiences strain; and he selects one or another mode of adaptation. The bearing of others' experience — their strains, their conformity and deviance, their success and failure — on ego's strain and consequent adaptations is comparatively neglected.

Consider first the concept of strain itself. It is a function of the degree of disjunction between goals and means, or of the sufficiency of means to the attainment of goals. But how imperious must the goals be, how uncertain their attainment, how incomplete their fulfillment, to generate strain? The relation between goals as components of that abstraction, culture, and the concrete goals of concrete role incumbents, is by no means clear and simple. One thing that is clear is that the level of goal attainment that will seem just and reasonable to concrete actors, and therefore the sufficiency of available means, will be relative to the attainments of others who serve as reference objects. Level of aspiration is not a fixed quantum, taken from the culture and swallowed whole, to lodge unchanged within our psyches. The sense of proportionality between effort and reward is not determined by the objective returns of effort alone. From the standpoint of the role sector whose rates of deviance are in question, the mapping of reference group orientations, the availability *to others* of access to means, and the actual distribution

of rewards are aspects of the social structure important for the determination of strain.[3]

Once we take explicit cognizance of these processes of comparison, a number of other problems unfold themselves. For example, others, whom we define as legitimate objects of comparison, may be more successful than we are by adhering to legitimate means. They not only do better than we do, but they do so "fair and square." On the other hand, they may do as well as we or even better by cutting corners, cheating, using illegitimate means. Do these two different situations have different consequences for the sense of strain, for attitudes toward oneself, for subsequent adaptations? In general, what strains does deviance on the part of others create for the virtuous? In the most obvious case ego is the direct victim of alter's deviance. Or ego's interests may be adversely but indirectly affected by the chicanery of a competitor — unfair trade practices in business, unethical advertising in medicine, cheating in examinations when the instructor grades on a curve. But there is a less obvious case, the one which, according to Ranulf,[4] gives rise to disinterested moral indignation. The dedicated pursuit of culturally approved goals, the eschewing of interdicted but tantalizing goals, the adherence to normatively sanctioned means — these imply a certain self-restraint, effort, discipline, inhibition. What is the effect of the spectacle of others who, though their activities do not manifestly damage our own interests, are morally undisciplined, who give themselves up to idleness, self-indulgence, or forbidden vices? What effect does the propinquity of the wicked have on the peace of mind of the virtuous?

In several ways, the virtuous can make capital out of this situation, can convert a situation with a potential for strain to a source of satis-

---

[3] See, for example, how Henry and Short explicitly incorporate reference group theory and relative deprivation into their theory of suicide. Andrew Henry and James F. Short, Jr., *Suicide and Homicide*, Glencoe, Ill.: The Free Press, 1954, pp. 56–59.

[4] Svend Ranulf, *Moral Indignation and Middle-Class Psychology: A Sociological Study*, Copenhagen: Levin and Munksgaard, 1938.

faction. One can become even more virtuous letting his reputation hinge on his righteousness, *building his self out of invidious comparison to the morally weak*. Since others' wickedness sets off the jewel of one's own virtue, and one's claim to virtue is at the core of his public identity, one may actually develop a stake in the existence of deviant others, and be threatened should they pretend to moral excellence. In short, another's virtue may become a source of strain! One may also join with others in righteous puritanical wrath to mete out punishment to the deviants, not so much to stamp out their deviant behavior, as to reaffirm the central importance of conformity as the basis for judging men and to reassure himself and others of his attachment to goodness. One may even make a virtue of tolerance and indulgence of others' moral deficiencies, thereby implicitly calling attention to one's own special strength of character. If the weakness of others is only human, then there is something more than human about one's own strength. On the other hand, one might join the profligate.

What I have said here is relevant to social control, but my concern at present is not with social control but with some of the ways in which deviance of others may aggravate or lighten the burdens of conformity and hence the strain that is so central to anomie theory.

The student of Merton will recognize that some of these points are suggested or even developed at some length here and there in Merton's own writing. Merton is, of course, one of the chief architects of reference group theory, and in his chapter on "Continuities in the Theory of Reference Groups and Social Structure," he has a section entitled "Nonconformity as a Type of Reference Group Behavior." [5] There he recognizes the problems that one actor's deviance creates for others, and he explicitly calls attention to Ranulf's treatment of disinterested moral indignation as a way of dealing with this problem. [6] In "Continuities in the Theory of Social Structure and Anomie," he describes how the deviance of some increases the others' vulnerability to deviance. [7] In short, my characterization of the earliest version of "Social Structure and Anomie" as "atomistic and individualistic" would be a gross misrepresentation if it were applied to the total corpus of Merton's writing on deviance. He has not, however, developed the role of comparison processes in the determination of strain or considered it explicitly in the context of anomie theory. And in general, Merton does not identify the complexities and subtleties of the concept strain as a problem area in their own right.

Finally, in connection with the concept strain, attention should be called to Smelser's treatment of the subject in his *Theory of Collective Behavior*. [8] Although Smelser does not deal with this as it bears on a theory of deviance, it is important here for two reasons. First, it is, to my knowledge, the only attempt in the literature to generate a systematic classification of types of strain, of which Merton's disjunction between goals and means is only one. The second reason is Smelser's emphasis that to account for collective behavior, one must *start with* strain, but one's theory must also specify a hierarchy of constraints, each of which further narrows the range of possible responses to strain, and the last of which rules out all alternatives but collective behavior. If the "value-added" method is sound for a theory of collective behavior, it may also be useful for a theory of deviance, starting from the concept strain, and constructed on the same model.

Now, *given strain*, what will a person do about it? In general, Merton's chief concern has been with the structural factors that account for variations in strain. On the matter of choice of solution, as on other matters, he has some perceptive observations, [9] but it has remained for others to develop these system-

[5] *Social Theory and Social Structure, op. cit.,* pp. 357–368.
[6] *Ibid.,* pp. 361–362.

[7] *Ibid.,* pp. 179–181.
[8] Neil J. Smelser, *Theory of Collective Behavior,* New York: The Free Press of Glencoe, 1963, esp. Ch. 3.
[9] *Social Theory and Social Structure, op. cit.,* p. 151.

144   ALBERT K. COHEN

atically. In particular, in the original version of his theory each person seems to work out his solution by himself, as though it did not matter what other people were doing. Perhaps Merton assumed such intervening variables as deviant role models, without going into the mechanics of them. But it is one thing to assume that such variables are operating; it is quite another to treat them explicitly in a way that is integrated with the more general theory. Those who continue the anomie tradition, however — most notably Merton's student, Cloward — have done much to fill this gap. Cloward, with Ohlin,[10] has accomplished this in large part by linking anomie theory with another and older theoretical tradition, associated with Sutherland, Shaw and McKay, and Kobrin — the "cultural transmission" and "differential association" tradition of the "Chicago school." Cloward and Ohlin also link anomie theory to a more recent theoretical development, the general theory of subcultures, and especially the aspect of the theory that is concerned with the emergence and development of new subcultural forms.[11] What these other theories have in common is an insistence that deviant as well as nondeviant action is typically not contrived within the solitary individual psyche, but is part of a collaborative *social* activity, in which the things that other people say and do give meaning, value, and effect to one's own behavior.

The incorporation of this recognition into anomie theory is the principal significance of Cloward's notion of illegitimate opportunity structures. These opportunity structures are going social concerns in the individual's milieu, which provide opportunities to learn and to perform deviant actions and lend moral support to the deviant when he breaks with conventional norms and goals.

This is the explicit link with the cultural transmission — differential association tradition. The argument is carried a step farther with the

recognition that, even in the absence of an already established deviant culture and social organization, a number of individuals with like problems and in effective communication with one another may join together to do what no one can do alone. They may provide one another with reference objects, collectively contrive a subculture to replace or neutralize the conventional culture, and support and shield one another in their deviance. This is the explicit link to the newer theory of subcultures.[12]

There is one more step in this direction that has not been so explicitly taken. Those who join hands in deviant enterprises need not be people with like problems, nor need their deviance be of the same sort. Within the framework of anomie theory, we may think of these people as individuals with quite variant problems or strains which lend themselves to a common solution, but a common solution in which each participates in different ways. I have in mind the brothel keeper and the crooked policeman, the black marketeer and his customer, the desperate student and the term paper merchant, the bookie and the wire services. These do not necessarily constitute solidary collectivities, like delinquent gangs, but they are structures of action with a division of labor through which each, by his deviance, serves the interests of the others. Theirs is an "organic solidarity," in contrast to the "mechanical solidarity" of Cloward and Ohlin's gangs. Some of Merton's own writing on functionalism — for example, his discussion of the exchange of services involved in political corruption — is extremely relevant here, but it is not explicitly integrated into his anomie theory.[13]

The Assumption of Discontinuity

To say that anomie theory suffers from the assumption of discontinuity is to imply that it treats the deviant act as though it were an abrupt change of state, a leap from a state of

[10] Cloward, *op. cit.*, and Richard A. Cloward and Lloyd E. Ohlin, *Delinquency and Opportunity, A Theory of Delinquent Gangs*, Glencoe, Ill.: The Free Press, 1960.
[11] *Ibid.*

[12] Albert K. Cohen, *Delinquent Boys, The Culture of the Gang*, Glencoe, Ill.: The Free Press, 1955, Ch. 3, and Merton, *Social Theory and Social Structure, op. cit.*, p. 179.
[13] *Social Theory and Social Structure, op. cit.*, pp. 71–82.

strain or anomie to a state of deviance. Although this overstates the weakness in Merton's theory the expression, "the assumption of discontinuity," does have the heuristic value of drawing attention to an important difference in emphasis between anomie theory and other traditions in American sociology, and to the direction of movement in anomie theory itself. Human action, deviant or otherwise, is something that typically develops and grows in a tentative, groping, advancing, backtracking, sounding-out process. People taste and feel their way along. They begin an act and do not complete it. They start doing one thing and end up by doing another. They extricate themselves from progressive involvement or become further involved to the point of commitment. These processes of progressive involvement and disinvolvement are important enough to deserve explicit recognition and treatment in their own right. They are themselves subject to normative regulation and structural constraint in complex ways about which we have much to learn. Until recently, however, the dominant bias in American sociology has been toward formulating theory in terms of variables that describe initial states, on the one hand, and outcomes, on the other, rather than in terms of processes whereby acts and complex structures of action are built, elaborated, and transformed. Notable exceptions are interaction process analysis,[14] the brand of action theory represented by Herbert Blumer,[15] and the descriptions of deviance by Talcott Parsons[16] and by Howard Becker.[17] Anomie theory has taken increasing cognizance of such processes. Cloward and Merton both point out, for example, that behavior may move through "patterned sequences of deviant roles" and from "one type of adaptation to another."[18] But this hardly does justice to the microsociology of the deviant act. It suggests a series of discontinuous leaps from one deviant state to another almost as much as it does the kind of process I have in mind.

Responses to Deviance

Very closely related to the foregoing point is the conception of the development of the act as a feedback, or, in more traditional language, interaction process. The history of a deviant act is a history of an interaction process. The antecedents of the act are an unfolding sequence of acts contributed by a set of actors. A makes a move, possibly in a deviant direction; B responds; A responds to B's responses, etc. In the course of this interaction, movement in a deviant direction may become more explicit, elaborated, definitive — or it may not. Although the act may be socially ascribed to only one of them, both ego and alter help to shape it. The starting point of anomie theory was the question, "*Given* the social structure, or ego's milieu, what will ego do?" The milieu was taken as more-or-less given, an independent variable whose value is fixed, and ego's behavior as an adaptation, or perhaps a series of adaptations, to that milieu. Anomie theory has come increasingly to recognize the effects of deviance upon the very variables that determine deviance. But if we are interested in a general theory of deviant behavior we must explore much more systematically ways of conceptualizing the *interaction* between deviance and milieu.[19] I suggest the following such lines of exploration.

If ego's behavior can be conceptualized in terms of acceptance and rejection of goals and means, the same can be done with alter's re-

[14] Robert F. Bales, *Interaction Process Analysis: A Method for the Study of Small Groups*, Cambridge: Addison-Wesley, 1950.

[15] Herbert Blumer, "Society as Symbolic Interaction," in Arnold M. Rose (ed.), *Human Behavior and Social Processes*, Boston: Houghton Mifflin, 1962, pp. 179–192.

[16] Talcott Parsons, *The Social System*, Glencoe, Ill.: The Free Press, 1951, Ch. 7.

[17] Howard S. Becker, *Outsiders: Studies in the Sociology of Deviance*, New York: The Free Press of Glencoe, 1963, esp. Ch. 2.

[18] Merton, *Social Theory and Social Structure*, *op. cit.*, p. 152; Cloward, *op. cit.*, p. 175; Cloward and Ohlin, *op. cit.*, pp. 179–184; Merton, "Conformity, Deviation, and Opportunity-Structures," *op. cit.*, p. 188.

[19] Dubin, *op. cit.*, esp. p. 151, and Merton's remarks on "typology of responses to deviant behavior," in his "Conformity, Deviation, and Opportunity-Structures," *op. cit.*, pp. 185–186.

sponses. Responses to deviance can no more be left normatively unregulated than deviance itself. Whose business it is to intervene, at what point, and what he may or may not do is defined by a normatively established division of labor. In short, for any given role — parent, priest, psychiatrist, neighbor, policeman, judge — the norms prescribe, with varying degrees of definiteness, *what* they are supposed to do and *how* they are supposed to do it when other persons, in specified roles, misbehave. The culture prescribes goals and regulates the choice of means. Members of ego's role set can stray from cultural prescriptions in all the ways that ego can. They may overemphasize the goals and neglect the normative restrictions, they may adhere ritualistically to the normatively approved means and neglect the goals, and so forth. I have spelled out the five possibilities on alter's side more fully elsewhere.[20] The theoretical value of applying Merton's modes of adaptation to responses to deviant acts is not fully clear; yet it seems worthy of exploration for at least two reasons.

First, *one* determinant of ego's response to alter's attempts at control, and of the responses of third parties whom ego or alter might call to their aid, is certainly the perceived legitimacy of alter's behavior. Whether ego yields or resists, plays the part of the good loser or the abused victim, takes his medicine or is driven to aggravated deviance, depends in part on whether alter has the right to do what he does, whether the response is proportional to the offense, and so on.

Normative rules also regulate the deviant's response to the intervention of control agents. How the control agent responds to the deviant, after the first confrontation, depends on his perception of the legitimacy of the deviant's response *to him*, and not only on the nature of the original deviant act. For example, this perceived legitimacy plays an important part in police dispositions of cases coming to their attention.

[20] Albert K. Cohen, "The Study of Social Disorganization and Deviant Behavior," in Robert K. Merton, Leonard Broom, and Leonard S. Cottrell, Jr. (eds.), *Sociology Today*, New York: Basic Books, 1959, pp. 464–465.

This approach also directs attention to strain in alter's role, the adequacy of *his* resources relative to the responsibilities with which he is charged by virtue of his role, and the illegitimate opportunities available to *him*. A familiar example would be the normative restrictions on the means police may consider effective to do the job with which they are charged, and variations in the availability to them of various illegitimate means to the same end.

The disjunction between goals and means and the choice of adaptations depend on the opportunity structure. The opportunity structure consists in or is the result of the actions of other people. These in turn are in part reactions to ego's behavior and may undergo change in response to that behavior. The development of ego's action can, therefore, be conceptualized as a series of responses, on the part of ego, to a series of changes in the opportunity structure resulting from ego's actions. More specifically, alter's responses may open up, close off, or leave unaffected legitimate opportunities for ego, and they may do the same to illegitimate opportunities. The following simplified table reduces the possibilities to four.

Responses of the Opportunity Structure to Ego's Deviance

	Legitimate opportunities	Illegitimate opportunities
Open up	I	II
Close off	III	IV

I. *Open up Legitimate Opportunities.* Special efforts may be made to find employment opportunities for delinquents and criminals. On an individual basis this has long been one of the chief tasks of probation officers. On a mass basis it has become more and more prominent in community-wide efforts to reduce delinquency rates.

Black markets may sometimes be reduced by making more of the product available in the legal market or by reducing the pressure on the legal supply through rationing.

Several years ago the Indiana University faculty had a high rate of violation of campus parking regulations, in part because of the disjunction between the demand for parking spaces and the supply. The virtuous left early for work and hunted wearily for legitimate parking spaces. The contemptuous parked anywhere and sneered at tickets. One response to this situation was to create new parking lots and to expand old ones. Since the new parking spaces were available to all, and not only to the former violators, this provides a clear instance where the virtuous — or perhaps the timid — as well as the deviants themselves are the beneficiaries of deviance.[21]

II. *Open up Illegitimate Opportunities.* Alter, instead of fighting ego, may facilitate his deviance by joining him in some sort of collusive illicit arrangement from which both profit. The racketeer and the law enforcement officer, the convict and the guard, the highway speeder and the traffic policeman, may arrive at an understanding to reduce the cost of deviance.

Alter, whether he be a discouraged parent, a law enforcement official, or a dean of students, may simply give up efforts systematically to enforce a rule and limit himself to sporadic, token gestures.

An important element in Cloward and Ohlin's theory of delinquent subcultures is that those who run the criminal syndicates are ever alert for promising employees, and that a certain number of those who demonstrate proficiency in the more juvenile forms of crime will be given jobs in the criminal organization.

III. *Closing off Legitimate Opportunities.* The example that comes most readily to mind is what Tannenbaum calls the "dramatization of evil."[22] A deviant act, if undetected or ignored, might not be repeated. On the other hand, others might react to it by publicly defining the actor as a delinquent, a fallen woman, a criminal. These definitions ascribe to him a social role, change his public image, and activate a set of appropriate responses. These responses may include exclusion from avenues of legitimate opportunity formerly open to him, and thus enhance the relative attractiveness of the illegitimate.

IV. *Closing off Illegitimate Opportunities.* This is what we usually think of first when we think about "social control." It includes increasing surveillance, locking the door, increasing the certainty and severity of punishment, cutting off access to necessary supplies, knocking out the fix. These measures may or may not achieve the intended effect. On the one hand, they make deviance more difficult. On the other hand, they may stimulate the deviant, or the deviant coalition, to ingenuity in devising new means to circumvent the new restrictions.

The table is a way of conceptualizing alter's actions. The same alter might respond simultaneously in different cells of the table, as may different alters, and these responses might reinforce or counteract one another. Responses might fall in different cells at different stages of the interaction process. In any case, as soon as we conceive of the opportunity structure as a dependent as well as an independent variable, this way of thinking suggests itself as a logical extension of the anomie schema.

Parsons' paradigm of social control is in his opinion applicable not only to deviance, but also to therapy and rehabilitative processes in general. According to this paradigm, the key elements in alter's behavior are support, permissiveness, denial of reciprocity, and rewards, judiciously balanced, and strategically timed and geared to the development of ego's behavior.[23] To exploit the possibilities of this and other paradigms of control, one must define more precisely these categories of alter's behavior, develop relevant ways of coding ego's responses to alter's responses, and investigate both theoretically and empirically the structure of extended interaction processes conceptualized in these terms.

Finally, the interaction process may be analyzed from the standpoint of its consequences for stability or change in the normative structure itself. Every act of deviance can be thought of as a pressure on the normative

[21] William J. Chambliss, *The Deterrent Influence of Punishment: A Study of the Violation of Parking Regulations,* M.A. thesis (sociology), Indiana University, 1960.

[22] Frank Tannenbaum, *Crime and the Community,* New York: Ginn, 1938, Ch. 7.

[23] *Op. cit.,* pp. 297–325.

structure, a test of its limits, an exploration of its meaning, a challenge to its validity. Responses to deviance may reaffirm or shore up the normative structure; they may be ritual dramatizations of the seriousness with which the community takes violations of its norms. Or deviance may prompt re-examination of the boundaries of the normatively permissible, resulting in either explicit reformulation of the rule or implicit changes in its meaning, so that the deviant becomes redefined as nondeviant, or the nondeviant as deviant. Thus deviance may be reduced or increased by changes in the norms.[24] These processes go on within the household, courts of law, administrative agencies, and legislative chambers, but also in the mass media, the streets, and the other forums in which "public opinion" is shaped. Although these processes may be punctuated by dramatic, definitive events, like the passage of a new law or the promulgation of a new set of regulations on allowable income tax deductions, the pressure of deviance on the normative structure and the responses of the normative structure to deviance constitute continuing, uninterrupted, interaction processes. One goal of deviance theory is to determine under what conditions feedback circuits promote change and under what conditions they inhibit change in the normative structure.

In this connection, one of Merton's most perceptive and fruitful distinctions is that between the "nonconformist" and other types of deviant.[25] Whereas the criminal and others typically *violate* the norms in pursuit of their own ends, but in no sense seek to *change* those norms (though such change might very well be an unanticipated consequence of their cumulative deviance), the nonconformist's objective is precisely to change the normative system itself. This distinction suggests, in turn, the concept of the "test case" (which need not be limited to the context of legal norms and

the formal judicial system) — *i.e.*, the act openly committed, with the intention of forcing a clarification or redefinition of the norms. What we must not overlook, however, is that *any* deviant act, whatever its intention, may, in a sense, function as a test case.

Deviance and Social Identity

There is another piece of unfinished business before anomie theory, and that is to establish a more complete and successful union with role theory and theory of the self. The starting point of Merton's theory is the means-ends schema. His *dramatis personae* are cultural goals, institutional norms, and the situation of action, consisting of means and conditions. The disjunction between goals and means provides the motive force behind action. Deviance is an effort to reduce this disjunction and re-establish an equilibrium between goals and means. It issues from tension; it is an attempt to reduce tension. Roles figure in this theory as a locational grid. They are the positions in the social structure among which goals, norms and means are distributed, where such disjunctions are located and such adaptations carried out.

Another starting point for a theory of deviant behavior grows out of the social theory of George Herbert Mead. This starting point is the actor engaged in an ongoing process of finding, building, testing, validating, and expressing a self. The self is linked to roles, but not primarily in a locational sense. Roles enter, in a very integral and dynamic way, into the very structure of the self. They are part of the categorical system of a society, the socially recognized and meaningful categories of persons. They are the kinds of people it is possible to be in that society. The self is constructed of these possibilities, or some organization of these possibilities. One establishes a self by successfully claiming membership in such categories.[26]

[24] Theodore M. Mills, "Equilibrium and the Processes of Deviance and Control," *American Sociological Review*, 24 (October 1959), pp. 671–679.

[25] Merton, *Social Theory and Social Structure, op. cit.*, pp. 360–368; Robert K. Merton and Robert A. Nisbet, *Contemporary Social Problems*, New York: Harcourt, Brace, 1961, pp. 725–728.

[26] George Herbert Mead, *Mind, Self, and Society*, Chicago: University of Chicago Press, 1934; Erving Goffman, *The Presentation of Self in Everyday Life*, New York: Doubleday Anchor, 1959, and *Stigma, Notes on the Management of Spoiled Identity*, Englewood Cliffs: Prentice-Hall, 1963.

To validate such a claim one must know the social meaning of membership in such roles: the criteria by which they are assigned, the qualities or behavior that function as signs of membership, the characteristics that measure adequacy in the roles. These meanings must be learned. To some degree, this learning may be accomplished before one has identified or even toyed with the roles. Such learning Merton has called anticipatory socialization. To some degree, however, it continues even after one has become more or less committed to a role, in the process of presenting one's self, experiencing and reading the feedback, and correcting one's notion of what it is to be that kind of person. An actor learns that the behavior signifying membership in a particular role includes the kinds of clothes he wears, his posture and gait, his likes and dislikes, what he talks about and the opinions he expresses — everything that goes into what we call the style of life. Such aspects of behavior are difficult to conceptualize as either goals or means; in terms of their relation to the role, at least, their function is better described as expressive or symbolic. But the same can be said even of the goals one pursues and the means one employs; they too may communicate and confirm an identity.

Now, *given* a role, and *given* the orientations to goals and to means that have been assumed because they are part of the social definition of that role, there may be a disjunction between goals and means. Much of what we call deviant behavior arises as a way of dealing with this disjunction. As anomie theory has been formally stated, this is where it seems to apply. But much deviant behavior cannot readily be formulated in these terms at all. Some of it, for example, is directly expressive of the roles. A tough and bellicose posture, the use of obscene language, participation in illicit sexual activity, the immoderate consumption of alcohol, the deliberate flouting of legality and authority, a generalized disrespect for the sacred symbols of the "square" world, a taste for marijuana, even suicide — all of these may have the primary function of affirming, in the language of gesture and deed, that one is a certain kind of person. The message-symbol rela-

tionship, or that of claim and evidence, seems to fit this behavior better than the ends-means relationship.

Sexual seduction, for example, may be thought of as illicit means to the achievement of a goal. The point is, however, that the seduction need not be an adaptation to the insufficiency of other means, a response to disjunction. One may cultivate the art of seduction because this sort of expertise is directly significant of a coveted role. Indeed, the very value and meaning of the prize are conferred by the means employed. One could, of course, say that the expertise is itself the goal, but then it is still a goal that expresses and testifies to a role. Finally, one could say that the goal of the act is to validate the role, and all these kinds of behavior are means to this end. I think this statement is plausible and can be defended. If it *is* the intent of anomie theory, then the language of tension reduction does not seem to fit very well. The relation I have in mind, between deviant act and social role, is like the relation between pipe and elbow patches and the professorial role. Like the professor's behavior, it is not necessarily a *pis aller*, a means that one has hit on after others have failed. It commends itself, it is gratifying, because it seems so right — not in a moral sense, but in the sense that it fits so well with the image one would like to have of oneself.

One important implication of this view is that it shifts the focus of theory and research from the disjunction and its resolution to the process of progressive involvement in, commitment to, and movement among social roles, and the processes whereby one learns the behavior that is significant of the roles. One may, like the child acquiring his sex identity, come to accept and identify with a role before he is quite clear what it means to be that sort of person, how one goes about being one. But once one has established the identity, he has an interest in learning these things and making use of that learning. Thus Howard Becker's dance band musicians arrive at that estate by various routes. For many of them, however, it is only as this identity is crystallizing that they fully learn what being a musician means within the world of musicians. They discover, so to speak, what they are, and what they are turns out to be highly unconventional people.[27] We seek roles for various reasons, some of them having little to do with tension reduction, and having found the role, come into unanticipated legacies of deviant behavior.

The same processes operate in movement in the other direction, toward restoration to conformity. They are most dramatically illustrated in religious conversion. As the sinner is born again, with a new identity fashioned out of new roles, whole bundles of behavior, not all of them deviant, are cast aside, and new bundles are picked up. Relatively little may be learned by examining, one at a time, the items these bundles contain, the sense in which they constitute means to ends, and their adequacy to their respective goals. The decisive event is the transformation of self and social identity. At that moment a wholesale transformation of behavior is determined.

Anomie theory is, perhaps, concerned with *one* structural source of deviance, while the ideas just presented are concerned with another. Neither one need be more faithful to reality than the other, and the defense of one need not be a challenge to the other. But those who are interested in the development of a general theory of deviance can hardly let matters stand at that. Is it possible to make any

[27] Howard S. Becker, *op. cit.*, Ch. 5.

general statements about the kinds of deviance that may be attributed to anomie and the kinds that may be attributed to role validation through behavior culturally significant of membership in the role? Or may two instances of *any* sort of deviant behavior, identical in their manifest or "phenotypic" content, differ in their sources or "genotypic" structure?

Ultimately, however, we must investigate the possible ways in which the two kinds or sources of deviance interact or interpenetrate. For example, does role symbolism function as a structural constraint on the choice of means, and instrumental or means-ends considerations as a structural constraint on the choice of expressive symbolism? Does behavior that originates as a characteristic adaptation to the anomie associated with a particular role, come in time to signify membership in that role and thereby to exercise a secondary or even independent attraction or repulsion, depending on one's orientation toward the role itself? Finally, is it possible that in any instance of deviant behavior, or, for that matter, *any* behavior, both processes are intertwined in ways that cannot be adequately described in terms of presently available modes of conceptualization? I suggest that we must bring the two schemes into more direct and explicit confrontation and try to evolve a formulation that will fuse and harness the power of both.

Differential Association

The theory of differential association is the outstanding attempt to formulate a theory consistent with the data on criminality and delinquency in terms of general propositions and without relying on assumptions of abnormality or peculiarity in the individual. The findings of research on rural-urban differences, regional differences, correctional institutions as "schools of crime," and ecological analyses of "delinquency areas," to name only a few, imply that delinquent behavior is the result of sociocultural influences on the individual and must be conceived as normal, learned behavior.

Proposing that the delinquent is to be explained by reference to the sociocultural circumstances in which he is placed and which are effective in determining his conduct, Sutherland provides a systematic statement of the process by which a person becomes delinquent. Delinquent behavior is viewed as the result of differential association with those who uphold pro-delinquent norms (see De Fleur and Quinney [1966]). The fundamental assumption underlying this etiological formulation is that the delinquent is a normal human being reared in a normal society; any significant behavioral differences between normal individuals are sociocultural or learned. According to Sutherland, delinquent behavior is learned in a process of symbolic interaction with other normal human beings. The process by which one becomes delinquent — the acquiring of attitudes favorable to delinquency and the learning of the appropriate behavior patterns — is no more normal or abnormal than the process by which one becomes a law-abiding citizen. The difference lies in the content, not the process of learning. The view that delinquency is ordinary learned behavior clearly rests on the psychological "laws of learning" applicable to all learned behavior.

This theory offers a positive proposition about the nature of the delinquent and the source of his delinquency (see Hartung [1965]). A conception of man as the product of his social experiences is implicit in this formulation. Sutherland focuses on the processes of learning, interaction, and communication; his essential ideas are that "criminal behavior is learned in interaction with other persons in a process of communication"; this learning occurs principally in primary groups; and specific motives, rationalizations, and attitudes are learned from two types of sources, those who do and those who do not uphold the legal codes as rules to be observed.

Sutherland referred to his sixth proposition as the "principle" of differential association; that this principle, as stated, is mechanistic cannot be denied (see the selection by Cressey in this section), but in their reformulation of Sutherland's theory De Fleur and Quinney (1966) avoid this problem. Suffice it to say that Sutherland was trying to communicate the idea that in a heterogeneous society two opposing definitions of what is expected and desirable in reference to legal codes exist; consequently, a person may receive contradictory conceptions. Sutherland's conception of society was phrased in terms of differential group organization; he saw society as containing groups organized both for and against criminal activities.

As stated in an address delivered in 1942, Sutherland saw the conflict between groups, or in "cultures," with reference to law and crime as the basic principle in the explanation of crime (1956:20). The crucial point is that in the type of social organization described as differential group organization, divergent subgroups possess alternative and inconsistent standards of conduct. As a result, an individual who is a member of one group has a high probability of learning to use legal means to achieve his goals whereas an individual in another group learns to achieve them illegally. It is this conception of society which leads Sutherland to suggest that when a boy becomes delinquent he does so because of differential association, that is, because of association in a group in which delinquent behavior patterns are presented and in relative isolation from groups upholding antidelinquent patterns.

The proposition that delinquent behavior is the result of differential association negates assertions that deviation from norms is simply a result of broken homes or emotional instability. Rather, the many factors or conditions utilized in multiple factor approaches are related to delinquent behavior only as they result in differential exposure to definitions favorable to violation of the law. According to Sutherland, it is not a delinquent's biological inferiority, mental deficiency, emotional instability, or physique that explain his behavior, but rather it is the frequency, duration, priority, and intensity of delinquent as opposed to nondelinquent associations. These "factors" cannot be dismissed summarily, however, for they may be important to the extent that they influence the boy's selection of companions and others' selection of him and hence his degree of exposure to the varying definitions of the legal norms.

The first formal statement of differential association appeared in the 1939 edition of Sutherland's text, *Principles of Criminology*. Sutherland altered the theory slightly in the 1947 edition, and in subsequent editions of the text Cressey did not modify the 1947 statement of the theory.

REFERENCES

Melvin L. De Fleur and Richard Quinney, "A Reformulation of Sutherland's Differential Association Theory and a Strategy for Empirical Verification," *The Journal of Research in Crime and Delinquency*, 3 (January 1966), pp. 1–22.

Frank E. Hartung, *Crime, Law and Society* (Detroit: Wayne State University Press, 1965).

Edwin H. Sutherland, "Development of the Theory," *The Sutherland Papers*, eds. Albert Cohen, Alfred Lindesmith, and Karl Schuessler (Bloomington, Ind.: Indiana University Press, 1956).

EDWIN H. SUTHERLAND
DONALD R. CRESSEY

The Theory of Differential Association

The following paragraphs state . . . a . . . theory of criminal behavior on the assumption that a criminal act occurs when a situation appropriate for it, as defined by the person, is present. The theory should be regarded as tentative, and it should be tested . . . by all other factual information and theories which are applicable.

The following statement refers to the process by which a particular person comes to engage in criminal behavior.

1. *Criminal behavior is learned.* Negatively, this means that criminal behavior is not inherited, as such; also, the person who is not already trained in crime does not invent criminal behavior, just as a person does not make mechanical inventions unless he has had training in mechanics.

2. *Criminal behavior is learned in interaction with other persons in a process of communication.* This communication is verbal in many respects but includes also "the communication of gestures."

3. *The principal part of the learning of criminal behavior occurs within intimate personal groups.* Negatively, this means that the impersonal agencies of communication, such as movies and newspapers, play a relatively unimportant part in the genesis of criminal behavior.

4. *When criminal behavior is learned, the learning includes (a) techniques of committing the crime, which are sometimes very* complicated, sometimes very simple; (b) the specific direction of motives, drives, rationalizations, and attitudes.

5. *The specific direction of motives and drives is learned from definitions of the legal codes as favorable or unfavorable.* In some societies an individual is surrounded by persons who invariably define the legal codes as rules to be observed, while in others he is surrounded by persons whose definitions are favorable to the violation of the legal codes. In our American society these definitions are almost always mixed, with the consequence that we have culture conflict in relation to the legal codes.

6. *A person becomes delinquent because of an excess of definitions favorable to violation of law over definitions unfavorable to violation of law.* This is the principle of differential association. It refers to both criminal and anti-criminal associations and has to do with counteracting forces. When persons become criminal, they do so because of contacts with criminal patterns and also because of isolation from anti-criminal patterns. Any person inevitably assimilates the surrounding culture unless other patterns are in conflict; a Southerner does not pronounce "r" because other Southerners do not pronounce "r." Negatively, this proposition of differential association means that associations which are neutral so far as crime is concerned have little or no effect on the genesis of criminal behavior. Much of the experience of a person is neutral in this sense, e.g., learning to brush one's teeth. This behavior has no negative or positive effect on criminal behavior except as it may be related to associations which are concerned with the legal codes. This neutral behavior is important especially

From *Principles of Criminology*, 7th Edition (Philadelphia: J. B. Lippincott, 1966). Used with permission of the publisher J. B. Lippincott.

as an occupier of the time of a child so that he is not in contact with criminal behavior during the time he is so engaged in the neutral behavior.

7. *Differential associations may vary in frequency, duration, priority, and intensity.* This means that associations with criminal behavior and also associations with anti-criminal behavior vary in those respects. "Frequency" and "duration" as modalities of associations are obvious and need no explanation. "Priority" is assumed to be important in the sense that lawful behavior developed in early childhood may persist throughout life, and also that delinquent behavior developed in early childhood may persist throughout life. This tendency, however, has not been adequately demonstrated, and priority seems to be important principally through its selective influence. "Intensity" is not precisely defined but it has to do with such things as the prestige of the source of a criminal or anti-criminal pattern and with emotional reactions related to the associations. In a precise description of the criminal behavior of a person these modalities would be stated in quantitative form and a mathematical ratio be reached. A formula in this sense has not been developed, and the development of such a formula would be extremely difficult.

8. *The process of learning criminal behavior by association with criminal and anti-criminal patterns involves all of the mechanisms that are involved in any other learning.* Negatively, this means that the learning of criminal behavior is not restricted to the process of imitation. A person who is seduced, for instance, learns criminal behavior by association, but this process would not ordinarily be described as imitation.

9. *While criminal behavior is an expression of general needs and values, it is not explained by those general needs and values since non-criminal behavior is an expression of the same needs and values.* Thieves generally steal in order to secure money, but likewise honest laborers work in order to secure money. The attempts by many scholars to explain criminal behavior by general drives and values, such as the happiness principle, striving for social status, the money motive, or frustration, have

been and must continue to be futile since they explain lawful behavior as completely as they explain criminal behavior. They are similar to respiration, which is necessary for any behavior but which does not differentiate criminal from non-criminal behavior.

It is not necessary, at this level of explanation, to explain why a person has the associations which he has; this certainly involves a complex of many things. In an area where the delinquency rate is high, a boy who is sociable, gregarious, active, and athletic is very likely to come in contact with the other boys in the neighborhood, learn delinquent behavior from them, and become a gangster; in the same neighborhood the psychopathic boy who is isolated, introverted, and inert may remain at home, not become acquainted with the other boys in the neighborhood, and not become delinquent. In another situation, the sociable, athletic, aggressive boy may become a member of a scout troop and not become involved in delinquent behavior. The person's associations are determined in a general context of social organization. A child is ordinarily reared in a family; the place of residence of the family is determined largely by family income; and the delinquency rate is in many respects related to the rental value of the houses. Many other aspects of social organization affect the kinds of associations a person has.

The preceding explanation of criminal behavior purports to explain the criminal and non-criminal behavior of individual persons. As indicated earlier, it is possible to state sociological theories of criminal behavior which explain the criminality of a community, nation, or other group. The problem, when thus stated, is to account for variations in crime rates and involves a comparison of the crime rates of various groups or the crime rates of a particular group at different times. The explanation of a crime rate must be consistent with the explanation of the criminal behavior of the person, since the crime rate is a summary statement of the number of persons in the group who commit crimes and the frequency with which they commit crimes. One of the best explanations of crime rates from this point of view is that a high crime rate is due to social disorganization. The term "social disorganization" is not entirely satisfactory and it seems preferable to substitute for it the term "differential social organization." The postulate on which this theory is based, regardless of the name, is that crime is rooted in the social organization and is an expression of that social organization. A group may be organized for criminal behavior or organized against criminal behavior. Most communities are organized both for criminal and anti-criminal behavior and in that sense the crime rate is an expression of the differential group organization. Differential group organization as an explanation of variations in crime rates is consistent with the differential association theory of the processes by which persons become criminals.

Two reactions to Sutherland's theory of differential association have been dominant. The theory has been severely criticized and discarded by many who consider it a poor alternative to psychogenic theories about the process by which individuals become delinquent. Those who adopt a psychogenic perspective generally view delinquency and criminality as medical problems. They accept the premise that these phenomena constitute disease and that offenders are "sick people" (see Hakeem [1958]); as a result, they neglect this two-edged theory, and, in fact, often consider sociocultural influences as of secondary importance.

On the other hand, many sociologists accept Sutherland's proposition that delinquent behavior is learned as a result of differential association with those who hold conflicting definitions of legal codes. Since they find the social psychological aspects of the theory quite acceptable, they use it, perhaps uncritically, as a description of the basic process involved in criminality and delinquency. Consequently, the sociological portion of the theory of differential association, which offers an explanation for the high- and low-delinquency rates of various categories and groups, is almost totally ignored.

In this selection Cressey summarizes the various criticisms lodged against differential association as an explanation of the process whereby individuals become delinquent, and he notes the attention Sutherland devoted to "epidemiology" or the distribution of criminal behavior. According to Cressey, there have been a number of erroneous interpretations of the theory, and he attributes some of these to ambiguities in Sutherland's statement. Each of the "literary errors" deserves careful attention. In addition, there have been several substantive criticisms.

The first basic criticism states that Sutherland's theory accounts for only one of several distinct types of criminality because it does not adequately consider personality traits. As Cressey observes, this is an important criticism because it suggests that an essential determinant of criminality is neglected. This criticism commonly involves a dualistic conception of criminality; criminality is conceived as a manifestation of differential association, personality, or both. Sutherland wrestled with the problem of the relation of personality traits and criminality for years. He was convinced that his basic principle, "personal traits have a causal relation to criminal behavior only as they affect a person's associations," was sound, although he recognized that perhaps it needed modification since "this proposition has been questioned more frequently and more vigorously than any other part of the theory" (Sutherland [1956:25]; see the selection by Voss in this section). Sutherland (1956:29) suggested that sociologists invade the province surrendered to psychiatrists in order to study such extreme cases as those involving "kleptomania, pyromania, the criminal behavior which is interpreted by psychoanalysis as symbolic incest, the psychotic criminal, the black sheep, and crimes committed under the influence of alcohol by persons who do not behave in [a] similar manner under other conditions." In view of this suggestion it is noteworthy that Cressey (1954) found differential association adequate to account for so-called "compulsive crimes."

Another basic criticism insists that the mechanistic ratio specified in the theory cannot be measured accurately. The principle of differential association conveys a mechanistic image of criminality: an individual is pushed toward criminality or law-abiding behavior according to a mathematical ratio of criminal and anticriminal associations. It is difficult to conceive this equation which involves "associations" and "definitions" in operational terms. Glueck (1956) suggests it is inconsistent to speak of a numerical excess of associations with criminal patterns while speaking of the duration, priority, and intensity of association with such patterns. As De Fleur and Quinney (1966) note, Sutherland emphasized the frequency, duration, priority, and intensity of delinquent, as opposed to nondelinquent, associations in an effort to suggest a more adequate level of quantification than the all-or-none level implied in the principle of differential association, but specification of these four modalities is not an essential part of his theory. In the final sections of his paper Cressey suggests that Sutherland used a "principle of normative conflict" to account for the distribution of high and low crime rates in a multigroup society and that differential association was suggested as the way in which normative conflict results in criminal behavior among certain individuals.

REFERENCES

Donald R. Cressey, "The Differential Association Theory and Compulsive Crimes," *Journal of Criminal Law, Criminology and Police Science*, 45 (May–June 1954), pp. 29–44.

Melvin L. De Fleur and Richard Quinney, "A Reformulation of Sutherland's Differential Association Theory and a Strategy for Empirical Verification," *The Journal of Research in Crime and Delinquency*, 3 (January 1966), pp. 1–22.

Sheldon Glueck, "Theory and Fact in Criminology," *The British Journal of Delinquency*, 7 (October 1956), pp. 92–109.

Michael Hakeem, "A Critique of the Psychiatric Approach to Crime and Correction," *Law and Contemporary Problems*, 23 (Autumn 1958), pp. 650–682.

Edwin H. Sutherland, "Development of the Theory," *The Sutherland Papers*, eds. Albert Cohen, Alfred Lindesmith, and Karl Schuessler (Bloomington, Ind.: Indiana University Press, 1956).

DONALD R. CRESSEY

Epidemiology and Individual Conduct: A Case from Criminology

A principal thesis of this paper is that a theory explaining social behavior in general, or any specific kind of social behavior, should have two distinct but consistent aspects. First, there must be a statement that explains the statistical distribution of the behavior in time and space (epidemiology), and from which predictive statements about unknown statistical distributions can be derived. Second, there must be a statement that identifies, at least by implication, the process by which individuals come to exhibit the behavior in question, and from which can be derived predictive statements about the behavior of individuals. Concentration on either the epidemiological segment or the individual conduct segment of a theoretical problem is sometimes necessary, but it is erroneous and inefficient to ignore the second segment, to turn it over to another academic discipline, or to leave its solution to a specialized set of workers within a single discipline.

In some cases, data on both aspects of a problem are not available, so that a two-edged theory is impossible. For example, my work on trust violation was concerned almost exclusively with the process by which one becomes a criminal, but such concentration was necessary because reliable data on the distribution of this type of crime was not available.[1] Should data become available, then the generalization about trust *violators* should be integrated with a generalization about variations in trust *violation*. In other cases, concentration on one phase of an explanation may be merely a matter of interest or time. However, it might also be due to an undesirable informal or formal division of labor — such as that between sociologists and psychiatrists, or that indicated by the recent development of a special Section on Social Psychology within the American Sociological Association.

The need for integrated theories of epidemiology and individual conduct is demonstrated in the work done on Merton's theory of deviant behavior. Over twenty years ago, Merton presented a sociological statement purporting, among other things, to account for an excess of property crimes in the working class population. However, he left unanswered (and to some extent unasked) the question of why only a rather insignificant proportion of working class persons become property offenders.[2] While a few sociologists paid attention to this theory about the epidemiology of crime, psychiatric theory that is quite unrelated to Merton's theory has continued to dominate explanation of individual cases of working class (and other) criminality.[3] Only in the last five years has there been a significant attempt to identify the processes by which the blocking of legitimate means for achieving success, posed by Merton, might "work" to produce the criminality of individual working class persons. Even here, the most significant efforts have concentrated on variations in socially structured opportunities for deviation, rather than on the social psychological mechanisms involved in individual cases.[4]

In an even more significant case, a sociologi-

From *Pacific Sociological Review*, 3 (Fall 1960), 47–58. Reprinted with permission of author and publisher.

[1] Donald R. Cressey, *Other People's Money*, Glencoe: The Free Press, 1953.

[2] Robert K. Merton, "Social Structure and Anomie," *American Sociological Review*, 3 (October 1938), pp. 672–682.

[3] Cf. Frank E. Hartung, "A Critique of the Sociological Approach to Crime and Correction," *Law and Contemporary Problems*, 23 (Autumn 1958), pp. 703–734.

[4] Richard A. Cloward, "Illegitimate Means, Anomie, and Deviant Behavior," *American Sociological Review*, 24 (April 1959), pp. 164–176; and Richard A. Cloward and Lloyd E. Ohlin, "Types of Delinquent Subcultures," unpublished manuscript, December 1958.

cal theory of the epidemiology of crime has been neglected because it has been viewed as only an alternative to psychiatric theories about the process by which individuals become criminals. The implications of Sutherland's "theory of differential association" for explaining the high and low crime rates of various categories of persons have been all but ignored, just as the implications of Merton's theory for explanation of individual conduct have been neglected. Yet it is clear, as we will show later, that when Sutherland introduced the idea of differential association, in 1939, he was concerned with both phases of the general problem in criminology: explaining the distribution of crime rates, and identifying the process by which a person becomes a criminal.[5] His idea has had a profound effect on criminological and sociological thought, despite the fact that it has become a center of controversy. Significantly, the controversy has concentrated on the capacity of the statement to portray accurately the process by which individuals become criminals, and its capacity to explain the distribution of crime and delinquency has scarcely been studied or discussed. Yet we shall see that, in a very real sense, Sutherland was trying to do for criminology what Darwin did for biology. Although such an observation might seem pretentious when the range of phenomena included in the scope of Darwin's theory is compared with the range included in Sutherland's, each man did try to state a principle accounting for the presence or absence of "deviant" phenomena, and then also tried to specify the process by which "deviancy" comes to be present in individual cases.

We shall return to this comparison after examining the theory of differential association and some of the criticisms of one of its parts.

Differential Association and Individual Criminality

Sutherland's theory of differential association can best be understood if only that part of it which has become the center of attention and which purports to explain individual criminality is considered first. The essential ideas here are that "criminal behavior is learned in interaction with persons in a pattern of communication," and that the specific direction of motives, drives, rationalizations, and attitudes — whether in the direction of criminality or anti-criminality — is learned from persons who define the legal codes as rules to be observed and from persons whose attitudes are favorable to violation of legal codes. "A person becomes delinquent because of an excess of definitions favorable to violation of law over definitions unfavorable to violation of law." [6] In modern society, the two kinds of definitions of what is expected and desired in reference to legal codes exist side by side, and a person might present contradictory definitions to another person at different times and in different situations. Sutherland called the process of receiving these two kinds of definitions "differential association," because what is learned in association with criminal behavior patterns is in competition with what is learned in association with anti-criminal behavior patterns. "When persons become criminals, they do so because of contacts with criminal behavior patterns and also because of isolation from anti-criminal patterns." The kind of social psychological process Sutherland seemed to have in mind will become clearer if we consider some of the details of his statement by reviewing both the principal interpretive errors apparently made by his readers and the principal criticisms advanced by his criminological colleagues.

Some Literary Errors

The statement of the theory of differential association is not clear. In two pages, Sutherland presented nine propositions, with little elaboration, that purport to explain both the epidemiology of crime and delinquency and the presence of criminality and delinquency in individual cases. It therefore is not surprising

---

[5] We do not mean to imply that this is the only general problem in criminology. In addition to the two phases of the general problem of etiology, criminologists are concerned with the sociology of criminal law and the sociology of punishment.

[6] For a complete statement of Sutherland's theory, see Edwin H. Sutherland and Donald R. Cressey, *Principles of Criminology*, 5th edition, New York: Lippincott, 1955, pp. 74–81. Unless otherwise identified, all quotations of Sutherland are from these pages.

that his words do not always convey the meaning he seemed to intend. Most significantly, as we shall see later, the statement gives the impression that there is little concern for explaining variations in crime and delinquency rates. This is a serious error in communication on Sutherland's part. In reference to the delinquent and criminal behavior of individuals, however, the difficulty in communication seems to arise as much from readers' failure to study the words presented as from the words themselves. Five principal errors, and a number of minor ones, have arisen because readers do not always understand what Sutherland seemed to be trying to say.

First, it is common to believe, or (perhaps necessarily) to assume momentarily, if only for purposes of research and discussion, that the theory is concerned only with contacts or associations with criminal and delinquent behavior patterns.[7] Vold, for example, says, "One

of the persistent problems that always has bedeviled the theory of differential association is the obvious fact that not everyone in contact with criminality adopts or follows the criminal pattern."[8] At first glance, at least, such statements seem to overlook or ignore the words "differential" and "excess" in Sutherland's presentation. After stating that a person becomes delinquent because of an *excess* of definitions favorable to violation of law over definitions unfavorable to violation of law, Sutherland continues by saying, "This is the principle of differential association. It refers to both criminal and anti-criminal associations and has to do with counter-acting forces." Thus, he does not say that persons become criminals because of associations with criminal behavior patterns; he says that they become criminals because of an *overabundance* of such associations, in comparison with associations with anti-criminal behavior patterns. Accordingly, it is erroneous to state or imply that the theory is invalid because a category of persons — such as policemen, prison workers, or criminologists — have had extensive association with criminal behavior patterns but yet are not criminals.

Second, it is commonly believed that Sutherland says persons become criminals because of an excess of associations with *criminals*.[9] Be-

[7] Robert G. Caldwell, *Criminology*, New York: Ronald Press, 1956, p. 182; Ruth S. Cavan, *Criminology*, 2nd edition, New York: Crowell, 1955, p. 701; Marshall B. Clinard, "The Process of Urbanization and Criminal Behavior," *American Journal of Sociology*, 48 (September 1942), pp. 202–213; "Rural Criminal Offenders," *American Journal of Sociology*, 50 (July 1944), pp. 38–45; "Criminological Theories of Violations of Wartime Regulations," *American Sociological Review*, 11 (June 1946), pp. 258–270; "The Sociology of Delinquency and Crime," in Joseph Gittler, editor, *Review of Sociology*, New York: Wiley, 1957, p. 477; and *Sociology of Deviant Behavior*, New York: Rinehart, 1957, p. 240; H. Warren Dunham and Mary Knauer, "The Juvenile Court in Its Relationship to Adult Criminality," *Social Forces*, 32 (March 1954), pp. 290–296; Mabel A. Elliott, *Crime in Modern Society*, New York: Harper & Bros., 1952, pp. 347–348; Sheldon Glueck, "Theory and Fact in Criminology," *British Journal of Delinquency*, 7 (October 1956), pp. 92–109; Robert E. Lane, "Why Businessmen Violate the Law," *Journal of Criminal Law and Criminology*, 44 (July–August 1953), pp. 151–165; Walter C. Reckless, *The Etiology of Delinquent and Criminal Behavior*, New York: Social Science Council, 1943, p. 60; James F. Short, Jr., "Differential Association and Delinquency," *Social Problems*, 4 (January 1957), pp. 233–239; and "Differential Association with Delinquent Friends and Delinquent Behavior," *Pacific Sociological Review*, 1 (Spring 1958), pp. 20–25; Harrison M. Trice, "Sociological Factors in Association with A.A.," *Journal of Criminal Law and Criminology*, 48 (November–December

1957), pp. 374–386; George B. Vold, *Theoretical Criminology*, New York: Oxford University Press, 1958, pp. 194–195.

[8] *Op. cit.*, p. 194.

[9] Harry Elmer Barnes and Negley K. Teeters, *New Horizons in Criminology*, 3rd edition, Englewood Cliffs, New Jersey: Prentice-Hall, 1959, p. 159; Caldwell, *op. cit.*, pp. 182–183; Cavan, *op. cit.*, p. 701; Clinard, "The Process of Urbanization and Criminal Behavior," *op. cit.*; "Rural Criminal Offenders," *op. cit.*, and "Criminological Theories of Violations of Wartime Regulations," *op. cit.*; Elliott, *op. cit.*, p. 274; Daniel Glaser, "The Sociological Approach to Crime and Correction," *Law and Contemporary Problems*, 23 (Autumn 1958), pp. 683–702; and "Differential Association and Criminological Prediction: "Problems of Measurement," paper read at the annual meetings of the American Sociological Association, Chicago, September, 1959; Glueck, *op. cit.*; Lane, *op. cit.*; Reckless, *op. cit.*, p. 60; Harry M. Shulman, "The Family and Juvenile Delinquency," *Annals of the American Academy of Political and Social Science*, 261 (January 1949), pp. 21–31; Donald R. Taft, *Criminology*, New York: Macmillan, 1956, p. 338.

cause of the manner in which the theory is stated, and because of the popularity of the "bad companions" theory of criminality in our society, this error is easy to make. Sutherland's proposal is concerned with ratios of associations with *patterns of behavior*, no matter what the character of the person presenting them. Throughout his formal statement, Sutherland uses terms such as "definitions of legal codes as favorable or unfavorable," "definitions favorable to violation of law over definitions unfavorable to violation of law," and "association with criminal and anti-criminal patterns." Thus, if a mother teaches her son that "Honesty is the best policy" but also teaches him, perhaps inadvertently, that "It is all right to steal a loaf of bread when you are starving," she is presenting him with an anti-criminal behavior pattern and a criminal behavior pattern, even if she herself is honest, noncriminal, and even anti-criminal. One can learn criminal behavior patterns from persons who are not criminals, and one can learn anti-criminal behavior patterns from hoods, professional crooks, habitual offenders, and gangsters.

Third, in periods of time ranging from five to twelve years after publication of the formal statement with the word "systematic" omitted, at least five authors have erroneously believed that the theory pertains to "systematic" criminal behavior only.[10] This error is not important to the substance of Sutherland's current statement of the theory, but discussing it does tell something about the nature of the theory. The first formal statement was qualified so that it pertained only to "systematic" criminal behavior, rather than to the more general category "criminal behavior."[11] Sutherland de-

leted the word "systematic" from the second version of his theory, which first appeared in the Fourth Edition of his *Principles of Criminology*, in 1947. He explained that it was his belief that all but "the very trivial criminal acts" were "systematic," but he deleted the word because some research workers were unable to identify "systematic criminals," and other workers considered only an insignificant proportion of prisoners to be "systematic criminals."[12] The theory now refers to all criminal behavior. Limitation to "systematic" criminality was made for what seemed to be practical rather than logical reasons, and it was abandoned when it did not seem to have practical utility. Yet, one author (Caldwell) has recently been as critical of the word "systematic" as was an early article that attacked the original statement containing the word "systematic."[13]

Fourth, it is commonplace to say that the theory is defective because it does not explain why persons have the associations they have.[14] Although such expressions are valuable statements of what is needed in criminological re-

---

[10] Caldwell, *op. cit.*, pp. 182–184; Cavan, *op. cit.*, p. 701; Elliott, *op. cit.*, p. 274; Richard R. Korn and Lloyd W. McCorkle, *Criminology and Penology*, New York: Holt, 1959, pp. 297–298; Vold, *op. cit.*, pp. 197–198.

[11] See Edwin H. Sutherland, *Principles of Criminology*, 3rd edition, New York: Lippincott, 1939, pp. 5–9. This statement proposed generally that systematic criminality is learned in a process of differential association but then went on to use "consistency" as one of the modes of affecting the impact of the various patterns presented in the process of association. Thus, "consistency" of the

behavior patterns presented was used as a general explanation of criminality, but "consistency" also was used to describe the process by which differential association takes place. Like the word "systematic," "consistency" was deleted from the next version of the theory.

[12] Edwin H. Sutherland, "Development of the Theory," in Albert K. Cohen, Alfred R. Lindesmith, and Karl F. Schuessler, editors, *The Sutherland Papers*, Bloomington: Indiana University Press, 1956, p. 21.

[13] Arthur L. Leader, "A Differential Theory of Criminality," *Sociology and Social Research*, 26 (September 1941), pp. 45–53.

[14] Glueck, *op. cit.*; Clarence R. Jeffery, "An Integrated Theory of Crime and Criminal Behavior," *Journal of Criminal Law and Criminology*, 49 (March–April 1959), pp. 533–552; Leader, *op. cit.*; Martin H. Neumeyer, *Juvenile Delinquency in Modern Society*, 2nd edition, New York: Van Nostrand, 1955, p. 152; James F. Short, Jr., "Differential Association as a Hypothesis: Problems of Empirical Testing," paper read at the annual meetings of the American Sociological Association, September 1959; Trice, *op. cit.*; S. Kirson Weinberg, "Theories of Criminality and Problems of Prediction," *Journal of Criminal Law and Criminology*, 45 (November–December 1954), pp. 412–429.

search, they are erroneous when applied to differential association. Sutherland recognized that determining why persons have the associations they have is a desirable problem for research, and we shall later see that when his theory is viewed as a principle that attempts to account for variations in crime rates it does deal in a general way with differential opportunities for association with an excess of criminal behavior patterns. Nevertheless, the fact that the "individual conduct" part of the theory does not pretend to account for a person's associations cannot be considered a defect in it:

It is not necessary, at this level of explanation, to explain why a person has the associations he has; this certainly involves a complex of things. In an area where the delinquency rate is high a boy who is sociable, gregarious, active, and athletic is very likely to come in contact with others boys in the neighborhood, learn delinquent behavior from them, and become a gangster; in the same neighborhood the psychopathic boy who is isolated, introvert, and inert may remain at home, not become acquainted with other boys in the neighborhood, and not become delinquent. In another situation, the sociable, athletic, aggressive boy may become a member of a scout troop and not become involved in delinquent behavior. The person's associations are determined in the general context of social organization.[15]

Fifth, other authors have erroneously taken "theory" to be synonymous with "bias" or "prejudice," and have condemned Sutherland's statement on this ground. For example, in connection with criticizing Sutherland for deleting "systematic" from the 1947 version of his theory, Caldwell has written that by 1947 "we had not acquired enough additional facts to enable [Sutherland] to explain all criminal behavior." [16] This statement does not clearly recognize that facts themselves do not explain anything, and that theory tries to account for the relationships between known facts, among other things. Confusion about the role of theory also is apparent in Clinard's statement that Sutherland's theory is "arbitrary," Glu-

eck's statement that "social processes are dogmatically shaped to fit into the prejudices of the pre-existing theory of 'differential association,'" and Jeffery's statement that "the theory does not differentiate between criminal and non-criminal behavior, since both types of behavior can be learned." [17] Such statements are not so much errors in interpretation of the differential association statement as they are errors regarding the role of theory, hypotheses, and facts in scientific research. Later, we will show that Sutherland's whole theory does organize and integrate known facts about crime. Here, we need only indicate that Merton, and many others, have dispelled the notion that sociological theory is arbitrarily imposed on the facts it seeks to explain.[18]

Additional errors stemming from the form of Sutherland's formal statement, from lack of careful reading of the statement, or from assumptions necessary to conducting research, have been made, but not with the frequency of the five listed above. Among these are confusion of the concept "definition of the situation" with the word "situation," [19] confusion of the notion that persons associate with criminal and anti-criminal behavior patterns with the notion that it is groups that associate on a differential basis,[20] belief that the theory is concerned principally with learning the *techniques* for committing crimes,[21] belief that the theory refers to learning of behavior patterns that are neither criminal nor anti-criminal in nature,[22] belief that "differential association," when used in reference to professional thieves,

[15] Sutherland and Cressey, *op. cit.*, p. 79.
[16] *Op. cit.*, p. 182.

[17] Clinard, *Sociology of Deviant Behavior, op. cit.*, p. 204; Glueck, *op. cit.*, p. 99; Jeffery, *op. cit.*, p. 537.
[18] Robert K. Merton, *Social Theory and Social Structure*, rev. edition, Glencoe: The Free Press, 1957, pp. 85–117.
[19] Milton L. Barron, *The Juvenile in Delinquent Society*, New York: Knopf, 1954, p. 101.
[20] Elliott, *op. cit.*, p. 274.
[21] Clinard, "Criminological Theories of Violations of Wartime Regulations," *op. cit.*
[22] Taft writes of differential association "with others who have become relative failures or criminals," but Sutherland's theory has nothing to say about association with "failures," unless "failures" and "persons presenting criminal behavior patterns" are used synonymously. *Op. cit.*, p. 338.

means maintaining "a certain necessary aloofness from ordinary people," [23] failure to recognize that the shorthand phrase "differential association" is equivalent to "differential association with criminal and anti-criminal behavior patterns," with the consequent assumption that the theory attempts to explain all behavior, not just criminal behavior,[24] and belief that the theory is concerned only with a raw ratio of associations between the two kinds of behavior patterns and does not contain the statement, explicitly made, that "differential association may vary in frequency, duration, priority, and intensity." [25]

Some Popular Criticisms of Differential Association

Identification of some of the defects that various critics have found in Sutherland's statement also should make his theory clearer. Five principal types of criticism have been advanced in the literature. It would be incorrect to assume that a criticism advanced by many readers is more valid or important than one advanced by a single reader, but commenting on every criticism would take us too far afield. We can only mention, without elaboration, some of the criticisms advanced by only one or two authors. It has been stated or implied that the theory of differential association is

defective because it omits consideration of free will,[26] is based on a psychology assuming rational deliberation,[27] ignores the role of the victim,[28] does not explain the origin of crime,[29] does not define terms such as "systematic" and "excess," [30] does not take "biological factors" into account,[31] is of little or no value to "practical men," [32] is not comprehensive enough because it is not interdisciplinary,[33] is not allied closely enough with more general sociological theory and research,[34] is too comprehensive because it applies to non-criminals,[35] and assumes that all persons have equal access to criminal and anti-criminal behavior patterns.[36] Some of these comments represent pairs of opposites, one criticism contradicting another, and others seem to be based on one or more of the errors described above. Still others are closely allied with the five principal types of criticism, and we shall return to them.

One popular form of "criticism" of differential association is not, strictly speaking, criticism at all. At least ten scholars have specu-

[26] Caldwell, op. cit., p. 182.

[27] Weinberg, op. cit.

[28] Clinard, "The Sociology of Delinquency and Crime, op. cit., p. 479.

[29] Jeffery, op. cit., p. 537.

[30] Leader, op. cit.; Caldwell, op. cit.; Marshall B. Clinard, "Criminological Research," in Robert K. Merton, Leonard Broom, and Leonard Cottrell, editors, Sociology Today, New York: Basic Books, 1959, pp. 510–513; Short, "Differential Association and Delinquency," op. cit.

[31] Barnes and Teeters, op. cit., p. 159; Caldwell, op. cit., p. 182; Gill, op. cit., pp. 289–291; Glueck, op. cit., pp. 98–99. Olof Kinberg, "Kritiska reflexioner över den differentiella associationhypotesen," Chapter 24, in Ivar Agge, Gunnar Boalt, Bo Gerle, Maths Heuman, Carl-Gunnar Janson, Olof Kinberg, Sven Rengby, Torgny Segerstedt, and Thorsten Sellin, Kriminologi, Stockholm: Wahlström and Widstrand, 1955, pp. 415–429.

[32] Barnes and Teeters, op. cit., p. 210.

[33] Ibid., p. 162; Caldwell, op. cit., p. 182; Gill, op. cit., p. 284; Glueck, op. cit., pp. 105, 108; Howard Jones, Crime and the Penal System, London: University Tutorial Press, 1956, p. 95.

[34] Clarence Schrag, "Review of Principles of Criminology," American Sociological Review, 20 (August 1955), pp. 500–501.

[35] Gill, op. cit., p. 284; Jeffery, op. cit., p. 537.

[36] Cloward, op. cit.; Short, "Differential Association as a Hypothesis," op. cit., p. 3.

[23] Walter C. Reckless, The Crime Problem, 2nd edition, New York: Appleton-Century-Crofts, 1955, p. 169. This kind of error may stem from Sutherland himself, for in his work on the professional thief he used the term "differential association" to characterize the members of the behavior system, rather than to describe the process presented in the first statement of his theory, two years later. See Edwin H. Sutherland, The Professional Thief, Chicago: University of Chicago Press, 1937, pp. 206–207.

[24] Howard B. Gill, "An Operational View of Criminology," Archives of Criminal Psychodynamics (October 1957), p. 284; Jeffery, op. cit.

[25] Clinard, "Criminological Theories of Violations of Wartime Regulations," op. cit. If these "modalities," as Sutherland called them, are ignored, then the theory would equate the impact of a behavior pattern presented once in a radio show with the impact of a pattern presented numerous times to a child who deeply loved and respected the donor. It does not so equate the patterns.

lated that some kinds of criminal behavior are exceptional to the theory. Thus, it has been said that the theory does not apply to rural offenders,[37] to landlords who violated OPA regulations,[38] to criminal violators of financial trust,[39] to "naive check forgers," [40] to white-collar criminals,[41] to perpetrators of "individual" and "personal" crimes,[42] to irrational and impulsive criminals,[43] to "adventitious" and/or "accidental" criminals,[44] to "occasional," "incidental," and "situational" offenders,[45] to murderers, non-professional shoplifters and non-career type of criminals,[46] to persons who commit crimes of passion,[47] and to men whose crimes were perpetrated under emotional stress.[48] It is significant that only the first five comments — those referring to rural offenders, landlords, trust violators, check forgers, and some white-collar criminals — are based on research. It also is significant that at least two

authors have simply stated that the theory is subject to criticism because there are exceptions to it; the kind of behavior thought to be exceptional is not specified.[49]

The fact that most of the comments are not based on research means that the "criticisms" actually are proposals for research. Should a person conduct research on a particular type of offender and find that the theory does not hold, a revision is called for, providing the research actually tested the theory, or part of it. As indicated, this procedure has been used in five instances, and these instances need to be given careful attention. But in most cases, there is no evidence that the kind of behavior said to be exceptional is exceptional. For example, we do not know that "accidental" or "incidental" or "occasional" criminals have not gone through the process specified by Sutherland. Perhaps it is assumed that some types of criminal behavior are "obviously exceptional." However, a theoretical analysis indicated that one type of behavior that appears to be obviously exceptional — "compulsive criminality" — is not necessarily exceptional at all.[50]

A second principal kind of criticism attacks the theory because it does not adequately take into account the "personality traits," "personality factors," or "psychological variables" in criminal behavior. This is real criticism, for it suggests that Sutherland's statement neglects an important determinant of criminality. Occasionally, the criticism is linked with the apparent assumption that some kinds of criminality are "obviously" exceptional. However, at least a dozen authors have proposed that Sutherland's statement is defective because it omits or overlooks the general role of personality traits in determining criminality.[51]

[37] Clinard, "The Process of Urbanization and Criminal Behavior," and "Rural Criminal Offenders," *op. cit.*

[38] Clinard, "Criminological Theories of Violations of Wartime Regulations," *op. cit.*

[39] Donald R. Cressey, "Application and Verification of the Differential Association Theory," *Journal of Criminal Law and Criminology*, 43 (May–June 1952), pp. 43–52.

[40] Edwin M. Lemert, "Isolation and Closure Theory of Naïve Check Forgery," *Journal of Criminal Law and Criminology*, 44 (September–October 1953), pp. 293–307.

[41] Clinard, *Sociology of Deviant Behavior, op. cit.*, p. 240; Korn and McCorkle, *op. cit.*, pp. 299–300.

[42] Marshall B. Clinard, "Criminal Behavior is Human Behavior," *Federal Probation*, 13 (March 1949), pp. 21–27; "Research Frontiers in Criminology," *British Journal of Delinquency*, 7 (October 1956), pp. 110–122; *Sociology of Deviant Behavior, op. cit.*, p. 229; and "Criminological Research," *op. cit.*, p. 512.

[43] Elliott, *op. cit.*, p. 402; Vold, *op. cit.*, pp. 197–198.

[44] Clinard, "Criminological Research," *op. cit.*, p. 511; Elliott, *op. cit.*, p. 402; Jeffery, *op. cit.*; Daniel Glaser, "Criminality Theories and Behavioral Images," *American Journal of Sociology*, 61 (March 1956), p. 441.

[45] Elliott, *op. cit.*, p. 402; Clinard, "Criminological Research," *op. cit.*, p. 512.

[46] *Ibid.*

[47] Jeffery, *op. cit.*

[48] Elliott, *op. cit.*, pp. 347–348.

[49] Barnes and Teeters, *op. cit.*, p. 159; Taft, *op. cit.*, p. 340.

[50] Donald R. Cressey, "The Differential Association Theory and Compulsive Crimes," *Journal of Criminal Law and Criminology*, 45 (May–June 1954), pp. 49–64.

[51] Barnes and Teeters, *op. cit.*, p. 159; Barron, *op. cit.*, p. 147; Caldwell, *op. cit.*, pp. 179, 182, 184; Clinard, "Criminological Theories of Violations of Wartime Regulations," *op. cit.*; "Sociologists and American Criminology," *Journal of Criminal Law and Criminology*, 41 (January–February 1951),

Sutherland took this kind of criticism seriously, and in an early period he stated that his theory probably would have to be revised to take account of personality traits.[52] Later he pointed out what he believed to be the fundamental weakness in his critics' argument: "Personality traits," and "personality" are words that merely specify a condition, like feeblemindedness, without showing the relationship between that condition and criminality. He posed three questions for advocates of "personality traits" as supplements to differential association: (1) What are the personality traits that should be regarded as significant? (2) Are there personal traits, to be used as supplements to differential association, which are not already included in the concept of differential association? (3) Can differential association, which is essentially a *process* of learning, be combined with personal traits, which are essentially the *product* of learning?[53]

Sutherland did not attempt to answer these questions, but the context of his discussion indicates his belief that differential association does explain why some persons with a trait like "aggressiveness" commit crimes, while other persons possessing the same trait do not. It also reveals his conviction that terms like "personality traits," "personality," and "psychogenic trait components" are (when used, with no further elaboration, to explain why a person becomes a criminal) synonyms for "unknown conditions."

Closely allied with the "personality trait" criticism is the assertion that Sutherland's statement does not adequately take into account the "response" patterns, "acceptance" patterns, and "receptivity" patterns of various individuals.[54] The essential notion here is that differential association emphasizes the social process of transmission but minimizes the individual process of reception. Stated in another way, the idea is that the theory of differential association deals only with external variables and does not take into account the meaning to the recipient of the various patterns of behavior presented to him in situations which are objectively quite similar but nevertheless variable, according to the recipient's perception of them. One variety of this type of criticism takes the form of asserting that criminals and non-criminals are sometimes reared in the "same environment" — criminal behavior patterns are presented to two persons, but only one of them becomes a criminal.

Sutherland was acutely aware of the social psychological problem posed by such concepts as "differential response patterns." Significantly, his proposed solution to the problem was his statement of the theory of differential association.[55] One of the principal objectives of the theory is to account for differences in individual responses to opportunities for crime and in individual responses to criminal behavior patterns presented. To illustrate, one person who walks by an unguarded and open cash register, or who is informed of the presence of such a condition in a nearby store,

---

pp. 549–577; "The Sociology of Delinquency and Crime," *op. cit.*; *Sociology of Deviant Behavior, op. cit.*, pp. 204–205, 229, 240–241; Gill, *op. cit.*, p. 286; Glueck, *op. cit.*, p. 97; Kinberg, *op. cit.*; Lane, *op. cit.*; Leader, *op. cit.*; S. F. Lottier, "Tension Theory of Criminal Behavior," *American Sociological Review*, 7 (December 1942), pp. 840–848; Neumeyer, *op. cit.*, pp. 152–153; Short, "Differential Association as a Hypothesis," *op. cit.*, p. 4; Vold, *op. cit.*, p. 197.

[52] Sutherland, "Development of the Theory," (1942) *op. cit.*, pp. 25–27.

[53] Edwin H. Sutherland, *White Collar Crime*, New York: Dryden, 1949, p. 272.

[54] John C. Ball, "Delinquent and Non-Delinquent Attitudes Toward the Prevalence of Stealing," *Journal of Criminal Law and Criminology*, 48 (September–October 1957), pp. 259–274; Caldwell, *op. cit.*, p. 182; Clinard, "The Process of Urbanization and Criminal Behavior," *op. cit.*; "Sociologists and American Criminology," *op. cit.*; *Sociology of Deviant Behavior, op. cit.*, pp. 240–241; and "Criminological Research," *op. cit.*; Glueck, *op. cit.*; Jeffery, *op. cit.*; Korn and McCorkle, *op. cit.*, p. 298; Leader, *op. cit.*; Neumeyer, *op. cit.*, p. 152; Reckless, *The Crime Problem, op. cit.*, p. 109; and *The Etiology of Delinquent and Criminal Behavior, op. cit.*, p. 62; Trice, *op. cit.*; Vold, *op. cit.*, p. 196; Weinberg, *op. cit.*

[55] See Edwin H. Sutherland, "Susceptibility and Differential Association," in Cohen, Lindesmith, and Schuessler, *op. cit.*, pp. 42–43. See also Solomon Kobrin, "The Conflict of Values in Delinquency Areas," *American Sociological Review*, 16 (October 1951), pp. 653–661.

may perceive the situation as a "crime committing" one, while another person in the identical circumstances may perceive the situation as one in which the owner should be warned against carelessness. The difference in these two perceptions, Sutherland held, is due to differences in the prior associations with the two types of definition of situation, so that the alternatives in behavior are accounted for in terms of differential association. The differential in "response pattern," or the difference in "receptivity" to the criminal behavior pattern presented, then, is accounted for by differential association itself.[56] Elsewhere, we have insisted that one of the greatest defects in Sutherland's theory is its implication that receptivity to any behavior pattern presented is determined by the patterns presented earlier, that receptivity to those early presentations was determined by even earlier presentations, and so on back to birth.[57] But this is an assertion that the theory cannot be tested, not an assertion that it does not take into account the "differential response patterns" of individuals.

If "receptivity" is viewed in a different way, however, the critics appear to be on firm ground.[58] Sutherland did not identify what constitutes a definition "favorable to" or "unfavorable to" the violation of law, but he recognized that the same objective definition might be "favorable" or "unfavorable," depending on the relationship between the donor and the recipient. Consequently, he said that differential associations may vary in "intensity," which was not precisely defined but "has to do with such things as the prestige of the source of a criminal or anti-criminal pattern and with emotional reactions to the associations." This attempt at what is now called "reference group theory" merely begs the question; tells us that some associations are to be given added *weight*, but it does not tell us how, or whether, early associations affect the *meaning* of later associations. If earlier associations determine whether a person will later identify specific behavior patterns as "favorable" or "unfavorable" to law violation, then these earlier associations determine the very meaning of the later ones, and do not merely give added weight to them. In other words, whether a person is prestigeful or not prestigeful to another may be determined by experiences that have nothing to do with criminality and anti-criminality. Nevertheless, these experiences affect the meaning (whether "favorable" or "unfavorable") of patterns later presented to the person and, thus, they affect his "receptivity" to the behavior patterns.[59]

A fourth kind of criticism is more damaging than the first three, for it insists that the ratio of learned behavior patterns used by Sutherland to explain criminality cannot be determined with accuracy in specific cases. A minimum of eight authors have stated this criticism in seven different articles.[60] Short, for example, has pointed out the extreme difficulty of operationalizing terms such as "favorable to" and "unfavorable to"; nevertheless, he has devised various measures of differential association and has used them in a series of significant studies. Glaser has argued that "the phrase 'excess of definitions' itself lacks clear denotation in human experience," and Glueck has asked, "Has anybody actually counted the number of definitions favorable to violation

---

[56] *Cf.* Ralph L. Beals, "Acculturation," in A. L. Kroeber, editor, *Anthropology Today*, Chicago: University of Chicago Press, 1953, pp. 621–641; and Richard Thurnwald, "The Psychology of Acculturation," *American Anthropologist*, 34 (October–December 1932), pp. 557–569.

[57] Cressey, "Application and Verification of the Differential Association Theory," *op. cit.*

[58] I am indebted to Albert K. Cohen for assistance with this paragraph and with other points. Also, I am grateful to the following persons for suggested modifications of the original draft: Daniel Glaser, Sheldon Glueck, Michael Hakeem, Frank Hartung, C. Ray Jeffery, Richard T. Morris, Melvin Seeman, James F. Short, Jr., and George B. Vold.

[59] This actually is the important point Vold was making in the quotation cited at footnote 8 above.

[60] Ball, *op. cit.*; Clinard, "Criminological Research," *op. cit.*; Cressey, "Application and Verification of the Differential Association Theory," *op. cit.*; Glaser, "Criminality Theories and Behavioral Images," *op. cit.*; Glueck, *op. cit.*, p. 96; Lane, *op. cit.*; Reckless, *The Etiology of Delinquent and Criminal Behavior, op. cit.*, p. 63; Schrag, *op. cit.*; Short, "Differential Association and Delinquency," *op. cit.*; "Differential Association as a Hypothesis," *op. cit.*

of law and definitions unfavorable to violation of law, and demonstrated that in the pre-delinquency experience of the vast majority of delinquents and criminals, the former exceeds the latter?" In my work on trust violation, I was unable with the methods at my disposal to get embezzlers to identify specific persons or agencies from whom they learned behavior patterns favorable to trust violation. My general conclusion was, "It is doubtful that it can be shown empirically that the differential association theory applies or does not apply to crimes of financial trust violation or even to other kinds of criminal behavior." [61] I have been severely taken to task for not revising Sutherland's statement in light of this conclusion.[62] My reasons for not doing so have to do with the difference in the theory of differential association considered as a general principle which organizes and makes good sense of the data on crime rates, as compared to the theory considered only as a statement of the precise mechanism by which a person becomes a criminal. As we shall see below, a principle accounting for the distribution of deviancy, or any other phenomenon, can be valid even if a presumably coordinate theory specifying the process by which deviancy occurs in individual cases is *incorrect*, let alone untestable.

The fifth kind of criticism states in more general terms than the first four that the theory of differential association over-simplifies the process by which criminal behavior is learned. Such criticism ranges from simple assertions that the learning process is more complex than the theory states or implies,[63] to the idea that the theory does not adequately take into account some specific type of learning process, such as differential identification.[64] Between these two extremes are assertions that the theory is inadequate because it does not allow for a process in which criminality seems

to be "independently invented" by the actor. I am one of the dozen authors who have advanced this kind of criticism,[65] and in this day of role theory, reference group theory, and complex learning theory, it would be foolhardy to assert that this type of general criticism is incorrect. But it is one thing to criticize the theory for failure to specify the learning process accurately and another to specify which aspects of the learning process should be included and in what way.[66] Clinard's and Glaser's attempts to utilize the process of identification, and Weinberg's, Sykes and Matza's, and my own efforts to utilize more general symbolic interactionist theory, seem to be the only published attempts that specifically substitute alternative learning processes for the mechanistic process specified by Sutherland. Even these attempts are, like Sutherland's statement, more in the nature of general indications of the kind of framework or orientation one should use in formulating a theory of criminality than they are statements of theory.

Differential Association and the Epidemiology of Crime

We have already indicated that Sutherland's short, formal statement emphasizes the problem of explaining variations in the criminality

[61] Cressey, "Application and Verification of the Differential Association Theory," *op. cit.*, p. 52.

[62] Caldwell, *op. cit.*, p. 185.

[63] See, for example, Ball, *op. cit.*

[64] See, for example, Clinard, "The Process of Urbanization and Criminal Behavior," *op. cit.*; and Glaser, "Criminality Theories and Behavior Images," *op. cit.*

[65] Caldwell, *op. cit.*, p. 183; Clinard, "The Sociology of Delinquency and Crime," *op. cit.*; and "Criminological Research," *op. cit.*; Cressey, "Application and Verification of the Differential Association Theory," *op. cit.*; and "The Differential Association Theory and Compulsive Crime," *op. cit.*; Daniel Glaser, "Review of *Principles of Criminology*," *Federal Probation*, 20 (December 1956), pp. 66–67; "The Sociological Approach to Crime and Correction," *op. cit.*; and "Differential Association and Criminological Prediction," *op. cit.*; Glueck, *op. cit.*, pp. 93, 97; Korn and McCorkle, *op. cit.*, p. 299; Leader, *op. cit.*; Short, "Differential Association as a Hypothesis," *op. cit.*; Gresham Sykes and David Matza, "Techniques of Neutralization: A Theory of Delinquency," *American Sociological Review*, 22 (December 1957), pp. 664–670; Weinberg, *op. cit.*

[66] Despite the fact that Sutherland described a learning process, it should be noted that he protected himself by saying, "The process of learning criminal and anti-criminal patterns involves all the mechanisms that are involved in any other learning."

of individuals but is designed to account for differences in crime rates as well. However, only a careful reader of the statement can discern that it is concerned with making sense of the gross facts about crime, rather than concentrating exclusively on individual criminality.[67] On the other hand, examination of Sutherland's writings clearly indicates that he was greatly, if not primarily, concerned with organizing and integrating the factual information about crime rates. In his account of how the theory of differential association developed, he made the following three points, which are sufficient to establish his concern for the epidemiology of crime.

More significant for the development of the theory were certain questions which I raised in class discussions. One of these questions was, Negroes, young-adult males, and city dwellers all have relatively high crime rates: What do these three groups have in common that places them in this position? Another question was, Even if feeble-minded persons have a high crime rate, why do they commit crimes? It is not feeble-mindedness as such, for some feeble-minded persons do not commit crimes. Later I raised another question which became even more important in my search for generalizations. Crime rates have a high correlation with poverty if considered by areas of a city but a low correlation if considered chronologically in relation to the business cycle; this obviously means that poverty as such is not an important cause of crime. How are the varying associations between crime and poverty explained? [68]

It was my conception that a general theory should take account of all the factual information regarding crime causation. It does this either by organizing the multiple factors in relation to each other or by abstracting them from certain common elements. It does not, or should not, neglect or eliminate any factors that are included in the multiple factor theory.[69]

The hypothesis of differential association seemed to me to be consistent with the principal gross findings in criminology. It explained why the Mollaccan children became progressively delinquent with length of residence in the deteriorated area of Los Angeles, why the city crime rate is higher than the rural crime rate, why males are more delinquent than females, why the crime rate remains consistently higher in deteriorated areas of cities, why the juvenile delinquency rate in a foreign nativity is high while the group lives in a deteriorated area and drops when the group moves out of the area, why second-generation Italians do not have the high murder rate their fathers had, why Japanese children in a deteriorated area of Seattle had a low delinquency rate even though in poverty, why crimes do not increase greatly in a period of depression. All of the general statistical facts seem to fit this hypothesis.[70]

It appears, then, that in writing about differential association Sutherland was trying to say, for example, that a high crime rate in urban areas can be considered the end product of social conditions that lead to a situation in which relatively large proportions of persons are presented with an excess of criminal behavior patterns. Similarly, the fact that the rate for all crimes is not higher in some urban areas than it is in some rural areas can be attributed to differences in conditions which affect the probabilities of exposure to criminal behavior patterns.[71] The important general

[67] One of Sutherland's own students, colleagues, and editors has said, "Much that travels under the name of sociology of deviant behavior or of social disorganization is psychology — some of it is very good psychology, but psychology. For example, Sutherland's theory of differential association, which is widely regarded as preeminently sociological, is not the less psychological because it makes much of the cultural milieu. It is psychological because it addresses itself to the question: How do people become the kind of individuals who commit criminal acts? A sociological question would be: What is it about the structure of social systems that determines the kinds of criminal acts that occur in these systems and the way in which such acts are distributed within these systems?" Albert K. Cohen, "The Study of Social Disorganization and Deviant Behavior," Chapter 21 in Robert K. Merton, Leonard Broom, and Leonard S. Cottrell, Jr., editors, *Sociology Today*, New York: Basic Books, 1959, p. 462.

[68] Sutherland, "Development of the Theory," *op. cit.*, p. 15.

[69] *Ibid.*, p. 18.

[70] *Ibid.*, pp. 19–20.

[71] *Cf.* Henry D. McKay, "Differential Association and Crime Prevention: Problems of Utilization," unpublished paper read at the annual meetings of the American Sociological Association, Chicago, September 1959.

point is that in a multi-group type of social organization, alternative and inconsistent standards of conduct are possessed by various groups, so that an individual who is a member of one group has a high probability of learning to use legal means for achieving success, or learning to deny the importance of success, while an individual in another group learns to accept the importance of success and to achieve it by illegal means. Stated in another way, there are alternative educational processes in operation, varying with groups, so that a person may be educated in either conventional or criminal means of achieving success. Sutherland sometimes called this situation "differential social organization" or "differential group organization," and he proposed that "Differential group organization should explain the crime rate, while differential association should explain the criminal behavior of a person. The two explanations must be consistent with each other." [72]

It should be noted that, in the quotations above, Sutherland referred to his statement as both a "theory" and a "hypothesis," and did not indicate any special concern for distinguishing between differential association as it applies to the epidemiology of crime and differential association as it applies to individual conduct. In order to avoid controversy about the essential characteristics of theories and hypotheses, we prefer to call differential association, as it is used in reference to crime rates, a "principle." Because sociology seems to be dominated by a logic and methodology derived from physics, through psychology, sociologists are reluctant to label a statement "theory" unless it is a generalization sufficiently detailed to permit derivation of predictive hypotheses that can be put to test by gathering *new* facts. Nevertheless, it might be argued that many "theories" in sociology are in fact principles that order *known* facts about rates — now called epidemiology — in some way, and that they only in very general ways specify directions for accumulation of new facts that might prove them wrong. Durkheim,

for example, invented what may be termed a "principle of group integration" to account for, organize logically, and integrate systematically the data on variations in suicide rates. He did not invent a theory of suicide, derive hypotheses from it, and then collect data to determine whether the hypotheses were correct or incorrect. He tried to "make sense" of known facts about rates, and the principle he suggested remains the most valuable idea available to persons who would understand the differences in the rates of suicide between Protestants and Jews, urban dwellers and rural dwellers, etc.

We suggest, similarly, that Sutherland's statement is a "principle of normative conflict" which proposes that high crime rates occur in societies and groups characterized by conditions that lead to the development of extensive criminalistic subcultures. Sutherland made some attempt to account for the origins of these subcultures,[73] but he did not concentrate on this problem any more than Durkheim concentrated on attempting to account for the fact that Jewish families seemed more closely integrated than non-Jewish families. He "made sense" of variations in crime rates by observing that modern societies are organized for crime as well as against it, and then observing further that crime rates are unequally distributed because of differences in the degree to which various categories of persons participate in this normative conflict.

Darwinism and Sutherlandism

The value of general principles like "normative conflict" can be further established by returning to a comparison of Darwin and Sutherland. Although Darwin's contribution is called the "theory of evolution" and Sutherland's is called the "theory of differential association," both had two distinct parts. There is a remarkable similarity in the goals of the two "theories," the logic on which they are based, and the defects in them. Darwin invented the principle of natural selection, with its implication of evolution, to account for the strange distribution of "deviant" biological specimens and the

[72] Sutherland, "Development of the Theory," *op. cit.,* p. 21.

[73] See Sutherland and Cressey, *op. cit.,* pp. 82–92.

forms of plant and animal life. Next, he tried to specify the process by which this principle of natural selection "works" in individual cases. Sutherland invented the principle of normative conflict to account for the strange distribution of high and low crime rates; he then tried to specify the mechanism by which this principle works to produce individual cases of criminality. The mechanism proposed is differential association:

The second concept, differential association, is a statement of [normative] conflict from the point of view of the person who commits the crime. The two kinds of culture impinge on him or he has association with the two kinds of cultures and this is differential association.[74]

Darwin had three principal advantages over Sutherland. First, his emphasis was on the "epidemiological" part of his theory, rather than on the "individual conduct" part. His principle of natural selection ordered a wide range of facts that had been minutely detailed by thousands of careful observers. He knew quite precisely what facts his principle had to fit. For at least a century prior to *Origin of Species*, observation of the wonders of nature had been almost a national pastime in England. Great numbers of persons who, like Darwin, had little formal training in science were recording observations of biological and physical phenomena.[75] In the fifty years before *Origin*, at least a half dozen persons, including Darwin's grandfather, tried to put order into all these data by formulating something like a principle of natural selection. After publication of *Origin of Species*, the principle became a "hit" because it stirred up religious controversy, but also because thousands of amateur scientists could, like the professionals, check it against their own small world of observations and agree or disagree.

In contrast, Sutherland presented his theory to a world that knew little about crime and cared little about understanding it. Twenty-five years ago, the study of crime probably was more popular than it is at present, but detailed, precise, observations were being made by only a handful of persons. As today, careful observations were being made largely by academic sociologists, and the amateurs in the field were more concerned with doing something about crime than they were in knowing about it. Moreover, much work in criminology was, and still is, sporadic and slipshod, so that we cannot be sure that the "facts" about crime are facts at all. Sutherland tried to induce order in what facts we have, sparse as they may be. His principle organized only a narrow range of observations which were not always valid, and which were known to only a handful of dedicated souls.

Moreover, Sutherland handicapped himself by presenting the principle as an appendage to a well-established textbook, and by not explicitly trying to show in a formal statement how the principle helped to integrate and organize the existing data on crime. He needed to confront the reader with an overwhelming number of valid observations that somehow seemed less likely to be mere happenstance occurrences after his principle was stated than they had seemed before it was stated. It seems likely that Sutherland did not try to promote his principle because of a characteristic he had in common with Darwin — extreme modesty. It is conceivable that he did not completely commit himself to his principle, in the form of a major publication like *Origin*, for the same reason that Darwin published four monographs on barnacles, none of them containing any reference to his principle, between the time he formulated the principle and the time he published it.[76] Sutherland was well aware

[74] Sutherland, "Development of the Theory," *op. cit.*, pp. 20–21.

[75] The popularity of scientific concern was a social movement growing out of Calvinism, which admonished its followers to observe God's laws by observing His works, the wonders of nature. Fashionable English ladies carried pocket microscopes, which they would train on flowers and insects while strolling through the garden. See Gerald Dennis Meyer, *The Scientific Lady in England, 1650–1750,* Los Angeles: The University of California Press, 1955.

[76] It is quite possible that Darwin never would have published his principle had it not been independently formulated by Alfred R. Wallace, who threatened to scoop him. See Garrett Hardin, *Nature and Man's Fate*, New York: Rinehart, 1959, pp. 42–45.

of the failure of previous theories about crime, and he did not want to get too committed to his own formulation.[77]

Second, it was to Darwin's advantage that *Origin of Species* eventually attracted the attention of his professional colleagues; Sutherland's theoretical work is still so unknown even among sociologists that in at least two instances the words "differential association" have been invented as concepts describing phenomena quite unrelated to crime.[78] Publication in a textbook, as compared to a monograph, probably had some effect on this difference. Also, there is a tendency among sociologists to think of criminology as a distinct discipline, rather than observing that criminologists like Sutherland are interested in data on crime for the same theoretical reasons that other sociologists are interested in data on industry, family life, and politics. Sutherland's principle remains unknown to almost all psychiatrists, psychologists, and social workers.

The third, and by far the most important, advantage Darwin had over Sutherland was a set of research workers who appeared on the scene to correct him as well as criticize him. In simple fact, Sutherland's Mendel, Fisher, and Wright have not appeared. It turned out that Darwin was quite wrong after all. His principle of natural selection became one of the most important ideas in the history of man, but it was founded on an erroneous conception of the mechanisms by which heredity takes place in individual cases. Darwin adhered to the incorrect but popular "paint pot" theory that viewed heredity as a blending process, and because of this adherence he eventually had to join the Lamarckian geneticists, holding that mysterious particles called "pangenes" are modified by environmental conditions and are then gathered together to form the hereditary elements of the sperm or egg.[79] Although Mendel "corrected" Darwin when he published his discovery in 1866, his work did not become known and understood until the turn of the century. Since then, research in genetics has given Darwin's principle what it most needed — mathematically precise statements of the process by which natural selection "works." What has remained of Darwin himself is his important first principle, the principle of natural selection, and not his ideas about genetics.

There are no known published accounts of research that would carefully quantify or in some other way induce exact precision in Sutherland's statement of the process by which normative conflict "works" to produce criminality in individual cases. The most significant work has been done by Daniel Glaser and James F. Short, Jr. Although critics agree, as we have indicated, that the differential association statement oversimplifies the process by which normative conflict "gets into" persons and produces criminality, an acceptable substitute that is consistent with the principle of normative conflict has not appeared.

The Value of Differential Association

We have suggested that Sutherland, like Darwin, tried to formulate a principle that would organize available factual information on a type of deviation and then tried to specify the process by which that principle operates in individual cases of deviation. Sutherland's critics have argued that his specification of the latter process is incorrect, just as Darwin's specification of the hereditary process was incorrect. But inaccuracy in specifying the mechanism for becoming a criminal does not necessarily negate the value of the general principle, as the history of Darwinism has shown.

As an organizing principle, normative conflict makes understandable most of the variations in crime rates discovered by various researchers and observers, and it also focuses

---

[77] Sutherland, "Development of the Theory," *op. cit.*, p. 17.

[78] Ronald Freedman, Amos H. Hawley, Werner S. Landecker, and Horace M. Miner, *Principles of Sociology*, 1st edition, New York: Holt, 1952, pp. 235–238; David Gold, "On Description of Differential Association," *American Sociological Review*, 22 (August 1957), pp. 448–450.

[79] Hardin, *op. cit.*, p. 118.

attention on crucial research areas.[80] In a publication . . . [that appeared in 1964], I have listed over thirty facts about the statistical distribution of crime by age, sex, race, nativity, size of community, and social class; and then examined the capacity of various criminological theories to integrate them logically.[81] The principle of normative conflict does not make good sense out of all the facts, but it seems to make better sense out of more of the facts than do any of the alternative theories. Probably we should not expect the principle to fit all the observations to which it might be applied. As the physicist-philosopher Phillipp Frank has said, "There is certainly no theory which is in complete agreement with all our observations. If we require complete agreement, we can certainly achieve it by merely recording the observations."[82]

On the other hand, it also seems safe to conclude that differential association is not a precise statement of the process by which one becomes a criminal. The idea that criminality is a consequence of an excess of intimate associations with criminal behavior patterns is valuable because, for example, it negates assertions that deviation from norms is simply a product of being emotionally insecure or living in a broken home, and then indicates in a general way why only some emotionally insecure persons and only some persons from broken homes commit crimes. Also, it directs attention to the idea that an efficient explanation of individual conduct is consistent with explanations of epidemiology. Yet the statement of the differential association process is not precise enough to stimulate rigorous empirical test, and it therefore has not been proved or disproved. This defect is shared with broader social psychological theory. As Schrag has pointed out, "The individual internalizes the norms of his group," and "Stimulus patterns that are active at the time of a response eventually acquire the capacity to elicit the response," are illustrations of assertions which cannot be confirmed or denied but which stand, at present, as substitutes for descriptions of the process by which persons learn social behavior.[83] Criminological theory can be no more precise than the general sociological theory and general social psychological theory of which it is a part.

It is important to observe, however, that the "individual conduct" part of Sutherland's statement does order data on individual criminality in a general way and, consequently, might be considered a principle itself. Thus, "differential association" may be viewed as a restatement of the principle of normative conflict, so that this one principle is used to account for the distribution of criminal and noncriminal behavior in both the life of the individual *and* in the statistics on collectivities. In this case, both individual behavior data and epidemiological rate data may be employed as indices of the variables in the principle, thus providing two types of hypotheses for testing it.[84] Glaser has recently shown that differential association makes sense of both the predictive efficiency of some parole prediction items and the lack of predictive efficiency of other items.[85] In effect, he tested the principle by

[80] *Cf.* Llewellyn Gross, "Theory Construction in Sociology: A Methodological Inquiry," Chapter 17 in Llewellyn Gross, editor, *Symposium on Sociological Theory*, Evanston: Row, Peterson, 1959, pp. 548–555.

[81] Donald R. Cressey, "Crime," Chapter 1 in Robert K. Merton and Robert A. Nisbet, editors, *Contemporary Social Problems*, New York: Harcourt, Brace & World, 1961, pp. 21–76. See also Donald R. Cressey, "The State of Criminal Statistics," *National Probation and Parole Association Journal*, 3 (July 1957), pp. 230–241.

[82] *Philosophy of Science*, Englewood Cliffs, New Jersey: Prentice-Hall, 1957, p. 353; quoted by Glaser, "Differential Association and Criminological Prediction," *op. cit.*

[83] Clarence Schrag, "Some Foundations for a Theory of Correction," Chapter 8 in Donald R. Cressey, editor, *The Prison: Studies in Institutional Organization and Change*, New York: Holt, Rinehart and Winston, 1961, pp. 309–357.

[84] I am indebted to Daniel Glaser for calling this point to my attention.

[85] "Differential Association and Criminological Prediction," *op. cit.* See also Daniel Glaser, "A Reconsideration of Some Parole Prediction Factors," *American Sociological Review*, 19 (June 1954), pp. 335–341; and "The Efficiency of Alternative Approaches to Parole Prediction," *American So-*

determining whether parole prediction procedures which could have proven it false actually failed to prove it false. First, he shows that a majority of the most accurate predictors in criminological prediction research are deducible from differential association theory while the least accurate predictors are not deducible at all. Second, he shows that this degree of accuracy does not characterize alternative theories. Finally, he notes that two successful predictors of parole violation — type of offense and non-criminal employment opportunities — are not necessarily deducible from the theory, and he suggests a modification that would take this fact into account.

Future research on differential association

might specify in more detail the mechanisms by which one becomes a criminal, but it probably will do so only if sociologists recognize the epidemiological principle with which the process is consistent. While it might be argued that Darwin's "theory of evolution" can only be illustrated, not tested, it is clear that genetics has been profoundly affected by Darwin's scientific desire to generalize broadly on his, and others' observations of the distribution of species.[86] Similarly, Sutherland's "theory of normative conflict" tends to be tautological and might not be testable. Nevertheless, it is a starting point for a theory of criminal epidemiology, and its counterpart, differential association, indicates in a general way the process which should be closely studied as a first step to development of efficient theory of individual criminal conduct.

ciological Review, 20 (June 1955), pp. 283–287; and Daniel Glaser and Richard F. Hangren, "Predicting the Adjustment of Federal Probationers," *National Probation and Parole Association Journal*, 4 (July 1958), pp. 258–267.

[86] *Cf.* Garrett Hardin, "The Competitive Exclusion Principle," *Science*, 131 (April 1960), pp. 1292–1298.

Self-Conception and Socialization

Sutherland's statement of the theory of differential association was an attempt to account for the occurrence of both delinquent and nondelinquent behavior. However, as the previous article by Cressey indicates, this theory has been criticized for a number of reasons. Perhaps the most frequent criticism is its failure to explain the existence of nondelinquents in high-delinquency areas, since only about one-fourth of the boys in such areas appear in the juvenile court (Clinard [1957:478]). Such criticism is partially answered by noting that only a small proportion of the offenders in these areas reach the court; the more inclusive police records in such areas indicate that almost two-thirds of the boys may be regarded as official delinquents (Kobrin [1951]). Some investigators are inclined to dismiss the remaining one-third under the assumption that they engage in delinquent activities but are successful in evading the police. Yet, this is part of the persistent fundamental criticism that the theory of differential association emphasizes the process of transmission of definitions or attitudes favorable to delinquency, but minimizes the individual process of reception.

To many, examination of the theory indicates an excessive emphasis on the process of transmission, in which the actor is depicted as the passive recipient of delinquent behavior patterns, and apparently little concern with the bases of choice on the part of the person in contact with patterns of delinquent behavior and definitions favorable to delinquency (see the article by Voss in this section). Recognition of components of differential response has been suggested to rectify this limitation in Sutherland's theory (Reckless [1943:62]; Cressey [1960:52]).

In a series of articles, Reckless and Dinitz and their co-workers have attacked the question: Why do many nondelinquent boys who reside in areas with high-delinquency rates remain nondelinquent? In attempting to account for these "good" boys, they suggested that a socially appropriate conception of self is the prime factor influencing a youth away from delinquency. Reckless and Dinitz selected for study boys who resided in areas of high-delinquency rates; these investigators apparently view "delinquency" as behavior which is learned from other delinquents in residential areas in which there presumably is an established tradition of delinquency. At least this appears to be a valid implication from their position, although it is never explicitly formulated in this way. Reckless and Dinitz hypothesized that differences in self-conception explain the delinquent youth in the area of low-delinquency rates as well as the "good" boy in high-rate areas. "Good" boys in high-rate areas escape involvement in delinquency through the insulating effect of having acquired socially appropriate self-concepts. In contrast, a socially inappropriate conception of self may turn the juvenile toward delinquency "in the sense that the young person has no internalized resistance to the confrontation of a bad neighborhood, bad home life, and bad companions" (Reckless, Dinitz, and Kay [1957:566]). The investigators apparently assume that all boys who reside in high-delinquency areas and who have socially inappropriate conceptions of self have equal opportunities to learn delinquent behavior patterns, norms, and supporting attitudes.

In the dialogue between sociologists and proponents of other orientations, sociologists have often been justifiably criticized for their failure to consider the important influence of the family. For a variety of reasons sociologists have placed greater emphasis on the influence of peers. Reckless and Dinitz' analysis of self-concepts offers a means, albeit indirect, of assessing the influence of parental socialization practices on the developing child. The family, after all, plays an important role in transmitting attitudes and values to the child.

In this paper Reckless and Dinitz review their pioneering research concerning the socialization and self-concepts of delinquents and nondelinquents. These investigations are addressed to one of the crucial questions in the area of delinquency — why do some persons who are exposed to prodelinquent norms and attitudes accept them while others do not?

REFERENCES

Marshall B. Clinard, "The Sociology of Delinquency and Crime," *Review of Sociology*, ed. Joseph B. Gittler (New York: John Wiley and Sons, Inc., 1957), pp. 465–499.

Solomon Kobrin, "The Conflict of Values in Delinquency Areas," *American Sociological Review*, 16 (October 1951), pp. 653–661.

Walter C. Reckless, *The Etiology of Delinquent and Criminal Behavior*, Social Science Research Council, Bulletin no. 50 (New York, 1943).

Donald R. Cressey, "Epidemiology and Individual Conduct: A Case from Criminology," *Pacific Sociological Review*, 3 (Fall 1960), pp. 47–58.

——, Simon Dinitz, and Barbara Kay, "The Self Component in Potential Delinquency and Potential Non-Delinquency," *American Sociological Review*, 22 (October 1957), pp. 566–570.

WALTER C. RECKLESS
SIMON DINITZ

Pioneering with Self-Concept as a Vulnerability Factor in Delinquency

This paper presents a retrospective assessment of a pioneering line of research on the self-concept as an insulator against delinquency. The authors were in search of a clue — a possible self-factor — which might shed light on what it is that steers youths in high delinquency areas of a large city away from involvement in delinquency. Certainly, criminologists and sociologists are well aware of the simple fact that a large percentage of adolescents in high delinquency areas manage to keep out of official trouble with the law, walk around the street-corner gang and avoid its so-called "subculture," stay in school rather than drop out, identify with the norms and values of the dominant society, and turn their backs on the availability of illegitimate means to ends in their neighborhood environment. What, then, are the components which enable adolescents to develop and maintain non-delinquent patterns of conduct despite the adversities of family, class position, and neighborhood?

It was decided that the best subjects for an initial inquiry would be the sixth-grade boys in high delinquency areas. Attention was focused on white sixth-grade boys, so as not to complicate the research design with race and sex variables. One might well ask: why sixth-grade boys? The answer is that they are approximately 12 years of age and are at the threshold of adolescence as well as the threshold of officially complained-upon delinquency. Complaints on boys for delinquency begin to increase at this age and keep on increasing through the succeeding years of adolescence. In addition, it begins to be feasible to interview

a child, at the age of 12, about himself and his world as he sees it. Attempts to obtain, by verbal interviews or pencil and paper inventories, subjective data from young children about themselves run into difficulty. This does not mean, however, that one cannot procure objective data from preadolescent children.

As a start, the authors in 1955 gained permission to ask sixth-grade teachers in predominantly white elementary schools in high delinquency areas of Columbus, Ohio — teachers who interact with their pupils the entire school day for an entire school year — to indicate from among the white boys in their classes those who would never get into trouble with the law. Despite the fact that most of the teachers were middle-class females, the authors maintain — and we think very rightly so — that they have a sense of the direction in which their pupils are going. Kvaraceus' work in developing a delinquency proneness measure certainly bears out our contention that teachers' behavior ratings, evaluations, or prognostications are quite accurate.[1]

A Close Look at Sampling and Procedure

Thirty sixth-grade teachers nominated 192 white boys in their classes who in their opinion would not experience police or juvenile court contact. The range was from 15 to 100 percent of the white boys in the 30 classes and the average per class was 6.4 boys.

The teachers at the time of making their nominations of the so-called "good boys" were asked to give their reasons for each nomination. They mentioned 1,033 reasons or 5.4 reasons per boy; 45 percent represented favorable personal characteristics, attitudes, and

Reprinted by special permission of the *Journal of Criminal Law, Criminology and Police Science* (Northwestern University School of Law), Copyright © 1967, Volume 58, Number 4.

[1] Kvaraceus, *Anxious Youth: Dynamics of Delinquency*, 102–108 (1966).

interests; 27 percent, one or more aspects of favorable home situations; 20 percent, participation in character-building youth organizations, religious activities, conforming in-school behavior, after-school employment; 7 percent, negative evaluations such as being excessively timid, naive, or overprotected so as to preclude involvement in delinquent behavior.

Sixteen of the 192 "good boys," constituting 8.3 percent of the teachers' nominees, turned out to have had, after clearance was made, previous contact with the police or the juvenile court. In 13 of the 16 cases, one or more members of the family had also had contact with the courts. Members of 42 additional families also had court contact, although the boys were not involved.

The authors eliminated these 16 boys, who already had contact with the law, from their "good boy" sample. In addition, when interviewers tried to locate the remaining 176 boys (out of the original 192), they could not find 51 boys, probably due in small part to wrong address, but in most part to removal of the family from the community in the interim of the several months between the teachers' nominations and the field follow-up. The project was left with a sample of 125 (192 minus 16 minus 51).[2]

A schedule was developed to be administered on an individual basis to each of the 125 good boys in their own homes. Among other formal scales and inventories included in the schedule were 50 items which attempted to assess the boy's perception of himself in relation to his family, friends, school, and possible involvement with the law. We called these items self-concept items, because the responses represented the boy's perception of himself in reference to the significant others in his immediate world.

Two research interviewers contacted the mother at home and obtained permission to interview her and her son. The one interviewer administered the schedule to the boy in one room; the other interviewer administered a specially prepared schedule to the mother in another room simultaneously.

The following school year, namely 1956, the authors returned to the same 30 sixth-grade classrooms and asked the teachers, most of whom were the same ones they interviewed in 1955, to nominate the white boys in their rooms, who would, in their opinion, almost certainly experience police or juvenile-court contact in the future.

The teachers named 108 white boys, constituting about 25 percent of the eligible boys. Twenty-four of the 108 nominated "bad boys" (23 percent) had already had contact with the police and juvenile court (as against 8.3 percent of the "good boy" nominees). In view of a much shorter time span between teacher nomination and home interview, we only lost 7 boys in the "bad boy" sample, reducing it to 101 cases. The interview schedules for the boy and the mother were the same in the 1956 101-bad-boy sample as in the 125-good-boy sample of the previous year.

The scores on the two directionally-oriented scales of the California Psychological Inventory (*De* scale and *Re* scale), which were included in the schedule administered to each boy, were different in the expected directions: significantly more favorable for the good boys than for the bad boys or more unfavorable for the bad boys than the good boys. Because the *De* scale of the CPI (now called the Socialization scale, measuring directionality toward and away from delinquency) and the *Re* scale of the CPI (measuring directionality toward social responsibility) are standardized scales, with national and even some international norms, the authors felt that the convincingly and significantly more favorable showing of the good, and the more unfavorable showing of the bad-boy sample, tended to validate the teacher's nominations. Likewise, these scale scores provided corroboration for the more favorable answers on the self-concept items received from the good than from the bad boys. In addition to these associations, the answers of the mothers to questions about their sons, paralleling virtually all of the questions used in the self-concept inventory for the boys, also added an additional dimension of

[2] Reckless, Dinitz & Murray, "Teacher Nominations and Evaluations of 'Good' Boys in High-Delinquency Areas," 57 *Elem. School J.*, 221 (1957).

validation. Thus, the teachers, the mothers, the *De* and *Re* Scales, and the boys' responses to the self-concept questions were highly consistent.

Follow-Up Four Years Later

Four years after initial contact (1959 for the good and 1960 for the bad boys), the authors set about determining how many of the boys were known to the juvenile court. Out of the total of 125 in the 1955 sample of good boys, they were able to locate and assess 103; out of the 101 in the 1956 sample of bad boys, 70. Incidentally, attrition was not related to scale scores or self-concept responses in either cohort. Those who remained in the community had scored neither better nor worse on the *De* and *Re* scales or on the self-concept responses than those who left.

Twenty-seven of the 70 bad boys (39 percent) had contact with the juvenile court for delinquency in the four-year follow-up period — not including the court contacts in the instance of 24 out of the original 101 sample, prior to our study. Each of the twenty-seven out of the traceable 70 bad boys averaged over 3 contacts with the juvenile court throughout the four-year period or from the time the boys were approximately 12 to the time they were 16 years of age.

In contrast, just four out of the 101 good boys who were followed had a one-time record in the juvenile court in the ensuing four-year period of follow-up — and only for very minor offenses. Ninety-nine of the 103 good boys were still in school, although half of them had passed legal age for drop-out. Of the 99 still in school, all but four impressed their teachers as unlikely to get into future difficulty. Their responses to the readministered self-concept items were quite favorable, just as favorable as they were four years previously and the mothers' evaluations were just as favorable as four years earlier.

There was a remarkable four-year cohort stability on all of the directional indicators in both the good- and bad-boy samples: self-concept projections, teachers' prognostications, mothers' evaluations, scores on the *De* and *Re* scales of the CPI.

Furthermore, the authors were able to compare the traceable 103 good, and the 70 bad boys, on the Nye-Short self-reporting delinquency check list (using 7 of the original Nye-Short items) and they found that the latter scored more unfavorably than the former. (This self-reporting check list was not available to us in 1955 and 1956.) Hence, "professed" involvement corroborated reported involvement in delinquency as well as the direction of the self-concept responses, and the teachers' expectations.

At this point it is important to duplicate the theoretical underpinning of our quest to discover what insulates a boy in the high delinquency areas against involvement in delinquency.

In our quest to discover what insulates a boy against delinquency in a high delinquency area, we believe we have some tangible evidence that a good self-concept, undoubtedly a product of favorable socialization, veers slum boys away from delinquency, while a poor self-concept, a product of unfavorable socialization, gives the slum boy no resistance to deviancy, delinquent companions, or delinquent subculture. We feel that components of the self strength, such as a favorable concept of self, act as an inner buffer or inner containment against deviancy, distraction, lure, and pressures. Our operational assumptions are that a good self-concept is indicative of a residual favorable socialization and a strong inner self, which in turn steers the person away from bad companions and street corner society, toward middle-class values, and to awareness of possibility of upward movement in the opportunity structure. Conversely, the poor concept of self is indicative of a residual unfavorable socialization (by 12 years of age probably not the result of participation in delinquency subculture) and indicative of weak inner direction (self or ego), which in turn does not deflect the boy from bad companions and street corner society, does not enable him to embrace middle-class values, and gives him an awareness of being cut off from upward movement in the legitimate opportunity system.

We feel that the selective operation of the

self element is not specified in the response to the models of behavior presented to the person by his associates in differential association theory (Sutherland) and is even less specified in delinquency subculture theory (Cohen), as well as "opportunity structure" theory (Cloward and Ohlin).[3]

Cross-Sectional Studies

In 1957, the authors administered 717 schedules to sixth-grade children in 24 classes in eleven elementary schools of Columbus, Ohio, chosen according to census tract indexes of socio-economic status as well as high and low delinquency. Eight of the schools (with 17 sixth-grade classes) served disadvantaged areas with high delinquency rates, while 3 served middle-class areas where delinquency rates were low. All the sixth-grade pupils present in class on the appointed day were administered a schedule. The schedule consisted of 46 items from the *De* scale, 38 items from the *Re* scale (both from the California Psychological Inventory which is a factor-analyzed version of the Minnesota Multiphasic Inventory), 56 self-concept items, plus certain social background items. During the administration of the inventories, the sixth-grade room teacher was interviewed elsewhere by a research assistant. With her cumulative record cards before her, the teacher rated each child in her class as either headed for trouble with the law, not sure, or not headed for trouble with the law.

Since the schedule was administered in school, a standard introductory statement requesting cooperation and allaying fears was used. On the front page of the schedule the following statement appeared in bold type: *Remember this is not a test. We simply want to know how you feel about things. There are no right or wrong answers. The right answer for you is how you feel about things.* Dr. Dinitz read aloud each question, reminding the pupils of the response pattern: true or false; yes or no.

Dr. Ernest Donald analyzed 354 boys' schedules from among the total of 717. Because the teachers nominated too few girls as headed for trouble with the law to warrant comparison, the Donald analysis applied only to white and colored sixth-grade boys in both the high and low delinquency areas of Columbus, Ohio, in 1957.[4] The various subgroups in the 1957 sample of 354 sixth-grade boys consisted of the subgroups shown in Table 1.

It was possible to relate the favorable and unfavorable responses on each of the 56 self-concept items with the dichotomous nominations of the sixth-grade teachers (headed for trouble with the law, including not sure, versus not headed for trouble with the law). Table 2 lists 16 of the 56 self-concept items, used in the 1957 schedule, which were found to be differentiated by teacher nomination at the .05 level of confidence and beyond (9 items at the .001; 3, at the .01; 1, at the .02; and 3, at the .05 level of confidence). Note that the items through number 39 were answered by yes or no; items 42 and 46 were answered by a response format of often, sometimes, never; item 50, as will be see on inspection, was answered by checking one out of three possibilities.

When the favorable and unfavorable responses on these 16 self-concept items were related to high and low scores on the *De* scale of the California Psychological Inventory (which also measures direction toward or away from delinquency), all but one item (number 25) reached the minimum .05 level of statistical significance. Certainly, there is corroboration here; teacher nomination, response to self-concept items, and scores on the *De* scale are going in the same direction.

Five of the 16 significant self-concept items according to teachers' nomination, as presented in Table 2, were discriminated by the race of the sixth-grade (1957) Columbus boys (items 2, 12, 23, 39, 52); seven, by high and low delinquency area (items 1, 2, 12, 25, 26, 27, and 39); 6, by I.Q. level, 94 and above, 93 and below (items 2, 17, 23, 27, 30, and 42); 1, by

---

[3] Dinitz, Scarpitti & Reckless, "Delinquency Vulnerability: A Cross Group and Longitudinal Analysis," 27 *Am. Sociol. Rev.,* 517 (1962).

[4] Donald & Dinitz, "Self Concept and Delinquency Proneness," *Interdisciplinary Problems of Criminology; Papers of the Am. Soc. of Criminol.,* 1964 (Reckless & Newman, Eds.), 49–59 (1965).

Table 1
The Sample of Sixth-Grade Boys, by Subgroups, Columbus, Ohio, 1957

Subgroup	Number
Teacher's nomination:	
Not headed for trouble (good)	222
Headed for trouble[a] (bad)	132
Race:	
White	234
Negro	120
Area:	
Low delinquency (good)	125
High delinquency (bad)	229
Nomination by race:	
Good white	155
Good Negro	67
Bad white	79
Bad Negro	53
Nomination by race by area:	
Good white (good)	86
Good white (poor)	69
Good Negro (poor)	67
Bad white (good)	39
Bad white (bad)	40
Bad Negro (bad)	53

[a] Including the teacher's evaluation of "not sure." The teacher rated each boy in terms of whether she thought he was headed for trouble with the law, not sure, or not headed for trouble with the law.[5]

reading achievement (item 17); and 7 by arithmetic achievement (1, 2, 11, 12, 24, 26, and 29).

After having spotted the 16 significant self-concept items, it was possible to obtain a total self-concept score on the 16. High total scores were in the unfavorable (delinquency) direction. When the mean (total) scores on the 16 self-concept items were computed for various subgroups of the sixth-grade boy sample (1957), the difference in the means for white and colored boys was (a) slight (although significant statistically); (b) somewhat larger for boys by type of area (again statistically significant); (c) not significant for white boys in high and in low delinquency areas; (d) significant for white boys in good areas and colored

Table 2
Significant Self-Concept Items According to Teacher Nomination, Associated with High and Low Scores on the De Scale of the California Psychological Inventory

Original schedule no.	Self-concept items
1	Will you probably be taken to juvenile court sometime?
2	Will you probably have to go to jail sometime?
6	If you found that a friend was leading you into trouble, would you continue to run around with him or her?
11	Do you plan to finish high school?
12	Do you think you'll stay out of trouble in the future?
17	Are grown-ups usually against you?
21	If you could get permission to work at 14 would you quit school?
23	Are you a big shot with your pals?
24	Do you think your teacher thinks you will ever get into trouble with the law?
25	Do you think your mother thinks you will ever get into trouble with the law?
26	Do you think if you were to get into trouble with the law, it would be bad for you in the future?
27	Have you ever been told that you were headed for trouble with the law?
39	Have most of your friends been in trouble with the law?
42	Do you confide in your father?
46	Do your parents punish you?
50	Do you think you are quiet _____ average _____ active _____.[6]

boys in bad areas; and (e) not significant for white boys and Negro boys (both) in areas of high delinquency.

By way of comparison, the mean self-concept score for boys with high *De* scores and that for boys with low *De* scores differed most of all and at a significance level of .00001.[7] In

[5] *Ibid.*, 50.

[6] *Ibid.*, 51.
[7] *Ibid.*, 52–53.

commenting on these findings relative to self-concept scores by various subgroups of the sixth-grade Columbus boys, Donald had this to say:

One is almost ready to hazard the guess that race and type of neighborhood, whatever they may signify in the accumulated socialization of 12-year-old boys, are relatively unimportant in determining self concepts. On the other hand, a large mean score difference on the self-concept items is found when the sixth-grade boys are divided by favorable and unfavorable direction of socialization as measured by the scores on the De scale. Evidently the big thing which determines the boy's self-concept orientation is something other than race and neighborhood. Might we say that it is the quality of family interaction and impact, apart from class and race, plus the impact of other supplementary relationships found within the child's world? [8]

Further details on the entire 717 (1957) "big run," giving the mean scores for girls as well as boys on the De and Re scales, I.Q., Reading Achievement, and Arithmetic Achievement, by sex, race, type of area, and teacher nomination were presented in a special article, published in 1958.[9] In addition, an analysis of 400 of the 717 (1957) sixth-grade children, girls as well as boys, all from high delinquency areas, was published in 1960.[10]

Soundings in Brooklyn and Akron

Prior to Donald's 1963 item analysis of the authors' self-concept items, using 354 schedules of sixth-grade boys in the 1957 Columbus, Ohio, sample, and establishing 16 discriminating items which could be summated into a total score, the authors received permission in 1959 to administer a schedule to 697 sixth-grade children in six elementary schools of Brooklyn, serving high, medium, and low delinquency areas. The object here was to deter-

mine whether the trends noted in Columbus applied to the more complex, heterogeneous, urban environment of New York.

The Brooklyn schedule consisted of 46 items of the De scale; 34 self-concept items, including 9 which deal with a general view that the child has of himself, 7 with his view of his home and parents, and 8 with his view of how his father deals with him (a sort of father rejection assessment), and 10 with his projection about getting into trouble with the law; and 7 items taken from the Nye-Short inventory of self-reported delinquency involvement. However, it was not possible to obtain the sixth-grade teachers' prognostications of delinquency vulnerability in the Brooklyn project.

The findings on the Brooklyn study were never published. It was expected, however, that the sixth-grade males would test more unfavorably than the sixth-grade females, Negro more than white, high-delinquency area more than low-delinquency area pupils, Puerto Rican sixth-graders about the same as Negro sixth-graders, on all or most of the measures in the schedule. The greatest over-all differences between the various subgroups among the 1959 Brooklyn sixth-grade pupils occurred in mean scores on the De scale, which measures direction toward and away from delinquency. The 10 self-concept items dealing with projected involvement with the law made less sharp distinctions than the De scale between the various subgroups, although practically all differences between the mean scores were significant. The mean subgroup scores on the self-concept items which focused on the father's rejection of the child were not significant, while most of the mean scores on the child's view of his home and parents did not distinguish the various subgroups in Brooklyn. The mean scores on the Nye-Short self-reported involvement in delinquency, likewise, for the most part did not differentiate the various subgroups. The authors wished that they could have gone into Brooklyn with a self-concept scale based on the 16 discriminating items which Donald analyzed and with more sophisticated measures of self-reported involvement.

The authors received considerable encour-

---

[8] Ibid., 54.

[9] Dinitz, Kay & Reckless, "Group Gradients in Delinquency Potential and Achievement Scores of Sixth Graders," 33 Am. J. Orthopsy., 598 (1958).

[10] Simpson, Dinitz, Kay & Reckless, "Delinquency Potential in Pre-Adolescents in High Delinquency Areas," 10 Br. J. Delinquency, 211 (1960).

agement from the results of a 1959 Akron, Ohio study made by Dr. Edwin L. Lively.[11] Lively administered the authors' Brooklyn schedule to 1171 pupils, boys and girls, in Akron: 192 in sixth-grade, 324 in seventh-grade, 325 in eighth-grade, and 300 in ninth-grade rooms, divided among schools serving lower and middle class neighborhoods as well as high and low delinquency areas. It was possible in this study to tell whether the mean scores by various subgroups (sex, race, high-low delinquency area, and teacher prognostication) had stability with increasing age in adolescence (roughly 12 through 15).

The mean scores on the *De* scale (now called the Socialization scale) of the CPI, the 10 self-concept items projecting involvement with the law, and the 7 items dealing with the child's view of his home, were quite stable throughout the four age samples (sixth, seventh, eighth, and ninth graders). The scores on the 8 items dealing with the child's view of his relations with his father (mostly rejection items) were not stable for the subgroups of the four age levels. The mean scores on the 7 self-reported involvements in delinquency increased with age (which trend seems logical).

Very interesting, as far as directional corroboration is concerned, is the fact that scores on the five instruments analyzed in the Akron study (*De* scale — now called Socialization scale, home items, law involvement items, father rejection items and self-reported delinquency) intercorrelated very well indeed ranging from +.27 to +.65, and at about the same levels of intercorrelation for each age sample: sixth, seventh, eighth and ninth grade.[12] (One should remind himself that if the coefficients of correlation had been in the high seventies, eighties, or nineties, he should suspect that any two measures which highly correlated would be assessing the same component of self.) This directional corroboration plus the

corroboration of stability with age gave reassurance to the authors that a self-factor seems to be involved in vulnerability toward or insulation against delinquency.

A disconcerting note, however, needs to be inserted at this point. The authors attempted to administer the Brooklyn schedule in representative sixth, seventh, eighth, and ninth grades of two large metropolitan school systems after the excellent results in Akron. But they were turned down in both instances, due to the political dynamite which could be caused by administering schedules to children. And just recently a new National Institute of Mental Health regulation requires that the principal investigators of research projects obtain parental permission before administering scales and inventories to school children.

Application to Prevention

In 1959, the authors were asked by the Columbus, Ohio, school system, to attempt some practical application of their findings. A demonstration on a very limited scale was undertaken to determine the feasibility of presenting appropriate models of behavior to sixth-grade boys, selected by teachers as headed for trouble. (Parental permission was obtained and the program occupied the last school period plus a half hour over school-closing time each day.) The main thrust of this demonstration was directed toward helping the vulnerable sixth-grade boy internalize effective models of behavior, thus building-up or strengthening his self-concept. The worker in charge of the model-building sessions was also trained to be a most significant other (adult) in the lives of the participants.

Three years of such limited demonstration projects led to the formulation of a large demonstration-research project, supported by grants from the National Institute of Mental Health, to discover whether appropriate presentation of realistic models of behavior in the classroom could "beef up" a vulnerable boy's self. The design followed the theory and procedures of our original work on the self-concept as the insulating agent against trends toward delinquency.

[11] Lively, Dinitz & Reckless, "Self Concept as a Predictor of Juvenile Delinquency," 32 *Am. J. Orthopsy.*, 1 (1962).
[12] Lively, "A Study of Teen-Age Socialization and Delinquency Insulation by Grade Levels" (a Ph.D. dissertation, Ohio State Univ. 1959, 70–71).

The authors selected eight junior high schools of the inner city of Columbus, Ohio, which served disadvantaged and high delinquency neighborhoods. These 8 junior high schools were fed pupils by 44 elementary schools. In May of 1963, the authors, after having received the go-ahead signal from the granting agency, asked the sixth-grade teachers of the 44 elementary schools to nominate the boys in their classes who, in their opinion were likely to get into trouble with the law and likely to drop out of school as well as the boys who were likely not to get into trouble with the law and likely to stay in school. In each school, the principal reviewed and confirmed the sixth-grade teacher's rating.

The over-all average was about 75 percent good; 25 percent bad boys. The following September when the boys reached the eight junior high schools, the nominated vulnerable ("bad") boys were randomly divided into two groups: an experimental, and a control group. The project also called for a continuing follow-up of a sample of 15 percent of the so-called "good" boys.

Preliminary data on the validity of these teacher-nominations of their students as vulnerable, doubtfully vulnerable or not vulnerable to later involvement with the law have been obtained. These data tend to support the contention that teacher-nominations are reasonably valid indicators of case outcomes of the 176 boys nominated as "good" (not vulnerable) in May, 1963; 154 or 87.5% had no contact with the police as of August, 1966. Of the unsure nominees, 69.4% avoided police contact in the comparable 3-year period, while just 53.7% of the nominated "bad" (vulnerable) boys were free of contact in the same three and one-fourth year time period.

The Columbus junior high schools at the time of the intervention demonstration operated "self-contained classes," which ran for three consecutive school periods (of forty minutes each) with the same teacher. In these self-contained classes, world geography, Ohio history, and English were taught in mixed groups, boys as well as girls. The project called for placing the experimental group (randomly split half of the vulnerable boys)

into an all-boy self-contained class of approximately 25 boys. It called also for retaining the other half of the vulnerable boys as well as the nonvulnerable boys in the regular mixed self-contained classes.

Permission was obtained from parents to gather the experimental group into a special all-boy section. When the boys and parents asked why, our reply was that Mr. Jones, the teacher, wanted Joe in his class and wanted an all-boy section.

Four male seventh-grade project teachers were selected by the authors (the principal investigators). They were specially trained to present "model" materials, as a youth development supplement to the regular diet of world geography, Ohio history, and English. They were trained also to play the role of the most significant adult in the lives of these boys in the experimental classes. They were involved in a summer tooling-up program, met with the project's research director each day after school, and with the project's consulting child psychiatrist each Saturday morning as a group.

Each of the four project teachers had two experimental self-contained classes: one in the morning at one junior high school and one in the afternoon at another junior high school. Thus, there was one experimental all-boy self-contained class in each of the 8 junior high schools serving children from disadvantaged, high-delinquency areas. The four project teachers worked with the research director in developing appropriate "lesson plans" to get on target of presenting models of behavior in an effective way. In addition, the project teachers, as a result of their Saturday morning discussions with the project's consulting psychiatrist, developed a class-room climate or atmosphere conducive to internalization of the regular class fare and the project's supplementation. The experimental group was found, on an average, to be reading at the fourth-grade level. Consequently, the project used seventh-grade materials written at a fourth-grade comprehension level and it availed itself of various reading-therapy procedures.

The youth-development supplementation (presentation of models of behavior) was fed into the experimental all-boy classes at the same time, in all eight groups — feeding in the same lesson plans — such as finding out something about the man on your city block who has the reputation of being the best worker so as to put on the board (on such and such day). During the first year of operation (1963–1964), the project teachers worked valiantly to develop lesson plans which had possibility of model takeover. These plans were standardized and used in the same way, to supplement the regular school fare, in two successive years, namely 1964–1965 and 1965–1966. During the last two years of the project, it was possible for the project teachers to use their after-school over-time for making home visits.

The demonstration-research design consisted of an experimental group and two control groups, in three cohorts, 1963–1964, 1964–1965, and 1965–1966. Standard information was accumulated on each boy. Certain inventories were administered to the three groups in September and again in May of each year, at the close of the school year. Available school information on reading and arithmetic achievement, absences, conduct, school performance, is being collected for the file. Yearly clearance (every year until 1970) of all three subgroups (the experimental group and the two control groups) is made through school records and through the files of the juvenile bureau of the police department in the summer of each follow-up year, to record truancy, non-attendance, and complaints for delinquency. Each yearly cohort will have four yearly clearances and by the time of the fourth clearance each boy will have passed his sixteenth birthday and will have had the legal opportunity to quit school and go to work.

Is the youth development supplement, in terms of presentation of appropriate models of behavior, strong enough preventive medicine? Does it reach the adolescent boy and presumably his self? Will the teacher-nominated vulnerable boys, who received Dr. Reckless and Dinitz's vitamins do better over a four-year period than their untreated first-cousins (also vulnerable boys) and even the teacher-nominated "good boys"? This is the question. The authors will have some answers in the fall of 1970.

Conclusion

It is no longer sufficient for sociologists who study criminal and delinquent behavior to call attention to the possible impact of disorganized and disadvantaged neighborhoods, family tensions and insufficiencies, bad companions and street-corner gangs, and the availability of illegitimate means to ends. Who responds to carriers of patterns of delinquency and crime? Who resists and goes the other way? We live in a society of alternates, where the self has more and more opportunities for acceptance or rejection of available confrontations. Consequently, sociologists as criminologists must join the search for the self-factors which determine direction of behavior or choice among alternates and in this endeavor they must work with their colleagues in psychology and psychiatry in an effort to discover what self-factors actually determine the direction of behavior and how they can be controlled.

The proposal herein has been to explore the self-concept as one important self-factor which controls the direction of the person. There is certainly some preliminary evidence in the authors' work to date, to indicate that the self-concept might be one of the important self-factors in determining the "drift" toward or away from delinquency and crime. The authors do not presume that such a self-factor would operate in instances of deep character and emotional disturbances. But for the large majority of unofficial and official offenders as well as effective conformers to the dominant norms of a democratic, industrial, urban, mobile society, it is certainly feasible to operate on the hypothesis that self-factors determine direction of behavior toward or away from delinquency and deviance in general.

The authors feel they uncovered some corroborating evidence, namely that the self-concept of an early adolescent might be one of the self-factors which controls directionality. Certainly, teachers' prognostications of sixth-grade boys — even the mothers' evaluations — plus the *De* scale (now called Socialization scale) indicate that directionality, toward or away from delinquent behavior, can be sensed and assessed. If, in the future, effective assessment of self-reported delinquency can be made, sociologists as well as behavioral-science researchers will have another effective instrument to gauge directionality of the youth.

It seems to the authors that these indicators of directionality toward or away from deviance point to the strong possibility of a favorable-to-unfavorable self-concept in the young person, which is acting as the controlling agent. Our large cross-sectional study in 1957 certainly indicated that self-concept factors, the teachers' prognostication of direction of the youth, and the *De* scale's assessment of direction were interrelated. And the authors, if they might be spared glibness, do not think it is the subtle "rub-off" of the teacher's sense of the individual youth's direction which causes an internalization of a favorable image of himself (although this might happen in rare instances). And in the 1955 and 1956 samples, when the mother's projections of direction in which the son was travelling were obtained, the authors did not feel that in the overwhelming majority of instances the mother's faith or lack of faith in the directional outcome of her boy was the "looking glass" which gave the boy his image (although this might happen in more instances than in the impact of the sixth-grade teacher's sense of direction on the boy). The authors believe that a youth in American society obtains his self-concepts from many experiential sources, inside and outside the home and school.

The findings from the Akron study point to stability of direction as assessed by teacher's nomination and other instruments of assessment. Here again, the authors' interpretation is that directional stability in comparable samples of the sixth, seventh, eighth and ninth grades reflects the operation of a self-factor. However, this is not as convincing evidence as if the same sample of children could be tested during four successive years of adolescence. Nevertheless, the authors felt they received indications of longitudinal stability in the operation of a self-factor in the four-year follow-up of the 1955 good-boy sample and the 1956 bad-boy sample.

Undoubtedly, there is a need for the development of an effective self-concept measure which can assess the direction toward or away from delinquency or deviant behavior generally. There is need also to develop measures of other self-factors which control directionality. When such factors are uncovered and when they are effectively measured, then it should be possible to chart workable programs to prevent delinquency and to re-enforce the components of self which enable the youth to be an effective conformer.

Certainly, the authors' experience in Brooklyn indicates that it is necessary to use much more discriminating instruments than the ones they used and it could very well be that much more sensitive instruments are needed to record differences in self development among sixth-graders in high, medium, and low delinquency areas as well as white, colored, and Puerto Rican sixth-graders than among sixth-grade white and colored adolescents in different areas of Columbus and Akron, Ohio.

In the meantime, more faith can be placed in the sixth-grade teacher's evaluations or her assessments of the directionality of her male pupils. Sophisticated studies could be made of the predictive efficacy of her ratings. More use could be made of her ratings, say in May of each year after 35 weeks of daily contact, for designing preventive programs or attempting individualized corrective therapy. More sophisticated effort should also be expended on attempting to develop improved measures of self-reported delinquency.

One of the most difficult tasks would be to follow a large stratified sample of children who were evaluated at the first-grade level by the Gluecks' family-factor prediction instrument, to obtain teacher's prognostication, a self-reported delinquency measure, and an assessment of self-concept at the sixth-grade level, and to make an official delinquency clearance on each youth in the sample at 18 years of age, no matter how many times he may have changed residence.

This paper provides a useful review and critique of the seminal research of Reckless and Dinitz on the variable of self-conception. In their analysis the authors divide the several investigations of Reckless and his associates into four parts. Critical assessments such as this, in which problems of sampling, measurement, interpretation, and theoretical linkage are raised, serve the highly useful function of alerting students to questions that deserve further attention. It is important to recognize that criticism of this type is not intended to detract from the importance of the initial investigations; one might well argue that the appearance of such a critique indicates that the writers, as well as their colleagues who review articles prior to their publication in journals, believe the research to be of sufficient importance to deserve careful scrutiny. The essential point is that Tangri and Schwartz regard self-concept as a variable with potential predictive utility, and they propose that the pioneering work of Reckless and Dinitz has opened the door to somewhat more sophisticated analysis with a research design which would permit assessment of the relative importance of self, structural, and cognitive variables.

SANDRA S. TANGRI

MICHAEL SCHWARTZ

Delinquency Research and the Self-Concept Variable

A wide variety of variables have been related to delinquency rates. These include demographic variables,[1] social structural variables,[2] variables having to do with perception of the social structures,[3] and occasionally personality variables.[4] In a recent paper by Himelhoch,[5]

Reprinted by special permission of the *Journal of Criminal Law, Criminology and Police Science* (Northwestern University School of Law), Copyright © 1967, Volume 58, Number 2.

[1] See especially Chilton, "Continuity in Delinquency Area Research: A Comparison of Studies for Baltimore, Detroit, and Indianapolis," 29 *Am. Soc. Rev.*, 71–83 (1964).

[2] For example, see Cloward & Ohlin, *Delinquency and Opportunity* (1960).

[3] See Short, Jr., Rivera & Tennyson, "Perceived Opportunities, Gang Membership and Delinquency," 30 *Am. Soc. Rev.*, 56–67 (1965).

[4] Reckless, Dinitz & Murray, "Self-Concept as an Insulator Against Delinquency," 21 *Am. Soc. Rev.*, 744–746 (1956).

[5] Himelhoch, "Delinquency and Opportunity:

the point is made, without much elaboration, that personality variables may indeed be necessary for an adequate prediction scheme in delinquency research. He makes a plea in his paper for multi-level analyses which ought to include at one time variables of structure, perception of structure, and personality.

A case can be made for engaging in such research on a number of counts. In the first place, while structural variables seem to be the primary focus in delinquency research carried on by sociologists, the results of their studies can by no means be taken as heartening. For example, in a recent paper by Westie and Turk, in which they examine the question of the relationship of social class to delinquency, they point out that it is quite possible to sup-

An End and a Beginning of Theory," Gouldner & Miller, Eds., *Applied Sociology*, 189–206 (1965).

port findings which indicate more delinquency in the lower class then the middle class, more delinquency in the middle class than the lower class, or no differences by class, on the basis of both current research and theory.[6] Similarly, those studies which relate demographic variables to delinquency rates do not by any means achieve the same results.

While some students of delinquency have been able to find that delinquents and non-delinquents have differing perceptions of the structure which they confront, in no case has it been determined that those perceptions precede delinquency or non-delinquency or are a consequence of delinquency or non-delinquency. That very criticism can be made of studies which claim to discriminate between delinquents and non-delinquents on the basis of personality measures, although studies of personality variables and delinquency are most uncommon in the sociological literature.

Apparently the major point, which is not made with the strength necessary in Himelhoch's paper, is that delinquency research has reached a stage where study designs ought to include variables at all of the levels we have mentioned, and that designs aimed at discriminating between groups are, at this stage, less important than are designs aimed at determining the amount of variance which can be accounted for in delinquency and non-delinquency by variables at a number of levels of analysis. In other words, we are now due for designs in delinquency research which are analysis of variance designs.

If the ambiguity and contradictions in our univariate forms of analysis are ever to be understood, then it seems that the analysis of variance design is one which ought to be employed. It does have the virtue of giving the reseacher an indication of the ways in which the interactions of variables from different levels of analysis combine to account for delinquency, and it seems that there is every indication that an understanding of the interaction effects of these variables may prove to be vastly more fruitful than a continued pursuit of univariate studies.

As Himelhoch has argued, however, sociologists concerned with delinquency research seem either to ignore variables at the level of personality, or to take them as given. Variables of personality seem to be in the domain of the psychologists and therefore out of the realm of the sociologist's competence or research concern. Perhaps that is a great error. There is available in our discipline a tradition of thought in the realm of personality and socialization which is not only respectable but also growing in measurement sophistication and applicability in empirical research. That is, of course, the tradition of symbolic interactionism.

Some sociologists have, in the past, investigated personality or self variables, keeping constant the social structural variables. Most important and impressive among these studies are the ones conducted by Professor Reckless and his associates, in which self-concept is viewed as a variable which seems effective in insulating boys against delinquency or in making them more vulnerable. Because this research has been so widely quoted and reprinted, and because it is practically the only research by sociologists in the area of delinquency which claims to handle variables of personality and self, it is wise, we believe, to undertake a thoroughgoing analysis of those researches, their designs, and the findings in order to determine what sociologists have been able to learn about delinquency and personality, as well as to determine what remains to be done in that area.

The behavior of the non-delinquent in a high delinquency area has occasioned a good deal of interest because of its possible implications for policies of social control. None of the studies by the Reckless group, however, draw such implications although they all claim to have discovered a crucial variable which differentiates delinquents and non-delinquents, and delinquents who have and have not been in contact with legal authorities as offenders. They do suggest that "self theory seems . . . to be the best operational basis for designing effective prevention and treatment measures."[7] This proposal is elaborated no further. As they

[6] Westie & Turk, "A Strategy for Research on Social Class and Delinquency," 56 J. Crim. L., C. & P. S., 454–462 (1965).

[7] Reckless, Dinitz & Kay, "The Self Component in Potential Delinquency and Non-Delinquency," 22 Am. Soc. Rev., 570 (1957).

state, the crucial variable is self-concept or "self-evaluation":

It is proposed that a socially appropriate or inappropriate concept of self and other is the basic component that steers the youthful person away from or toward delinquency and that those appropriate or inappropriate concepts represent differential response to various environments and confrontations of delinquent patterns.[8]

In this discussion we shall review the methodology and detailed results of several studies, and attempt to evaluate the extent to which these impose certain restrictions on the broad interpretation quoted above.

The Original Study: Self-Concept as an Insulator Against Delinquency [9]

This was the first of the series of articles on the problem and deals exclusively with the boys whom we shall refer to as "good boys."

For this study, all thirty sixth-grade teachers in schools located in the highest white delinquency areas of Columbus, Ohio, were asked to nominate those white boys who would not, in their opinion, ever experience police or juvenile court contact; and the teachers were asked to give their reasons. Half of those eligible were nominated (i.e., 192). Of those, 51 students (27.3%) could not be located because of summer vacation. Of the remaining 141 boys, sixteen (11.3%) already had records and were eliminated from the sample. This left 125 "good boys" — and their mothers — who were interviewed. Each boy was administered the delinquency proneness (DE) and social responsibility (RE) scales of Gough's California Personality Inventory (CPI); a questionnaire on his occupational preference (the data from which do not appear among the results); and each was asked questions about his concept of himself, his family, and his interpersonal relations.

The results obtained for the "good boys" were: (1) Low scores on the DE scale and high scores on the RE scale; (2) "self-evaluations" which were law-abiding and obedient;

and (3) very favorable perceptions of family interaction, and lack of resentment of close family (mother) supervision; (4) these families were maritally, residentially, and economically stable. The authors concluded: "Insulation against delinquency is an ongoing process reflecting internalization of non-delinquent values and conformity to the expectations of significant others."

Critique

1. The first and obvious problem is that, without knowing parallel results on a control group of so-called "bad boys," we cannot conclude that these results actually differentiate the two populations. Since this comparison is subsequently made at the time of a later study, we shall postpone further discussion of this issue.

2. Insofar as the term "insulation" implies present and/or future predictiveness as to actual delinquent behavior, the following difficulties arise:

(a) It is perhaps a truism to point out that court records do not contain evidence of all law-violating behavior, and particularly in the case of minors. Therefore, it is probably safe to guess that the previous offenders constituting 11.3% of the "good boys" is an underestimate. It is about half the proportion of previous offenders later found among the "bad boys."

(b) Since these boys were only 12 years old at this time, it would be more reasonable to look for a correlation between present "self-concept" and future "delinquency." Most of these boys (99 out of 125) were relocated in school four years later (at age 16), and four of them had been in "contact" with the police or juvenile court or both, one time each during the intervening years. Even this interval might be questioned as to whether it provides an adequate time span in which to validate actual "insulation." Together with the 16 "good boys" who were eliminated for this reason from the original sample, this makes 20 boys, or 14.4% of the 141 nominated "good boys" who were originally located.

(c) What is required is a comparison of the proportion of "contacts" among those scoring like "good boys" and those scoring like "bad

[8] *Ibid.*, p. 569.
[9] Reckless, Dinitz & Murray, *op. cit. supra* note 4.

boys" on the DE and RE scales from both actual groups of "good boys" and "bad boys" as
nominated by the teachers. The analysis is not
made anywhere, and is precluded by the exclusion of the 16 "contact" cases fom the study
of "good boys."

3. There is some clarification needed as to
the use of teachers' nominations in this design.
We have already seen that there is not a perfect correlation between the teachers' evaluations of the boys and their actual (non-) delinquency, as operationally defined in this study.

(a) If the authors wanted to investigate that
relationship, they would not have eliminated
11.3% of the "good boys" who had already experienced "contact" with juvenile court or police. Such an investigation would have shed an
interesting sidelight on why, in spite of being
capable of making a good impression, these
boys also had police or court records. What if
they had turned out to have relatively positive
self-concepts instead of relatively negative
ones — contrary to the author's later assumption? We would be in a much better position
to evaluate the authors' conclusion if they had
elected to gather these data. On the other
hand, it must be pointed out that the authors
were presumably not interested in investigating
this relationship. From their point of view, it
could be argued that there is no need for a
perfect correlation. The assumption is only
that you have a little better chance of getting
a pure non-delinquent sample if you have two
criteria; that the delinquent who can slip by
one of them is less likely to slip by both.

(b) Nevertheless, the margin of uncertainty
about the meaning of the teachers' nominations
is magnified by the fact that only one-half of
the eligible students were nominated. Who are
the remaining boys? We wonder how many of
those not nominated as "good boys" and with no
"contact" experience would have been found to
have poor self-concepts? And how many of
these would have had "contact" with the police
or juvenile court? Conversely, we wonder how
many of those not nominated but with no
"contact" would have been found to have
poor self-concepts. The magnitudes involved
are certainly great enough to reverse or eliminate the reported relationships.

The fact remains, however, that if we are
really interested in determining the effect of
the self-concept upon delinquency vulnerability, then we ought not look for delinquent
and non-delinquent groups, but rather for
groups with clearly good and clearly bad self-
concepts. How those would be distributed between later delinquent and non-delinquent
groups would better determine the effect of
self-concept as the independent variable, upon
delinquency as the dependent one. Clearly, a
major issue in much of this research has to do
with the delineation of the experimental variables. If self-concept is an "insulator against delinquency," this implies that self-concept is an
independent variable. But the research causes
confusion because self-concept is treated as the
dependent variable.

(c) There is some reason to feel uneasy also
about the fairly high percentage (27.3%) of
"good boys" who could not be located (i.e.,
51 out of 192). This is particularly so when we
compare the similar percentage for the "bad
boys" nominated in the later study: 6.5% (or
7 out of 108). Thus, the original population of
"good boys" (192) has been reduced by 34.9%
(51 + 16 = 67), whereas no comparable shrinkage occurred in the "bad boy" population.

4. Our most serious concern, however, is
with the instruments used to evaluate self-
concept.

(a) In terms of the most elementary Meadian
psychology, the relationship between frame of
reference and self-evaluation, i.e., the correlation between teachers' nominations and the
boys' responses to CPI items is not surprising.
The CPI items obviously are drawn from a
middle-class frame of reference, as are the
teachers' impressions. They do not sample
from an alternative frame of reference, in
which positive instead of negative values might
be placed on the same response. But we do not
know whether a revised scoring procedure in
itself could be sensibly interpreted. Therefore,
we would prefer to substitute a less culture-
bound measure such as the semantic differential, in which the individual is free to operate
in terms of any (unspecified) frame of reference. (We will have more to say about this
problem presently, in some general comments.)

(b) Viewed in this light, one might hypothesize that because of this frame of reference, boys who are nominated as "good" will continue to test positive on the CPI, until they are caught in a delinquent act, at which time — and not until — the middle-class frame of reference would operate to devalue their behavior, and supposedly that part of their self-concept. Unfortunately, no such separate analysis was made.

The "Good Boys" Four Years Later [10]

Some of the questions raised in the previous section about the interpretation of the "insulation" of the "good boys" in these studies may now be answered. Of the original 125 on whom data had been collected, only 103 boys (82.4%) were relocated, now age 16, but only 99 of them were still in school. The others were not retested. These boys' homeroom teachers were again requested to nominate the boys as (a) ones who would not experience difficulty with the law, (b) ones who would get into trouble, or (c) ones about whom the teacher was unsure, and why. Each of the boys was again checked through police and juvenile court files "for official or unofficial violation behavior in the intervening years," and their school records were checked. Their mothers or mother-surrogates were again interviewed.

The results were as follows: Ninety-five of the boys were again nominated by their teachers as unlikely to get into trouble with the law. The reasons indicated "quietness," "good family," and "good student." Four of these boys had become known to the police or juvenile court, or both — one time each during the intervening years. Ninety-six boys were enrolled in the academic program, although they showed a more or less normal distribution scholastically and in attendance (in which respect there had been no significant change over time). Ninety-eight expected to finish high school. Ninety-one remained aloof from boys in trouble with the law. The families of these boys, who were found in the original study to be typical of the families in the school

areas in terms of father's occupation, were not nearly as residentially mobile as anticipated. (A separate analysis comparing the respondents who remained in the high delinquency areas with those who had achieved upward mobility revealed no significant difference on any of the indices included.) The boys' responses on the tests "and, apparently, in behavior as well," were consistent with their earlier performances.

On an additional measure, the Short-Nye seven-item scale of admitted delinquent behavior, "The good boys appear almost angelic." The authors question, however, the reliability of this result because they were unable to replicate the Short-Nye scale in any of their own more recent studies and because of the lack of anonymity of the boys, ". . . and their younger age." The boys' reports on their families were again favorable, somewhat more so than previously.

Critique

1. Now it is somewhat more clear that self-concept is the independent variable and that delinquency is the dependent one. At least it is clear if one keeps the first paper in mind. Of greatest interest is the finding that most of the "good boys" located again are still in school (99/103 = 96.1%), and all but three are in the academic program. We wonder if this might not imply that the factor differentiating good from bad boys is ability to perform adequately in school. Glueck's findings on comparative intelligence between the normal and reformatory population would tend to support this interpretation: "It will be seen that the reformatory population contains a considerable excess of dull, borderline, and feebleminded groups." [11]

2. There are, however, several reasons why this interpretation may be unwarranted:

(a) The later studies do not give information on how many of the "bad boys" similarly remained in school (and in an academic program).

(b) Even if we found the proportion to be radically different, it would be quite reasonable to argue that this was because of their

[10] Scarpitti, Murray, Dinitz & Reckless, "The 'Good' Boy in a High Delinquency Area: Four Years Later," 25 *Am. Soc. Rev.*, 555–558 (1960).

[11] Glueck, S. & E., *Five Hundred Criminal Careers*, 156 (1939).

delinquency, lack of motivation, rejection by their teachers, or any one of a number of other factors than intelligence *per se*. However, it might have been helpful for narrowing the possible interpretations to have such a measure, providing it too wasn't class-biased.

(c) Of the boys still in school, half were still in the compulsory attendance age bracket.

3. In the relocation of the "good boys," 22 of the original sample were lost. Although this is three times as many as were lost from the "bad boy" sample, because of the fact that the original nominees from the population were almost 50% more for the "good boys" than for the "bad boys," it means in effect that the retested samples were approximately in the same proportions to the original populations for both groups: 99/141 = 70.2% of the "good boys" and 70/101 = 69.3% of the "bad boys."

4. We are also faced again with the questionable interpretation of the teachers' nominations. Why were they again asked to nominate each boy as a likely or unlikely candidate for trouble?

(a) In this case they were not choosing the boys out of the total class; if they had, perhaps fewer would have been nominated as "good boys."

(b) We do not know whether the four "good boys" still in school but not renominated were nominated as likely to get into trouble, or whether in their case the teacher was "unsure" (an additional category not previously used).

(c) It is interesting to point out that the four boys who had police or court contact in the intervening years are not these four (who were *not* renominated), but are among those the teachers again nominated as unlikely to get into trouble.

(d) It is not clear whether these are the only boys out of those relocated who had been "in trouble," or whether they are the only ones out of those still in school. If the latter is the case, and it appears to be, then there remains some question about the "insulation" of the four boys *not* in school.

(e) We are left with 95 "good boys" (67.4%) out of the original 141 nominated and tested about whom we can say with some (but not absolute) confidence that they have not been delinquent. Because of the unfortunate reporting of data, we cannot determine the comparable figure for the "bad boys." We know there were 20 offenders among the original "good boys" at the end of the study, but we don't know how many there were among the "bad boys" (because some of the earlier and later offenders may be the same boys).

The Self Component in Potential Delinquency and Non-Delinquency;[12] A Self-Gradient Among Potential Delinquents[13]

The sample of potential delinquents were nominated a year after the "good boy" study by 37 sixth-grade teachers in the same 20 schools in a white high delinquency area in Columbus, Ohio. Approximately one-fourth (108) of those eligible were nominated as "headed for police and juvenile court contact." Apparently population growth in the area had increased the white sixth-grade population by about 13% (from ca. 384 to ca. 432) and the number of sixth-grade teachers by 23% (from 30 to 37) (There may have been a greater increase in the area's Negro population than in its white population). Only seven of these boys could not be located; the remaining 101, and their mothers, were interviewed. A check of the police and juvenile court files revealed that 24 of these twelve-year-old boys (23%) were already on record for previous offenses which ranged from charges of incorrigibility to theft.

The results, when compared with the first study, were as follows: The "bad boy" scores

. . . were significantly higher on the DE and lower on the RE scales than those made by the "good boys" of the first study. Indeed, this mean delinquency vulnerability score was higher than that achieved by any of the nondelinquents and non-disciplinary sample subjects treated in other studies. Similarly, the mean social responsibility score was lower than those recorded in other studies for all

[12] Reckless, Dinitz & Kay, *op. cit. supra* note 7.
[13] Dinitz, Reckless & Kay, "A Self-Gradient Among Potential Delinquents," 49 *J. Crim. L., C. & P. S.*, 230–233 (1958).

but prisoners, delinquents, and school disciplinary cases. These scores seem to validate the judgments of the teachers in selecting these boys as ones who would get into future difficulties with the law.

Not only do these scales appear to differentiate between the potentially delinquent and nondelinquent, but even more importantly they were found to discriminate within the sample of nominated delinquents between those boys who had and those who had not experienced previous court contact. . . . These differences between the contact and non-contact groups on both sides were statistically significant.[14]

Critique

(We shall not repeat the points already discussed as parts of the preceding sections.)

1. Adding to the confusion of possible interpretations already mentioned is the fact that the samples were not "designed" in a parallel manner. It will be recalled that in order to isolate "a truly non-delinquent group" for the first study, the investigators discarded sixteen cases (11.3%) of the "good boys" who could be located. This procedure would lead one to think that the interest was in fact correlating certain psychological patterns with behavioral patterns. However, we find that in the second study no such "purity" is attempted, and the 77 boys (76.8% of the 101 "bad boys" located) who did *not* have records for previous offenses were retained in the sample. Had the parallel operation been carried out, the "truly delinquent" group would have been considerably smaller, thus altering the statistical results of the measure. However, it should be pointed out that this type of attrition would have led to more, rather than less, significant results. The problem, therefore, is not the validity of the statistics, but rather the *interpretation* in comparing two non-parallel groups.

2. The second most critical point to make is that there is further contamination of variables due to the fact that the teachers' knowledge of the boys' involvement with the law "undoubtedly influenced" their nominations. Therefore, we have neither an independent "nomination variable" nor independent behavior variable.

(We shall subsequently discuss the possible contamination of the third and critical variable, the test and interview responses.)

3. Although it is not possible to infer *a priori* whether any bias in sampling occurred because of the increase in number of teachers participating (37 as against 30 in the first study), it should be noted that there were large teacher differences in the number of "bad boys" nominated. In some classrooms 60% of the eligible boys were nominated, whereas nine teachers nominated no one. (There was an average of 11.7 white boys per class, out of whom an average of 2.9 were nominated as headed for trouble.) These differences may reflect school policy to segregate potential disrupters, but we do not know.

We should point out that the statement that "these scores seem to validate the judgment of the teachers in selecting these boys as ones who would get into future difficulties with the law" implies some "validation" of the teachers' nominations against the nominees' later (future) actual behavior. This interpretation clearly may be unwarranted insofar as the only relationship being described is that teachers' nominations succeeded in creating two groups (at two different times) whose average scores on the DE and RE scales were significantly different. Moreover, we do not know how many of the same teachers were involved in both tests.

5. With respect to the comparisons of the "contact cases" and "non-contact cases," the conclusion that "it is apparent that the contact cases in many respects seem to be confirmed in their delinquent self-concepts to a greater extent than are the others" is justified in light of the results. What is not warranted, however, is the investigators' projected *evaluation* of the self-concept as a negative one to the boys being studied. A delinquent self-concept is not necessarily a negative concept.

Delinquency Vulnerability [15]

The follow-up study four years later of the "bad boys" succeeded in relocating 70 boys,

---

[14] *Ibid.*, p. 231.

[15] Dinitz, Scarpitti & Reckless, "Delinquency Vulnerability: A Cross-Group and Longitudinal Analysis," 27 *Am. Soc. Rev.*, 515–517 (1962).

now 16 years old. We know nothing of how many were in school or in an academic program, and there is no report of a second set of teachers' nominations. Twenty-seven (38.6%) of these seventy boys "had had serious and frequent contact with the court during the four-year interlude. These 27 boys averaged slightly more than three contacts with the court, involving separate complaints for delinquency." However, we do not know how many (if any) of these 27 are the same boys (24 of them) who had already had records at the time of the first testing, or whether they are different boys from the original population. As was mentioned earlier, both the "good" and "bad" follow-up samples are approximately the same proportion of the originally located, but untested, nominee groups. The "good" group lost 11.3% of its boys before testing began because of their delinquency records, whereas none of the located "bad boys" was dropped. The "bad" group, on the other hand, diminished proportionately more in size between the first and second testing, which may be considered more serious because it was an *uncontrolled* shrinkage of the *tested* population. The result is that the "good" follow-ups constitute 82.4% of their originally tested group and the "bad" follow-up constitute only 69.3% of theirs. Results of the second follow-up indicated that the "bad boys" mean score on the DE scale had not changed (it was 23.6 and at second testing was 23.4), and was still significantly "worse" than the "good boys" (whose mean score was 14.2, and at the second testing 13.6). The authors also note that "whereas the individual scores of the 70 'bad' boys on the DE scale at age 16 correlated with their scores at 12 years of age to the extent of $r = .78$," the "coefficient of correlation (r) of the DE scores for the boys in the 'good' cohort at 16 and at 12 years of age was only .15." They do not attempt to give any explanation for this difference in the groups' longitudinal stability. Certainly this is a most important finding and requires further understanding.

General Comments

There are criticisms which pertain to the series of studies as a whole, and which are so important as to restrict severely the authors' interpretations given, even if all the foregoing is deemed irrelevant or incorrect. Of major concern to us are the measures which were used to define operationally the boys' self-concepts. In the first place, it is not made quite clear in the original studies whether the conclusions with regard to self-concept are based on the Gough (DE and RE) CPI Scales, or whether the conclusion is based on the boys' answers to questions about their expectations of getting into trouble, or whether it was based on attitude items such as whether "any real trouble persons have with the law can be 'fixed' if they know the right people," whether it had to do with their descriptions of their home life or the degree to which they and their mothers (or mother-surrogates) seemed to agree.

It would be helpful in deciding which items are appropriate to a self-concept measure to differentiate between questions of *fact* and questions of *evaluation*. It is our opinion that only the latter is relevant to self-concept. Therefore, insofar as the boy states facts as he perceives them about his present behavior, the age and delinquency of his companions, "activity level" (whatever that is), whether he relies more on his friends or his parents for advice, etc., he tells us nothing about whether he thinks these are good or bad things, i.e., how these reflect on him personally and in his own judgment. Even in his judgment about the likelihood of his getting into trouble in the future, we do not know whether (1) this is self-criticism, (2) a badge of bravado, or (3) whether the prediction is accurate.

If we look at the operational definitions which are more ambiguously stated in the later studies, we see that they consist primarily of these kinds of statements:

On a nine-item quasi-scale or inventory, which measures the boys' favorable or unfavorable *projections of self in reference to getting into trouble with the law,* the cohort of 103 sixteen-year-old insulated slum boys showed an average score of 15.8. In this instance, the inventory was scored from 10 for the most favorable answers to 19 for the most unfavorable answers on all nine items. The 70 vulnerable

16-year-old slum boys scored an average of 18.9 on this quasi-scale.[16]

Could not these results be regarded as a statistically reasonable prediction by the boys of future events based on their respective past histories? Could it not be possible that the "bad boys" take some pride in their "record" and consider it a necessary adjunct to their self-image to be "tough" and "in trouble"?

Later in the same article quoted above, the following operational definition is given:

Regarding favorable or unfavorable concepts of self as measured by responses to questions such as "up to now, do you think things have gone your way?" or "do you feel that grown ups are usually against you?" or "do you expect to get an even break from people in the future?" there was no major change in the percentage distribution of the responses of the two cohorts at age 12 and at age 16. The good cohort had a very high percentage of favorable responses and the bad cohort a low percentage of favorable responses. On all three questions listed above, the percentage of favorable responses for the 103 good boys at age 16 was 90. For the 70 bad boys at 16 the percentage of favorable responses on the first of the above listed questions was 50; on the second, 29; on the third, 30.[17]

It is reasonable again to ask whether the "bad boys" responses are not simply realistic reflections of the fact that these same boys ". . . who had already been in trouble with the law defined themselves significantly more often than the others as likely candidates for getting into future difficulties with the police and the courts." [18]

Does it not reflect the fact that their mothers think so too; and that their teachers think so? Is it not just another way of saying that their "family affectional relationships" are not satisfactory? But, does it also necessarily mean that these boys have no recourse but to accept these negative evaluations of *these* others *as their own evaluations of themselves?* We would argue that this is not the case, but that

these boys look elsewhere for positive self-reflection, and that they may find it in their friends, which is the meaning of their seeking advice from friends more than from parents. A major problem appears to be that the authors may have selected sets of others for the boys, i.e., mother and teacher, both of whom are not significant "others" from the boys' own points of view.[19]

In summary, we would say that these studies have demonstrated:

1. That there is a certain amount of agreement between teachers and parents on the likelihood of certain boys getting into trouble; it has not demonstrated that this consensus agrees with either present or future actual experience.

2. That boys are aware of the judgments their elders make of them; it has not demonstrated the boys' acceptance of these evaluations of them as their own.

3. That this is true for the so-called "good boys" as well as the "bad boys"; and we still do not know whether the former think well of themselves and the latter do not.

The primary problem that is raised by Reckless' treatment of self is this: from any collection of questionnaire or interview responses, what kinds of conclusions can we draw about the self? It is not enough to say that these responses represent the subject's self. Since almost anything one can say may have some bearing on the self, we must have rules for extracting that aspect or implication of the statement relevant to self; otherwise we have no basis for distinguishing self from non-self, for everything is self. And that is the trouble with these studies. If everything is self, then self becomes another word for everything and its value is destroyed! A general hodgepodge of items from the CPI, questions asked of mother, son and teacher all thrown into the pot of self seems to destroy the meaning of self for research usage.

Vastly improved measurement in all of sociology is necessary. But adequate self-con-

---

[16] *Ibid.*, p. 516. (Emphasis added.)

[17] *Ibid.*, p. 517.

[18] Dinitz, Reckless & Kay, *op. cit. supra* note 7, at p. 232.

[19] Schwartz & Tangri, "A Note on Self-Concept As an Insulator Against Delinquency," 30 *Am. Soc. Rev.*, 922–926 (1965).

cept measurement is a dire necessity. We do not wish, however, to belabor the point. This research represents an important contribution to delinquency theory as well as to general social psychology. The papers have been reprinted in numbers of books of readings. It has been our experience that teachers, school administrators, public officials concerned with youth problems and others are very much aware of the Reckless *et al.* studies and in some cases try to operate in terms of these findings. But it would seem that there are some problems with this work which require adequate investigation. Nevertheless, Professor Reckless has opened an important door.

Our second comment in general has to do with the interpretation of the correspondence between the two studies. It will be remembered that the two cohorts were examined a year apart and taken from the same schools. They were not done contemporaneously. This may have had the advantage of avoiding invidious comparisons between the two groups of boys. However, in order to have confidence in the lack of bias on the part of the *investigators who administered the tests and interviewed the parents,* we would have to know whether or not they knew which cohort they were interviewing. In light of the fact that the data on the students in the good cohort were published soon after the data on the bad cohort were collected, (which means, in effect, that the results were known sometime earlier), and considering the fact that all these studies have been done by substantially the same group of investigators, we are inclined to believe that the investigators' own interviewers knew which cohort was which *while they were collecting data.*

Finally, we would point out that a theoretical link is missing from this research. Why should poor self-concept leave the individual vulnerable to delinquency? It might be argued, for example, that a poor self-concept ought to produce behavior more in conformity with the demands of significant others like mother or teacher. Or does poor self-concept lead to rejecting the rejectors and subsequent attributions of significance to those others who prove rewarding to the self (say, delinquent peers)?

Is it enough to indicate that more nominated "bad boys" than "good boys" become delinquent, even though the number of "bad boys" who become delinquent is less than 50% of the total nominated. In short, we are not yet convinced that "self-concept" is a major contributor to the variance in delinquent behavior. No small part of our skepticism arises from the atheoretical orientation of the Reckless work.

Even if all the foregoing criticism of this research were to be determined to be incorrect, the fact of the matter is that until this same form of research is undertaken in a somewhat more sophisticated way and a design is formed which includes not only self variables but also structural and cognitive (such as perception of structure) variables, and until the interaction effects from all of these levels as well as the main effects of each are understood, then it will continue to be impossible to develop predictive accuracy with reference to juvenile delinquency.

On the basis of the research on the self-concepts and socialization of delinquents and nondelinquents reviewed in the two preceding selections, Reckless (1961, 1967) has proposed containment theory as a new theory of delinquency and crime. Reckless (1961:44–45) describes the key ingredients in his explanation in these words: "Inner containment consists mainly of self components, such as self-control, good self-concept, ego strength, well-developed superego, high frustration tolerance, high resistance to diversions, high sense of responsibility, goal orientation, ability to find substitute satisfactions, tension-reducing rationalizations, and so on," whereas "outer containment represents the structural buffer in the person's immediate social world which is able to hold him within bounds. It consists of such items as a presentation of a consistent moral front to the person, institutional reinforcement of his norms, goals, and expectations, the existence of a reasonable set of social expectations, effective supervision and discipline (social controls), provision for reasonable scope of activity (including limits and responsibilities) as well as for alternatives and safety-valves, opportunity for acceptance, identity, and belongingness. Such structural ingredients help the family and other supportive groups contain the individual."

If it is not apparent in the foregoing quotations, in Reckless' (1967:469 ff.) elaboration of containment theory it is evident that Reckless accepts Sutherland's premise that illegal and unconventional patterns of behavior coexist with legal and conventional patterns of behavior in industrial societies. Outer or external containment, in this view, is the "holding power" of society, and particularly of primary groups within the society, to restrict the behavior of members to conformity with the group's norms by means of integrating and thereby sustaining the individual. Simply stated, the person who feels that he belongs and is accepted is more likely to develop a favorable conception of himself and to conform to societal expectations. The complement of external containment is inner containment, and a key component is a favorable self-concept. As Reckless (1967:475) phrases it, "The person who perceives of himself as reliable, honest, helpful, co-operative, or unassuming, is most likely to be that way."

In this selection Voss argues that the work of Reckless and Dinitz on the socialization and self-concepts of "good" boys and "potential" delinquents offers the basis for a test and extension of the theory of differential association. This position is based on recognition that these investigators, like Sutherland, emphasized socialization processes; to explain the non-delinquent, Reckless and Dinitz rely on the same mechanisms Sutherland employed to explain the delinquent. In the analysis of data obtained in Honolulu it was found that the joint effects of the measures of differential association and socialization account for delinquent behavior, defined according to official and unofficial criteria, more fully than does the separate effect of either measure.

One other point deserves mention. In the previous selection the authors criticize Reckless and Dinitz on methodological grounds and observe that their research lacks a theoretical link. This paper provides such a link and reveals that many reject Sutherland's theory as a naïve oversimplification of a complex problem. Part of the explanation for the difference in response to Sutherland and Reckless may lie in the fact that Sutherland presents a mechanistic image of delinquency in a "closed system," which Reckless "opens" to allow individual choice.

REFERENCES

    Walter C. Reckless, *The Crime Problem*, 4th ed. (New York: Appleton-Century-Crofts, 1967).

————, "A New Theory of Delinquency and Crime," *Federal Probation*, 25 (December 1961), pp. 42–46.

HARWIN L. VOSS

Differential Association and Containment Theory: A Theoretical Convergence

One of the crucial questions in the study of delinquent behavior is: Why do some persons who are exposed to pro-delinquent definitions of norms accept them while others do not? Sutherland's statement of the theory of differential association constitutes a classic attempt to answer this question. This theory has influenced criminology, and has become the center of a continuing controversy concerning its capacity to depict accurately the process by which individuals become delinquent.[1] Considerable attention has been devoted to the theory: among others, Cressey,[2] Glaser,[3] McKay,[4] and De Fleur and Quinney[5] have examined the theoretical implications of Sutherland's formulation, while Reiss and Rhodes,[6] Short,[7] and Voss[8] have made efforts to test the theory, or at least implications of it. Yet, a considerable body of research which deals in part with differential association is not generally recognized as bearing on Sutherland's formulation. This is the work of Reckless, Dinitz, and their co-workers concerning the socialization and self-concepts of "good" boys and "potential" delinquents.[9]

    From *Social Forces*, June 1969, pp. 381–391. Reprinted by permission.

[1] Cressey has summarized the criticism lodged against the theory of differential association. Cf. Donald R. Cressey, "Epidemiology and Individual Conduct: A Case from Criminology," *Pacific Sociological Review*, 3 (Fall 1960), pp. 47–58.

[2] Donald R. Cressey, "The Differential Association Theory and Compulsive Crimes," *Journal of Criminal Law, Criminology and Police Science*, 45 (May–June 1954), pp. 29–40.

[3] Daniel Glaser, "Criminality Theories and Behavioral Images," *American Journal of Sociology*, 61 (March 1956), pp. 433–444.

[4] Henry D. McKay, "Differential Association and Crime Prevention: Problems of Utilization," *Social Problems*, 8 (Summer 1960), pp. 25–37.

[5] Melvin L. De Fleur and Richard Quinney, "A Reformulation of Sutherland's Differential Association Theory and a Strategy for Empirical Verification," *Journal of Research in Crime and Delinquency*, 3 (January 1966), pp. 1–22.

[6] Albert J. Reiss, Jr. and A. Lewis Rhodes, "An Empirical Test of Differential Association Theory," *Journal of Research in Crime and Delinquency*, 1 (January 1964), pp. 5–18.

[7] James F. Short, Jr., "Differential Association and Delinquency," *Social Problems*, 4 (January 1957), pp. 233–239; "Differential Association with Delinquent Friends and Delinquent Behavior," *Pacific Sociological Review*, 1 (Spring 1958), pp. 20–25; and "Differential Association as a Hypothesis: Problems of Empirical Testing," *Social Problems*, 8 (Summer 1960), pp. 14–25.

[8] Harwin L. Voss, "Differential Association and Reported Delinquent Behavior: A Replication," *Social Problems*, 12 (Summer 1964), pp. 78–85.

[9] Walter C. Reckless, Simon Dinitz, and Ellen Murray, "Self-Concept as an Insulator Against Delinquency," *American Sociological Review*, 21 (December 1956), pp. 744–746; "Teacher Nominations and Evaluations of 'Good' Boys in High Delinquency Areas," *Elementary School Journal*, 57 (January 1957), pp. 221–223; "The 'Good' Boy in a High Delinquency Area," *Journal of Criminal Law, Criminology and Police Science*, 48 (June 1957), pp. 18–25; Walter C. Reckless, Simon Dinitz, and Barbara Kay, "The Self-Component in Potential Delinquency and Potential Non-Delinquency," *American Sociological Review*, 22 (Oc-

In this paper data are presented to support the argument that the work of Reckless and Dinitz offers the basis for a test of the theory of differential association. An attempt is made to combine their analysis of socialization with a previous effort to test empirically the quantitative aspects of differential association. It is hypothesized that taken together, the measures of differential association and socialization proposed, respectively, by Short and Reckless and Dinitz, account for delinquent behavior more fully than does the influence of either measure treated singly. In this analysis the dependent variable is delinquent behavior; the separate and joint effects of the measures of differential association and socialization are examined. In terms of previous research this is an effort to bridge the narrow gap between the work focused specifically on differential association and the investigation of the socialization of law-abiding and delinquent boys which also constitutes a test of Sutherland's formulation.

Qualitative and Quantitative Dimensions of Differential Association

The theory of differential association sets forth an explanation of delinquent behavior and by implication accounts for non-delinquent behavior. The principle of differential association provides that one will become delinquent if, in his interpersonal relations, there is an *excess* of definitions favorable to the violation of law. As Hartung observes, "The word 'excess,' which by itself might seem to imply that lawfulness is a mere summation by lawful experience, suggests that there are two aspects to the process of becoming criminal, namely, the qualitative and the quantitative." [10]

Short explored the latter by pursuing the implication of Sutherland's suggestion that the influence of association with others, and with

patterns of behavior, is a function of the frequency, duration, priority, and intensity of lawful and criminal associations. [11] He found that adolescents who associate extensively with delinquent friends report more delinquent behavior than those whose contacts with delinquent peers are minimal. [12] Replication of this research produced similar findings; however, the degree of association between the various indices of differential association and reported delinquent behavior was not high. [13]

Quite independently of Sutherland's framework, Reckless and Dinitz have studied both the quantitative and the qualitative aspects of differential association in their examination of the socialization and self-concepts of potential delinquents and non-delinquents. The assertion that their research may be conceived as a test of Sutherland's position is based on recognition that these investigators, like Sutherland, emphasize socialization processes. If the theory of differential association accounts for the learning of delinquent behavioral patterns and the symbolic justification for such action, Reckless and Dinitz demonstrate that the same theoretical mechanisms may be used to account for the occurrence of non-delinquency. In attempting to explain why many non-delinquent boys residing in areas of high delinquency rates remain non-delinquent they suggest that good boys escape involvement in delinquency through the insulating effect of having acquired socially appropriate self-concepts. This is, in effect, an explanation of non-delinquency, as Reckless recognizes in his discussion of "containment theory." [14] This explanation offers an interesting inversion of Sutherland's formulation.

In his effort to explain delinquent behavior Sutherland emphasized the primary group setting and focused on the processes of learning,

---

tober 1957), pp. 566–570; and "A Self-Gradient Among Potential Delinquents," *Journal of Criminal Law, Criminology and Police Science*, 49 (September–October 1958), pp. 230–233.

[10] Frank E. Hartung, *Crime, Law and Society* (Detroit: Wayne State University Press, 1965), p. 16.

[11] Edwin H. Sutherland and Donald R. Cressey, *Principles of Criminology* (7th ed.; Philadelphia: J. B. Lippincott, 1966), p. 82.

[12] Short, "Differential Association as a Hypothesis," p. 18.

[13] Voss, *op. cit.*

[14] Walter C. Reckless, *The Crime Problem* (3d ed.; New York: Appleton-Century-Crofts, 1961), pp. 335–360.

communication, and interaction; significantly, these are the same processes that are used in attempts to account for the emergence of the self-concept. The standard theory of the formation of the self-concept is that described by Cooley in terms of the "looking-glass self." In this view the self-concept is acquired socially; through the processes of communication and interaction taking place in primary group settings a person learns to think of himself in particular ways, i.e., he acquires a self-concept. Reckless and Dinitz adopt this orientation toward the self-concept. They suggest that a boy's concept of self is "acquired in his primary group relationships," [15] that is, interaction with "significant figures in his milieu such as a mother, a relative, a priest, a settlement-house worker, a teacher." [16] The impact of such persons underscores the meaning of the qualifier *differential* in Sutherland's formulation. In Reckless and Dinitz' terms, an adolescent acquires, or has acquired, a self-concept as a good boy in interaction with others who respond to him as a good boy. The others in this case are those who are active agents of socialization upholding non- or anti-delinquent norms. While Sutherland emphasized the acquisition of definitions favorable or unfavorable to violation of law, Reckless and Dinitz stress that "concept of self and other contains the impact of life on the person as he has internalized his experience, . . . it consists of the residues of attitudes and meanings accumulated . . . in interpersonal relations." [17] Like many others, Reckless and Dinitz apparently hold a highly limited view of differential association, namely, differential association refers only to association with delinquent peers. Yet, to explain the good boy they ultimately rely on the same *mechanisms* in order as those which Sutherland employed to explain the delinquent.

There appears to be a simple explanation for the failure to recognize the correspondence between the research of Reckless and Dinitz and Sutherland's theory. Sutherland stressed the crucial importance of the *process* of differential association (or pro-delinquent socialization) in the acquisition of definitions favorable or unfavorable to violation of law, while Reckless and Dinitz emphasized the acquisition of "socially appropriate" and "socially inappropriate" self-conceptions, or the *products* of socialization processes. It is evident that emphases on processes and products are not the same, and in their emphasis on self-concepts Reckless and Dinitz underplay the importance of socialization processes.[18] In devoting attention to self-concepts the investigators point to the importance of the qualitative dimension of differential association and consider a social psychological variable Sutherland ignored; this provides a basis for explication of Sutherland's position. Yet, Reckless and Dinitz were not solely concerned with self-concepts; with the exception of the *18* items they constructed to measure conception of self, Gough's *So* or *Socialization* scale served as their basic instrument.[19] In their concern with socialization Reckless and Dinitz examined, albeit in a broader perspective, the very processes Sutherland emphasized.

In pursuing Sutherland's suggestion regarding quantification Short emphasized the "negative" side of the quantitative dimension of differential association. As a measure of the impact of socialization processes, the *So* scale may be used to tap the "positive" side of this

[15] Reckless, Dinitz, and Kay, *American Sociological Review*, p. 567.

[16] Reckless, Dinitz, and Murray, "Self-Concept as an Insulator Against Delinquency," p. 746.

[17] Reckless, Dinitz, and Kay, *American Sociological Review*, p. 570.

[18] Quay notes the crucial importance of socialization processes rather than the variable of self-concept in Reckless and Dinitz' research. Herbert C. Quay, "Personality and Delinquency," in *Juvenile Delinquency*, Herbert C. Quay, ed. (Princeton, New Jersey: D. Van Nostrand Co., 1965), p. 148.

[19] Tangri and Schwartz observe that in the original studies it is not completely clear whether the conclusions with regard to self-concept are based on the scales developed by Gough or the boys' answer to questions pertaining to their expectations, attitudes, home life, or their agreement with their mothers. Sandra S. Tangri and Michael Schwartz, "Delinquency Research and the Self-Concept Variable," *Journal of Criminal Law, Criminology and Police Science*, 58 (June 1967), p. 188.

quantitative dimension.[20] The analysis in this paper is directed to the question of whether behavioral outcomes are accounted for more fully in terms of the measures of differential association and socialization than by examination of only "positive" or "negative" aspects of the quantitative dimension of differential association. After a brief introduction of the data this question and some of the implications of bringing together the theory of Sutherland and the research of Reckless and Dinitz are pursued.

The Data

The data were gathered by the administration of anonymous questionnaires to a *15.5* percent simple random sample of seventh grade students in the junior high schools of Honolulu, Hawaii. The information provided by the *284* male respondents is analyzed in this paper.

To measure the socialization of the seventh graders, the self-referent items employed by Reckless and Dinitz were included in the questionnaire.[21] Following Reckless and Dinitz, *45* of the *64* items in the *So* scale developed by Gough were used to measure the impact of socialization. Responses were scored according to Gough's instructions, and a corrected score of *36* was established as a cutting point to differentiate those who were "vulnerable" or "insulated" on the basis of this measure.[22]

The items Short developed to measure frequency, duration, priority, and intensity, the

variables specified by Sutherland, and the "general components" of differential association were included in the questionnaire. The derivation of a scale measure of differential association from these items has been described elsewhere; the scale was dichotomized and the resulting categories were treated as most and least associative.[23] All efforts to operationalize complex social processes, e.g., differential association, have limitations, including the present attempt. These will be made explicit in the discussion.

There is as yet little agreement among investigators concerning the definition of delinquent behavior that is to be used in research. Consequently, both official and unofficial criteria are utilized. The first unofficial criterion is a scale measure of self-reported delinquent behavior which was dichotomized to maximize the difference between the public school sample and the institutionalized male delinquents in Hawaii's training school; on the basis of this criterion, *43* of the seventh grade boys are defined as delinquent. Because some of the acts included in the Nye-Short delinquency check list, from which the items in the delinquency scale were derived, are of a minor, petty nature, a measure of the seriousness of self-reported behavior was developed in an effort to overcome the criticism that self-reports do not treat "real crime."[24] Chart 1 shows the acts and the frequency required for inclusion as a serious offense. According to this self-reported or unofficial criterion, a respondent is defined as delinquent if he reports with the required frequency three or more acts defined as serious; *31* boys are defined as delinquent on the basis of this criterion. The third criterion of delinquent behavior was based on official contact.[25] Of the *284* boys, *83* of them were

---

[20] Gough's *So* scale was developed as a measure of social maturity and delinquency proneness. This is an additive, not a unidimensional scale; while some of the *So* items may reflect attitudes favorable or unfavorable to violation of the law, others concern role-taking skills, attitudes toward one's family, degree of self-confidence and emotional stability, and scholastic adjustment. With regard to positive influences, it should be noted that in his later research Short attempted to investigate associational patterns hypothesized to be delinquency inhibiting and neutral with respect to delinquency. Cf. Short, "Differential Association and Problems of Empirical Testing."

[21] These items were used with the written permission of Professor Reckless.

[22] Harrison G. Gough, "Theory and Measurement of Socialization," *Journal of Consulting Psychology*, 24 (February 1960), pp. 23–30.

[23] Voss, *op. cit.*

[24] Harwin L. Voss, "Socio-Economic Status and Reported Delinquent Behavior," *Social Problems*, 13 (Winter 1966), pp. 314–324.

[25] The names of the respondents were checked against the records of the Honolulu Police Department in January 1961, approximately a year and a half after the questionnaires were administered. The method and purpose of identifying the anonymous respondents has been discussed elsewhere. Harwin L. Voss, "Ethnic Differentials in Delin-

Chart 1

Delinquent Acts and Frequency of Reporting Required for Definition as Serious

Delinquent act	Minimum frequency required
Skipped school without an excuse	very often
Had a fist fight with another person	very often
"Run away" from home	twice
Placed on school probation or expelled from school	once
Taken little things (worth less than $2) that did not belong to you	once
Taken things of medium value (between $2 and $50)	once
Taken things of large value (over $50)	once
Taken part in "gang fights"	three times
Bought or drank beer, wine, or liquor without your parents' consent	very often
Purposely damaged or destroyed public or private property	several times
Had sex relations with a person of the opposite sex	once

Chart 2

Serious and Petty Acts Resulting in Official Police Contact

Nature of the act

Serious	Petty and non-delinquent
Burglary	Traffic
Larceny and theft	Jaywalking
Auto theft (malicious conversion)	Bicycle[a]
Disorderly conduct	Street trade (permit obtained)
Vagrancy (unlawful premises)	
Incorrigible or runaway	Victim
Truancy	Neglect
Assault	Dependency
Weapons (concealed)	Not stated
Sex offense	
Fraud	
Gambling	

a "Packing" or riding double; no tag; no lights; no brakes; riding bike on sidewalk; stop sign; wrong side of street.

known to the police for a variety of reasons, including application for a permit to engage in a street trade, i.e., to shine shoes or to "hawk" newspapers. Again, offenses were divided into serious and petty categories as shown in Chart 2. Boys known to the police for two or more serious offenses are defined as delinquent. According to this official criterion, *17* boys are defined as delinquent.

The Findings

The first step in the analysis is to examine separately the positive and negative aspects of differential association, as operationalized by Reckless and Dinitz and by Short. The data presented in Table 1 demonstrate the associa-

quency in Honolulu," *Journal of Criminal Law, Criminology and Police Science*, 54 (September 1963), pp. 322–327.

tion between differential association, as operationalized in this investigation, and the three criteria of delinquent behavior. In each instance, a larger proportion of the delinquent boys are found in the most associative than in the least associative category; the reverse obtains among the non-delinquents. The percentage differences range from *10* to *28* percent, and are all in the expected direction. The statistical tests of significance indicate a minimal likelihood that the observed relationships are due to chance. The association between differential association and delinquent behavior, as measured by the *phi* coefficient, is stronger for the unofficial measures of delinquent behavior than it is for official delinquent behavior; the degree or strength of association is highest where the contrived measure of seriousness of self-reported delinquent behavior is employed as the criterion of delinquent behavior. In general, however, it is evident that the boys who associate extensively with delinquent friends are more highly involved in delinquent activities, whether of the self-reported or officially recorded varieties, than those whose association with delinquent friends is minimal. This conclusion holds not only for both self-reported measures of delinquent behavior but also for delinquent behavior officially recorded by the police.

In Table 2 the association between socialization, as measured by Gough's *So* scale, and the three criteria of delinquent behavior is shown. There is a significant association between the measure of socialization and each measure of the dependent variable, delinquent behavior. Again, the percentage differences are all in the expected direction, and in size range from 6 to 17 percent. As observed with differential association, the strength of association is highest where the measure of seriousness of self-reported delinquent behavior is utilized.

Tables 1 and 2 show the relations between each of the independent variables and delinquent behavior. The analysis to this point is comparable to the treatment accorded these measures in the past, i.e., each is considered separately. Comparison of Tables 1 and 2 reveals, first of all, that both differential association and socialization are significantly related to the various measures of delinquent behavior. Looking at the comparable subtables, one finds that a higher proportion of the most associative than of the vulnerable boys are delinquent, i.e., the percentage differences are greater in Table 1. The values of *phi* are also larger than in Table 2. This suggests that differential association is more highly related to delinquent behavior than is the more broadly conceived measure of socialization. However, in each of the pairs of subtables a higher proportion of the delinquent boys are vulnerable than are most associative. This important difference in outcome occurs because 65 boys are classified as most associative, but 127 are categorized as vulnerable. The restricted number of boys who associate extensively with delinquent peers leads to higher percentage differences and higher *phi* values, but in obtaining these advantages, more of the delinquent boys are missed.

At this point the analysis is directed to the question of whether behavioral outcomes are accounted for more fully in terms of the joint effects than by either the positive or negative dimensions of differential association considered thus far. Because differential association and socialization are viewed as coextensive, no assumption concerning order in time has been made. Consequently, selection of either of the bivariate relationships previously presented as the "original relation" would be arbitrary and the use of multivariate analysis to specify the conditions for or the contingencies of the relationship would be inappropriate. Therefore, in Table 3 the boys are separated into four relatively homogeneous subgroups in terms of socialization and differential association. The separate and joint effects of the two independent variables can be determined by comparing the proportions of delinquent boys in each of these categories. In the first category of Table 3*A*, in which both differential association and socialization are in the direction predictive of delinquent behavior, 44.2 percent of the boys are delinquent. The figure in this cell is approximately 30 percentage points higher than in the second and third categories in which only one of the measures is in the direction predictive of delinquency.

The results are even more striking in subtable 3*B*. In this case the measure of delinquent behavior is more satisfactory, or at least overcomes some of the difficulties inherent in the use of self-reports; and, 46.5 percent of the boys who are vulnerable and associate extensively with delinquent peers are delinquent. In contrast, only 3 percent of the boys who are in the fourth or optimum category are delinquent. Few of the boys are delinquent who only associate with delinquent peers or are only classified as vulnerable on the basis of their score on the measure of socialization.

The results in Table 3*C* are in the same direction as those in 3*A* and 3*B*, but only 18.6 percent of the boys in the first category are delinquent. The measures employed do not adequately differentiate those who are and are not known to the police. The response of law enforcement officials to delinquent behavior is a variable not included in this analysis. It is evident that variables which help to explain involvement in delinquent behavior do not account for the response of officials to that behavior.

Only in the first subtable is the proportion of delinquents higher in the fourth category, in which neither variable is in the direction

Table 1

Differential Association and Criteria of Delinquency

	Differential association			
	Most associative		Least associative	
	Number	Percentage	Number	Percentage
A. Self-reported delinquent behavior				
Delinquent	22	33.8	21	9.6
Non-delinquent	43	66.2	198	90.4
	$\chi^2 = 21.31$ $P < .001$		$\phi = .29$ $Q = .66$	
B. Serious self-reported delinquent behavior				
Delinquent	21	32.3	10	4.6
Non-delinquent	44	67.7	209	95.4
	$\chi^2 = 36.83$ $P < .001$		$\phi = .37$ $Q = .82$	
C. Official delinquent behavior				
Delinquent	9	13.8	8	3.7
Non-delinquent	56	86.2	211	96.3
	$\chi^2 = 7.50$ $P < .01$		$\phi = .18$ $Q = .62$	

predictive of delinquency, than in the second or third categories in which one of the variables is in the direction predictive of delinquency. While the differences are minimal, this indicates the occurrence of a distinct possibility with self-reports — a boy may indicate he has experienced conventional socialization and does not associate with delinquent peers, yet can report a sufficient number of delinquent acts on an anonymous questionnaire to be classified as a delinquent. Further research is necessary to determine whether this type of boy is reporting trivial acts or behavior officials would deem sufficient to warrant official action.

Support has been found for the hypothesis

Table 2

Socialization and Criteria of Delinquency

	Socialization			
	Vulnerable		Insulated	
	Number	Percentage	Number	Percentage
A. Self-reported delinquent behavior				
Delinquent	26	20.5	17	10.8
Non-delinquent	101	79.5	140	89.2
	$\chi^2 = 4.41$ $P < .05$		$\phi = .13$ $Q = .36$	
B. Serious self-reported delinquent behavior				
Delinquent	26	20.5	5	3.2
Non-delinquent	101	79.5	152	96.8
	$\chi^2 = 19.70$ $P < .001$		$\phi = .28$ $Q = .77$	
C. Official delinquent behavior				
Delinquent	12	9.4	5	3.2
Non-delinquent	115	90.6	152	96.8
	$\chi^2 = 3.85$ $P < .05$		$\phi = .13$ $Q = .52$	

Table 3

Differential Association, Socialization, and Criteria of Delinquency

Differential association: socialization	Most associative vulnerable		Most associative insulated		Least associative vulnerable		Least associative insulated	
	Number	Percentage	Number	Percentage	Number	Percentage	Number	Percentage
A. Self-reported delinquent behavior								
Delinquent	19	44.2	3	13.6	7	8.3	14	10.4
Non-delinquent	24	55.8	19	86.4	77	91.7	121	89.6
B. Serious self-reported delinquent behavior								
Delinquent	20	46.5	1	4.5	6	7.1	4	3.0
Non-delinquent	23	53.5	21	95.5	78	92.9	131	97.0
C. Official delinquent behavior								
Delinquent	8	18.6	1	4.5	4	4.8	4	3.0
Non-delinquent	35	81.4	21	95.5	80	95.2	131	97.0

that the joint effects of differential association and socialization, as operationalized by previous investigators, account for delinquent behavior more fully than does the separate effect of either variable. In each of the three subtables the joint effect of the measures is considerably greater than the separate effect of either. Comparison of the separate effects, as shown in the second and third categories, reveals that there is little to choose — differential association appears to be slightly stronger in the first subtable, weaker in the second subtable, and no different in the third. One point deserves comment. Only *22* of the *157* insulated boys, or *14* percent, associate extensively with delinquent peers. In contrast, *43* of the *127* vulnerable boys, or *34* percent, have such contacts. The insulated boys, in general, appear relatively more isolated from pro-delinquent norms, at least as these are available through association with delinquents.

Only one question remains: To what extent is it necessary to utilize both measures to account for delinquent behavior? This question requires comparison of the results presented in Table 3 with those in Tables 1 and 2. Such a comparison indicates that the proportion of delinquents obtained with both measures is somewhat higher than that observed when differential association and socialization are examined independently. Stated differently, *33.8* percent of the most associative boys are delinquent (Table *1A*); *20.5* percent of the vulnerable boys are delinquent (Table *2A*); but of the boys who are vulnerable and associate extensively with delinquent peers *44.2* percent (Table *3A*) are delinquent according to the measure based on self-reports. The measures of differential association and socialization are not identical, but they do overlap considerably. This indicates that the research of Reckless and Dinitz on socialization may properly be conceived as a test of Sutherland's formulation. In summary, this analysis demonstrates that behavioral outcomes are accounted for more fully by the use of measures of differential association and socialization than by the use of either measure independently.

Discussion

What does the research of Reckless and Dinitz suggest regarding Sutherland's theory? Is drastic and dramatic revision necessary? In this paper it is argued that the research of Reckless and Dinitz in part offers a test of the theory of differential association, but also suggests a possible explication of Sutherland's position. After a comment on the operational definition of differential association, the implications of bringing together the theory of differential association and the research of Reckless and Dinitz are pursued.

The operational definition of differential association proposed by Short and utilized in this research provides a measure of differential interaction, and is not necessarily a true index of differential association. While differential interaction with persons who favor violation of the law implies selective or differential exposure to pro-delinquent definitions of norms, only differential interaction *with* delinquent peers is measured in this research. To the extent that favorable definitions result from extensive association with delinquents this approach is adequate. Yet, as Cressey observes, "one can learn criminal behavior patterns from persons who are not criminals, and one can learn anti-criminal behavior patterns from hoods, professional crooks, habitual offenders, and gangsters." [26] Operationalization of differential association in terms of association with *friends* is a limitation of this study, but the fact that negative influences, i.e., differential association with friends *defined as delinquent,* are considered, is overcome by inclusion of Gough's *So* scale. This scale provides a broad measure of positive influences, or exposure to favorable definitions of cultural norms. Efforts to operationalize complex theoretical positions demand the taking of considerable liberties; it is recognized that these measures do not fully represent Sutherland's position.

Use of the terms insulation and vulnerability in the analysis may be misleading. As used in this paper, conventional socialization or insulation against delinquency is conceived as an on-going sociocultural process in which a juvenile accepts conventional norms and conforms to the expectations of significant others who uphold conventional norms and engage in non-delinquent behavior.[27] Vulnerability to delinquency may be conceived as the same kind of process; the process resulting in vulnerability is distinguished by the acceptance of delinquent norms and conformity to the expectations of those who uphold delinquent norms.

The interpretation of the research of Reckless and Dinitz concerning socialization as providing a rough indication of the positive aspects of differential association, or the "definitions unfavorable to violation of law," does not require revision of Sutherland's formulation. Recognition of the essential similarity in the positions adopted by Sutherland and by Reckless and Dinitz should, however, serve to clarify the fact that Sutherland was emphasizing *one* of the outcomes of the process of socialization, namely, a favorable or unfavorable view of the law. As De Fleur and Quinney observe, differential association "is a special case of the socialization process which occurs in the context of primary groups through symbolic interaction." [28]

Reckless and Dinitz did not confine their attention to the process of socialization; they also emphasized the importance of particular kinds of self-concepts. The position accepted in this paper is that differential association, or the process in which one acquires definitions favorable or unfavorable to violation of the law, is coextensive with the process in which one's self-conception is developed. This does not imply that differential association and self-conception are identical. This interpretation may be clarified by a brief comment on the definition of self-conception. Although a variety of definitions have been suggested, general agreement might be reached on the definition suggested by Kinch: "The self-concept is that organization of qualities that the individual attributes to himself." [29] This definition implies that the self-concept is multifaceted, one quality or dimension of which pertains to the individual's view of himself as a conventional, law-abiding person or as a delinquent. Also included within the self-concept are views of one's physical attributes, as

---

[26] Cressey, "Epidemiology and Individual Conduct," p. 49.

[27] Cf. Reckless, Dinitz, and Murray, "Self-Concept as an Insulator Against Delinquency," p. 746.

[28] De Fleur and Quinney, *op. cit.,* p. 21.

[29] John W. Kinch, "A Formalized Theory of the Self-Concept," *American Journal of Sociology,* 68 (January 1963), p. 481.

the terms handsome, ugly, unattractive, obese, and skinny denote. One also has a view of himself as bright, average, or dull intellectually. These examples of facets of the person's self-concept could easily be multiplied, but these are sufficient to indicate that the concept of self refers to a set of beliefs a person holds about himself. In addition to these cognitive elements, the individual also has attitudes toward himself, i.e., he may be satisfied or dissatisfied with the self-image constructed on the basis of these beliefs.

Although Sutherland was justified in his reluctance to incorporate in his theory the notion that certain unspecified personality traits are relevant in explaining delinquent behavior,[30] the research of Reckless and Dinitz suggests the relevance of the social psychological variable, self-conception. If it is possible to integrate this variable in Sutherland's theory, this would provide an important explication of his position.

The development of a person's self-concept begins in his early socialization; once a person can differentiate himself as an object, the "self" becomes an element in the definition of any situation faced thereafter. It may be recalled that the theory of differential association is stated "on the assumption that a criminal act occurs when a situation appropriate for it, as defined by the person, is present." [31] Sutherland presumably had in mind the "differential response" of different persons to an "identical" situation, e.g., that of the average citizen and the patrolman on his beat when passing a box of apples in front of a store. Another example may be more appropriate. To some, a drunk in a dark alley is an object of pity; to others, he is merely a disgusting sight, but to still others, he is a prime target for jack-rolling. In this sense, the acceptability of a delinquent act to the person may be viewed as dependent upon its compatibility with the person's self-conception.[32] Particular kinds of self-concepts

may serve the function of forestalling offenses, because the actor does not define himself as the kind of person who can roll a drunk, rob a service station, or take a pickup to a hotel room, but does define himself as one who can cheat on his income tax or accept an undercharge in a store.

This perspective seemingly overcomes one limitation of Sutherland's theory. As it is stated, the theory implies that, given an appropriate setting, violation results "automatically" among those with a negative set concerning the law as a body of rules. Because the system of law supports the existing social structure, this position implies that delinquents are necessarily alienated from the social system. Such a view does not appear to be entirely reasonable. While a few members of the society may have a generally negative view of all laws, few persons violate *all* laws. While some delinquents are versatile, there are indications that many of them, like many "law-abiding citizens," selectively violate the law.[33] A juvenile may learn to violate a variety of traffic regulations from his otherwise saintly father; on this basis alone one would not anticipate the juvenile's involvement in an armed robbery. In short, the learning which occurs in primary groups may be more specific than is suggested by Sutherland's formulation; [34] a person may learn favorable attitudes toward

---

conceives of himself in relation to others. Those boys identified as insulated who engage in delinquent activities may be expected to rationalize, using one or more of the "techniques of neutralization," in order to reconcile the discrepancy between their self-concepts and their behavior. Gresham M. Sykes and David Matza, "Techniques of Neutralization: A Theory of Delinquency," *American Sociological Review*, 22 (December 1957), pp. 664–670.

[33] Marshall B. Clinard, *Sociology of Deviant Behavior* (rev. ed.; New York: Holt, Rinehart & Winston, 1963), pp. 172–174.

[34] This reference is to Sutherland's formulation; the manner in which he states his position suggests that one has either a favorable or unfavorable view of law violation and his reference to definitions is easily overlooked. In their analysis of differential association in terms of set theory De Fleur and Quinney maintain that the revised version of Sutherland's theory is highly specific. De Fleur and Quinney, *op. cit.*

---

[30] Albert Cohen, Alfred Lindesmith, and Karl Schuessler (eds.), *The Sutherland Papers* (Bloomington: Indiana University Press, 1956), pp. 25–26.

[31] Sutherland and Cressey, *op. cit.*, p. 80.

[32] Sykes and Matza suggest that delinquency results, in part, from the way in which a person

particular kinds of offenses, rather than a generalized negative set toward the law. This is by no means a simple issue. A father who confines his violations of the law to speeding and other traffic offenses, the padding of his expense account, cheating on his income tax, and bribery of the tax assessor is often appalled that his son generalized from such carefully rationalized behavior to violation of the law of which the father does not approve. The question of whether learning is specific or is commonly generalized to related activities is a very old one; social psychologists have debated the issue whether attitudes are general or specific for some time. There is little point in entering the lists with regard to attitudes toward the law.

As utilized herein, self-conception is not excluded from Sutherland's formulation and may be considered as an important explication of the assumption on which the theory is phrased. Integration of self-conception in this manner does not require revision of Sutherland's viable theory.

Summary

It is argued that the work of Reckless and Dinitz offers the basis for a test and explication of the theory of differential association.

This position is based on recognition that these investigators, like Sutherland, emphasized socialization processes; to explain the non-delinquent, Reckless and Dinitz rely on the same mechanisms Sutherland employed to explain the delinquent.

In the analysis it was found that the joint effects of differential association and socialization, as operationalized by Short and Reckless and Dinitz, account for delinquent behavior more fully than does the separate effect of either variable. While the measures overlap considerably, the use of both accounts for delinquent behavior, defined according to official and unofficial criteria, more fully than does either measure treated singly.

The use of Gough's *So* scale helps to overcome some of the limitations in previous efforts to operationalize differential association. Acceptance of the view that differential association, or the process in which one acquires definitions favorable or unfavorable to violation of the law, is coextensive with the process in which one's self-conception is developed, does not require revision of Sutherland's viable theory. Rather, the social psychological variable of self-conception may be used to explicate the assumption on which Sutherland's theory is phrased.

The Labeling Perspective

The authors of this selection suggest that labeling is particularly relevant to the study of delinquency, and they implicitly treat delinquency as a type of deviant behavior. To understand their position, a review of some of the ideas of Lemert is necessary. Although written as a textbook, Lemert's *Social Pathology* (1951) presented a theory of deviant behavior which led to the contemporary emphasis on the importance of the labeling process. According to Lemert (1951:75), a person may violate norms, but these remain primary deviations "as long as they are rationalized or otherwise dealt with as functions of a socially acceptable role." Thus, a deviant act may not affect a person's conception of self or lead to adoption of a deviant role; juveniles may commit delinquent acts without becoming committed to a delinquent career or being regarded by themselves or others as delinquents. Lemert (1951:76) points out, however, that if the deviant acts are repeated and these acts are visible to family, friends, or authorities, and if there is a severe societal reaction, a person may assume a deviant role: "*When a person begins to employ his deviant behavior or a role based upon it as a means of defense, attack, or adjustment to the overt and covert problems created by the consequent societal reaction to him, his deviation is secondary.*" The disapproval and isolation experienced by the person may be more important in explaining his subsequent behavior than the original "causes" of his deviant acts (Lemert [1967:17]).

In Lemert's view one deviant act rarely results in a sufficiently strong societal reaction to lead to secondary deviation, and he expresses doubt whether exposure, temporarily, to a severe punitive reaction would be sufficient for such a transition, unless the experience were highly traumatic. Lemert (1951:76–77) suggests that "most frequently there is a progressive reciprocal relationship between the deviation of the individual and the societal reaction, with a compounding of the societal reaction out of the minute accretions in the deviant behavior, until a point is reached where ingrouping and outgrouping between society and the deviant is manifest. At this point a stigmatizing of the deviant occurs in the form of name calling, labeling, or stereotyping. The sequence of interaction leading to secondary deviation is roughly as follows: (1) primary deviation; (2) social penalties; (3) further primary deviation; (4) stronger penalties and rejections; (5) further deviation, perhaps with hostilities and resentment beginning to focus upon those doing the penalizing; (6) crisis reached in the tolerance quotient, expressed in formal action by the community stigmatizing of the deviant [Van Vechten (1940:39) defined the tolerance quotient as "a ratio between the behavior in objective terms and the community's willingness to tolerate it, with the critical point for each case where the community in its corporate capacity goes into action."]; (7) strengthening of the deviant conduct as a reaction to the stigmatizing and penalties; (8) ultimate acceptance of deviant social status and efforts at adjustment on the basis of the associated role." From Lemert's position a number of writers, including Becker, Kitsuse, Erickson, and the authors of this selection, have correctly inferred that the societal reaction to deviant acts and labeling of the actor as a deviant may have important consequences for subsequent deviation.

REFERENCES

Edwin M. Lemert, *Human Deviance, Social Problems, and Social Control* (Englewood Cliffs, N.J.: Prentice-Hall, Inc., 1967).
——, *Social Pathology* (New York: McGraw-Hill Book Co., Inc., 1951).
Courtlandt C. Van Vechten, "The Tolerance Quotient as a Device for Defining Certain Social Concepts," *American Journal of Sociology*, 46 (July 1940), pp. 35–39.

STANTON WHEELER
LEONARD S. COTTRELL, JR.

The Labeling Process

Delinquency-prevention activities include all efforts expended before the juvenile's behavior has brought him to the attention of such official agencies as the police and the courts, while adjudicative and correctional activities are those that ensue after the youth's contact with these agencies. Important problems emerge at the meeting of the preventive and adjudicative agencies.

A traditional view of the relationship between delinquents and official agencies is that the latter are primarily passive responders to the active behavior or misbehavior of juveniles. The police exist, among other reasons, to detect delinquency, and the courts to adjudicate the cases of those who are detected. Both are reactions to deviant behavior.

From Stanton Wheeler and Leonard S. Cottrell, Jr., *Juvenile Delinquency: Its Prevention and Control* (New York: Russell Sage Foundation, 1966), pp. 22–27. Reprinted by permission.

A variety of social science theory and evidence leads to the conclusion that such agencies may play a far more important role than is ordinarily ascribed to them. The evidence suggests that official response to the behavior in question may initiate processes that push the misbehaving juveniles toward further delinquent conduct, and, at least, make it more difficult for them to re-enter the conventional world. This hypothesis is based upon the concept of labeling and a theory of its consequences.[1]

[1] Recent relevant works include: Eliot Freidson, "Disability as Social Deviance," in Marvin B. Sussman, editor, *Sociology and Rehabilitation*, American Sociological Association and Vocational Rehabilitation Administration, 1965; Howard S. Becker, *Outsiders: Studies in the Sociology of Deviance*, Free Press of Glencoe, New York, 1963; Edwin M. Lemert, *Social Pathology*, McGraw-Hill, Inc., 1951; and John I. Kitsuse, "Societal Reaction to Deviant Behavior: Problems of

The assumption is that the public responds to a person informally and in an unorganized way unless that person has been defined as falling into a clear category. The official labeling of a misbehaving youth as delinquent has the effect of placing him in such a category. This official stamp may help to organize responses different from those that would have arisen without the official action. The result is that the label has an important effect upon how the individual is regarded by others. If official processing results in an individual's being segregated with others so labeled, an additional push toward deviant behavior may result. Their association with others who are similarly defined may make the category "delinquent" or "criminal" much more salient for them as well as for others' views of them. In other words, the individual begins to think of himself as delinquent, and he organizes his behavior accordingly.

This argument is particularly relevant to the field of delinquency, even though it has been extended to a variety of other forms of deviant behavior. Its special relevance for delinquency is twofold. First, since delinquency is so broadly defined, discretion is necessary in deciding which cases should be officially handled and which dismissed. Most youths may be involved in minor forms of misbehavior during their teens. This means that the official decision to categorize certain youths as delinquent may provide the important cue for public reactions. The second aspect is the nature of the delinquent act itself. There is a very important distinction between engaging in a delinquent *act* and following a delinquent *career* organized around the repetitive commission of such acts. Given the relatively minor, episodic, and perhaps situationally induced character of much delinquency, many who have engaged in minor forms of delinquency once or twice may grow out of this pattern of behavior as they move toward adulthood. For these, the labeling theorists argue, a concerted policy of doing nothing may be more helpful than active intervention, if the long-range goal is to reduce the probability of repetition of the acts. If the labeling hypothesis is correct, official intervention may further define the youth as delinquent in the eyes of neighbors, family members, and peers, thus making it more difficult for him to resume conventional activities.

The counterargument to this view takes two forms. First, if the offender is ignored, he may continue to offend for the same reason he began. The assumption here is that delinquency brings the youth some return and that it will continue to do so unless he is apprehended. It is precisely this argument that provides support for those persons interested in early identification and treatment of problem children.[2] If we assume that their deviant behavior is not a relatively superficial form of expression of adolescence, but symptomatic of something deep within them, some form of official reaction is essential. It is beneficial for the welfare of the delinquent, as well as for the community, that the deviant behavior be dealt with immediately, before it grows worse.

The second strand of the counterargument is that the process of official police handling in court adjudication may have a deterrent effect on the youths so processed. The youths do not want to be treated like delinquents and hence will refrain from further delinquent acts. This argument justifies intervention on much different grounds from the former one,

---

Theory and Method," in Howard S. Becker, editor, *The Other Side: Perspectives on Deviance*, Free Press of Glencoe, New York, 1964, pp. 87–102. But the idea is not new in its application to delinquency. Frank Tannenbaum treated it under the concept of "the dramatization of evil" in *Crime and the Community*, Columbia University Press, New York, 1938.

[2] The early identification theme appears most clearly in conjunction with the prediction efforts associated with the work of the Gluecks and the tests carried out by the New York City Youth Board. See Eleanor T. Glueck, "Efforts to Identify Delinquents," *Federal Probation*, vol. 24, June, 1960, pp. 49–56. The identification efforts have been subject to detailed criticisms. See, for example, Alfred J. Kahn, "Public Policy and Delinquency Prediction: The Case of the Premature Claims," *Crime and Delinquency*, vol. 11, July, 1965, pp. 217–228; Jackson Toby, "An Evaluation of Early Identification and Intensive Treatment Programs for Predelinquents," *Social Problems*, vol. 13, no. 2, 1965, pp. 160–175.

and entails very different assumptions about the nature of delinquent motivations. Indeed, it is the standard argument for the deterrent impact of punishment. As such, it more often appears in arguments about adult crime and penal sanctions. But, although it is a distinctly secondary theme as applied to delinquency, it is still frequently voiced and forms a part of the public concern for dealing too leniently with delinquents.

These competing rationales for official actions are difficult to test empirically. Indeed, as yet there is very little systematic knowledge regarding reactions of offenders to varying types of sanctions. Conceivably, some delinquents refrain from committing further delinquent acts without official sanctions or labeling processes, while others may refrain only after such inhibition. But what are the conditions under which these various alternatives will occur? No other single question in the field of delinquency prevention and control seems so important and so deserving of careful investigation.

Social policy formation, however, may not be able to wait for the results of such research, and it is necessary to formulate a position on these issues without the carefully gathered and assessed data that would support a more clearcut choice for one or another alternative. The choice seems clear: in the absence of evidence on the beneficial effects of official contacts, every effort should be made to avoid the use of a formal sanctioning system and particularly the official pronouncement of delinquency. Such a position is justified on grounds of the potentially damaging effects of the labeling process. The primary reason for use of the official sanctions should be the seriousness of the conduct and its potential damage to the community.

A concomitant effort must be devoted to developing new forms of controlling youthful misbehavior without relying on the traditional agencies that usually process deviants. If the school system, for example, can develop programs for truants and potential dropouts, it might be possible to avoid the potentially negative effects of processing offenders by the police and courts. Further, if cases normally coming before the courts can be handled by police referral to family and neighborhood institutions and child welfare agencies, a similar benefit may result. Currently, about one-fourth of all cases handled by the juvenile courts are youth offenses that have no parallel in adult crime: curfew violation, running away from home, ungovernability, and related types of activity. Many of these activities, and perhaps many of the more minor forms of delinquency, could be handled without official court contact.

The aim in all such cases would be to avoid a possibly premature labeling of a young person as delinquent or deviant, except in cases where the action is so repetitive or so clearly dangerous to the community that really major efforts are required. Adherence to such a policy would considerably reduce the number of cases that now come before the juvenile courts. It would clearly be necessary, for at least many of such cases, to provide supportive services at the family and neighborhood level. The goal of all such services would be to keep the juvenile functioning in the family and community as long as possible without recourse to the official sanctioning systems.[3]

The same logic should apply at each point in the process of delinquency control. If it is necessary to take official actions, efforts should first be made to leave the offenders in the community. The burden of proof, any time official intervention occurs, must be on the side of those who feel that the intervention is clearly necessary for the safety of the community and the welfare of the juvenile.

This position is fortified by two features of delinquency control as currently practiced. First, it is not at all clear that doing something

[3] A different and in some ways more radical suggestion has been offered in the British White Paper on "The Child, The Family, and the Young Offender," published by Great Britain Home Office, London, Her Majesty's Stationery Office, 1965. It recommends that all persons under sixteen years of age be removed from the jurisdiction of the court and placed under local welfare authorities. Family councils, operating on a county level and composed of social workers and others with experience in handling children, would work with parents in devising courses of treatment for the juveniles coming before them.

is better than doing nothing, or that doing one thing is better than doing another. This is a hard fact that simply must be faced. Indeed, we are finally beginning to understand that any intervention has the possibility of harm as well as help, and it is conceivable that the actions of even the well-meaning helpers do as much harm as good. At least in the absence of strong evidence that they are effective, there is reason to guard against intervening in the life of the child or family. In the past such interventions have often been justified less on grounds of the severity of misconduct of a child than on grounds of the seeming problems and pathologies within his family. While it is important not to underestimate the problems of parental and family pathology, it seems similarly important not to overestimate the power of current therapeutic techniques.

Second, the current trends toward professionalization in the field of delinquency prevention and control services may lead toward a broader category of persons being defined as "in need of service" than in the past. For there is at least a modicum of evidence that the more sophisticated personnel become, the greater is their tendency to see symptoms of problem behavior, and therefore the greater the tendency to engage in some form of intervention. It is the very feeling of confidence in the sophisticated techniques of modern intervention methods that may serve as justification for placing children in special therapeutic settings, in residential treatment centers, and in institutions thought to be beneficial for them. Thus a study of police relations with juveniles suggests that the more professionalized police system formally charges a larger percentage of the juvenile population with delinquency. A study of judges suggests that those with more therapeutically oriented attitudes were somewhat more willing to commit children to institutions, and an authority on youth correctional systems who has surveyed them around the country is left with the strong feeling that it is the states with the most professional services that implicate the largest number of children in the official agencies and institutions.[4]

In the absence of greater evidence as to their effectiveness, the wisest policy is to refrain from implicating children in the delinquency control apparatus insofar as possible, and to invoke that apparatus only when it is clear that the conduct of the juvenile in question requires it for the protection of the community. There seems to be support for this position from many of those involved in judicial and correctional work. This is not to argue that professionalism is harmful. Rather, it is to argue simply that intervention techniques, if justified on grounds of therapeutic effectiveness, should be demonstrated to be successful before they are widely employed.

[4] James Q. Wilson, "The Police and the Delinquent in Two Cities," in Stanton Wheeler, editor, *Controlling Delinquents*, published by John Wiley & Sons, Inc., New York, 1968; Stanton Wheeler, "Legal Justice and Mental Health in the Care and Treatment of Deviants," paper presented at meetings of the American Orthopsychiatric Association, San Francisco, April, 1966.

Treating delinquency and crime as subclasses of deviant behavior, Gibbs contrasts the older conceptions of "deviant behavior" with the conception proposed by the interactionists. The latter, who emphasize societal reaction to deviance and are sometimes referred to as the "labeling school," take as their point of departure the work of Lemert (1951). (See the introduction to the previous selection).

Gibbs raises a number of questions which the proponents of the "new conception" of deviant behavior have not, as yet, adequately answered.

According to Gibbs, the ultimate goal of Becker, Kitsuse, and Erickson, the leading proponents of the new perspective in deviance, is not clear. He questions whether the perspective is intended to be a theory of deviant behavior or a conceptual analysis of it. If it is proposed as an explanation of deviant behavior, then, as Gibbs observes, the interactionists do not offer an explanation for variation in the incidence of deviant acts nor do they explain why some persons commit a given act while others do not. Gibbs' third major question, why a given act is considered deviant or criminal in some societies, but not in others, remains unanswered in alternative perspectives and theories, although Becker (1963:147–163) has commented on the role of "moral entrepreneurs" in the enactment of rules.

Among the interactionists "deviant behavior" is defined according to reactions to it, although the question of what kind of reaction identifies behavior as deviant remains unanswered. Gibbs clearly prefers to define a "deviant act" as "behavior which is contrary to a norm or rule." Gibbs does not suggest that his definition of "deviance" is "right" and that of the interactionists is "wrong." Nor does he suggest that answers to the questions he posed about the interactionist perspective cannot be derived from this "new conception." His purpose, and the reason his paper is included in this volume, is to indicate the questions which must be answered if the new conception is to develop and thus to serve as a useful perspective in the study of deviance in general and delinquency in particular.

REFERENCES

Howard S. Becker, *Outsiders* (New York: The Free Press of Glencoe, 1963).

Edwin M. Lemert, *Social Pathology* (New York: McGraw-Hill Book Co., Inc., 1951).

JACK P. GIBBS

Conceptions of Deviant Behavior: The Old and the New

The ultimate end of substantive theory in any science is the formulation of empirical relations among classes of phenomena, e.g., X varies directly with Y, X is present if and only if Y is present. However, unless such propositions are arrived at by crude induction or sheer intuition, there is a crucial step before the formulation of a relational statement. This step can be described as the way the investigator comes to perceive or "think about" the phenomena under consideration. Another way

From *Pacific Sociological Review*, 9 (Spring 1966), 9–14. Reprinted by permission of author and publisher.

to put it is the development of a "conception."

There is no clear-cut distinction between, on the one hand, a conception of a class of phenomena and, on the other, formal definitions and substantive theory. Since a conception emphasizes the predominant feature of a phenomenon, it is not entirely divorced from a definition of it; but the former is not identical with the latter. Thus, for example, the notion of exploitation looms large in the Marxian conception of relations among social classes; but exploitation is or may be only one feature of class relations, and it does not serve as a formal definition of them. Further, in certain fields, particularly the social sciences, a conception often not only precedes but also gives rise to operational definitions. As the case in point, if an operational definition of social class relies on the use of "reputational technique," the investigator's conception of social class is in all probability non-Marxian.

What has been said of the distinction between definitions and conceptions holds also for the relation between the latter and substantive theory. A conception may generate a particular theory, but it is not identical with it. For one thing, a conception contains definitional elements and is therefore partially tautological, which means that in itself a conception is never a clear-cut empirical proposition. Apart from its tautological character, a conception is too general to constitute a testable idea. Nonetheless, a conception may generate substantive theory, and it is certainly true that theories reflect conceptions. Durkheim's work is a classic illustration. His theory on suicide clearly reflects his view of society and social life generally.

In a field without consensus as to operational definitions and little in the way of systematic substantive theory, conceptions necessarily occupy a central position. This condition prevails in most of the social sciences. There, what purport to be definitions of classes of phenomena are typically general and inconsistent to the point of lacking empirical applicability (certainly in the operational sense of the word). Moreover, what passes for a substantive theory in the social sciences is more often than not actually a loosely formulated conception. These observations are not intended to deride the social sciences for lack of progress. All fields probably go through a "conceptions" stage; it is only more apparent in some than in others.

Of the social sciences, there is perhaps no better clear-cut illustration of the importance of conceptions than in the field identified as criminology and the study of deviant behavior. As we shall see, the history of the field can be described best in terms of changing conceptions of crime, criminals, deviants, and deviation. But the purpose of this paper is not an historical account of major trends in the field. If it is true that conceptions give rise to formal definitions and substantive theory, then a critical appraisal of conceptions is important in its own right. This is all the more true in the case of criminology and the study of deviant behavior, where conceptions are frequently confused with substantive theories, and the latter so clearly reflect the former.

Older Conceptions

In recent years there has been a significant change in the prevailing conception of deviant behavior and deviants. Prior to what is designated here as the "new perspective," it commonly was assumed that there is something inherent in deviants which distinguishes them from non-deviants.[1] Thus, from Lombroso to Sheldon, criminals were viewed as biologically distinctive in one way or another.[2] The inadequacies of this conception are now obvious. After decades of research, no biological characteristic which distinguishes criminals has been discovered, and this generalization applies even to particular types of criminals (e.g., murderers, bigamists, etc.). Consequently, few theorists now even toy with the notion that all criminals are atavistic, mentally defective, constitutionally inferior. But the rejection of the biological conception of crime stems from more than research findings. Even casual observation and mild logic cast doubt on the idea. Since legislators are not geneticists, it is difficult to see how they can pass laws in such a way as to create "born criminals." Equally important, since most if not all "normal" persons have violated a law at one time or another,[3] the assertion that criminals are so by heredity now appears most questionable.

Although the biological conception generally

[1] Throughout this paper crime is treated as a sub-class of deviant behavior. Particular issues may be discussed with reference to crime, but on the whole the observations apply to deviant behavior generally.

[2] Although not essential to the argument, it is perhaps significant that the alleged biological differentiae of criminals have been consistently viewed as "pathological" in one sense or another.

[3] See Edwin H. Sutherland and Donald R. Cressey, *Principles of Criminology*, 6th ed., Chicago: J. B. Lippincott, 1960, p. 39.

has been rejected, what is here designated as the analytic conception of criminal acts largely has escaped criticism. Rather than view criminals acts as nothing more or less than behavior contrary to legal norms, the acts are construed as somehow injurious to society. The shift from the biological to the analytical conception is thus from the actors to the characteristics of their acts, with the idea being that some acts are inherently "criminal" or at least that criminal acts share intrinsic characteristics in common.

The analytical conception is certainly more defensible than the biological view, but it is by no means free of criticism. Above all, the "injurious" quality of some deviant acts is by no means conspicuous, as witness Durkheim's observation:

. . . There are many acts which have been and still are regarded as criminal without in themselves being harmful to society. What social danger is there in touching a tabooed object, an impure animal or man, in letting the sacred fire die down, in eating certain meats, in failure to make the traditional sacrifice over the grave of parents, in not exactly pronouncing the ritual formula, in not celebrating holidays, etc.? [4]

Only a radical functionalism would interpret the acts noted by Durkheim as literally injuring society in any reasonable sense of the word. The crucial point is that, far from actually injuring society or sharing some intrinsic feature in common, acts may be criminal or deviant because and only because they are proscribed legally and/or socially. The proscription may be irrational in that members of the society cannot explain it, but it is real nonetheless. Similarly, a law may be "arbitrary" in that it is imposed by a powerful minority and, as a consequence, lacks popular support and is actively opposed. But if the law is consistently enforced (i.e., sanctions are imposed regularly on violators), it is difficult to see how it is not "real."

The fact that laws may appear to be irrational and arbitrary has prompted attempts to define crime independently of legal criteria, i.e., analytically. The first step in this direction was Garofalo's concept of natural crime — acts which violate prevailing sentiments of pity and probity.[5] Garofalo's endeavor accomplished very little. Just as there is probably no act which is contrary to law universally, it is equally true that no act violates sentiments of pity and probity in all societies. In other words, cultural relativity defeats any attempt to compile a list of acts which are crimes universally. Also, it is hard to see why the violation of a rigorously enforced traffic regulation is not a crime even though unrelated to sentiments of pity and probity. If it is not a crime, what is it?

The search for an analytic identification of crime continued in Sellin's proposal to abandon legal criteria altogether in preference for "conduct norms." [6] The rationale for the proposal is simple. Because laws vary and may be "arbitrary" in any one society, a purely legal definition of crime is not suited for scientific study. But Sellin's observations on the arbitrariness of laws apply in much the same way to conduct norms. Just as the content of criminal law varies from one society to the next and from time to time, so does the content of extra-legal norms. Further, the latter may be just as arbitrary as criminal laws. Even in a highly urbanized society such as the United States, there is evidently no rationale or utilitarian reason for all of the norms pertaining to mode of dress. True, there may be much greater conformity to conduct norms than to some laws, but the degree of conformity is hardly an adequate criterion of the "reality" of norms, legal or extra-legal. If any credence whatever can be placed in the Kinsey report, sexual taboos may be violated frequently and yet remain as taboos. As a case in point, even if adultery is now common in the United States, it is significant that the participants

[4] Emile Durkheim, *The Division of Labor in Society*, trans. George Simpson, Glencoe, Illinois: The Free Press, 1949, p. 72.

[5] Raffaele Garofalo, *Criminology*, Boston: Little, Brown and Co., 1914, Chapter I.

[6] Thorsten Sellin, *Culture Conflict and Crime*, New York: Social Science Research Council, Bulletin 41, 1938.

typically attempt to conceal their acts. In brief, just as laws may be violated frequently and are "unreal" in that sense, the same applies to some conduct norms; but in neither case do they cease to be norms. They would cease to be norms if and only if one defines deviation in terms of statistical regularities in behavior, but not even Sellin would subscribe to the notion that normative phenomena can or should be defined in statistical terms.

In summary, however capricious and irrational legal and extra-legal norms may appear to be, the inescapable conclusion is that some acts are criminal or deviant for the very simple reason that they are proscribed.

The New Conception

Whereas both the pathological and the analytical conception of deviation assume that some intrinsic feature characterizes deviants and/or deviant acts, an emerging perspective in sociology flatly rejects any such assumption. Indeed, as witness the following statements by Kitsuse, Becker, and Erikson, exactly the opposite position is taken.

Kitsuse:

Forms of behavior *per se* do not differentiate deviants from non-deviants; it is the responses of the conventional and conforming members of the society who identify and interpret behavior as deviant which sociologically transform persons into deviants.[7]

Erikson:

From a sociological standpoint, deviance can be defined as conduct which is generally thought to require the attention of social control agencies — that is conduct about which "something should be done." Deviance is not a property *inherent in* certain forms of behavior; it is a property *conferred upon* these forms by the audiences which directly or indirectly witness them. Sociologically, then, the critical variable in the study of deviance is the social *audience* rather than individual *person*, since it is the audience which eventually decides whether or not any given action or

actions will become a visible case of deviation.[8]

Becker:

From this point of view, deviance is *not* a quality of the act a person commits, but rather a consequence of the application by others of rules and sanctions to an "offender." The deviant is one to whom that label has successfully been applied; deviant behavior is behavior that people so label.[9]

The common assertion in the above statements is that acts can be identified as deviant or criminal only by reference to the character of reaction to them by the public or by the official agents of a politically organized society. Put simply, if the reaction is of a certain kind, then and only then is the act deviant. The crucial point is that the essential feature of a deviant or deviant act is *external* to the actor and the act. Further, even if the act or actors share some feature in common other than social reactions to them, the feature neither defines nor completely explains deviation. To take the extreme case, even if Lombroso had been correct in his assertion that criminals are biologically distinctive, the biological factor neither identifies the criminal nor explains criminality. Purely biological variables may explain why some persons commit certain acts, but they do not explain why the acts are crimes. Consequently, since criminal law is spatially and temporally relative, it is impossible to distinguish criminals from non-criminals (assuming that the latter do exist, which is questionable) in terms of biological characteristics. To illustrate, if act X is a crime in society A but not a crime in society B, it follows that, even assuming Lombroso to have been correct, the anatomical features which distinguish the criminal in society A may characterize the non-criminal in society B. In both societies some persons may be genetically predisposed to commit act X, but the act is a crime in one society and not in the other. Accordingly, the generalization that all persons

---

[7] John I. Kitsuse, "Societal Reaction to Deviant Behavior: Problems of Theory and Method," *Social Problems*, 9 (Winter 1962), p. 253.

[8] Kai T. Erikson, "Notes on the Sociology of Deviance," *Social Problems*, 9 (Spring 1962), p. 308.

[9] Howard S. Becker, *Outsiders*, New York: Free Press of Glencoe, 1963, p. 9.

with certain anatomical features are criminals would be, in this instance, false. True, one may assert that the "born criminal" is predisposed to violate the laws of his own society, but this assumes either that "the genes" know what the law is or that the members of the legislature are geneticists (i.e., they deliberately enact laws in such a way that the "born criminal" will violate them). Either assumption taxes credulity.

The new perspective of deviant behavior contradicts not only the biological but also the analytical conception. Whereas the latter seeks to find something intrinsic in deviant or, more specifically, criminal acts, the new conception denies any such characterization. True, the acts share a common denominator — they are identified by the character of reaction to them — but this does not mean that the acts are "injurious" to society or that they are in any way inherently abnormal. The new conception eschews the notion that some acts are deviant or criminal in all societies. For that matter, the reaction which identifies a deviant act may not be the same from one society or social group to the next. In general, then, the new conception of deviant behavior is relativistic in the extreme.

Criticism of the New Perspective

The new perspective of deviant behavior is much more consistent not only with what is known about deviant behavior but also with contemporary sociological principles generally. However, while containing a fundamentally sound idea, the new perspective leaves some crucial questions unanswered. For one thing, it is not clear whether the perspective is intended to be a "substantive theory" of deviant behavior (i.e., an explanation of the phenomenon) or a conceptual treatment of it. Consider, again, statements by Becker, Kitsuse, and Erikson:

Becker:
. . . *Social groups create deviance by making the rules whose infraction constitute deviance*, and by applying those rules to particular people and labeling them as outsiders.[10]

10 *Op. cit.*, p. 9.

Kitsuse and Cicourel:
. . . *Rates of deviant behavior* are produced by *the actions taken by persons in the social system* which define, classify and record certain behaviors as deviant.[11]

Erikson:
. . . Transactions taking place between deviant persons on the one side and agencies of control on the other are boundary maintaining mechanisms. They mark the outside limits of the area in which the norm has jurisdiction, and in this way assert how much diversity and variability can be contained within the system before it begins to lose its distinct structure, its unique shape.[12]

Now these statements appear to be something more than definitions. However, if regarded as explanations of deviant behavior, these and other similar observations do not provide adequate answers to three major questions: (1) Why does the incidence of a particular act vary from one population to the next? (2) Why do some persons commit the act while others do not? (3) Why is the act in question considered deviant and/or criminal in some societies but not in others?

The assertion that deviation is created or produced by the character of reactions to behavior (see statements by Becker and Kitsuse above) implies an answer to the question on incidence. But are we to conclude that the incidence of a given act is in fact a constant in all populations and that the only difference is in the quality of reactions to the act? Specifically, given two populations with the same kind of reaction to a particular type of act, can the new perspective explain why the incidence of the act is greater in one population than in the other? Not at all! On the contrary, even if two populations have the same legal and social definition of armed robbery and even if instances of the crime are reacted to in exactly the same way, it is still possible for the armed robbery rate to be much higher in one population than in the other. Reaction to deviation may influence the rate of deviation in

11 John I. Kitsuse and Aaron Cicourel, "A Note on the Uses of Official Statistics," *Social Problems*, 11 (Fall 1963), p. 135.
12 *Op. cit.*, p. 310.

that certain kinds of reaction may have a deterrent effect, but the deterrent quality of reaction has not been examined systematically by Becker, Kitsuse, or Erikson, primarily because they view reaction in terms of *identifying* deviant behavior. Actually, apart from identifying deviation, the new conception presents a sophisticated framework for the study of deterrence as an aspect of reaction to deviant behavior. All three of the advocates are sensitive to the importance of the deviant's response to reaction, and it would not be inconsistent for them to devote more attention to the possibility that some kinds of reaction have consequences beyond identifying behavior as deviant.

What has been said of the new perspective with regard to explaining variation in the incidence of deviant acts also applies to the second major question: Why do some persons commit a given act while others do not? The point is that the new perspective does not generate an answer to this question. For example, the fact that the reaction to armed robbery may involve incarceration hardly explains why some but not all persons commit the act. Again, the quality of reaction (or the probability of reaction) may have a differential deterrent effect, a possibility which is relevant in attempting to answer the question; but, as noted before, the new perspective exhibits little concern not only with deterrence but also with etiological factors generally. The lack of concern with etiological factors suggests that Becker, Erikson, and Kitsuse actually are seeking a theory not about deviant behavior *per se* but rather about reactions to deviant behavior (i.e., why does the quality of reaction vary from place to place and time to time?). In any event, the three persons closely associated with the perspective have not explicitly stated that they are seeking such a theory.

It is not at all clear whether Becker is pursuing a theory about deviant behavior or a theory about reactions to deviation. If it is the latter, then his focus on deviants rather than reactors is puzzling. Kitsuse is concerned with reaction to deviant behavior as a process, but he views reaction not only as a criterion of deviant behavior but also (evidently) as the decisive factor in relation to incidence. As such, he is apparently seeking a theory about deviant behavior and not reactions to it. Erikson's "functionalist" position could be construed as a theory about deviant behavior, or reactions, or both. However, even if reactions to deviation do serve a "function" — boundary maintenance — a functional interpretation hardly explains why the quality of reaction varies from one society to the next. Further, with reference to incidence, are we to conclude that social boundaries are maintained or demarcated if and only if the rate of deviant behavior is high?

Even if deviant acts are defined in terms of reactions to behavior, the identification does not and cannot explain why a given act is considered deviant and/or criminal in some but not all societies (the third major question). After all, a certain kind of reaction may identify behavior as deviant, but it obviously does not explain why the behavior is deviant.

The danger in evaluating the work of Becker, Erikson, and Kitsuse is that of prematurely rejecting what is a most promising approach to the study of deviant behavior. The danger can be avoided if it is clearly understood that they have formulated what is essentially a conception. As such, it contains both definitions and elements of substantive theory, and the development of the latter would be furthered considerably by making the distinction explicit. Finally, since a conception precedes substantive theory, it would be most unrealistic to demand testable empirical propositions at this stage. The only justifiable criticism on this point is that the three men have not specified their goal adequately, i.e., whether they are seeking an explanation of deviant behavior or of reaction to it. The fact that it may be both testifies to the fertility of the conception, but it is all the more reason to treat the distinction seriously.

Reaction as a Criterion of Deviation

The point stressed continually by the new perspective is that acts are identified as deviant by the character of reactions to them. Whatever the merits of this position, it is not free of criticism. For one thing, Becker, Erikson, and Kitsuse have never specified exactly what kind of reaction identifies deviant acts. Becker constantly refers to deviants as persons labelled as "outsiders," but this term is Becker's, not that of the man on the street. For that matter, the public may be more familiar with the meaning of the term "deviant" than with "outsider."

When we turn to concrete cases of reactions supposedly indicative of deviant acts, there are some rather curious results. Kitsuse, for example, found reactions of students to persons identified by the students as homosexuals to be "generally mild." [13] These reactions may or may not be representative of the public generally; nonetheless, two significant questions are posed. First, are we to conclude, because of the mildness of the reaction, that homosexuals are not deviants after all? Second, how "harsh" must the reaction be before the behavior is to be construed as deviant? More generally, since "mild" and "harsh" are subjective terms, exactly what "kind" of reaction identifies deviant acts or deviance? Some of Becker's observations are puzzling in this connection. As a case in point: "Whether an act is deviant, then, depends on how other people react to it. You can commit clan incest and suffer no more than gossip as long as no one makes a public accusation. . . ." [14] Why is it that gossip does not qualify as a reaction which identifies deviant behavior?

The failure of Becker, Erikson, and Kitsuse to specify the kind of reactions which identify deviation is further complicated by the contradictions in their own position. The contradictions stem from the fact that a deviant act can be defined as behavior *which is contrary to a norm or rule.* One type of norm is simply what the members of a social unit think conduct "ought" or "ought not" be. For example, on this basis it is probably true that the act of joining the Communist party is "deviant" in American society, even though the quality of reaction to it in a particular instance may be problematical. This conception of deviation enables one to treat deviant acts and reactions to them as conceptually distinct. But this is not

so from the viewpoint of Becker, Erikson, and Kitsuse, because deviant behavior for them *is defined in terms of reactions to it.* On the other hand, while advocates of the new perspective do recognize the "norm" conception of deviation, they do not consistently reject it. Witness, for example:

Becker:
An even more interesting kind of case is found at the other extreme of *secret deviance.* Here an improper act is committed, yet no one notices it or reacts to it as a violation of the rules. [15]

Kitsuse and Cicourel:
We wish to state explicitly that the interpretation of official statistics proposed here *does not* imply that the forms of behavior which the sociologist might define and categorize as deviant (e.g., Merton's modes of adaptation) have no factual basis or theoretical importance. [16]

Erikson:
There are societies in which deviance is considered a natural pursuit for the young, an activity which they can easily abandon when they move through defined ceremonies into adulthood. There are societies which give license to large groups of persons to engage in deviant behavior for certain seasons or on certain days of the year. And there are societies in which special groups are formed to act in ways "contrary" to the normal expectations of the culture. [17]

Now all of these statements admit, in one way or another, that deviant behavior can be identified in terms of norms, but the authors do not come to grips with the problem and take a consistent stand on the issue. Thus, if deviant behavior is defined in terms of reactions to it, then Becker cannot speak properly of "secret deviance." If behavior defined as deviant by sociologists in reference to the prevailing social norms is "real," then in what sense can one maintain, as Kitsuse does elsewhere, that behavior is deviant if and only if there is a certain kind of reaction to it. Finally, in the case of Erikson, how can the behavior

[13] *Op. cit.,* p. 256.
[14] *Op. cit.,* p. 11.

[15] *Op. cit.,* p. 20.
[16] *Op. cit.,* pp. 138–139.
[17] *Op. cit.,* p. 313.

of "large groups of persons" be identified as deviant when they have been given a "license" to engage in it? To be consistent, Becker, Kitsuse, and Erikson would have to insist that behavior which is contrary to a norm is not deviant unless it is discovered and there is a particular kind of reaction to it. Thus, if persons engage in adultery but their act is not discovered and reacted to in a certain way (by the members of the social unit), then it is not deviant! Similarly, if a person is erroneously thought to have engaged in a certain type of behavior and is reacted to "harshly" as a consequence, a deviant act has taken place!

The extreme position of Becker, Erikson, and Kitsuse is also apparent when attempting to explain why reaction to deviant behavior is not purely random and idiosyncratic. One could argue that a satisfactory explanation cannot be given without making reference to norms, but this concept evidently is not altogether welcome in the new perspective. Finally, apart from the issue of norms, the new perspective negates a significant empirical question: Why do reactions to deviant behavior vary from place to place and time to time? An answer to this question from the new perspective necessarily would be at least partially tautological because deviant behavior is defined in terms of reactions to it.

As the tone of the above criticism suggests, this writer differs with Becker, *et al.*, on the issue of identifying deviant behavior. My preference is to identify deviant acts by reference to norms, and treat reaction to deviation as a contingent property. However, this preference reflects nothing more than opinion, and the ultimate evaluation of the new conception on this point must await an assessment of substantive theory generated by it. Accordingly, no claim is made that Becker, Erikson, and Kitsuse are "wrong." Rather, the criticism is that (1) they have not specified exactly what kind of reaction identifies behavior as deviant and (2) they have failed to take a consistent stand on a particular conceptual issue.

Overview

The major trend in the study of crime and deviant behavior has been in the direction of a distinctly "social" conception of the subject matter. Whereas Lombroso thought of criminals in biological terms and later positivists sought to discover intrinsic features of criminal acts, the new perspective conceives of both in terms of the quality of social reaction to behavior. Accordingly, whether or not a person or an act is criminal or deviant is a matter of the way in which the public and/or officials react.

The relativistic criterion of deviation introduced by the new perspective is in keeping with contemporary sociological principles. Further, a social conception of the phenomenon promises to generate substantive theories that are distinctly sociological in outlook. But the new conception has left at least four crucial questions unanswered. First, what elements in the scheme are intended to be definitions rather than substantive theory? Second, is the ultimate goal to explain deviant behavior or to explain reactions to deviation? Third, is deviant behavior to be identified exclusively in terms of reaction to it? Fourth, exactly what kind of reaction identifies behavior as deviant?

No claim is made that the advocates of the new conception are unable to answer the above questions, nor that their answers would be wrong. The only point is that the questions must be answered if the new conception is to develop and receive the constructive attention that it deserves.

Section
Four

SUBCULTURAL
DELINQUENCY

Status Deprivation

In his monumental study of 1,313 gangs in Chicago, Thrasher (1927) depicted the origin of the gang in the spontaneous play activities of children and described gang members as engaging both in legal and illegal activities; in Thrasher's view, involvement in delinquency provided the boys with fun and excitement. Thrasher recognized that clique or group formation is a common phenomenon of adolescence, and he argued that gangs become integrated through conflict with other segments of the society. Thrasher (1927:57) defined the gang as follows: "The gang is an interstitial group originally formed spontaneously, and then integrated through conflict. It is characterized by the following types of behavior: meeting face to face, milling, movement through space as a unit, conflict, and planning. The result of this collective behavior is the development of tradition, unreflective internal structure, *esprit de corps*, solidarity, morale, group awareness, and attachment to a local territory." Thrasher's acceptance of the now discarded "social disorganization" perspective led him to view the gang as a symptom of disorganization in the slum. This view, unfortunately, allows one to infer that the gang is a pathological form of human association—a view consistent with the common-sense meaning of the term "gang" as a collectivity whose members engage in delinquent acts. Nevertheless, Thrasher's definition has served either implicitly or explicitly as the definition of the concept "gang" in theoretical works and in many studies conducted over the past four decades.

Although Thrasher referred to "gangs" as interstitial groups in his definition, he did not insist that gangs are found only in interstitial areas, because he recognized the existence of gangs outside the transitional zone. His point is that the location of the gang is primarily in the interstitial or slum areas of the city. It is important to recognize that Thrasher (1927:58–76) distinguished several types of gangs: (1) the diffuse and loosely organized groups; (2) the group solidified through conflict to the point that it is "a well-integrated fighting machine" which "presents a solid front against its foes" (1927:61); (3) the conventionalized type which takes the form of an athletic or recreational club, or if the group is not conventionalized with the passage of time, it may become (4) the criminal type devoted to "habitual crime." Given conditions favorable to its continued existence, a gang evolves from type 1 to type 2 and then to either type 3 or 4. Stated differently, the age of gang members is correlated with the type of gang. Thrasher, then, provides the classical view of delinquent gangs.

With the appearance of Cohen's *Delinquent Boys* in 1955 a new era in the study of delinquency began. To a considerable extent, research and theorizing since that date are an outgrowth of his work. Like earlier writers, Cohen accepted as an initial premise the existence of the "delinquent subculture," a system of beliefs and values or a "way of life" traditional among boys' gangs in large American cities. Stated simply, the delinquent subculture is the "culture" of the "gang." Rather than dealing with the old question of how a child becomes involved in or "takes over" that subculture, Cohen posed for himself different questions. Why is there a delinquent subculture in the boys' milieu? Why does a subculture, with its particular content, arise and persist in some neighborhoods of our cities, but not in others? Cohen concluded that juvenile delinquency and the delinquent subculture are concentrated among working-class boys; although based on a variety of studies, this inference has not gone unchallenged, as may be recalled from the first section of this volume.

After developing a general theory of subcultures, Cohen explained the delinquent subculture as a group product which emerges from the interaction of working-class males who, by virtue of the similarity of their positions in the social structure, face similar problems of adjustment. Cohen does not suggest that the delinquent subculture arises because working-class boys have problems; he assumes, rather, that all human action, including delinquent behavior, is an effort to solve problems. The problems of adjustment of these working-class boys are largely problems of status and self-respect, and these arise because the socialization of working-class children does not prepare them to meet the standards of the larger culture. These standards are manifestations of the dominant American value system and in the middle class socialization is deliberately directed toward their inculcation. Consequently, in competition with middle-class peers, the working-class boy is more likely to find himself on the lower rungs of the status hierarchy. One might infer that working-class boys would be likely, therefore, to avoid "status competition" with middle-class rivals. However, our system of compulsory education suggests at least one setting, the school, in which this is likely to occur. Cohen (1955:112–115) cites three reasons why status in school, to the extent it is controlled by the teacher, is awarded according to middle-class standards. In addition to the "structural imperatives" of the school, which include the need for order and discipline, the teacher is, by origin or orientation, typically a middle-class person. Further, the middle-class board of education, the middle-class parents, and many of the working-class parents expect teachers to inculcate middle-class manners and skills in the students.

The working-class boy is neither fully prepared nor properly motivated to perform according to middle-class standards. Therefore, argues Cohen (1955:119), "to the degree to which he values middle-class status, either because he values the good opinion of middle-class persons or because he has to some degree internalized middle-class standards himself, he [the working-class boy] faces a problem of adjustment and is in the market for a 'solution.'" The delinquent subculture provides a solution which justifies "the free expression of aggression against the sources of his frustration" (1955: 132). This solution is in the form of an alternative status system offering criteria of status which working-class boys *can* meet: "The hallmark of the delinquent subculture is the explicit and wholesale repudiation of middle-class standards and the adoption of their very antithesis" (1955:129). Cohen assumes that participants in the delinquent subculture are ambivalent about middle-class norms, and this threatens the stability of their delinquent adaptation. He therefore introduces the psychological concept of "reaction formation" to explain their exaggerated response in the form of malicious and negativistic delinquent actions.

REFERENCE

Frederic M. Thrasher, *The Gang* (Chicago: University of Chicago Press, 1927).

ALBERT K. COHEN

The Origin and Nature of the Delinquent Subculture

In the following pages we present a portrait of the delinquent subculture. In presenting a thumbnail description of any widely distributed subculture it is impossible to do full justice to the facts, for no brief account can deal with all the varieties and nuances which actually exist. The subcultures of the medical profession, the professional gambler or the jitterbug have many local versions, as does the delinquent subculture. Nonetheless, it is possible, for each of these subcultures, to draw a picture which represents certain themes or traits which run through all the variants. This "ideal-typical" or "full-blown" picture will be fully realized in some of the variants and only approximated, in various degrees, in others. This much, however, may be said for our description of the delinquent subculture. It is a real picture, drawn from life. It is the picture most familiar to students of juvenile delinquency,

especially those who, like the group worker, encounter the delinquent gang in its natural habitat, the streets and alleys of our cities. It is the picture that stands out most prominently in the literature of juvenile delinquency. Compare it to a generalized picture of a pear, in which the distinctively pearlike features are accentuated. Many pears will look very like our picture; others will only approximate it. However, if our picture is truly drawn, it will give us a good idea of the shape which distinguishes pears in general from other fruits. This is the kind of validity which we claim for our portrait of the delinquent subculture.

The Content of the
Delinquent Subculture

The common expression, "juvenile crime," has unfortunate and misleading connotations. It suggests that we have two kinds of criminals, young and old, but only one kind of crime. It suggests that crime has its meanings and its motives which are much the same for young and old; that the young differ from the old as the apprentice and the master differ at the same trade; that we distinguish the young from the old only because the young are less "set in their ways," less "confirmed" in the same criminal habits, more amenable to treatment and more deserving, because of their tender age, of special consideration.

The problem of the relationship between juvenile delinquency and adult crime has many facets. To what extent are the offenses of children and adults distributed among the same legal categories, "burglary," "larceny," "vehicle-taking," and so forth? To what extent, even when the offenses are legally identical, do these acts have the same meaning for children and adults? To what extent are the careers of adult criminals continuations of careers of juvenile delinquency? We cannot solve these problems here, but we want to emphasize the danger of making facile and unproven assumptions. If we assume that "crime is crime," that child and adult criminals are practitioners of the same trade, and if our assumptions are false, then the road to error is wide and clear. Easily and unconsciously, we may impute a whole host of notions concerning the nature of crime and its causes, derived from our knowledge and fancies about adult crime, to a large realm of behavior to which these notions are irrelevant. It is better to make no such assumptions; it is better to look at juvenile delinquency with a fresh eye and try to explain what we see.

What we see when we look at the delinquent subculture (and we must not even assume that this describes *all juvenile* crime) is that it is *non-utilitarian, malicious* and *negativistic.*

We usually assume that when people steal things, they steal because they want them. They may want them because they can eat them, wear them or otherwise use them; or because they can sell them; or even — if we are given to a psychoanalytic turn of mind — because on some deep symbolic level they substitute or stand for something unconsciously desired but forbidden. All of these explanations have this in common, that they assume that the stealing is a means to an end, namely, the possession of some object of value, and that it is,

in this sense, rational and "utilitarian." However, the fact cannot be blinked — and this fact is of crucial importance in defining our problem — that much gang stealing has no such motivation at all. Even where the value of the object stolen is itself a motivating consideration, the stolen sweets are often sweeter than those acquired by more legitimate and prosaic means. In homelier language, stealing "for the hell of it" and apart from considerations of gain and profit is a valued activity to which attaches glory, prowess and profound satisfaction. There is no accounting in rational and utilitarian terms for the effort expended and the danger run in stealing things which are often discarded, destroyed or casually given away. A group of boys enters a store where each takes a hat, a ball or a light bulb. They then move on to another store where these things are covertly exchanged for like articles. Then they move on to other stores to continue the game indefinitely. They steal a basket of peaches, desultorily munch on a few of them and leave the rest to spoil. They steal clothes they cannot wear and toys they will not use. Unquestionably, most delinquents are from the more "needy" and "underprivileged" classes, and unquestionably many things are stolen because they are intrinsically valued. However, a humane and compassionate regard for their economic disabilities should not blind us to the fact that stealing is not merely an alternative means to the acquisition of objects otherwise difficult of attainment.[1]

---

[1] See H. M. Tiebout and M. E. Kirkpatrick, "Psychiatric Factors in Stealing," *American Journal of Orthopsychiatry*, II (April 1932), 114–123, which discusses, in an exceptionally lucid manner, the distinction between motivating factors which center around the acquisition of the object and those which center around the commission of the act itself.

The non-utilitarian nature of juvenile delinquency has been noted by many students. ". . . While older offenders may have definitely crystallized beliefs about profitable returns from anti-social conduct, it is very clear that in childhood and in earlier youth delinquency is certainly not entered into as a paying proposition in any ordinary sense." William Healy and Augusta F. Bronner, *New Light on Delinquency and Its Treatment* (New Haven: Yale University Press, 1936), p. 22. "The juvenile property offender's thefts,

Can we then account for this stealing by simply describing it as another form of recreation, play or sport? Surely it is that, but why is this form of play so attractive to some and so unappealing to others? Mountain climbing, chess, pinball, number pools and bingo are also different kinds of recreation. Each of us, child or adult, can choose from a host of alternative means for satisfying our common "need" for recreation. But every choice expresses a preference, and every preference reflects something about the chooser or his circumstances that endows the object of his choice with some special quality or virtue. The choice is not self-explanatory nor is it arbitrary or random. Each form of recreation is distributed in a characteristic way among the age, sex and social class sectors of our population. The explanation of these distributions and of the way they change is often puzzling, sometimes fascinating and rarely platitudinous.

By the same logic, it is an imperfect answer to our problem to say: "Stealing is but another way of satisfying the universal desire for status." Nothing is more obvious from numberless case histories of subcultural delinquents that they steal to achieve recognition and to avoid isolation or opprobrium. This is an important insight and part of the foundation on which we shall build. But the question still haunts us: "Why is stealing a claim to status in one group and a degrading blot in another?"

If stealing itself is not motivated by rational, utilitarian considerations, still less are the manifold other activities which constitute the delinquent's repertoire. Throughout there is a kind of *malice* apparent, an enjoyment in the discomfiture of others, a delight in the defiance of taboos itself. Thrasher quotes one gang delinquent:

> We did all kinds of dirty tricks for fun. We'd see a sign, "Please keep the streets clean," but we'd tear it down and say, "We don't feel like keeping it clean." One day we put a can of glue in the engine of a man's car. We would always tear things down. That would make us laugh and feel good, to have so many jokes.[2]

The gang exhibits this gratuitous hostility toward nongang peers as well as adults. Apart from its more dramatic manifestations in the form of gang wars, there is keen delight in terrorizing "good" children, in driving them from playgrounds and gyms for which the gang itself may have little use, and in general in making themselves obnoxious to the virtuous. The same spirit is evident in playing hookey and in misbehavior in school. The teacher and her rules are not merely something onerous to be evaded. They are to be *flouted*. There is an element of active spite and malice, contempt and ridicule, challenge and defiance, exquisitely symbolized, in an incident described to the writer by Mr. Henry D. McKay, of defecating on the teacher's desk.[3]

---

at least at the start, are usually 'for fun' and not for gain." Paul Tappan, *Juvenile Delinquency* (New York: McGraw-Hill Book Company, 1949), p. 143. "Stealing, the leading predatory activity of the adolescent gang, is as much a result of the sport motive as of a desire for revenue." Frederic M. Thrasher, *The Gang*, 2d rev. ed. (Chicago: University of Chicago Press, 1936), p. 143. "In its early stages, delinquency is clearly a form of play." Henry D. McKay, "The Neighborhood and Child Conduct," *Annals of the American Academy of Political and Social Science*, CCLXI (January 1949), 37. See also Barbara Bellow, Milton L. Blum, Kenneth B. Clark, *et al.*, "Prejudice in Seaside," *Human Relations*, I (1947), 15–16 and Sophia M. Robison, Nathan Cohen and Murray Sachs, "An Unsolved Problem in Group Relations," *Journal of Educational Psychology*, XX (November 1946), 154–162. The last cited paper is an excellent description of the non-utilitarian, malicious and negativistic quality of the delinquent subculture and is the clearest statement in the literature that a satisfactory theory of delinquency must make sense of these facts.

[2] Frederic M. Thrasher, *op. cit.*, pp. 94–95.

[3] To justify the characterization of the delinquent subculture as "malicious" by multiplying citations from authorities would be empty pedantry. The malice is evident in any detailed description of juvenile gang life. We commend in particular, however, the cited works of Thrasher, Shaw and McKay and Robison *et al.* One aspect of this "gratuitous hostility" deserves special mention, however, for the benefit of those who see in the provision of facilities for "wholesome recreation" some magical therapeutic virtue. "On entering a playground or a gym the first activity of gang members is to disrupt and interrupt whatever activities are going on. Nongang members flee, and when the coast is clear the gang plays desultorily on the apparatus or carries on horseplay." Sophia

All this suggests also the intention of our term "negativistic." The delinquent subculture is not only a set of rules, a design for living which is different from or indifferent to or even in conflict with the norms of the "respectable" adult society. It would appear at least plausible that it is defined by its "negative polarity" to those norms. That is, the delinquent subculture takes its norms from the larger culture but turns them upside down. The delinquent's conduct is right, by the standards of his subculture, precisely *because* it is wrong by the norms of the larger culture.[4] "Malicious" and "negativistic" are foreign to the delinquent's vocabulary but he will often assure us, sometimes ruefully, sometimes with a touch of glee or even pride, that he is "just plain mean."

In describing what might be called the "spirit" of the delinquent culture, we have suggested also its *versatility.* Of the "antisocial" activities of the delinquent gangs, stealing, of course, looms largest. Stealing itself can be, and for the gang usually is, a diversified occupation. It may steal milk bottles, candy, fruit, pencils, sports equipment and cars; it may steal from drunks, homes, stores, schools and filling stations. No gang runs the whole gamut but neither is it likely to "specialize" as do many adult criminal gangs and "solitary" delinquents. More to our point, however, is the fact that stealing tends to go hand-in-hand with "other property offenses," "malicious mischief," "vandalism," "trespass," and truancy. This quality of versatility and the fusion of versatility and malice are manifest in the following quotation:

We would get some milk bottles in front of the grocery store and break them in somebody's hallway. Then we would break windows or get some garbage cans and throw them down someone's front stairs. After doing all this dirty work and running through alleys and yards, we'd go over to a grocery store. There, some of the boys would hide in a hallway while I would get a basket of grapes. When the man came after me, why the boys would jump out of their places and each grab a basket of grapes.[5]

Dozens of young offenders, after relating to the writer this delinquent episode and that, have summarized: "I guess we was just ornery." A generalized, diversified, protean "orneriness," not this or that specialized delinquent pursuit seems best to describe the vocation of the delinquent gang.[6]

---

[5] Clifford R. Shaw and Henry D. McKay, *Social Factors in Juvenile Delinquency,* Vol. II of National Commission on Law Observance and Enforcement, *Report on the Causes of Crime* (Washington: U.S. Government Printing Office, 1931), p. 18.

[6] *Federal Probation,* XVIII (March 1954), 3–16 contains an extremely valuable symposium on vandalism, which highlights all of the characteristics we have imputed to the delinquent subculture. In the belief that no generalization can convey the flavor and scope of this subculture as well as a simple but massive enumeration, we quote at length from Joseph E. Murphy's contribution, pp. 8–9:

Studies of the complaints made by citizens and public officials reveal that hardly any property is safe from this form of aggression. Schools are often the object of attack by vandals. Windows are broken; records, books, desks, typewriters, supplies, and other equipment are stolen or destroyed. Public property of all types appears to offer peculiar allurement to children bent on destruction. Parks, playgrounds, highway signs, and markers are frequently defaced or destroyed. Trees, shrubs, flowers, benches, and other equipment suffer in like manner. Autoists are constantly reporting the slashing or releasing of air from tires, broken windows, stolen accessories. Golf clubs complain that benches, markers, flags, even expensive and difficult-to-replace putting greens are defaced, broken or uprooted. Libraries report the theft and destruction of books and other equipment. Railroads complain of and demand protection from the destruction of freight car seals, theft of property, willful and deliberate throwing of stones at passen-

---

Robison *et al., op. cit.,* p. 159. See, to the same effect, the excellent little book by Kenneth H. Rogers, *Street Gangs in Toronto* (Toronto: The Ryerson Press, 1945), pp. 18–19.

[4] Shaw and McKay, in their *Social Factors in Juvenile Delinquency,* p. 241, come very close to making this point quite explicitly: "In fact the standards of these groups may represent a complete reversal of the standards and norms of conventional society. Types of conduct which result in personal degradation and dishonor in a conventional group serve to enhance and elevate the personal prestige and status of a member of the delinquent group."

Another characteristic of the subculture of the delinquent gang is *short-run hedonism*. There is little interest in long-run goals, in planning activities and budgeting time, or in activities involving knowledge and skills to be acquired only through practice, deliberation and study. The members of the gang typically congregate, with no specific activity in mind, at some street corner, candy store or other regular rendezvous. They "hang around," "rough-housing," "chewing the fat," and "waiting for something to turn up." They may respond impulsively to somebody's suggestion to play ball, go swimming, engage in some sort of mischief, or do something else that offers excitement. They do not take kindly to organized and supervised recreation, which subjects them to a regime of schedules and im-

personal rules. They are impatient, impetuous and out for "fun," with little heed to the remoter gains and costs. It is to be noted that this short-run hedonism is not inherently delinquent and indeed it would be a serious error to think of the delinquent gang as dedicated solely to the cultivation of juvenile crime. Even in the most seriously delinquent gang only a small fraction of the "fun" is specifically and intrinsically delinquent. Furthermore, short-run hedonism is not characteristic of delinquent groups alone. On the contrary, it is common throughout the social class from which delinquents characteristically come. However, in the delinquent gang it reaches its finest flower. It is the fabric, as it were, of which delinquency is the most brilliant and spectacular thread.[7]

---

ger car windows, tampering with rails and switches. Vacant houses are always the particular delight of children seeking outlets for destructive instincts; windows are broken, plumbing and hardware stolen, destroyed, or rendered unusable. Gasoline operators report pumps and other service equipment stolen, broken, or destroyed. Theatre managers, frequently in the "better" neighborhoods, complain of the slashing of seats, willful damaging of toilet facilities, even the burning of rugs, carpets, etc.

Recently the Newark *Evening News*, commenting editorially on the problem of vandalism in New York City housing projects, stated "housing authorities complain of the tearing out of steel banisters, incinerator openings, and mail boxes, damaging of elevators, defacing walls, smashing windows and light bulbs, stealing nozzles of fire hoses, destroying trees and benches on the project's grounds and occasionally plundering and setting fire to parked cars. Moreover, gangs have terrorized not only tenants but also the three hundred unarmed watchmen hired to protect the property."

This quotation places "stealing" in the context of a host of other manifestations of the protean "orneriness" of which we have spoken. The implication is strong that the fact that an object is "stolen" rather than destroyed or damaged is, from the standpoint of motivation, almost incidental. J. P. Shalloo, *ibid.*, pp. 6–7, states in a forceful way the problem which this creates for criminological theory: "Delinquency and crime are, and have been regarded as, purposeful behavior. But wanton and vicious destruction of property both public and private by teen-age hoodlums reveals

no purpose, no rhyme, no reason. . . . These are not the actions of thoughtless youth. These are actions based upon a calculated contempt for the rights of others. . . ."

It is widely believed that vandalism, on the scale we know it today, is a relatively recent phenomenon. Douglas H. MacNeil, *ibid.*, p. 16, observes that, although vandalism is a form of delinquency which has been neglected by social scientists, there is little reason to believe that it has increased spectacularly, if at all, in recent years. Apparently it is and it has been for many years part and parcel, indeed the very spirit, of the delinquent subculture.

In connection with the versatility of the delinquent subculture, it should be noted that truancy is also institutionalized in the delinquent gang. In Lester E. Hewitt and Richard L. Jenkins (eds.), *Fundamental Patterns of Maladjustment* (published by The State of Illinois, no date), p. 94, habitual truancy as found to have a tetrachoric coefficient of correlation of .10 with the "unsocialized aggressive" syndrome, -.08 with the "overinhibited behavior" syndrome and .75 with the "socialized delinquent" syndrome. These findings are of special interest because the latter syndrome corresponds closely to what we have called the delinquent subculture. For summaries of studies on the relationship between truancy and other forms of delinquency see Norman Fenton, *The Delinquent Boy and the Correctional School* (Claremont, California: Claremont Colleges Guidance Center, 1935), pp. 66–69 and William Kvaraceus, *Juvenile Delinquency and the School* (Yonkers-on-Hudson: World Book Company, 1945), pp. 144–146.

[7] See the splendid report on "Working with a Street Gang" in Sylvan S. Furman (ed.), *Reach-*

Another characteristic not peculiar to the delinquent gang but a conspicuous ingredient of its culture is an emphasis on *group autonomy*, or intolerance of restraint except from the informal pressures within the group itself. Relations with gang members tend to be intensely solidary and imperious. Relations with other groups tend to be indifferent, hostile or rebellious. Gang members are unusually resistant to the efforts of home, school and other agencies to regulate, not only their delinquent activities, but any activities carried on within the group, and to efforts to compete with the gang for the time and other resources of its members. It may be argued that the resistance of gang members to the authority of the home may not be a result of their membership in gangs but that membership in gangs, on the contrary, is a result of ineffective family supervision, the breakdown of parental authority and the hostility of the child toward the parents; in short, that the delinquent gang recruits members who have already achieved autonomy. Certainly a previous breakdown in family controls facilitates recruitment into delinquent gangs. But we are not speaking of the autonomy, the emancipation of *individuals*. It is not the individual delinquent but the gang that is autonomous. For many of our subcultural delinquents the claims of the home are very real and very compelling. The point is that the gang is a separate, distinct and often irresistible focus of attraction, loyalty and solidarity. The claims

of the home versus the claims of the gang may present a real dilemma, and in such cases the breakdown of family controls is as much a casualty as a cause of gang membership.[8]

What the Delinquent Subculture Has to Offer

The delinquent subculture, we suggest, is a way of dealing with the problems of adjustment we have described. These problems are chiefly status problems: certain children are denied status in the respectable society because they cannot meet the criteria of the respectable status system. The delinquent subculture deals with these problems by providing criteria of status which these children *can* meet.

This statement is highly elliptical and is based upon a number of assumptions whose truth is by no means self-evident. It is not, for example, self-evident that people whose status positions are low must necessarily feel deprived, injured or ego-involved in that low status. Whether they will or not depends upon several considerations.

We remarked earlier that our ego-involvement in a given comparison with others depends upon our "status universe." "Whom do we measure ourselves against?" is the crucial question. In some other societies virtue may consist in willing acceptance of the role of peasant, low-born commoner or member of an inferior caste and in conformity to the expectations of that role. If others are richer, more nobly-born or more able than oneself, it is by the will of an inscrutable Providence and not to be imputed to one's own moral defect. The sting of status inferiority is thereby removed or mitigated; one measures himself only against those of like social position. We have suggested, however, that an important feature of American "democracy," perhaps of the Western European tradition in general, is the tendency to measure oneself against "all comers." This means that, for children as for adults, one's sense of personal worth is at stake in status comparisons with all other persons,

---

ing the Unreached (New York: New York City Youth Board, 1952), pp. 112–121. On this quality of short-run hedonism we quote, p. 13:

> One boy once told me, "Now, for example, you take an average day. What happens? We come down to the restaurant and we sit in the restaurant, and sit and sit. All right, say, er . . . after a couple of hours in the restaurant, maybe we'll go to a poolroom, shoot a little pool, that's if somebody's got the money. O. K., a little pool, come back. By this time the restaurant is closed. We go in the candy store, sit around the candy store for a while, and that's it, that's all we do, man."

See also Barbara Bellow *et al.*, *op. cit.*, pp. 4–15, and Ruth Topping, "Treatment of the Pseudo-Social Boy," *American Journal of Orthopsychiatry*, XIII (April 1943), p. 353.

[8] The solidarity of the gang and the dependence of its members upon one another are especially well described in Barbara Bellow *et al.*, *op. cit.*, p. 16 and Sophia Robison *et al.*, *op. cit.*, p. 158.

at least of one's own age and sex, whatever their family background or material circumstances. It means that, in the lower levels of our status hierarchies, whether adult or juvenile, there is a chronic fund of motivation, conscious or repressed, to elevate one's status position, either by striving to climb within the established status system or by redefining the criteria of status so that one's present attributes become status-giving assets. It has been suggested, for example, that such typically working-class forms of Protestantism as the Holiness sects owe their appeal to the fact that they reverse the respectable status system; it is the humble, the simple and the dispossessed who sit at the right hand of God, whereas worldly goods, power and knowledge are as nothing in His eyes. In like manner, we offer the view that the delinquent subculture is one solution to a kindred problem on the juvenile level.

Another consideration affecting the degree of privation experienced in a given status position is the "status source." A person's status, after all, is how he stands in somebody's eyes. Status, then, is not a fixed property of the person but varies with the point of view of whoever is doing the judging. I may be revered by some and despised by others. A crucial question then becomes: "Whose respect or admiration do I value?" That *you* think well or ill of me may or may not *matter* to me.

It may be argued that the working-class boy does not *care* what middle-class people think of him, that he is ego-involved only in the opinions of his family, his friends, his working-class neighbors. A definitive answer to this argument can come only from research designed to get at the facts. This research, in our opinion, is yet to be done. There is, however, reason to believe that most children are sensitive *to some degree* about the attitudes of *any persons* with whom they are thrown into more than the most superficial kind of contact. The contempt or indifference of others, particularly of those like schoolmates and teachers, with whom we are constrained to associate for long hours every day, is difficult, we suggest, to shrug off. It poses a problem with which one may conceivably attempt to cope

in a variety of ways. One may make an active effort to change himself in conformity with the expectations of others; one may attempt to justify or explain away his inferiority in terms which will exculpate him; one may tell oneself that he really doesn't care what these people think; one may react with anger and aggression. But the least probable response is simple, uncomplicated, honest indifference. If we grant the probable truth of the claim that most American working-class children are most sensitive to status sources on their own level, it does not follow that they take lightly rejection, disparagement and censure from other status sources.

Even on their "own" social level, the situation is far from simple. The "working class," we have repeatedly emphasized, is not culturally homogeneous. Not only is there much diversity in the cultural standards applied by one's own working-class neighbors and kin so that it is difficult to find a "working-class" milieu in which "middle-class" standards are not important. In addition, the "working-class" culture we have described is, after all, an ideal type; most working-class *people* are culturally ambivalent. Due to lack of capacity, of the requisite "character structure" or of "luck," they may be working-class in terms of job and income; they may have accepted this status with resignation and rationalized it to their satisfaction; and by example, by class-linked techniques of child training and by failure to support the middle-class agencies of socialization they may have produced children deficient in the attributes that make for status in middle-class terms. Nevertheless, all their lives, through all the major media of mass indoctrination — the schools, the movies, the radio, the newspapers and the magazines — the middle-class powers-that-be that manipulate these media have been trying to "sell" them on middle-class values and the middle-class standard of living. Then there is the "propaganda of the deed," the fact that they have seen with their own eyes working-class contemporaries "get ahead" and "make the grade" in a middle-class world. In consequence of all this, we suspect that few working-class parents unequivocally repudiate as intrinsically worthless middle-class objectives. There is good reason to believe that the modesty of working-class aspirations is partly a matter of trimming one's sails to the available opportunities and resources and partly a matter of unwillingness to accept the discipline which upward striving entails.

However complete and successful one's accommodation to an humble status, the vitality of middle-class goals, of the "American dream," is nonetheless likely to manifest itself in his aspirations for his children. His expectations may not be grandiose, but he will want his children to be "better off" than he. Whatever his own work history and social reputation may be, he will want his children to be "steady" and "respectable." He may exert few positive pressures to "succeed" and the experiences he provides his children may even incapacitate them for success; he may be puzzled at the way they "turn out." But whatever the measure of his own responsibility in accounting for the product, he is not likely to judge that product by unadulterated "corner-boy" standards. Even "corner-boy" parents, although they may value in their children such corner-boy virtues as generosity to friends, personal loyalty and physical prowess, are likely also to be gratified by recognition by middle-class representatives and by the kinds of achievement for which the college-boy way of life is a prerequisite. Even in the working-class milieu from which he acquired his incapacity for middle-class achievement, the working-class corner-boy may find himself at a status disadvantage as against his more upwardly mobile peers.

Lastly, of course, is that most ubiquitous and inescapable of status sources, oneself. Technically, we do not call the person's attitudes towards himself "status" but rather "self-esteem," or, when the quality of the self-attitude is specifically moral, "conscience" or "superego." The important question for us is this: To what extent, if at all, do boys who are typically "working-class" and "corner-boy" in their overt behavior evaluate themselves by "middle-class," "college-boy" standards? For our overt behavior, however closely it conforms to one set of norms, need not argue against the existence or effectiveness of alternative and conflicting norms. The failure of our own behavior to conform to our own expectations is an elementary and commonplace fact which gives rise to the tremendously important consequences of guilt, self-recrimination, anxiety and self-hatred. The reasons for the failure of self-expectations and overt conduct to agree are complex. One reason is that we often internalize more than one set of norms, each of which would dictate a different course of action in a given life-situation; since we can only *do* one thing at a time, however, we are forced to choose between them or somehow to compromise. In either case, we fall short of the full realization of our own expectations and must somehow cope with the residual discrepancy between those expectations and our overt behavior.

We have suggested that corner-boy children (like their working-class parents) internalize middle-class standards to a sufficient degree to create a fundamental ambivalence towards their own corner-boy behavior. Again, we are on somewhat speculative ground where fundamental research remains to be done. The coexistence within the same personality of a corner-boy and a college-boy morality may appear more plausible, however, if we recognize that they are not simple antitheses of one another and that parents and others may in all sincerity attempt to indoctrinate both. For example, the goals upon which the college-boy places such great value, such as intellectual and occupational achievement, and the college-boy virtues of ambitiousness and pride in self-sufficiency are not as such disparaged by the corner-boy culture. The meritoriousness of standing by one's friends and the desire to have a good time here and now do not by definition preclude the desire to help oneself and to provide for the future. It is no doubt the rule, rather than the exception, that most children, college-boy and corner-boy alike, would like to enjoy the best of both worlds. *In practice*, however, the substance that is consumed in the pursuit of one set of values is not available for the pursuit of the other. The sharpness of the dilemma and the degree of the residual discontent depend upon a number of things, notably, the intensity with which both sets of norms have been internalized, the extent to which the life-situations which one encounters compel a choice between them, and the abundance and appropriateness of the skills and resources at one's disposal. The child of superior intelligence, for example, may find it easier than his less gifted peers to meet the demands of the college-boy standards without failing his obligations to his corner-boy associates.

It is a plausible assumption, then, that the working-class boy whose status is low in middle-class terms *cares* about that status, that this status confronts him with a genuine problem of adjustment. To this problem of adjustment there are a variety of conceivable responses, of which participation in the creation and the maintenance of the delinquent subculture is one. Each mode of response entails costs and yields gratifications of its own. The circumstances which tip the balance in favor of the one or the other are obscure. One mode of response is to desert the corner-boy for the college-boy way of life. To the reader of Whyte's *Street Corner Society* the costs are manifest. It is hard, at best, to be a college-boy and to run with the corner-boys. It entails great effort and sacrifice to the degree that one has been indoctrinated in what we have described as the working-class socialization process; its rewards are frequently long-deferred; and for many working-class boys it makes demands which they are, in consequence of their inferior linguistic, academic and "social" skills, not likely ever to meet. Nevertheless, a certain proportion of working-class boys accept the challenge of the middle-class status system and play the status game by the middle-class rules.

Another response, perhaps the most common, is what we may call the "stable corner-boy response." It represents an acceptance of the corner-boy way of life and an effort to make the best of a situation. If our reasoning is correct, it does not resolve the dilemmas we have described as inherent in the corner-boy position in a largely middle-class world, although these dilemmas may be mitigated by an effort to disengage oneself from dependence upon middle-class status-sources and by

withdrawing, as far as possible, into a sheltering community of like-minded working-class children. Unlike the delinquent response, it avoids the radical rupture of good relations with even working-class adults and does not represent as irretrievable a renunciation of upward mobility. It does not incur the active hostility of middle-class persons and therefore leaves the way open to the pursuit of some values, such as jobs, which these people control. It represents a preference for the familiar, with its known satisfactions and its known imperfections, over the risks and the uncertainties as well as the moral costs of the college-boy response, on the one hand, and the delinquent response on the other.

What does the delinquent response have to offer? Let us be clear, first, about what this response is and how it differs from the stable corner-boy response. The hallmark of the delinquent subculture is the explicit and wholesale repudiation of middle-class standards and the adoption of their very antithesis. *The corner-boy culture is not specifically delinquent.* Where it leads to behavior which may be defined as delinquent, *e.g.*, truancy, it does so not because nonconformity to middle-class norms *defines* conformity to corner-boy norms but because conformity to middle-class norms *interferes with* conformity to corner-boy norms. The corner-boy plays truant because he does not like school, because he wishes to escape from a dull and unrewarding and perhaps humiliating situation. But truancy is not defined as intrinsically valuable and status-giving. The member of the delinquent subculture plays truant because "good" middle-class (and working-class) children do not play truant. Corner-boy resistance to being herded and marshalled by middle-class figures is not the same as the delinquent's flouting and jeering of those middle-class figures and active ridicule of those who submit. The corner-boy's ethic of reciprocity, his quasi-communal attitude toward the property of in-group members, is shared by the delinquent. But this ethic of reciprocity does not sanction the deliberate and "malicious" violation of the property rights of persons outside the in-group. We have observed that the differences between the

234 ALBERT K. COHEN

corner-boy and the college-boy or middle-class culture are profound but that in many ways they are profound differences in emphasis. We have remarked that the corner-boy culture does not so much repudiate the value of many middle-class achievements as it emphasizes certain other values which make such achievements improbable. In short, the corner-boy culture temporizes with middle-class morality; the full-fledged delinquent subculture does not.

It is precisely here, we suggest, in the refusal to temporize, that the appeal of the delinquent subculture lies. Let us recall that it is characteristically American, not specifically working-class or middle-class, to measure oneself against the widest possible status universe, to seek status against "all comers," to be "as good as" or "better than" anybody — anybody, that is, within one's own age and sex category. As long as the working-class corner-boy clings to a version, however attenuated and adulterated, of the middle-class culture, he must recognize his inferiority to working-class and middle-class college-boys. The delinquent subculture, on the other hand, permits no ambiguity of the status of the delinquent relative to that of anybody else. In terms of the norms of the delinquent subculture, defined by its negative polarity to the respectable status system, the delinquent's very nonconformity to middle-class standards sets him above the most exemplary college-boy.

Another important function of the delinquent subculture is the legitimation of aggression. We surmise that a certain amount of hostility is generated among working-class children against middle-class persons, with their airs of superiority, disdain or condescension and against middle-class norms, which are, in a sense, the cause of their status-frustration. To infer inclinations to aggression from the existence of frustration is hazardous; we know that aggression is not an inevitable and not the only consequence of frustration. So here too we must feel our way with caution. Ideally, we should like to see systematic research, probably employing "depth interview" and "projective" techniques, to get at the relationship between status position and aggressive

dispositions toward the rules which determine status and toward persons variously distributed in the status hierarchy. Nevertheless, despite our imperfect knowledge of these things, we would be blind if we failed to recognize that bitterness, hostility and jealousy and all sorts of retributive fantasies are among the most common and typically human responses to public humiliation. However, for the child who temporizes with middle-class morality, overt aggression and even the conscious recognition of his own hostile impulses are inhibited, for he acknowledges the *legitimacy* of the rules in terms of which he is stigmatized. For the child who breaks clean with middle-class morality, on the other hand, there are no moral inhibitions on the free expression of aggression against the sources of his frustration. Moreover, the connection we suggest between status-frustration and the aggressiveness of the delinquent subculture seems to us more plausible than many frustration-aggression hypotheses because it involves no assumptions about obscure and dubious "displacement" of aggression against "substitute" targets. The target in this case is the manifest cause of the status problem.

It seems to us that the mechanism of "reaction-formation" should also play a part here. We have made much of the corner-boy's basic ambivalence, his uneasy acknowledgement, while he lives by the standards of his corner-boy culture, of the legitimacy of college-boy standards. May we assume that when the delinquent seeks to obtain unequivocal status by repudiating, once and for all, the norms of the college-boy culture, these norms really undergo total extinction? Or do they, perhaps, linger on, underground, as it were, repressed, unacknowledged but an ever-present threat to the adjustment which has been achieved at no small cost? There is much evidence from clinical psychology that moral norms, once effectively internalized, are not lightly thrust aside or extinguished. If a new moral order is evolved which offers a more satisfactory solution to one's life problems, the old order usually continues to press for recognition, but if this recognition is granted, the applecart is upset. The symptom of this obscurely felt, ever-present threat is clinically known as "anxiety," and the literature of psychiatry is rich with devices for combatting this anxiety, this threat to a hard-won victory. One such device is reaction-formation. Its hallmark is an "exaggerated," "disproportionate," "abnormal" intensity of response, "inappropriate" to the stimulus which seems to elicit it. The unintelligibility of the response, the "over-reaction," becomes intelligible when we see that it has the function of reassuring the actor against an *inner* threat to his defenses as well as the function of meeting an external situation on its own terms. Thus we have the mother who "compulsively" showers "inordinate" affection upon a child to reassure herself against her latent hostility and we have the male adolescent whose awkward and immoderate masculinity reflects a basic insecurity about his own sex-role. In like manner, we would expect the delinquent boy who, after all, has been socialized in a society dominated by a middle-class morality and who can never quite escape the blandishments of middle-class society, to seek to maintain his safeguards against seduction. Reaction-formation, in his case, should take the form of an "irrational," "malicious," "unaccountable" hostility to the enemy within the gates as well as without: the norms of the respectable middle-class society.[9]

If our reasoning is correct, it should throw some light upon the peculiar quality of "property delinquency" in the delinquent subculture. We have already seen how the rewardingness of a college-boy and middle-class way of life depends, to a great extent, upon general respect for property rights. In an urban society, in particular, the possession and display of property are the most ready and public badges of reputable social class status and are, for that reason, extraordinarily ego-involved. That property actually is a reward for middle-class morality is in part only a plausible fiction, but in general there is certainly a relationship between the practice of that morality and the possession of property. The middle-classes have, then, a strong interest in scrupulous regard for property rights, not only because property is "intrinsically" valuable but because the full enjoyment of their status requires that that status be readily recognizable and therefore that property adhere to those who earn it. The cavalier misappropriation or destruction of property, therefore, is not only a diversion or diminution of wealth; it is an attack on the middle-class where their egos are most vulnerable. Group stealing, institutionalized in the delinquent subculture, is not just a way of *getting* something. It is a means that is the antithesis of sober and diligent "labor in a call-

[9] No single strand of our argument concerning the motivation of the delinquent subculture is entirely original. All have been at least adumbrated and some quite trenchantly formulated by others.

The idea that aggressive behavior, including crime and delinquency, are often reactions to difficulties in achieving status in legitimate status systems has been remarked by many, although the systematic linkage between the particular status problems we have described and social class position has not been well developed in the literature. Caroline B. Zachry, for example, in *Emotion and Conduct in Adolescence* (New York: D. Appleton-Century Company, 1940), pp. 187, 200–209, 245–246, has a thoughtful discussion of the ego-damage resulting from inability to compete effectively in school and of the function of aggressive behavior in maintaining self-esteem. Arthur L. Wood, in "Social Disorganization and Crime," *Encyclopedia of Criminology* (New York: Philosophical Library, 1949), pp. 466–471, states that the highest crime rates tend to occur in those minority culture groups "which have become acculturated to the majority-group patterns of behavior, but

due to hostility toward them they have failed to succeed in competition for social status." Robert B. Zajonc, in "Aggressive Attitudes of the 'Stranger' as a Function of Conformity Pressures," *Human Relations*, V (1952), 205–216, has experimentally tested the general hypothesis, although not in connection with delinquency or crime, that a "need to conform" with a pattern of behavior coupled with inability to conform successfully generates hostile attitudes towards that pattern.

The general notion of negativism as an ego-salving type of reaction-formation, which plays such an important part in the theory we have outlined, is common in the psychoanalytical literature. It has been brilliantly developed with specific reference to criminality in a paper by George Devereux, "Social Negativism and Criminal Psychopathology," *Journal of Criminal Psychopathology*, I (April 1940), 322–338 and applied to other behavior problems in George Devereux and Malcolm E. Moos, "The Social Structure of Prisons, and the Organic Tensions," *Journal of Criminal Psychopathology*, IV (October 1942) 306–324.

ing." It expresses contempt for a way of life by making its opposite a criterion of status. Money and other valuables are not, as such, despised by the delinquent. For the delinquent and the non-delinquent alike, money is a most glamorous and efficient means to a variety of ends and one cannot have too much of it. But, in the delinquent subculture, the stolen dollar has an odor of sanctity that does not attach to the dollar saved or the dollar earned.

This delinquent system of values and way of life does its job of problem-solving most effectively when it is adopted as a group solution. We have stressed in our chapter on the general theory of subcultures that the efficacy of a given change in values as a solution and therefore the motivation to such a change depends heavily upon the availability of "reference groups" within which the "deviant values" are already institutionalized, or whose members would stand to profit from such a system of deviant values if each were assured of the support and concurrence of the others. So it is with delinquency. We do not suggest that joining in the creation or perpetuation of a delinquent subculture is the only road to delinquency. We do believe, however, that for most delinquents delinquency would not be available as a response were it not socially legitimized and given a kind of respectability, albeit by a restricted community of fellow-adventurers. In this respect, the adoption of delinquency is like the adoption of the practice of appearing at the office in open-collar and shirt sleeves. Is it much more comfortable, is it more sensible than the full regalia? Is it neat? Is it dignified? The arguments in the affirmative will appear much more forceful if the practice is already established in one's milieu or if one senses that others are prepared to go along if someone makes the first tentative gestures. Indeed, to many of those who sweat and chafe in ties and jackets, the possibility of an alternative may not even occur until they discover that it has been adopted by their colleagues.

This way of looking at delinquency suggests an answer to a certain paradox. Countless mothers have protested that their "Johnny" was a good boy until he fell in with a certain bunch. But the mothers of each of Johnny's companions hold the same view with respect to their own offspring. It is conceivable and even probable that some of these mothers are naive, that one or more of these youngsters are "rotten apples" who infected the others. We suggest, however, that all of the mothers may be right, that there is a certain chemistry in the group situation itself which engenders that which was not there before, that group interaction is a sort of catalyst which releases potentialities not otherwise visible. This is especially true when we are dealing with a problem of status-frustration. Status, by definition, is a grant of respect from others. A new system of norms, which measures status by criteria which one can meet, is of no value unless others are prepared to apply those criteria, and others are not likely to do so unless one is prepared to reciprocate.[10]

We have referred to a lingering ambivalence in the delinquent's own value system, an ambivalence which threatens the adjustment he has achieved and which is met through the mechanism of reaction-formation. The delinquent may have to contend with another ambivalence, in the area of his status sources. The delinquent subculture offers him status *as against* other children of whatever social level, but it offers him this status *in the eyes of* his fellow delinquents only. To the extent that

[10] The distinguished criminologist, Sutherland, apparently had this in mind when he wrote: "It is not necessary that there be bad boys inducing good boys to commit offenses. It is generally a mutual stimulation, as a result of which each of the boys commits delinquencies which he would not commit alone." Edwin H. Sutherland, *Principles of Criminology* (New York: J. B. Lippincott Company, 1947), p. 145. Having made the point, however, Sutherland failed to develop its implications, and in his general theory of criminal behavior the function of the group or the gang is not collectively to *contrive* delinquency but merely to *transmit* the delinquent tradition and to provide protection to the members of the group. Fritz Redl, on the other hand, in "The Psychology of Gang Formation and the Treatment of Juvenile Delinquents," *The Psychoanalytic Study of the Child*, Vol. I (New York: International Universities Press, 1945), pp. 367–377, has developed at considerable length the ways in which the group makes possible for its members behavior which would otherwise not be available to them.

there remains a desire for recognition from groups whose respect has been forfeited by commitment to a new subculture, his satisfaction in his solution is imperfect and adulterated. He can perfect his solution only by rejecting as status sources those who reject him. This too may require a certain measure of reaction-formation, going beyond indifference to active hostility and contempt for all those who do not share his subculture. He becomes all the more dependent upon his delinquent gang. Outside that gang his status position is now weaker than ever. The gang itself tends toward a kind of sectarian solidarity, because the benefits of membership can only be realized in active face-to-face relationships with group members.

This interpretation of the delinquent subculture has important implications for the "sociology of social problems." People are prone to assume that those things which we define as evil and those which we define as good have their origins in separate and distinct features of our society. Evil flows from poisoned wells; good flows from pure and crystal fountains. The same source cannot feed both. Our view is different. It holds that those values which are at the core of "the American way of life," which help to motivate the behavior which we most esteem as "typically American," are among the major determinants of that which we stigmatize as "pathological." More specifically, it holds that the problems of adjustment to which the delinquent subculture is a response are determined, in part, by those very values which respectable society holds most sacred. The same value system, impinging upon children differently equipped to meet it, is instrumental in generating both delinquency and respectability.

Kitsuse and Dietrick remind us that it is incorrect to interpret Cohen's explanation of the content and distribution of the delinquent subculture as a theory of juvenile delinquency. They then offer three substantive criticisms of his theory of the delinquent subculture. With appropriate textual exegesis they observe that the evidence is equivocal for Cohen's proposition that working-class boys are oriented to achieve status in the middle-class system. They question whether introduction of the concept "reaction formation" is warranted, and they suggest that Cohen's description of "delinquent subculture" is not independent of the theory he proposed to explain it. These criticisms point to empirical ambiguities and logical inconsistencies in Cohen's work.

In addition to these substantive criticisms Kitsuse and Dietrick say that the theory is an historical construction, and as it is stated, a test of the theory is impossible other than through historical reconstruction (see O'Donnell [1967] for such an attempt with respect to the addict subculture). If the theory is inherently untestable, either directly or through the derivation of hypotheses, then it will remain merely plausible and the substantive criticisms of the theory are primarily of academic interest. The heuristic value of Cohen's explanation of the origin of the delinquent subculture lies, Kitsuse and Dietrick suggest, in the clues it offers to explain the continuation of that subculture, and the propositions regarding maintenance of the delinquent subculture that Kitsuse and Dietrick derive from the theory deserve careful attention.

REFERENCE

John A. O'Donnell, "The Rise and Decline of a Subculture," *Social Problems*, 15 (Summer 1967), pp. 73–84.

JOHN I. KITSUSE

DAVID C. DIETRICK

Delinquent Boys: A Critique

One of the most provocative theoretical formulations concerning juvenile delinquency is that contained in Albert K. Cohen's *Delinquent Boys: The Culture of the Gang*.[1] The reviews of Cohen's monograph are enthusiastic in their praise,[2] and one textbook has already incorporated the theory of the delinquent subculture as the major framework for the discussion of juvenile delinquency.[3] Sykes and Matza, Wilensky and Lebeaux, Merton, and Kobrin and Finestone [4] have questioned various propositions and implications of Cohen's thesis, but their discussions are limited to rather specific issues. In view of the impressive reception

which has greeted Cohen's work, his theory of the delinquent subculture deserves a more detailed and systematic examination.

The primary concern of Cohen's inquiry is stated clearly and repeatedly throughout the study: the theoretical task is to explain the content and distribution of the delinquent subculture. Cohen offers his theory to fill a gap in the cultural transmission theories of delinquency which assert that individuals become delinquent because they learn the values, attitudes, and techniques of the delinquent group. The theory of the delinquent subculture attempts to account for the content of what the delinquent learns. Thus, Cohen does *not* purport to present a theory of delinquency.

Although Cohen is explicit about the limited and specific nature of the problem he is addressing, his theory has been interpreted and discussed as a theory of juvenile delinquency.[5] Indeed, the psychological terms in which Cohen couches his discussion and the logic of his thesis invite such an interpretation. In this paper, therefore, Cohen's thesis is critically examined both as a theory of the delinquent subculture and as a theory of delinquency. We contend that (1) Cohen does not present adequate support, either in theory or in fact, for his explanation of the delinquent subculture, (2) the methodological basis of the theory renders it inherently untestable, (3) the theory is ambiguous concerning the relation between the *emergence* of the subculture and its *mainte-*

From *American Sociological Review*, April 1959, pp. 208–215. Reprinted by permission of the American Sociological Association.

[1] Glencoe, Ill.: Free Press, 1955.

[2] See reviews by Frank E. Hartung, *American Sociological Review*, 20 (December 1955), pp. 751–752; Donnell M. Poppenfort, *American Journal of Sociology*, 62 (July 1956), pp. 125–126; Hermann Mannheim, *British Journal of Sociology*, 7 (June 1956), pp. 147–152; Max Benedict, *The British Journal of Delinquency*, 7 (October 1956), pp. 323–324; Gilbert Shapiro, *Dissent*, 3 (Winter 1956), pp. 89–92.

[3] Jessie Bernard, *Social Problems at Midcentury*, New York: Dryden, 1957, Chapter 18.

[4] See, respectively, Gresham M. Sykes and David Matza, "Techniques of Neutralization," *American Sociological Review*, 22 (December 1957), pp. 664–670; Harold Wilensky and Charles Lebeaux, *Industrial Society and Social Welfare*, New York: Russell Sage Foundation, 1958, Chapter 9; Robert K. Merton, *Social Theory and Social Structure*, Glencoe, Ill.: Free Press, 1957, pp. 177–179; and Solomon Kobrin and Harold Finestone, "A Proposed Framework for the Analysis of Juvenile Delinquency," presented at the meeting of the American Sociological Society, August 1958.

[5] See, e.g., Bernard, *op. cit.*; Marshall B. Clinard, *Sociology of Deviant Behavior*, New York: Rinehart, 1957, pp. 182–183.

nance, and (4) the theory should include an explanation of the persistence of the subculture if it is to meet an adequate test. In the following section, we remain close to Cohen's statements and analyze them for their internal consistency.

The Theory of the Delinquent Subculture

Cohen addresses himself to the task of constructing a theory which will explain two sets of "known facts": first, the content of what he calls the "delinquent subculture," which is characterized by maliciousness, non-utilitarianism, and negativism; and, second, the concentration of that subculture among the male, working-class segment of the population.[6]

The propositions in Cohen's theory may be stated briefly as follows:

1. The working-class boy faces a characteristic problem of adjustment which is qualitatively different from that of the middle-class boy.
2. The working-class boy's problem is one of "status-frustration," the basis of which is systematically generated by his early exposure to the working-class pattern of socialization.
3. The working-class boy's socialization handicaps him for achievement in the middle-class status system.
4. Nevertheless, he is thrust into this competitive system where achievement is judged by middle-class standards of behavior and performance.
5. Ill-prepared and poorly motivated, the working-class boy is frustrated in his status aspirations by the agents of middle-class society.
6. The delinquent subculture represents a "solution" to the working-class boy's problem for it enables him to "break

clean" with the middle-class morality and legitimizes hostility and aggression "without moral inhibitions on the free expression of aggression against the sources of his frustration."[7]
7. Thus, the delinquent subculture is characterized by non-utilitarian, malicious, and negativistic values as "an attack on the middle-class where their egos are most vulnerable. . . . It expresses contempt for a way of life by making its opposite a criterion of status."[8]

The Working-Class Boy's Problem

What are the logic and the evidence presented in support of Cohen's theory? He begins by noting the class differentials in the socialization experience of the child which handicaps the working-class boy in his competition for status in the middle-class system. For example: the working-class boy's social and cultural environment does not systematically support the middle-class ethic of ambition to get ahead; he is not socialized in techniques of discipline and hard work; his behavior is oriented to immediate satisfactions rather than to future goals. Thus, the working-class boy is not socialized to middle-class norms. "To this extent he is less likely to identify with these norms, to 'make them his own,' and to be able to conform to them easily and 'naturally.' "[9]

What then is the basis for the working-class boy's fundamental ambivalence toward the middle-class system that seeks and finds a solution in the delinquent subculture? His ambivalence, according to Cohen, is due to the fact that, in American society, children are compared with "all comers" by a single standard of performance which embodies the norms of the middle class. Neither the working-class boy nor his parents can ignore or deny the dominance of middle-class norms for they comprise the code of "the distinguished people who symbolize and represent the local and national communities with which the children iden-

---

[6] Cohen, *op. cit.,* pp. 36–44. It should be noted that Cohen's assertion that the *delinquent subculture* is concentrated in the working-class is based on an inference from data, not specifically classified with respect to their subcultural character, which suggest the concentration of *delinquency* in that social stratum.

[7] *Ibid.,* p. 132.
[8] *Ibid.,* p. 134.
[9] *Ibid.,* p. 97.

tify." [10] Confronted by the obvious dominance and prestige of middle-class values, the working-class boy is drawn to the "American Dream."

We note a persistent ambiguity in Cohen's statements. The working-class boy faces a problem of adjustment "to the degree to which he values the good opinion of middle-class persons or because he has to some degree internalized middle-class standards himself. . . ." [11] On the other hand, Cohen acknowledges, "it may be argued that the working-class boy does not *care* what middle-class people think of him." [12] He suggests, and rightly so, that this is an empirical question. Nevertheless, Cohen proceeds to develop his thesis with the assertion that "there is, however, reason to believe that most children are sensitive *to some degree* about the attitudes of *any persons* with whom they are thrown into more than the most superficial kind of contact." [13]

Cohen's reasons for rejecting the argument that the working-class boy may not care what middle-class people think (which is crucial for his theory) are not convincing. Indeed, his statements about the working-class boy's socialization lend strong support to the contrary view.[14] If there are in fact class differences in socialization, surely they may be expected to insulate the working-class boy from the re-

sponses of middle-class people. Furthermore, it would appear that the working-class boy's problem is a minor one if it depends on "the degree to which he values middle-class persons" or if it rests upon the argument that he is "sensitive *to some degree*" about the attitudes of others. On the strength of his statements, the rejected proposition seems equally plausible, namely, that the working-class boy is *not* oriented to status in the middle-class system. As Cohen himself suggests, "satisfactory emotional relationships with his peers are likely to be more important" for the working-class boy than for his middle-class counterpart.

The Reaction-Formation Concept

Cohen's explanation of the distinctive content of the delinquent subculture and "what it has to offer" to the working-class boy is anchored in the concept of "reaction-formation." His use of this psychological concept deserves careful examination, for reaction-formation provides the key to his explication of the non-utilitarian, malicious, and negativistic character of the delinquent subculture.

A reaction-formation is a psychological mechanism which "attempts to deny or to repress some impulses, or to defend the person against some instinctual danger. . . . The original opposite attitudes still exist in the unconscious." [15] In the context of Cohen's argument, the "impulse" is the working-class boy's desire for middle-class status which, if expressed, would only be frustrated. Therefore, the reaction-formation is instituted against it.

Is the ambivalence described by Cohen sufficient warrant for the introduction of this psychological concept? Cohen states that the reaction-formation in the case of the working-class boy who responds to the delinquent subculture "should take the form of an 'irrational,' 'malicious,' and 'unaccountable' hostility to the enemy within the gates as well as without: the norms of the respectable middle-class society." He suggests: "the unintelligibility of the response, the 'overreaction,' becomes intelligible when we see that it has the function of reassuring the actor against an *inner* threat to his

10 *Ibid.*, p. 87.
11 *Ibid.*, p. 119.
12 *Ibid.*, p. 123, Cohen's emphasis.
13 *Ibid.*, p. 123, Cohen's emphases.
14 Thus Cohen states, "In general, the working-class person appears to be more dependent upon and 'at home' in primary groups [presumably among his own social class] and to avoid secondary, segmental relationships more than the middle-class person." (*Ibid.*, p. 97) Again, "The working-class child is more often thrown upon his own or the company of an autonomous group of peers." (p. 100) He suggests further that "At the same time, it seems likely, although this aspect of differential socialization has not been so well explored, that the working-class child is more dependent emotionally and for the satisfaction of many practical needs upon his relationships to his peer groups. . . . Satisfactory emotional relationships with his peers are likely to be more important, their claims to be more imperious, and the rewards they offer to compete more effectively with parental [and we might add, teacher] expectations." (p. 101)

15 Otto Fenichel, *Psychoanalytic Theory of Neurosis*, New York: Norton, 1945, p. 151.

defenses as well as the function of meeting an external situation on its own terms. . . . We would expect the delinquent boy, who, after all, has been socialized in a society dominated by a middle-class morality and who can never quite escape the blandishments of middle-class society, to seek to maintain his safeguards against seduction." [16]

Clearly, Cohen's use of reaction-formation assumes that the delinquent boy is *strongly and fundamentally ambivalent* about status in the middle-class system, and that he "cares" so intensely about improving his status within the system that he is faced with a genuine problem of adjustment. Cohen's theory stands on this assumption which is, by his own admission, on "somewhat speculative ground where fundamental research remains to be done." [17]

Cohen's description of the social and cultural conditions of the working-class boy is a tenuous base from which to posit the internalization of middle-class values. A more reasonable and obvious question is: How under such conditions are such values significantly communicated to the working-class boy at all? According to Cohen, in his daily encounters with the middle-class system, the working-class boy suffers humiliation, shame, embarrassment, rejection, derision, and the like as a consequence of his family background. Similarly, in the settlement houses, recreation centers, and other welfare agencies, the working-class boy is exposed to the "critical or at best condescending surveillance of people who are 'foreigners' to his community and who appraise him in terms of values *which he does not share.* . . . To win favor of the people in charge he must change his habits, his values, his ambitions, his speech and his associates. Even were these things possible, the game might not be worth the candle. So, having sampled what they have to offer, he turns to the street or to his 'clubhouse' in a cellar where 'facilities' are meager but human relations more satisfying." [18] In this description of the working-class boy's perceptions of the middle-class system, the implication is clear that it is not that the work-

ing-class boy's status aspirations are frustrated (that is, he is motivated but is unable to achieve prestigeful status in the middle-class system), but rather that he does not want to strive for status in the system, and that he resents the intrusion of "foreigners" who seek to impose upon him an irrelevant way of life.

Cohen's image of the working-class boy, who admittedly is extremely dependent upon his gang, standing alone to face humiliation at the hands of middle-class agents is difficult to comprehend. To add to this picture of the pre-teen and teen-ager an intense desire to gain status in the middle-class system, which when frustrated provides sufficient basis for a reaction-formation response, is to overdraw him beyond recognition. Even in "Elmtown," to which Cohen refers, it is difficult to conceive of the working-class boy exposed to the middle-class environment unprotected by the support of his peer group. When we realize that Cohen's formulation applies, presumably, more directly to schools in urban areas which are predominantly working-class in composition, confusion is compounded.

Again, *why* does Cohen insist upon the working-class boy's ambivalence toward the middle-class system? His discussion of alternative subcultural responses among working-class boys to the problem of status-frustration may provide a clue. He specifies three modes of response: that of the college-boy, of the "stable corner-boy," and the delinquent boy response. The college-boy deserts the corner-boy way of life and accepts the "challenge of the middle-class status system," conforming to its rules.[19] The stable corner-boy culture "does not so much repudiate the value of middle-class achievements as it emphasizes certain other values which make such achievements improbable. . . . The corner-boy culture temporizes the middle-class morality." [20] It is the delinquent response, legitimized by the subculture, that represents the reaction-formation of a wholehearted repudiation of middle-class morality.

It would appear that, of the three categories of respondents, the working-class boys who

[16] Cohen, *op. cit.*, p. 133, Cohen's emphasis.
[17] *Ibid.*, p. 127.
[18] *Ibid.*, p. 117, emphasis added.
[19] *Ibid.*, p. 128.
[20] *Ibid.*, p. 130.

find a solution in the delinquent subculture are those who are faced with the most serious problems of status-frustration and ambivalence. The logic of the reaction-formation thesis leads us to conclude that, of the three modes of adjustment, the delinqent boys' is an expression of the *most serious* problems of status-frustration and ambivalence. We must assume that the intensity of the hostility and aggression against the middle-class system is a measure of status-frustration and ambivalence.

Theoretically, the college-boy is equally ambivalent about the middle-class system, yet Cohen does not invoke the concept of reaction-formation to account for *his* (the college-boy's) rejection of (or reaction against) working-class values. If the price of the working-class boy's accommodation to the middle-class system is that he must "change his habits, his values, his ambitions, his speech and his associates," would not the college-boy response entail more than an acceptance of the challenge to compete within the system on its own terms? [21]

The Description of the Delinquent Subculture

Cohen's emphasis upon the "positive" aspect of the college-boy response contrasts with his stress upon the "negative" aspect of the delinquent response, which leads him, we suggest, to describe the delinquent subculture as an irrational, malicious attack on the middle-class system. This raises the more fundamental question about his *description* of the subculture, "the facts to be explained."

"Non-utilitarian," "malicious," and "negativistic" are, we suggest, interpretive categories of description which are not independent of Cohen's explanation of the delinquent subculture. For example, the imputation of intent, implicit in his description of malice, is open to serious doubt.[22] We do not deny that subcul-

ture delinquency is marked by such distinctive characteristics as the systematic extortion of money from younger, defenseless children. What is at issue here is the interpretation of this kind of delinquent behavior, an interpretation directed systematically at the middle-class as a consequence of the frustration of ambivalent status aspirations.

It is important that we keep apace the facts. Cohen's description of the delinquent subculture does not fit the behavior of contemporary delinquent gangs.[23] They are not engaged in replacing one stolen hat with another from store to store, or delighting in the terrorizing of "good" children by driving them from playgrounds and gyms. The delinquents whose activities are organized by a delinquent subculture are attending to more serious enterprises. There is no absence of rational, calculated, utilitarian behavior among delinquent gangs, as they exist today. To describe the activities of such gangs as non-utilitarian, malicious, and negativistic gives the misleading view that they somehow represent a child's angry outbursts against the injustices of a world he never made.

It is also important to guard against the tendency to apply different standards for interpreting the behavior of class-differentiated groups. There is ample evidence in the daily press that middle-class adolescents are engaged in the kinds of activities that Cohen cites to support his description of the working-class delinquent subculture. To be sure, such reports appear less frequently under banner headlines than do the exploits of working-class delinquents; and middle-class delinquency does not prompt, as does working-class delinquency, edi-

---

[21] *Ibid.*, p. 127.

[22] Martha M. Eliot, Chief of the Children's Bureau, has observed, "We are too inclined to make vandalism a catch-all phrase which imputes to the vandal hostile antagonisms toward society, then to compound the catch-all by saying that vandals, by and large, are teen-agers. But if teen-agers are vandals, why are they any more so than children of any age?" "What is Vandalism?" *Federal Probation*, 18 (March 1954), p. 3.

[23] See, e.g., Sam Glane, "Juvenile Gangs in East Side Los Angeles," *Focus*, 29 (September 1950), pp. 136–141; Dale Kramer and Madeline Karr, *Teen-Age Gangs*, New York: Henry Holt, 1953; Stacy V. Jones, "The Cougars — Life with a Brooklyn Gang," *Harper's Magazine*, 209 (November 1954), pp. 35–43; Paul C. Crawford, Daniel I. Malamud, and James R. Dumpson, *Working with Teen-Age Gangs*, New York: New York Welfare Council, 1950; Harrison E. Salisbury, "The Shook-Up Generation," *New York Times*, March 24–30, 1958; Dan Wakefield, "The Gang That Went Good," *Harper's Magazine*, 216 (June 1958), pp. 36–43.

torial clamor for a radical and thorough revision of programs of control. For example, acts of vandalism committed by college boys on the facilities rented for fraternity dances and other occasions occur with annual regularity.[24] In view of the great probability that such instances of middle-class gang delinquency are substantially under-reported, it would be an arbitrary preconception to dismiss them as no more than scattered and rare occurrences.

The Test of Cohen's Theory

In the preceding discussion we argue that, first, Cohen does not present adequate support for his formulation of "the working-class boy's problem," second, his description of the working-class boy's ambivalence toward the middle-class system does not warrant the use of the reaction-formation concept, and, third, his description of the delinquent subculture, the "facts" to which his theory is addressed, is open to question. While these criticisms are presented as logical ambiguities and inconsistencies in Cohen's statements, it may be maintained nevertheless that empirical research demonstrates the validity of his major thesis. In turning to this question, we suspend the criticisms formulated above, and examine the methodology of Cohen's theory.

The Historical Method and Empirical Research

What, then, are the research directives of the theory of the delinquent subculture?

[24] One Southern California college fraternity has depleted a long list of rental facilities where their patronage is no longer solicited. The last dance held by this fraternity was the scene of a minor riot which required a force of thirty regular and reserve police officers to control. Acts of vandalism included ripping fixtures from the walls, entering the ballroom dripping with water from the swimming pool, tearing radio antennae from police cars, etc. Lest this example be dismissed as institutionalized saturnalia, other instances may be cited which the community was less willing to view as mere pranks. In Los Angeles, a group of high school seniors of undisputedly middle-class families committed an "unprovoked" act of setting fire to a school building. In another case, several middle-class adolescents in Glendale, California were convicted for stomping on the hoods and roofs of automobiles in that city. And so on.

When this problem is analyzed, Cohen's methodology presents numerous difficulties, for his theory is an historical construction addressed to the explanation of the *emergence* of an existing subculture and its *present* concentration among the working-class male population. Furthermore, the basic propositions of this explanation utilize concepts which require data about the psychological characteristics of past populations.

Cohen's use of the present indicative in the development of his theory is misleading, for the interpretation of the rise of the delinquent subculture requires historical data. It is not that the working-class boy *is* ambivalent about middle-class values; the theory requires only that at some unspecified time when the delinquent subculture emerged, the working-class boy *was* ambivalent about middle-class values.

Subculture Maintenance and Motivation

There is no objection *per se* to a plausible explanation that cannot be tested if the explanation is viewed as an heuristic device for the generating of hypotheses. If then a direct test of Cohen's theory through the measurement of deduced empirical regularities is not possible as a practical matter, is it feasible to approach the problem from a functional point of view? The question may be phrased: what are the necessary conditions for the maintenance of the delinquent subculture? On this question, Cohen's statements are quite explicit. Commenting on the fact that his theory is not concerned with the processes by which one boy becomes delinquent while another does not, Cohen writes:

We have tried to show that a subculture owes its existence to the fact that it provides a solution to certain problems of adjustment shared among a community of individuals. However, it does not follow that for every individual who participates these problems provide the sole or sufficient source of motivation. Indeed, there may be some participants to whose motivation these problems contribute very little. . . . Our delinquent subculture . . . is not a disembodied set of beliefs and practices but is "carried" and supported by groups with distinctive personnel. A position in this organization or affiliation with this or that particular member may offer other satisfactions which help to account for the participation of certain members but do not help to explain the content of the culture in which they participate.[25]

An implication of this statement is that the maintenance of the delinquent subculture is not wholly dependent upon the motivational structure which explains its emergence. Not *every* individual who participates in the delinquent subculture need be so motivated and, for some, such motivation may be peripheral if not irrelevant. Clearly an investigation of the motivations which lead individuals to participate in the delinquent subculture does not constitute even an indirect test of the theory. For the statement may be read to mean that once the subculture is established, it can be maintained by the behavior of individuals who bring a diverse range of motivations to the gangs which embody the delinquent subculture. Thus, functionally, the delinquent subculture requires another explanation.

The Double Dilemma: Theory and Method

The theoretical significance of Cohen's explanation of the emergence of the delinquent subculture, however, lies precisely in its relevance for an explanation of the maintenance of that subculture. Were this not so, the theory could be dismissed as merely plausible and untestable or as incapable of generating hypotheses about regularities other than the pre-existing "facts" which it explains. We suggest that the statement quoted above presents a methodological dilemma by divorcing the dynamics of the etiology of the delinquent subculture from the dynamics of its maintenance. Cohen is correct of course in asserting that, theoretically, the former does not necessarily require the same motivational dynamics as the latter. However, the ambiguity of his statement lies in his implicit concession that *some* of the participants in the subculture must have the characteristic motivational structure posited in the theory.

The research dilemma posed by Cohen's theory is two-fold. Methodologically, the historical method relies upon data concerning the

25 Cohen, *op. cit.*, p. 148.

psychological dynamics of a population which are difficult if not impossible to obtain. Theoretically, the motivational dynamics posited as necessary for the *emergence* of the delinquent subculture is considered either (a) independent of the motivational dynamics necessary for the *maintenance* of the subculture, or (b) dependent upon it in some unspecified relationship.

In view of these difficulties, it may be fruitful to turn the problem around and ask: What are the consequences of participation in the delinquent subculture for the motivational structure of the participants? This question places the theory of the delinquent subculture in its proper relation to the value-transmission theories of delinquency, and directs us to examine the heuristic value of Cohen's theory. Viewing his theory from this perspective, the following propositions about the maintenance of the delinquent subculture may be stated:

1. The individual learns the values of the delinquent subculture through his participation in gangs which embody that subculture.
2. The motivations of individuals for participating in such gangs are varied.
3. The malicious, non-utilitarian, and negativistic behavior which is learned through participation in the subculture is met by formal negative sanctions, rejection, and limitation of access to prestigeful status within the middle-class system.
4. Thus, participation in the delinquent subculture creates similar problems for all its participants.
5. The participants' response to the barriers raised to exclude them from status in the middle-class system (that is, the "problem") is a hostile rejection of the standards of "respectable" society and an emphasis upon status within the delinquent gang.
6. The hostile rejection response reinforces the malicious, non-utilitarian, and negativistic norms of the subculture.

The formulation suggested here relates Cohen's explanation of the emergence of the delinquent subculture with an explanation of its maintenance. It hypothesizes that the delinquent subculture persists because, once established, it creates for those who participate in it, the very problems which were the bases for its emergence. It is possible to derive the further hypothesis that the motivational structure of the participants of the subculture displays characteristics similar to those described by Cohen.

Conclusions

In this paper, we have critically examined Cohen's monograph for its implications for theory and method. The problems raised in the first part of our critique cannot be resolved by logical argumentation. Indeed, we have suggested that insofar as they are consequences of the historical method, research to test the validity of Cohen's statements, as a practical matter, is impossible. If, however, the theory of the delinquent subculture is read for its heuristic value, its significance for theory and research is not limited to the field of juvenile delinquency, but extends to the more general problem of the dynamics of subcultural maintenance.

Delinquency and Opportunity

In *Delinquency and Opportunity*, the source of this selection, Cloward and Ohlin are concerned with those forms of delinquent behavior resulting "from the performance of social roles *specifically provided and supported by delinquent subcultures*" (1960:9). The delinquent subculture, they suggest, is distinguished from other deviant subcultures by the central place accorded to specifically delinquent behavior; and they define a "delinquent subculture" as *"one in which certain forms of delinquent activity are essential requirements for the performance of the dominant roles supported by the subculture"* (1960:7). Toby (1961) suggests that gang delinquency as defined by Cloward and Ohlin may amount to no more than 10 percent of the cases handled by American juvenile courts, and he raises the as yet unanswered question whether the etiological process postulated by the authors is also relevant to other types of delinquency.

Writing in the Mertonian tradition, Cloward and Ohlin, like Cohen, take the class system as their point of departure. They propose the following central hypothesis: "The disparity between what lower-class youth are led to want and what is actually available to them is the source of a major problem of adjustment. Adolescents who form delinquent subcultures, we suggest, have internalized an emphasis upon conventional goals. Faced with limitations on legitimate avenues of access to these goals, and unable to revise their aspirations downward, they experience intense frustrations; the exploration of nonconformist alternatives may be the result" (1960:86).

Cloward and Ohlin propose that youth in slums accept the equalitarian ideology of American society in which they are promised a fair share of the good things in life, but they recognize that ethnic and class barriers will prevent them from realizing their aspirations for money and the things money will buy. The result of the anticipation of failure is "alienation," which is defined as "a process of withdrawal of attributions of legitimacy from established social norms" (1960:110). In addition to being "freed from commitment to and belief in the legitimacy of certain aspects of the existing organization of means" (1960:110), the disenchanted youth must seek support from others to develop a collective, rather than an individual, solution to their adjustment problems. They also have to develop "appropriate means for handling the problems of guilt and fear" (1960:110) which may result from engaging in deviant acts; Cloward and Ohlin suggest that this may be accomplished by the development of a set of rationalizations or "a supporting structure of beliefs and values that provide advance justification for deviant conduct" (1960:132). Finally, the members of a newly emerging subculture "must face no obstacles to the possibility of joint problem-solving" (1960:110).

In the cited quotation from Cloward and Ohlin (1960:86) the authors do not propose that deprivation *will* result in the evolution of delinquent subcultures, but that it *may*. Their position is that adolescents whose paths to conventional goals are blocked and who simultaneously find illegitimate avenues open are the ones who become gang delinquents. For some years it has been recognized that legitimate opportunities are limited for some youth; Cloward and Ohlin argue that illegitimate opportunities are not, as sometimes assumed, equally available to all. Thus, whether the feeling of unjust deprivation results in the development of a delinquent subculture depends on the availability of illegitimate means as does the type of subculture which may emerge.

Cloward and Ohlin propose that three major types of delinquent subculture are encountered among lower-class adolescent males in metropolitan areas: (1) criminal, (2) conflict, and (3) retreatist. Their description of these three types is included in this selection. Differentiating between integrated and unintegrated slums, Cloward and Ohlin suggest that the social milieu affects the nature of the deviant response. They speculate that in integrated slums youngsters can associate on an intimate and stable basis with sophisticated offenders, and the adult criminals serve as role models and as sources of criminal values and skills. In such a setting the criminal subculture emerges. In unintegrated areas, characterized by vertical and geographic mobility, transiency, and instability and epitomized by massive housing projects, criminal role models and opportunity structures are not available. In such areas youth "are relatively deprived of *both* conventional and criminal opportunity" (1960:172), and conflict subcultures emerge in which the manipulation of violence serves as a route to status or "rep" (reputation). Finally, it is hypothesized that participants in the third type, the retreatist subculture, are "double-failures," or failures in the use of *both* legitimate and illegitimate means. Cloward and Ohlin do not believe that all double failures will become retreatists: "It may be that those who become retreatists are incapable of revising their aspirations downward to correspond to reality" (1960:184).

REFERENCE

Jackson Toby, "Delinquency and Opportunity," *The British Journal of Sociology*, 12 (September 1961), pp. 282–289.

RICHARD A. CLOWARD
LLOYD E. OHLIN

Differential Opportunity and Delinquent Subcultures

The Availability of Illegitimate Means

Social norms are two-sided. A prescription implies the existence of a prohibition, and vice versa. To advocate honesty is to demarcate and condemn a set of actions which are dishonest. In other words, norms that define legitimate practices also implicitly define illegitimate practices. One purpose of norms, in fact, is to delineate the boundary between legitimate and illegitimate practices. In setting this boundary, in segregating and classifying various types of behavior, they make us aware not only of behavior that is regarded as right and proper but also of behavior that is said to be wrong and improper. Thus the criminal who engages in theft or fraud does not invent a new way of life; the possibility of employing alternative means is acknowledged, tacitly at least, by the norms of the culture.

This tendency for proscribed alternatives to be implicit in every prescription, and vice versa, although widely recognized, is nevertheless a reef upon which many a theory of delinquency has foundered. Much of the criminological literature assumes, for example, that one may explain a criminal act simply by accounting for the individual's readiness to employ illegal alternatives of which his culture, through its norms, has already made him generally aware. Such explanations are quite unsatisfactory, however, for they ignore a host of questions regarding the *relative availability* of illegal alternatives to various potential criminals. The aspiration to be a physician is hardly enough to explain the fact of becoming a physician; there is much that transpires between the aspiration and the achievement. This is no less true of the person who wants to be a successful criminal. Having decided

that he "can't make it legitimately," he cannot simply choose among an array of illegitimate means, all equally available to him. . . . It is assumed in the theory of anomie that access to conventional means is differentially distributed, that some individuals, because of their social class, enjoy certain advantages that are denied to those elsewhere in the class structure. For example, there are variations in the degree to which members of various classes are fully exposed to and thus acquire the values, knowledge, and skills that facilitate upward mobility. It should not be startling, therefore, to suggest that there are socially structured variations in the availability of illegitimate means as well. In connection with delinquent subcultures, we shall be concerned principally with differentials in access to illegitimate means within the lower class.

Many sociologists have alluded to differentials in access to illegitimate means without explicitly incorporating this variable into a theory of deviant behavior. This is particularly true of scholars in the "Chicago tradition" of criminology. Two closely related theoretical perspectives emerged from this school. The theory of "cultural transmission," advanced by Clifford R. Shaw and Henry D. McKay, focuses on the development in some urban neighborhoods of a criminal tradition that persists from one generation to another despite constant changes in population.[1] In the theory of "differential association," Edwin H. Sutherland described the processes by which criminal values are taken over by the individual.[2]

[1] See esp. C. R. Shaw, *The Jack-Roller* (Chicago: University of Chicago Press, 1930); Shaw, *The Natural History of a Delinquent Career* (Chicago: University of Chicago Press, 1931); Shaw et al., *Delinquency Areas* (Chicago: University of Chicago Press, 1929); and Shaw and H. D. McKay, *Juvenile Delinquency and Urban Areas* (Chicago: University of Chicago Press, 1942).

[2] E. H. Sutherland, ed., *The Professional Thief* (Chicago: University of Chicago Press, 1937); and

He asserted that criminal behavior is learned, and that it is learned in interaction with others who have already incorporated criminal values. Thus the first theory stresses the value systems of different areas; the second, the systems of social relationships that facilitate or impede the acquisition of these values.

Scholars in the Chicago tradition, who emphasized the processes involved in learning to be criminal, were actually pointing to differentials in the availability of illegal means — although they did not explicitly recognize this variable in their analysis. This can perhaps best be seen by examining Sutherland's classic work, *The Professional Thief.* "An inclination to steal," according to Sutherland, "is not a sufficient explanation of the genesis of the professional thief." [3] The "self-made" thief, lacking knowledge of the ways of securing immunity from prosecution and similar techniques of defense, "would quickly land in prison; . . . a person can be a professional thief only if he is recognized and received as such by other professional thieves." But recognition is not freely accorded: "Selection and tutelage are the two necessary elements in the process of acquiring recognition as a professional thief. . . . A person cannot acquire recognition as a professional thief until he has had tutelage in professional theft, *and tutelage is given only to a few persons selected from the total population.*" For one thing, "the person must be appreciated by the professional thieves. He must be appraised as having an adequate equipment of wits, front, talking-ability, honesty, reliability, nerve and determination." Furthermore, the aspirant is judged by high standards of performance, for only "a very small percentage of those who start on this process ever reach the stage of professional thief. . . ." Thus motivation and pressures toward deviance do not fully account for deviant behavior any more than motivation and pressures toward conformity account for conforming behavior. The individual must have access to a learning environment and, once having been

trained, must be allowed to perform his role. Roles, whether conforming or deviant in content, are not necessarily freely available; access to them depends upon a variety of factors, such as one's socioeconomic position, age, sex, ethnic affiliation, personality characteristics, and the like. The potential thief, like the potential physician, finds that access to his goal is governed by many criteria other than merit and motivation.

What we are asserting is that access to illegitimate roles is not freely available to all, as is commonly assumed. Only those neighborhoods in which crime flourishes as a stable, indigenous institution are fertile criminal learning environments for the young. Because these environments afford integration of different age-levels of offenders, selected young people are exposed to "differential association" through which tutelage is provided and criminal values and skills are acquired. To be prepared for the role may not, however, ensure that the individual will ever discharge it. One important limitation is that more youngsters are recruited into these patterns of differential associations than the adult criminal structure can possibly absorb. Since there is a surplus of contenders for these elite positions, criteria and mechanisms of selection must be evolved. Hence a certain proportion of those who aspire may not be permitted to engage in the behavior for which they have prepared themselves.

Thus we conclude that access to illegitimate roles, no less than access to legitimate roles, is limited by both social and psychological factors. We shall here be concerned primarily with socially structured differentials in illegitimate opportunities. Such differentials, we contend, have much to do with the type of delinquent subculture that develops.

Learning and Performance Structures

Our use of the term "opportunities," legitimate or illegitimate, implies access to both learning and performance structures. That is, the individual must have access to appropriate environments for the acquisition of the values and skills associated with the performance of a particular role, and he must be supported in the performance of the role once he has learned it.

Sutherland, *Principles of Criminology*, 4th Ed. (Philadelphia: Lippincott, 1947).

[3] All quotations in this paragraph are from *The Professional Thief, op. cit.*, pp. 211–13. Emphasis added.

Tannenbaum, several decades ago, vividly expressed the point that criminal role performance, no less than conventional role performance, presupposes a patterned set of relationships through which the requisite values and skills are transmitted by established practitioners to aspiring youth:

It takes a long time to make a good criminal, many years of specialized training and much preparation. But training is something that is given to people. People learn in a community where the materials and the knowledge are to be had. A craft needs an atmosphere saturated with purpose and promise. The community provides the attitudes, the point of view, the philosophy of life, the example, the motive, the contacts, the friendships, the incentives. No child brings those into the world. He finds them here and available for use and elaboration. The community gives the criminal his materials and habits, just as it gives the doctor, the lawyer, the teacher, and the candlestick-maker theirs.[4]

Sutherland systematized this general point of view, asserting that opportunity consists, at least in part, of learning structures. Thus "criminal behavior is learned" and, furthermore, it is learned "in interaction with other persons in a process of communication." However, he conceded that the differential-association theory does not constitute a full explanation of criminal behavior. In a paper circulated in 1944, he noted that "criminal behavior is partially a function of opportunities to commit [i.e., to perform] specific classes of crime, such as embezzlement, bank burglary, or illicit heterosexual intercourse." Therefore, "while opportunity may be partially a function of association with criminal patterns and of the specialized techniques thus acquired, it is not determined entirely in that manner, and consequently differential association is not the sufficient cause of criminal behavior." [5]

To Sutherland, then, illegitimate opportunity included conditions favorable to the performance of a criminal role as well as conditions favorable to the learning of such a role (differential associations). These conditions, we suggest, depend upon certain features of the social structure of the community in which delinquency arises.

Differential Opportunity: A Hypothesis

We believe that each individual occupies a position in both legitimate and illegitimate opportunity structures. This is a new way of defining the situation. The theory of anomie views the individual primarily in terms of the legitimate opportunity structure. It poses questions regarding differentials in access to legitimate routes to success-goals; at the same time it assumes either that illegitimate avenues to success-goals are freely available or that differentials in their availability are of little significance. This tendency may be seen in the following statement by Merton:

Several researches have shown that specialized areas of vice and crime constitute a "normal" response to a situation where the cultural emphasis upon pecuniary success has been absorbed, but where there is little access to conventional and legitimate means for becoming successful. The occupational opportunities of people in these areas are largely confined to manual labor and the lesser white-collar jobs. Given the American stigmatization of manual labor *which has been found to hold rather uniformly for all social classes*, and the absence of realistic opportunities for advancement beyond this level, the result is a marked tendency toward deviant behavior. The status of unskilled labor and the consequent low income cannot readily compete *in terms of established standards of worth* with the promises of power and high income from organized vice, rackets and crime. . . . [Such a situation] leads toward the gradual attenuation of legitimate, but by and large ineffectual, strivings and the increasing use of illegitimate, but more or less effective, expedients.[6]

The cultural-transmission and differential-

---

[4] Frank Tannenbaum, "The Professional Criminal," *The Century*, Vol. 110 (May–Oct. 1925), p. 577.

[5] See A. K. Cohen, Alfred Lindesmith, and Karl Schuessler, eds., *The Sutherland Papers* (Bloomington, Ind.: Indiana University Press, 1956), pp. 31–35.

[6] R. K. Merton, *Social Theory and Social Structure*, Rev. and Enl. Ed. (Glencoe, Ill.: Free Press, 1957), pp. 145–46.

association tradition, on the other hand, assumes that access to illegitimate means is variable, but it does not recognize the significance of comparable differentials in access to legitimate means. Sutherland's "ninth proposition" in the theory of differential association states:

Though criminal behavior is an expression of general needs and values, it is not explained by those general needs and values since noncriminal behavior is an expression of the same needs and values. Thieves generally steal in order to secure money, but likewise honest laborers work in order to secure money. The attempts by many scholars to explain criminal behavior by general drives and values, such as the happiness principle, striving for social status, the money motive, or frustration, have been and must continue to be futile since they explain lawful behavior as completely as they explain criminal behavior.[7]

In this statement, Sutherland appears to assume that people have equal and free access to legitimate means regardless of their social position. At the very least, he does not treat access to legitimate means as variable. It is, of course, perfectly true that "striving for social status," "the money motive," and other socially approved drives do not fully account for either deviant or conforming behavior. But if goal-oriented behavior occurs under conditions in which there are socially structured obstacles to the satisfaction of these drives by legitimate means, the resulting pressures, we contend, might lead to deviance.

The concept of differential opportunity structures permits us to unite the theory of anomie, which recognizes the concept of differentials in access to legitimate means, and the "Chicago tradition," in which the concept of differentials in access to illegitimate means is implicit. We can now look at the individual, not simply in relation to one or the other system of means, but in relation to both legitimate and illegitimate systems. This approach permits us to ask, for example, how the relative availability of illegitimate opportunities affects the resolution of adjustment problems leading to deviant behavior. We believe that the way in which these problems are resolved may depend upon the kind of support for one or another type of illegitimate activity that is given at different points in the social structure. If, in a given social location, illegal or criminal means are not readily available, then we should not expect a criminal subculture to develop among adolescents. By the same logic, we should expect the manipulation of violence to become a primary avenue to higher status only in areas where the means of violence are not denied to the young. To give a third example, drug addiction and participation in subcultures organized around the consumption of drugs presuppose that persons can secure access to drugs and knowledge about how to use them. In some parts of the social structure, this would be very difficult; in others, very easy. In short, there are marked differences from one part of the social structure to another in the types of illegitimate adaptation that are available to persons in search of solutions to problems of adjustment arising from the restricted availability of legitimate means.[8] In this sense, then, we can think of individuals as being located in two opportunity structures — one legitimate, the other illegitimate. Given limited access to success-goals by legitimate means, the nature of the delinquent response that may result will vary according to the availability of various illegitimate means.[9]

[7] *Principles of Criminology, op. cit.,* pp. 7–8.

[8] For an example of restrictions on access to illegitimate roles, note the impact of racial definitions in the following case: "I was greeted by two prisoners who were to be my cell buddies. Ernest was a first offender, charged with being a 'hold-up' man. Bill, the other buddy, was an old offender, going through the machinery of becoming a habitual criminal, in and out of jail. . . . The first thing they asked me was, 'What are you in for?' I said, 'Jack-rolling.' The hardened one (Bill) looked at me with a superior air and said, 'A hoodlum, eh? An ordinary sneak thief. Not willing to leave jack-rolling to the niggers, eh? That's all they're good for. Kid, jack-rolling's not a white man's job.' I could see that he was disgusted with me, and I was too scared to say anything" (Shaw, *The Jack-Roller, op. cit.,* p. 101).

[9] For a discussion of the way in which the availability of illegitimate means influences the adaptations of inmates to prison life, see R. A. Cloward, "Social Control in the Prison," *Theoretical Studies of the Social Organization of the Prison,* Bulletin No. 15 (New York: Social Science Research Council, March 1960), pp. 20–48.

Varieties of Delinquent Subculture

There appear to be three major types of delinquent subculture typically encountered among adolescent males in lower-class areas of large urban centers. One is based principally upon criminal values; its members are organized primarily for the pursuit of material gain by such illegal means as extortion, fraud, and theft. In the second, violence is the keynote; its members pursue status ("rep") through the manipulation of force or threat of force. These are the "warrior" groups that attract so much attention in the press. Finally, there are subcultures which emphasize the consumption of drugs. The participants in these drug subcultures have become alienated from conventional roles, such as those required in the family or the occupational world. They have withdrawn into a restricted world in which the ultimate value consists in the "kick." We call these three subcultural forms "criminal," "conflict," and "retreatist," respectively.[10]

These shorthand terms simply denote the *principal* orientation of each form of adaptation from the perspective of the dominant social order; although one can find many examples of subcultures that fit accurately into one of these three categories, subcultures frequently appear in somewhat mixed form. Thus members of a predominantly conflict subculture may also on occasion engage in systematic theft; members of a criminal subculture may sometimes do combat in the streets with rival gangs. But this should not obscure the fact that these subcultures tend to exhibit essentially different orientations.

The extent to which the delinquent subculture organizes and controls a participant's allegiance varies from one member to another. Some members of the gang are almost totally immersed in the perspectives of the subculture and bring them into play in all their contacts; other segregate this aspect of their lives and maintain other roles in the family, school, and church. The chances are relatively slight, however, that an adolescent can successfully segregate delinquent and conforming roles for a long period of time. Pressures emanate from the subculture leading its members to adopt unfavorable attitudes toward parents, school teachers, policemen, and other adults in the conventional world. When he is apprehended for delinquent acts, the possibility of the delinquent's maintaining distinctly separate role involvements breaks down, and he is confronted with the necessity of choosing between law-abiding and delinquent styles of life. Since family, welfare, religious, educational, law-enforcement, and correctional institutions are arrayed against the appeal of his delinquent associates, the decision is a difficult one, frequently requiring either complete acceptance or complete rejection of one or the other system of obligations.[11]

At any one point in time, however, the extent to which the norms of the delinquent subculture control behavior will vary from one member to another. Accordingly, descriptions of these subcultures must be stated in terms of the fully indoctrinated member rather than the average member. Only in this way can the distinctiveness of delinquent styles of life be made clear. It is with this understanding that we offer the following brief empirical characterizations of the three main types of delinquent subculture.

The Criminal Pattern

The most extensive documentation in the sociological literature of delinquent behavior patterns in lower-class culture describes a tradition which integrates youthful delinquency with adult criminality.[12] In the central value orientation of youths participating in this tradition, delinquent and criminal behavior is ac-

---

[10] It should be understood that these terms characterize these delinquent modes of adaptation from the reference position of conventional society; they do not necessarily reflect the attitudes of members of the subcultures. Thus the term "retreatist" does not necessarily reflect the attitude of the "cat." Far from thinking of himself as being in retreat, he defines himself as among the elect.

[11] Tannenbaum summarizes the community's role in this process of alienation by the phrase "dramatization of evil" (Frank Tannenbaum, *Crime and the Community* [New York: Columbia University Press, 1938], pp. 19–21). . . .

[12] See especially references, *op. cit., supra,* notes 1 and 2; and E. H. Sutherland, *White Collar Crime* (New York: Dryden Press, 1949).

cepted as a means of achieving success-goals. The dominant criteria of in-group evaluation stress achievement, the use of skill and knowledge to get results. In this culture, prestige is allocated to those who achieve material gain and power through avenues defined as illegitimate by the larger society. From the very young to the very old, the successful "haul" — which quickly transforms the penniless into a man of means — is an ever-present vision of the possible and desirable. Although one may also achieve material success through the routine practice of theft or fraud, the "big score" remains the symbolic image of quick success.

The means by which a member of a criminal subculture achieves success are clearly defined for the aspirant. At a young age, he learns to admire and respect older criminals and to adopt the "right guy" as his role-model. Delinquent episodes help him to acquire mastery of the techniques and orientation of the criminal world and to learn how to cooperate successfully with others in criminal enterprises. He exhibits hostility and distrust toward representatives of the larger society. He regards members of the conventional world as "suckers," his natural victims, to be exploited when possible. He sees successful people in the conventional world as having a "racket" — *e.g.*, big businessmen have huge expense accounts, politicians get graft, etc. This attitude successfully neutralizes the controlling effect of conventional norms. Toward the in-group the "right guy" maintains relationships of loyalty, honesty, and trustworthiness. He must prove himself reliable and dependable in his contacts with his criminal associates although he has no such obligations toward the out-group of noncriminals.

One of the best ways of assuring success in the criminal world is to cultivate appropriate "connections." As a youngster, this means running with a clique composed of other "right guys" and promoting an apprenticeship or some other favored relationship with older and successful offenders. Close and dependable ties with income-producing outlets for stolen goods, such as the wagon peddler, the junkman, and the fence, are especially useful. Furthermore, these intermediaries encourage

and protect the young delinquent in a criminal way of life by giving him a jaundiced perspective on the private morality of many functionaries in conventional society. As he matures, the young delinquent becomes acquainted with a new world made up of predatory bondsmen, shady lawyers, crooked policemen, grafting politicians, dishonest businessmen, and corrupt jailers. Through "connections" with occupants of these half-legitimate, half-illegitimate roles and with "big shots" in the underworld, the aspiring criminal validates and assures his freedom of movement in a world made safe for crime.

The Conflict Pattern [13]

The role-model in the conflict pattern of lower-class culture is the "bopper" who swaggers with his gang, fights with weapons to win a wary respect from other gangs, and compels a fearful deference from the conventional adult world by his unpredictable and destructive assaults on persons and property. To other gang members, however, the key qualities of the bopper are those of the successsful warrior. His performance must reveal a willingness to defend his personal integrity and the honor of the gang. He must do this with great courage and displays of fearlessness in the face of personal danger.

The immediate aim in the world of fighting gangs is to acquire a reputation for toughness and destructive violence. A "rep" assures not only respectful behavior from peers and threatened adults but also admiration for the

[13] For descriptions of conflict groups, see Harrison Salisbury, *The Shook-up Generation* (New York: Harper & Bros., 1958); *Reaching the Unreached*, a Publication of the New York City Youth Board, 1952; C. K. Myers, *Light the Dark Streets* (Greenwich, Conn.: Seabury Press, 1957); Walter Bernstein, "The Cherubs Are Rumbling," *The New Yorker*, Sept. 21, 1957; Sam Glane, "Juvenile Gangs in East Side Los Angeles," *Focus*, Vol. 29 (Sept. 1959), pp. 136–41; Dale Kramer and Madeline Karr, *Teen-Age Gangs* (New York: Henry Holt, 1953); S. V. Jones, "The Cougars — Life with a Brooklyn Gang," *Harper's*, Vol. 209 (Nov. 1954), pp. 35–43; P. C. Crawford, D. I. Malamud, and J. R. Dumpson, *Working with Teen-Age Gangs* (New York Welfare Council, 1950); Dan Wakefield, "The Gang That Went Good," *Harper's*, Vol. 216 (June 1958), pp. 36–43.

physical strength and masculinity which it symbolizes. It represents a way of securing access to the scarce resources for adolescent pleasure and opportunity in underprivileged areas.

Above all things, the bopper is valued for his "heart." He does not "chicken out," even when confronted by superior force. He never defaults in the face of a personal insult or a challenge to the integrity of his gang. The code of the bopper is that of the warrior who places great stress on courage, the defense of his group, and the maintenance of honor.

Relationships between bopping gang members and the adult world are severely attenuated. The term that the bopper uses most frequently to characterize his relationships with adults is "weak." He is unable to find appropriate role-models that can designate for him a structure of opportunities leading to adult success. He views himself as isolated and the adult world as indifferent. The commitments of adults are to their own interests and not to his. Their explanations of why he should behave differently are "weak," as are their efforts to help him.

Confronted by the apparent indifference and insincerity of the adult world, the ideal bopper seeks to win by coercion the attention and opportunities he lacks and cannot otherwise attract. In recent years the street-gang worker who deals with the fighting gang on its own "turf" has come to symbolize not only a recognition by conventional adult society of the gang's toughness but also a concession of opportunities formerly denied. Through the alchemy of competition between gangs, this gesture of attention by the adult world to the "worst" gangs is transformed into a mark of prestige. Thus does the manipulation of violence convert indifference into accommodation and attention into status.

The Retreatist Pattern

Retreatism may include a variety of expressive, sensual, or consummatory experiences, alone or in a group. In this analysis, we are interested only in those experiences that involve the use of drugs and that are supported by a subculture. We have adopted these limita-

tions in order to maintain our focus on subcultural formations which are clearly recognized as delinquent, as drug use by adolescents is. The retreatist preoccupation with expressive experiences creates many varieties of "hipster" cult among lower-class adolescents which foster patterns of deviant but not necessarily delinquent conduct.

Subcultural drug-users in lower-class areas perceive themselves as culturally and socially detached from the life-style and everyday preoccupations of members of the conventional world. The following characterization of the "cat" culture, observed by Finestone in a lower-class Negro area in Chicago, describes drug use in the more general context of "hipsterism." [14] Thus it should not be assumed that this description in every respect fits drug cultures found elsewhere. We have drawn heavily on Finestone's observations, however, because they provide the best descriptions available of the social world in which lower-class adolescent drug cultures typically arise.

The dominant feature of the retreatist subculture of the "cat" lies in the continuous pursuit of the "kick." Every cat has a kick — alcohol, marijuana, addicting drugs, unusual sexual experiences, hot jazz, cool jazz, or any combination of these. Whatever its content, the kick is a search for ecstatic experiences. The retreatist strives for an intense awareness of living and a sense of pleasure that is "out of this world." In extreme form, he seeks an almost spiritual and mystical knowledge that is experienced when one comes to know "it" at the height of one's kick. The past and the future recede in the time perspective of the cat, since complete awareness in present experience is the essence of the kick.

The successful cat has a lucrative "hustle" which contrasts sharply with the routine and discipline required in the ordinary occupational tasks of conventional society. The many varieties of the hustle are characterized by a rejection of violence or force and a preference for manipulating, persuading, outwitting, or "conning" others to obtain resources for experiencing the kick. The cat begs, borrows,

[14] Harold Finestone, "Cats, Kicks and Color," *Social Problems*, Vol. 5 (July 1957), pp. 3–13.

steals, or engages in some petty con-game. He caters to the illegitimate cravings of others by peddling drugs or working as a pimp. A highly exploitative attitude toward women permits the cat to view pimping as a prestigeful source of income. Through the labor of "chicks" engaged in prostitution or shoplifting, he can live in idleness and concentrate his entire attention on organizing, scheduling, and experiencing the esthetic pleasure of the kick. The hustle of the cat is secondary to his interest in the kick. In this respect the cat differs from his fellow delinquents in the criminal subculture, for whom income-producing activity is a primary concern.

The ideal cat's appearance, demeanor, and taste can best be characterized as "cool." The cat seeks to exhibit a highly developed and sophisticated taste for clothes. In his demeanor, he struggles to reveal a self-assured and unruffled manner, thereby emphasizing his aloofness and "superiority" to the "squares." He develops a colorful, discriminating vocabulary and ritualized gestures which express his sense of difference from the conventional world and his solidarity with the retreatist subculture.

The word "cool" also best describes the sense of apartness and detachment which the retreatist experiences in his relationships with the conventional world. His reference group is the "society of cats," an "elite" group in which he becomes isolated from conventional society. Within this group, a new order of goals and criteria of achievement are created. The cat does not seek to impose this system of values on the world of the squares. Instead, he strives for status and deference within the society of cats by cultivating the kick and the hustle. Thus the retreatist subculture provides avenues to success-goals, to the social admiration and the sense of well-being or oneness with the world which the members feel are otherwise beyond their reach.

Cloward and Ohlin's theory of delinquency and opportunity is examined in terms of its logical, operational, and empirical adequacy in this selection. Schrag observes that Cloward and Ohlin developed a typology of gangs in an effort to explain norm violations sanctioned by delinquent subcultures, and that the theorists do not propose a general theory of delinquency. This distinction has an important implication — in a test of the theory, the units of observation must be organized gangs and their norms of nonconformity, not individual delinquents and their delinquent acts.

Schrag attempts to identify the fundamental premises in Cloward and Ohlin's argument. One set of postulates concerns opportunity structures in an urban industrial society. According to variations in legitimate and illegitimate opportunity structures, three types of communities are identified, and the distinctive type of delinquency to be anticipated in each of these is noted. Another set of postulates permits identification of those persons who are most likely to participate in gangs. Schrag concludes that on logical grounds the theory is generally sound, although it does not adequately explain retreatism.

Assessing the operational adequacy of the theory, Schrag observes that complex concepts are employed, but operational definitions of these concepts are lacking. In constructing a theory in an empirical science, rules must be formulated to link theoretical concepts with empirical data; Cloward and Ohlin's theory is weak in this regard and, consequently, is subject to a variety of interpretations. Schrag also raises a number of questions concerning the empirical adequacy of the theory. A theory must, after all, fit the available empirical evidence. Although it may be necessary to alter the claims of the theory, it clearly constitutes an important contribution to our understanding of delinquency as well as having implications for the prevention and control of delinquency.

CLARENCE SCHRAG

Delinquency and Opportunity: Analysis of a Theory

Three things can legitimately be asked of any empirical theory.[1] First, the theory should have sound logical structure. That is, its postulates should be connected in such a manner that a number of claims or assertions can be derived from them by means of logical inference or deduction. Second, the theory should have operational significance. Some of its terms should be related by rule to observable data so that its meaning is clear and its claims can be tested by evidence and experience. Third, the theory should have high congruence with the world of experience. Its major claims should be generally consistent with the preponderance of relevant factual evidence. When these three requirements are met, the theory can be used successfully for pragmatic purposes.[2] We propose, then, to examine the theory of delinquency and opportunity in terms of three sets of criteria, namely, its logical, operational, and empirical adequacy.

The opportunity theory devotes little attention to personality traits or situational pressures. It, therefore, is not intended as a general explanation of delinquent acts or of the careers of individual offenders. Rather, it employs socio-cultural variables in developing a typology of gangs aimed at the explanation of norm violations that are sanctioned by organized gangs or delinquent subcultures. Consequently, the units of observation in any realistic test of the theory are organized gangs and their norms of nonconformity instead of individual offenders and their delinquent acts.[3]

Group sanctioned nonconformity, according to the theory, is found primarily in certain types of delinquent gangs that are indigenous to lower class neighborhoods in large urban industrial societies. Disparity between cultural goals and socially structured opportunities for their achievement creates special problems of adjustment for youthful members of the lower social classes and makes them particularly susceptible to the adoption of noncomformist strategies of achievement. The precise pattern of nonconformity that is most likely to be adopted in any given neighborhood depends chiefly upon the relative accessibility of alternative opportunity structures, illegitimate as well as legitimate. Norms of nonconformity, in

From *Sociology and Social Research*, 46 (January 1962), pp. 167–175. Reprinted by permission of *Sociology and Social Research*, University of Southern California, Los Angeles, California 90007.

[1] The book by Richard A. Cloward and Lloyd E. Ohlin, *Delinquency and Opportunity: A Theory of Delinquent Gangs* (Glencoe: The Free Press, 1960) should be judged exclusively on the merits of the opportunity theory. It provides an excellent digest and collation of much of the sociological literature on delinquency, and the importance of its evaluative commentary can be detached largely from any considerations regarding the adequacy of the theory therein presented.

[2] Cf. Gustav Bergman, *Philosophy of Science* (Madison: University of Wisconsin Press, 1957); Philipp Frank, *Modern Science and Its Philosophy* (Cambridge: Harvard University Press, 1949); Carl G. Hempel and Paul Oppenheim, "Studies in the Logic of Explanation," *Philosophy of Science*, 15 (April–June 1948), 135–46.

[3] Richard A. Cloward and Lloyd E. Ohlin, *op. cit.*, especially the Introduction.

other words, reflect the balance of power and the degree of integration between legitimate and illegitimate systems of opportunity. This is the essential argument of the theory.[4]

I. Logical Adequacy of Postulates and Theorems

Since the style of presentation throughout the book in question is discursive and exploratory rather than definitive, identification of the fundamental premises of the argument is partly a matter of conjecture. What follows should therefore be regarded simply as one reader's effort to reconstruct the main argument. It does seem, however, that the major claims of the theory can be fairly clearly and easily developed if a limited number of propositions are accepted as basic postulate-sets.[5]

We begin with a series of postulate-sets dealing with opportunity structures in urban industrial societies.[6]

1. Emphasis on middle class goals, especially those involved in economic achievement, is widespread. This means that members of the lower classes generally endorse those cultural goals that are highly valued in the broader community. While some differences can be found among lower class members with respect to their attitudes toward middle class membership and their desire to improve their economic position, it is not necessary for us to assume any wide discrepancies in the major goals of lower class and middle class youth.

2. There exists in any organized community a system of regulated and legitimated avenues toward the attainment of cultural goals. However, unorganized neighborhoods can also be found, especially among recent immigrants who have diverse cultural backgrounds.

3. Access to legitimate means of achievement varies among the social classes and, in general, to the disadvantage of lower class members. Furthermore, perceived disadvantage, regardless of the accuracy of the perception, is for lower class youth the functional equivalent of objectively verified disadvantage in that it has the same effect on overt behavior.

4. Within any given neighborhood there may or may not be an organized system of illegitimate opportunities. Should an illegitimate opportunity structure exist, it may be either integrated with the legitimate system or unintegrated. When the systems are integrated, it may be expected that the illegitimate system will have established procedures for the recruitment of young participants, for the indoctrination of recruits in the employment of illegitimate means, and for the eventual absorption of recruits into a system of illegitimate occupations for adults. Conversely, where legitimate and illegitimate opportunity structures are not integrated, it may be assumed that the aforementioned devices for social control of nonconformists do not occur.

The above postulate-sets enable us to identify three main types of communities classified on the basis of their legitimate and illegitimate opportunity structures.

Type I communities are those in which the legitimate system holds the balance of power to the virtual exclusion of organized illegitimate opportunities. In such communities, because of the absence of culturally sanctioned nonconformity, delinquency should be an infrequent, sporadic, unorganized activity among isolated individuals. Type II communities are those in which legitimate and illegitimate opportunity structures are integrated in a symbiotic manner so that access to either system provides fairly good prospects for goal achievement. The balance of power may fluctuate somewhat, but neither system is likely to be capable or desirous of eliminating the other. Here delinquency should be highly organized, instrumental, and subject to some control by both normative systems. Delinquency, in effect, may serve as an apprenticeship for adult ca-

[4] *Ibid.*, Chapter 7.

[5] Any given theory, of course, is subject to a variety of reconstructions. We have not attempted here to develop a minimum set of terms and postulates, but have tried to retain some of the language and context of the original statement. A relatively loose reconstruction seems advisable at this time because certain logical and empirical issues need to be resolved before a more formal reconstruction is necessary or useful. Our basic premises, or postulate-sets, are neither primitive in logical sense nor parsimonious. They are aimed at the clarification of certain problems believed to be inherent in the original theory.

[6] *Op. cit.*, 16–17, 77–107, 144–86.

reers in illegitimate occupations. Type III communities are those in which legitimate and illegitimate opportunity systems are not integrated. Access to the illegitimate system provides few career opportunities and limited prospects for the attainment of cultural goals. It serves only as a temporary means for the achievement of highly restricted objectives. Delinquency in these communities consequently should be expressive, violent, contagious, and organized around unconventional objectives.

We now have a theoretical mechanism for predicting the occurrence of two kinds of organized gangs described by Cloward and Ohlin. Specifically, criminal gangs should be found most frequently in Type II communities, whereas conflict gangs should occur chiefly in communities of Type III. At the same time, the unorganized and solitary delinquencies expected in Type I communities fall outside the scope of the Cloward-Ohlin discussion, since these offenses presumably are not sanctioned by any local subculture. Thus, our reconstruction of the theory is somewhat broader than the initial statement of it.[7]

However, the theory as thus far developed fails to explain the apparent fact that even in Type II and Type III communities a large number of young persons who belong to the lower classes do not become involved in the activities of delinquent gangs. The assumptions about relative access to illegitimate means may tell us what type of gang is likely to be found in any given type of community, but they do not enable us to identify the lower class members who are most likely to participate in gang activities. In addition, the theory thus far makes no special reference to the retreatist gangs that supposedly are found most frequently in communities of Type II and Type III. Some added postulates are needed, then, to identify probable gang participants and to explain retreatist behavior.

The following postulates deal with these problems by attempting to explain variations in susceptibility to involvement in illegitimate subcultures among lower class members.[8]

5. Susceptibility to involvement in delinquent gangs is greatest among those members of the lower classes who are alienated from the legitimate system, who blame the social system rather than themselves for their adjustment problems, and who in general deny the pragmatic efficacy of legitimate norms.

6. Alienation from conventional norms has two major socio-cultural sources. First, some persons may perceive considerable discrepancy between (a) the formal or official criteria for achievement, such as hard work, ability, or initiative, and (b) the pragmatic or operative criteria, such as luck, being "in the know," or "having the right contacts." These persons may not challenge the moral validity of the official criteria but they are likely to deny the practical significance of these criteria. Second, achievement in certain cases may be limited by highly visible barriers such as race and place of residence, indicating that discrimination sometimes occurs in the application of achievement criteria. It follows that alienation will be highest among those persons who feel that they are capable of meeting the official criteria for achievement but who regard themselves as being unjustly deprived because of the operation of extraneous pragmatic factors.

7. Withdrawal of legitimacy from conventional norms minimizes guilt feelings among nonconformists, facilitates the legitimization of delinquent norms, and provides a foundation for the development of delinquent subcultures. These added postulates enable us to formulate a large number of theorems relating delinquency with racial, religious, residential, educational, occupational, and other social variables that are associated with access to legitimate and illegitimate opportunity systems. Again, they imply certain connections between delinquency and attitudinal variables, such as the degree of potency assigned to conventional norms, prevalence of guilt feelings, amount of extrapunitiveness, attachment to deviant subcultures, and so on. They likewise suggest some preventive or ameliorative programs aimed at control of delinquency by modification of the opportunity structure or by revision of the way in which the opportunity structure is perceived in some segments of the community.

[7] *Ibid.*, Chapter 7.
[8] *Ibid.*, 110–39, and Chapters 4, 5, and 8.

Many of these theorems are left unstated by the authors, of course, but it seems clear that the theory has considerable deductive potential and that it is rich in its implications for social control. In this sense the theory is a rather distinctive contribution to sociological literature.

Some difficulties remain, however, in the attempted explanation of retreatist behavior. Essentially the argument is that retreatists are "double failures" who are unsuccessful in both legitimate and illegitimate realms of endeavor. Because of internal inhibitions or external discriminatory factors, retreatists are unwilling or unable to utilize existing opportunity structures. They therefore remove themselves from the arena of competition by adopting an escapist posture.[9] Now, the main logical problem involved in this formulation is that internal and external factors associated with double failure are not clearly enough identified for us to anticipate instances of retreatism. Thus, retreatism, in effect, is a residual category rather than a dependent variable in the theoretical system.[10]

II. Operational Adequacy of the Theory

The operational adequacy of a theory, of course, is determined on the basis of criteria that are entirely different from those considered in assessing logical adequacy. Here we are interested in operational definitions or correspondence rules that relate theoretical concepts to the data of observation and experience.[11] In the absence of correspondence rules, a theory is likely to be ambiguous and untestable when applied to the realm of human experience. Consequently the formulation of rules for relating empirical materials to theoretical concepts is an essential and integral part of the process of theory construction in empirical science.

Since the definitions employed in opportunity theory are primarily contextual rather than operational, the theory must be interpreted chiefly in a commonsense manner. Many of the concepts, such as perception of opportunity, denial of legitimacy, double failure, and elimination of guilt, for example, are complex and difficult to handle empirically. There is no precise indication as to how the authors have related these concepts to reliable research evidence.

We encounter some special difficulties in attempting to utilize the notion of gang culture or delinquent subculture, a key concept in opportunity theory. How well organized does a gang have to be before it falls within the scope of the theory? We might argue that an organized gang can be recognized in terms of social traits such as stable membership, spatial localization, dissentient norms regarding legitimate means, devices for the neutralization of guilt feelings and sense of responsibility, and relative consensus in support of certain unconventional or illegitimate activities. Presumably, only gangs that possess these traits come under the theory. But these are precisely the traits that the theory is intended to explain. Now, in order to explain gang organization, we need to discover the independent factors that are predictive of organization. Obviously, the same set of factors cannot be used both to identify organized gangs and to explain the fact of their organization. It follows that if organized gangs are selected on the basis of the criteria mentioned, then the theory is in this respect circular and logically impotent.

There are two main ways out of the dilemma concerning the identification of organized gangs. First, it may be possible to define gang organization independently of the variables that are included in the empirical claims of the theory. Second, it may be argued that opportunity theory applies to all gangs regardless of the degree of their organization. While Cloward and Ohlin are not clear in their definition, it appears that their students who have done

---

[9] *Ibid.*, 178–86.

[10] The theory is of little help in the prediction of retreatism. It seems doubtful that the empirical claims concerning retreatism are accurate. See Part III below.

[11] See Bergman, *op. cit.*, 37–38, 71–72, 89. Also, Frank, *op. cit.* A more technical discussion is found in C. G. Hempel, "The Theoretician's Dilemma," in H. Feigl, M. Scriven, and G. Maxwell, *Minnesota Studies in the Philosophy of Science* (Minneapolis: University of Minnesota Press, 1958), 37–98.

research on delinquent gangs have used some combination of these two solutions to the problem.[12]

A rather similar difficulty is involved in the definition of opportunity. If differentials in opportunity are responsible for variations in gang organization, then opportunity structures must be identified independently of gangs or delinquent subcultures. However, research on opportunity theory suggests that the kind of gang organization observed in a community is accepted as evidence of the kind of opportunity structure in that community.[13] This strategy for observing opportunity structures, of course, deprives the theory of much of its explanatory potential.

In summary, much work remains to be done on the formulation of correspondence rules connecting concepts with observational data if the theory of opportunity is to be applied realistically to concrete situations. Until these rules are evident the claims of the theory are likely to be somewhat controversial because they are subject to a variety of interpretations. Further refinements are needed to clarify the kinds of gangs and communities that fall legitimately within the scope of the theory and to demonstrate the utility of opportunity differentials as an independent variable in the explanation of gang organization.

III. Empirical Adequacy of the Theory

Several further questions of adequacy are encountered when the theory of opportunity is checked against available empirical evidence.[14] To illustrate, the theory implies that the existence of criminal, conflict, and retreatist gangs is determined by the relative accessibility and the degree of integration of legitimate and illegitimate opportunity structures in the local neighborhood. Thus, in any given neighborhood a certain kind of gang organization should predominate over other types of gangs, and in any given gang a certain pattern of unconventional behavior should prevail. It appears that neither of these claims is entirely satisfactory.

For example, neighborhoods with high delinquency rates are frequently characterized by a diversity of gang organizations rather than by the dominance of any single form.[15] Again, many gangs do not exhibit the degree of cultural integration suggested by the theory. They often adopt distinctive titles, special items of apparel, and other symbols of identity long before they have a stabilized membership or any high degree of organizational autonomy. Fluid membership, spatial mobility, and considerable versatility with respect to objectives and internal organization are characteristic of many of our delinquent gangs. It may therefore be advisable either to modify the claims of the theory or clearly to restrict its application to certain identifiable neighborhoods that are organized on the basis of highly specialized illegitimate opportunities.

---

[12] Cf. Irving Spergel, "An Exploratory Research in Delinquent Subculture," *The Social Service Review*, 35 (March 1961), 33–47. Spergel (p. 37) selected the "worst or most delinquent" gangs in three carefully chosen neighborhoods.

[13] Spergel, *ibid.*, 36. "Three kinds of neighborhoods were selected: two with reputations for high-level racket activity, a second type noted for the productivity of violent fighting gangs, and a third accepted as rather ordinary, except for the extensive but not alarming involvement of its delinquent youth in acts of car theft or 'joy-riding' and burglary." After selecting in this manner the neighborhoods to be investigated, Spergel concluded that in the racketeering neighborhoods the legitimate and illegitimate opportunity systems were integrated because "The racketeer played a variety of significant economic and social roles in the neighborhood. He was the sponsor and subsidizer of legitimate and illegitimate business enterprises. He was helpful when others were in trouble by raising bail money and making appropriate 'payoffs'" (p. 38). The conflict neighborhood was partly integrated. However, various types of rackets were in operation in all three neighborhoods.

[14] The main sources of information are Spergel, *op. cit.*, and Delbert S. Elliott, *Delinquency, Opportunity, and Patterns of Orientations*, Ph.D. Dissertation, University of Washington, 1961. The latter is a study of delinquency in Seattle, Washington. However, no gangs possessing the degree of organization described by Cloward and Ohlin were observed in Seattle.

[15] This seems to be the case in Seattle and also, to some extent, in the New York study reported by Spergel, *op. cit.*, 39–41.

In addition, the theory holds that major goals and objectives are much the same for gang members and nonmembers, that members deny the legitimacy of conventional norms and attach considerable legitimacy to nonconformist standards, and that members show little evidence of guilt with respect to their transgressions. On each of these points available evidence, although by no means conclusive, throws some doubt on the claims of the theory. Thus, distinctive differences have been found in the goals and aspirations of delinquents and nondelinquents,[16] while many recidivistic delinquents exhibit reliable evidence of guilt and attachment to legitimate norms.[17] Perhaps the issue depends largely on the definition of gang culture, but in any event its resolution appears at present to be uncertain.

Likewise, the theory maintains that the route to retreatism is "double failure," that illegitimate opportunities are severely restricted for retreatists, and that retreatism is not an effective avenue toward achievement. The evidence is that there are several alternative paths to retreatism and that retreatism by no means prohibits access to opportunity or achievement by illegitimate means.[18]

However, the great merit of opportunity theory is that it identifies an important and hitherto largely neglected factor in the genesis of deviant behavior. Delinquents clearly perceive limited opportunities in the legitimate system, they are sensitive to artificial barriers against achievement, and they estimate their prospects for success as being better in illegitimate or semilegitimate occupations.[19] This, by the way, seems to be as true for solitary offenders as for gang members. Consequently, the theory of opportunity, while it may be uncertain in some of its corollary arguments, appears to be on solid ground in attempting to explain delinquent organizations in terms of variations in perceived accessibility of legitimate and illegitimate opportunity systems.

---

[16] Spergel, *op. cit.*, 41–42, and Elliott, *op. cit.*, Chapter 4.

[17] Elliott, *op. cit.*, Chapters 5 and 6.

[18] Spergel, *op. cit.*, states, for example, that "some drug addicts from the racket subcultural area had access to certain organized criminal opportunities . . . It was not at all clear that drug use or addiction was always a vocational liability and a necessary handicap or that it impeded in every case the development of a highly proficient burglar or shoplifter" (p. 43).

[19] Spergel, *op. cit.*, 41–42, and Elliott, *op. cit.*, Chapters 4 and 7.

Alternative Interpretations
and Critiques

As might be expected, Cohen's provocative theoretical formulation regarding the content and distribution of the delinquent subculture stimulated a number of critiques. In one of these assessments Sykes and Matza remark that juvenile delinquents experience guilt when apprehended, accord respect to law-abiding persons, distinguish between those who are "fair game" for victimization and those who are not, and are by no means immune from demands for conformity. On these bases they question a central proposition in Cohen's theory: delinquency is based on values and norms antithetical to those of the larger culture.

Rather than positing that delinquents are indifferent to the expectations of the society, Sykes and Matza suggest that delinquents have in fact internalized the norms and values of the dominant culture. However, delinquents have at their disposal a number of justifications or rationalizations which neutralize the internalized norms and external demands for conformity and thereby protect them from guilt or self-condemnation — at least until they are caught. Sykes and Matza recognize that these rationalizations are operative prior to the commission of a delinquent act; they do not use the concept "rationalization" simply as a post facto justification for one's behavior. To the extent that the work of Sykes and Matza presents a theory of juvenile delinquency — or, as they phrase it, "an alternative or modified explanation for a large portion of juvenile delinquency" — it is best viewed as an extension of Sutherland's position, rather than as a modification of Cohen, because, as Kitsuse and Dietrick indicated in the previous selection, Cohen did not present a theory of delinquency.

GRESHAM M. SYKES

DAVID MATZA

Techniques of Neutralization: A Theory of Delinquency

In attempting to uncover the roots of juvenile delinquency, the social scientist has long since ceased to search for devils in the mind or stigma of the body. It is now largely agreed that delinquent behavior, like most social behavior, is learned and that it is learned in the process of social interaction.

The classic statement of this position is found in Sutherland's theory of differential association, which asserts that criminal or delinquent behavior involves the learning of (a) techniques of committing crimes and (b) motives, drives, rationalizations, and attitudes favorable to the violation of law.[1] Unfortunately, the specific content of what is learned — as opposed to the process by which it is learned — has received relatively little attention in either theory or research. Perhaps the single strongest school of thought on the nature of this content has centered on the idea of a delinquent sub-culture. The basic characteristic of the delinquent sub-culture, it is argued, is a system of values that represents an inversion of the values held by respectable, law-abiding society. The world of the delinquent is the world of the law-abiding turned upside down and its norms constitute a countervailing force directed against the conforming social order. Cohen[2] sees the process of developing a delinquent sub-culture as a matter of building, maintaining, and reinforcing a code for behavior which exists by opposition, which stands in point by point contradiction to dominant values, particularly those of the middle class. Cohen's portrayal of delinquency is ex-

ecuted with a good deal of sophistication, and he carefully avoids overly simple explanations such as those based on the principle of "follow the leader" or easy generalizations about "emotional disturbances." Furthermore, he does not accept the delinquent sub-culture as something given, but instead systematically examines the function of delinquent values as a viable solution to the lower-class, male child's problems in the area of social status. Yet in spite of its virtues, this image of juvenile delinquency as a form of behavior based on competing or countervailing values and norms appears to suffer from a number of serious defects. It is the nature of these defects and a possible alternative or modified explanation of a large portion of juvenile delinquency with which this paper is concerned.

The difficulties in viewing delinquent behavior as springing from a set of deviant values and norms — as arising, that is to say, from a situation in which the delinquent defines his delinquency as "right" — are both empirical and theoretical. In the first place, if there existed in fact a delinquent sub-culture such that the delinquent viewed his illegal behavior as morally correct, we could reasonably suppose that he would exhibit no feelings of guilt or shame at detection or confinement. Instead, the major reaction would tend in the direction of indignation or a sense of martyrdom.[3] It is true that some delinquents do react in the latter fashion, although the sense of martyrdom often seems to be based on the fact that

---

From *American Sociological Review*, December 1957, pp. 664–670. Reprinted by permission of the American Sociological Association.

[1] E. H. Sutherland, *Principles of Criminology*, revised by D. R. Cressey, Chicago: Lippincott, 1955, pp. 77–80.

[2] Albert K. Cohen, *Delinquent Boys*, Glencoe, Ill.: The Free Press, 1955.

[3] This form of reaction among the adherents of a deviant subculture who fully believe in the "rightfulness" of their behavior and who are captured and punished by the agencies of the dominant social order can be illustrated, perhaps, by groups such as Jehovah's Witnesses, early Christian sects, nationalist movements in colonial areas, and conscientious objectors during World Wars I and II.

others "get away with it" and indignation appears to be directed against the chance events or lack of skill that led to apprehension. More important, however, is the fact that there is a good deal of evidence suggesting that many delinquents *do* experience a sense of guilt or shame, and its outward expression is not to be dismissed as a purely manipulative gesture to appease those in authority. Much of this evidence is, to be sure, of a clinical nature or in the form of impressionistic judgments of those who must deal first hand with the youthful offender. Assigning a weight to such evidence calls for caution, but it cannot be ignored if we are to avoid the gross stereotype of the juvenile delinquent as a hardened gangster in miniature.

In the second place, observers have noted that the juvenile delinquent frequently accords admiration and respect to law-abiding persons. The "really honest" person is often revered, and if the delinquent is sometimes overly keen to detect hypocrisy in those who conform, unquestioned probity is likely to win his approval. A fierce attachment to a humble, pious mother or a forgiving, upright priest (the former, according to many observers, is often encountered in both juvenile delinquents and adult criminals) might be dismissed as rank sentimentality, but at least it is clear that the delinquent does not necessarily regard those who abide by the legal rules as immoral. In a similar vein, it can be noted that the juvenile delinquent may exhibit great resentment if illegal behavior is imputed to "significant others" in his immediate social environment or to heroes in the world of sport and entertainment. In other words, if the delinquent does hold to a set of values and norms that stand in complete opposition to those of respectable society, his norm-holding is of a peculiar sort. While supposedly thoroughly committed to the deviant system of the delinquent sub-culture, he would appear to recognize the moral validity of the dominant normative system in many instances.[4]

In the third place, there is much evidence that juvenile delinquents often draw a sharp line between those who can be victimized and those who cannot. Certain social groups are not to be viewed as "fair game" in the performance of supposedly approved delinquent acts while others warrant a variety of attacks. In general, the potentiality for victimization would seem to be a function of the social distance between the juvenile delinquent and others and thus we find implicit maxims in the world of the delinquent such as "don't steal from friends" or "don't commit vandalism against a church of your own faith."[5] This is all rather obvious, but the implications have not received sufficient attention. The fact that supposedly valued behavior tends to be directed against disvalued social groups hints that the "wrongfulness" of such delinquent behavior is more widely recognized by delinquents than the literature has indicated. When the pool of victims is limited by considerations of kinship, friendship, ethnic group, social class, age, sex, etc., we have reason to suspect that the virtue of delinquency is far from unquestioned.

In the fourth place, it is doubtful if many juvenile delinquents are totally immune from the demands for conformity made by the dominant social order. There is a strong likelihood that the family of the delinquent will agree with respectable society that delinquency is wrong, even though the family may be engaged in a variety of illegal activities. That is, the parental posture conducive to delinquency is not apt to be a positive prodding. Whatever may be the influence of parental example, what might be called the "Fagin" pattern of socialization into delinquency is prob-

---

[4] As Weber has pointed out, a thief may recognize the legitimacy of legal rules without accepting their moral validity. Cf. Max Weber, *The Theory of Social and Economic Organization*

(translated by A. M. Henderson and Talcott Parsons), New York: Oxford University Press, 1947, p. 125. We are arguing here, however, that the juvenile delinquent frequently recognizes *both* the legitimacy of the dominant social order and its moral "rightness."

[5] Thrasher's account of the "Itschkies" — a juvenile gang composed of Jewish boys — and the immunity from "rolling" enjoyed by Jewish drunkards is a good illustration. Cf. F. Thrasher, *The Gang*, Chicago: The University of Chicago Press, 1927, p. 315.

ably rare. Furthermore, as Redl has indicated, the idea that certain neighborhoods are completely delinquent, offering the child a model for delinquent behavior without reservations, is simply not supported by the data.[6]

The fact that a child is punished by parents, school officials, and agencies of the legal system for his delinquency may, as a number of observers have cynically noted, suggest to the child that he should be more careful not to get caught. There is an equal or greater probability, however, that the child will internalize the demands for conformity. This is not to say that demands for conformity cannot be counteracted. In fact, as we shall see shortly, an understanding of how internal and external demands for conformity are neutralized may be crucial for understanding delinquent behavior. But it is to say that a complete denial of the validity of demands for conformity and the substitution of a new normative system is improbable, in light of the child's or adolescent's dependency on adults and encirclement by adults inherent in his status in the social structure. No matter how deeply enmeshed in patterns of delinquency he may be and no matter how much this involvement may outweigh his associations with the law-abiding, he cannot escape the condemnation of his deviance. Somehow the demands for conformity must be met and answered; they cannot be ignored as part of an alien system of values and norms.

In short, the theoretical viewpoint that sees juvenile delinquency as a form of behavior based on the values and norms of a deviant sub-culture in precisely the same way as law-abiding behavior is based on the values and norms of the larger society is open to serious doubt. The fact that the world of the delinquent is embedded in the larger world of those who conform cannot be overlooked nor can the delinquent be equated with an adult thoroughly socialized into an alternative way of life. Instead, the juvenile delinquent would appear to be at least partially committed to the dominant social order in that he frequently

exhibits guilt or shame when he violates its proscriptions, accords approval to certain conforming figures, and distinguishes between appropriate and inappropriate targets for his deviance. It is to an explanation for the apparently paradoxical fact of his delinquency that we now turn.

As Morris Cohen once said, one of the most fascinating problems about human behavior is why men violate the laws in which they believe. This is the problem that confronts us when we attempt to explain why delinquency occurs despite a greater or lesser commitment to the usages of conformity. A basic clue is offered by the fact that social rules or norms calling for valued behavior seldom if ever take the form of categorical imperatives. Rather, values or norms appear as *qualified* guides for action, limited in their applicability in terms of time, place, persons, and social circumstances. The moral injunction against killing, for example, does not apply to the enemy during combat in time of war, although a captured enemy comes once again under the prohibition. Similarly, the taking and distributing of scarce goods in a time of acute social need is felt by many to be right, although under other circumstances private property is held inviolable. The normative system of a society, then, is marked by what Williams has termed *flexibility;* it does not consist of a body of rules held to be binding under all conditions.[7]

This flexibility is, in fact, an integral part of the criminal law in that measures for "defenses to crimes" are provided in pleas such as nonage, necessity, insanity, drunkenness, compulsion, self-defense, and so on. The individual can avoid moral culpability for his criminal action — and thus avoid the negative sanctions of society — if he can prove that criminal intent was lacking. *It is our argument that much delinquency is based on what is essentially an unrecognized extension of defenses to crimes, in the form of justifications for deviance that are seen as valid by the delinquent but not by the legal system or society at large.*

These justifications are commonly described

[6] Cf. Solomon Kobrin, "The Conflict of Values in Delinquency Areas," *American Sociological Review,* 16 (October 1951), pp. 653–661.

[7] Cf. Robin Williams, Jr., *American Society,* New York: Knopf, 1951, p. 28.

as rationalizations. They are viewed as following deviant behavior and as protecting the individual from self-blame and the blame of others after the act. But there is also reason to believe that they precede deviant behavior and make deviant behavior possible. It is this possibility that Sutherland mentioned only in passing and that other writers have failed to exploit from the viewpoint of sociological theory. Disapproval flowing from internalized norms and conforming others in the social environment is neutralized, turned back, or deflected in advance. Social controls that serve to check or inhibit deviant motivational patterns are rendered inoperative, and the individual is freed to engage in delinquency without serious damage to his self image. In this sense, the delinquent both has his cake and eats it too, for he remains committed to the dominant normative system and yet so qualifies its imperatives that violations are "acceptable" if not "right." Thus the delinquent represents not a radical opposition to law-abiding society but something more like an apologetic failure, often more sinned against than sinning in his own eyes. We call these justifications of deviant behavior techniques of neutralization; and we believe these techniques make up a crucial component of Sutherland's "definitions favorable to the violation of law." It is by learning these techniques that the juvenile becomes delinquent, rather than by learning moral imperatives, values or attitudes standing in direct contradiction to those of the dominant society. In analyzing these techniques, we have found it convenient to divide them into five major types.

The Denial of Responsibility. In so far as the delinquent can define himself as lacking responsibility for his deviant actions, the disapproval of self or others is sharply reduced in effectiveness as a restraining influence. As Justice Holmes has said, even a dog distinguishes between being stumbled over and being kicked, and modern society is no less careful to draw a line between injuries that are unintentional, i.e., where responsibility is lacking, and those that are intentional. As a technique of neutralization, however, the denial of responsibility extends much further than the claim that de-

viant acts are an "accident" or some similar negation of personal accountability. It may also be asserted that delinquent acts are due to forces outside of the individual and beyond his control such as unloving parents, bad companions, or a slum neighborhood. In effect, the delinquent approaches a "billiard ball" conception of himself in which he sees himself as helplessly propelled into new situations. From a psychodynamic viewpoint, this orientation toward one's own actions may represent a profound alienation from self, but it is important to stress the fact that interpretations of responsibility are cultural constructs and not merely idiosyncratic beliefs. The similarity between this mode of justifying illegal behavior assumed by the delinquent and the implications of a "sociological" frame of reference or a "humane" jurisprudence is readily apparent.[8] It is not the validity of this orientation that concerns us here, but its function of deflecting blame attached to violations of social norms and its relative independence of a particular personality structure.[9] By learning to view himself as more acted upon than acting, the delinquent prepares the way for deviance from the dominant normative system without the necessity of a frontal assault on the norms themselves.

The Denial of Injury. A second major technique of neutralization centers on the injury or harm involved in the delinquent act. The criminal law has long made a distinction between crimes which are *mala in se* and *mala prohibita* — that is between acts that are wrong in themselves and acts that are illegal but not immoral — and the delinquent can make the same kind of distinction in evaluating the wrongfulness of his behavior. For the delinquent, however, wrongfulness may turn on the question of whether or not anyone has clearly

[8] A number of observers have wryly noted that many delinquents seem to show a surprising awareness of sociological and psychological explanations for their behavior and are quick to point out the causal role of their poor environment.

[9] It is possible, of course, that certain personality structures can accept some techniques of neutralization more readily than others, but this question remains largely unexplored.

been hurt by his deviance, and this matter is open to a variety of interpretations. Vandalism, for example, may be defined by the delinquent simply as "mischief" — after all, it may be claimed, the persons whose property has been destroyed can well afford it. Similarly, auto theft may be viewed as "borrowing," and gang fighting may be seen as a private quarrel, an agreed upon duel between two willing parties, and thus of no concern to the community at large. We are not suggesting that this technique of neutralization, labelled the denial of injury, involves an explicit dialectic. Rather, we are arguing that the delinquent frequently, and in a hazy fashion, feels that his behavior does not really cause any great harm despite the fact that it runs counter to law. Just as the link between the individual and his acts may be broken by the denial of responsibility, so may the link between acts and their consequences be broken by the denial of injury. Since society sometimes agrees with the delinquent, e.g., in matters such as truancy, "pranks," and so on, it merely reaffirms the idea that the delinquent's neutralization of social controls by means of qualifying the norms is an extension of common practice rather than a gesture of complete opposition.

The Denial of the Victim. Even if the delinquent accepts the responsibility for his deviant actions and is willing to admit that his deviant actions involve an injury or hurt, the moral indignation of self and others may be neutralized by an insistence that the injury is not wrong in light of the circumstances. The injury, it may be claimed, is not really an injury; rather, it is a form of rightful retaliation or punishment. By a subtle alchemy the delinquent moves himself into the position of an avenger and the victim is transformed into a wrong-doer. Assaults on homosexuals or suspected homosexuals, attacks on members of minority groups who are said to have gotten "out of place," vandalism as revenge on an unfair teacher or school official, thefts from a "crooked" store owner — all may be hurts inflicted on a transgressor, in the eyes of the delinquent. As Orwell has pointed out, the type of criminal admired by the general public

has probably changed over the course of years and Raffles no longer serves as a hero; [10] but Robin Hood, and his latter day derivatives such as the tough detective seeking justice outside the law, still capture the popular imagination, and the delinquent may view his acts as part of a similar role.

To deny the existence of the victim, then, by transforming him into a person deserving injury is an extreme form of a phenomenon we have mentioned before, namely, the delinquent's recognition of appropriate and inappropriate targets for his delinquent acts. In addition, however, the existence of the victim may be denied for the delinquent, in a somewhat different sense, by the circumstances of the delinquent act itself. Insofar as the victim is physically absent, unknown, or a vague abstraction (as is often the case in delinquent acts committed against property), the awareness of the victim's existence is weakened. Internalized norms and anticipations of the reactions of others must somehow be activated, if they are to serve as guides for behavior; and it is possible that a diminished awareness of the victim plays an important part in determining whether or not this process is set in motion.

The Condemnation of the Condemners. A fourth technique of neutralization would appear to involve a condemnation of the condemners or, as McCorkle and Korn have phrased it, a rejection of the rejectors.[11] The delinquent shifts the focus of attention from his own deviant acts to the motives and behavior of those who disapprove of his violations. His condemners, he may claim, are hypocrites, deviants in disguise, or impelled by personal spite. This orientation toward the conforming world may be of particular importance when it hardens into a bitter cynicism directed against those assigned the task of enforcing or expressing the norms of the dominant society. Police, it may be said, are corrupt, stupid, and brutal. Teach-

---

[10] George Orwell, *Dickens, Dali, and Others,* New York: Reynal, 1946.
[11] Lloyd W. McCorkle and Richard Korn, "Re-socialization Within Walls," *The Annals of the American Academy of Political and Social Science,* 293 (May 1954), pp. 88–98.

ers always show favoritism and parents always "take it out" on their children. By a slight extension, the rewards of conformity — such as material success — become a matter of pull or luck, thus decreasing still further the stature of those who stand on the side of the law-abiding. The validity of this jaundiced viewpoint is not so important as its function in turning back or deflecting the negative sanctions attached to violations of the norms. The delinquent, in effect, has changed the subject of the conversation in the dialogue between his own deviant impulses and the reactions of others; and by attacking others, the wrongfulness of his own behavior is more easily repressed or lost to view.

The Appeal to Higher Loyalties. Fifth, and last, internal and external social controls may be neutralized by sacrificing the demands of the larger society for the demands of the smaller social groups to which the delinquent belongs such as the sibling pair, the gang, or the friendship clique. It is important to note that the delinquent does not necessarily repudiate the imperatives of the dominant normative system, despite his failure to follow them. Rather, the delinquent may see himself as caught up in a dilemma that must be resolved, unfortunately, at the cost of violating the law. One aspect of this situation has been studied by Stouffer and Toby in their research on the conflict between particularistic and universalistic demands, between the claims of friendship and general social obligations, and their results suggest that "it is possible to classify people according to a predisposition to select one or the other horn of a dilemma in role conflict." [12] For our purposes, however, the most important point is that deviation from certain norms may occur not because the norms are rejected but because other norms, held to be more pressing or involving a higher loyalty, are accorded precedence. Indeed, it is the fact that both sets of norms are believed in that gives meaning to our concepts of dilemma and role conflict.

The conflict between the claims of friendship and the claims of law, or a similar dilemma, has of course long been recognized by the social scientist (and the novelist) as a common human problem. If the juvenile delinquent frequently resolves his dilemma by insisting that he must "always help a buddy" or "never squeal on a friend," even when it throws him into serious difficulties with the dominant social order, his choice remains familiar to the supposedly law-abiding. The delinquent is unusual, perhaps, in the extent to which he is able to see the fact that he acts in behalf of the smaller social groups to which he belongs as a justification for violations of society's norms, but it is a matter of degree rather than of kind.

"I didn't mean it." "I didn't really hurt anybody." "They had it coming to them." "Everybody's picking on me." "I didn't do it for myself." These slogans or their variants, we hypothesize, prepare the juvenile for delinquent acts. These "definitions of the situation" represent tangential or glancing blows at the dominant normative system rather than the creation of an opposing ideology; and they are extensions of patterns of thought prevalent in society rather than something created *de novo*.

Techniques of neutralization may not be powerful enough to fully shield the individual from the force of his own internalized values and the reactions of conforming others, for as we have pointed out, juvenile delinquents often appear to suffer from feelings of guilt and shame when called into account for their deviant behavior. And some delinquents may be so isolated from the world of conformity that techniques of neutralization need not be called into play. Nonetheless, we would argue that techniques of neutralization are critical in lessening the effectiveness of social controls and that they lie behind a large share of delinquent behavior. Empirical research in this area is scattered and fragmentary at the present time, but the work of Redl,[13] Cressey,[14] and others has supplied a body of significant data that has done much to clarify the theoretical issues and

[12] See Samuel A. Stouffer and Jackson Toby, "Role Conflict and Personality," in *Toward a General Theory of Action*, edited by Talcott Parsons and Edward A. Shils, Cambridge: Harvard University Press, 1951, p. 494.

[13] See Fritz Redl and David Wineman, *Children Who Hate*, Glencoe: The Free Press, 1956.
[14] See D. R. Cressey, *Other People's Money*, Glencoe: The Free Press, 1953.

enlarge the fund of supporting evidence. Two lines of investigation seem to be critical at this stage. First, there is need for more knowledge concerning the differential distribution of techniques of neutralization, as operative patterns of thought, by age, sex, social class, ethnic group, etc. On *a priori* grounds it might be assumed that these justifications for deviance will be more readily seized by segments of society for whom a discrepancy between common social ideals and social practice is most apparent. It is also possible however, that the habit of "bending" the dominant normative system — if not "breaking" it — cuts across our cruder social categories and is to be traced primarily to patterns of social interaction within the familial circle. Second, there is need for a greater understanding of the internal structure of techniques of neutralization, as a system of beliefs and attitudes, and its relationship to various types of delinquent behavior. Certain techniques of neutralization would appear to be better adapted to particular deviant acts than to others, as we have suggested, for example, in the case of offenses against property and the denial of the victim. But the issue remains far from clear and stands in need of more information.

In any case, techniques of neutralization appear to offer a promising line of research in enlarging and systematizing the theoretical grasp of juvenile delinquency. As more information is uncovered concerning techniques of neutralization, their origins, and their consequences, both juvenile delinquency in particular and deviation from normative systems in general may be illuminated.

In this selection the author explicitly defines "delinquency" in behavioral terms; he uses specific types of behavior or acts which could result in legal action as the referent of the term "delinquent." Miller's thesis is that the motivation for the delinquent acts of members of lower-class corner groups or "gangs" consists largely of efforts to conform to the standards and values of the lower-class community. Rejecting Cohen's position on the delinquent subculture, he argues that lower-class gang delinquency is best understood not as a reaction to middle-class norms but as a positive effort to achieve that which is valued in the distinctive lower-class cultural milieu.

In describing lower-class culture, Miller emphasizes three structural elements — the female-based household, serial monogamy, and age-graded one-sex peer groups — and a distinctive pattern of focal concerns. Among the "hard core" of the lower class, a particular form of the family, the female-based household, serves as the unit of child-rearing, whereas serial monogamy is the common pattern of mating. A system of age-graded one-sex peer groups is directly related to the prevalence of female-based households. The one-sex peer group, Miller assumes, is the most significant "relational unit" or primary group for male and female adolescents and adults (for a penetrating description of a corner group see Liebow [1967]). Since membership in such a group is restricted to one sex and to persons within a limited age range, adolescent street-corner groups are simply the adolescent version of this typical form of grouping in the lower class, and what is commonly called the "delinquent gang" is, according to Miller, a subtype or variant of the adolescent street-corner group.

The focal concerns of the corner groups reflect those of the cultural milieu, and Miller vividly portrays the focal concerns of lower-class culture — trouble, toughness, smartness, excitement, fate, and autonomy. Adolescents and adults differ somewhat in the relative importance of these concerns, and Miller specifies two additional "concerns" important for adolescents, belonging and status.

REFERENCE

Elliot Liebow, *Tally's Corner* (Boston: Little, Brown, 1967).

WALTER B. MILLER

Lower Class Culture as a Generating Milieu of Gang Delinquency

The etiology of delinquency has long been a controversial issue, and is particularly so at present. As new frames of reference for explaining human behavior have been added to traditional theories, some authors have adopted the practice of citing the major postulates of each school of thought as they pertain to delinquency, and going on to state that causality must be conceived in terms of the dynamic interaction of a complex combination of variables on many levels. The major sets of etiological factors currently adduced to explain delinquency are, in simplified terms, the physiological (delinquency results from organic pathology), the psychodynamic (delinquency is a "behavioral disorder" resulting primarily from emotional disturbance generated by a defective mother-child relationship), and the environmental (delinquency is the product of disruptive forces, "disorganization," in the actor's physical or social environment).

This paper selects one particular kind of "delinquency" [1] — law-violating acts committed by members of adolescent street corner groups in lower class communities — and attempts to show that the dominant component of motivation underlying these acts consists in a directed attempt by the actor to adhere to forms of behavior, and to achieve standards of value as they are defined within that community. It takes as a premise that the motivation of behavior in this situation can be approached most productively by attempting to understand the nature of cultural forces impinging on the acting individual as they are perceived *by the actor himself* — although by no means only that segment of these forces of which the actor is consciously aware — rather than as they are perceived and evaluated from the reference position of another cultural system. In the case of "gang" delinquency, the cultural system which exerts the most direct influence on behavior is that of the lower class community itself — a long-established, distinctively patterned tradition with an integrity of its own — rather than a so-called "delinquent subculture" which has arisen through conflict with middle class culture and is oriented to the deliberate violation of middle class norms.

The bulk of the substantive data on which the following material is based was collected in

From *Journal of Social Issues*, 14, no. 3 (1958), 5–19. Reprinted by permission.

[1] The complex issues involved in deriving a definition of "delinquency" cannot be discussed here. The term "delinquent" is used in this paper to characterize behavior or acts committed by individuals within specified age limits which if known to official authorities could result in legal action. The concept of a "delinquent" individual has little or no utility in the approach used here; rather, specified types of *acts* which may be committed rarely or frequently by few or many individuals are characterized as "delinquent."

connection with a service-research project in the control of gang delinquency. During the service aspect of the project, which lasted for three years, seven trained social workers maintained contact with twenty-one corner group units in a "slum" district of a large eastern city for periods of time ranging from ten to thirty months. Groups were Negro and white, male and female, and in early, middle, and late adolescence. Over eight thousand pages of direct observational data on behavior patterns of group members and other community residents were collected; almost daily contact was maintained for a total time period of about thirteen worker years. Data include workers' contact reports, participant observation reports by the writer — a cultural anthropologist — and direct tape recordings of group activities and discussions.[2]

Focal Concerns of Lower Class Culture

There is a substantial segment of present-day American society whose way of life, values, and characteristic patterns of behavior are the product of a distinctive cultural system which may be termed "lower class." Evidence indicates that this cultural system is becoming increasingly distinctive, and that the size of the group which shares this tradition is increasing.[3]

[2] A three year research project is being financed under National Institutes of Health Grant M–1414, and administered through the Boston University School of Social Work. The primary research effort has subjected all collected material to a uniform data-coding process. All information bearing on some seventy areas of behavior (behavior in reference to school, police, theft, assault, sex, collective athletics, etc.) is extracted from the records, recorded on coded data cards, and filed under relevant categories. Analysis of these data aims to ascertain the actual nature of customary behavior in these areas, and the extent to which the social work effort was able to effect behavioral changes.

[3] Between 40 and 60 percent of all Americans are directly influenced by lower class culture, with about 15 percent, or twenty-five million, comprising the "hard core" lower class group — defined primarily by its use of the "female-based" household as the basic form of child-rearing unit and of the "serial monogamy" mating pattern as the primary form of marriage. The term "lower class culture" as used here refers most specifically to the way of life of the "hard core" group; system-

The lower class way of life, in common with that of all distinctive cultural groups, is characterized by a set of focal concerns — areas or issues which command widespread and persistent attention and a high degree of emotional involvement. The specific concerns cited here, while by no means confined to the American lower classes, constitute a distinctive *patterning* of concerns which differs significantly, both in rank order and weighting from that of American middle class culture. The following chart presents a highly schematic and simplified listing of six of the major concerns of lower class culture. Each is conceived as a "dimension" within which a fairly wide and varied range of alternative behavior patterns may be followed by different individuals under different situations. They are listed roughly in order of the degree of *explicit* attention accorded each, and, in this sense represent a weighted ranking of concerns. The "perceived alternatives" represent polar positions which define certain parameters within each dimension. As will be explained in more detail, it is necessary in relating the influence of these "concerns" to the motivation of delinquent behavior to specify *which* of its aspects is oriented to, whether orientation is *overt* or *covert, positive* (conforming to or seeking the aspect), or *negative* (rejecting or seeking to avoid the aspect).

The concept "focal concern" is used here in preference to the concept "value" for several interrelated reasons: (1) It is more readily derivable from direct field observation. (2) It is descriptively neutral — permitting independent consideration of positive and negative valences as varying under different conditions, whereas "value" carries a built-in positive valence. (3) It makes possible more refined analysis of subcultural differences, since it reflects actual behavior, whereas "value" tends to wash out in-

atic research in this area would probably reveal at least four to six major subtypes of lower class culture, for some of which the "concerns" presented here would be differently weighted, especially for those subtypes in which "law-abiding" behavior has a high overt valuation. It is impossible within the compass of this short paper to make the finer intracultural distinctions which a more accurate presentation would require.

tracultural differences since it is colored by notions of the "official" ideal.

Trouble: Concern over "trouble" is a dominant feature of lower class culture. The concept has various shades of meaning; "trouble" in one of its aspects represents a situation or a kind of behavior which results in unwelcome or complicating involvement with official authorities or agencies of middle class society. "Getting into trouble" and "staying out of trouble" represent major issues for male and female, adults and children. For men, "trouble" frequently involves fighting or sexual adventures while drinking; for women, sexual involvement with disadvantageous consequences. Expressed desire to avoid behavior which violates moral or legal norms is often based less on an explicit commitment to "official" moral or legal standards than on a desire to avoid "getting into trouble," e.g., the complicating consequences of the action.

The dominant concern over "trouble" involves a distinction of critical importance for the lower class community—that between "law-abiding" and "non-law-abiding" behavior. There is a high degree of sensitivity as to where each person stands in relation to these two classes of activity. Whereas in the middle class community a major dimension for evaluating a person's status is "achievement" and its external symbols, in the lower class, personal status is very frequently gauged along the law-abiding–non-law-abiding dimension. A mother will evaluate the suitability of her daughter's boyfriend less on the basis of his achievement potential than on the basis of his innate "trouble" potential. This sensitive awareness of the opposition of "trouble-producing" and "non-trouble-producing" behavior represents both a major basis for deriving status distinctions, and an internalized conflict potential for the individual.

As in the case of other focal concerns, which of two perceived alternatives — "law-abiding" or "non-law-abiding" — is valued varies according to the individual and the circumstances; in many instances there is an overt commitment to the "law-abiding" alternative, but a covert commitment to the "non-law-abiding." In certain situations, "getting into trouble" is overtly recognized as prestige-conferring; for example, membership in certain adult and adolescent primary groupings ("gangs") is contingent on having demon-

Chart 1
Focal Concerns of Lower Class Culture

Area		Perceived alternatives (state, quality, condition)
1. *Trouble:*	law-abiding behavior	law-violating behavior
2. *Toughness:*	physical prowess, skill; "masculinity"; fearlessness, bravery, daring	weakness, ineptitude; effeminacy; timidity, cowardice, caution
3. *Smartness:*	ability to outsmart, dupe, "con"; gaining money by "wits"; shrewdness, adroitness in repartee	gullibility, "con-ability"; gaining money by hard work; slowness, dull-wittedness, verbal maladroitness
4. *Excitement:*	thrill; risk, danger; change, activity	boredom; "deadness," safeness; sameness, passivity
5. *Fate:*	favored by fortune, being "lucky"	ill-omened, being "unlucky"
6. *Autonomy:*	freedom from external constraint; freedom from superordinate authority; independence	presence of external constraint; presence of strong authority; dependency, being "cared for"

strated an explicit commitment to the law-violating alternative. It is most important to note that the choice between "law-abiding" and "non-law-abiding" behavior is still a choice *within* lower class culture; the distinction between the policeman and the criminal, the outlaw and the sheriff, involves primarily this one dimension; in other respects they have a high community of interests. Not infrequently brothers raised in an identical cultural milieu will become police and criminals respectively.

For a substantial segment of the lower class population "getting into trouble" is not in itself overtly defined as prestige-conferring, but is implicitly recognized as a means to other valued ends, e.g., the covertly valued desire to be "cared for" and subject to external constraint, or the overtly valued state of excitement or risk. Very frequently "getting into trouble" is multi-functional, and achieves several sets of valued ends.

Toughness: The concept of "toughness" in lower class culture represents a compound combination of qualities or states. Among its most important components are physical prowess, evidenced both by demonstrated possession of strength and endurance and athletic skill; "masculinity," symbolized by a distinctive complex of acts and avoidances (bodily tatooing; absence of sentimentality; non-concern with "art," "literature," conceptualization of women as conquest objects, etc.); and bravery in the face of physical threat. The model for the "tough guy" — hard, fearless, undemonstrative, skilled in physical combat — is represented by the movie gangster of the thirties, the "private eye," and the movie cowboy.

The genesis of the intense concern over "toughness" in lower class culture is probably related to the fact that a significant proportion of lower class males are reared in a predominantly female household, and lack a consistently present male figure with whom to identify and from whom to learn essential components of a "male" role. Since women serve as a primary object of identification during pre-adolescent years, the almost obsessive lower class concern with "masculinity" probably resembles a type of compulsive reaction-formation. A concern over homosexuality runs like a persistent thread through lower class culture. This is manifested by the institutionalized practice of baiting "queers," often accompanied by violent physical attacks, an expressed contempt for "softness" or frills, and the use of the local term for "homosexual" as a generalized pejorative epithet (e.g., higher class individuals or upwardly mobile peers are frequently characterized as "fags" or "queers"). The distinction between "overt" and "covert" orientation to aspects of an area of concern is especially important in regard to "toughness." A positive overt evaluation of behavior defined as "effeminate" would be out of the question for a lower class male; however, built into lower class culture is a range of devices which permit men to adopt behaviors and concerns which in other cultural milieus fall within the province of women, and at the same time to be defined as "tough" and manly. For example, lower class men can be professional short-order cooks in a diner and still be regarded as "tough." The highly intimate circumstances of the street corner gang involve the recurrent expression of strongly affectionate feelings towards other men. Such expressions, however, are disguised as their opposite, taking the form of ostensibly aggressive verbal and physical interaction (kidding, "ranking," roughhousing, etc.).

Smartness: "Smartness," as conceptualized in lower class culture, involves the capacity to outsmart, outfox, outwit, dupe, "take," "con" another or others, and the concomitant capacity to avoid being outwitted, "taken," or duped oneself. In its essence, smartness involves the capacity to achieve a valued entity — material goods, personal status — through a maximum use of mental agility and a minimum use of physical effort. This capacity has an extremely long tradition in lower class culture, and is highly valued. Lower class culture can be characterized as "non-intellectual" only if intellectualism is defined specifically in terms of control over a particular body of formally learned knowledge involving "culture" (art, literature, "good" music, etc.), a generalized perspective on the past and present conditions of our own and other societies, and other areas of knowledge imparted by formal educational institutions. This particular type of mental attainment is, in general, overtly disvalued and frequently associated with effeminacy; "smartness" in the lower class sense, however, is highly valued.

The lower class child learns and practices the use of this skill in the street corner situation. Individuals continually practice duping and outwitting one another through recurrent card games and other forms of gambling, mutual exchanges of insults, and "testing" for mutual "con-ability." Those who demonstrate competence in this skill are accorded considerable prestige. Leadership roles in the corner group are frequently allocated according to demonstrated capacity in the two areas of "smartness" and "toughness"; the ideal leader combines both, but the "smart" leader is often accorded more prestige than the "tough" one — reflecting a general lower class respect for "brains" in the "smartness" sense.[4]

The model of the "smart" person is represented in popular media by the card shark, the professional gambler, the "con" artist, the promoter. A conceptual distinction is made between two kinds of people: "suckers," easy marks, "lushes," dupes, who work for their money and are legitimate targets of exploitation; and sharp operators, the "brainy" ones, who live by their wits and "getting" from the suckers by mental adroitness.

Involved in the syndrome of capacities related to "smartness" is a dominant emphasis in lower class culture on ingenious aggressive repartee. This skill, learned and practiced in the context of the corner group, ranges in form from the widely prevalent semi-ritualized teasing, kidding, razzing, "ranking," so characteristic of male peer group interaction, to the highly ritualized type of mutual insult interchange known as "the dirty dozens," "the dozens," "playing house," and other terms. This highly patterned cultural form is practiced on its most advanced level in adult male Negro society, but less polished variants are found throughout lower class culture — practiced, for example, by white children, male and female, as young as four or five. In essence, "doin' the dozens" involves two antagonists who vie with each other in the exchange of increasingly inflammatory insults, with incestuous and perverted sexual relations with the mother a dominant theme. In this form of insult interchange, as well as on other less ritualized occasions for joking, semi-serious, and serious mutual invective, a very high premium is placed on ingenuity, hair-trigger responsiveness, inventiveness, and the acute exercise of mental faculties.

Excitement: For many lower class individuals the rhythm of life fluctuates between periods of relatively routine or repetitive activity and sought situations of great emotional stimulation. Many of the most characteristic features of lower class life are related to the search for excitement or "thrill." Involved here are the highly prevalent use of alcohol by both sexes and the widespread use of gambling of all kinds — playing the numbers, betting on horse races, dice, cards. The quest for excitement finds what is perhaps its most vivid expression in the highly patterned practice of the recurrent "night on the town." This practice, designated by various terms in different areas ("honky-tonkin' "; "goin' out on the town"; "bar hoppin' "), involves a patterned set of activities in which alcohol, music, and sexual adventuring are major components. A group or individual sets out to "make the rounds" of various bars or night clubs. Drinking continues progressively throughout the evening. Men seek to "pick up" women, and women play the risky game of entertaining sexual advances. Fights between men involving women, gambling, and claims of physical prowess, in various combinations, are frequent consequences of a night of making the rounds. The explosive potential of this type of adventuring with sex and aggression, frequently leading to "trouble," is semi-explicitly sought by the individual. Since there is always a good likelihood that being out on the town will eventuate in fights, etc., the practice involves elements of sought risk and desired danger.

---

[4] The "brains-brawn" set of capacities are often paired in lower class folk lore or accounts of lower class life, e.g., "Brer Fox" and "Brer Bear" in the Uncle Remus stories, or George and Lennie in *Of Mice and Men*.

Counterbalancing the "flirting with danger" aspect of the "excitement" concern is the prevalence in lower class culture of other well established patterns of activity which involve long periods of relative inaction, or passivity. The term "hanging out" in lower class culture refers to extended periods of standing around, often with peer mates, doing what is defined as "nothing," "shooting the breeze," etc. A definite periodicity exists in the pattern of activity relating to the two aspects of the "excitement" dimension. For many lower class individuals the venture into the high risk world of alcohol, sex, and fighting occurs regularly once a week, with interim periods devoted to accommodating to possible consequences of these periods, along with recurrent resolves not to become so involved again.

Fate: Related to the quest for excitement is the concern with fate, fortune, or luck. Here also a distinction is made between two states — being "lucky" or "in luck," and being unlucky or jinxed. Many lower class individuals feel that their lives are subject to a set of forces over which they have relatively little control. These are not directly equated with the supernatural forces of formally organized religion, but relate more to a concept of "destiny," or man as a pawn of magical powers. Not infrequently this often implicit world view is associated with a conception of the ultimate futility of directed effort towards a goal: if the cards are right, or the dice good to you, or if your lucky number comes up, things will go your way; if luck is against you, it's not worth trying. The concept of performing semi-magical rituals so that one's "luck will change" is prevalent; one hopes that as a result he will move from the state of being "unlucky" to that of being "lucky." The element of fantasy plays an important part in this area. Related to and complementing the notion that "only suckers work" (Smartness) is the idea that once things start going your way, relatively independent of your own effort, all good things will come to you. Achieving great material rewards (big cars, big houses, a roll of cash to flash in a fancy night club), valued in lower class as well as in other parts of American culture, is a recurrent theme in lower class

fantasy and folk lore; the cocaine dreams of Willie the Weeper or Minnie the Moocher present the components of this fantasy in vivid detail.

The prevalence in the lower class community of many forms of gambling, mentioned in connection with the "excitement" dimension, is also relevant here. Through cards and pool which involve skill, and thus both "toughness" and "smartness"; or through race horse betting, involving "smartness"; or through playing the numbers, involving predominantly "luck," one may make a big killing with a minimum of directed and persistent effort within conventional occupational channels. Gambling in its many forms illustrates the fact that many of the persistent features of lower class culture are multi-functional — serving a range of desired ends at the same time. Describing some of the incentives behind gambling has involved mention of all of the focal concerns cited so far — Toughness, Smartness, and Excitement, in addition to Fate.

Autonomy: The extent and nature of control over the behavior of the individual — an important concern in most cultures — has a special significance and is distinctively patterned in lower class culture. The discrepancy between what is overtly valued and what is covertly sought is particularly striking in this area. On the overt level there is a strong and frequently expressed resentment of the idea of external controls, restrictions on behavior, and unjust or coercive authority. "No one's gonna push *me* around," or "I'm gonna tell him he can take the job and shove it. . . ." are commonly expressed sentiments. Similar explicit attitudes are maintained to systems of behavior-restricting rules, insofar as these are perceived as representing the injunctions, and bearing the sanctions of superordinate authority. In addition, in lower class culture a close conceptual connection is made between "authority" and "nurturance." To be restrictively or firmly controlled is to be cared for. Thus the overtly negative evaluation of superordinate authority frequently extends as well to nurturance, care, or protection. The desire for personal independence is often expressed in such terms as "I don't need *nobody* to take care of me. I can take care of myself!" Actual patterns of behavior, however, reveal a marked discrepancy between expressed sentiment and what is covertly valued. Many lower class people appear to seek out highly restrictive social environments wherein stringent external controls are maintained over their behavior. Such institutions as the armed forces, the mental hospital, the disciplinary school, the prison or correctional institution, provide environments which incorporate a strict and detailed set of rules defining and limiting behavior, and enforced by an authority system which controls and applies coercive sanctions for deviance from these rules. While under the jurisdiction of such systems, the lower class person generally expresses to his peers continual resentment of the coercive, unjust, and arbitrary exercise of authority. Having been released, or having escaped from these milieux, however, he will often act in such a way as to insure recommitment, or choose recommitment voluntarily after a temporary period of "freedom."

Lower class patients in mental hospitals will exercise considerable ingenuity to insure continued commitment while voicing the desire to get out; delinquent boys will frequently "run" from a correctional institution to activate efforts to return them; to be caught and returned means that one is cared for. Since "being controlled" is equated with "being cared for," attempts are frequently made to "test" the severity or strictness of superordinate authority to see if it remains firm. If intended or executed rebellion produces swift and firm punitive sanctions, the individual is reassured, at the same time that he is complaining bitterly at the injustice of being caught and punished. Some environmental milieux, having been tested in this fashion for the "firmness" of their coercive sanctions, are rejected, ostensibly for being too strict, actually for not being strict enough. This is frequently so in the case of "problematic" behavior by lower class youngsters in the public schools, which generally cannot command the coercive controls implicitly sought by the individual.

A similar discrepancy between what is overtly and covertly desired is found in the area of dependence-independence. The pose of tough rebellious independence often assumed by the lower class person frequently conceals powerful dependency cravings. These are manifested primarily by obliquely expressed resentment when "care" is not forthcoming rather than by expressed satisfaction when it is. The concern over autonomy-dependency is related both to "trouble" and "fate." Insofar as the lower class individual feels that his behavior is controlled by forces which often propel him into "trouble" in the face of an explicit determination to avoid it, there is an implied appeal to "save me from myself." A solution appears to lie in arranging things so that his behavior will be coercively restricted by an externally imposed set of controls strong enough to forcibly restrain his inexplicable inclination to get in trouble. The periodicity observed in connection with the "excitement" dimension is also relevant here; after involvement in trouble-producing behavior (assault, sexual adventure, a "drunk"), the individual will actively seek a locus of imposed control (his wife, prison, a restrictive job); after a given period of subjection to this control, resentment against it mounts, leading to a "break away" and a search for involvement in further "trouble."

Focal Concerns of the Lower Class Adolescent Street Corner Group

The one-sex peer group is a highly prevalent and significant structural form in the lower class community. There is a strong probability that the prevalence and stability of this type of unit is directly related to the prevalence of a stabilized type of lower class child-rearing unit — the "female-based" household. This is a nuclear kin unit in which a male parent is either absent from the household, present only sporadically, or, when present, only minimally or inconsistently involved in the support and rearing of children. This unit usually consists of one or more females of child-bearing age and their offspring. The females are frequently related to one another by blood or marriage ties, and the unit often includes two or more generations of women, e.g., the mother and/or aunt of the principal child-bearing female.

The nature of social groupings in the lower

class community may be clarified if we make the assumption that it is the *one-sex peer unit* rather than the two-parent family unit which represents the most significant relational unit for both sexes in lower class communities. Lower class society may be pictured as comprising a set of age-graded one-sex groups which constitute the major psychic focus and reference group for those over twelve or thirteen. Men and women of mating age leave these groups periodically to form temporary marital alliances, but these lack stability, and after varying periods of "trying out" the two-sex family arrangement, gravitate back to the more "comfortable" one-sex grouping, whose members exert strong pressure on the individual *not* to disrupt the group by adopting a two-sex household pattern of life.[5] Membership in a stable and solidary peer unit is vital to the lower class individual precisely to the extent to which a range of essential functions — psychological, educational, and others — are not provided by the "family" unit.

The adolescent street corner group represents the adolescent variant of this lower class structural form. What has been called the "delinquent gang" is one subtype of this form, defined on the basis of frequency of participation in law-violating activity; this subtype should not be considered a legitimate unit of study per se, but rather as one particular variant of the adolescent street corner group. The "hanging" peer group is a unit of particular importance for the adolescent male. In many cases it is the most stable and solidary primary group he has ever belonged to; for boys reared in female-based households the corner group provides the first real opportunity to learn essential aspects of the male role in the context of peers facing similar problems of sex-role identification.

The form and functions of the adolescent corner group operate as a selective mechanism in recruiting members. The activity patterns

of the group require a high level of intra-group solidarity; individual members must possess a good capacity for subordinating individual desires to general group interests as well as the capacity for intimate and persisting interaction. Thus highly "disturbed" individuals, or those who cannot tolerate consistently imposed sanctions on "deviant" behavior, cannot remain accepted members; the group itself will extrude those whose behavior exceeds limits defined as "normal." This selective process produces a type of group whose members possess to an unusually high degree both the *capacity* and *motivation* to conform to perceived cultural norms, so that the nature of the system of norms and values oriented to is a particularly influential component of motivation.

Focal concerns of the male adolescent corner group are those of the general cultural milieu in which it functions. As would be expected, the relative weighting and importance of these concerns pattern somewhat differently for adolescents than for adults. The nature of this patterning centers around two additional "concerns" of particular importance to this group — concern with "belonging," and with "status." These may be conceptualized as being on a higher level of abstraction than concerns previously cited, since "status" and "belonging" are achieved *via* cited concern areas of Toughness, etc.

Belonging: Since the corner group fulfills essential functions for the individual, being a member in good standing of the group is of vital importance for its members. A continuing concern over who is "in" and who is not involves the citation and detailed discussion of highly refined criteria for "in-group" membership. The phrase "he hangs with us" means "he is accepted as a member in good standing by current consensus"; conversely, "he don't hang with us" means he is not so accepted. One achieves "belonging" primarily by demonstrating knowledge of and a determination to adhere to the system of standards and valued qualities defined by the group. One maintains membership by acting in conformity with valued aspects of Toughness, Smartness, Autonomy, etc. In those instances where con-

[5] Further data on the female-based household unit (estimated as comprising about 15 percent of all American "families") and the role of one-sex groupings in lower class culture are contained in Walter B. Miller, "Implications of Urban Lower Class Culture for Social Work," *Social Service Review,* 1959, 33, No. 3.

forming to norms of this reference group at the same time violates norms of other reference groups (e.g., middle class adults, institutional "officials"), immediate reference group norms are much more compelling since violation risks invoking the group's most powerful sanction: exclusion.

Status: In common with most adolescents in American society, the lower class corner group manifests a dominant concern with "status." What differentiates this type of group from others, however, is the particular set of criteria and weighting thereof by which "status" is defined. In general, status is achieved and maintained by demonstrated possession of the valued qualities of lower class culture — Toughness, Smartness, expressed resistance to authority, daring, etc. It is important to stress once more that the individual orients to these concerns *as they are defined within lower class society;* e.g., the status-conferring potential of "smartness" in the sense of scholastic achievement generally ranges from negligible to negative.

The concern with "status" is manifested in a variety of ways. Intra-group status is a continued concern, and is derived and tested constantly by means of a set of status-ranking activities; the intra-group "pecking order" is constantly at issue. One gains status within the group by demonstrated superiority in Toughness (physical prowess, bravery, skill in athletics and games such as pool and cards), Smartness (skill in repartee, capacity to "dupe" fellow group members), and the like. The term "ranking," used to refer to the pattern of intra-group aggressive repartee, indicates awareness of the fact that this is one device for establishing the intra-group status hierarchy.

The concern over status in the adolescent corner group involves in particular the component of "adultness," the intense desire to be seen as "grown up," and a corresponding aversion to "kid stuff." "Adult" status is defined less in terms of the assumption of "adult" responsibility than in terms of certain external symbols of adult status — a car, ready cash, and, in particular, a perceived "freedom" to drink, smoke, and gamble as one wishes and to come and go without external restrictions. The de-

sire to be seen as "adult" is often a more significant component of much involvement in illegal drinking, gambling, and automobile driving than the explicit enjoyment of these acts as such.

The intensity of the corner group member's desire to be seen as "adult" is sufficiently great that he feels called upon to demonstrate qualities associated with adultness (Toughness, Smartness, Autonomy) to a much greater degree than a lower class adult. This means that he will seek out and utilize those avenues to these qualities which he perceives as available with greater intensity than an adult and less regard for their "legitimacy." In this sense the adolescent variant of lower class culture represents a maximization or an intensified manifestation of many of its most characteristic features.

Concern over status is also manifested in reference to other street corner groups. The term "rep" used in this regard is especially significant, and has broad connotations. In its most frequent and explicit connotation, "rep" refers to the "toughness" of the corner group as a whole relative to that of other groups; a "pecking order" also exists among the several corner groups in a given interactional area, and there is a common perception that the safety or security of the group and all its members depends on maintaining a solid "rep" for toughness vis-a-vis other groups. This motive is most frequently advanced as a reason for involvement in gang fights: "We *can't* chicken out on this fight; our rep would be shot!"; this implies that the group would be relegated to the bottom of the status ladder and become a helpless and recurrent target of external attack.

On the other hand, there is implicit in the concept of "rep" the recognition that "rep" has or may have a dual basis — corresponding to the two aspects of the "trouble" dimension. It is recognized that group as well as individual status can be based on both "law-abiding" and "law-violating" behavior. The situational resolution of the persisting conflict between the "law-abiding" and "law-violating" bases of status comprises a vital set of dynamics in determining whether a "delinquent" mode of behavior will be adopted by a group, under what circumstances, and how persistently. The determinants of this choice are evidently highly complex and fluid, and rest on a range of factors including the presence and perceptual immediacy of different community reference-group loci (e.g., professional criminals, police, clergy, teachers, settlement house workers), the personality structures and "needs" of group members, the presence in the community of social work, recreation, or educational programs which can facilitate utilization of the "law-abiding" basis of status, and so on.

What remains constant is the critical importance of "status" both for the members of the group as individuals and for the group as a whole insofar as members perceive their individual destinies as linked to the destiny of the group, and the fact that action geared to attain status is much more acutely oriented to the fact of status itself than to the legality or illegality, morality or immorality of the means used to achieve it.

Lower Class Culture and the Motivation of Delinquent Behavior

The customary set of activities of the adolescent street corner group includes activities which are in violation of laws and ordinances of the legal code. Most of these center around assault and theft of various types (the gang fight; auto theft; assault on an individual; petty pilfering and shoplifting; "mugging"; pocketbook theft). Members of street corner gangs are well aware of the law-violating nature of these acts; they are not psychopaths, nor physically or mentally "defective"; in fact, since the corner group supports and enforces a rigorous set of standards which demand a high degree of fitness and personal competence, it tends to recruit from the most "able" members of the community.

Why, then, is the commission of crimes a customary feature of gang activity? The most general answer is that the commission of crimes by members of adolescent street corner groups is motivated primarily by the attempt to achieve ends, states, or conditions which are valued, and to avoid those that are disvalued within their most meaningful cultural milieu, through those culturally available avenues which appear as the most feasible means of attaining those ends.

The operation of these influences is well illustrated by the gang fight — a prevalent and characteristic type of corner group delinquency. This type of activity comprises a highly stylized and culturally patterned set of sequences. Although details vary under different circumstances, the following events are generally included. A member or several members of group A "trespass" on the claimed territory of group B. While there they commit an act or acts which group B defines as a violation of its rightful privileges, an affront to their honor, or a challenge to their "rep." Frequently this act involves advances to a girl associated with group B; it may occur at a dance or party; sometimes the mere act of "trespass" is seen as deliberate provocation. Members of group B then assault members of group A, if they are caught while still in B's territory. Assaulted members of group A return to their "home" territory and recount to members of their group details of the incident, stressing the insufficient nature of the provocation ("I just *looked* at her! Hardly even said anything!"), and the unfair circumstances of the assault ("About *twenty* guys jumped just the *two* of us!"). The highly colored account is acutely inflammatory; group A, perceiving its honor violated and its "rep" threatened, feels obligated to retaliate in force. Sessions of detailed planning now occur; allies are recruited if the size of group A and its potential allies appears to necessitate larger numbers; strategy is plotted, and messengers dispatched. Since the prospect of a gang fight is frightening to even the "toughest" group members, a constant rehearsal of the provocative incident or incidents and the essentially evil nature of the opponents accompanies the planning process to bolster possibly weakening motivation to fight. The excursion into "enemy" territory sometimes results in a full scale fight; more often group B cannot be found, or the police appear and stop the fight, "tipped off" by an anonymous informant. When this occurs, group members express disgust and disappointment; secretly there is much relief; their honor has been avenged without incurring injury;

often the anonymous tipster is a member of one of the involved groups.

The basic elements of this type of delinquency are sufficiently stabilized and recurrent as to constitute an essentially ritualized pattern, resembling both in structure and expressed motives for action classic forms such as the European "duel," the American Indian tribal war, and the Celtic clan feud. Although the arousing and "acting out" of individual aggressive emotions are inevitably involved in the gang fight, neither its form nor motivational dynamics can be adequately handled within a predominantly personality-focused frame of reference.

It would be possible to develop in considerable detail the processes by which the commission of a range of illegal acts is either explicitly supported by, implicitly demanded by, or not materially inhibited by factors relating to the focal concerns of lower class culture. In place of such a development, the following three statements condense in general terms the operation of these processes:

1. *Following cultural practices which comprise essential elements of the total life pattern of lower class culture automatically violates certain legal norms.*

2. *In instances where alternate avenues to similar objectives are available, the non-law-abiding avenue frequently provides a relatively greater and more immediate return for a relatively smaller investment of energy.*

3. *The "demanded" response to certain situations recurrently engendered within lower class culture involves the commission of illegal acts.*

The primary thesis of this paper is that the dominant component of the motivation of "delinquent" behavior engaged in by members of lower class corner groups involves a positive effort to achieve states, conditions, or qualities valued within the actor's most significant cultural milieu. If "conformity to immediate reference group values" is the major component of motivation of "delinquent" behavior by gang members, why is such behavior frequently referred to as negativistic, malicious, or rebellious? Albert Cohen, for example, in

Delinquent Boys (Glencoe: Free Press, 1955) describes behavior which violates school rules as comprising elements of "active spite and malice, contempt and ridicule, challenge and defiance." He ascribes to the gang "keen delight in terrorizing 'good' children, and in general making themselves obnoxious to the virtuous." A recent national conference on social work with "hard-to-reach" groups characterized lower class corner groups as "youth groups in conflict with the culture of their (*sic*) communities." Such characterizations are obviously the result of taking the middle class community and its institutions as an implicit point of reference.

A large body of systematically interrelated attitudes, practices, behaviors, and values characteristic of lower class culture are designed to support and maintain the basic features of the lower class way of life. In areas where these differ from features of middle class culture, action oriented to the achievement and maintenance of the lower class system may violate norms of middle class culture and be perceived as deliberately non-conforming or malicious by an observer strongly cathected to middle class norms. This does not mean, however, that violation of the middle class norm is the dominant component of motivation; it is a by-product of action primarily oriented to the lower class system. The standards of lower class culture cannot be seen merely as a reverse function of middle class culture — as middle class standards "turned upside down"; lower class culture is a distinctive tradition many centuries old with an integrity of its own.

From the viewpoint of the acting individual, functioning within a field of well-structured cultural forces, the relative impact of "conforming" and "rejective" elements in the motivation of gang delinquency is weighted preponderantly on the conforming side. Rejective or rebellious elements are inevitably involved, but their influence during the actual commission of delinquent acts is relatively small compared to the influence of pressures to achieve what is valued by the actor's most immediate reference groups. Expressed awareness by the actor of the element of rebellion often represents only that aspect of motivation of which he is explicitly conscious; the deepest and most compelling components of motivation — adherence to highly meaningful group standards of Toughness, Smartness, Excitement, etc. — are often unconsciously patterned. No cultural pattern as well-established as the practice of illegal acts by members of lower class corner groups could persist if buttressed primarily by negative, hostile, or rejective motives; its principal motivational support, as in the case of any persisting cultural tradition, derives from a positive effort to achieve what is valued within that tradition, and to conform to its explicit and implicit norms.

Differentiating between motivational and social-control theories, Briar and Piliavin examine the explanation of delinquency in relation to the delinquent subculture. Listing five problems common to motivational theories, the authors suggest the importance of situationally induced motives to engage in such behavior; however, they state that constraints against that behavior must also be considered. Specifically, they view the processes of social control in terms of commitments to conformity. Although such commitments can develop from a number of sources, it is suggested that parent-child relationships are critically important. In the final section of the paper the authors examine the congruence of their views with what is known empirically about delinquency.

SCOTT BRIAR
IRVING PILIAVIN

Delinquency, Situational Inducements, and Commitment to Conformity

In recent years a theory of delinquency, the delinquent subculture thesis, has been advanced which has had an enormous influence on delinquency prevention and control programs throughout the United States. In the present paper we will show: first, that the subculture thesis, and the general class of theories of which it is a part, are unable to account satisfactorily for crucial aspects of the phenomena of delinquency; and second, that these phenomena can be better explained by an alternative class of formulations currently categorized as social control theories, when

From *Social Problems* (Summer 1965), Vol. 13, no. 1, pp. 35–45. Reprinted by permission of the Society for the Study of Social Problems.

these theories are modified in ways suggested below.

The subculture theory of delinquency along with some of the theories it is intended to supersede — such as psychoanalytic theory and the adolescent rebellion thesis — belong to the class of what may be termed motivational theories of delinquency. These theories regard the illegal acts of delinquents as the product of some enduring disposition or combination of dispositions unique to these youths. While motivational theories differ widely on the nature and precise etiology of these dispositions, they follow a common logic regarding the development of these dispositions and their role in delinquent behavior. In brief, these dispositions are seen as: (1) deriving from certain interpersonal and/or social conditions which delinquents experience; (2) essentially permanent aspects of the personality and/or value framework of delinquent boys; and (3) forces which propel them into illegal behavior.

Despite their numerous differences, however, all motivational theories of delinquency have incurred common problems. First, the etiological factors they postulate do not operate uniformly. That is, many boys subjected to experiences which presumably should give rise to delinquency-producing dispositions do not acquire them. Second, many boys who exhibit these dispositions do not appear among identified delinquents. Third, the great majority of identified delinquents apparently become law-abiding in late adolescence and early adulthood — a fact which motivational theories of delinquency cannot explain, with their assumptions on the enduring nature of delinquency-producing dispositions. Fourth, even if we grant, despite the above problems,[1] that delinquent behavior is in some fashion and to some degree a product of enduring dispositions, we still face the unexplained fact that only a small portion of boys who are members of delinquent gangs or who are designated delinquent by juvenile courts have those characteristics predicted for them by contemporary motivational theories of delinquency. Finally, motivational theories of delinquency do not account for the well documented fact that the vast majority of boys engage in delinquent behavior to some degree.

To avoid the above problems, defenders of these theories have (1) indicated that various factors may mitigate the influence of delinquency-producing dispositions, (2) suggested that forces other than those so far identified may also lead boys to commit illegal acts, and (3) argued that the delinquent behavior of so-called non-delinquents is accidental, prankish, or otherwise understandable in terms not applicable to true delinquents.[2] These arguments, however, imply a cumbersome multi-factor theory of delinquency whose obvious defects have led some theorists to doubt whether etiological explanations of the phenomena are in fact possible.[3]

Situationally Induced Motives to Deviate

Those who argue for a radical distinction between delinquent and non-delinquent traits attempt to justify it on the basis of the apparent differentials in the frequency of various types of delinquent activity among "delinquents" (or a particular class of delinquents) and "non-delinquents." Having established such differentials, these theorists argue that the infractions of "delinquents" are different in origin from those of "non-delinquents." More concise and less questionable, however, is the assumption that the delinquent acts of both non-delinquents and delinquents are conditioned largely by common factors. This assumption provides the basic premise for the formulation to follow.

Because delinquent behavior is typically episodic, purposive, and confined to certain situations,[4] we assume that the motives for such be-

[1] Presumably these problems can be dealt with by the introduction of additional factors which either augment or constrain the influence of those factors considered basic to the development of delinquent-producing dispositions and/or the operation of the dispositions themselves. However, to our knowledge, no systematic effort has been made to identify these ancillary conditions and their operation.

[2] This interpretation is not shared by Bloch and Niederhoffer who, in acknowledging the universality of delinquent behavior, attribute it to adolescent identity crisis. But as Cloward and Ohlin point out, this view of delinquency fails to account for apparent differentials in illegal activities among various identifiable adolescent subgroupings. Herbert Bloch and Arthur Niederhoffer, *The Gang: A Study in Adolescent Behavior* (New York: Philosophical Library, 1958), p. 17; Richard A. Cloward and Lloyd E. Ohlin, *Delinquency and Opportunity* (Glencoe, Ill.: The Free Press, 1960), pp. 50–55.

[3] David Matza, *Delinquency and Drift* (New York: John Wiley & Sons, 1964), pp. 33–67.

[4] Borrowing from Kohn and Williams, we define a situation as ". . . a series of interactions, located in space and time, and perceived by the participants as an event: in this usage 'situation' is a delimiting term, cutting out from the flow of experience a particular series of interpersonal actions which are seen by the participants as a describable event, separable from preceding and succeeding events, constraining the participants to act in par-

havior are frequently episodic, oriented to short-term ends, and confined to certain situations. That is, rather than considering delinquent acts as solely the product of long-term motives deriving from conflicts or frustrations whose genesis is far removed from the arenas in which the illegal behavior occurs, we assume these acts are prompted by short-term situationally induced desires experienced by all boys to obtain valued goods, to portray courage in the presence of, or be loyal to peers, to strike out at someone who is disliked, or simply to "get kicks." [5]

The influence of currently experienced situations on individuals' attitudes and behaviors has been emphasized in numerous sociological and social-psychological studies. In brief, these studies indicate that situational factors can confront actors with conflicts, opportunities, pressures, and temptations which may influence the actors' actions and views. Many of these studies, especially those conducted under "real-life" conditions, have focused on highly patterned situations of long duration, such as the social structure of an industrial plant, a hospital ward, or a housing project.[6] On the

other hand, several theoretical writings,[7] material from some case studies,[8] and a large number of experimental studies in social psychology indicate that situationally induced stimuli of relatively short duration also can affect, to varying extents, the values and behaviors of those exposed to these stimuli. In the words of Lewin:

It is a simple fact, but still not sufficiently recognized in psychology and sociology, that the behavior of a person depends above all upon his momentary position. Often, the world looks very different before and after an event which changes the region in which a person is located.[9]

But even granting that short-term situationally induced stimuli can influence individuals, we question whether or not such stimuli are sufficient to effect deviant behavior. There is some evidence to suggest that they are. Cressey, for example, has shown that the criminal violation of financial trust can be viewed as a narrow goal-oriented response to a situationally induced financial problem:

Trusted persons become trust violators when

---

ticular ways and having its own unique consequences." Melvin L. Kohn and Robin M. Williams, "Situational Patterning in Intergroup Relations," *American Sociological Review*, 21 (April 1956), p. 164.

[5] We are suggesting here that the situations which delinquents find tempting and exciting are similar, in spirit, to those which attract the nondelinquent. As Matza has pointed out, the teen-age culture is "a conventional version of the delinquent tradition. Here we find an emphasis on fun and adventure: a disdain for scholastic effort; the more or less persistent involvement in 'tolerated' status offenses like drinking, gambling, occasional truancy, 'making out' in the sense of sexual conquest, driving cars before the appropriate age, smoking, swearing, and staying out late. . . . Aggression is considerably tempered, but there is a persistent concern with the credentials on [sic] masculinity and femininity." David Matza, "Subterranean Traditions of Youth," *Annals of the American Academy of Political and Social Science*, 338 (November 1961), p. 116.

[6] See for example: Leon Festinger, Stanley Schachter, and Kurt Back, *Social Pressures in Informal Groups* (New York: Harper, 1950); Morton Deutsch and Mary E. Collins, *Interracial Housing: A Psychological Evaluation of a Social*

Experiment (Minneapolis: Univ. of Minnesota Press, 1951); Neal Gross, Ward S. Mason, Alexander W. McEachern, *Explorations in Role Analysis* (New York: John Wiley & Sons, 1958); Kurt Lewin, Ronald Lippett, and Ralph K. White, "Patterns of Aggressive Behavior in Experimentally Created 'Social Climates,'" *Journal of Social Psychology*, 10 (1939), pp. 271–299; Seymour Lieberman, "The Effects of Changes in Roles on the Attitudes of Role Occupants," *Human Relations*, 9 (1950), pp. 385–403; Alvin Gouldner, *Patterns of Industrial Bureaucracy* (Glencoe, Ill.: The Free Press, 1954); Peter G. Garabedian, "Social Roles and Processes of Socialization in the Prison Community," *Social Problems*, 11 (Fall 1963), pp. 139–152; Alfred Stanton and Morris Schwartz, *The Mental Hospital* (New York: Basic Books, 1954); Peter Blau, "Structural Effects," *American Sociological Review*, 25 (1960), pp. 178–193.

[7] Kurt Lewin, *Field Theory in Social Science* (New York: Harper & Brothers, 1951); George C. Homans, *Social Behavior: Its Elementary Forms* (New York: Harcourt, Brace and World, 1961), pp. 46–47, 51–82.

[8] Gouldner, *op. cit.*, pp. 83–85; Kohn and Williams, *op. cit.*, pp. 164–174.

[9] Lewin, *op. cit.*, p. 137.

they conceive of themselves as having a financial problem which is nonsharable, have the knowledge or awareness that this problem can be secretly resolved by violation of the position of financial trust, and are able to apply to their own conduct in that situation verbalizations which enable them to adjust their conceptions of themselves as trusted persons with their conceptions of themselves as users of the entrusted funds or property.[10]

Additional support for the notion that situationally induced stimuli of short duration can lead to illegal behavior is provided by self-reports from gang members:

When we were shoplifting we always made a game of it. For example we might gamble on who could steal the most caps in a day, or who could steal in the presence of a detective and then get away. This was the best part of the game. . . . It was the fun I wanted, not the hat.[11]

I was walkin' uptown with a couple of friends, and we run into Magician and them there. They asked us if we wanted to go to a fight, and we said "Yes." When they asked me if I wanted to go to a fight, I couldn't say, "No." I mean I could say, "No," but for old-time's sake, I said, "Yes." [12]

You see, man, it's not that I'm against anyone else, I'm just "all for me." Our stealing did have a utilitarian motive. Sometimes we stole something we actually liked and wanted and stealing always proved we had guts. . . . [But] most of the time I didn't even have stealing on my mind. . . .
What have we done? We're just trying to have some fun. We don't want to be like those middle class guys. We are no mamma's boys.[13]

Thus, there is considerable basis for assuming that the immediate situation in which a

youth finds himself can play an important role in his decision to engage in delinquent behavior. Obviously, however, this is not to say that the situation offering inducement or pressure to a youth to deviate will necessarily lead him to take such action. For one thing, situationally induced motives vary in intensity. Furthermore, their expression depends on a variety of contingencies, such as the ease with which the motivated behavior can be carried out, the risks involved, and the press or attractiveness of other activities.[14] Finally, whether or not the motives to deviate are situationally induced, the behavioral expression of them depends on the degree to which the individuals experiencing the motives also experience constraints against that behavior.

Constraints on Deviance:
The Concept of Commitment

Three dominant views can be identified in motivational theories of delinquency regarding (1) the nature of the influences which constrain individuals from engaging in delinquent behavior, and (2) the conditions under which these influences are neutralized.

In delinquent sub-culture theories, the basic constraint against the exercise of deviant motives is allegiance to the dominant values of the larger society. Depending on the particular theorist, a youth's freedom from this constraint entails allegiance to an oppositional system of values by means of either a type of reaction-formation,[15] a more or less rational process of decision-making,[16] or socialization

---

[10] Donald R. Cressey, "The Criminal Violation of Financial Trust," *American Sociological Review*, 15 (December 1950), p. 742.

[11] Clifford R. Shaw, "Juvenile Delinquency — A Group Tradition," *Bulletin of the State University of Iowa*, No. 23, N.S. No. 700, 1933, p. 8.

[12] Lewis Yablonsky, *The Violent Gang* (New York: Macmillan, 1962), p. 13.

[13] Comments of an ex-gang leader as quoted in Sophia M. Robison, *Juvenile Delinquency* (New York: Holt, Rinehart and Winston, 1960), pp. 134–137.

[14] It should be emphasized, however, that while many situational contingencies of this sort fall in the class of phenomena often considered "accidental," these events do not occur randomly. For example, boys living in slums are more likely to encounter experiences which can evoke motives to deviate in certain ways than are their middle class counterparts. To illustrate: the slum youth is more likely to find drunks sleeping in doorways, to see wares displayed in open counters on the sidewalk, to meet adult criminals, and to come under police surveillance than is the youth living in a middle class neighborhood.

[15] Albert K. Cohen, *Delinquent Boys: The Culture of the Gang* (Glencoe, Ill.: The Free Press, 1955).

[16] Richard A. Cloward and Lloyd E. Ohlin, *op. cit., passim.*

to a cultural tradition differing from that of the large society.[17]

A second type of constraint involves internalization of parental prohibitions and demands — in other words, the development of a super-ego. Freedom from this constraint is seen largely as the product of parental failure to socialize children properly. Such failure may result from a variety of conditions, ranging from parental failure to articulate conventional values to lack of the kind of familial atmosphere in which such values, even if articulated, can be incorporated by children.[18]

There are, however, important limitations in these two formulations of the constraining influences on deviant behavior. For one thing, empirical studies have failed to find a strong oppositional or autonomous value system among delinquent gang youth as predicted by delinquent sub-culture theorists.[19] Moreover, considerable evidence indicates that moral concerns, such as would be expected from the operation of the super-ego, are neither the only nor necessarily the major factors in constraining persons from engaging in or legitimizing illegal behavior.[20]

A third formulation of the constraints against delinquency, deriving from the writings of social control theorists, overcomes these limitations to some extent. This formula-

tion stresses the importance of social institutions such as the family, the school, and law enforcement as instruments of control on the delinquent motives of boys. Presumably all boys are subject to these motives;[21] however, they express them in overt behavior only when, for whatever reason, the controlling potential of these institutions is not realized. A considerable literature has developed attempting to specify the conditions under which this occurs. Thus the absence of family controls has been linked to parental rejection, ineffectuality, and neglect;[22] and the deficiency of controls within the school has been traced, among other things, to its failure to be oriented to the capabilities and interests of students.[23] But while social control theory can account for much delinquency, it, too, suffers limitations, since the nature of the processes by which social control is exercised and the sequential patterning of these processes have not been specified. Thus, for example, social control theories are ambiguous regarding the relationship between "inner controls" and external (or social) controls; moreover, they are unable to account for some of the phenomena of delinquency, such as the eventual conventionalization of many delinquent boys.

These problems can be eliminated by viewing the central processes of social control as "commitments to conformity." By this term we mean not only fear of the material deprivations and punishments which might result from being discovered as an offender but also apprehension about the deleterious consequences of such a discovery on one's attempts to maintain a consistent self image, to sustain valued relationships, and to preserve current and future statuses and activities. A youth with

[17] Walter Miller, "Lower Class Culture as a Generating Milieu of Gang Delinquency," *Journal of Social Issues*, 14, No. 3 (1958), pp. 5–19.

[18] Kate Friedlander, *The Psychoanalytic Approach to Juvenile Delinquency* (New York: International Universities Press, 1947).

[19] Robert A. Gordon, James F. Short, Jr., Desmond S. Cartwright, and Fred L. Strodtbeck, "Values and Gang Delinquency: A Study of Street-Corner Groups," *American Journal of Sociology*, 69 (1963), pp. 109–128.

[20] Solomon Rettig and Harve E. Rawson, "The Risk Hypothesis in Predictive Judgements of Unethical Behavior," *Journal of Abnormal and Social Psychology*, 66 (March 1963), pp. 243–248; Helen Merrell Lynd, *On Shame and the Search for Identity* (New York: Harcourt, Brace, and Co., 1958); David P. Ausubel, "Relationships Between Shame and Guilt in the Socializing Process," *Psychological Review*, 62 (1955), pp. 378–390; Justin Aronfreed, "The Nature, Variety, and Social Patterning of Moral Responses to Transgression," *Journal of Abnormal and Social Psychology*, 63 (1961), pp. 223–240.

[21] However, it must be admitted that the nature of these motives is not well articulated by social control theorists.

[22] F. Ivan Nye, *Family Relationships and Delinquent Behavior* (New York: John Wiley & Sons, 1958); William McCord and Joan McCord, *Origins of Crime* (New York: Columbia University Press, 1959).

[23] Jackson Toby and Marcia L. Toby, *Low School Status as a Predisposing Factor in Subcultural Delinquency* (New Brunswick, N.J.: Rutgers University, no date, mimeographed); Cohen, *op. cit.*, pp. 112–116.

strong commitments to conformity is less likely to engage in deviant acts than is one for whom these commitments are minimal, given that both experience motives to deviate in the same degree. The cumulative strength of one's various commitments is not to be equated with motives to deviate. Commitment refers instead to the *probability* that such motives will be acted upon when they are experienced. Even persons with strong commitments to conformity experience motives to engage in criminal acts, and they may perform such acts when their commitments do not appear to be threatened (for example, under conditions of low visibility) or when the motives to deviate are very strong.

The role of commitments of the type discussed here is not new to sociological or psychological discussion. For example, Goode has stated that interpersonal commitments are fundamentally important in understanding conformity within modern urban society:

. . . In a secularized society, with perhaps weak commitment to norms or role emotion, role or norm conformity may depend far more on the greater sensitivity of ego to alter's response than it does in other types of societies. This is not to assert that high sensitivity is inversely correlated with high intensity of role commitment or emotion. Rather when there is low intensity there must be a correlative increase of sensitivity to "alter opinion" or to "community opinion" (outsiders related to alter and ego) if role obligations are to be met generally.[24]

A more general formulation of the concept of commitment has been put forth recently by Becker:

First, the individual is in a position in which his decision with regard to some particular line of action has consequences for other interests and activities not necessarily related to it. Second, he has placed himself in that position by his own prior actions. A third element is present though so obvious as not to be apparent: the committed person must be aware . . . (of these other interests) and must recognize that

his decision in this case will have ramifications beyond it.[25]

The applicability of this formulation for socially disapproved as well as conventional behaviors is suggested by one of Becker's examples:

A middle class girl can find herself committed to a consistently chaste line of behavior by the sizable bit of her reputation that middle class culture attaches to virginity for females. A girl who is a member of a social class where virginity is less valued could not be committed in this way; and except for a few puritanical enclaves in our society, boys cannot acquire commitments of this kind at all, for male virginity has little value. . . .[26]

If commitments to, or stakes in, conformity play an important role in determining a youth's capability for deviance, they also are significant in at least two other respects. First, they affect the stance the youth takes *vis-à-vis* adult authority figures. The boy with high commitments to conformity is by definition committed to maintaining and achieving desired statuses as well as to obtaining the approval of those whose love and protection he regards as important. Those aims, however, will also lead this youth to defer to the judgments of adult authorities, to accord these adults respect during social intercourse, and to be fearful, contrite, and ashamed when they confront him with his misdeeds. The low stake boy, however, is less likely to manifest these attributes. Because the disapproval of these adults entails less cost for him than for the high stake youth, he is not as constrained to defer to or show respect for adults.

Secondly, stakes in conformity will influence the youth's choice of friends. Those boys who have high stakes will tend not to befriend peers whose stakes are low since the latter are more likely to "get into trouble." Boys with low stakes, on the other hand, will tend to avoid those who are "chicken" and to seek out those

---

[24] William J. Goode, "Norm Commitment and Conformity to Role-Status Obligations," *American Journal of Sociology*, 66 (November 1960), pp. 246–258.

[25] Howard S. Becker, "Notes on the Concept of Commitment," *American Journal of Sociology*, 66 (July 1960), pp. 35–36. See also Howard S. Becker, "Personal Change in Adult Life," *Sociometry*, 27 (1964), pp. 40–53.
[26] Becker, "Notes on the Concept of Commitment," *op. cit.*, p. 39.

with congruent interests and freedom to act. These processes are not different logically from those involved in the formation of most youth groups. Just as athletes, daters, and music lovers cluster together,[27] so do those with similar commitments to conformity.[28]

Acquiring or losing stakes in conformity does not take place only through a sudden or cataclysmic event, nor is it an irreversible process. Boys who for a considerable period have had high commitments to maintaining a conventional appearance, and whose deviance is rare and circumspect, may, for a variety of reasons, gradually have these commitments reduced and become more active and visible in their illegal activities. Conversely, many of those whose stakes in conformity have been low may encounter experiences which serve to increase their stakes, leading them in turn to more conventional behavior.

Some Bases for Commitments
to Conformity

A variety of conditions can serve as bases for the development of commitments to conformity, including, among others, belief in God, affection for conventionally behaving peers, occupational aspirations, ties to parents, desire to perform well in school, and fear of the material deprivations and punishments associated with arrest. Among the most important, if not, in fact, the most important of these conditions is the relationship of the youth to his parents. In most families, parental sanctions and the withdrawal of love implied in their use are effective instruments for maintaining parental authority. Because of his dependence on and affection for his parents, the child conforms to their expectations in order to obtain their approval. In some families, however, parents fail to exercise authority. The punitive parent who does not reward conformity with affection thereby may undermine the basis for voluntary compliance by his child.[29] The parent who is overwhelmed by current responsibilities and problems may ignore his children, leaving them to fend for themselves and to define alone their relations with the outside world. Some parents who love their children and who are loved by them may caution their children against many things but then fail to enforce these expectations. They thus behave toward their children more as friends and siblings than as authorities, and their desires, therefore, are compromised because control is not exercised. Finally, some parents are unable to be effective authorities because they lack the economic and social statuses which their children equate with legitimate authorities.[30] The unemployed male, for example, may be seen as inferior not only by his peers but by his children, thus undermining his claim to parental authority. These examples obviously do not exhaust the various conditions which can lead children to develop autonomy from parental expectations. Moreover, these conditions do not necessarily represent steady states. Parents who are fully able to cope with infants and toddlers may be far less capable of dealing with more active, less dependent, and more perceptive school-age children. Also, a variety of crises and tragedies may vitiate parents' competence to operate as adult authorities, regardless of the adequacy with which they formerly performed these tasks.

It is likely that failure to develop conformity commitments through the desire to satisfy parental expectations reduces the probability that the youth will develop such commitments in other social contexts. As a case in point, the desire to achieve in school is in many instances

---

[27] James S. Coleman, *The Adolescent Society* (New York: The Free Press, 1962), pp. 173–219.
[28] This argument derives from that of Merton and Lazersfeld on value homophyly. Paul F. Lazersfeld and Robert K. Merton, "Friendship as Social Process" in Monroe Berger, Theodore Abel, and Charles H. Page (eds.), *Freedom and Control in Modern Society* (New York: Van Nostrand, 1954), pp. 18–66.

[29] While the threat of severe physical punishment and material deprivation can constrain the child's behavior at home, it is not as likely to control his behavior in other social contexts as less severe parental sanctions. Moreover, severe punishment may lower the child's reliance on parental guidance. Albert Bandura and Richard H. Walters, *Adolescent Aggression* (New York: Ronald Press, 1959); Albert Bandura and Richard H. Walters, *Social Learning and Personality Development* (New York: Holt, Rinehart and Winston, 1963).
[30] Donald G. McKinley, *Social Class and Family Life* (New York: The Free Press, 1964), pp. 92–93, 152–191.

the product of parents' expectations that their child perform well in the classroom and of the child's concern for fulfilling these expectations.[31] Should either or both of these conditions be lacking, then the chances of developing commitments based on academic aspirations are reduced. Similar considerations hold in the conformity commitments arising from fear of the consequences of arrest. Most youth regard arrest as a fearful experience because they believe, among other things, that (1) it can alter their public image adversely, and (2) it exposes them to punishment, deprivation, and the moral indignation of parents, friends, and officials. Those youths, then, whose behavior is not governed by parental evaluations, lack an important basis for developing concern about the consequences of arrest.

Nevertheless, the failure of children to develop commitments to conformity through a desire to fulfill parental expectations need not necessarily preclude the development of such commitments in other ways. For example, the desire to achieve in school, which can provide a potent incentive for conventional behavior, may develop in response to praise from teachers, respect from friends, and the anticipation of future pay-offs for school achievement, even in the absence of strong commitments to perform in accord with parental expectations. Furthermore, loss of commitments in arenas outside the home may precede and lead to loss of commitments within the family. Again, using the school as an example, some youths with high commitments to parental expectations may nevertheless be disinterested in and perform poorly in school or may be apprehended as offenders. If as a result they experience severe and enduring parental criticism, their commitments to parental authority may diminish.

Congruence with Empirical Data on Delinquency

As noted above, little evidence is available which provides a direct test of the basic

propositions in the model presented here. However, we can examine the congruence between this model and what is known empirically about delinquency. Obviously, even if considerable congruence is found, it cannot be interpreted as a demonstration of the validity of these propositions; nevertheless, it does suggest their plausibility.

First, the conditions for lack of commitment to conformity are more prevalent among lower class than middle class youth. "The lower class individual is more likely to have been exposed to punishment, lack of love, and a general atmosphere of tension and aggression snce early childhood." [32] Furthermore, his parents devote less time to supervising his activities,[33] are less trusting of him,[34] and are less likely to be viewed by him as legitimate authorities.[35] Consequently, and consistent with empirical findings, the lower class youth, lacking these bases for commitment, will engage in more frequent, more visible, and more severely punished delinquent behavior than their middle class peers.

Second, since this formulation does not regard delinquent acts as the product of enduring motives, nor as completely determined by

---

[31] David C. McClelland, John W. Atkinson, Russell A. Clark, and Edgar L. Lowell, *The Achievement Motive* (New York: Appleton-Century-Crofts, 1953); McKinley, *op. cit.,* p. 96.

[32] Seymour Martin Lipset, "Democracy and Working-Class Authoritarianism," *American Sociological Review*, 24 (August 1959), p. 495. See, too, Urie Bronfenbrenner, "Socialization and Social Class Through Time and Space," in Eleanor E. Maccoby, Thomas M. Newcomb, and E. L. Hartley (eds.), *Readings in Social Psychology* (New York: Holt, 1958), pp. 400–425, and Genevieve Knupfer, "Portrait of the Underdog," *Public Opinion Quarterly*, 11 (Spring 1947), pp. 103–114.

[33] Eleanor E. Maccoby, "Effects Upon Children of Their Mothers' Working," in Norman W. Bell and Ezra Vogel (eds.), *A Modern Introduction to the Family* (Glencoe, Ill.: The Free Press, 1960), pp. 521–533.

[34] Ivan Nye, "Adolescent-Parent Adjustment — Socio-Economic Level as a Variable," *American Sociological Review*, 16 (June 1951), pp. 341–349; George Psathas, "Ethnicity, Social Class, and Adolescent Independence from Parental Control," *American Sociological Review*, 22 (August 1957), pp. 415–423.

[35] McKinley, *op. cit.,* pp. 92–93, 156–157; Albert Reiss, "Delinquency as the Failure of Personal and Social Controls," *American Sociological Review*, 16 (April 1951), pp. 196–207.

stable characteristics of boys and their situations, it is consistent with the observation that delinquent behavior is an episodic and typically noncompulsive activity.[36]

Third, the present framework can account for the fact that virtually all middle class and lower class boys engage in some delinquent activities and that some middle class boys are serious delinquents while many lower class boys are not. As indicated earlier, even boys with strong commitments to their parents' expectations, who perform well and aspire to good performance in school, and who fear the punishments associated with arrest and detention, will commit delinquent acts if the rewards are sufficient, visibility is low, and the act can be rationalized or justified so as not to denigrate the youth's self-image.[37] Furthermore, in some middle class families, parent-child relationships are not always so benign as to rule out the possibility that parental authority will fail to be acknowledged. Nor are lower class parents uniformly so punishing, rejecting, or incapable that they fail, even in high delinquency areas, to be effective authority figures *vis-à-vis* their children. Similar considerations apply to children's commitments to academic performance and fear of the consequences ensuing from arrest and detention.

Fourth, this formulation explains the evident reduction in delinquent activities among late adolescents and young adults. Specifically, during these years some delinquents obtain jobs; others marry; and for all, the penalties for offending behavior greatly increase. Such events increase commitments to conformity. Furthermore, insofar as employment takes boys off the streets and provides them with money, they are less likely to experience motives to commit illegal acts for gain.

Fifth, the group nature of many delinquent activities and the norms of these groups are not nearly as compelling as some theorists have assumed.[38] This is not to suggest that the expectations of gang members do not influence individuals considerably, nor that those delinquent gang members with more than minimal commitments to conformity will not forego these commitments on occasion in response to the demands of their peers. On the other hand, adolescents in general frequently give priority to peer expectations over those emanating from other sources.[39] What is distinctive about delinquent gang members is that a greater proportion of their activities involve illegal acts. This can be accounted for by the argument that members of delinquent gangs, at the time of their recruitment, already lack strong commitments to conformity.[40]

Sixth, the model provides a conceptual basis for understanding the hostile and/or coolly indifferent and unconcerned demeanor which many delinquent boys display toward adult authority figures such as teachers, police, and correctional workers.[41] The boy with a high stake in conformity is by definition committed to meeting conventional expectations in order to maintain and achieve desired statuses as well

[36] David Matza, *op. cit.*, pp. 22, 26–30.

[37] Sykes and Matza have pointed out that such "techniques of neutralization" are used by so-called confirmed delinquents. Their use by other youths who offend seems therefore quite probable. [Greshman M. Sykes and David Matza, "Techniques of Neutralization: A Theory of Delinquency," *American Sociological Review*, 22 (December 1957), pp. 664–670.] Moreover, as Matza points out in *Delinquency and Drift* (*op. cit.*, pp. 90–91), "the delinquent by using these techniques of neutralization, is able to consider himself not responsible for his acts, a self-conception which is confirmed, perhaps surpassed by views held in certain quarters of conventional society." In this way, the delinquent is able to preserve an image of himself as an essentially law-abiding person who is being treated unfairly. This at least suggests that the delinquent does not necessarily see himself as more delinquent than the so-called non-delinquent.

[38] Matza, *op. cit.*, pp. 38–40.

[39] James S. Coleman, *The Adolescent Society* (New York: The Free Press, 1961), pp. 138–141, 172; Joseph Stone and Joseph Church, *Childhood and Adolescence* (New York: Random House, 1957), pp. 288–292.

[40] Albert Cohen considers this possibility but rejects it in favor of the notion that the offenses of delinquent gang members are group compelled. No empirical evidence is given, however, for his conclusions. Albert K. Cohen, *op. cit.*, pp. 31–32.

[41] Irving Piliavin and Scott Briar, "Police Encounters with Juveniles," *American Journal of Sociology*, 70 (September 1964), pp. 206–214; Frederic M. Thrasher, *The Gang*, abridged edition (Chicago: University of Chicago Press, 1963), pp. 270–273.

as to obtain the approval of those whose love and protection he regards as important. These aims, however, will also lead this youth to defer to the judgments of adult authorities, to accord these adults respect during social intercourse and to be fearful, contrite and ashamed when they confront him with his misdeeds. The low stake boy, however, is less likely to manifest these attributes. Because the approval of these adults carries for him less significance than for the high stake youth, he is not as constrained to defer to or show respect for adults.[42]

Finally, the present model permits a more complete explanation of the phenomenon known as secondary deviance. The theory of secondary deviance holds that the experience of being labeled and treated as a deviant has self-fulfilling consequences.

[Branding and] treating a person as though he were generally deviant . . . sets in motion several mechanisms which conspire to shape the person in the image people have of him.
Put . . . generally, the point is that the treatment of deviants denies them the ordinary means of carrying on the routines of everyday life open to most people. Because of this denial the deviant must of necessity develop illegitimate routines.[43]

Secondary deviance theory, however, has not been able to account for the fact that many boys who are labeled delinquent by the courts apparently do not continue their deviant behavior. An explanation of this phenomenon consistent with the thesis of this paper is that the effects of labeling a youth delinquent are a function of his pre-existing commitments to conformity. For the high stake boy, arrest is likely to lead to a reconfirmation of conventional behavior. He will "toe the line" more rigorously in order to (1) regain and maintain the respect and affection of those who expect

him to behave conventionally and (2) increase his chances of achieving conventional goals. For the low stake boy, however, arrest may remove one of the few remaining constraints against his exercise of deviant behavior. That is, for the boy who is not committed to parental expectations of conformity and who has little interest in school achievement, etc., one of the few bases for his conformity may be his fear of the experiences he will go through during arrest, trial, and incarceration. But typically these experiences are not as depriving as anticipated, and in encountering them the low stake boys may find they need not be feared. For these boys, then, this source of commitment to conformity has, in effect, been reduced, and the probability of their committing further delinquencies is enhanced.

Conclusion

The formulation presented in this paper is essentially a probabilistic one. It views delinquency as the product of commitments to conformity, situationally induced motives to deviate, and a variety of contingencies. This framework is consistent with the empirical data on delinquency and, in fact, accounts for some aspects of this phenomena — such as its presence among most youth and its decline in early adulthood — which are not accounted for by other theoretical models.

For example, one implication of Cloward and Ohlin's delinquent sub-culture thesis is that lower class boys will reduce their delinquent activities if they perceive that opportunities for employment will be provided them when they become adults. In our view, however, employment opportunities do not become a salient influence on the day to day behavior of delinquent boys until they develop commitments and needs that make full-time work a valued activity. Moreover, such commitments ordinarily do not occur until late adolescence and early adulthood. Younger boys, those in the age group with the highest rate of delinquent behavior, are not affected by job market conditions; rather, their behavior is influenced, as we have argued above, by more mundane situational considerations. For these boys, therefore, it is necessary to provide bases for

[42] It is important to note in this regard that delinquents do respect and work well for some teachers and that they do not hate all policemen. The attributes of liked and respected officials are discussed in Carl Werthman and Irving Piliavin, "Delinquency and Alienation from Authority" (in process).
[43] Howard S. Becker, *Outsiders* (New York: The Free Press, 1963), pp. 34–35.

conformity commitments which are more immediately relevant than future employment opportunities. While a variety of such bases could be developed, one suggestion by way of example would involve the use of money wages to boys on the condition that they keep out of trouble. The effectiveness of such wages would not depend on long-term efforts by professionals in order to develop boys' aspirations and alleviate their interpersonal problems; consequently, if such wages are effective at all, their impact should be immediate. In any event, the idea of paying boys to conform is sufficiently intriguing to merit study and experimentation.

In his critique Bordua uses the classic view of "gang delinquency," as found in Thrasher's *The Gang*, as a background against which he evaluates three contemporary positions in which status deprivation, opportunity structure, and lower-class culture are emphasized by Cohen, Cloward and Ohlin, and Miller, respectively. According to Bordua, the theories of Cohen and of Cloward and Ohlin emphasize "irrationalism" and depend on an equilibrium model — points stressed by Quinney in an earlier selection (see Section II). The lives of gang members are characterized by desperation, and not a quiet desperation at that, rather than by the attraction and fun Thrasher saw delinquency as offering. Central to Cohen's argument is the assumption that lower-class youth, whom Cohen consistently refers to as "working class," have so internalized middle-class status criteria and antidelinquency norms that they are ambivalent about their delinquent activities. Three outcomes or "mobility stances" — College Boy, Corner Boy, and Delinquent Boy — are noted, but Cohen's failure to treat "internalized resistance to delinquency" as a variable means that Cohen has no explanation for some boys' choice of a "delinquent solution" rather than a College- or Corner-Boy stance.

Cloward and Ohlin treat subcultural delinquency as the result of a particular mobility stance; in their argument delinquent subcultures arise among the boys who possess the means to achieve success goals but who seek economic advancement, not middle-class status. For the most part Cloward and Ohlin do not treat internalization of norms as a variable; Bordua suggests, the inability to lower aspirations, which Cloward and Ohlin emphasize, may be related to the strength of internalized prohibitions. Bordua states another possibility — gang boys may be those who never had very strong internal prohibitions.

In contrast, Miller does not employ the equilibrium model derived from the Parsonian paradigm, nor does he assume prior internalization of antidelinquency norms. In the second section of his paper Bordua caustically observes that sociologists are willing to view delinquency as a reaction to stress as long as the source of stress is located in the class structure and not in the family. Of the three views he examines, it is only in Miller's statement that the family plays a part in the etiology of gang delinquency. Although

Cohen attributes the working-class boys' "inadequate socialization" to their families, he does not emphasize experiences in the family, and Cloward and Ohlin almost completely ignore the family. Bordua attributes the limited emphasis on the family to "the struggle with psychology." Bordua then turns to "the formula" used in contemporary theories of gang delinquency in which "problems of adjustment" owing to class position lead to subcultural "solutions." In devoting attention to class position the theorists ignore or underplay the importance of other attributes of the "population at risk." Bordua poses five important questions about this approach; among them is the importance of race — intergroup hostilities cannot be ignored in gauging the likelihood of gang violence.

Finally, Bordua comments on the use of time in the theories and discusses a number of implications of the handling of the time dimension. Cloward and Ohlin use the "methodological present," but the present is in effect an indicator of what the future must have been anticipated to be at some time in the past. Stated differently, in Cloward and Ohlin's view, gang boys, whose past was spent in anticipating the future so as to produce the present, possess an uncanny ability to foresee the future correctly. The theorists' unusual use of time is related to their search for a plausible problem of adjustment to which delinquency might be a response but results in their positing of "the prealienated boy." One of the implications of the use of time in the development of theory which Bordua discusses is the key problem of the relationship between personal characteristics and associational patterns. Although it may be theoretically inconvenient, this problem is crucial in delinquency theory. Bordua suggests, for example, that the working-class socialization Cohen describes might well lead to delinquency; in this case conflict with middle-class standards would be a consequence rather than a source of delinquency.

DAVID J. BORDUA

Some Comments on Theories of Group Delinquency

This paper is part of an effort to organize and evaluate delinquency theory and research.[1] It will concentrate on current theories of group delinquency especially the "status deprivation"

Originally published in Vol. 32, no. 2 of *Sociological Inquiry* (Spring 1962). Reprinted by permission.

[1] For a treatment of American theory in an historical format see David J. Bordua, *Delinquency Theory and Research In The United States: Major Trends Since 1930* (Mimeo., 1957); "Hauptrichtungen in Theorie und Erforschung der Jugendkriminalität in den USA seit 1930," *Kölner Zeitschrift für Soziologie und Sozialpsychologie*, Sonderheft 2 (1957), pp. 156–88; *La Delinquencia Juvenil en Los Estados Unidos,* Santiago, Chile: Editoriale Andres Bello, 1959. For discussion of theories of group delinquency in a more comparative, systematic view see David J. Bordua, *Sociological Theories and Their Implications For Juvenile Delinquency*, Children's Bureau, Juvenile Delinquency: Facts and Facets, No. 2; Washington, D.C.: U.S. Government Printing Office, 1960. For the immediate background to the present paper see David J. Bordua, "Delinquent Subcultures: Sociological Interpretations of Gang Delinquency," *The Annals*, 338 (November 1961), pp. 119–136.

approach of Albert K. Cohen, the "opportunity structure" approach of Richard A. Cloward and Lloyd E. Ohlin and the "lower class culture" approach of Walter B. Miller.[2] No attempt will be made to review these positions in detail.[3] The paper will concentrate on larger issues raised by these interpretations and other theoretical and research materials will be discussed only secondarily.

Equilibrium and Irrationalism

As compared with the discussion of gangs and gang delinquency by Thrasher and others of the "Chicago School," current theories have shifted in an "irrationalist" direction. Gang boys are driven, not attracted. Their life is

characterized by desperation rather than fun.[4] This is especially true of the status deprivation of Cohen and the opportunity limitation of Cloward and Ohlin.

The stresses to which lower class delinquent "subcultures" are a response are of two sorts. Stress derives from the deprivation visited upon the young by class position and stress derives from guilt over violating the law. Thus, psychically, the delinquent subculture is both created by and creative of desperation.

These two sources of stress — deprivations associated with class position and guilt over internalized norms — appear in slightly different forms in the theories under discussion. In *Delinquent Boys* the prime source of stress is the sensitivity of working (lower?) class boys to the middle class measuring rod. Secondarily the content of the delinquent subculture must also deal with the guilt generated by the delinquent resolution of the status deprivation problem. The "psychic style" of the delinquent subculture then derives from an overdetermined reaction formation to the loss of self-esteem in terms of the middle class measuring rod plus the provocative aggression employed to justify the hostility, aggression and deviance necessitated by the solution of the status deprivation problem. Thus derogation produces hostility, hostility produces guilt, guilt produces provocation, provocation produces counteraggression and so on. All of this presupposes — indeed, make no sense without — a high degree of internalization not only of the middle class status measuring criteria but also of the norms specifically prohibiting theft, property destruction, violence, etc. This assumption that internalization of anti-delinquency norms can be taken for granted I call the implicit moral equilibrium model.

Since Cohen's discussion of the sensitivity of the working class boy to middle class criteria is so central to his argument as well as to much of the criticism of his argument it may be worth somewhat extended treatment here. The key postulate is as follows.[5]

In summary, it may confidently be said that

[2] Albert K. Cohen, *Delinquent Boys: The Culture of the Gang*, Glencoe, Illinois: The Free Press, 1955; Albert K. Cohen and James F. Short, Jr., "Research in Delinquent Subcultures," *Journal of Social Issues*, 14 (1958), pp. 20–36; Richard A. Cloward and Lloyd E. Ohlin, *Delinquency and Opportunity*, Glencoe, Illinois: The Free Press, 1960; Richard A. Cloward, "Illegitimate Means, Anomie and Deviant Behavior," *American Sociological Review*, 24 (April 1959), pp. 164–176. The following papers are all by Walter B. Miller, "Lower Class Culture as a Generating Milieu of Gang Delinquency," *Journal of Social Issues*, 14 (1958), pp. 5–19; "Preventive Work With Street Corner Groups: Boston Delinquency Project," *The Annals*, 322 (March 1959), pp. 97–106; "Implications of Urban Lower Class Culture for Social Work," *The Social Service Review*, 33 (September 1959), pp. 219–236. See also William C. Kvaraceus and Walter B. Miller, *Delinquent Behavior: Culture and The Individual*, Washington, D.C.: National Education Association, 1959.

[3] The originals should of course be referred to. Among them the book by Cloward and Ohlin contains the most thorough review of the other interpretations. For the most complete discussion of the work of Albert K. Cohen see Harold L. Wilensky and Charles N. Lebeaux, *Industrial Society and Social Welfare*, New York: Russell Sage Foundation, 1958, Chapter 9. For a discussion of the "opportunity structure" approach of Cloward and Ohlin which sets it in the larger context of delinquency theory in general see Jackson Toby (Privately circulated review, 1961). For a treatment of the limitations of "subculture" theories as well as an attempt to develop a more generally applicable approach see Walter C. Reckless, "A New Theory of Delinquency and Crime," *Federal Probation*, XXV (December 1961), pp. 42–46. See also Bordua, "Delinquent Subcultures: Sociological Interpretations of Gang Delinquency," *op. cit.*

[4] Bordua, "Delinquent Subcultures: Sociological Theories of Gang Delinquency," *op. cit.*, p. 136.

[5] Cohen, *op. cit.*, p. 119. Italics added.

the working-class boy, particularly if his training and values be those we have here defined as working-class, is more likely than his middle class piers (sic!) to find himself at the bottom of the status hierarchy whenever he moves in a middle-class world, whether it be of adults or of children. *To the degree to which he values middle-class status, either because he values the good opinion of middle-class persons or because he has to some degree internalized middle-class standards himself, he faces a problem of adjustment and is in the market for a "solution."*

But why should the working class boy value middle class status or the good opinion of middle class persons? Cohen gives the following general reasons.[6] (a) Children are generally sensitive to the attitudes of others with whom they are in more than superficial contact. (b) Working class culture is an ideal type and most working class people are culturally ambivalent due to the impact of the mass media and the example of working class contemporaries who have gotten ahead. (c) Working class parents may accommodate to low status but are likely to project their aspirations onto their children even if only to the extent that they will want their children to be steady and respectable. (d) Corner-boy children internalize middle class standards to a sufficient degree to be ambivalent about their corner-boy behavior.

Essentially, then, the delinquent subculture derives from a particular resolution of this ambivalence. The College Boy commits himself to upward mobility, the Corner Boy accepts defeat and withdraws from the struggle, the Delinquent Boy overturns and attacks the middle class norms. Why one solution rather than another? More crucially why are not all Corner Boys Delinquent Boys and *vice versa?* This question is made even more crucial by Cohen's notion that the delinquent solution is superior in the calculus of psychic gains and losses because the Corner Boy solution requires acceptance of felt inferiority.

As long as the psychic life of the delinquent boy is presumed to be exhausted by his orientation to "middle class values" in the status aspiration sense the question is unanswerable.

If the theory requires only three responses to objective working class position — College Boy, Corner Boy, Delinquent Boy — and does not stipulate why the choices are made then it cannot be a theory of delinquency.

At the very minimum the theory must include as an independent element rather than as just part of the loose package of "middle class values" differential internalization of the norms specifically prohibiting delinquency. Thus the Corner Boy presumably cannot engage in serious and substantial delinquency because of the success with which he has been socialized with respect to theft, etc. But since the degree of internalization is presupposed in the implicit moral equilibrium model employed by Cohen and by Cloward and Ohlin it cannot enter the theory as a variable. Thus there is nothing in Cohen's theory that dictates that *anyone* become delinquent. The College Boy-Corner Boy distinction could be exhaustive.

The Cloward and Ohlin formulation relative to choice of adaptation to lower class position and gang formation is less subject to this criticism because it at least conceives mobility stance and orientation to norms governing theft, etc., separately. When Cohen sees the delinquent subculture as in effect a type of mobility stance, Cloward and Ohlin treat subcultural delinquency as an outcome of a particular mobility stance. Thus internalization of norms against theft, etc., is conceptualized separately but by and large still not treated variably. Again as in Cohen the best indication of the importance of this consequence of the implicit moral equilibrium model is given in the treatment of the relationship of aspiration, frustration and non-conformity.[7]

Adolescents who form delinquent subcultures, we suggest, have internalized an emphasis upon conventional goals. Faced with limitations on legitimate avenues of access to these goals, *and unable to revise their aspirations downward,* they experience intense frustrations; the exploration of nonconformist alternatives *may* be the result.

But what can account for this inability to revise aspirations downward? Certainly one force would be the strength of internalized prohibitions against illegal activity.

[6] *Ibid.,* pp. 123–127.

[7] Cloward and Ohlin, *op. cit.,* p. 86. Italics added.

Again in a long section on defenses against guilt Cloward and Ohlin deal with the significance of rationalization processes in enabling the delinquent to circumvent his own internal prohibitions.[8] It is quite possible, of course, that what distinguishes gang boys from others is the fact that gang boys may not have had very strong internal prohibitions to begin with. In which case the necessity to break through the moral barriers might not be so great and the "irrationalism" of the subculture not so necessary theoretically.

The implicit equilibrium model makes handling the individual differences problem especially difficult in the work of Cohen and Cloward and Ohlin. Both of these theories — though in different ways — define the problem of individual differences as essentially a problem of mobility stance. Cohen seems to come out better here since individuals are seen as varying in the degree to which they possess the means to avoid opprobrium at the hands of middle class representatives. Cloward and Ohlin seem to argue that it is from the ranks of those who *do* possess the means to reach success goals but who *do not* seek status advance — only economic advancement — that the developers of delinquent subcultures will arise. Neither approach produces much leverage on the matter of individual differences.[9]

All this is not to say that deprivations are unimportant in slum gang delinquency or that problems of overcoming internalized prohibitions do not exist but simply to argue that the moral equilibrium model be made explicit and the degree to which internalized resistance to delinquency is present be made a variable.[10]

[8] *Ibid.*, pp. 130 ff.
[9] It is fashionable with some sociological theorists to claim with an air of superior virtue that they are interested in rates of deviance and not in individual differences. It may be useful therefore to point out that a rate is an operation in arithmetic and not *necessarily* an operation in sociological theory.
[10] For a brilliant commentary on the taking of internalization for granted see Dennis Wrong, "The Oversocialized Conception of Man," *American Sociological Review*, 26 (April 1962), pp. 183–193. Wrong traces some of the questionable uses of what I have called the implicit moral equilibrium model to uncritical adaptations of the Parsonian interaction paradigm which posits an equilibrium based upon the "complimentarity of

Thus it seems quite simple to point out that the degree of stress necessary to produce candidates for delinquent subcultures will vary with the degree of anti-delinquency internalization that has occurred.

Not all delinquency theory or even all theories of gang delinquency proceed from this implicit assumption of prior internalization. Notable among gang theories which do not is that of Thrasher which stresses rather the attractiveness of much delinquent activity and the weakness of social control and therefore of internalized prohibitions against delinquency.[11] Since Miller's "lower-class culture" approach locates the primary motivation for delinquency in the "pulls" of lower class culture rather than in the "pushes" of deprivation and since lower class culture automatically legitimates certain forms of delinquency Miller's boys seem less pressed and driven. Perhaps staid old Boston casts her shadow even here and these are gang delinquents Brahmin style.

For Miller lower class culture *per se* constitutes a weakened form of social and internal control over delinquency and there is no moral equilibrium notion implicit or otherwise.

The Struggle with Psychology

Concern for the variable of strength of internalization at a given point in time naturally

expectations" as an analytic convenience though not necessarily an empirical reality. The Parsonian statement leads directly to the idea that deviance must be produced by some disturbance of equilibrium on the social level and sufficient stress to overcome previous internalization on the personality level. Thus deviance is psychically "overdetermined" and "compulsive" precisely because of the necessity to repress "conformative need-dispositions." (Parsons, *The Social System*, Glencoe, Illinois: The Free Press, 1951, esp. pp. 254 ff.) All of this flows from the model but of course the real issue is the degree to which this model fits any particular situation. Parsons himself would doubtless urge close attention to the problem of "system reference," i.e., to the fact that the total society may be in a stable state which includes persisting levels of deviance and even fairly uncomplicated deviant motivation and "definitions of the situation" in some segments of the population. This seems especially true with respect to delinquency which is more an irritating gadfly than a serious threat to the social order.
[11] Frederick M. Thrasher, *The Gang*, Chicago: The University of Chicago Press, 1927.

leads to an interest in life history materials and in the biography of the individual seen as a succession of social influences. This interest in turn leads naturally to the family. Unfortunately discussion of the family in recent sociological theory of group delinquency seems to be distinguished more by a desire to avoid "psychologizing" than by a desire to understand delinquency.

One of the traditional concerns of sociological theories of delinquency has been to avoid what sociologists have viewed as the overly simple ideas of some extreme psychologistic and psychiatric positions which see delinquency as a response to stresses produced by experience in the family.[12] These "psychic disturbance" viewpoints have emphasized the high levels of tension underlying delinquency with the tension arising primarily from experiences in the family.

Current sociological thinking seems willing to accept the view of delinquency as a stress reaction providing only that the source of stress is the class structure and not the family. Thus Cohen declares that "the family is not the world" and reduces family experience to its role as a source of conflict with middle class dominated institutions. Cloward and Ohlin ignore the family almost completely. Walter Miller, alone of the three, hypothesizes that the family in lower class culture can be in itself a source of stress and tension the resolution of which is part of the etiological process.

Leaving Miller aside we might caricature the current state of sociological theory of gang delinquency as resting its implicit case against psychology largely on the following grounds:

1. If a lower class boy is humiliated by his teacher that is social class and admissible. If he is humiliated by his father that is child psychology and inadmissible.

2. If a boy is hostile because of deprivation of legitimate means to success goals it leads to "alienation" which is sociological and admis-

sible. If a boy is hostile because of deprivation of love and affection in his family it leads to "disturbance" which is psychological and inadmissible.

3. If many families whose heads have similar occupations deprive boys similarly that makes the deprivation "patterned" and part of a "class culture" and it does not hurt.

The first two points need no elaboration but the third does. The struggle with psychology has been historically linked with concepts like "family disorganization" or "family inadequacy" insofar as these features of family life were seen as sources of stress rather than as sources of weak acculturation or norm transmission. As a consequence sociological theorists seem to have decided that if delinquency is a stress response the stress cannot come from the family because that would imply that the family was "inadequate" and the psychiatric nose would be in the sociological tent.

An alternative solution to this dilemma is to conceive of the "disorganized" or "inadequate" family as a class-linked cultural form, i.e., as a form of *organization* rather than *disorganization* with the implication that if a particular form of family structure is common or subcultural then it does not have to be seen as a source of stress.

Of the three bodies of theory we are considering, only Miller seems to have escaped this peculiar trap. He vociferously protests against the view that the "female-based-household" is a disorganization of the conventional family structure in American society and insists that it is the appropriate family form for lower class life. Nevertheless he also sees the female-based-household as a source of anxiety and conflict centering around masculine identity.[13] It seems likely that Miller's ability to deal with the family as *both* "organized" and a source of stress derives from the fact that he is an anthropologist rather than a sociologist. Psychology has entered modern anthropology through the "culture and personality" avenue rather than through the "personal pathology" avenue through which it entered (or threatened to enter) sociological criminology. Culture and Personality theory emphasizes the

---

[12] The benchmark study is of course William Healy and Augusta F. Bronner, *New Light on Delinquency and Its Treatment*, New Haven: Yale University Press, 1936. A general discussion of this literature is in Guy E. Swanson, *Emotional Disturbances and Juvenile Delinquency* (unpublished doctoral dissertation, Division of the Social Sciences, University of Chicago, 1948).

[13] Miller, "Lower Class Culture as a Generating Milieu of Gang Delinquency," *op. cit.*

patterning of personal stress and conflict *normal* rather than abnormal in a society and highlights the role of family socialization as at least one proximate cause of such patterning.

In sum, in the struggle with psychology sociological theorists seem to accept and reject psychological ideas concerning lower class gang delinquency in very complex ways, which sometimes confuse social system and personality system levels of analysis with the issue of whether rates, groups or individuals are the appropriate dependent variables, which tend to accept delinquency as a response to stress providing only that stress does not occur in the family and which tend to implicitly accept the notion that a stress producing family must be disorganized, while conversely if disorganized families are common they cannot be stress producing.

Two other consequences of the struggle with psychology warrant brief mention. First is the use of the term "internalization" as a concept in theories of group delinquency. Seldom if ever is there a sophisticated discussion of what "internalization" means on a personality system level — the most crucial one. What gets internalized, in what role relationships with what intrapersonal consequences? Questions like this are seldom asked much less answered. Partly this is because of the implicit moral equilibrium model and partly it is because of a proclivity for homemade psychology. Thus for example the Freudian axiom that internalization of norms also requires internalization of the originally external relationship to the norm enforcer with all that implies is completely scanted.[14]

Second, we should point out how lower class urban slum life is seldom seen as in itself a source of stress but becomes so only when this life condition (or these life chances) clash with cultural (or structural) barriers. But this takes us over into the next topic, the formula.

The Formula

The formula dictates that the motivation derived from class position lead to the formation of a subculture. The terms of the formula then are "class," "problem of adjustment" (motive)

and "subculture." We would like to comment on each briefly.

The focus on class position to the near exclusion of other social attributes of the population at risk raises some important questions. The first and most obvious is how much should be attributed to class position *per se* and how much to other characteristics of the populations occupying positions of low economic status. Despite the assimilation process and other social changes the occupants of the lowest occupational segments of the urban labor force are still very heavily rural migrants, immigrants, Negroes or other minority groups. The various theories deal with this fact in different ways, none too satisfactory. Miller, for example, posits a lower class culture which, however, is "less applicable to certain ethnic groups, such as the Italians and Chinese."[15] Cloward and Ohlin discuss racial and ethnic origin differences in the types of delinquent subcultures found in different neighborhoods but do not seem sensitive to the possibility that race, ethnicity or rural origin may be heavily involved in the "problem of adjustment" to which the delinquent subcultures are solutions.[16]

The concentration of immigrant, migrant and minority populations has several implications for the theories of group delinquency. First, race and ethnicity are criteria of social ranking that operate independently, to some degree, of objective class position or of correlative ranking criteria such as education. Race especially is a major criterion according to which prestige, self-esteem and economic life chances are distributed even with levels of talent and education controlled.[17]

---

[14] Again see Dennis Wrong, *op. cit.*, for a discussion of this and similar issues.

[15] Kvaraceus and Miller, *op. cit.*, p. 63 fn. There are of course other examples of groups who while objectively lower class in occupational position have not manifested "lower class culture." Among them are Jews, Japanese, and Greeks.

[16] Cloward and Ohlin, *op. cit.*, p. 29 fn.

[17] There is a copious literature on the subject. For the general matter of differing criteria of social ranking see Gerhard Lenski, "Status Crystallization: A Non-Vertical Dimension of Social Status," *American Sociological Review*, 19 (1954), pp. 405–13. See also the general treatment and the review of the literature by Leonard Broom, "Social Differentiation and Stratification," Chapter 19 in Robert K. Merton, Leonard Broom, and Leon-

Second, different groups located similarly in objective occupational terms differ greatly in the cultural "stance" they take toward the desirability of upward mobility and in the traditional fund of skills with which they are equipped for the task. They also differ in family structure and in many other ways.[18] Third, groups that are overrepresented at the lower end of the occupational scale often bring with them traditions which are differentially likely to produce crime and delinquency. Thus migrants from the South, both white and Negro, are likely to bear with them the traditions of extreme individualism and violence which may be directly productive of crime or act as facilitators of violence in the northern, urban setting. The Latin American tradition of Machismo is a similar import.[19]

Fourth, groups that are heavily rural in origin at least for a time continue to manifest elements of rural culture that can be highly maladaptive in an urban environment.[20] Fifth, the ethnic and racial heterogeneity of the objectively lower class northern urban population gives a special cast to the "struggle for life" of the slum, which tends to accentuate the likelihood of gang violence based on intergroup hostilities. This intergroup conflict has traditionally extended from struggle over housing in the slum to struggle over control of municipal governments and may reasonably be supposed to set an environmental context supportive of street gang life.

In addition to the problems of the ethnic, racial and rural composition of the lower class urban population we should mention the prob-

ard C. Cottrell, Jr., eds., *Sociology Today*, New York: Basic Books, Inc., 1959. For material more directly in the area of slum life and delinquency see St. Clair Drake and Horace R. Cayton, *Black Metropolis*, New York: Harcourt, Brace, and Company, 1945. Drake and Cayton show the complex interactions of race, economic status and rural origins that are involved in the varying adaptations of Negroes in Chicago's Black Belt. See also William F. Whyte, *Street Corner Society*, Chicago: University of Chicago Press, 1943, pp. 272–276.

It is indeed odd that all the theorists we are considering acknowledge their debt to Whyte but overlook the fact that one of the key features of the youth situation in his Boston slum was that they were *Italian* not just poor. The college boy-corner boy distinction made famous by Whyte has been taken over presumably because it fits into the almost totally class oriented more recent analyses but the implications of ethnicity have not.

[18] Cohen's relative emphasis on the cultural features of working class life allows considerable flexibility here as is shown in the discussion by Wilensky and Lebeaux, *op. cit.* But even Cohen seems to think of class as the source of the diverse cultural systems sustained by working class populations. He makes no serious attempt to analyze the sources of cultural systems which are linked to but only partly produced by working class position. Because of their "structuralist" emphasis Cloward and Ohlin have much more difficulty handling this problem.

[19] The discussion of violence by these theorists, especially Cohen and Cloward and Ohlin merits much more attention than it can be given in this paper. It is sufficient to point out here that present position in the northern, urban labor force is not the only determinant of the use, enjoyment and

positive evaluation of violence manifested in some lower class groups. For a brilliant analysis of the role of violence as rooted in the tradition of the rural south see W. J. Cash, *The Mind of the South*, Garden City, New York: Doubleday and Company, Inc., 1941, esp. pp. 55–56 and 412 ff. It is also doubtful that violence by urban, lower class Negroes can be attributed solely to class position. On this point see Marvin E. Wolfgang, *Patterns in Criminal Homicide*, Philadelphia: University of Pennsylvania Press, 1958, pp. 36–46.

[20] For national sample data concerning the socio-economic status, political participation, sense of political efficacy and participation in formal organizations of farm-reared elements in the non-farm population see Ronald Freedman and Deborah Freedman, "Farm-Reared Elements in the Nonfarm Population," *Rural Sociology*, 21 (March 1956), pp. 50–61. Fifteen percent of the population age 21 or more in the twelve largest metropolitan areas in 1952 were farm-reared. Recomputation from the Freedman and Freedman tables shows that in those metropolitan areas the farm-reared constituted 24% of those who had completed only grade school or less and 27% of those with family incomes of less than $2,000.

For evidence that at least one important feature of lower class life can be attributed to the over-concentration of rural migrants see David Goldberg, "The Fertility of Two-Generation Urbanites," *Population Studies*, XII (March 1959), pp. 214–222. Goldberg found that inverse relations between fertility and occupation, education and income were due to the distribution of farm migrants. Additionally he found that farm migrants as compared to two-generation urbanites had larger numbers of children with controls for occupation, income, education, religion, and race.

lem of "drift" as it affects current emphasis on class. The processes of sorting and sifting of populations which have characterized the American city for generations are likely to result in the concentration at the bottom of the status heap of individuals and families who, for a wide variety of reasons, have been unable to make the grade in the mobility struggle. Included among these downward selection criteria are attributes of individual and family functioning that are likely to result in a highly disproportionate concentration of "problem families" in certain slum areas. Indeed, insofar as it constitutes an adaptation inimical to economic stability serious gang delinquency itself may be a source of downward drift or failure of upward movement.[21]

These considerations affect the three theoretical positions somewhat differently. For Cohen's status deprivation position it means that the conflicting demands of working class and middle class cultural systems should perhaps be seen in terms of a working or lower class system only partially derived from class position itself. For Miller's concept of "lower class culture" these considerations imply much more care in attributing this cultural system to class and also much more attention to variability based on racial and other grounds. For Cloward and Ohlin they imply a less exclusive emphasis on denial of economic opportunity as a function of economic position and much more consideration of the impact especially of race.[22] For the general problem of class and delinquency they mean more awareness of the complex historical processes that operate to distribute groups and individuals of different backgrounds through the economic order.[23]

As we have mentioned elsewhere, the concept group has to a considerable extent given way to the concept "subculture" in the analysis of group delinquency.[24] While "subculture" is a useful concept and has been usefully used it nevertheless raises some problems. Since some of these problems are closely linked to motivational formulations, especially those of Cohen and Cloward and Ohlin, we will treat the motive and subculture terms of the formula together.

The pairing of motive or "problem of ad-

[21] One of the greatest needs in delinquency theory is to somehow bring together the literature emphasizing class cultures with the literature based on analysis of the family. One of the ways to begin would be for the more "sociological" theorists to deal seriously with the drift problem and the related problems of how family structure variables interact with neighborhood culture, class barriers to advancement and other more "social structural" factors. A good beginning would be to allow theoretical room for a variety of social sources of "problems of adjustment." The drift problem is likely to affect different groups differently with native white, Anglo-Saxon, multigeneration slum dwellers more likely to have serious family difficulties. For evidence that early delinquency may be a source of later lack of upward mobility see Lee N. Robbins, Harry Gyman and Patricia O'Neal, "The Interaction of Social Class and Deviant Behavior" (Paper read at American Sociological Association Meetings, 1961).

The literature on the ecological concentration of "multi-problems families" is also relevant. For a discussion and review of this literature see Harry M. Shulman, *Juvenile Delinquency In American Society*, New York: Harper and Brothers, 1961, pp. 397–401. For a related and insightful study of the impact of family patterns on delinquency in Britain see H. C. Wilson, "Juvenile Delinquency in Problem Families in Cardiff," *British Journal of Delinquency*, 9 (1953), pp. 94–105.

[22] I have elsewhere indicated that the Cloward and Ohlin position seems plausible only for lower class Negroes under some urban conditions. See Bordua, "Delinquent Subcultures: Sociological Theories of Gang Delinquency," *op. cit.*, p. 135 fn. The fact that the northern urban slum gang problem is increasingly a Negro problem has been a kind of "hidden agenda" until very recently. See National Committee for Children and Youth, *Social Dynamite*, Washington, D.C.: The Committee, 1961; and Charles E. Silberman, "The City and The Negro," *Fortune* (March 1962).

[23] That the situation with respect to "class" theories of delinquency is a highly complex one can be seen in the studies that have tried to sort out socio-economic and other determinants of census tract variations in delinquency rates. See Bernard Lander, *Towards An Understanding of Juvenile Delinquency*, New York: Columbia University Press, 1954. Lander's conclusions are by and large supported by two other American studies. See Kenneth Polk, "Juvenile Delinquency and Social Areas," *Social Problems*, 5 (Winter 1957–58), pp. 214–217; David J. Bordua, "Juvenile Delinquency and 'Anomie': An Attempt at Replication," *Social Problems*, VI (Winter 1959), pp. 230–238.

[24] Bordua, "Delinquent Subcultures: Sociological Interpretations of Gang Delinquency," *op. cit.*, p. 122, fn.

justment" and subculture leads to an attempt to "understand" the personal significance of the subculture in terms of positionally derived problems of adjustment which are antecedent to the group formation process itself. Thus it is in his role in the class structure rather than in his role in the street group that the subculture becomes of primary relevance to the psychic life of the "culture carrier." Conversely the content of the subculture is derived largely or wholly from the motives or problems of adjustment stemming from the slum boy's individual position in the class structure. In short, there is strong pressure here toward a simple isomorphism of culture content and problem of adjustment. The complex society of street groupings characteristic of slum life is given little or no culture creating potential of its own. The group is simply the instrument that translates the individual discontent into the collective solution.[25]

This isomorphism of culture and motives neglects several possible alternatives. First, the

[25] See John I. Kitsuse and David C. Dietrick, "'Delinquent Boys': A Critique," *American Sociological Review*, 24 (April 1959), pp. 208–214. Kitsuse and Dietrick point up the peculiar fact that where class based problems of adjustment are concerned the working class boy is seen as ". . . standing alone to face humiliation at the hands of middle class agents . . ." (*ibid.*, p. 211). Cloward and Ohlin adopt a somewhat different version of the isomorphism notion by conceiving the problem of adjustment as deriving from a two step procedure where economic gain oriented adolescents are deprived of legitimate and/or illegitimate opportunities. Thus there are different versions of the common problem of adjustment each with its appropriate subculture. In the case of the "criminal subculture" based on anticipation of adult criminal careers, however, it is hard to discover why there need be a "problem of adjustment" at all rather than simply a combination of attractive criminal opportunities and variable socialization into conventional norms. (Cloward and Ohlin, *op. cit.*, p. 161 ff.)

Thus the implicit equilibrium model requires that there must be *a* problem, the struggle with psychology and "the formula" emphasis on class dictates that it be a *common* problem related to mobility striving even across very different racial, familial and neighborhood contexts, and the emphasis on subculture dictates that the collective solution be isomorphic with the motivating problem.

motives satisfied by adherence to the group's culture may vary over time. Second, the motives satisfied by maintaining membership in the group may vary considerably among the members, i.e., the situational generalization of goals may be a better analytic model than the common problem of adjustment and its correlative common culture.[26]

Finally in connection with the formula we should mention the relation between the first two terms, i.e., class and motive. Much of this is implicit in the previous analysis. The struggle with psychology excludes family mediated effects. The implicit moral equilibrium model requires that the link be a "problem"; the emphasis on motive and subculture rather than on group rules out the peer group system. The only remaining link is a direct attitudinal, cognitive or evaluational one. This seems to underlie Cohen's difficulty over why the working class boy is sensitive to the middle class measuring rod. It also underlies Cloward and Ohlin's concentration on the Mertonian means-goals discrepancy as well as their endowing of their gang boys with a rather remarkable degree of anticipatory prescience.

Time and Birds of a Feather

Although it has largely been adumbrated in earlier sections of the paper it seems worthwhile to consider briefly the matter of time and some implications of the way it is handled theoretically.

In the case of the Cloward and Ohlin formulation especially we see the peculiar operation of what may be termed the methodological present. In their theory the present is produced by past anticipations of the future. When this use of the methodological present is combined with the overwhelming tendency

[26] See the treatment of the profit motive in Talcott Parsons, *op. cit.*, p. 243 ff. This problem is dealt with by Cohen in his notion that only the "common core" of motivation need really be supplied by the "common problem of adjustment" (Cohen, *op. cit.*, page 148). See the criticism of this "common core" idea in Kitsuse and Dietrick, *op. cit.*, pp. 213–214. We might add that "common core" is hard to specify empirically. Does it mean the motivation common to the core members? If so who would the core members be? The leaders? The longest term members?

for the theory to be postdictive rather than predictive the result is to use the present as the sole indicator of what future must have been anticipated in the past and by whom. This is the most grievous result of the tendency to formulate the theoretical problem in terms of "facts the theory must fit" and to embark on a hunt for plausible "problems of adjustment" which must exist in a peculiarly atemporal world. Thus not only must subculture be isomorphic with the past and the past consists of anticipations of a future that has not yet arrived.

This peculiar use of time by Cloward and Ohlin relates also to their penchant for formulations in terms of anticipatory socialization which endows their delinquents with a capacity to foresee the future with an almost uncanny accuracy. Thus the gang boys' past has been spent presumably anticipating the future so as to produce the present. *Nothing else has been going on.* Nothing else *can* go on since the implicit moral equilibrium model precludes consideration of differential socialization into conventional norms, the struggle with psychology precludes consideration of the family and the formula requires that the social context be forced into the rubric of class position.

One outcome of all this is the production of a highly specialized type of problem of adjustment characteristic of boys who want a lot of money but do not aspire to the middle class life style and who, because they possess all the attributes formally required for success, respond to their anticipation of failure with hostility directed toward the system rather than towards themselves.[27] They have all the criteria for advancement except a rather crucial one — they do not want to do it our way. For some strange reason they reject school, a massive opportunity structure. In short the theory is led to posit a *deus ex machina* — the prealienated boy.

The combination of the methodological present and the postdictive nature of their theory leads Cloward and Ohlin into a rather odd use of the doctrine of "functional equivalence" in the following quotation.[28]

[27] Cloward and Ohlin, *op. cit.*, pp. 110–126.
[28] *Ibid.*, p. 86, fn. Italics added.

The young acquire definitions of the availability of success-goals from older persons with whom they interact. *For our purposes "actual" and "anticipated" failure to improve one's social position are functional equivalents.*

Since the processes whereby different boys first are affected by failure — actual or anticipated — are different, and therefore the outcomes should be different, the two are not *causally* equivalent. Since in large part the distinction between Cohen's approach and that of Cloward and Ohlin can be reduced to the issue of when the problem of adjustment manifests itself in an individual's life history, the two are not *theoretically* equivalent. Since the success of any delinquency prevention program suggested by opportunity structure theory will be profoundly affected by when and in what socio-emotional context opportunity blockage is met or learned, the two are not practically equivalent.[29]

It is only possible to make such a statement concerning "functional equivalence" if methodological time is assumed to represent real time, i.e., if formal, analytical categories are confused with social history or individual biography in the real world.[30]

[29] For evidence that school maladjustment can begin very early and be a complex resultant of class, race, sex and family structure see Martin Deutsch, *Minority Group and Class Status as Related to Social and Personality Factors in School Achievement*, Monograph No. 2, The Society For Applied Anthropology; Ithaca, New York: The Society, 1960.
[30] This is not to argue that "abstract," atemporal theory is not valuable in general or in the area of gang delinquency but only to point out that any theory must specify the historical or biographical parameter values appropriate at any given time point. In the case of theories bearing on individual biography especially it is necessary to be aware that the temporal *ordering* of events as well as their biographical *timing* may change the parameters drastically. This section of the paper could perhaps have been framed in the now familiar rhetoric of the "conflict" between functionalist and historicist explanations except that the larger argument often seems more trouble than help. There are several publications broadly in this larger frame that are particularly helpful. In connection with general theoretical problems involved in analyzing deviant behavior see Dennis Wrong, *op. cit.*, and Reinhard Bendix, "The Image of Man

The theoretical use of time bears on what is probably the key theoretical problem in the literature on lower-class, urban, male delinquency — the problem of the relationship of personal characteristics and associational patterns. While it has often been involved in the arguments over "psychological" vs. "sociological" explanations of delinquency it is also a crucial problem within the two disciplines. The most famous controversy centering on this problem is the one between the Gluecks and Sutherland.[31] We do not propose to review the controversy here although it has often seemed to us that sociological theorists sometimes seem determined to ignore the whole matter as being theoretically inconvenient. That this problem of personal characteristics and associational patterns constitutes a central if not the central problem in delinquency theory was explicitly recognized by Sutherland who was not satisfied with the state of affairs represented by differential association theory.[32] In rejecting the differential association approach and the whole area of "criminal learning" the Gluecks were led to the following comment.[33]

So far as delinquency is concerned, then, "birds of a feather flock together." This tendency is a much more fundamental fact than the theory that accidental differential association of non-delinquents with delinquents is the basic cause of crime.

Whatever sociologists may think of its resolution in the work of the Gluecks there is little question that the treatment of developmental process both at the individual and group levels lies at the heart of the matter.[34] Indeed in its simplest form the issue boils down to how much feathering precedes how much flocking.

Cohen's description of the "mutual conversion" process makes a major contribution here since it enables consideration of flocking and feathering in terms of complex feedback mechanisms.[35] Unfortunately however the operation of the implicit moral equilibrium model leads Cohen to largely ignore the delinquency producing consequences of what he describes as working class socialization independent of the conflict with the middle class measuring rod. If working class socialization (in some families, at least) has the characteristics described by Cohen then the lack of regard for property may lead to theft and property destruction, the tolerance for physical aggression may lead to

---

in the Social Sciences: The Basic Assumptions of Present-Day Research," *Commentary*, 11 (1951), pp. 187–92. For a discussion of the current state of the "conflict" which includes an eminently sensible conclusion see Seymour Martin Lipset and Neil Smelser, "Change and Controversy in Recent American Sociology," *British Journal of Sociology*, XII (March 1961), pp. 45–47.

[31] Actually between the Gluecks and sociologists who took up the cudgels in defense of differential association theory and the "area approach." For the Gluecks' most trenchant criticism see Sheldon Glueck, "Theory and Fact in Criminology," *British Journal of Delinquency*, 7 (1956), pp. 92–109. This paper is also reprinted in Sheldon Glueck, *The Problem of Delinquency*, Cambridge, Mass.: The Riverside Press, 1959. For a series of articles on differential association theory see *Social Problems*, 8 (Summer 1960).

[32] Edwin H. Sutherland, "The Relation Between Personal Traits and Associational Patterns," in Walter C. Reckless, ed., *The Etiology of Delinquent and Criminal Behavior*, Social Science Research Council Bulletin 50, New York: Social Science Research Council, 1943, pp. 131–137.

[33] Sheldon and Eleanor Glueck, *Unravelling Juvenile Delinquency*, Cambridge, Mass.: Harvard University Press, 1950, p. 164.

[34] Sociological criticism both theoretical and methodological of the work of the Gluecks often is well taken but seems to have led to an agreement to ignore their findings. The results in *Unravelling Juvenile Delinquency* agree fairly well with those of comparable control group studies. See the summary in William C. Kvaraceus, *The Community and The Delinquent*, Yonkers-On-Hudson, New York: The World Book Company, 1954, Chapter 4. The exaggerated claims for their delinquency prediction instruments is perhaps the weakest point in the Gluecks' work. For a discussion of the current experiment in New York City see David J. Bordua, *Prediction and Selection of Delinquents*, Children's Bureau, Juvenile Delinquency: Facts and Facets, No. 17; Washington, D.C.: U.S. Government Printing Office, 1961.

It should perhaps be pointed out that the struggle with psychology as a genus includes the struggle with the Gluecks as an important species. It should also be pointed out that no one as yet seems to have solved the problem of interrelating theoretical work of the sort being considered in this paper with the form and results of the control group researches.

[35] Cohen, *op. cit.*, p. 61.

assault, the bad language may lead to disorderly conduct at an early age.[36] For some youngsters at least conflict with the middle class measuring rod may be a consequence rather than a source of delinquency.

Despite Cohen's considerable clarification of the issue, the literature is still quite unclear as to whether acts, personal-attitudinal states, group roles or collective values are the appropriate dependent variable. This unclarity partly at least derives from a lack of detailed attention to developmental sequence since both the forms of individual commitment and the forms of grouping will vary developmentally.

The concept of "parent subculture" introduced by Cohen and Short implies a recognition of age-graded variations in the structural and cultural characteristics of group delinquency although they do not develop the notion very fully.[37] The idea that different forms of group delinquency would characterize different ages is a central feature of Thrasher's discussion.[38] Indeed his discussion of the varieties of group forms and their "natural histories" seems to largely cover some recent theoretical counterpoints to the approaches we have been considering. Pfautz's statement that Thrasher saw the gang as "an organized social group" is an only partially correct construction of Thrasher's analysis.[39] It would be more appropriate to say that Thrasher used "gang" as a generic term, distinguishing different types of grouping by using such terms as "diffuse" and "solidified" as in the following quotation.[40]

If conditions are favorable to its continued existence, the gang tends to undergo a sort of natural evolution from a diffuse and loosely organized group into the solidified unit which represents the matured gang and which may take several forms. It sometimes becomes a specialized delinquent type such as the criminal gang, but usually it becomes conventionalized and seeks incorporation into the structure of the community, imitating some established social pattern such as a club. . . .

Much of the theoretical controversy over what "the gang" is really like seems partly a matter of semantics, partly a lack of willingness to deal with wide ranges of variability in slum group life and mostly a matter of a determined unwillingness to do the necessary job of sociographic description of slum life.

[36] *Ibid.*, p. 97 ff.

[37] Albert K. Cohen and James F. Short, Jr., "Research in Delinquent Subcultures," *Journal of Social Issues*, 14 (1958), pp. 20–26.

[38] Thrasher, *op. cit.*, esp. Chs. III and IV. See also Bordua, "Delinquent Subcultures: Sociological Theories of Gang Delinquency," *op. cit.*

[39] Harold M. Pfautz, "Near-Group Theory and Collective Behavior: A Critical Reformulation," *Social Problems*, 9 (Fall 1961), pp. 167–74. The reference to Thrasher is on page 170. See also Lewis Yablonsky, "The Delinquent Gang as a Near-Group," *Social Problems*, 7 (Fall 1959), pp. 108–117. Certainly of all the forms of group deviance in the slums the so-called "bopping gang" has proven most capable of serving as a theoretical projective test.

[40] Thrasher, *op. cit.*, page 58.

Empirical Analyses

In this paper Short and his co-workers report the results of their effort to test empirically certain aspects of the theoretical position of Cloward and Ohlin. The data reported in this selection were obtained in interviews with gang and nongang boys. The nongang "controls" were selected from YMCA's, boys' clubs, settlement houses, park district field houses, and other agencies serving youth in the areas where the gangs were located (Short and Strodtbeck [1965:15]). Also interviewed were members of sixteen "delinquent gangs" in Chicago to which detached workers were assigned. The size of these collectivities ranged from sixteen to sixty-eight, and membership was defined on the basis of the detached workers' judgments regarding who should be considered as members (Short, Tennyson, and Howard [1963]). These respondents constitute neither an enumeration of all members of gangs in Chicago nor a random sample of gang members; rather, they are boys who were the object of special concern in the YMCA's program of detached workers because the gangs in which they participated were, in contrast with other "gangs" in existence, particularly troublesome to the community. This methodological point must be kept in mind in evaluating the contribution of this research.

One of the important "findings" reported elsewhere by Short, Tennyson, and Howard (1963) is that numerous conflict-oriented gangs were located in Chicago, but groups oriented to criminal activities and drug-using groups proved to be difficult to locate. Although many boys had experimented with heroin and "pills," and marihuana smoking was found in several groups, it took the investigators more than a year to locate a drug-oriented group, that is, one in which the major activities or normative emphasis of the group centered on drug use. Again, "criminal" activity was extensive, but the researchers failed to find a criminally oriented gang. This suggests that the recent theoretical emphasis on specialization in particular types of delinquent activities — as in Cloward and Ohlin's differentiation of conflict, criminal, and retreatist subcultures — may lack empirical counterparts.

Using the variables of race, class, and gang membership to differentiate categories, the investigators in this selection compare the respondents' perceptions of legitimate and illegitimate opportunities as well as other elements of the "opportunity structure." Calculation of mean or average scores for the responses to the questions pertaining to various aspects of the opportunity structure revealed similar trends — gang boys perceive themselves as having fewer legitimate opportunities than do nongang boys, but, as expected, the gang boys are more likely to perceive illegitimate opportunities as open than are other boys. A search of police records permitted the investigators to calculate official delinquency rates for the six categories of respondents. The ranking or ordering of the race-class-gang status categories on official delinquency rates was found to correspond more closely to the ordering of these categories on perceptions of legitimate opportunities than to their ranking on perceptions of illegitimate opportunities; this finding is consistent with the researchers' assumption that illegitimate opportunities intervene after legitimate opportunities are appraised and found wanting. The investigators conclude that Cloward and Ohlin's theory is appropriately addressed to the social distribution of delinquent subcultures, but they propose that to account for the entry of some boys into delinquent gangs and to explain the behavior of the boys within the context of a subculture requires one to consider group process as well as variables on the personality level.

REFERENCES

James F. Short, Jr., and Fred Strodtbeck, *Group Process and Gang Delinquency* (Chicago: The University of Chicago Press, 1965).

——, Ray A. Tennyson, and Kenneth I. Howard, "Behavior Dimensions of Gang Delinquency," *American Sociological Review*, 28 (June 1963), pp. 411–428.

JAMES F. SHORT, JR.
RAMON RIVERA
RAY A. TENNYSON

Perceived Opportunities, Gang Membership, and Delinquency

Not since the advent of psychoanalysis has a theory had such impact on institutionalized delinquency control as the theory, explicit or

From *American Sociological Review*, February 1965, pp. 56–67. Reprinted by permission of the American Sociological Association.

This research is supported by grants from the Behavior Science Study Section of the National Institute of Mental Health (M-3301 and MH-07158); the Office of Juvenile Delinquency and Youth Development, Welfare Administration, U.S. Department of Health, Education, and Welfare in cooperation with the President's Committee on Juvenile Delinquency and Youth Crime (#62220); the Ford Foundation; and the Research Committee of Washington State University.

implied, in *Delinquency and Opportunity*.[1] Given the impetus of major foundation and federal support, the theory has been extensively adopted as a rationale for action programs in many areas of the country. There is some danger that, like psychoanalysis, "opportunity structure theory" may be rationalized and elaborated so rapidly and extensively as to discourage, if not render impossible, empirical testing, pragmatic validation, or dem-

[1] Richard A. Cloward and Lloyd E. Ohlin, *Delinquency and Opportunity: A Theory of Delinquent Gangs*, New York: Free Press of Glencoe, 1960.

onstration of worth by any other criterion of "good theory." *Delinquency and Opportunity* has been widely praised for its theoretical integration, e.g., as "a logically sound deductive system that is rich in its implications for delinquency causation and control," but the same critic also notes that "examined in terms of its logical, operational, and empirical adequacy, the theory poses a number of questions concerning the accuracy of some of its postulates and theorems." [2] Our paper will bring data to bear on certain aspects of the opportunity structure paradigm as we operationalized it in a study of delinquent gangs in Chicago.

Table 1 reproduces in paradigm form the principal elements of "opportunity structure theory" concerning *criminal* and *conflict* subcultures. It subdivides the "Innovation" category of Merton's deviance paradigm, referring to acceptance (internalization) of culturally prescribed success goals and rejection (incomplete internalization) of institutional norms or culturally prescribed means, by those for whom legitimate means to success goals are restricted.[3] To this the paradigm adds Cloward's four sets of defining conditions for the relative availability of illegitimate means to success goals,[4] and the two hypothesized types of "collective response among delinquents" produced by the preceding conditions.[5]

In our research in Chicago we have attempted to measure variables specified in this paradigm and to investigate their interrelations. For this purpose we have studied lower-class "delinquent gangs" involved in a "detached worker" program of the YMCA of Metropolitan Chicago, control groups of lower-class nongang boys from the same neighborhoods as the gang boys, and middle-class nongang boys.[6] Elements of the paradigm were operationalized in terms of the *perceptions* reported by the boys studied.[7] In this paper we direct attention to perceptions of legitimate and illegitimate opportunities by Negro and white lower-class gang and nongang boys and middle-class boys of both races, and to the relations among these perceptions. Detailed discussion of the relation of perceived opportunities and patterns of behavior derived from self-reports and, for gang boys only, from detached-worker ratings, is deferred for later presentation.[8]

[2] Clarence Schrag, "Delinquency and Opportunity: Analysis of a Theory," *Sociology and Social Research*, 46 (January 1962), pp. 167–75.

[3] Robert K. Merton, *Social Theory and Social Structure*, New York: Free Press of Glencoe, 1958, Ch. 4.

[4] Richard A. Cloward, "Illegitimate Means, Anomie, and Deviant Behavior," *American Sociological Review*, 24 (April 1959), pp. 164–76.

[5] Cloward and Ohlin use a different theoretical rationale to explain "retreatist" subcultures, but our data are not relevant specifically to this aspect of the theory. See Cloward and Ohlin, *op. cit.*, pp. 25–27, 178 ff.

[6] Selection and description of study populations and other characteristics of the research program are described in previous publications and in greatest detail in Short and Strodtbeck's book. See James F. Short, Jr., Fred L. Strodtbeck, and Desmond Cartwright, "A Strategy for Utilizing Research Dilemmas: A Case from the Study of Parenthood in a Street Corner Gang," *Sociological Inquiry*, 32 (Spring 1962), pp. 185–202; James F. Short, Jr., "Street Corner Groups and Patterns of Delinquency: A Progress Report," *American Catholic Sociological Review*, 24 (Spring 1963), pp. 13–32; and James F. Short, Jr., and Fred L. Strodtbeck, *Group Process and Gang Delinquency* (Chicago: The University of Chicago Press, 1965), esp. Ch. 1.

[7] Cloward and Ohlin refer to "common perceptions" of opportunities, and Schrag explains that one of the basic postulates of the theory is that "perceived disadvantage, regardless of the accuracy of the perception, is for lower-class youth the functional equivalent of objectively verified disadvantage in that it has the same effect on overt behavior" (Schrag, *op. cit.*, p. 168). This is not to deny the importance of *objective* opportunities, legitimate and illegitimate. The former can be demonstrated to be greater for whites than for Negroes, and for middle- than for lower-class persons. It is more difficult to demonstrate gang-nongang differences except in terms of the cumulative *effects* — school performance, relations with the police, etc. — which favor nongang boys. Differences in objective illegitimate opportunities are similarly difficult to demonstrate, though the illegal enterprises are more likely to be present in a lower-class than in a middle-class environment.

[8] Behavior factors based on detached-worker ratings of gang boys are reported in James F. Short, Jr., Ray A. Tennyson, and Kenneth I. Howard, "Behavior Dimensions of Gang Delinquency," *American Sociological Review*, 28 (June 1963), pp. 411–428. Self-reported behavior factors are presented in Short and Strodtbeck, *op. cit.*, Ch. 7.

Table 1

Social Context and Modes of Delinquent Behavior: A Paradigm

Structural features	Type of subculture	
	Criminal	Conflict
I. *Independent variable*	(Integrated areas)	(Unintegrated areas)
A. Culturally prescribed success goals	Internalized	Internalized
B. Availability of legitimate means to success goals	Limited; hence intense pressures toward deviant behavior	Limited; hence intense pressures toward deviant behavior
II. *Intervening variables*		
A. Institutional norms	Incomplete internalization	Incomplete internalization
B. Availability of illegal means to success goals	Available	Unavailable
1. Relations between adult carriers of conventional and criminal values	Accommodative; each participates in value system of other	Conflicted; neither group well organized; value systems implicit, and opposed to one another
2. Criminal learning structure	Available; offenders at different age levels integrated	Unavailable; attenuated relations between offenders at different age levels
3. Criminal opportunity structure	Stable sets of criminal roles graded for different ages and levels of competence; continuous income; protection from detection and prosecution	Unarticulated opportunity structure; individual rather than organized crime; sporadic income; little protection from detection and prosecution
4. Social control	Strong controls originate in *both* legitimate and illegal structures	Diminished social control; "weak" relations between adults and adolescents
III. *Dependent variable*		
A. Expected type of collective response among delinquents	Pressures toward deviance originate in limited accessibility to success goals by legitimate means, but are ameliorated by opportunities for access by illegal means. Hence, delinquent behavior is rational, disciplined, and crime-oriented	Pressures toward deviance originate in blocked opportunity by *any* institutionalized system of means. Hence, delinquent behavior displays expressive conflict patterns

Data reported elsewhere established different levels of aspiration among the boys studied, but they show that regardless of race, class, or gang membership, mean levels of both occupational and educational aspirations considerably exceed fathers' achieved levels of occupation and education.[9] In this sense the independent variable — internalization of culturally prescribed success goals — may be said to have a positive value among all the boys studied. For

[9] See James F. Short, Jr., "Gang Delinquency and Anomie," in Marshall B. Clinard (ed.), *Deviant Behavior and Anomie*, New York: Free Press of Glencoe, 1964; see also Jonathan Freedman and Ramon Rivera, "Education, Social Class, and Patterns of Delinquency," paper read at the an-

the first intervening variable in the paradigm, however — internalization of institutional norms — our gang members boys are less positive than the other boys studied. With "values" data from semantic differential scales, we established the fact that all groups assign equally high value and degree of legitimacy to such "middle-class" images as "Someone who works for good grades at school" and "Someone who likes to read good books" — again indicating that certain values are common to all groups — but gang boys of both races hold more positive attitudes toward *deviant* images than do the other boys.[10] These deviant images represented hypothesized "delinquent subcultures"; e.g., conflict ("Someone who is a good fighter with a tough reputation"), criminal ("Someone who knows where to sell what he steals" and "Someone who has good connections to avoid trouble with the law"), and retreatist ("Someone who makes easy money by pimping and other illegal hustles" and "Someone who gets his kicks by using drugs"). Middle-class boys generally attribute to these deviant images a lower value and less legitimacy, as we expected.

This paper is concerned with other elements in the paradigm, based on data from one part of an extensive interview schedule administered by specially trained interviewers to more than 500 boys in the six categories (race by class status and gang membership) under study. Respondents were instructed to indicate whether each of a series of statements was true of the "area where your group hangs out." In this way we hoped to measure perceptions of relatively specific legitimate and illegal opportunities. Perceptions of legitimate means to success goals, for example, were sampled by a series of statements concerning the *educational* and *occupational* orientations, abilities, and prospects for "guys in our area." We hoped by the impersonal referent to avoid the personalized ambitions and expectations which were the subject of inquiry in another part of the interview and thus to obtain measures referring to the boys' perceptions of general opportunities for legitimate and illegal achievement in their respective areas.

Aspects of the availability of illegal means to success goals to which attention was directed concerned the relative integration of the carriers of criminal and noncriminal values (in terms of the respectability of persons making money illegally and the orientation of local police toward law violation); adult "connections" and opportunities for learning and abetting criminal activities; the availability of criminal role models; and the probability of successful criminal enterprise in the area. Finally, because Cloward and Ohlin stress the importance of these matters for social control, perceptions of appropriate adult role models and their interest and sincerity concerning the problems of adolescents were also covered. The list of statements is in Table 2, together with the percentage of boys in each group answering "true." [11]

In most cases responses to the statements concerning open legitimate opportunities and adult helpfulness form a gradient: gang boys are least likely to answer "true," followed by nongang and then by middle-class boys of each race. For negatively stated legitimate opportunity questions, and for the two negative adult power ("clout") statements, this gradient is reversed.[12] White gang boys generally are more sanguine than Negro gang boys about occupational opportunities and adult "clout," while Negroes tend to be slightly more optimistic concerning education and adult helpful-

---

nual meetings of the American Sociological Association, 1962. Elliott's study of "200 delinquent and nondelinquent boys attending two adjoining high schools in a large West Coast city" supports these findings. See Delbert S. Elliott, "Delinquency and Perceived Opportunity," *Sociological Inquiry*, 32 (Spring 1962), pp. 216–27.

[10] The data are reported in Robert A. Gordon, James F. Short, Jr., Desmond S. Cartwright, and Fred L. Strodtbeck, "Values and Gang Delinquency: A Study of Street Corner Groups," *American Journal of Sociology*, 69 (September 1963), pp. 109–128.

[11] In the interview schedule the statements were not labeled according to which "opportunity structures" were being studied, and they were arranged in different order.

[12] Elliott, *op. cit.*, finds that delinquents consistently perceive lower opportunities for educational and occupational "success" than do nondelinquents. For evidence of other gradients among boys in the present study, see Gordon, *et al.*, *op. cit.*, and Short and Strodtbeck, *op. cit.*

ness. For all these areas, white middle-class boys have the most *open* view of "opportunities."

Conversely, gang boys are more likely to perceive illegitimate opportunities as open than are other boys, and these perceptions are held by more Negro than white boys in each stratum. The latter finding is somewhat surprising, in view of the acknowledged white domination of organized crime in Chicago. Informal observation suggests that vice organized on a large scale does flourish in Negro communities, and that "independent entrepreneurship" in such forms as small (and large) policy wheels, marijuana peddling, street-walking prostitutes, pool sharks, professional burglars and robbers, and the like, is more common in lower-class Negro than in lower-class white communities.[13] In any case, illegitimate opportunities appeared to be open to more Negro than white boys.

To reduce these data further, we assigned an opportunity structure score to each item. Except for items 17(A) and 18(A) answers were scored 2, 1, or 0, with 2 assigned to *open* opportunity perceptions, whether legitimate or illegitimate. Thus, for questions in Table 2 followed by (−), a "true" answer received a 0, "Don't know," a 1, and "False," a 2. The reverse procedure was applied to questions followed by (+).

Statements 17(A) and 18(A) are difficult to score. At first we assumed that a positive response to these questions indicated that illegitimate opportunities were perceived as closed. Boys were asked these questions only if they had already responded positively to questions 17 and 18. Thus, a "true" response to the statement that "A lot of these guys who make money illegally do not operate alone. They have to answer to people above them who are calling the shots," was taken to mean that the "really big" hoodlums were not available as role models; hence, to this extent illegitimate opportunities for "making it big" were perceived as closed. On the other hand, a boy might answer *false* to this statement on the grounds that those who were making money illegally were involved in such petty pursuits

as not to warrant concern or control by the syndicate, or, particularly in the case of middle-class white boys, illegal pursuits might be in the nature of white-collar crime and so not subject to syndicate control. In the latter case, a "false" answer still would be consistent with an *open* perception of opportunity, while in the former it would not. Answers to "elite criminal opportunities" questions are the only exceptions to the observed gradient for perceptions of illegitimate opportunities, suggesting that boys within each class of respondents may have interpreted these questions less uniformly than they did the others.

Before answers to these questions are dismissed as invalid, however, they should be examined more carefully. Note that responses to questions 17(A) and 18(A) follow a pattern: more Negro than white boys say that people in their areas who make money illegally have to "answer to people above them." Unfortunately the question did not specify where these "higher ups" lived or whether they were visible to the boys. We may infer, however, that a higher proportion of persons making money illegitimately in the white areas were among the "higher ups" in organized crime than was the case in Negro neighborhoods.

The middle-class boys' answers to the entire set of four "elite" questions are especially interesting. Negro middle-class boys are far more likely to indicate that local area people have "a chance of really making it big in the rackets" and far less likely to say that locals do not "make big money in the rackets." Drake and Cayton [14] and Frazier [15] have described important criminal and otherwise "shady" elements in the Negro middle class. Frazier, in particular, indicates that influential segments of the "black bourgeoisie" are "recruited from the successful underworld Negroes, who have gained their money from gambling, prostitution, bootlegging, and the 'numbers.'" [16] Frazier attributes the flashy consumption patterns of the new Negro mid-

[13] See Short and Strodtbeck, *op. cit.*, esp. Ch. 5, "Racial Differentials in Gang Behavior."

[14] St. Clair Drake and Horace R. Cayton, *Black Metropolis: A Study of Negro Life in a Northern City*, New York: Harper and Row, 1962, Vol. II.
[15] E. Franklin Frazier, *Black Bourgeoisie*, New York: Collier Books, 1962.
[16] *Ibid.*, p. 109.

Table 2

Percentage of Boys Answering "True" to Opportunity Structure Questions, by Race, Class, and Gang Status

Interviewer: "Once again I want you to think about the area where your group hangs out. I'm going to read a few statements to you, and all you have to do is say 'True' or 'False' after each statement. If you think the statement is true about the area, say 'True'; if you don't think it's true, say 'False.'"	Percentage answering "true"					
	Negro			*White*		
	Lower class gang N = 206	*Lower class non-gang* N = 89	*Middle class* N = 26	*Lower class gang* N = 90	*Lower class non-gang* N = 79	*Middle class* N = 53
Legitimate educational opportunities						
1. In our area it's hard for a young guy to stay in school. (−)[a]	48.5	28.1	7.7	52.2	21.5	0.0
2. Most kids in our area like school. (+)	43.2	49.4	80.8	32.2	60.8	94.3
3. Most of the guys in our area will graduate from high school. (+)	30.6	44.9	96.2	32.2	65.8	100.0
4. In our area, there are a lot of guys who want to go to college. (+)	37.4	47.2	84.6	16.7	44.3	98.1
5. College is too expensive for most of the guys in the area. (−)	75.7	76.4	53.8	80.0	65.8	7.5
6. As far as grades are concerned, most of the guys in our area could get through college without too much trouble. (+)	46.6	43.8	50.0	43.3	40.5	73.6
Legitimate occupational opportunities						
7. It's hard for a young guy in our area to get a good paying honest job. (−)	77.2	62.9	46.2	56.7	31.6	9.4
8. Most of the guys in the area will probably get good paying honest jobs when they grow up. (+)	51.9	59.6	61.5	65.6	79.7	92.5
9. For guys in this area honest jobs don't pay very well. (−)	56.3	47.2	26.9	40.0	22.8	3.8
10. Guys in this area have to have connections to get good paying jobs. (−)	53.9	51.7	30.8	56.7	44.3	22.6
11. In this area it's hard to make much money without doing something illegal. (−)	54.9	38.2	23.1	37.8	13.9	0.0
Integration of the carriers of criminal and non-criminal values						
12. Some of the most respectable people in our area make their money illegally. (+)	44.2	19.1	15.4	24.4	10.1	3.8
13. The police in this area get paid off for letting things happen that are against the law. (+)	51.5	37.1	30.8	42.2	36.7	20.8
Criminal learning structures						
14. There are connections in this area for a guy who wants to make good money illegally. (+)	57.8	49.4	38.5	47.8	35.4	5.7

Table 2 (*Continued*)

| | *Percentage answering "true"* | | | | | |
| | Negro | | | White | | |
	Lower class gang N = 206	Lower class non-gang N = 89	Middle class N = 26	Lower class gang N = 90	Lower class non-gang N = 79	Middle class N = 53
15. Young guys can learn a lot about crime from older people in the area. (+)	75.2	66.3	34.6	52.2	35.4	11.3
16. There are adults in this area who help young guys make money illegally. (+)	59.2	49.4	30.8	42.2	26.6	15.1
Visibility of criminal careers						
17. In this area there are some people who make their living by doing things that are against the law. (+)	83.0	73.0	69.2	70.0	60.8	30.2
18. Some of the young guys in our area will be making a living someday by doing things that are against the law. (+)	83.0	79.8	73.1	75.6	59.5	39.6
Elite criminal opportunities						
17. (A) A lot of these guys who make money illegally do not operate alone. They have to answer to people above them who are calling the shots. (−)	62.6	62.9	65.4	45.6	40.5	18.9
18. (A) A lot of these guys won't be operating alone either. They'll have to answer to people above them who'll be calling the shots. (−)	70.4	70.8	65.4	62.2	53.2	30.2
19. A guy from this area has a chance of really making it big in the rackets. (+)	45.1	30.3	34.6	35.6	24.1	3.8
20. None of the people who make big money in the rackets live in this area. (−)	54.4	66.3	38.5	56.7	75.9	60.4
Adult "clout"						
21. Not many really successful people live in this area. (−)	63.6	59.6	19.2	42.2	26.6	0.0
22. Adults in this area haven't much clout (pull). (−)	55.3	42.7	23.1	48.9	48.1	13.2
Adult helpfulness						
23. There are adults in this area who help young guys get jobs. (+)	82.5	93.3	92.3	78.9	89.9	94.3
24. Adults in the area do a lot to help young guys keep out of trouble. (+)	67.0	91.0	61.5	50.0	73.4	88.7

ª Signs in parentheses indicate the "valence" of a "True" answer relative to the opportunity structure area indicated.

Table 3
Mean Opportunity Structure Scores, by Race, Class, and Gang Status

Aspect of opportunity structure [a]	Negro			White		
	Lower class gang N = 206 [b]	Lower class non-gang N = 89	Middle class N = 26	Lower class gang N = 89	Lower class non-gang N = 75	Middle class N = 53
Legitimate educational (0–12)	4.8	5.7	9.0	3.8	6.4	11.2
Legitimate occupational (0–10)	4.2	5.2	6.6	5.4	7.3	9.1
Integration of carriers of criminal and noncriminal values (0–4)	2.1	1.4	1.2	1.5	1.0	0.5
Criminal learning structures (0–6)	4.0	3.6	2.3	3.0	2.2	0.7
Visibility of criminal careers (0–4)	3.4	3.2	3.0	3.0	2.5	1.4
Criminal opportunities (0–10)	4.7	4.0	4.6	4.7	4.3	4.6
Adult *clout* (0–4)	1.5	1.9	3.0	2.0	2.4	3.7
Adult helpfulness (0–4)	3.0	3.7	3.2	2.6	3.2	3.7
Criminal opportunities (0–4)	1.8	1.2	1.8	1.5	1.0	0.9
Summary scores						
Legitimate educational and occupational opportunities (0–22)	9.0	11.0	15.6	9.3	13.7	20.2
Illegitimate opportunities (0–24)	14.3	12.3	11.0	12.1	10.0	7.2
Illegitimate opportunities less inclusive (0–18)	11.4	9.5	8.2	9.0	6.7	3.5
Adult power and helpfulness (0–8)	4.5	5.6	6.2	4.7	5.6	7.4

[a] Figures in parentheses indicate the possible range for each score.

[b] Ns vary slightly for some scores, due to nonresponse. Scores are based in each case on the number of boys who actually gave meaningful responses.

dle class to the influence of these elements and contrasts this way of life with that of the old upper and middle classes who "erected an impenetrable barrier between themselves and Negroes who represented the 'sporting' and criminal world." [17] The white middle-class boys, who were chosen precisely because they were the "cream" of YMCA Hi-Y clubs, are very unlikely to be exposed to this sort of community influence. Such differences as these, if they are real, should find expression in other data from these subjects.[18]

[17] *Ibid.*, pp. 109–110.

[18] We were first alerted to differences between our Negro and white middle-class boys when they came to our offices for testing, and later by analysis of semantic differential data. See Gordon, *et al.*, *op. cit.* It should be emphasized that primary data for this paper represent perceptions rather than objective measures of opportunities or of the communities in which these boys live. Other investi-

These ambiguities in interpretation led us to score "elite" criminal opportunities in two ways — with and without questions 17(A) and 18(A). When they were included, we followed our original assumptions, adjusting the scoring so that if either question was not asked, implying closed opportunities, the boy was scored zero for the question; if the question was asked and a "true" answer recorded,

gators have emphasized the extent to which middle-class Negroes are like their white counterparts in terms of the character and stability of their institutions and their community leadership, and in interracial situations. Life styles, interaction patterns with whites, and leadership among middle-class Negroes vary greatly, however. See, for example, the discussion in Robin M. Williams, Jr., *et al.*, *Strangers Next Door: Ethnic Relations in American Communities*, New York: Prentice-Hall, 1964, esp. Chs. 7–10; also James Q. Wilson, *Negro Politics: The Search for Leadership*, New York: The Free Press of Glencoe, 1960.

Table 4

Mean Opportunity Structure Scores Known to the Police,
by Race, Class, and Gang Status [a]

Legitimate educational and occupational opportunities (0 to 22)	Perception of illegitimate opportunities (less inclusive) (0 to 18)	Perception of adult power and helpfulness (0 to 8)	Total opportunities score [b] (−18 to 30)	Mean number of offenses known to police, per boy
NG (9.0)	NG (11.4)	NG (4.5)	NG (2.1)	NG (3.14)
WG (9.3)	NLC (9.5)	WG (4.7)	WG (5.0)	WG (2.73)
NLC (11.0)	WG (9.0)	NLC (5.6)	NLC (7.1)	NLC (0.47)
WLC (13.7)	NMC (8.2)	WLC (5.6)	WLC (12.6)	WLC (0.31)
NMC (15.6)	WLC (6.7)	NMC (6.2)	NMC (13.6)	NMC (0.06)
WMC (20.2)	WMC (3.5)	WMC (7.4)	WMC (24.1)	WMC (0.02)

[a] NG stands for Negro gang members, NLC for Negro lower-class boys, and so on.

[b] Total Opportunities Score is designed to reflect both legitimate and illegitimate pressures toward delinquency. It is obtained by adding together legitimate educational and occupational opportunities and adult power and helpfulness scores, and from this sum subtracting illegitimate opportunity scores. Hence it should be negatively correlated with delinquency.

a score of 1 was given; "undecided" was scored 2, and "false," 3.

Table 3 presents mean opportunity structure scores, by race, class, and gang status of respondents. The trends apparent in Table 2 appear here, also.

In addition, it is clear that for *legitimate* opportunities, gang-nongang and middle-class differences *within* racial categories are greater than the Negro-white differences for each of the three gang and class strata. For *illegitimate* opportunities, differences between races are greater than within-race differences.

Perceived Opportunities and an
Official Delinquency Rate

In Table 4, ranking on each of the summary opportunity scores is compared with the official delinquency rates of the six race-by-class-by-gang-status groups.[19] As far as the *ordering* of the six groups is concerned, perception of *legitimate* opportunities is more strongly associated with delinquency rates than is perception of illegitimate opportunities. This is con-

[19] These rates refer to the mean number of offenses known to the police, per boy, in each group. Data are based on John M. Wise, "A Comparison of Sources of Data as Indexes of Delinquent Behavior," M.A. thesis, University of Chicago, 1962.

sistent with the assumption that perceived legitimate opportunities are independent variables, while perceived illegitimate opportunities intervene, after legitimate opportunities have been appraised and found wanting. Legitimate achievement tends to be the universal standard in our culture, highly valued even by very deviant individuals.[20] Note, however, that *within* racial categories, perception of illegitimate opportunities does order the groups according to official delinquency rates.

Official delinquency rates measure the hypothesized dependent variables only in a very gross sense. The gang-nongang distinction probably measures participation in delinquent subcultural activity, and adding the middle-class–lower-class division permits a test of the theory in terms somewhat broader than it was originally set forth. Here the theory holds up well: gang boys of both races perceive greater restrictions on legitimate opportunities than do nongang boys in the same neighborhoods or middle-class boys. Thus, the *negative* pressure toward deviance is greater for gang boys. Within each racial group, gang boys perceive better illegitimate opportunities; hence the greater "pull" toward deviance. While perceived adult power and helpfulness,

[20] See Gordon, *et al., op. cit.*

combined, rank the groups very much as do official delinquency rates, adult power alone turns out, as predicted, to be negatively related to delinquency, while helpfulness, which may be exercised by carriers of criminal as well as noncriminal values, is related inconsistently to delinquency among Negro boys.

Adult power and helpfulness are both hypothesized by Cloward and Ohlin to be negatively related to the emergence and maintenance of conflict subcultures. "The term that the bopper uses most frequently to characterize his relationships with adults is 'weak'. . . . He views himself as isolated and the adult world as indifferent. The commitments of adults are to their own interests and not to his. Their explanations of why he should behave differently are 'weak,' as are their efforts to help him." [21] This description holds up well with respect to "clout." Gang boys score lower than the others and Negro gang boys — by far our most conflict oriented [22] — score lowest of all. But helpfulness scores are comparatively high for all groups, and they are lowest for the less conflict-oriented white gang boys.[23]

Differences between nongang and gang boys on both scores are sufficient to suggest that these factors are important in selection for gang membership, though their relation to a particular type of delinquent subculture — con-

[21] Cloward and Ohlin, op. cit., pp. 24–25.

[22] For documentation, see Short, Tennyson, and Howard, op. cit., and Short and Strodtbeck, op. cit., esp. Chs. 1, 5, and 9. It was in large part because they were involved in gang fighting that most of the Negro gangs received the attention of newspapers, police, and the Program for Detached Workers with which this research program was associated. Close observation of the gangs over periods ranging from several months to more than three years suggests that nearly all the Negro gangs had at one time been more involved in "conflict subcultures" than had any of the white gangs. Finally, detailed analysis of behavior ratings by detached workers indicates greater conflict involvement by Negro than white gangs.

[23] These findings are consistent with boys' ratings of a series of adult roles in the same interview. See James F. Short, Jr., Ramon Rivera, and Harvey Marshall, "Adult-Adolescent Relations and Gang Delinquency: An Empirical Report," Pacific Sociological Review (Fall 1964).

flict — is inconsistent with the theory. The previously noted higher illegitimate opportunity scores registered by the Negro boys are also inconsistent, but the greater visibility and availability of petty criminal activities in lower-class Negro communities may account for this. Similarly, the comparatively low Negro middle-class scores on clout and helpfulness are consistent with Frazier's descriptions of the superficial show put on by Negro middle-class "society," which he regards as a somewhat futile attempt to compensate for status insecurities relative to whites.[24]

The hypothesis that perceived adult power is inversely related to gang conflict is essentially a social control argument. But helpfulness, when exercised by illegitimate adults, may be conducive to involvement in a criminal subculture. To investigate this possibility, we examined the relation between perceptions of various types of opportunities.

The Relation Between Legitimate and Illegitimate Opportunities

The product-moment correlations between opportunity scores, for all boys and for gang boys only, by race, are in Table 5. Legitimate opportunity scores tend to be positively correlated with one another, as are illegitimate opportunity scores, and between legitimate and illegitimate scores correlations are negative. There are exceptions to this general pattern, however; for example, perceptions of legitimate educational and occupational opportunities are significantly correlated for all groups except white gang boys. The low correlation in the latter group suggests that perceptions of legitimate educational and occupational opportunities often are not mutually reinforcing.

The relation between adult power and perceived illegitimate opportunities suggests greater "integration" of the carriers of criminal and conventional values in white neighborhoods: the correlations are low but positive among white boys, and negative among Negroes. For both races, adult helpfulness is negatively correlated with illegitimate opportunities.

Correlations between perceived illegitimate

[24] Frazier, op. cit.

Table 5
Correlations among Opportunity Structure Scores, by Race [c]

	Legitimate educational		Legitimate occupational		Adult clout		Adult helpfulness		Criminal, noncriminal integration		Criminal learning opportunities		Visibility of criminal careers		Criminal opportunities elite (less inclusive)		Criminal opportunities elite (inclusive)	
	W [a]	N [b]	W	N	W	N	W	N	W	N	W	N	W	N	W	N	W	N
Legitimate educational	**1.00**		.48	.38	.45	.34	.35	.27	-.36	-.17	-.49	-.22	-.42	-.23	-.27	-.13	-.06	-.03
Legitimate occupational	*.13*	*.34*	**1.00**		.42	.35	.28	.28	-.26	-.32	-.31	-.37	-.26	-.30	-.25	-.23	-.10	-.08
Adult clout	*.10*	*.22*	*.28*	*.37*	**1.00**		.29	.29	-.14	-.25	-.13	-.23	-.19	-.23	.04	-.01	.10	.05
Adult helpfulness	*.23*	*.32*	*.23*	*.35*	*.19*	*.32*	**1.00**		-.23	-.26	-.19	-.15	-.26	-.14	-.27	-.21	-.19	-.13
Criminal, noncriminal integration	*-.26*	*-.19*	*-.18*	*-.33*	*.05*	*-.23*	*-.27*	*-.29*	**1.00**		.49	.51	.37	.32	.46	.32	.20	.14
Criminal learning opportunities	*-.26*	*-.20*	*-.15*	*-.31*	*.16*	*-.22*	*-.20*	*-.19*	*.59*	*.52*	**1.00**		.54	.43	.52	.27	.19	-.02
Visibility of criminal careers	*-.28*	*-.27*	*-.17*	*-.39*	*.10*	*-.22*	*-.34*	*-.16*	*.37*	*.34*	*.46*	*.37*	**1.00**		.38	.21	.00	-.14
Criminal opportunities elite (less inclusive)	*-.21*	*-.18*	*-.24*	*-.25*	*.24*	*-.04*	*-.32*	*-.24*	*.60*	*.31*	*.64*	*.29*	*.49*	*.23*	**1.00**		.73	.70
Criminal opportunities elite (inclusive)	*-.03*	*-.05*	*-.15*	*-.07*	*.19*	*.01*	*-.23*	*-.15*	*.32*	*.08*	*.41*	*-.03*	*.16*	*-.10*	*.74*	*.66*	**1.00**	

[a] White: p < .05 = .13 (all boys) and .21 (gang boys); p < .01 = .18 (all boys) and .27 (gang boys)
[b] Negro: p < .05 = .11 (all boys) and .14 (gang boys); p < .01 = .14 (all boys) and .18 (gang boys)
[c] Italicized coefficients below the diagonal represent gang boys only; coefficients above the diagonal represent all boys, including gang members.

opportunities are higher for white boys, particularly those involving the criminal *elite* measures. Thus, while white boys perceive illegitimate opportunities as less available than do Negro boys, "integration" as we have operationalized it is actually more characteristic of white than Negro gang areas. Negro gang boys perceive illegitimate opportunities as relatively open, but they tend to perceive illegitimate adults as neither powerful nor helpful. White gang boys, however, tend to perceive illegitimate adults as powerful but not very helpful. A similar pattern occurs in data from another section of the interview, in which boys were asked to indicate four characteristics of several adult roles in their local areas. Among Negro gang boys, 38 percent, compared with 53 percent of white gang boys, felt that adults making money illegally have "a lot of clout," while only about one boy in five in both racial groups felt that such adults are "interested in the problem of teen-agers." Lower-class nongang boys consistently rated legitimate adult roles higher than gang boys did on scales reflecting their interest in and degree of contact with teen-agers, their "clout," and the extent to which they are considered "right guys." [25]

In the present analysis, the relations between various opportunity scores reveal no significant or consistent differences that explain behavioral differences between gang and nongang lower-class boys. The most striking differences are between middle-class Negro boys and all other groups in the correlation between adult helpfulness and perceived elite criminal opportunities. This correlation is positive for both elite scores (.34 for the more inclusive measure, .20 for the less inclusive measure) among Negro middle-class boys, but both correlations are negative in all other groups. Adult clout was also correlated positively with the two elite criminal opportunity scores among Negro middle-class boys (.22 and .30), and among white gang members, but negatively in the other groups. Again, reference to Frazier's perceptive analysis is pertinent.[26]

Summary

Legitimate occupational opportunities are perceived as available less often by gang than by nongang boys, and most often by middle-class boys. White boys are more likely than Negro boys to perceive such opportunities as available, in each of the strata examined. With respect to legitimate educational opportunities, the same pattern occurs, except that the racial difference does not occur among gang boys. Race and class-by-gang-status gradients are both present concerning adult clout, but not perceived adult helpfulness, among lower-class boys. These data are consistent with the apparently greater *protest* orientation of white as compared with Negro gang boys.[27] Gradients within racial groups are consistent with inferences from the Cloward and Ohlin theory.

Differences in perceptions of illegitimate opportunities reverse most of those found for legitimate opportunities, as expected. These differences are inconsistent with the greater conflict orientation of Negro gang boys, but when adult clout is correlated with criminal opportunity scores, and other data are introduced, "integration" of criminal opportunities and between criminal and legitimate opportunities is greater for white than for Negro boys. Even for white gang boys, however, the negative correlations between adult helpfulness and criminal opportunity scores, and their small positive correlations with adult clout suggest a low degree of "integration" between the carriers of criminal and conventional values.[28]

The logic of the theory clearly presumes that perceptions of opportunities *precede* involvement in delinquency, while our data reflect perceptions "after the fact." We cannot fully resolve this problem. Evidence concerning the relation of *individual* gang boys' perceptions of opportunities to their behavior as individuals, is relevant, however, and its mention permits brief discussion of the somewhat different causal model that has emerged from the larger study of which this paper is a par-

[25] A more detailed report of these data is in Short, Rivera, and Marshall, *op. cit.*

[26] Frazier, *op. cit.*

[27] See Short, Tennyson, and Howard, *op. cit.*, and Short and Strodtbeck, *op. cit.*, Ch. 5.

[28] This, perhaps, explains why we had such difficulty locating criminal gangs. See Short and Strodtbeck, *op. cit.*, Chs. 1 and 9.

tial report. Correlations between opportunity scores and theoretically relevant behavior scores for individual gang boys are low. For example, *conflict factor scores*, consisting of a combination of individual and gang fighting (with and without weapons), assault, and carrying concealed weapons, are not systematically related to perceptions of either legitimate or illegitimate opportunity scores. That is, boys with high scores do not have lower opportunity scores.[29] It seems unlikely, therefore, that data reported in this paper reflect the boys' efforts to rationalize delinquent behavior by "blaming" the lack of opportunity. Although this does not solve the problem of temporal order, it is presumptive evidence against an alternative interpretation based on the assumption of "after-the-fact" (of delinquency or gang membership) influences on perception.

Our argument is not that the latter are unimportant. Other data from our study suggest that social structure influences the development of ethnic, class, life-cycle, and perhaps "delinquent" subcultures with relatively distinctive content. Social structural theories are therefore appropriately applied to the social distribution of many phenomena — to delinquency "rates" rather than to individual episodes or degrees of involvement in delinquency. It is to the question of "rates" or the social distribution of delinquent subcultures, that the Cloward and Ohlin theory is addressed — appropriately. To account for selection into subcultures — into gang membership, for example — from the youngsters available, and for individual behavior within the context of a subculture, requires reference to "levels" of explanation other than social structure.[30]

We have found it necessary to invoke personality level variables, as Inkeles suggested,[31] and *group process* considerations, to explain delinquent behavior *within* our gangs.[32] The give and take of interaction among gang boys, and between gang boys and others; a variety of role relations within the gang and status considerations related to these roles and to opportunities present in situations of the moment — these are prime determinants of what happens in the gang, of who becomes involved in what type of behavior, and with whom.[33] This *level* of explanation "washes out" variations in perceptions of opportunities related to social structure as a major determinant of individuals' behavior in the gang context.

---

[29] Derivation of the scores is detailed in Short, Tennyson and Howard, *op. cit.* Full presentation of the data concerning individual opportunity perception and behavior is beyond the scope of this paper.

[30] See David Bordua's critique of social structural theories in this regard. David Bordua, "Delinquent Subcultures: Sociological Interpretations of Gang Delinquency," *Annals of the American Academy of Political and Social Science*, 338

(November 1961), and his *Sociological Theories and Their Implications for Juvenile Delinquency*, Children's Bureau, Juvenile Delinquency: Facts and Facets, No. 2, Washington, D.C.: Government Printing Office, 1960. See, also, Short and Strodtbeck, *op. cit.*, and James F. Short, Jr., "Social Structure and Group Processes in Explanations of Gang Delinquency," paper read at the Fifth Social Psychology Symposium, University of Oklahoma, 1964, Muzafer Sherif and Carolyn Sherif, (eds.), *Problems of Youth: Transition to Adulthood in a Changing World*, Chicago: Aldine Pub. Co., 1965, pp. 155–158.

[31] Alex Inkeles, "Personality and Social Structure," Ch. 11 in *Sociology Today*, Robert K. Merton, Leonard Broom, and Leonard S. Cottrell, Jr. (eds.), New York: Basic Books, 1959. From the present study, see Robert A. Gordon and James F. Short, Jr., "Social Level, Social Disability, and Gang Interaction," Ch. 10 in Short and Strodtbeck, *op. cit.*

[32] See, esp., Short, "Gang Delinquency and Anomie," *op. cit.*; Short and Strodtbeck, *op. cit.*, and by the same authors, "The Response of Gang Leaders to Status Threats: An Observation on Group Process and Delinquent Behavior," *American Journal of Sociology*, 68 (March 1963), pp. 571–579, and "Why Gangs Fight," *Trans-Action*, 1 (September–October 1964), pp. 25–29; and Strodtbeck and Short, "Aleatory Risks v. Short-Run Hedonism in Explanation of Gang Action," *Social Problems* (Fall 1964).

[33] The point is made in more general theoretical terms in Albert K. Cohen, "The Sociology of the Deviant Act: Anomie Theory and Beyond," *American Sociological Review*, 30 (February 1965), pp. 5–14.

Since the publication of Shaw and McKay's research, Thrasher's classic study of *The Gang*, and Sutherland's theory of differential association, many sociologists have taken the position that to become delinquent neither requires a juvenile to be "different" from other juveniles, nor are defects of personality, intelligence, or physique needed; rather, children learn delinquent patterns of conduct in association with others. Shaw and McKay found that juveniles usually committed their delinquent acts in the company of one or more persons, and this indication of the social nature of delinquency, Lerman suggests, led to the inference that the delinquents were members of gangs. Thrasher depicted the origin of the gang in the spontaneous play activities of children, and he noted that "gangs" become integrated through conflict with other segments of the society. Sutherland theorized that the learning of techniques for the commission of offenses, as well as the supporting attitudes and rationalizations, occurs principally within primary groups. In *Delinquent Boys*, Cohen equated his concept "delinquent subculture" with the concept "gang." He wrote that "when we speak of a delinquent subculture, we speak of a way of life that has somehow become traditional among certain groups in American society. These groups are the boys' gangs that flourish most conspicuously in the 'delinquency neighborhoods' of our large American cities" (1955:13). According to Cohen, the gang is "the culture-bearer *par excellence* of the delinquent subculture" (1955:43). He offered an explanation, it may be recalled, of the origin of the delinquent subculture as a group "product" — another way of saying that delinquency is neither an inborn disposition nor the invention of a particular child. Similarly, in *Delinquency and Opportunity*, Cloward and Ohlin defined the delinquent subculture with respect to the delinquent gang. The opening line in their first chapter reads, "This book is about delinquent gangs, or subcultures, as they are typically found among adolescent males in lower-class areas of large urban centers" (1960:1).

In this selection Lerman challenges the view that subcultural delinquency is predominantly gang delinquency. Lerman argues against use of the usual methods of investigating subcultural phenomena because these result in the study of biased samples; he suggests advantages of survey methods. According to Lerman, the concepts "subculture" and "gang" are not synonymous, and participation in subcultural delinquency is not restricted to members of gangs. The existence of a subculture, he says, implies a relationship between shared symbols, such as deviant values and speech, and behavioral consequences, but the cultural aspect, "symbolic deviance," must be distinguished from the social dimension of "interaction patterns." The social units most frequently used by subcultural participants in their delinquencies are the pair and triad, and approximately half of the boys rated high on subcultural indicators report association in pairs or triads. Thus, Lerman proposes that the social boundaries of a subculture are described most accurately as a network of pairs, triads, and groups with or without names.

Later commentary and debate between Short (1968) and Lerman (1968), which is not included here, suggest the important point that the "gang" may be an "occasional grouping." Many boys commonly associate in pairs, triads, or other small groups. It is when they leave their area, or "turf," or when the threat of a "rumble," or fight, arises from the intrusion of outsiders in their area that the "gang" is operative. In these instances the gang may be cohesive, but the effective social units on a daily basis are smaller cliques or subgroups. Short also comments that among the gangs studied in Chicago, pairs and triads constituted the most common patterns of "hanging out" of known gang members. Lerman's paper carries an important implication for the distinction Yablonsky (1962) draws between "core" and "peripheral" gang members. As Lerman (1968) observes, the so-called "peripheral members" may simply be pairs and triads that occasionally participate in the activities of the larger collectivity, the gang.

REFERENCES

Richard A. Cloward and Lloyd E. Ohlin, *Delinquency and Opportunity: A Theory of Delinquent Gangs* (Glencoe, Ill.: The Free Press, 1960).

Albert K. Cohen, *Delinquent Boys: The Culture of the Gang* (Glencoe, Ill.: The Free Press, 1955).

Paul Lerman, "Reply," *American Journal of Sociology*, 73 (January 1968), pp. 515–517.

James F. Short, Jr., "Comment on Lerman's 'Gangs, Networks, and Subcultural Delinquency,'" *American Journal of Sociology*, 73 (January 1968), pp. 513–515.

Lewis Yablonsky, *The Violent Gang* (New York: The Macmillan Co., 1962).

PAUL LERMAN

Gangs, Networks, and Subcultural Delinquency

Since the ground-breaking studies of Shaw and McKay,[1] and particularly since the publication of Cohen's *Delinquent Boys*,[2] many American sociologists have insisted that a significant manifestation of masculine youthful misconduct is the "tradition," "way of life," or "subculture" of deviant peer groups and that the most serious forms of officially known male juvenile delinquency can be described as distinctively subcultural phenomena. The usual method of describing and "proving" the existence of a distinct way of life among delinquents has been by means of case studies of street gangs. Cohen,[3] Miller,[4] and Cloward and Ohlin,[5] for example, offer as their supporting data anecdotes, participant-observation reports, impressions of gang workers, journalistic writings, and excerpts from interviews with gang members.

These and other theorists have tended to assume that peer-based delinquency is predomi-

From *American Journal of Sociology*, 73 (July, 1967), pp. 63–72. Reprinted by permission.

Adapted from Paul Lerman, "Issues in Subcultural Delinquency" (unpublished doctoral dissertation, Columbia University, 1966). The study was conducted under the auspices of the Columbia University School of Social Work, Mobilization for Youth Research Project, Dr. Richard A. Cloward, project director. It was funded by the National Institute of Mental Health (Contract MH-01178-01). A special grant by the Ford Foundation made my participation in the construction of the survey instrument possible.

[1] Clifford R. Shaw and Henry D. McKay, *Juvenile Delinquency and Urban Areas* (Chicago: University of Chicago Press, 1942).

[2] Albert K. Cohen, *Delinquent Boys* (Glencoe, Ill.: Free Press, 1955).

[3] *Ibid.*

[4] Walter B. Miller, "Lower Class Culture as a Generating Milieu of Gang Delinquency," *Journal of Social Issues*, XIV (Summer 1958), pp. 5–19.

[5] Richard A. Cloward and Lloyd E. Ohlin, *Delinquency and Opportunity* (Glencoe, Ill.: Free Press, 1960).

320   PAUL LERMAN

nantly gang delinquency. It is the contention of this paper — supported by empirical evidence — that this assumption hinders our understanding of deviant youth subcultures.

The concept "subculture" refers to shared symbols, not to a specific type of interaction pattern. From the point of view of this paper, a delinquent subculture can be said to exist if a relationship is found between shared symbols (deviant values and deviant speech, or argot) and behavior that is potentially noticeable by officials. The social context of this shared deviance can be quite varied and should be addressed empirically and theoretically.

In the following pages, we shall first consider the tendency to view the gang as the sole subcultural unit, drawing on published studies for support of our position that the gang has been overemphasized. The second half of the paper empirically examines various interaction patterns as they are related to deviant indicators.

The findings reported are based on information derived from a survey of youth residing in randomly selected household units of a portion of New York City's Lower East Side.[6] The original target group consisted of 706 boys and girls aged ten to nineteen years; interviews were completed with 555 youth, a rate of 79 percent. Processing of the entire sample through the official police files disclosed that interviewed boys, even with age controlled, were as likely to be "delinquent" as their non-cooperative peers.

Viewing the Gang as the Sole Subcultural Unit

As long as sociologists were interested in mapping the social distribution of rates of delinquency, the problem of defining the social boundaries of a juvenile "tradition" of deviant conduct was easily handled by utilizing ecological units of a city.[7] The boundaries of a

deviant "way of life" were regarded as coterminous with those of geographical areas high in delinquency, and "inner" or "interstitial" areas were compared to "outer" areas. The social patterns of interaction were further inferred from Shaw's findings that 81 percent of the youthful offenders brought to the Juvenile Court of Chicago were likely to commit officially proscribed acts with one or more persons rather than alone.[8] Since the phenomenon of gangs was in evidence then as it is now, it was inferred from the social character of juvenile misconduct that offenders were likely to be members of gangs. Thus many sociologists tended to conceive of the subcultural boundaries as synonymous with gang membership, and studies of gangs within "inner" zones of the city became increasingly prominent. Thrasher's classic work[9] epitomizes this gang-study tradition.

Both Cohen and Cloward-Ohlin cite Shaw's early findings on offenders' tendencies to be deviant with peers as the major evidence for regarding gangs as the appropriate unit of concern. However, there are no reports in the literature of studies demonstrating that peer-oriented offenders known to the police are predominately members of gangs. A study by Wattenberg and Balistrieri, using the four-member group as a definition of "gang," found that only 47 percent of a male youth population "interviewed on complaint" by the police of Detroit could be clearly classified as gang members.[10] There is, then, a lack of explicit empirical evidence to support the assumption that gang boundaries of membership tend to coincide with the boundaries of symbolic participation in a delinquent subculture.

Perhaps the reason that the literature has not consistently distinguished between subcul-

[6] For further details about the sample and a copy of the questionnaire used, see *A Proposal for the Prevention and Control of Delinquency by Expanding Opportunities* (New York: Mobilization for Youth, Inc., December 9, 1961), Appendixes R4 and R5.

[7] See the brief review of early European and American studies in Shaw and McKay, *op. cit.*, pp. 1–14.

[8] Clifford R. Shaw, "Juvenile Delinquency — a Case History," *Bulletin of the State University of Iowa*, No. 24, N.S. No. 701 (1933), pp. 1–3.

[9] Frederick M. Thrasher, *The Gang* (Chicago: University of Chicago Press, 1927). A modern example of this tradition can be found in James F. Short, Jr., and Fred L. Strodtbeck, *Group Process and Gang Delinquency* (Chicago: University of Chicago Press, 1965).

[10] William W. Wattenberg and James J. Balistrieri, "Gang Membership and Juvenile Misconduct," *American Sociological Review*, XV (December 1950), 744–52.

tural and interactional dimensions lies in the nature of the samples used. In the main, the samples have not been drawn from a cross-section of a lower-class community but have consisted of segments from rather special populations: cases known on complaint to the police; adjudicated delinquents; institutionalized boys; or groups of concern to social agencies and demonstration projects. In a sense, these descriptions of the subculture may be based on a sampling artifact that yields a disproportionate number of "gang" members.

Although more appropriate sampling designs can help us to avoid factual error, we also need to evolve a theoretical framework that permits us to deal with the variety of collective forms that have already been noted in the literature. Even the writings that tend to reify the gang exhibit an awareness of "amorphous coalitions of cliques," [11] of groups with loose "ties" and limited cohesion,[12] and of the existence of disagreements among gang participants regarding who is and who is not a member.[13] The failure of gangs to conform to a preconception of "group" has been noted particularly by Scott and by Richards.[14]

Yablonsky has used the term "near-group" to deal with the findings that emerged from his study of thirty New York City gangs.[15] Whether or not we accept his term, it is evident that it is an attempt to delineate the loose associational form that others have noted. As characteristics of the "near-groups" engaging in conflict activities, Yablonsky lists the following: diffuse role definitions, limited cohesion, impermanence, minimal consensus on norms, shifting membership, disturbed leadership, and limited definitions of membership

expectations. Because of their failure to appreciate these factors, he claims, gang workers enter the field with certain distortions, namely, that the gang has a measurable number of members, that the role of a member is specified, that there is a consensus of understood gang norms among gang members, and that gang leadership is clear and entails a flow of authority and direction of action.

Yablonsky's finding that gangs do not always match preconceived stereotypes is valuable. He errs, however, in assuming that loose associational forms are in some way pathological and that "normal" associational forms of adolescents have to be modeled after a classical group.

As a matter of fact, both adolescents and adults have many acceptable phrases that are used in everyday speech to describe loose associational types: for example, the "horsey set," the "jet set," the "bowling crowd," the "beatniks." All these associational forms seem to share fluidity of membership, ill-defined roles, limited cohesion, and other characteristics noted by Yablonsky. However, these forms need not become fully organized or contain "disturbed" leadership personnel.

The observation that a loose associational form lacks classic group attributes should not blind us to the social and cultural regularities that *can* be found:

1. The participants share a common set of values and activities — but enactments can be performed individually *or* in groupings, as long as there is an appreciative audience.
2. There are implicit or explicit criteria for evaluating whether the values are expressed appropriately or inappropriately and the activities carried out well, indifferently, or badly.
3. Participants can gain favorable evaluations for performing the activities well or for giving effective verbal expression to the shared values.
4. The activities are often accompanied by stylistic embellishments that enable those "in the know" to determine whether participants are "square" or "hip." Argot is one means of accomplishing this end.
5. Many of the participants are in effective interaction with others in the collectivity, and

---

[11] Albert K. Cohen and James F. Short, Jr., "Research in Delinquent Subcultures," *Journal of Social Issues*, XIV (Summer 1958), 25.

[12] Cloward and Ohlin, *op. cit.*, p. 179.

[13] Irving Spergel, *Racketville, Slumtown, Haulburg* (Chicago: University of Chicago Press, 1964), pp. 66–68.

[14] Peter Scott, "Gangs and Delinquent Groups in London," *British Journal of Delinquency*, VII (July 1956), 8–21; Catherine V. Richards, *Breaking through Barriers* (Chicago: Welfare Council of Metropolitan Chicago, 1959).

[15] Lewis Yablonsky, "The Delinquent Gang as a Near-Group," *Social Problems*, VII (Fall 1959), 108–17.

there exists some communication structure by means of which participants can be "clued in." Argot is also useful in carrying out this purpose.

6. There may be influentials and style setters who are acknowledged as such.

7. Cliques can be recognized, but the total association population is less identifiable, and the membership boundaries are vague.

It is clear that this phenomenon can be described according to two distinct analytic dimensions: cultural and social. The cultural dimension refers to the shared symbols (i.e., values and argot) and the behavior consonant with these symbols. The social dimension refers to the patterns of interaction that distinguish participants from non-participants. Differentiation of youth who share consonant symbols from youth who do not share these symbols demarcates the *subcultural boundaries*. Differentiation of interacting participants from non-participants demarcates the *social boundaries*. The two are not synonymous, since the referents can be adequately distinguished. However, they are related, since actors need symbols for purposes of interaction, and symbols cannot be shared except in an interaction context. But symbols can be shared in a variety of interaction contexts, and a prior assumption concerning the associational form necessary for the symbol sharing is unwarranted and open to empirical doubt.

Where membership boundaries are vague but interaction regularities can be identified, the concept of "network" may be found useful. Bott notes, in her discussion of "open" and "closed" family networks, that this concept has been used in studies of personal influence, voting behavior, interpersonal relations, and kinship systems.[16] Utilization of this broader concept does *not* preclude the possibility that groups are one of the types of social unit comprising a network. However, it permits us to recognize that pairs and triads are also units in a network.

The observation that pairs and triads are important collectivities used by youth would not

be surprising to Thrasher. Present-day theorists, stressing the prescriptive requirements of gang membership, might ponder his conclusion that:

The two- and three-boy relationship is often much more important to the individual boy than his relationship to the gang. In such cases a boy would doubtless forego the gang before he would give up his special pal or pair of pals. . . .[17]

Interaction Patterns Among Peers

Our empirical analysis of the interaction patterns of urban slum youth will rely solely on the actor's point of view. This approach, although not the only possible way of studying peer associations in a slum area, provides a necessary corrective to the prevalent tendency to single out gangs for attention to the exclusion of other possible types of social unit. Gathering responses for a random population in an extensive geographical area can provide the data necessary for a comparison of subcultural participants and more conforming youth. By treating "interaction" and "subculture" as separate variables, we not only can further delinquency research but can study associational patterns of youth for their own intrinsic interest.

To elicit information concerning their interaction patterns, survey respondents were asked: (1) what type of social unit (a regular group, one or two others, or "myself") they "usually go around with"; (2) whether their regular social unit, if any, had a name; and (3) how much of their leisure time (all, most, or some) was spent with friends. (Youth who reported themselves as "loners" were not asked this question.)

Developmental Aspects of Peer Interaction Patterns

The actors' perceptions of the type of social unit they were part of are presented in Table 1, for four age groupings of boys.

Until the age of fourteen or fifteen, the dominant pattern appears to be the pair or triad; a regular group is second, and a small minority (11–12 percent) perceive themselves as "loners." At age fourteen to fifteen, there is

[16] Elizabeth Bott, "Norms and Ideology: The Normal Family," in Norman W. Bell and Ezra F. Vogel (eds.), *The Family* (Glencoe, Ill.: Free Press, 1960), pp. 435–52.

[17] Thrasher, *op. cit.*, p. 322.

Table 1

Responses to "Who Do You Usually Go Around With?" by Age (N = 276)

Usual interaction pattern	Age			
	10–11	12–13	14–15	16–19
Self[a]	12%	12%	11%	24%
One or two others	57	56	42	46
Regular group	31	32	47	30
N	67	84	62	63

a Includes 4 DK (don't know) and NA (no answer) boys.

a shift in the direction of associating with a regular group; this pattern slightly surpasses the pair and triad in popularity. At age sixteen to nineteen, there is a movement away from the regular-group pattern toward the unit of the "loner"; the pair and triad types, however, are still dominant.

Data pertaining to the types of social units are only one indication of associational patterns. Another measure is the likelihood that the social unit possesses a public name. The information depicted in Table 2 indicates that the groups are almost as nameless as the pairs and trios that are the favored type of associational pattern.

Although there are some age differences, the significant finding is the low percentage of groups with a name at all age ranges. It is unlikely that reluctance to identify the group name, if it exists, could account wholly for this finding.

Table 3, which shows the reported frequency of interaction with friends, supports the previous findings that the oldest age group tends to move away from collective interaction with peers.

In general, the three measures of interaction suggest that the associational patterns usually projected for youth in slum areas are in need of revision. Except for boys aged fourteen to fifteen, the pair or triad is the favored associational form, and at age fourteen to fifteen this pattern competes on an equal basis with the regular-group form. Group names are not common as perceived and reported by youth. To further undermine the ideal image, the percentage of youth reporting that they spend

Table 2

Percentage of Boys Who Responded That Their Social Unit Had a Name, by Age (N = 276)

Age	Group has name
10–11	1%
N = 67	
12–13	5%
N = 84	
14–15	8%
N = 62	
16–19	10%
N = 63	

"all" their leisure time with peers is quite small, except at the girl-avoiding age of ten to eleven.

These findings do not mean that boys refrain from association with others. However, not all their time is taken up with regular peer life. That a sizable proportion spend "some" or "most" of their time with friends certainly indicates the ready availability of an interaction context for shared symbols.

Interaction Patterns and the Acquisition of Argot

Once interaction variables have been analytically distinguished from symbolic variables and measured separately, it becomes possible to explore the interaction contexts that facilitate the acquisition of shared symbols.

In the study reported here, shared deviant symbols refer to values (e.g., admiration of toughness and the ability to keep one's mouth shut to the cops, enjoying kicks) and language (i.e., argot). Boys who ranked high in shared deviant values and in knowledge of the argot peculiar to various illegal activities were found to be highest in the number, frequency, and variety of self-reported deviant acts, as well as in the likelihood of being recorded in police files or admitting to being "stopped" by the police. A combined index of "bopping" and drug argot knowledge [18] was found to be espe-

[18] The final index of argot knowledge was obtained after analyzing responses to a list of twenty argot words used in the interview. The word list contained five words for each of the following referents: organized rackets, unorganized crimes, interpersonal aggression (bopping), and drug ac-

Table 3

Frequency of Interaction with Peers by Age (N = 232) [a]

Amount of leisure time usually spent with friends	Age			
	10–11	12–13	14–15	16–19
All	22%	8%	9%	6%
Most	33	43	47	34
Some	45	49	43	60
N	58	74	53	47

[a] Excludes 40 "self" boys and 4 DK and NA boys.

cially effective in discriminating boys who were high in these measures of behavioral deviance, as well as boys ranking high in shared deviant values. In Tables 4, 5, and 6, this index is used alone to highlight the usefulness of distinguishing between symbolic and interaction variables. In the remaining tables, we use a subcultural typology to refer to high knowledge of argot *and* high ranking in shared deviant values to broaden our exposition of the idea that subcultural delinquency refers to shared symbolic as well as behavioral deviance.

Two interaction conditions will be explored in relation to the index of bop-drug argot knowledge: (1) a group, with and without a name, versus a pair or triad versus self; and (2) degrees of frequency of interaction with peers. Although only a small percentage of boys reported that their group had a name, it is instructive to classify youth by this variable so as to approximate the interaction pattern that has been studied most extensively (i.e., gangs), while comparing it to other types that have been found to exist. We concentrate on fourteen- to nineteen-year-olds because this is the age when boys are most likely to know argot.

Table 4 clearly indicates that association

tivities. Only the interrelated indexes of bopping and drug argot knowledge fulfilled the minimal subcultural test, that there exists a strong relationship between shared values and language. For a fuller discussion and a historical review of empirical studies of argot, see Paul Lerman, "Issues in Subcultural Delinquency," (unpublished doctoral dissertation, Columbia University, 1966).

Table 4

Relationship of Interaction Patterns and Combined Argot Index, 14- to 19-Year-Old Boys (N = 124)

Combined argot index [a]	Usual interaction pattern			
	Regular group		Pair or triad	Self
	Name	No name		
$\bar{B}$-$\bar{D}$	18%	36%	42%	77%
B or D	18	28	23	5
BD	64	36	35	18
N	11	36	55	22

[a] $\bar{B}$-$\bar{D}$ means knows *neither* bopping nor drug words; B or D means knows at least one bopping *or* one drug word; BD means knows at least one bopping *and* one drug word.

with a regular group that has a name is the condition likely to yield the greatest knowledge of argot. If the group does not have a name, however, the argot-knowledge profile of participants is quite similar to that for participants in pairs or triads. Since these two interaction classifications include the largest number of boys, the findings are of some relevance. Apparently, boys who associate with others in any form are superior to "loners" in their knowledge of combined argot.

Table 5 presents the relationship between the amount of time usually spent with peers and the combined bop-drug index for two age-ranges.

At both ages the boys who interact all or most of the time with friends have only a slight advantage in argot knowledge: at age fourteen to fifteen, the BD category yields a difference of only 10 percent, and at age sixteen to nineteen, the difference is virtually negligible. Evidently, frequency of interaction as measured by peer reports is less salient as a facilitating condition for knowledge of argot than the mere fact of association with others.

Interaction Patterns as Social Boundaries

We use measures of interaction as independent variables not only because this enables us to investigate the facilitating effects of vari-

Table 5
Relationship of Frequency of Interaction with Peers and Combined Argot Index by Age (N = 100)

	Age and frequency of interaction			
	14–15 years		*16–19 years*	
Combined argot index	*All or most*	*Some*	*All or most*	*Some*
$\bar{B}$-$\bar{D}$	50%	43%	21%	32%
B or D	23	39	21	11
BD	27	17	58	57
N	30	23	19	28

Table 6
Relationship of Combined Argot Index and Interaction Patterns (N = 276)

Usual interaction pattern	*Combined argot index*		
	$\bar{B}$-$\bar{D}$	B or D	BD
Self	18%	7%	9%
Pair or triad	51	56	45
Regular group with no name	28	33	30
Regular group with name	3	5	16
N	177	43	56

ous interaction conditions but also because high rates of peer interaction are reported at an early age (e.g., only 12 percent "loners" are reported at ages ten to eleven and twelve to thirteen). However, it is also useful to answer the following question: What types of social unit are found among boys who are high on measures of shared symbols? Stated in this form, the interaction patterns are treated as dependent variables. Table 6 presents the data relevant to an exploration of this interesting issue, using knowledge of argot as the symbolic indicator.

Table 6 reveals important differences both among and within argot categories. Differences among argot categories refer to interaction patterns that are most likely to distinguish between subcultural participants and non-participants. Differences within argot categories (particularly the high one, *BD*) can refer to the degree of heterogeneity or homogeneity of the interaction patterns of boys who are likely to be subcultural participants.

Compared to boys who are ignorant of argot ($\bar{B}$-$\bar{D}$), knowledgeable boys (*BD*) are more likely to interact in a regular group with a name (16 percent versus 3 percent); more likely to interact in a regular group, with or without a name (46 percent versus 31 percent); and therefore less likely to be loners (9 percent versus 18 percent).

In terms of differences within the most knowledgeable argot category, it is interesting to note that the two types of collective

pattern have an equal chance of being used; 46 percent of the high-argot boys report membership in a regular group, and 45 percent report association with pairs or triads.[19] This result suggests that *subcultural boundaries and interaction boundaries are, in fact, distinct phenomena.* The social boundaries of youth sharing argot as deviant symbols can best be conceived, therefore, as a *network* of pairs, triads, and regular groups, with and without a name.

Recognition of these smaller social units imbedded in the interaction pattern of a network does not mean negation of the earlier findings. Membership in a group with a publicly identifiable name still constitutes a facilitating condition for the acquisition of shared symbols. However, the argot community is broader than any particular informal associational pattern used by peers. In short, subculture does not refer only to gangs but cross-cuts the social boundaries of specific groups, pairs, and triads.

Interaction Patterns with Deviant Associates

Our contention that undue emphasis on regular groups (e.g., "gangs") hinders our understanding of peer-based delinquency is supported by another line of analysis. In addition to being questioned about their everyday, informal interaction patterns, respondents were asked whether most of the illegal acts they re-

[19] These findings fit in remarkably well with the finding reported by Wattenberg and Balistrieri, *op. cit.*, that about 47 percent of youth known to the police on complaint were "gang" members.

Table 7
*Interaction Pattern of Deviance
by Age (N = 276)*

Interaction pattern of deviance	Age			
	10–11	*12–13*	*14–15*	*16–19*
Self	55%	51%	61%	65%
Pair or triad	25	32	19	22
Regular group	0	6	6	6
DK, NA, or DNA[a]	19	11	13	6
N	67	84	62	63

[a] "Don't know," "no answer," or "does not apply."

Table 8
*Relationship of Subcultural Typology and
Interaction Pattern of Deviance (N = 276)*

Interaction pattern of deviance	Subcultural typology			
	Very low	*Low*	*Medium*	*High to very high*
Self	73%	59%	55%	38%
Pair or triad	14	21	29	43
Regular group	1	3	3	13
DK, NA, or DNA	11	16	13	6
N	70	91	62	53

ported had been done alone, with one or two others, or with a regular group. The results of this measure of peer partners in delinquent acts are shown in Table 7 for four age groupings of males. Boys who reported no deviant acts were placed in the "DK, NA, or DNA" category; however, even if such boys were excluded, the results of Table 7 would be substantially as reported.

Starting at age twelve to thirteen, boys report a regular group as one type of associational context for deviant activities, but the percentage is quite small and does not increase with age. The general message conveyed by these data is that a majority of youth at all ages engage in illegal behavior alone, rather than with others. However, if youth are classified according to a combined index of argot *and* shared values (the subcultural typology referred to earlier) a quite different image emerges, as shown in Table 8.

Table 8 reveals that the high subcultural boys comprise the only category in which "lone-wolf" deviance is reported as the minor type. The favored mode of collective participation for these boys is the pair or triad. It should be noted, however, that high subcultural boys are also the ones most likely to use a group.

These findings lend further support to the contention of this paper and earlier studies that subcultural delinquency is a form of shared, collective deviance. However, in supporting the view that the pair or triad, not the group or gang, is the social unit most frequently used

by subcultural boys in their deviance, the results of this study contradict the conclusion of earlier studies that peer-based deviance is predominantly gang delinquency.

*The Interaction Pattern and
Police Contact*

We have noted earlier that the subcultural typology has proved capable of distinguishing boys who are highest on indexes of behavioral deviance. A critical issue for adherents of the traditional "gang" point of view is whether interaction measures have any social relevance in the sense that they improve on the utility of indexes of shared symbolic deviance. If the level of subcultural participation is controlled, does it matter whether the actors are members of regular groups or are linked to the network via a pal or two? Table 9 indicates that membership in a deviant symbolic network is the critical variable for being noticed by the police; the type of "usual" interaction unit does not seem to affect the likelihood of having one's name in the official police files *or* of admitting to having been stopped by a policeman. Were age also controlled, the conclusion would be similar regarding this combined measure of police contact.

Summary and Conclusions

If we accept the actor's point of view as the basis for defining the social unit of peer activities, youth in urban slum areas tend to associate in pairs and triads even more than in regular groups. Although membership in a group

Table 9

Index of Police Contact [a] *for Boys,*
Classified by Both Subcultural Involvement
and Interaction Pattern ($N = 236$)

Usual interaction pattern [b]	Subcultural typology	
	Low-medium	High-very high
Pair or triad	12%	52%
N	113	27
Regular group	11%	59%
N	74	22

[a] Boys are classified as having been in contact with the police if (1) their names were found recorded in the official files of the New York City Police Department; and/or (2) they admitted to having been stopped by the police for any of the items in the list of self-reports.

[b] The rate of police contact for the 40 loners, who are excluded from this table, is 10%.

with a name is a facilitating condition for learning argot, even the boys rated high in subcultural indicators are about evenly divided in their preference for pairs or triads versus regular groups. The data clearly support the view that "subculture" and "gang" are not synonymous.

This conclusion is also supported by analysis of patterns of interaction with deviant associates in illegal acts. Although high subcultural boys are the least likely to report "lone-wolf" activities, it is clear that only in a minority of

cases is a regular group the unit for illegal activities. Not only are the everyday social units of high subcultural boys composed of diverse types of collectivities, but partners in deviance appear to be chosen on the basis of palship rather than group criteria. The social unit of a subculture, then, is most accurately described as a network of pairs, triads, groups with names, and groups without names. This perspective is quite useful in interpreting interaction patterns based on a cross-section of low-income youth, as well as in dealing with descriptive findings based on more restrictive samples.

It is important to remember that the perspective being advanced is supported by empirical data generated by survey techniques. It has been suggested that "gang" boys are reluctant to identify themselves as regular group members when interviewed by a strange adult. This may be so. However, potential gang boys should also be reluctant to admit their knowledge of argot, reports of misconduct, the values of their friends, and contacts with the police. The fact that they respond to these indicators of deviance — and that the consistency of responses increases with age — certainly suggests that the survey method is capable of "tapping" symbolic and behavioral variables of interest to subcultural researchers. It appears unreasonable to conclude that likely subcultural participants will tell us about their varied modes of deviance but will not disclose their interaction patterns to the same degree.

Examining the available empirical evidence, Empey raises three fundamental questions regarding contemporary theories of delinquency. The first is related to the implications of the body of research in which self-reports are used as an alternative to reliance on official statistics (see Section I). Empey correctly interprets these studies as suggesting that the presumed inverse relationship between delinquent behavior and social class, so evident in data obtained from official sources, may be less "potent" than has been assumed. He points to the need for analysis of differences in delinquent behavior within classes as well as between classes.

Empey's second question concerns the dimensions of group delinquency.

He asks what forces hold delinquent groups together. Identification of the source of group cohesiveness is important because of its implications both for our causal models and for social control.

Finally, Empey inquires whether the delinquent subculture stands in opposition to middle-class standards or is part of a widespread deviant tradition. Cohen and Short (1958) refer to Cohen's description of "the" delinquent subculture in *Delinquent Boys* as the "parent male subculture"; and they suggest that the offspring of this subculture may include several variants — the conflict-oriented subculture, the drug-addict subculture, semi-professional theft, and a subculture they distinguish on theoretical rather than empirical grounds, the middle-class delinquent subculture. In this selection Empey indicates that there is more empirical support for the notion of an amorphous "parent" subculture than for the idea of highly focused delinquent subcultures. Pointing out that empirical evidence is needed on adolescents' acceptance of the legitimacy of conventional patterns and the extent to which they also participate in a more amorphous tradition of deviance, Empey also suggests investigation of a representative sample of adolescents to determine the effects of official processing.

REFERENCE

Albert K. Cohen and James F. Short, Jr., "Research in Delinquent Subcultures," *The Journal of Social Issues*, vol. 14, no. 3 (1958), pp. 20–37.

LA MAR T. EMPEY

Delinquency Theory and Recent Research

Attempts to explain delinquency traditionally have been concerned with two fundamental sets of data: (1) evidence from official sources that delinquency is concentrated most heavily among lower-class juveniles [1] and (2) evidence that the delinquent act is typically a group phenomenon, not a solitary enterprise.[2] The result has been a number of influential theories

From *Journal of Research in Crime and Delinquency*, January 1967, pp. 28–42. Reprinted by permission.

[1] For examples see Ernest W. Burgess, "The Economic Factor in Juvenile Delinquency," *Journal of Criminal Law, Criminology and Police Science*, May–June 1952, pp. 29–42; Joseph W. Eaton and Kenneth Polk, *Measuring Delinquency: A Study of Probation Department Referrals* (Pittsburgh: University of Pittsburgh Press, 1961), p. 4; Clifford R. Shaw and Henry D. McKay, *Juvenile Delinquency and Urban Areas* (Chicago: University of Chicago Press, 1942); and Albert K. Cohen's analysis of several studies in *Delinquent Boys: The Culture of the Gang* (Glencoe: Free Press, 1955), pp. 37–44.

[2] For examples see William Healy and Augusta F. Bronner, *New Light on Delinquency and Its Treatment* (New Haven: Yale University Press, 1936), p. 52; Sheldon and Eleanor Glueck, *Delinquents in the Making* (New York: Harper, 1952), p. 89; Clifford R. Shaw and Henry D. McKay, "Social Factors in Juvenile Delinquency," *Report on the Causes of Crime* (Washington: National Commission on Law Observance and Enforcement, 1931), pp. 195–96; Joseph D. Lohman, *Juvenile Delinquency* (Cook County: Office of the Sheriff, 1957), p. 8; Norman Fenton, *The Delinquent Boy and the Correctional School* (Claremont: Claremont Colleges Guidance Center, 1935), as quoted by Karl G. Garrison, *Psychology of Adolescence* (New York: Prentice-Hall, 1956), p. 350; and Peter Scott, "Gangs and Delinquent Groups in London," *British Journal of Delinquency*, July 1956, pp. 4–26.

which, despite many differences, have a common theme,[3] viz., that delinquency is primarily the product of provincial, lower-class gangs whose members share a common subculture. The factors which set delinquents apart from nondelinquents are thought to be their face-to-face interactions within gangs, the deviant norms and beliefs which the gangs engender, and the group rewards and publicity which the gangs provide.

Comparatively little attention has been paid to middle-class delinquency, principally because middle-class delinquency has not been considered serious, either in frequency or in form.[4] However, a growing number of empirical studies question both the basic facts which the theories must encompass and the theoretical constructs themselves. This paper reviews some of the questions that have been raised.

Social Class and Delinquency

The accuracy of official statistics regarding the relationship of social class to delinquency has long been a bone of contention. Many people have argued that official records are biased.[5]

The reason, they say, that lower-class juveniles are overrepresented in delinquency statistics is simply that official agencies are more inclined to record the offenses of lower-class offenders. But can this conclusion be substantiated by fact or is it, as Cohen asks, the product of "egalitarian proclivities and sentimental humanitarianism"?[6]

*Universality of Inverse Relation
between Class and Delinquency*

The first issue that reflects on Cohen's question has to do with the universality of the supposed inverse relation between social class and delinquency. On one hand, the Short and Strodtbeck studies of delinquent gangs in Chicago tended to support official findings. Lower-class gang boys *were* the most delinquent. They were followed, in turn, by lower-class nongang boys and then by middle-class boys. These differences held up for both Negro and white respondents, although Negro gang members were not so different from their Negro middle-class peers as were white gang boys from white middle-class peers.[7]

On the other hand, most studies of undetected delinquency in smaller cities and towns have not found significant differences among adolescents from different classes,[8] and those which have, have reported differences which are not nearly so strong as those indicated by

---

[3] Cohen, *op. cit. supra* note 1; Richard A. Cloward and Lloyd E. Ohlin, *Delinquency and Opportunity: A Theory of Delinquent Gangs* (Glencoe: Free Press, 1960); Walter B. Miller, "Lower Class Culture as a Generating Milieu of Gang Delinquency," *Journal of Social Issues,* Summer 1958, pp. 5–19. See also Frederic M. Thrasher, *The Gang: A Study of 1,313 Gangs in Chicago,* abridged and with a new introduction by James F. Short, Jr. (Chicago: University of Chicago Press, 1963); and Lewis Yablonsky, *The Violent Gang* (New York: Macmillan, 1962).

[4] For some discussions of the subject see Ralph W. England, Jr., "A Theory of Middle-Class Delinquency," *Journal of Criminal Law, Criminology and Police Science,* April 1960, pp. 535–40; Herbert A. Bloch and Arthur Niederhoffer, *The Gang: A Study of Adolescent Behavior* (New York: Philosophical Library, 1958); Cohen, *op. cit. supra* note 1, pp. 88–91; William C. Kvaraceus and Walter B. Miller, *Delinquent Behavior, Culture and the Individual* (Washington: National Education Association, 1959), pp. 77–84.

[5] Austin L. Porterfield, *Youth in Trouble* (Fort Worth: Leo Potishman Foundation, 1946), *passim;* Milton A. Barron, *The Juvenile in Delinquent Society* (New York: Alfred A. Knopf, 1956), p. 32; Lloyd Warner and Paul S. Lunt, *The Social Life of a Modern Community* (New Haven: Yale University Press, 1941), p. 427; and William C.

Kvaraceus, *What Research Says to the Teacher: Juvenile Delinquency* (Washington: National Education Association, 1958), pp. 331–32.

[6] Cohen, *op. cit. supra* note 1, p. 42.

[7] James F. Short, Jr. and Fred L. Strodtbeck, *Group Process and Gang Delinquency* (Chicago: University of Chicago Press, 1965), pp. 164–71.

[8] F. Ivan Nye, James F. Short, Jr., and V. J. Olsen, "Socio-Economic Status and Delinquent Behavior," *American Journal of Sociology,* January 1958, pp. 318–29; John P. Clark and Eugene P. Wenninger, "Socio-Economic Class and Area as Correlates of Illegal Behavior Among Juveniles," *American Sociological Review,* December 1962, pp. 826–34; Robert Dentler and Lawrence J. Monroe, "Early Adolescent Theft," *American Sociological Review,* October 1961, pp. 733–43; and Porterfield, *op. cit. supra* note 5. An exception is Albert J. Reiss, Jr., and Albert L. Rhodes, "The Distribution of Juvenile Delinquency in the Social Class Structure," *American Sociological Review,* October 1961, pp. 730–32.

official data.[9] For example, Gold, in a Michigan study, found a statistically significant, inverse relation between class and delinquency, but the strength of the relationship was extremely slight, a coefficient of —.12.[10] The degree of variance which could be explained by this relationship would be small indeed.

Empey and Erickson report similar findings from Utah.[11] The degrees of association between social class and three different delinquency scales were: for *general* theft, —.20; for *serious* theft, —.17; and for *common* delinquency, —.17. They discovered further that the inverse relationship was due more to a small amount of delinquency among upper-class respondents than it was to an excessive amount of delinquency among lower-class respondents. The lower- and middle-class groups did not differ significantly from each other while the degree of difference between each of them and the upper-class group was considerable.

Actual Violation vs. Apprehension

Empirical studies have indicated that the amount of undetected delinquency is great.[12] The degree of apprehension is extremely low, somewhere between 3 and 5 percent of all self-reported offenses. Yet, when apprehension does occur, officials are more likely to record and process lower-class youngsters.[13]

The picture is further confused by the fact that the police and other officials are charged by juvenile court law to respond to poor home and family conditions, neglect, truancy, and other factors which may come to light when some "predatory" act is detected. Their interest is often solicitous rather than punitive, but since these factors are more often associated with lower-class than middle-class juveniles, the former are more inclined to be processed legally. These two conditions distort the idea of the epidemiological character of delinquency and probably lend credence to the notion of an inverse relation between class and delinquency.

Seriousness

There are many who feel that the offenses of lower-class youngsters are more likely to be serious. Ohlin, for example, maintains that middle-class delinquency is "petty" in comparison with lower-class delinquency.[14] The inclination to violate the law, he believes, is more deeply ingrained in the lower-class youngster who therefore possesses a greater potential for the development of a criminal career. The evidence pertinent to this question is limited but that which is available is not entirely supportive of Ohlin's position.

The Myerhoffs, in their observations of middle-class "gangs" in Los Angeles, reported that the violations of these "gangs" were often more "mischievous" than violent.[15] However, violence is not the only dimension of seriousness. Included in these "mischievous" acts was the frequent and regular theft of articles that

[9] LaMar T. Empey and Maynard L. Erickson, "Hidden Delinquency and Social Status," *Social Forces*, June 1966, pp. 546–54; and Martin Gold, "Undetected Delinquent Behavior," *Journal of Research in Crime and Delinquency*, January 1966, pp. 27–46.

[10] Gold, *op. cit. supra* note 9, pp. 40–43.

[11] Empey and Erickson, *op. cit. supra* note 9, pp. 549–50. See also Maynard L. Erickson and LaMar T. Empey, "Class Position, Peers and Delinquency," *Sociology and Social Research*, April 1965, pp. 271–72.

[12] Maynard L. Erickson and LaMar T. Empey, "Court Records, Undetected Delinquency and Decision-Making," *Journal of Criminal Law, Criminology and Police Science*, December 1963, pp. 456–69; Fred J. Murphy, M. Shirley, and Helen L. Witmer, "The Incidence of Hidden Delinquency," *American Journal of Orthopsychiatry*, October 1946, pp. 686–96; Gold, *op. cit. supra* note 9; and Porterfield, *op. cit. supra* note 5.

[13] Gold found that the police were more likely to record lower-class offenders; see Gold, *op. cit.*

supra note 9, p. 38. Empey and Erickson found that low-class adolescents were overrepresented in a training school in proportion to the offenses they reported having committed; see Empey and Erickson, *op. cit. supra* note 9.

[14] Lloyd E. Ohlin, *The Development of Opportunities for Youth* (New York: Youth Development Center, Syracuse University, 1960), pp. 8–9; and Cloward and Ohlin, *op. cit. supra* note 3, p. 12.

[15] Howard L. and Barbara G. Myerhoff, "Field Observations of Middle-Class Gangs," *Social Forces*, March 1964, pp. 328–36. See also Andrew Greely and James Casey, "An Upper-Middle-Class Deviant Gang," *American Catholic Sociological Review*, Spring 1963, pp. 33–41.

were by no means small nor inexpensive: radios, phonographs, car accessories, television sets, all usually taken from employers or personal acquaintances.

Such findings were corroborated by Empey and Erikson in a more systematic enumeration of offenses in a *nonmetropolitan* center.[16] They found that, while the more serious forms of delinquency were less common among all class groups, such violations as grand theft, forgery, breaking and entering, destroying property, and even arson, when they did occur, were more often committed by middle- than lower-class juveniles. This rather surprising finding held true whether the self-reported data came from boys with no official record or boys who were incarcerated in a training school.[17] Middle-class groups in both populations were the ones who rated disproportionately high on these kinds of offenses.

Even with respect to violence, Karacki and Toby found fighting gangs that did not come from economically deprived homes.[18] These gangs placed emphasis on many of the characteristics traditionally associated with lower-class delinquent groups: physical aggression, loyalty to peers, and immediate gratification. Shanley located a similar group of middle- and upper-class boys in the suburbs of Los Angeles who had patterns of police contact which were as extensive and serious as samples of adjudicated delinquents from lower-class neighborhoods.[19] Finally, other analyses suggest that

particular patterns of delinquency may be associated as much with differences in place of residence — rural, urban, or type of neighborhood — as with social class position.[20]

In summary, these findings suggest that the inverse relationship between social class and delinquency may be less potent than has been traditionally assumed and that we should search for other determinants;[21] social class by itself may be a poor clue. The behavior of some middle-class groups suggests that we might discover as many differences *within* classes regarding delinquency as we now discover between them. In other words, instead of using a two- or three-celled table to compare lower-, middle-, and upper-class groups across the board, we should use four- or six-celled tables to compare the delinquent acts of various groups within, as well as between, classes.[22] More precise distinctions of this type might provide better clues to the nature of delinquency than do gross comparisons between classes.

Dimensions of Group Delinquency

What about the second set of facts which theory must fit — the proposition that delinquency is typically a group phenomenon? The available evidence has a paradoxical quality which illustrates both the complexity of the subject and the meagerness of our information.

There are few findings which question seriously the basic proposition that delinquency is

[16] Empey and Erickson, *op. cit. supra* note 9, pp. 551–54.

[17] Albert H. Herskovitz, Murray Levene, and George Spivak, "Anti-Social Behavior of Adolescents from Higher Socio-Economic Groups," *Journal of Nervous and Mental Diseases*, November 1959, pp. 1–9. They found no sharply different patterns between middle- and low-class incarcerated offenders and little variation in the seriousness of their offenses.

[18] Larry Karacki and Jackson Toby, "The Uncommitted Adolescent: Candidates for Gang Socialization," *Sociological Inquiry*, Spring 1962, pp. 203–15.

[19] Fred J. Shanley, "Middle-Class Delinquency as a Social Problem," paper presented at the Annual Meetings of the Pacific Sociological Association, Salt Lake City, April 1965, p. 2. An article in *Life* magazine was also devoted to the extensive drug use and other delinquent patterns

of middle-class groups on Sunset Strip in Hollywood. The Strip is also the locale of the heaviest concentration of "gay" (homosexual) hangouts in the city; see *Life*, August 26, 1966, pp. 75–83.

[20] Irving Spergel, *Racketville, Slumtown, Haulburg: An Exploratory Study of Delinquent Subcultures* (Chicago: University of Chicago Press, 1964); and Clark and Wenninger, *op. cit. supra* note 8.

[21] Identification with particular sets of peers is one that has appeared. See Erickson and Empey, *op. cit. supra* note 11, pp. 272–81.

[22] Miller, for example, noted differences in theft behavior among three different groups, all *within* the lower class. See Walter B. Miller, "Theft Behavior in City Gangs," *Juvenile Gangs in Context: Theory, Research and Action*, Malcolm W. Klein and Barbara G. Myerhoff, eds. (New York: Prentice-Hall, 1967).

typically a group phenomenon. Most studies, including some which use self-reported data, place the incidence of group delinquency somewhere between 60 and 90 percent of the total.[23] It may be that with more systematic data this range will be extended, since some offenses — defying parents or running away — are by nature less likely to be group-related than others. However, the group aspects of delinquency seem to be well established with a modal figure of about 75 percent.

What is not well established is a consensus regarding the nature of delinquent groups — their cohesiveness, their structural qualities, their subcultural characteristics. The most commonly used term to refer to delinquent groups has been the word "gang." The term has been so overworked and is so imprecise that its use in scientific discourse may well be questioned. An examination of evidence relative to the cohesiveness and structural qualities of delinquent groups illustrates the elusiveness of the "gang" and other group concepts.

Group Cohesiveness

Conflicting themes run through the literature regarding cohesiveness. The first theme, exemplified most clearly by Thrasher and the Chicago school, emphasizes the idea that delinquent groups are characterized by *internal* cohesion — *esprit de corps*, solidarity, cooperative action, shared tradition, and a strong group awareness.[24] Despite the qualifications which Thrasher placed on this theme — and he did qualify it — there is no denying that a traditional perspective has developed emphasizing the romantic quality of delinquent gangs, the free and easy life, the joint commitments of members to one another. The key to this theme is its emphasis upon the culture-generating qualities and attractiveness of the peer group.

The second theme, as Bordua notes, is irrationalistic and deterministic in its emphasis.

"Gang boys are driven," he notes, "not attracted. Their lives are characterized by desperation rather than fun." [25] Such theories as those of Cohen,[26] Cloward and Ohlin,[27] and Miller [28] emphasize the idea that lower-class children are downgraded in both the child and the adult status hierarchies of our middle-class institutions. They are ill-prepared by family background and cultural heritage to achieve successfully and, as a consequence, their lives are characterized by frustration, negativistic retaliation, alienation, and radical separation from conventional successes and satisfactions. This theme is much less romantic in its emphasis than the first and implies, not internal attraction, but external pressure as the source of gang cohesion.

It is the role of the individual youngster in the social structure, not his role in the street group, that is of primary significance. He is alienated before he enters the group, not because of it. The group is simply the instrument that translates his individual discontent into a collective solution.[29] By implication, the group can do little to remedy his sensitivity to the middle-class measuring rod, to provide him with the material and social satisfactions to which he aspires.

The fundamental question, then, asks what the forces are that hold delinquent groups together. Are they the group rules and loyalties which emerge from gratifying relationships within the group, as the first theme suggests, or are they due to the position of gang boys in the class structure as suggested by the second theme?

First of all, we are confronted with the apparent fact that, if the delinquent group were not rewarding to the individual, it would cease to exist. In this vein, Short and Strodtbeck

[23] See note 2 of this paper for relevant studies. Unpublished data in our possession on self-reported delinquency, both from Utah and California, confirm this figure.

[24] Thrasher, *op. cit. supra* note 3, pp. 40–46. See also Short's discussion of this theme in his introduction to the abridged edition, *passim*.

[25] David J. Bordua, "Some Comments on Theories of Group Delinquency," *Sociological Inquiry*, Spring 1962, pp. 245–46; see also David J. Bordua, "A Critique of Sociological Interpretations of Gang Delinquency," *Annals of the American Academy of Political and Social Science*, November 1961, pp. 120–36.

[26] Cohen, *op. cit. supra* note 1.

[27] Cloward and Ohlin, *op. cit. supra* note 3.

[28] Miller, *op. cit. supra* note 3.

[29] Bordua, *op. cit. supra* note 25, pp. 252–57.

have observed that when it comes to assuming adult roles — occupation and marriage — ". . . the lure of the gang may spell disaster." [30] Even when challenging jobs are obtained for them, when the pay is good or when gang members are married and have children, the lure of the street is not easily forgotten and any inclination to return to it is supported by the gang. The implication, of course, is one of *internal* cohesiveness and attraction: gang membership has much to offer. However, as might be expected, there are other interpretations.

. . . Klein and Crawford argue that *internal* sources of lower-class gang cohesion are weak.[31] Group goals which might be unifying are minimal, membership stability is low, loyalty is questionable, and even the names of gangs — Gladiators, Vice Lords, Egyptian Kings — are unifying only when external threat is present. When the threat is diminished, cohesion is diminished. It is their feeling that were it not for the external pressures of police and other officials, the threats of rival groups, or the lack of acceptance by parents and employers, many delinquent gangs would have nothing to unify them. By themselves, such gangs do not develop the kinds of group goals and instrumentally oriented activities which are indicative of much organization.

Group Cohesion and Delinquent Acts

The commission of delinquent acts seems to illustrate this lack of organization. One of the most striking things about them is not their planned and patterned characteristics but their episodic and highly situational character.[32] One would think that if delinquent groups were highly cohesive or highly structured this would not be the case. Yet, most delinquent acts are more spontaneous than planned and, even

though they involve groups, they rarely involve all members of a gang acting together.

Even complex crimes reveal considerable spontaneity and what Matza calls "shared misunderstanding." [33] Thrasher describes three college students who began to phantasize about robbing a post-office.[34] Subsequent interviews with them revealed that none of them wanted to be involved in the actual robbery but the more they talked the deeper they became involved, each hoping, actually believing, that the others would call a halt to this crazy phantasy but each reluctant, on his own, to "chicken out." The result was that, in a state of almost total individual disbelief, they robbed the post-office and found themselves in legal custody.

Careful observation of delinquents reveals countless repetitions of this phenomenon — the wandering kinds of interaction that lead to delinquent acts and the mixed rather than solidary motivations that accompany them. Even in regard to fighting, as Miller points out, "A major objective of gang members is to put themselves in the posture of fighting without actually having to fight." [35]

Group Cohesion and Member Interaction

Observations of delinquent gangs led Short and Strodtbeck, like Klein and Crawford, to depreciate nostalgic references to "that old gang of mine" and to deny the image of the delinquent gang as a carefree and solidary group. They report that such an interpretation may derive more from the projections of middle-class observers than from the realities that dominate street life.[36] They document this interpretation with a considerable amount of data.

They found that, compared with others, gang boys were characterized by a long list of "social disabilities": unsuccessful school adjustment, limited social and technical skills, a low capacity for self-assertion, lower intelligence

[30] Short and Strodtbeck, *op. cit. supra* note 7, pp. 221–34.

[31] Malcolm W. Klein and Lois Y. Crawford, "Groups, Gangs and Cohesiveness," *Journal of Research in Crime and Delinquency*, January 1967, pp. 63–75.

[32] Many works allude to this phenomenon. For examples see Thrasher, *op. cit. supra* note 3; Short and Strodtbeck, *op. cit. supra* note 7; and Yablonsky, *op. cit. supra* note 3.

[33] David Matza, *Delinquency and Drift* (New York: Wiley, 1964), pp. 35–59.

[34] Thrasher, *op. cit. supra* note 3, pp. 300–03.

[35] Walter B. Miller, "Violent Crimes in City Gangs," *Annals of the American Academy of Political and Social Science*, March 1965, p. 110.

[36] Short and Strodtbeck, *op. cit. supra* note 7, p. 231.

scores, and also a tendency to hold other gang members in low esteem.[37] Interaction within the gang seemed to be characterized by an omnipresent tone of aggression as a result of these disabilities and the insecurities they engendered.

This account is complemented by Matza's use of the term "sounding," which refers to the incessant plumbing and testing through insult by delinquent boys of one another's status and commitment to delinquency.[38] Miller speaks of the "focal concerns" of lower-class gang culture as toughness, smartness, and excitement.[39] Whatever the terms, it appears that delinquent boys are under constant pressure to protect status and assert masculinity.

While this pressure to project a particular image may not be qualitatively different from many of the highly stylized kinds of interaction found in a host of other status-conscious groups, the point is that such interaction is not characteristic, at least hypothetically, of *primary* groups. Primary groups, ideally, are supposed to provide warmth and support. With the constant "sounding" that goes on in delinquent groups it is questionable whether lower-class gangs are conducive to close friendships.[40]

The picture that is painted suggests that gang members, like inmates in a prison, are held together, not by feelings of loyalty and solidarity, but by forces much less attractive. It is not that structure is lacking but that it is defensive and highly stylized, not supportive. Group members stay together simply because they feel they have more to lose than to gain by any breach in their solidarity. While they may appear to the outsider to be dogmatic, rigid, and unyielding in their loyalty to each other, the sources of this loyalty are not internal but external. Remove the pressure and you remove the cohesion.

Seeming to comment on this very point, Short and Strodtbeck report that they "find the capacity of lower-class gangs to elaborate

and enforce norms of reciprocity is very much below what might be required to sustain the group if alternative forms of gratification were available." [41] Similarly, Matza argues that the majority of delinquents are not strongly committed either to delinquent groups or to a criminal career but are "drifters" who are held together by a kind of pluralistic ignorance.[42] When in the company of others, the boy is inclined to attribute to them a greater commitment to delinquent relationships and values than he has himself.

These points of view indicate the need for more direct investigation of delinquent group cohesiveness *per se* and for the study of middle-class as well as lower-class groups. Our lack of information is so great that we do not have even an adequate baseline from which to begin; that is, we know very little about the cohesiveness and inherent gratifications of adolescent groups in general. Therefore, until we can establish a baseline, it will be difficult either to generalize about delinquent groups or to compare them with other groups. Furthermore, the possible lack of cohesiveness in delinquent groups raises questions regarding the nature of delinquent subculture. If delinquent groups are not cohesive and internally gratifying, can it be expected that delinquents, especially those in the lower class, have either the personal motivation or the organizational skills to promote and maintain a deviant subculture which is in total opposition to prevailing values?

Delinquent Subculture

Such theorists as Cloward and Ohlin have defined the subcultural concept in narrow terms.[43] They see a delinquent subculture as unique and as autonomous. Organization around a specific delinquent activity, they say, distinguishes a delinquent subculture from other subcultures. Such behaviors as truancy, drunkenness, property destruction, or theft are legally delinquent activities but these they would not include as characteristic of a delin-

[37] *Ibid.*, ch. 10 and 12.
[38] Matza, *op. cit. supra* note 33, pp. 53–55.
[39] Miller, *op. cit. supra* note 3, p. 519.
[40] Short and Strodtbeck, *op. cit. supra* note 7, p. 233. See also Lewis Yablonsky, "The Delinquent Gang as a Near-Group," *Social Problems*, Fall 1959, pp. 108–17.

[41] Short and Strodtbeck, *op. cit. supra* note 7, p. 280.
[42] Matza, *op. cit supra* note 33, pp. 27–30, 56.
[43] Cloward and Ohlin, *op. cit. supra* note 3, p. 7.

quent subculture unless they were the focal activities around which the dominant beliefs and roles of a group were organized.

The narrowness and rigor of their postulates regarding criminal, retreatist, and conflict-oriented subcultures characterize the logical structure of their theory but do these postulates accurately characterize delinquent groups and subculture? Are they this focused? Are they this unique and autonomous?

When Short and his associates set about trying to study these kinds of subcultures, they had extreme difficulty in locating them.[44] They found a number of gangs in which marijuana smoking was rather common and in which there was experimentation with heroin and pills, but it took more than a year of extensive inquiries among police and local adults to locate a clearly drug-oriented group. They never did find a full-blown criminal group. Consequently, they concluded that their failure casts doubt on the generality of the Cloward-Ohlin postulates.[45]

Short, *et al.*, had no difficulty in locating a number of gangs who were well-known for their conflict, toughness, and fighting but one still must question what it means to say that the "focal" concern of gangs is conflict. The bulk of even the most delinquent boys' time is spent in nondelinquent activity and their delinquent acts make up a long list of different offenses.[46] How precise can we be, then, in referring to the characteristics of a "conflict" subculture or gang?

In observing "typical," "tough" city gangs over a two-year period, Miller found that assault was *not* the most dominant form of activity.[47] In fact, two-thirds of the male gang members who were observed were not known to have engaged in *any* assaultive crimes over the two-year period and 88 percent did not appear in court on such a charge. Similarly, Klein and his colleagues in Los Angeles have found that less than 10 percent of the recorded

offenses for gang members are assaultive.[48] Instead, the *frequency* with which adolescents commit a long list of different offenses seems to better characterize their commitments to delinquency than their persistent adherence to a particular offense pattern.[49] There seems to be limited empirical support for the idea of autonomous and highly focused delinquent subcultures and somewhat more support for the notion of a ubiquitous, "parent" subculture of delinquency in which there is a "garden-variety" of delinquent acts.[50]

A ubiquitous, but amorphous, subculture would be more consistent with the notion of weak internal bonds in delinquent groups and highly situational delinquent acts than with the idea of internally cohesive groups who participate in planned and highly patterned delinquent activities. Furthermore, if delinquent subculture is not highly focused and autonomous, question is raised regarding its relation to the larger culture.

Subculture: Contraculture or Infraculture?

Most contemporary theory has suggested that lower-class delinquent subculture is *contra*culture[51] in which status is gained by demonstrated opposition to prevailing middle-class standards.[52] Theories of middle-class delinquency suggest that the delinquent group is a collective response to adolescent efforts to establish sexual identity and to deal with frustrations attendant on the transition from childhood to adulthood.[53] But does this mean that a

[44] Short and Strodtbeck, *op. cit. supra* note 7, pp. 10–13.

[45] *Ibid.*, p. 13.

[46] Short, Introduction in Thrasher, *op. cit. supra* note 3, pp. xlvii–xlviii.

[47] Miller, *op. cit. supra* note 35, pp. 105, 111.

[48] Malcolm W. Klein, Youth Studies Center, University of Southern California, Personal Communication, September 1966.

[49] Erickson and Empey, *op. cit. supra* note 12, pp. 465–69; and Gold, *op. cit. supra* note 9, pp. 27–46.

[50] Albert K. Cohen and James F. Short, Jr., "Research in Delinquent Subcultures," *Journal of Social Issues*, Summer 1958, pp. 20–36.

[51] J. Milton Yinger, "Contraculture and Subculture," *American Sociological Review*, October 1960, pp. 625–35.

[52] Cohen, *op. cit. supra* note 1; Cloward and Ohlin, *op. cit. supra* note 3; and Miller, *op. cit. supra* note 3.

[53] England, *op. cit. supra* note 4; Bloch and Niederhoffer, *op. cit. supra* note 4.

middle-class delinquent group is, like a lower-class gang, the instrument that translates individual discontent into a delinquent *contra*culture?

Matza takes issue with the notion of *contra*-culture on any class level and emphasizes a subtle but important distinction. He argues that "there is a subculture of delinquency but it is not a delinquent subculture." [54] American culture, he believes, is not a simple puritanism exemplified by the middle class. Instead, it is a complex and pluralistic culture in which, among other cultural traditions, there is a "subterranean" tradition — an *infra*culture of delinquency.[55]

This *infra*culture does not represent ignorance of the law nor even general negation of it; instead, it is a complex relationship to law in a *symbiotic* rather than an oppositional way. It is not a separate set of beliefs which distinguishes delinquents from other youth, or youth from adults; it is that part of the overall culture which consists of the personal, more deviant, and less-publicized version of officially endorsed values. The two sets of traditions — conventional and deviant — are held simultaneously by almost everyone in the social system and, while certain groups may be influenced more by one than the other, both determine behavior to a considerable degree.

Daniel Bell's analysis of crime as an American way of life is probably a good illustration of Matza's point.[56] Bell notes that Americans are characterized by an "extremism" in morality, yet they also have an "extraordinary" talent for compromise in politics and a "brawling" economic and social history. These contradictory features form the basis for an intimate and symbiotic relationship between crime and politics, crime and economic growth, and crime and social change, not an oppositional relationship. The tradition of wanting to "get ahead" is no less an ethic than wanting to observe the law.

Crime has been a major means by which a variety of people have achieved the American success ideal and obtained respectability, if not for themselves, for their children. The basic question, therefore, is whether this deviant tradition contributes more than we realize to the behavior of younger as well as older people. Rather than delinquent subculture being uniquely the property of young people, it may have roots in the broader culture.

Empirical investigation of the matter would seem to involve two questions: (1) the extent to which adolescents legitimate official, conventional patterns and (2) the extent to which they simultaneously participate in, or espouse in some way, deviant patterns. With reference to the first question both Kobrin [57] and Gordon *et al.*[58] suggest that adolescents from all strata are inclined to legitimate official patterns. The gang members they studied did not seem to be alienated from the goals of the larger society and ". . . even the gang ethic, is not one of 'reaction formation' *against* widely shared conceptions of the 'good' life." Gang, low-class and middle-class boys, Negro and white ". . . *evaluated images representing salient features of the middle-class styles of life equally high.*" [59] This finding confirmed that of Gold in Michigan with a much different population [60] and led to the conclusion that ". . . if the finding is valid, three separate theoretical formulations [Cohen, Miller, and Cloward-Ohlin] fail to make sufficient allow-

---

54 Matza, *op. cit. supra* note 33, p. 33; and David Matza and Gresham M. Sykes, "Juvenile Delinquency and Subterranean Values," *American Sociological Review*, October 1961, pp. 712–19.

55 The idea of *infra*culture was suggested by J. A. Pitt-Rivers, *The People of the Sierra* (Chicago: University of Chicago Press, 1961), who referred to "infrastructure" rather than "infraculture."

56 Daniel Bell, *The End of Ideology* (Glencoe: Free Press, 1959), pp. 115–36.

57 Solomon Kobrin, "The Conflict of Values in Delinquency Areas," *American Sociological Review*, October 1951, pp. 653–61.

58 Robert A. Gordon, James F. Short, Jr., Desmond F. Cartwright, and Fred L. Strodtbeck, "Values and Gang Delinquency," *American Journal of Sociology*, September 1963, pp. 109–28, as reproduced in Short and Strodtbeck, *op. cit. supra* note 7, ch. 3.

59 Short and Strodtbeck, *op. cit. supra* note 7, pp. 271, 59. Italics theirs.

60 Martin Gold, *Status Forces in Delinquent Boys* (Ann Arbor: University of Michigan, Institute for Social Research, 1963).

ance for the meaningfulness of middle-class values to members of gangs." [61] In fact, given the strength of the findings, one wonders whether we are correct in referring to official values as "middle-class" values or whether we should be using some more inclusive term.

The second question, regarding the simultaneous possession of deviant patterns, presents a more confused picture. A curious omission in our conjectures and research has been our failure to examine the extent to which deviant values are widely transmitted to young people. Several elaborate theories hypothesize that all children, including those in the lower class, are conditioned by official, "middle-class" stimuli. They watch television, listen to the radio, go to the movies, read the ads, and attend middle-class dominated schools; as a consequence, they acquire common desires for status, recognition, and achievement. Despite these conjectures, we have not had similar conjectures regarding the possible transmission of deviant patterns.

Kvaraceus and Miller have suggested that middle-class delinquency represents an upward diffusion of lower-class attitudes and practices; [62] but are lower-class patterns all that are diffused? To what extent are children on all class levels conditioned not just by lower-class values but by mass stimuli which emphasize violence, toughness, protest, kicks, and expedience? These are certainly important aspects of our "brawling" American history, a part of our cultural tradition. If we pay too little heed to them then we may be inclined to overemphasize the narrowness and autonomy of delinquent subculture, especially as the sole possession of the lower class. It is seductively easy to overemphasize the uniqueness of problem people and thereby to obscure their similarities to non-problem people. For example, studies of self-reported delinquency reveal that the extent of hidden law violation is widespread,[63] so widespread, indeed, that Murphy, Shirley, and Witmer were led to remark that "even a

moderate increase in the amount of attention paid to it by law enforcement authorities could create the semblance of a 'delinquency wave' without there being the slightest change in adolescent behavior." [64] This finding, coupled with the questionable strength of the theory of an inverse relationship between social class and delinquency, suggests that, unless we are to assume that deviant traditions actually predominate, they must occupy a symbiotic tie of some kind with conformist traditions.

Conventional Values and Deviance

In order to investigate the matter further, several factors should be considered. One important factor is the nature of adult-youth relationships. What perspectives, for example, are transmitted from adults to youth? Is the youthful search for "kicks" or the irresponsible acquisition of wealth and leisure profoundly different from adult desires for the same things or, rather, a projection of them? A double standard for judging adult and youthful behavior is certainly not uncommon and could be far more influential than a double standard distinguishing between the sexes. Personal access to various adult role models, as contrasted to a vague and abstract relationship with them, would likely affect the selection of deviant or conformist behavior. The absence of a strong personal relationship would make the juvenile more dependent upon the images projected by such secondary sources as the movies or television.

A second important factor has to do with the relative valences of delinquent and conformist values for different populations of adolescents. How do they balance? Short and Strodtbeck found that, while conventional prescriptions were generally accepted, subterranean, deviant values were accepted differentially. While gang boys were as willing as lower- and middle-class nongang boys to legitimate official *pre*scriptions, they were not as inclined to support official *pro*scriptions.[65]

[61] Short and Strodtbeck, *op. cit. supra* note 7, p. 74.
[62] Kvaraceus and Miller, *op. cit. supra* note 4, pp. 77–79.
[63] Erickson and Empey, *op. cit. supra* note 12; and Gold, *op. cit. supra* note 9.
[64] Murphy, Shirley, and Witmer, *op. cit. supra* note 12.
[65] Short and Strodtbeck, *op. cit. supra* note 7, pp. 59–76.

This particular research failed to explore other important aspects of the issue.

Besides obtaining some indication of the general valences of both deviant and conventional values, we need to explore their valences in various specific contexts. We know, for example, that if changes in group context or social situation occur, both behavior and the espousal of particular values are likely to change also. The citizen who is in favor of racial equality in a general way is often one of the first to sell his home when integration occurs in his neighborhood. Specific considerations alter his behavior. Similarly, the delinquent boy, when placed in the context of having to exercise leadership over his peers in a conventional setting, will often act remarkably like a conventional adult. His actions are surprisingly stereotyped, a response not to norms in general but to norms as they apply in a specific context.

In studying the relative valences of conventional and deviant *pro*scriptions we also need to compare not only lower-class gang boys with others, as Short and Strodtbeck did, but excessively delinquent boys from other classes with their peers as well. We need a better indication of the extent to which deviant values are diffused either throughout the entire class structure or through subgroups on all class levels.

Finally, we need more careful study of the way official and societal responses to juvenile behavior contribute to definitions of delinquency and delinquent subcultures, either by overemphasizing their uniqueness or by contributing to their development. Becker argues that the process by which some juveniles but not others are labeled may be as crucial in defining the problem as the behavior of the juveniles themselves.[66] For example, as mentioned earlier, there are those who think that the coalescence and persistence of delinquent gangs may be due as much to external pressure from official and other sources as to the internal gratifications and supposedly unique standards of those groups.

[66] Howard S. Becker, *Outsiders: Studies in the Sociology of Deviance* (Glencoe: Free Press, 1963), ch. 1.

The contribution which could be made by a study of official systems — the police, the courts, the correctional agencies — would be clarification of the total *gestalt* to which officials respond: how legal statutes, official policies, and perceptual cues affect the administration of juvenile justice.[67] It seems apparent that official and societal reactions to juveniles are due not entirely to criminalistic behavior but also (1) to acts which, if committed by adults, would not warrant legal action and (2) to a number of "social disabilities" that are popularly associated with deviance: unkempt appearance, inappropriate responses due to lack of interpersonal skills, and educational deficiencies.[68]

These are characteristics which traditionally have been more closely associated with lower-than middle-class juveniles and are characterized in legal terms by truancy, dependency, or incorrigibility. It would be important to learn the extent to which these identifying characteristics, as contrasted to demonstrably delinquent *values*, contribute to the definition of some groups, but not others, as seriously delinquent. Since only a small fraction of their time and attention is devoted to law violation, even among the most seriously delinquent, the meanings which these juveniles assign to themselves are usually far less sinister than the meanings which officials assign to them.

Conclusion

It seems apparent that, in order to complete the picture of the total phenomenon, we need a series of related studies which would, first,

[67] See Irving Piliavin and Scott Briar, "Police Encounters with Juveniles," *American Journal of Sociology*, September 1964, pp. 206–15; Joseph D. Lohman, James T. Carey, Joel Goldfarb, and Michael J. Rowe, *The Handling of Juveniles From Offense to Disposition* (Berkeley: University of California, 1965); and Nathan Goldman, *The Differential Selection of Juvenile Offenders for Court Appearance* (National Research and Information Center, National Council on Crime and Delinquency, 1963).

[68] For conflicting evidence, see A. W. McEachern and Riva Bouzer, "Factors Related to Disposition in Juvenile Police Contacts," *Juvenile Gangs in Context*, Klein and Myerhoff, eds., *op. cit. supra* note 22.

identify a representative population of adolescents, their class positions, their value-beliefs and commitments, various measures of delinquent acts (self-reported and official), their symptoms of disability, and their group affiliations; and, second, follow these adolescents through the institutional paths — educational, economic, or correctional — along which they are routed by officials. Which juveniles are processed legally and on what criteria? In what ways are they the same or different from nonprocessed juveniles in terms of values, class position, group affiliations, actual delinquent acts, and so on.

Given such research we might then be in a better position to know not only what the consequences are for those who are apprehended and processed by legal and correctional institutions but also what the consequences are for those who are *not* processed. This would most certainly apply to middle-class as well as lower-class juveniles. Hopefully, we might gain better insight into the total mosaic composed of delinquent values, actual behavior, and official reaction. Are delinquent values widely shared and is delinquent behavior common? Does legal or semilegal processing contribute to the solidification of delinquent groups? Is there differential treatment of juveniles based not on actual behavioral or value differences but on other identifying characteristics? Information of this type would help to indicate whether delinquent subculture is *contra*culture or *infra*culture.

We are only recently becoming aware of the extent of the symbiotic and mutually supporting characteristics of official and client roles in a long list of social systems; for example, policeman-offender, captor-captive, teacher-pupil, therapist-patient, caseworker-client. These are inextricably tied together by a host of traditional expectations and definitions. Change one and you are likely to change the other. We need to know more clearly the extent to which these definitions and the systems of which they are a part make delinquency and delinquents appear to be what they are, as well as the standards, beliefs, and behavior which may be unique to delinquents. Interactive relations between and among juveniles and official agencies may be as important as the behavior exhibited by juveniles in delimiting delinquency for purposes of both etiological inquiry and social control.

Section
Five

SOCIETAL RESPONSES
TO DELINQUENCY

The Police, Probation,
and Court

As specialized courts for children, the purpose, philosophy, and methods of handling offenders in juvenile courts were, at least theoretically, to be dissimilar from those of the criminal court. The broad objective underlying establishment of these courts was the substitution of "individualized justice" for the concept prevailing in the criminal court that the punishment should fit the crime. The goal of the court was rehabilitation, and the guiding philosophy was that the "wayward child" should be protected and rehabilitated, rather than exposed to a harsh criminal court.

To this end procedural informality was substituted for the adversary system, and in making a decision regarding disposition, considerable attention was devoted to the social report prepared on the basis of investigation of the juvenile's background. Hearings were not only informal, they were also closed to the public. If reporters were admitted, they were generally admonished to refrain from using names or in any way identifying the juvenile publicly. Probation officers, who were to conduct social investigations and supervise persons on probation, were to serve collectively as the juvenile-court judge's "right hand man." Thus, children were neither to be treated as criminals nor dealt with by the process employed for criminals.

Unfortunately, in their desire to substitute an "informal hearing" for the adversary system of the criminal courts, the proponents of the juvenile court justified their omission of specific procedural requirements on the ground that more specific procedures would be established through appellate decisions. Impelled by humanitarian zeal, these reformers virtually ignored procedural issues. Yet the higher courts were not often called upon to review procedures; it was not until the mid-sixties that the United States Supreme Court examined the procedures used in juvenile courts.

This is not to suggest that questions were not raised about the operation of the courts (see the next selection, entitled "Procedural Justice for the Juvenile"). After the founding of the juvenile courts, a number of questions were indeed raised. These included, but were not confined to, questions regarding the constitutionality of the proceedings. These inquiries finally reached the Supreme Court in the cases of *Kent v. United States* and *In re Gault* (see the selection by Neigher in this section). Although written prior to the Gault decision, this selection provides a valuable description of the origin and operation of the juvenile court and assessment of the conception of the juvenile court prevailing at the time of the Gault decision. It provides, then, a description of the context in which the Gault decision was made.

It may be recalled that in the operation of the juvenile court almost half the cases are handled informally, that is, without the filing of a petition (see Perlman's article in Section I). The major phases of official handling involve (1) the filing of a petition, (2) arraignment, (3) detention, (4) social investigation, and (5) a hearing for adjudication and disposition. Although it is technically a "petition in the child's behalf," the filing of a petition is analogous to the filing of a complaint in the criminal court. The petition, usually written by an intake or probation officer, specifies the reasons for court referral; and the juvenile is informed of these allegations in an initial hearing or arraignment.

After the initial hearing, the child may be released in the custody of his parents, who are then responsible for his later appearance in court, or he may be held in custody in a detention facility. Tappan (1958:39) observes that "some judges employ detention quite unnecessarily as a standard practice of 'cold storage' for the child, not uncommonly on the premise that the brief period of institutional 'treatment' may be all that he will require and that if his problems prove to be minor or non-existent, the detention may act as a harmless warning against getting into trouble in the future."

Comparable to the pre-sentence investigation of a criminal court, the social investigation conducted by a probation officer fits the court's purpose of determining "treatment requirements." In the hearing on the delinquency petition, the social information reported by the probation officer is essentially the basis for the decision as to whether or not the juvenile should be adjudicated, that is, found to be a delinquent. As this selection indicates, juvenile-court judges have broad discretionary power in disposing of cases; they may use warnings or fines, arrange for restitution, place the juvenile on probation, refer the child to a social agency, or commit the juvenile to an institution.

REFERENCE

Paul W. Tappan, *Comparative Survey of Juvenile Delinquency, Part 1. North America* (New York: United Nations, 1958), p. 39.

THE PRESIDENT'S COMMISSION ON
LAW ENFORCEMENT AND ADMINISTRATION OF JUSTICE

The Administration of Juvenile Justice

Juvenile courts are judicial tribunals that deal in special ways with young people's cases. They exist in all jurisdictions. The cases they deal with include delinquency (conduct in violation of the criminal code and also truancy, ungovernability, and certain conduct illegal only for children), neglect, and dependency. The young people they deal with are those below a designated age, usually set between 16 and 21; their authority extends until the youth reaches his majority. They differ from adult criminal courts in a number of basic respects, reflecting the philosophy that erring children should be protected and rehabilitated rather than subjected to the harshness of the criminal system. Thus they substitute procedural informality for the adversary system, emphasize investigation of the juvenile's background in deciding upon dispositions, rely heavily on the social sciences for both diagnosis and treatment, and in general are committed to rehabilitation of the juvenile as the predominant goal of the entire process.

The juvenile court has become the primary judicial agency for dealing with juvenile criminality, the single most pressing and threatening aspect of the crime problem in the United States. One in every nine children will be referred to juvenile courts for an act of delinquency before his 18th birthday. Considering boys alone, the ratio rises to one in every six.[1] Arrests of persons under 18 for serious crimes increased 47 percent in 1965 over 1960; the increase in that age group population for the same period was 17 percent. In 1965, persons under 18 referred to juvenile court constituted 24 percent of all persons charged with forcible rape, 34 percent of all persons charged with robbery, 52 percent of all persons charged with burglary, 45 percent of all persons charged with larceny, 61 percent of all persons charged with auto theft.[2] It is apparent that responsibility for meeting the problems of crime rests more heavily on no other judicial institution. The subsequent pages of this chapter seek to offer a series of interlocking proposals addressed to the basic deficiencies in the operation of the juvenile courts as functioning agencies in the total crime prevention effort. The essence of the proposals is as follows:

The formal sanctioning system and pronouncement of delinquency should be used only as a last resort.

In place of the formal system, dispositional alternatives to adjudication must be developed for dealing with juveniles, including agencies to provide and coordinate services and procedures to achieve necessary control without unnecessary stigma. Alternatives already available, such as those related to court intake, should be more fully exploited.

The range of conduct for which court intervention is authorized should be narrowed, with greater emphasis upon consensual and informal means of meeting the problems of difficult children.

From the President's Commission on Law Enforcement and Administration of Justice, "The Administration of Juvenile Justice," in *Juvenile Delinquency and Youth Crime* (Washington, D.C.: U.S. Government Printing Office, 1967), pp. 1–9. *Note:* After the work on this chapter was completed, but before its publication, the Supreme Court on May 15, 1967, decided *In re Gault*, dealing with procedural protection in juvenile proceedings. Time has not permitted the revision of this chapter to reflect that decision. Furthermore, this chapter presents in greater detail the discussion at pp. 78–89 of the Commission's general report, *The Challenge of Crime in a Free Society*, issued in February 1967, which was referred to by the Court in *Gault* and much of which is of as great or greater relevance since the *Gault* decision. Therefore, the chapter is included here although unrevised.

[1] Children's Bureau, U.S. Dep't HEW, stat. ser. no. 83, *Juvenile Court Statistics — 1964*, at 1.
[2] 1965 *FBI Uniform Crime Reports*, 23.

The cases that fall within the narrowed jurisdiction of the court and filter through the screen of prejudicial, informal disposition methods would largely involve offenders for whom more vigorous measures seem necessary. Court adjudication and disposition of those offenders should no longer be viewed solely as a diagnosis and prescription for cure, but should be frankly recognized as an authoritative court judgment expressing society's claim to protection. While rehabilitative efforts should be vigorously pursued in deference to the youth of the offenders and in keeping with a general commitment to individualized treatment of all offenders, the incapacitative, deterrent, and condemnatory aspects of the judgment should not be disguised.

Accordingly, the adjudicatory hearing should be consistent with basic principles of due process. Counsel and evidentiary restrictions are among the essential elements of fundamental fairness in juvenile as well as adult criminal courts.

Development of the Idea of the Juvenile Court

The juvenile court emerged from the confluence of several streams of thought and practice, some of them centuries old, others relatively recent responses to changing social conditions.

The best known source of the idea of the juvenile court is summed up in the Latin phrase, *parens patriae*. From feudal days the English chancery court has exercised protective jurisdiction over all the children of the realm on behalf of the *pater patriae*, the King. While the chancery court traditionally had broad authority over the welfare of children, its jurisdiction was exercised almost exclusively on behalf of minors whose property rights were jeopardized, on the theory that it lacked the means with which to provide for impoverished, neglected minors. When the English legal system was transplanted to the United States, the chancery court's activities were extended to include protection of minors in danger of personal as well as property injury, and it is as inheritor of the chancery court's protective powers that the juvenile court in this country has most commonly been justified against constitutional attack.

The chancery court, however, dealt only with neglected and dependent children, not with children accused of criminal law violations, and the historical basis of the present-day juvenile court's delinquency jurisdiction has been a matter of some dispute. One opinion is that the institution of the juvenile court owes more to the criminal law than to chancery;[3] other writers give the common law of crimes at least part of the credit.[4] The common law had long presumed a child under 7 years incapable of felonious intent and therefore unable to be held criminally responsible, and a child between 7 and 14 years similarly incapable unless shown able to understand the consequences of his actions. It has been suggested, however, that the older adolescent now included in the juvenile court's province cannot really be considered without legal responsibility and that, while it may be historically correct to ascribe the juvenile court's delinquency jurisdiction to the criminal law, "its logical justification seems to lie in the recognition of the failure of the older criminal courts to prevent crime and in the experimentation in judicial methods and procedure."[5]

A somewhat different view of the court's origins is that "these courts have developed as part and reflection of the growth of contemporary administrative and quasi-judicial tribunals"[6] and that the *parens patriae* theory is the *ex post facto* justification offered for practices that in fact originated with the modern juvenile court. Similarly the Children's Bureau of the Department of Health, Education, and Welfare, emphasizing the uniqueness of juvenile court procedures, has characterized them as special statutory creations rather than direct descendants of chancery.[7]

[3] Pound, *Interpretations of Legal History*, 134–35 (1923).

[4] Glueck & Glueck, *One Thousand Juvenile Delinquents* (1934); Lou, *Juvenile Courts in the United States* (1927).

[5] Lou, *op. cit. supra* note 4, at 7.

[6] Tappan, *Juvenile Delinquency*, 169 (1949); Tappan, "Judicial and Administrative Approaches to Children With Problems," in *Justice for the Child*, 144, 146 (Rosenheim ed. 1962).

[7] U.S. Dep't HEW, Children's Bureau Pub. no. 346, *Standards for Specialized Courts Dealing with Children*, 55 (1954).

Although the 19th century movement for reform in treatment of children was a natural enough development in the humanizing of the criminal law, it may well have been accelerated and intensified by the social conditions then prevailing. Both industrialization and immigration were bringing people into cities by the thousands, with resulting overcrowding, disruption of family life, increase in vice and crime, and all the other destructive factors characteristic of rapid urbanization. Truancy and delinquency rose rapidly, and civic-minded men and women worried about the exposure of children to tobacco, alcohol, pornography, and street life in general. With the growing concern over environmental influences came the desire to rescue children and restore them to a healthful, useful life.[8] In addition, throughout the 19th century there was a rising concern about official treatment of children — the growth of what has been called the spirit of social justice.[9] The ascending social sciences, with their optimistic claims to diagnose and treat the problems underlying deviance, seemed to provide the ideal tool for implementing the dual goals of treating wayward children humanely and offsetting their deleterious surroundings. Philanthropic men and women such as the members of the Chicago Women's Club, emancipated intellectual feminists like the Hull House group, and professional penologists and reformers joined forces to achieve recognition of the greater vulnerability and salvageability of children — first in establishing separate institutions for youth and substituting noninstitutional supervision wherever feasible, then in adopting physically separate court proceedings, and finally in altering the very philosophy underlying judicial handling of children.

Thus, whatever its historical basis, the scene was set for the juvenile court's arrival by a variety of reforms that immediately preceded it. The growing trend was early evidenced in the founding of such institutions as New York City's House of Refuge (1825), in which children were to be separated from adult offenders and given corrective treatment rather than punishment. State reform and industrial schools for juveniles followed, the first in Massachusetts in 1847, all of them aimed at teaching youths discipline and an honest trade and instilling dedication to advancement through hard work. The development of probation as a substitute for confinement in criminal cases, which began in Massachusetts in 1880, reflected the growing belief in application of the social sciences, through treatment and supervision, as a means of preventing further criminality.

Awareness of the brutality of incarcerating children with adult criminals led to efforts to separate them before and during trial as well. In 1861 the mayor of Chicago was authorized to appoint a commissioner to hear and decide minor charges against boys between 6 and 17 years and to place them on probation or in a reformatory, power which the judges received in 1867. In 1869 a Massachusetts statute provided for the presence in court of an agent of the State in cases where the child might be committed to the State reformatory; the agent was also charged with finding foster homes in suitable cases and paying subsequent visits to them. A law of 1870 required separate hearing of children's cases in Suffolk County (Boston) and authorized a representative of the Commonwealth to investigate cases, attend trials, and protect children's interests. The separate trial statute was extended throughout the Commonwealth in 1872, followed in 1877 by provision for separate sessions, dockets, and court records in juvenile cases. New York established separate trials, dockets, and records in 1892. Rhode Island in 1898 instituted segregation of children under 16 awaiting trial, separate arraignments and trials, special dockets and records, and presence at juvenile proceedings of public and private agents to protect the interests of the child.

But the reformers were not yet satisfied. Judge Julian Mack, a well-known early juvenile court judge, commented years later on the juvenile court's development out of the general movement to reform the treatment

---

[8] See generally Platt, "The Child Savers: The Emergence of the Juvenile Court in Chicago," 1966 (unpublished thesis, Univ. of Cal., Berkeley, Cal.).

[9] Lou, *op. cit. supra* note 4, at 1.

of children: "What we did not have was the conception that a child that broke the law was to be dealt with by the State as a wise parent would deal with a wayward child." [10]

The juvenile court, then, was born in an aura of reform, and it spread with amazing speed. The conception of the delinquent as a "wayward child" first specifically came to life in April 1899, when the Illinois legislature passed the Juvenile Court Act, creating the first statewide court especially for children. It did not create a new court; it did include most of the features that have since come to distinguish the juvenile court. The original act and the amendments to it that shortly followed brought together under one jurisdiction cases of dependency, neglect, and delinquency — the last comprehending incorrigibles and children threatened by immoral associations as well as criminal lawbreakers. Hearings were to be informal and nonpublic, records confidential, children detained apart from adults, a probation staff appointed. In short, children were not to be treated as criminals nor dealt with by the processes used for criminals.

A new vocabulary symbolized the new order: Petition instead of complaint, summons instead of warrant, initial hearing instead of arraignment, finding of involvement instead of conviction, disposition instead of sentence. The physical surroundings were important too: They should seem less imposing than a courtroom, with the judge at a desk or table instead of behind a bench, fatherly and sympathetic while still authoritative and sobering. The goals were to investigate, diagnose, and prescribe treatment, not to adjudicate guilt or fix blame. The individual's background was more important than the facts of a given incident, specific conduct relevant more as symptomatic of a need for the court to bring its helping powers to bear than as prerequisite to exercise of jurisdiction. Lawyers were unnecessary — adversary tactics were out of place, for the mutual aim of all was not to contest or object but to determine the treatment plan best for the child. That plan was to be devised by the increasingly popular psychologists and psychiatrists; delinquency was

[10] Addams, *My Friend, Julia Lathrop*, 137 (1935).

thought of almost as a disease, to be diagnosed by specialists and the patient kindly but firmly dosed. Even the judicial role began to attract extralegal specialists, men and women aware of and interested in the social and scientific developments of the day, and government-supported professional personnel and services expanded and replaced the amateur volunteers.

Within a dozen years 22 states had followed the example of Illinois, and by 1925 there were juvenile courts in every State but 2. Today there is a juvenile court act in every American jurisdiction, including the District of Columbia, with approximately 2,700 courts hearing children's cases. The alacrity with which State after State followed the Illinois example, however, must be considered in the context of the developing reform movement sketched above; the Illinois act was in many respects the reflection of an idea already widespread and the consolidation of previous efforts to realize it.

Furthermore, the mere passage of a juvenile court statute does not automatically establish a tribunal of the sort the reformers contemplated. A U.S. Children's Bureau survey in 1920 found that only 16 percent of all so-called juvenile courts in fact had separate hearings for children and an officially authorized probation service and recorded social information on children brought to court.[11] A similar survey conducted by the Children's Bureau and this Commission in 1966 revealed significant gaps still existing between ideal and actual court structures, practices, and personnel. Indeed, it has been observed that "there is nothing uniform" in the operations of children's courts and that:

in the analysis of their procedures, confusion has come from a common inclination to picture them as uniform throughout the country and to idealize them: to describe optimium [sic] practices (or, at least, procedures conceived ideal by the analyst) as though they were characteristic.[12]

In fact, more children's courts than not are staffed by judges and other personnel who

[11] Tappan, *Juvenile Delinquency*, 173 (1949).
[12] *Id.*, at 179.

spend much of their time on civil, criminal, and other nonjuvenile matters, and many children's courts are unlike other courts only by virtue of their separate and more private hearings. Even among those few more specialized courts for children there are great differences in method, depending both on statutes and on the views and values of those in charge.

The Juvenile Court in Operation [13]

The structure of the juvenile court and its position or status in the State's organizational pattern vary among and even within States. Relatively few are separate, independent courts. Most are part of a circuit, district, superior, county, common pleas, probate, or municipal court. In a few jurisdictions, family courts have been established to deal with both children's and domestic relations cases. Even where the jurisdiction of children's cases is in a court that is organizationally part of a larger system, however, the judge assigned to hear children's cases often operates his court quite independently.

Although there is variation among and in some instances within States in the jurisdiction of the courts hearing children's cases, jurisdiction generally includes delinquency, neglect, and dependency. Delinquency comprises cases of children alleged to have committed an offense that if committed by an adult would be a crime. It also comprises cases of children alleged to have violated specific ordinances or regulatory laws that apply only to children, such as curfew regulations, school attendance laws, restrictions on use of alcohol and tobacco; and children variously designated as beyond control, ungovernable, incorrigible, runaway, or in need of supervision — according to national juvenile court statistics, the latter two groups account for over 25 percent of the total number of delinquent children appearing before children's courts and between 25 and 30 percent of the population of State

institutions for delinquent children.[14] In addition to cases of delinquent, neglected, and dependent children, children's courts may deal with other types of actions involving children: Adoption, termination of parental rights, appointment of a guardian of the person of a minor, custody, contributing to delinquency or neglect, nonsupport.

In some States major offenses such as capital crimes are excluded from the juvenile court's jurisdiction. In other States the jurisdiction of the juvenile court is concurrent with that of the criminal court in more serious offenses.

Age, objective and readily ascertainable, has traditionally served to delimit the population subject to juvenile court jurisdiction. At present the upper age jurisdiction of juvenile courts varies from 16 to 21. Eighteen is the upper limit recommended by the Children's Bureau, and it has gained acceptance in about two-thirds of the States. In the remaining one-third the age is 16, 17, or 21 — different, in some, for boys and girls. In the one or two States in which it is 21, jurisdiction above 18 is concurrent with the criminal court, and in practice youths over 18 are almost invariably referred to the criminal court.

But age is inevitably arbitrary and fails to take account of individual differences in maturity, past and present conduct, and other factors relevant to choosing between juvenile and adult court handling of a given youth. About 40 States therefore provide for waiver or transfer by the juvenile court to the adult court, thus giving the juvenile court some discretion and flexibility in exercising its jurisdiction. Waiver laws vary greatly. Nearly half attach no conditions to the judge's exercise of discretion. In about a third of the States, waiver is authorized for any offense but only of a youth above a specified age, the lowest being 13. In a fifth of the States, waiver is permitted without regard to age but only for specified offenses, or with both age and offense limitations; the lowest age is 14 and the offense must usually amount to a felony. In one or two States, less stringent waiver criteria are

---

[13] This section draws heavily on a paper on the history and problems of the juvenile court prepared for the Commission by William H. Sheridan, Assistant Director of the Division of Juvenile Delinquency Service, Children's Bureau, U.S. Dep't of Health, Education, and Welfare.

[14] Children's Bureau, U.S. Dep't HEW, stat. ser. no. 83, *Juvenile Court Statistics — 1964*, stat. ser. no. 85, *Juvenile Court Statistics — 1965*.

provided when a child already under supervision or care for a previous offense is alleged to have committed an additional one.

Written criteria to guide the judge in deciding whether or not to waive are rare. Where they do exist, they are general: "not amenable to treatment in juvenile court," "not a fit subject" for juvenile court jurisdiction. Many State statutes heretofore have required no hearing or findings on the issue of waiver, a situation changed expressly in the District of Columbia, and called into question elsewhere, by the recent Supreme Court decision that a juvenile is entitled to a hearing, the assistance of counsel, access to social records, and a statement of reasons for the judge's decision to waive.[15]

The statutes establishing juvenile courts contain few if any specific procedural requirements. Many provide simply that the hearing shall be conducted in an "informal manner," a degree of generality that reflects the juvenile court proponents' desire to eliminate adversary aspects of adjudication and that was justified on the ground that more specific procedures would gradually be established through appellate decisions and formalized rules of court. In practice, however, upper court rulings have proved rare and have provided few guidelines, often instead reflecting but not resolving basic differences from State to State, and few formalized rules have developed.

Most juveniles who appear in juvenile court are sent there by the police. Extensive screening and informal adjustment by the police on the street and in the police station significantly reduce the number of apprehended juveniles referred to court; these practices are discussed in detail elsewhere in this report. Parents, social agencies, and others may also have direct recourse to the court.

Juvenile court statutes frequently provide that when a complaint is received, the court shall make a preliminary inquiry to determine whether the interests of the child or the public require court action. The inquiry may vary from a cursory investigation to a full-fledged social study involving contact with numerous persons and agencies in the community. It

may include a hearing at which the child, his parents, and, rarely, a lawyer representing the child are present. In many juvenile courts, especially the larger metropolitan ones, the preliminary screening function, known as intake, is performed by a special division of the probation department. Depending upon his judgment as to basis for court jurisdiction, sufficiency of evidence, and desirability of court action, the intake officer may dismiss the case, authorize the filing of a petition, or in many courts dispose of the case by "informal adjustment." In many juvenile courts approximately half the cases referred there are informally adjusted at intake — by referral to another agency, by continuation on "informal probation," or in some other way.[16]

The intake officer also determines whether a juvenile should be detained pending court action. In about one-fifth of the jurisdictions the right to bail is extended by statute to juveniles. In most jurisdictions a juvenile taken into custody by the police has no right to bail but is to be released to his parents or other suitable person unless no such individual can be found or the juvenile is believed to present a serious threat of immediate danger to himself or the community. The intake officer, having decided to authorize the filing of a petition, may continue the detention of a juvenile already detained, order him released, or order detention of a juvenile previously at large.

Where a petition is filed, the juvenile then appears before the judge for an initial hearing (arraignment). If the juvenile denies involvement, there may be, immediately or subsequently, an adjudication hearing. In most jurisdictions, as under the Standard Juvenile Court Act, there is no right to jury trial in juvenile court.[17] In keeping with the desired informality and noncombativeness of the court's proceedings, evidentiary rules are not strictly adhered to and hearsay and unsworn testimony

---

[15] *Kent* v. *United States*, 383 U.S. 541 (1966).

[16] Children's Bureau, U.S. Dep't HEW, stat. ser. no. 83, *Juvenile Court Statistics* — 1964; stat. ser. no. 85, *Juvenile Court Statistics* — 1965.

[17] Standard Juvenile Court Act § 19, 5 *N.P.P.A.J.* (1959), printed in *Nat'l Probation & Parole Ass'n, Standard Juvenile Court Act* (6th ed. 1959) [hereinafter referred to as Standard Juvenile Court Act].

may be received and considered. The standard of proof varies, but it is generally lower than the proof beyond a reasonable doubt required in the adult criminal court. In most juvenile courts there is no prosecutor; in some the case is presented by a police or probation officer. Appearance of a lawyer for the child, while still the exception, is less unusual than it once was. By virtue of recent legislation at least a third of the States now provide by statute for notice of right to counsel, assignment of counsel, or both; court rules reach the same result in other States. Great variation remains in practice, however, as to the time and manner of informing parents and child of the right to counsel, time and method of appointment of counsel, and extent and nature of counsel's participation in the proceedings.

In accordance with their emphasis on protecting and helping juveniles, many courts exclude from proceedings all except persons with a specific interest in them. Where newspaper reporters are admitted, they are generally requested to refrain from using names or otherwise making the juvenile publicly identifiable. Perhaps partly because of the consequent lack of public surveillance and more because of the absence of attorneys and records, juvenile court actions are rarely appealed, a circumstance that has reinforced the informality within as well as the variations among courts.

The disposition hearing is conducted separately from the adjudication proceeding in some courts. In many, however, it is held at the same time or is separate only in the minority of cases in which the allegations of the petition are at issue. In determining disposition, the court places great reliance on the social and clinical report (similar to the presentence investigation report in adult criminal court) prepared by the probation officer to whom the case has been assigned for social study (an assignment made in some courts before and in others not until after a hearing has been held on contested allegations in the petition). The social study embodies the juvenile court's emphasis on inquiring into the child's background and its attempt to apply the social and behavioral sciences to diagnosing and dealing with the problems behind his errant conduct.

Social information is of prime importance — even more important, in the view of some, than the circumstances of the specific events on which the court's jurisdiction in a given case is based. That view is reflected in the fact that in many jurisdictions the social reports, in theory a guide to disposition, in practice are given to the judge before the adjudication hearing. On the question of disclosing material in the social reports to parties and their lawyers, practices again vary among courts.

Most juvenile court judges have broad discretion in disposing of cases, being empowered to dismiss the case, warn the juvenile, fine him, place him on probation, arrange for restitution, refer him to an agency or treatment facility, or commit him to an institution. The length of institutional commitment is usually indefinite and in most States cannot extend beyond the juvenile's 21st birthday. Commitment of a young child may thus amount to a relatively lengthy term; recently developed standards therefore recommend that commitment be for an indefinite period not to exceed 3 years, renewable during minority on a finding that the child's welfare or the community's protection requires further institutionalization.[18]

There is as much variation in the structure and organization of agencies administering services and facilities for delinquent children as there is in the structure of courts, with the consequence that responsibility for a child often shifts back and forth among courts and a variety of public and private agencies, both State and local. A recent plan developed in response to that problem and already implemented in about a third of the States vests responsibility for the administration and expansion of a State's control and treatment program in a single State agency to which all children adjudged in need of care are committed.[19]

In about 10 States the juvenile court is authorized to commit juveniles directly to insti-

[18] Sheridan, U.S. Dep't HEW, Children's Bureau pub. no. 437, *Standards for Juvenile and Family Courts,* 82–83 (1966) [hereinafter cited as Standards for Juvenile and Family Courts].

[19] *Cal. Welf. & Inst'ns Code* § 1000 (1961).

tutions for adult offenders. In another third of the States a child committed by the juvenile court to an institution for delinquent children may be administratively transferred to an institution for adults convicted of crime. According to a recent report, more than 500 children were so transferred in 1962.[20] Appellate decisions are in conflict on the constitutionality of the practice.

In 1963 the National Council of Juvenile Court Judges sponsored a biographical survey of judges exercising juvenile court jurisdiction, to which responses were received from 1,564 judges (estimated at 70 percent of those appreciably involved in juvenile matters).[21] Of the total number replying, 71 percent had received law degrees — 95 percent for those serving jurisdictions with population over 1 million; 48 percent had received no undergraduate degree. The average age was 53 years, the average salary (for full-time judges) $12,493.15. Almost 75 percent had been elected to office, a third of them after an initial interim appointment; 62 percent had previously been elected to another public office. Of the full-time judges in the group, 72 percent spent a quarter or less of their time on juvenile matters. The most prevalent previous occupation (73.7 percent) was practicing law, for an average of 9 years. A third of the full-time judges said there were no probation officers or social workers available to their courts; 83 percent reported no regularly available psychologists or psychiatrists.

The juvenile court judge's right-hand man is the probation officer. Probation, it will be recalled, is one of the several 19th century developments that conjoined in the juvenile court movement and embodies the ideal of individualized, rehabilitative diagnosis and treatment. Probation officers serve as investigators into the juvenile's all-important social history, establish a link between the legally trained or lay judge and the social scientists who guide him, and provide a vehicle for disposition with supervision but without institutionalization. Probation, therefore, was and still is central to the juvenile court's special functions, and its limitations are inseparable from the juvenile court's own shortcomings. Probation workers, trained in the social sciences and working with juveniles who have been adjudicated as well as with preadjudication court referrals, are commonly classified as corrections rather than court personnel and accordingly are considered more exhaustively in the report of the Commission's Task Force on Corrections. What follows, since it is essential for a full view of the court itself, is a brief general description of the current state of juvenile probation services.

Juvenile probation is provided for by statute in every State, and 31 States have probation services in each county — 74 percent of all counties in the United States.[22] In 165 counties spread among 4 States, however, there are no juvenile probation services at all. Probation is administered by courts in 32 States, by State correctional agencies in 5, by State public welfare departments in 7, by other State agencies in 4, and by other agencies in 3. Since State and county civil service and merit systems usually apply only to administrative employees, probation officers in court-administered (judicial branch) departments generally are not under civil service regulations; of the 235 agencies surveyed by this Commission, less than half (47 percent) reported merit or civil service coverage.

Regardless of their organizational niche, juvenile court probation officers serve two major functions: making social studies of cases referred to the court and supervising juveniles placed on probation. Their duties may in addi-

[20] Sheridan, U.S. Dep't HEW, Children's Bureau pub. no. 415, *Delinquent Children in Penal Institutions*, 5 (table 2) (1964).

[21] Center for the Behavioral Sciences, Geo. Wash. Univ., *Judges Look at Themselves: Profile of the Nation's Juvenile Court Judges* (prepared for Nat'l Council of Juv. Ct. Judges, 1965); McCune & Skoler, "Juvenile Court Judges in the United States," 11 *Crime & Delinquency*, 121 (1965).

[22] This and the following information are taken from the national survey of corrections conducted for the Commission by the National Council on Crime and Delinquency and printed as appendix A of the Report of the Commission's Task Force on Corrections. The data from the survey appear also in a separate pamphlet entitled *Correction in the United States* (1966).

tion entail intake functions such as screening cases referred to the court and determining the necessity for detention, administering the juvenile detention facility, and managing the court's probation department and court-attached diagnostic and treatment services (clinics, camps, halfway houses, community residential facilities).

The number of juveniles touched by probation activities is very large and still increasing. In one recent year 192,000 written social studies were made of children referred to court. In the same year, 189,000 were placed on probation. In 1966, at the time of the nationwide survey of corrections services conducted by this Commission, approximately 223,800 children were under probation supervision for periods varying from 3 to 36 months.

Juvenile probation services cost an estimated $75,916,000 a year. Notwithstanding the size of that figure, salaries are low and caseloads high. Median salary for probation officers among the 235 agencies in the survey sample was between $5,000 and $6,000 (ranging from $1,500 to $11,000). Caseloads among the same 235 agencies averaged between 71 and 80 supervision cases (excluding social studies, which take at least half the time of most probation officers). Only two-tenths of 2 percent of all children on probation were, at the time of the survey, in caseloads of fewer than 20 supervision cases; 10.6 percent were in caseloads of over 100.

Given those meager salaries and burdensome workloads (even apart from the unpopularity of corrections work, a situation attributable in part to the field's limited mobility), it is hardly surprising that probation departments cannot compete successfully for the best educated in the social service field. While 74 percent of the departments surveyed required a bachelor's degree, a master's degree in social work or an allied social science is a prerequisite for employment in only 4 percent. Nor is the lack of advanced education made up by inservice training programs; 52 percent of the sample departments reported no such program, and of those with one, only 21 percent meet more frequently than once a month. Despite minimal education and experience requirements, how-

ever, juvenile courts report frequent resignations and long-lived staff vacancies.

With the exception of the Youth Services Bureau, the service agency described subsequently, the recommendations made in this chapter deal chiefly with specific institutions of juvenile justice – the police and, particularly, the juvenile court – and do not directly confront underlying issues of organization and coordination among the court and community and other agencies. In fact, the court is vitally influenced by a number of such issues, some unique to its purposes and functions, others shared by many other public and private institutions.

One of the court's better known dilemmas is the multiplicity of its mandates. While its most usual image is as a benevolent redirector of straying children – a role it is expected to fulfill with a minimum of stigma and resulting disability – it is also expected to protect the community from offenders often apparently as dangerous as those with whom the adult criminal court deals.

A less obvious source of difficulty is the court's inferior position in the court hierarchy of most jurisdictions. The consequences of its low position include low regard by lawyers, judges, and social workers; great dependence on the support of local government, local organizations, and often the local electorate for funds, clients, support; and the vulnerability to criticism that accompanies dependence.

Its lack of independence further complicates the typical juvenile court's already intricate relationships with other organizations. Increasingly the juvenile court has been looked to as provider of the social services to which local government has become more and more committed. To carry out even a portion of these obligations, it must not only dilute severely its own activities, especially its judicial ones, but must also rely heavily on good will and more tangible forms of assistance from many local groups, among them police, schools, welfare agencies. That reliance increases the court's vulnerability to pressure both in a given case and as to general operating policies.

Underlying and intensifying all of those difficulties is the court's lack of resources. Procedures for finding facts, gathering and recording information, and other essential tasks are cumbersome and antiquated. The struggle to carry out service functions with inadequate staff and facilities detracts from judicial responsibilities, with the result that neither is fully performed.

These issues, while not within the scope of this material, are of significant influence on the operation of many juvenile courts, and any effort to improve the court requires that they be given careful consideration. They are more fully discussed in "The Juvenile Court as an Institution," a paper written by Robert D. Vinter for this Commission. [Published as an Appendix to The President's Commission on Enforcement and Administration of Justice, *Juvenile Delinquency and Youth Crime* (Washington, D.C.: U.S. Government Printing Office, 1967).]

An Assessment of the Juvenile
Court Today

Studies conducted by the Commission, legislative inquiries in various States, and reports by informed observers compel the conclusion that the great hopes originally held for the juvenile court have not been fulfilled. It has not succeeded significantly in rehabilitating delinquent youth, in reducing or even stemming the tide of juvenile criminality, or in bringing justice and compassion to the child offender. To say that juvenile courts have failed to achieve their goals is to say no more than what is true of criminal courts in the United States. But failure is most striking when hopes are highest.

One reason for the failure of the juvenile courts has been the community's continuing unwillingness to provide the resources — the people and facilities and concern — necessary to permit them to realize their potential and prevent them from taking on some of the undesirable features typical of lower criminal courts in this country. In few jurisdictions, for example, does the juvenile court judgeship enjoy high status in the eyes of the bar, and while there are many juvenile court judges of outstanding ability and devotion, many are not. One crucial presupposition of the juvenile

court philosophy — a mature and sophisticated judge, wise and well-versed in law and the science of human behavior — has proved in fact too often unattainable. A recent study of juvenile court judges reported above [23] revealed that half had not received undergraduate degrees; a fifth had received no college education at all; a fifth were not members of the bar. Almost three-quarters devote less than a quarter of their time to juvenile and family matters, and judicial hearings often are little more than attenuated interviews of 10 or 15 minutes' duration. The National Council on Crime and Delinquency states that the family court in Cook County (Chicago), Ill., averages a little over 15 minutes per hearing — about half the time the council estimates is needed for proper consideration of the issues.[24] A recent California State study concluded:

Based upon estimates furnished by juvenile court judges, the average time spent on a juvenile court case is approximately 10 to 15 minutes. . . . An appropriate question is whether the beneficent values of the juvenile court hearing implied by the philosophy expressed in the law can be achieved in the abbreviated time which most juvenile courts devote to each case. To what extent, for example, can a judge make a significant impact on the errant child and his parents in what is almost an assembly line judicial process? A corollary question is whether the juvenile court judge can actually explore in a brief hearing the behavioral complexities presented by each case? [25]

Other resources are equally lacking. The survey of juvenile court judges reveals the scarcity of psychologists and psychiatrists — over half a century after the juvenile court movement set out to achieve the coordinated application of the behavioral and social sciences to the misbehaving child. Where clinics

[23] Center for the Behavioral Sciences, *op. cit.* *supra* note 21; McCune & Skoler, *supra* note 21, at 121.

[24] NCCD, *The Cook County Family (Juvenile) Court and Arthur J. Audy Home*, 28–29 (1963). See Barron, *The Juvenile in Delinquent Society*, ch. 15 (1954).

[25] Cal. Gov.'s Special Study Comm'n on Juvenile Justice, *A Study of the Administration of Juvenile Justice in California*, pt. 2, at 16 (1960).

exist, their waiting lists usually are months long and frequently they provide no treatment but only diagnosis. And treatment, even when prescribed, is often impossible to carry out because of the unavailability of adequate individual and family casework, foster home placement, treatment in youth institutions. Despite general acceptance of the fact that many children who cannot adjust successfully in their own homes could do so in another community setting without requiring incarceration, only 99 of the 235 agencies in the sample studied by the Commission use foster homes, and only 10 operate group homes.[26]

The dispositional alternatives available even to the better endowed juvenile courts fall far short of the richness and the relevance to individual needs envisioned by the court's founders. In most places, indeed, the only alternatives are release outright, probation, and institutionalization. Probation means minimal supervision at best. A large percentage of juvenile courts have no probation services at all, and in those that do, caseloads typically are so high that counseling and supervision take the form of occasional phone calls and perfunctory visits instead of the careful, individualized service that was intended. Institutionalization too often means storage — isolation from the outside world — in an overcrowded, understaffed, high-security institution with little education, little vocational training, little counseling or job placement or other guidance upon release. Programs are subordinated to everyday control and maintenance. Children spend weeks in limbo-like detention, awaiting bed space. Professor Glueck quotes a well-informed penologist:

There are things going on, methods of discipline being used in the State training schools of this country that would cause a warden of Alcatraz to lose his job if he used them on his prisoners. There are practices that are a daily occurrence in some of our State training schools that are not permitted in the prisons

or penitentiaries of the same States. There are many States in which this discipline is more humane, more reasonable, in the prison than it is in the State training school.[27]

But it is of great importance to emphasize that a simple infusion of resources into juvenile courts and attendant institutions would by no means fulfill the expectations that accompanied the court's birth and development. There are problems that go much deeper. The failure of the juvenile court to fulfill its rehabilitative and preventive promise stems in important measure from a grossly overoptimistic view of what is known about the phenomenon of juvenile criminality and of what even a fully equipped juvenile court could do about it. Experts in the field agree that it is extremely difficult to develop successful methods for preventing serious delinquent acts through rehabilitative programs for the child. There is no shortage of theories of the etiology of delinqency. They range from the intrapsychic to the sociological, from the genetic to the anthropological, even to theories turning upon analyses of body types and structures. Some have looked for basic, generalized explanations of all delinquency. Some have noted the enormous variety in the types of conduct officially denominated delinquency as well as in the types of juveniles found to be delinquents and have begun to suggest narrower explanations differentiating among kinds of deviant behavior. But fundamentally delinquency is behavior, and until the science of human behavior matures far beyond its present confines, an understanding of those kinds of behavior we call delinquency is not likely to be forthcoming. Study and research tend increasingly to support the view that delinquency is not so much an act of individual deviancy as a pattern of behavior produced by a multitude of pervasive societal influences well beyond the reach of the actions of any judge, probation officer, correctional counselor, or psychiatrist.

[26] NCCD, Correction in the United States, 64–65 (prepared for President's Comm'n on Law Enforcement and Administration of Justice, 1966), printed as appendix A of the Report of the Task Force on Corrections.

[27] MacCormick, "The Essentials of a Training School Program, Matching Scientific Advance With Human Progress," 15 (NCJCJ Conference, May 1950), quoted in Glueck, "Some 'Unfinished Business' in the Management of Juvenile Delinquency," 15 *Syracuse L. Rev.*, 628, 630 (1964).

The same uncritical and unrealistic estimates of what is known and can be done that make expectation so much greater than achievement also serve to justify extensive official action and to mask the fact that much of it may do more harm than good. Official action may actually help to fix and perpetuate delinquency in the child through a process in which the individual begins to think of himself as delinquent and organizes his behavior accordingly. That process itself is further reinforced by the effect of the labeling upon the child's family, neighbors, teachers, and peers, whose reactions communicate to the child in subtle ways a kind of expectation of delinquent conduct. The undesirable consequences of official treatment are heightened in programs that rely on institutionalizing the child. The most informed and benign institutional treatment of the child, even in well-designed and staffed reformatories and training schools, thus may contain within it the seeds of its own frustration and itself may often feed the very disorder it is designed to cure.

The limitations, both in theory and in execution, of strictly rehabilitative treatment methods, combined with public anxiety over the seemingly irresistible rise in juvenile criminality, have produced a rupture between the theory and the practice of juvenile court dispositions. While statutes, judges, and commentators still talk the language of compassion, help, and treatment, it has become clear that in fact the same purposes that characterize the use of the criminal law for adult offenders — retribution, condemnation, deterrence, incapacitation — are involved in the disposition of juvenile offenders too. These are society's ultimate techniques for protection against threatening conduct; it is inevitable that they should be used against threats from the young as well as the old when other resources appear unavailing. As Professor Francis Allen has acutely observed:

In a great many cases the juvenile court must perform functions essentially similar to those exercised by any court adjudicating cases of persons charged with dangerous and disturbing behavior. It must reassert the norms and standards of the community when con-fronted by seriously deviant conduct, and it must protect the security of the community by such measures as it has at its disposal, even though the available means may be unsatisfactory when viewed either from the standpoint of the community interest or of the welfare of the delinquent child.[28]

The difficulty is not that this compromise with the rehabilitative idea has occurred, but that it has not been acknowledged. Juvenile court laws and procedures that can be defended and rationalized solely on the basis of the original optimistic theories endure as if the vitality of those theories were undiluted. Thus, for example, juvenile courts retain expansive grounds of jurisdiction authorizing judicial intervention in relatively minor matters of morals and misbehavior, on the ground that subsequent delinquent conduct may be indicated, as if there were reliable ways of predicting delinquency in a given child and reliable ways of redirecting children's lives. Delinquency is adjudicated in informal proceedings that often lack safeguards fundamental for protecting the individual and for assuring reliable determinations, as if the court were a hospital clinic and its only objective were to discover the child's malady and to cure him. As observed by Mr. Justice Fortas, speaking for the Supreme Court in Kent v. United States, "there may be grounds for concern that the child receives the worst of both worlds: that he gets neither the protections accorded to adults nor the solicitous care and regenerative treatment postulated for children." [29, 30]

What emerges, then, is this: In theory the juvenile court was to be helpful and rehabilitative rather than punitive. In fact the distinction often disappears, not only because of the absence of facilities and personnel but also because of the limits of knowledge and technique. In theory the court's action was to affix no stigmatizing label. In fact a delinquent is generally viewed by employers, schools, the armed services — by society generally — as a criminal. In theory the court was to treat children guilty

28 Allen, *The Borderland of Criminal Justice*, 53 (1964).
29 383 U.S. 541, 556 (1966).
30 [See the following selection.]

of criminal acts in noncriminal ways. In fact it labels truants and runaways as junior criminals.

In theory the court's operations could justifiably be informal, its findings and decisions made without observing ordinary procedural safeguards, because it would act only in the best interest of the child. In fact it frequently does nothing more nor less than deprive a child of liberty without due process of law — knowing not what else to do and needing, whether admittedly or not, to act in the community's interest even more imperatively than the child's. In theory it was to exercise its protective powers to bring an errant child back into the fold. In fact there is increasing reason to believe that its intervention reinforces the juvenile's unlawful impulses. In theory it was to concentrate on each case the best of current social science learning. In fact it has often become a vested interest in its turn, loath to cooperate with innovative programs or avail itself of forward-looking methods.

Nevertheless, study of the juvenile courts does not necessarily lead to the conclusion that the time has come to jettison the experiment and remand the disposition of children charged with crime to the criminal courts of the country. As trying as are the problems of the juvenile courts, the problems of the criminal courts, particularly those of the lower courts, which would fall heir to much of the juvenile court jurisdiction, are even graver; and the ideal of separate treatment of children is still worth pursuing. What is required is rather a revised philosophy of the juvenile court based on the recognition that in the past our reach exceeded our grasp. The spirit that animated the juvenile court movement was fed in part by a humanitarian compassion for offenders who were children. That willingness to understand and treat people who threaten public safety and security should be nurtured, not turned aside as hopeless sentimentality, both because it is civilized and because social protection itself demands constant search for alternatives to the crude and limited expedient of condemnation and punishment. But neither should it be allowed to outrun reality. The juvenile court is a court of law, charged like other agencies of criminal justice with protecting the community against threatening conduct. Rehabilitating offenders through individualized handling is one way of providing protection, and appropriately the primary way in dealing with children. But the guiding consideration for a court of law that deals with threatening conduct is nonetheless protection of the community. The juvenile court, like other courts, is therefore obliged to employ all the means at hand, not excluding incapacitation, for achieving that protection. What should distinguish the juvenile from the criminal courts is greater emphasis on rehabilitation, not exclusive preoccupation with it.

In this selection the President's Commission describes some of the procedural differences between juvenile and criminal courts and the reasons for rejection of the adversary system in favor of informal, flexible proceedings. Also discussed are some of the early challenges to the legality of the juvenile court and the response of the Pennsylvania Supreme Court, which became an authoritative expression of the higher courts' receptivity to the juvenile delinquency laws on the grounds that the proceedings (1) were civil, not criminal, and (2) were an extension of equity, a system of law which originated in the early chancery proceedings. According to Tappan (1949: 169), a distinct court and jurisdiction of chancery (so-named because it was presided over by the lord chancellor) appeared in the fifteenth century in

England, and the Crown exercised the power of *parens patriae*, or the power of guardianship to protect children. The current reaction to the juvenile court's philosophy may be viewed as part of the widespread concern about protection of the rights of persons in the face of governmental intervention in their lives; hence, the President's Commission suggests six special considerations which are involved in the questions being raised about the operation of the juvenile court. Juvenile-court proceedings must be brought into closer harmony with the requirements of due process, but to make the juvenile court a replica of the criminal court would be, in the Commission's view, a serious error.

REFERENCE

Paul W. Tappan, *Juvenile Delinquency* (New York: McGraw-Hill Book Co., Inc., 1949).

THE PRESIDENT'S COMMISSION ON
LAW ENFORCEMENT AND ADMINISTRATION OF JUSTICE

Procedural Justice for the Juvenile

The original humanitarian philosophy of the juvenile court was believed to require a significant change in the manner in which courts made their determinations about which children to deal with and how to deal with them. In place of the rigorous formalities of the criminal law there was to be substituted a wholly informal and flexible procedure under which, by gentle and friendly probing by judge, social worker, parent, and child, the roots of the child's difficulties could be exposed and informed decisions made as to how best to meet his problems. The rejection of the formalities of criminal procedure was explained on the grounds that they were not needed in juvenile court proceedings and that they would be destructive of the goals of those proceedings.

They were not needed because the objective of the whole process was to help the child ad-

From the President's Commission on Law Enforcement and Administration of Justice, "Procedural Justice for the Juvenile," in *Juvenile Delinquency and Youth Crime* (Washington, D.C.: U.S. Government Printing Office, 1967), pp. 28–31.
[This selection was written prior to the Supreme Court's decision *In re Gault*.]

just to himself and his environment. Punishment for wrongdoing, the rationale of the criminal law, was foreign to juvenile court philosophy. Hence there was no need for traditional criminal procedures designed to shield an innocent accused against punishment, any more than these procedures would be appropriate in medical diagnosis and treatment of physical or psychological ailments.

They were destructive for several reasons. First, the formal process — charges, jury trials, representation by counsel, evidentiary restrictions, motions and countermotions, the privilege against self-incrimination — was inescapably identified with the criminal law, the atmosphere and presuppositions of which it was the objective of the juvenile court movement to eliminate in dealing with child offenders. Second, adversary procedures for determining whether a person committed a criminal act with a criminal state of mind were not useful for ascertaining the full picture of the child's behavior, including not only the conduct that brought him to court but the whole pattern of his prior behavior and relationships. Third, criminal procedures would put the child on one side and the court on the other, creating a tone of combat and contentiousness that would destroy the sought after cooperation of the child in the common effort to help him.

The statutes faithfully reflected this philosophy. Typically they provided (as many still do), "The court may conduct the hearing in an informal manner and may adopt any form of procedure in such cases which it deems best suited to ascertain the facts," [1] or, "The hearing of any matter involving a child shall be informal, and the judge shall, in chambers, without the intervention of a jury, inquire into the facts. . . ." [2] What this meant in practice varied greatly, depending upon the attitudes of the judges, the resources available, and the volume of the caseload. But in the vast majority of cases, parents and child would be notified of the basis of the proceeding in vague and general terms, the child would appear without counsel, the probation officer would report to the court what his inquiries disclosed, the judge would ask the child such questions as he thought necessary, witnesses would be brought in where the judge thought it useful to do so, and the judge would make his finding.

That radical departure from traditional modes of inquiry of course elicited constitutional challenges in the courts. But the courts proved receptive to the spirit of the juvenile delinquency laws. On the ground that the proceedings were civil and not criminal, were an extension of equity's authority to deal compassionately with children, and were addressed to the salvation rather than the punishment of the child, the courts sustained these laws against challenges based on the due process clause and the specific guarantees of Federal and State bills of rights.[3] An opinion of the Pennsylvania Supreme Court of 1905, which came to be regarded as an authoritative expression of this point of view, provides a sobering lesson of changing fashions in ideas about dealing with children: So much of wish and ideal and so little of fact and hard experience go into these ideas that those of one generation often seem to the next as quaint as its clothes. The following quotation from that opinion was reproduced with apparent acceptance in a discussion of the child offender in one of the Wickersham Commission reports in 1931.[4]

The appellant child, said the court:

could not have been without due process of law for the constitutional guaranty is that no one charged with a criminal offense shall be deprived of life, liberty, or property without due process of law. To save a child from becoming a criminal, or from continuing in a career of crime, to end in mature years in public punishment and disgrace, the legislature surely may provide for the salvation of such a child, if its parents or guardian be unable or unwilling to do so. . . . The natural parent needs no process to temporarily deprive his child of its liberty . . . to save it and to shield it from the consequences of persistence in a career of waywardness, nor is the State, when compelled, as parens patriae, to take the place of the father for the same purpose, required to adopt any process as a means of placing its hands upon the child to lead it into one of its courts. When the child gets there and the court, with the power to save it, determines on its salvation, it . . . is immaterial how it got there. The act simply provides how children who ought to be saved may reach the court to be saved. If experience should show that there ought to be other ways for it to get there, the legislature can, and undoubtedly will, adopt them and they will never be regarded as undue processes for depriving a child of its liberty or property as a penalty for crime committed. . . . [T]he act is not for the trial of a child charged with a crime, but is mercifully to save it from such an ordeal, with the prison or penitentiary in its wake, if the child's own good and the best interests of the State justify such salvation.[5]

Occasionally, dissenting voices protested either the unfairness [6] or the leniency [7] of the juvenile court's methods, and courts sometimes

---

[1] Utah Code Ann. § 55–10–26 (1953).

[2] Ariz. Rev. Stat. Ann. § 8–229 (1956).

[3] See cases cited in *Pee v. United States*, 274 F.2d 556, 561–62 (D.C. Cir. 1959).

[4] Nat'l Comm'n on Law Observance and Enforcement, *Report on the Child Offender in the Federal System of Justice*, 28 (1931).

[5] *Commonwealth v. Fisher*, 213 Pa. 48, 53, 54 (1905).

[6] E.g., Lindsey, "The Juvenile Court Movement From a Lawyer's Standpoint," 52 *The Annals*, 140 (1914).

[7] E.g., Note, *Juvenile Court v. Criminal Court*, 21 *Ill. L. Rev.*, 375 (1926).

admonished the importance of adhering to principles of basic fairness in dealing informally and flexibly with the child.[8] But the prevailing spirit was one of sympathy and encouragement in the nurturing of a noble experiment in the administration of justice.

In recent years, however, commencing roughly in the period following the Second World War, there has been a mounting reaction, termed by one juvenile court judge a "legal renaissance." [9] This has been based in some measure upon rejection of the whole philosophy of the juvenile court as a denial, in the face of an increasing challenge of juvenile criminality, of the uses of deterrence and moral condemnation.[10] In larger part, however, the reaction has come from those concerned about potential arbitrariness and unfairness and unfettered judicial discretion in dealing with human lives. The reaction has been manifested on a broad front. Scholarly commentators have been virtually unanimous in decrying the injustices and harmfulness of completely abandoning procedural protections. Only rarely in recent years is a voice heard in praise of the old ways.[11] Legislative studies in a variety of States reflect the same judgment.[12]

As a recent California special study commission concluded:

The results of virtually all of these studies — both in California and in other States — have been fairly uniform. While the court's rehabilitative objectives and protective philosophy are uniformly endorsed, considerable question has been raised as to whether the court as presently constituted is providing sufficient legal safeguards.[13]

Recent amendments of the juvenile court laws in a number of States, including New York and California, manifest a growing legislative acceptance of this view.[14]

Organizations generally identified with humane philosophies of correction, including the National Council on Crime and Delinquency, the National Council of Juvenile Court Judges, and the Children's Bureau of the Department of Health, Education, and Welfare, have endorsed like positions on procedural fairness in the juvenile courts.[15] Nor have the courts been passive in the call for a return to a greater measure of procedural regularity in the juvenile courts. Both State and Federal courts have increasingly sustained, on grounds either of statutory interpretation or of constitutional requirement, claims based upon failure to advise of the right to counsel, denial of the right to confrontation, and like matters.[16] The Supreme Court, which had been silent on the various issues raised by the juvenile court since

---

[8] E.g., *People v. Lewis*, 260 N.Y. 171, 183 N.E. 353 (1932).

[9] Ketcham, "Legal Renaissance in the Juvenile Court," 60 *NW. U.L. Rev.*, 585 (1965).

[10] See e.g., Judge Oliphant dissenting in *State v. Monahan*, 15 N.J. 34, 59, 104 A.2d 21, 36 (1954):

Infants under the age of 21 years, according to statistics, perpetrate a high percentage of the heinous crimes committed throughout the country, and the situation has reached such serious proportions that it is a threat to the public welfare and safety of law-abiding citizens. . . . [T]he time has come to examine the underlying philosophy of the treatment of juvenile offenders.

A Chief Justice of England, Lord Goddard, in Giles, *Children and the Law*, Foreword (1959), admonished "justices to remember that the sending of children for examination by psychiatrists may do more harm than good, as it is so apt to make children think they are interesting cases when they are only naughty boys or girls."

[11] See Alexander, "Constitutional Rights in the Juvenile Court," in *Justice for the Child*, 82 (Rosenheim ed. 1962).

[12] 6 Wis. Legislative Council, *Conclusions and Recommendations of the Child Welfare Commis-*

sion pt. 1 (1955); Minn. Legislative Interim Comm'n, *Report on Public Welfare Laws* (1959); Ore. Legislative Interim Comm'n on Judicial Administration, *Juvenile Law* pt. 2 (1959); Cal. Report pts. 1, 2; N.Y. Report pts. 1, 2.

[13] Cal. Report pt. 2, at 3.

[14] E.g., N.Y. Family Ct. Act §§ 111–1019 (1966); Cal. Welf. & Inst'ns Code §§ 500–914 (Supp. 1966). See Standard Juvenile Court Act § 19.

[15] See, e.g., *Standards for Juvenile and Family Courts*, ch. 4; NCCD, *Guides for Juvenile Court Judges*, ch. 9 (1963) (prepared in cooperation with NCJCJ).

[16] See, e.g., *Shioutakon v. District of Columbia*, 236 F.2d 666 (D.C. Cir. 1956) (right to counsel); *Black v. United States*, 355 F.2d 104 (D.C. Cir. 1965) (right to appointment of counsel in waiver proceedings); *Watkins v. United States*, 343 F.2d 278 (D.C. Cir. 1964) (right to see child's social records).

its inception wrote an opinion in March 1966 raising serious question that the Court will continue its policy of aloofness. In *Kent v. United States*,[17] the Court reversed an order of the District of Columbia juvenile court waiving a juvenile to the criminal court, on the grounds that the court had failed to grant a hearing, to provide counsel access to records, and to state reasons for its order. While the Court rested its decision upon an interpretation of the District of Columbia juvenile court statute, it made clear that the result was reached by reading the statute "in the context of constitutional principles relating to due process and the assistance of counsel." [18] Furthermore, the Court has agreed to review in the October 1966 term a far-reaching challenge to the constitutionality of the entire Arizona juvenile court law.[19]

What are the reasons for this widespread disaffection with the original philosophy of the juvenile court as to legal protections? In a fundamental sense the reaction is only one manifestation of much broader concern about protection of the rights of persons threatened with State intervention in their daily lives, particularly those who live in poverty at the margin of American life.[20] This larger concern is seen in growing availability of legal assistance for the poor, in public defender and bail reform programs, in constitutional decisions on the right to counsel and equal protection and the privilege against self-incrimination. But there are special considerations applicable to the juvenile court that are of immediate importance.

First, efforts to help and heal and treat, if they are to have any chance of success, must be based on an accurate determination of the facts — the facts of the immediate conduct that led to the filing of the petition and also the facts of the child's past conduct and relationships. The point is made vivid by an occurrence in California in which a person convicted of a sexual offense was committed as a sexual psychopath and was subjected to psychiatric examination and diagnosis on the assumption that he had actually committed the sexual act for which he had originally been convicted.[21] In fact, as later established, he was the victim of misidentification. As one observer comments:

Thus, the mistake as to the facts not only resulted in an improper conviction but rendered invalid the psychiatric judgment of the defendant's personality and propensities. However advanced our techniques for determining what an individual is, we have not yet approached the point at which we can safely ignore what he has done. What he has done may often be the most revealing evidence of what he is.[22]

Mistakes and misapprehensions concerning the defendant and his conduct can and do survive even a formal criminal trial. But the essential attributes of a judicial trial — an adversary proceeding in which the defendant is represented by counsel who may present his own witnesses and cross-examine others, before a judge whose judgment is undisturbed by having to shift roles, as he proceeds, from prosecutor to defense counsel to judge — are the best guarantee our system has been able to devise for assuring reliable determinations of fact.[23]

Second, we are committed to the value of individual self-determination and freedom. The fact that the state's motives are beneficent and designed to provide what, at least in its view, the child and its parents need should not be allowed to obscure the fact that, in taking a child from his parents or placing him in an institution or even subjecting him to probation and supervision, the state is invoking its power to interfere with the lives of individuals as

---

[17] 383 U.S. 541 (1966).

[18] *Id.*, at 557.

[19] *In re Gault*, 99 Ariz. 180, 407 P.2d 760 (1965), *cert. granted*, 384 U.S. 997 (1966).

[20] Other manifestations of this concern include the nationwide bail reform movement, encouraged by the Department of Justice's 1964 Conference on Bail and Criminal Justice, and the neighborhood law offices, supported by the Office of Economic Opportunity, to provide legal assistance for indigents.

[21] See Hacker & Frym, "The Sexual Psychopath Act in Practice: A Critical Discussion," 43 *Calif. L. Rev.*, 766 (1955).

[22] Allen, *The Borderland of Criminal Justice*, 19 (1964).

[23] See Handler, "The Juvenile Court and the Adversary System: Problems of Function and Form," 1965, *Wis. L. Rev.*, 7, 29.

they choose to lead them. While the interests of society in helping people in trouble and in protecting itself may require this intervention, its interest in keeping faith with its commitment to the individual requires that it first establish its right to intervene in a procedure that affords the affected individual every resource necessary for his own protection.

Third, the experience of more than half a century has made clear that, despite the hopes and best efforts of those involved in the juvenile courts, being adjudicated delinquent has become as stigmatizing as being convicted as a criminal. In the minds of the child, the family, and the community, including schools, the Government, the Armed Forces, and future employers, the label of juvenile delinquent imposes a severe and grievous disadvantage upon the child.

Fourth, as was developed earlier in this report, it has proven to be true for a variety of reasons that the promise of the juvenile courts to help the child, to rehabilitate him, to lead him into a healthy and constructive life has not been kept. This has been partly because of lack of community support, but also because of considerations beyond society's power to alter. Therefore, the major rationale for the withdrawal of procedural safeguards ceases to exist.

For, to the extent that restraints are imposed upon the freedom of an individual for rehabilitative purposes, only the real possibility of accomplishing these purposes justifies them. Without it, not only are the restraints immoral and pointless, they establish a precedent dangerous to the whole community.[24]

As Mr. Justice Fortas observed, speaking for the majority of the Supreme Court in *Kent v. United States:*

While there can be no doubt of the original laudable purpose of juvenile courts, studies and critiques in recent years raise serious questions as to whether actual performance measures well enough against theoretical purpose to make tolerable the immunity of the process from the reach of constitutional guaranties applicable to adults. There is much evidence

that some juvenile courts, including that of the District of Columbia, lack the personnel, facilities, and techniques to perform adequately as representatives of the state in a parens patriae capacity, at least with respect to children charged with law violation. There is evidence, in fact, that there may be grounds for concern that the child receives the worst of both worlds: That he gets neither the protections accorded to adults nor the solicitous care and regenerative treatment postulated for children.[25]

Fifth, it follows naturally from the circumstances just outlined that the juvenile court system is not single-mindedly devoted to the welfare and needs of the child offender, but rather has the same purposes that mark the criminal law. As was indicated earlier in this report, the overwhelming limitations on our ability to make inroads into the phenomenon of increasing juvenile criminality through programs of individual rehabilitation make it inevitable that the juvenile courts, like the criminal courts, resort to the traditional means of providing social protection to the community, limited and unproved though they be — deterrence, condemnation, and incapacitation.[26] To the extent this is so, the justification for abandoning the protective procedural guarantees associated with due process of law disappears.

[25] 383 U.S. 541, 555–56 (1964).

[26] See the revealing observations of Judge Ketcham in "Legal Renaissance in the Juvenile Court," 60 *NW. U.L. Rev.*, 585, 593 (1965): [T]he great challenge to juvenile courts in the second half of the twentieth century is not the orphan or the neglected child, but the aggressive, youthful offender (often referred to as the young criminal). Society rightfully demands that his predatory violence be halted. Yet, existing procedures for the rehabilitation of these youths are both uncertain and expensive. In such circumstances, to require a juvenile court judge to prosecute, defend, and adjudicate such older youths and then, acting as both the substitute parent and the conscience of the community, to order a disposition designed to protect other citizens and rehabilitate the youth — all without benefit of counsel — may be asking too much. Dogged insistence upon "going it alone" and following the warm-hearted but unrealistic principle that "there is no such thing as a bad boy" may, in fact, place the juvenile court philosophy in imminent danger of being "swept away by the tide of history."

[24] Kadish, Book Review, 78 *Harv. L. Rev.*, 907, 908 (1965).

Sixth, there has been increasing feeling on the part of sociologists and social welfare people that the informal procedures, contrary to the original expectation, may themselves constitute a further obstacle to effective treatment of the delinquent. The feeling is based in part upon the often observed sense of injustice engendered in the child by seemingly all-powerful and challengeless exercise of authority by judges and probation officers, based, in the child's eyes, on inconsistency, hypocrisy, favoritism, and whimsy.[27] It is based also upon the atmosphere of the proceedings, which instills in the child a feeling that he is being treated as a "nonperson" incapable of making decisions as to his own welfare and future, and engenders in him a regression and diminution of self-respect.[28] And it is based upon the destruction of trust and cooperation — the avowed goals of the informal process — in what has been described as "authoritarian professionalism and pious intimacy in a courtroom setting." [29] As in most matters dealing with juve-

nile delinquency, there is no reliable evidence as to whether or how accurate these observations are. But the increasing doubts they cast upon the basic suppositions of the original juvenile court philosophy cannot be disregarded.

These challenges to the departure from procedural regularity in the juvenile courts make the case for bringing juvenile court procedures into closer harmony with our fundamental commitments to due process of law. What is entailed is not abandonment of the unique qualities of the juvenile court or adoption of the precise model of the criminal trial in all its particulars. To pursue single-mindedly the goal of procedural justice without regard to the often competing goal of the child's welfare would be to commit the error of the past in reverse, for the great defect of the early juvenile court movement was that it did pursue the welfare goal with just such single-mindedness, to the exclusion of much that is involved in the concept of justice. What is entailed is accommodation of both goals by establishing procedures permitting the court effectively to pursue humane and rehabilitative aims within the framework of a system that recognizes the indispensability of justice in any coercive governmental venture into the lives of individuals. This should in no sense mean compromising our concern to protect the child. It was the necessary and useful insight of the original juvenile court laws that children require protection from the criminal law — from the atmosphere of guilt and condemnation, the association with adult criminals, the highly formalized ritual of the criminal trial. But we have now learned that children need protection fully as much against the coercive, though often beneficent, regimes that the juvenile court laws have substituted for the criminal law.

---

[27] See Matza, *Delinquency and Drift*, 136 (1964).

[28] See Studt, "The Client's Image of the Juvenile Court," in *Justice for the Child*, 200 (Rosenheim ed. 1962).

[29] Platt, "The Child Savers: The Emergence of the Juvenile Court in Chicago," 1966 (unpublished thesis, Univ. of Cal., Berkeley, Cal.). See Handler, *op. cit. supra* note 23, at 20–21, drawing on findings in Halleck, "The Impact of Professional Dishonesty on Behavior of Disturbed Adolescents," *Social Work,* April 1963, p. 48:

Dr. Halleck argues that there are several ways in which professionals attempt to deceive adolescents and that such attempts not only are not successful but may actually perpetuate or even precipitate rebellious behavior. Deceitful attempts include the fact that the adolescent is required to see the professional, a person paid by the community to control and modify the behavior of the child, but who nevertheless insists that his only interest is to help the child; the professional cannot guarantee confidentiality although he attempts to create the contrary impression; he tells the adolescent that everything will be fine if he will only conform to community norms; he makes pious statements that adults control aggressiveness (usually referring to sexual aggressiveness) and that success is dependent on restraint; he encourages ambitions and achievements

that are not possible for adolescents; the adolescent is often struggling to free himself from threatening and harmful adult relationships and establish safer peer relationships, but the professional, from a position of great power, nevertheless urges the adolescent to expose himself to an adult in a situation where the adolescent has little reason to expect true intimacy.

Terry focuses his attention on the criteria employed by the police, probation department, and juvenile court in a midwestern city in sanctioning juvenile offenders. A variety of bases for differential treatment of offenders have been suggested, and Terry uses these to formulate an extensive series of hypotheses. Because many juveniles are eliminated from the legal-judicial process, Terry analyzed a "universe" of police cases. Of 9,023 offenses known to the police, 775 were referred to the probation department, and 246 of these offenses eventually were brought to the attention of the juvenile court. Terry found that the severity of the sanction accorded juvenile offenders was not related to the power of the juvenile or to the social distance between the delinquent and agents of social control. Although a common presumption has been that juveniles from the lower class, and especially those who are members of a minority group, are discriminated against by agents of social control, Terry found that minority status, socioeconomic status, and the delinquency rate of the juvenile's area of residence were relatively unimportant in terms of the sanctions accorded juvenile offenders. However, at each level of the legal process the amount of deviance engaged in by the individual was significantly related to the severity of the sanction employed.

In the midwestern city in which Terry did his research the police utilize essentially legalistic criteria in making decisions regarding disposition, whereas the juvenile court employs a wider variety of criteria than either the police or the probation department. Agencies of social control do not use the more severe sanctions available to them until the juvenile demonstrates, by committing additional delinquent acts, that application of these sanctions is warranted. Before services are offered the juvenile he generally must have committed several serious offenses and be relatively old. This, Terry observes, has a practical implication: counselors and probation officers handle delinquents whose careers are well under way but may not be reaching others who might profit from their efforts.

ROBERT M. TERRY

The Screening of Juvenile Offenders

Students of deviant behavior are increasingly coming to recognize that deviance is not a quality that inheres in either the person who engages in the behavior or in the behavior itself. Instead, deviance resides in the definitions that are imposed on the behavior and the deviant is a person who has been so labeled.[1] This "interactionist" conceptualization has important implications for the study of crime and delinquency in that actions taken by members of the social audience constitute phenomena to be explained rather than simply to be taken for granted.[2]

The theoretical significance of interactionism is exemplified by Lemert's theory of deviance, wherein emphasis is placed upon accounting for the processes which lead to systematic deviant behavior as a function of adopting a deviant role.[3] Briefly, the development of career deviance is regarded as being dependent

upon the societal reactions to one's deviant behavior. By reacting to a person's deviant behavior, the social audience accords deviant statuses and thereby structures the internal and external limits upon the individual's choice of roles in such a way that few alternatives to the deviant role exist for the "deviant." Where deviant statuses are accorded, the deviant role simply becomes the subjective aspect of the societal reaction.[4] Thus, the understanding of career deviance is dependent upon an understanding of the reasons for and variations in the societal reactions to deviant behavior on the part of social audiences.

Agencies that are designed to deal with problems of deviance are especially relevant members of the social audience. This is most obviously the case with respect to what may be called "primary" agencies of social control, or those agencies which have as the primary basis for their existence the functions of identifying, defining, and sanctioning deviant behavior. The police, probation departments, parole departments, courts, and correctional institutions are examples of such agencies with respect to violations of legal norms. Acting as the community's official representatives they not only determine, to a large extent, the broader reactions to legal deviations, but also act to change the individual's status by means of applying deviant definitions. Thus, their identification, definition, and sanctioning of an individual as deviant provides a basis upon which family members, peers, employers, neighbors, and others may rely in according status to the individual. Since this is the case, the actions taken by these agencies are of significance in that the individual may be defined and reacted to primarily with respect to his deviant status, and his behavior will be expected to coincide with this status.

Reprinted by Special Permission of the *Journal of Criminal Law, Criminology and Police Science* (Northwestern University School of Law), Copyright © 1967, Volume 58, Number 2.

The original aspects of the research upon which this paper is based were supported by a University Fellowship at the University of Wisconsin.

[1] A number of recent sociological works have emphasized this approach and its significance. See, e.g., Becker, *Outsiders* (1963); Becker, ed., *The Other Side* (1964); Goffman, *Asylums* (1961); Kitsuse, "Societal Reactions to Deviant Behavior: Problems of Theory and Method," 9 *Social Problems*, 247–256 (1962); Mechanic, "Some Factors in Identifying and Defining Mental Illness," 46 *Mental Hygiene*, 66–74 (1962); Scheff, "The Role of the Mentally Ill and the Dynamics of Mental Disorder: A Research Framework," 26 *Sociometry*, 436–453 (1963).

[2] See, especially, Wheeler, "Criminal Statistics: A Reformulation of the Problem," unpublished paper read at the meetings of the American Statistical Association, Philadelphia, September, 1965.

[3] Lemert, "Some Aspects of a General Theory of Sociopathic Behavior," 16 *Proceedings of Meetings of Pacific Sociological Society*, State College of Wash., 1–28 (1948).

[4] Lemert, *Social Pathology*, 76 (1951).

Problem

As part of the broader study of societal re-actions to deviance, this research focuses pri-marily upon the bases for according sanctions of varying severity to juveniles whose behavior has been identified and defined as delinquent. Specifically, we will be concerned with the severity of sanctions accorded juveniles who become involved in the legal-judicial process designed to deal with juvenile offenders by three relevant kinds of social audiences: (1) the police; (2) the probation department; (3) the juvenile court.[5] Each of these agencies ac-cord sanctions, which take the form of disposi-tions, to offenders for having engaged in de-linquent behavior.

The sanctioning of juvenile offenders ap-pears to be a most appropriate area for this type of research in that the identification and definition of juveniles as delinquents is not strictly limited by legal definitions or statutory considerations, but is at the relative discretion of those who, as members of the social audi-ence, find themselves disposed to identify and define juvenile behavior as such. In addition, no penal sanctions are attached to juvenile offenses. In fact, *theoretically*, juvenile offend-ers are not sanctioned for their deviant behav-ior, but are "helped" or "treated" by having certain kinds of dispositions accorded them. The selection of dispositions in any particular case is, legally speaking, to be guided only by the "best interests of the child." Therefore, discretion is built into juvenile codes in such a way as to allow relatively complete freedom of action (with respect to dispositions) by the primary agencies of social control.[6]

The specific problem, then, with which we will be concerned in this research may be stated as follows in the form of a question: *What are the criteria utilized by the police, the probation department, and the juvenile court in the sanctioning of juvenile offenders?*

Numerous suggestions as to the criteria uti-lized exist in the theoretical and research liter-ature on crime and delinquency although sound

empirical research is sparse.[7] Generally, these hypothesized relationships maintain that the severity of the societal reaction varies signifi-cantly with such things as the nature of the behavior engaged in, the offender's past record of misbehavior, salient personal and social char-acteristics such as how old the offender is, where he lives, his race, etc., and the situational circumstances in which offenses are com-mitted.[8] Taking these suggestions as the basis for departures, we have formulated a series of major hypotheses concerning variations in the societal reaction to deviant behavior and have formulated relevant sub-hypotheses which will provide an indication not only of the adequacy of the major hypotheses but will also enable specification of some of the criteria utilized by control agencies in sanctioning juvenile of-fenders.

1: The severity of the societal reaction is positively related to the degree of the devi-ance.

1.1: The severity of dispositions accorded juvenile offenders is positively related to the seriousness of the offense committed.[9]

---

[5] This is generally referred to as the screening process.

[6] In other words, lay-social as well as technical-impersonal criteria are legitimate.

[7] While most of these studies lack a theoretical framework, they provide useful perspectives on the problem at hand. See Green, *Judicial Attitudes in Sentencing* (1961); Foote, "Vagrancy-Type Law and Its Administration," 104 *U. Pa. L. Rev.,* 603–650 (1956); La Fave, "The Police and Non-enforcement of the Law – Part II," 1962 *U. Wis. L. Rev.,* 188–238 (1962); Mannheim, Spencer, and Lynch, "Magisterial Policy in the London Juvenile Courts," 8 *Brit. J. Crim.,* 13–33, 119–138 (1957); Piliavin and Briar, "Police Encounters with Juveniles," 70 *Am. J. Sociol.,* 206–214 (1964); Shannon, "Types and Patterns of Delinquency Referral in a Middle-sized City," 4 *Brit. J. Crim.,* 24–36 (1963); Goldman, *The Differential Selection of Juvenile Offenders for Court Appearance* (1963); Kinney, Klem, and Myers, "Selective Fac-tors Involved in Differential Treatment of Youth-ful Offenders at the Juvenile Court of Cook County" (unpublished thesis, University of Chi-cago, 1951).

[8] See, especially, Lemert, *supra* note 4 at 51–53, 55–68; Scheff, *supra* note 1 at 452; Mechanic, *supra* note 1 at 66–74; Erikson, "Notes on the Sociology of Deviance," 9 *Social Problems,* 308 (1962).

[9] Delinquent offenses are classified as being one of nine types. Questionnaires were submitted to

2: The severity of the societal reaction is positively related to the amount of deviance engaged in by the individual.

2.1: The severity of dispositions accorded juvenile offenders is positively related to the number of previous offenses committed.[10]

3: The severity of the societal reaction is negatively related to the power of the deviant.

3.1: The severity of dispositions accorded juvenile offenders is negatively related to the socio-economic status of the offender.[11]

4: The severity of the societal reaction is positively related to the social distance between the deviant and agents of social control.

4.1: The severity of dispositions accorded juvenile offenders is positively related to the degree of minority status of the offender.[12]

5: The severity of the societal reaction is positively related to the "unfavorability" of the situation in which the offense is committed.

5.1: The severity of dispositions accorded juvenile offenders is negatively related to the number of individuals involved in an offense.[13]

5.2: The severity of dispositions accorded juvenile offenders is positively related to the degree of involvement with offenders of the opposite sex.[14]

5.3: The severity of dispositions accorded juvenile offenders is positively related to the degree of involvement with adult offenders.[15]

5.4: The severity of dispositions accorded juvenile offenders is positively related to the formality of the social control function of the complainant.[16]

6: The severity of the societal reaction is positively related to the "unfavorability" of the place in which the deviance is committed.

6.1: The severity of dispositions accorded juvenile offenders is positively related to the degree of commercial/industrial development of the area in which the offense is committed.[17]

---

personnel of the police Juvenile Bureau and the County Probation Department in order to ascertain the seriousness with which they regarded each of these types of offenses. The result was the following ranking of offenses from least serious to most serious: (1) disorderly conduct; (2) liquor offenses; (3) incorrigibility; (4) theft excluding auto theft; (5) sex offenses; (6) assault and violent property damage; (7) burglary; (8) auto theft; (9) homicide and robbery.

[10] The number of previous offenses committed was ranked in five categories: (1) no previous offenses; (2) 1–2 previous offenses; (3) 3–4 previous offenses; (4) 5–6 previous offenses; (5) 7 or more previous offenses.

[11] Socio-economic status was measured by the use of the Minnesota Scale for Paternal Occupations and yielded the following ranks: (1) lower status; (2) middle status; (3) upper status. Lower status consists of classes V, VI, and VII of the Minnesota Scale, middle status consists of classes III and IV, and upper status consists of classes I and II. See *The Minnesota Scale for Paternal Occupations* (undated pamphlet).

[12] The following ranks of ethnic groupings are used as measures of the degree of minority status: (1) Anglos; (2) Mexican-Americans; (3) Negroes. Anglos include all Caucasians with the exception of Mexican-Americans. Being a Mexican-American is regarded as less of a minority status than being a Negro on the basis of several things: (1) We are measuring social distance between deviants and agents of social control. Several Mexican-Americans are members of the community's agencies of social control, while no Negroes are so employed. (2) There is less discrimination in the community under study against Mexican-Americans than against Negroes. Negroes were not, during the period under study, permitted to stay in the com-

munity's major hotels, to eat in a number of establishments, and were more segregated in terms of housing.

[13] The following categories were used: (1) one offender; (2) 2–3 offenders; (3) 4–5 offenders; (4) 6 or more offenders.

[14] The following ranks were used as measures of the degree of involvement with the opposite sex: (1) offense committed alone or with companions of the same sex; (2) offense committed with companions of the opposite sex.

[15] The degree of involvement with adult offenders is measured by the following ranks: (1) offense committed alone or with juvenile companions; (2) offense committed with adult companions.

[16] The formality of the social control function of the complainant in an offense was measured by the following ranks: (1) family member or relative of the offender; (2) neighbor of the offender; (3) other citizen; (4) business or employee of a business; (5) employee of a public agency (e.g., teacher, principal, recreation department playground leader, mayor, etc.); (6) police.

[17] School districts constitute the basis for establishing areas. The degree of commercial/industrial development within these school districts was ascertained by dividing the total amount of land utilized for public buildings, businesses, light and

7: The severity of the societal reaction is positively related to the "unfavorability" of the deviant's personal and social biography.[18]

7.1: The severity of dispositions accorded juvenile offenders is positively related to the "maleness" of the offender.[19]

7.2: The severity of dispositions accorded juvenile offenders is positively related to the age of the offender.[20]

7.3: The severity of dispositions accorded juvenile offenders is positively related to the delinquency rate of the area in which the offender resides.[21]

The dependent variables, designed to provide indications of the severity of the societal reaction to deviant behavior on the part of primary agencies of social control, consist of the dispositions accorded juvenile offenders by each of the agencies.[22] In order of increasing severity, police dispositions consist of: (1) release; (2) referral to a social or welfare agency; (3) referral to the County Probation Department; (4) referral to the State Department of Public Welfare. Probation department sanctions consist of: (1) release; (2) placement under informal supervision; (3) referral to the juvenile court; (4) waiver to the criminal court. Although a number of dispositions are possible by juvenile court judges, only two are utilized by the juvenile court judge in the community under study in this research: (1) formal supervision; (2) commitment to an institution.

Data and Procedures

The site of this research is a heavily-industrialized Midwestern city of slightly less than 100,000. The primary agencies of social control are probably typical of those in other cities of this size. The police Juvenile Bureau utilizes full-time officers in the handling of juvenile offenders. A three person probation department, one of whom is a female, carries out both intake and supervisory functions as an arm of the juvenile court. Finally, the juvenile court judge is also a judge of the Municipal Court and devotes two half-days a week to juvenile matters.

The principal sources of data utilized consist of police records on file in the Juvenile Bureau covering the period from January 1, 1958, through December 31, 1962. These records provided information with respect to most of the variables utilized, but the records of the County Probation Department were used for information concerning the dispositions accorded by the probation department and the juvenile court. In addition, city directories provided the chief source for obtaining parental occupations, and information provided by the Board of Education and City Planning Department was used in delineating and characterizing areas within the community.[23]

---

heavy industry, and railroads by the total amount of land within the school districts. Due to changes in school district boundaries, several of these districts were combined. The school districts in which offenses occurred were recorded. The final result is a ranking of nine areas in terms of the degree of their commercial/industrial development.

[18] Goffman argues that the individual's biography is composed of both past and present events and characteristics which function so as to establish the individual's identity. Of special relevance here is what he calls "social identity," or those attributes which are observable by others and which thereby provide a basis for categorization of the individual as a particular "kind" of person. Certainly one's age, sex, and place of residence are of primary importance in making such categorizations. Although none of these variables is inherently linked to the unfavorability dimension of our major hypothesis, the theoretical literature in deviant behavior rather clearly indicates that being a male, an older juvenile, and residing in high-delinquency areas tend to be viewed as unfavorable "attributes" by agents of social control. See Goffman, *Stigma*, 1–104 (1963).

[19] The "maleness" of the offender was obtained by ranking the nominal variable sex as follows: (1) female; (2) male.

[20] Age was measured by ascertaining the offender's age at the time of the offense. Since relatively few young juveniles engage in delinquent behavior, some of the younger ages were combined. This resulted in the following ranking: (1) 6–8; (2) 9–10; (3) 11–12; (4) 13; (5) 14; (6) 15; (7) 16; (8) 17.

[21] Utilizing school districts as the basis for establishing areas, the delinquency rates of the areas were computed and ranked from lowest to highest. Several school districts were combined due to boundary changes during the period under study, the result being a ranking of nine areas.

[22] See the excellent discussion of dispositions accorded juveniles by control agencies in *Wisconsin Handbook for Juvenile Court Services* (1959).

[23] For extensive discussions of the adequacy of the data see Terry, "The Screening of Juvenile Offenders: A Study in the Societal Reaction of

Since the screening process operates in such a way as to eliminate the vast majority of juvenile offenders from the legal-judicial process before reaching the juvenile court stage, a universe of offenses was utilized in preference to a sample. This insured that enough cases would be included at later stages in the process in order to permit adequate statistical manipulation.[24]

The result is a "universe" of 9,023 juvenile offenses at the police level. Of these offenses, 775 were referred to the County Probation Department and 246 of these were eventually referred to the juvenile court. The necessity for utilizing a universe rather than a sample should be obvious.

Since much of our data is ordinal, the principal statistical measure used is Kendall's rank correlation coefficient, tau.[25] This measure permits more extensive statistical analyses than other rank order correlation coefficients in that it is generalizable to a partial coefficient ($tau_{xy.z}$).[26]

Since we are not, strictly speaking, utilizing a sample, however, the problem of the significance of relationships we may find becomes important. Since we are not generalizing from a

Table 1

Distribution of Dispositions

	N	%
Police department		
Released	8,014	88.8
Referred to social or welfare agency	180	2.0
Referred to county probation department	775	8.6
Referred to state department of public welfare	54	0.6
Total	9,023	100.0
Probation department		
Released	229	29.5
Informal supervision	243	31.4
Referred to juvenile court	246	31.7
Waiver to criminal court	57	7.4
Total	775	100.0
Juvenile court		
Formal supervision	94	38.2
Institutionalized	152	61.8
Total	246	100.0

sample to a universe, the usual testing of hypotheses as being "statistically significant" does not apply. Therefore, some arbitrary criterion must be selected in order that unimportant findings may be dealt with accordingly.

Previous research into the study of the societal reactions to deviant behavior indicates that the relationships that may be found to exist are frequently of relatively small magnitude. This may be due to the fact that a large number of independent variables may be of importance. In view of this, *we will reject all hypotheses when $-.10 < tau < +.10$, except when the matrix indicates that the direction of the relationship is consistent for each category of the independent variable despite the introduction of control variables.* This criterion does not appear to be overly stringent.

Results

The data presented in Table 1 demonstrate that the vast majority of offenses committed do not result in formal action by control agents. In fact, a significant majority of offenses result in the release of the offender by the police and thereby never eventuate in juvenile court hear-

---

Deviant Behavior" (unpublished dissertation, University of Wisconsin, 1965).

[24] A number of types of offenders and/or offenses were eliminated from the universe. These include: (1) non-residents of the city, since the police lacked jurisdiction over these individuals; (2) traffic offenses, which were subjected to procedural handling which differed from that governing the handling of other offenses; (3) "offenders" under the age of six, since these children are regarded as being too young to engage in what could be considered delinquent behavior; (4) information types of offenses which, although recorded by the police, consisted of contacts with the police as a result of being a victim, providing information concerning offenses and/or offenders, being wrongly accused of delinquent behavior, or being suspected of having committed delinquent acts.

[25] See Kendall, *Rank Correlation Methods* (1948); Siegel, *Nonparametric Statistics*, 213–229 (1956).

[26] We will use partialling techniques only when two independent variables are significantly related to each other and when at least one is significantly related to the dependent variable. See Zetterberg, *On Theory and Verification in Sociology*, 61–66 (1963).

Table 2

Relationships Between the Independent Variables and the Severity of Sanctions Accorded Juvenile Offenders

Hypothesis number	Independent variable	Police	Probation	Juvenile court
1.1	Seriousness of offense committed	.35	.18	—.12[a]
2.1	Number of previous offenses committed	.25	.16	.28
3.1	Socio-economic status	—.04[a]	—.02[a]	—.09[a]
4.1	Degree of minority status	.02[a]	.01[a]	.04[a]
5.1	Number of individuals involved	—.06[a]	—.01[a]	—.17
5.2	Degree of involvement with offenders of the opposite sex	.04[a]	—.04[a]	.06[a]
5.3	Degree of involvement with adults	.09	.07[a]	.15
5.4	Formality of the social control function of the complainant	.01[a]	.03[a]	.08[a]
6.1	Degree of commercial/industrial development of area in which offense occurs	.05[a]	.06[a]	.10
7.1	"Maleness"	—.05[a]	.07[a]	—.11[b]
7.2	Age	.18	.18	.11
7.3	Delinquency rate of area of residence	.01[a]	.04[a]	.03[a]

[a] Hypothesis rejected.
[b] Hypothesis rejected and alternate hypothesis substituted.

ings, intake procedures on the part of the probation department, or action by any other agencies.

The relationships between our independent variables and the severity of dispositions at each of the levels of the screening process are summarized in Table 2. It is readily apparent that most of the sub-hypotheses must be rejected in that the relevant correlation coefficients do not meet our criteria for significance. Furthermore, some variation is evident among those hypotheses that are not rejected when agencies are compared with one another.

At the police level of screening, significant relationships in the hypothesized direction are evident between the seriousness of the offense committed, the number of previous offenses committed, and the age of the offender and the severity of sanctions. These relationships are generally independent from the influence of the remaining variables. The degree of involvement with adults approaches significance and retains a consistency of direction although reduced in magnitude when age is controlled (Table 3). The related sub-hypothesis is therefore not rejected. Each of the remaining sub-hypotheses is rejected at the police level.

At the probation department level of screening the findings are similar, although only three of the sub-hypotheses are supported and, where support exists, it is less significant than the support evident at the police level. Only the seriousness of the offense committed, the number of previous offenses committed, and the age of the offender are significantly related to the severity of sanctions accorded by the probation department. Again, these relationships are not substantially affected when the remaining independent variables are controlled. All of the remaining sub-hypotheses must be rejected.

At the juvenile court, a wider variety of criteria appear to be utilized and several variables that appear to be unimportant at earlier stages in the screening process become significant at the juvenile court stage. Significant relationships in the hypothesized direction are evident between the number of previous offenses committed, the number of individuals involved in an offense, the degree of involvement with adults, the age of the offender, and the degree of commercial/industrial development in the area in which the offense occurs and the severity of dispositions accorded. Although several of these relationships are affected when control variables are introduced (Table 3), the status of the related hypotheses remains unaltered.

Finally, a significant *negative* relationship exists between the "maleness" of the offender and the severity of juvenile court dispositions (tau = −.11). Three of our independent variables affect this relationship when used as controls (Table 3). These reflect the tendency for females to be overrepresented in terms of involvement with both the opposite sex and adults and, at the same time, to have less serious records of previous delinquent behavior than males. The first two detract from the importance of the variable as a possible criterion while the latter indicated that the "maleness" of the offender is of even greater importance than is superficially apparent.[27] The sub-hypothesis is rejected and replaced by an alternate hypothesis which posits a negative relationship between the "maleness" of the offender and the severity of juvenile court sanctions.

Each of the remaining sub-hypotheses is rejected. Especially noteworthy is the negative relationship between seriousness of offense committed and the severity of juvenile court dispositions. Although this negative relationship is substantial, the positing of the alternate hypothesis does not seem plausible. Rather, the relationship that exists appears to be a function of the broad categories used in measuring the seriousness of offense committed. Also, since the independent variable in question has been utilized as a criterion by both the police and the probation department, it is probable that the types of offenses which reach the juvenile court tend to be similar in seriousness.[28] This similarity does not become evident

Table 3
Significant Effects of Control Variables [a]

	Police	Juvenile court
Number of previous offenses		
"Maleness" controlled	.22	.31
Age controlled	.22	—
Involvement with adults		
Age controlled	.05	.13
"Maleness" controlled	—	.12
Age		
Number of previous offenses controlled	.12	—
Involvement with adults controlled	.16	.09
Involvement with opp. sex controlled	—	.09
"Maleness"		
Involvement with adults controlled	—	−.07
Involvement with opp. sex controlled	—	−.08
Number of previous offenses controlled	—	−.18

[a] Significant independent variables at the probation department level are unaffected by the introduction of control variables.

in terms of the broad categories used. It should also be pointed out that while the relationship between the socio-economic status of the offender and the severity of juvenile court disposition approaches significance (tau = −.09), this relationship appears to be a function of differences in prior records of delinquent behavior on the part of offenders of varying statuses. When the number of previous offenses committed is controlled, for example, the relationship in question becomes negligible (tau$_{xy\,.z}$ = −.02).

Conclusions

The status of the major hypotheses is summarized in Table 4. Consistently negative evidence leads to the rejection of two of our major hypotheses at each of the levels of the

[27] Our data do not permit us to account for this negative finding. Speculatively, however, the harsher handling of females might indicate that appearance in the juvenile court by females is regarded with more disdain since such appearances tend to be incompatible with common conceptions of the female role.

[28] While the three least serious offenses comprise 65% and the three most serious offenses comprise 6% of all offenses appearing in the police records, the three least serious offenses comprise only 9% of the offenses that appear in the juvenile court

and the three most serious offenses comprise over 66% of the offenses appearing in the juvenile court records.

screening process. The severity of the societal reaction does not appear to be a function of either the power of the deviant or the social distance that exists between the deviant and agents of social control. These findings are significant in and of themselves in view of the vast amount of criminological literature that has taken the hypothesized relationships for granted.[29]

Only one of the major hypotheses is completely and consistently supported at the three stages of the legal-judicial process. This would seem to indicate that the severity of the societal reaction is a function, at least in part, of the amount of deviance engaged in by the offender. Also relevant, but less clearly so, are the degree of the deviation, the unfavorability of the personal and social biography of the deviant, the place in which the deviance is committed, and the unfavorability of the situation in which the deviance is committed. Each of these was supported to some extent at one or more of the stages of the screening process. At the same time, however, they are subject to qualification in that they were not consistently supported by: (1) each of the sub-hypotheses utilized as indicators of the major hypothesis and/or (2) tests of the sub-hypotheses at each of the three stages of the screening process. As they are stated, some of them appear to be too vague to be of much use in the study of the societal reaction.

Generally speaking, the severity of sanctions accorded juvenile offenders varies considerably from agency to agency. The police appear to utilize basically legalistic criteria in making disposition decisions. The variables that are regarded as criteria are the same as those which could be expected to guide their handling of adult offenders as well. In other words, the police appear to interpret the "best interests of the child" in terms of criteria also used when dealing with adult offenders.

While similar variables were found to be significant at the probation department level, they apparently do not possess the same de-

---

[29] Nearly any criminology, delinquency, or social problems text may serve as a reference to the fact that lower-status offenders, Negroes and Mexican-Americans, and males are thought to be discriminated against by agents of social control.

Table 4
Status of Major Hypotheses

Status	Police	Probation	Juvenile court
Supported	Amount Degree	Amount Degree	Amount Place
Partially supported	Biography Situation	Biography	Biography Situation
Not supported	Power Distance Place	Power Distance Place Situation	Power Distance Degree

gree of explanatory power. That is, those relationships which were found to be significant were of relatively small magnitude. While these variables may be regarded as legalistic in orientation, it seems reasonable to assume that other variables, untapped in this research, are of greater significance. Given the emphasis in contemporary social work upon family-related variables as being of crucial importance in delinquency causation and treatment, the use of these variables might provide a useful manner of approaching the screening process as carried out at the probation department level.[30]

The juvenile court judge utilizes a broader range of criteria than do either the police or the probation department. The criteria used tend to be partially legally based, but they are also significantly dependent upon the situation in which the offense is committed and the unfavorability of the personal and social biography of the offender. This seems to indicate an attempt at the "individualization" of sanctions by the juvenile court and, at the same time, an attempt to find criteria that are relevant given the previous decisions made in terms of legalistic criteria by the police and the probation department. Given that the number of previous offenses committed, age, degree of involvement with adult offenders, and number of individuals involved in an offense constitute some of the criteria utilized, the juvenile court's sanctioning of delinquent behavior may be indicative of a concern with

---

[30] See, e.g., Kinney, Klem, and Myers, *supra* note 7.

the *extensiveness* of the individual's involvement in delinquent activities.

The variations that exist between agencies may be a function of the differences in orientation which characterize the agents of social control. If the police, probation officers, and juvenile court judges vary in terms of their conceptions of delinquency causation, delinquency prevention, and the rehabilitation of delinquents, we may expect corresponding variations in their reactions to delinquent behavior. On the other hand, variations may be due in large part to the characteristics of the offenders who appear before each of the agencies. Thus, the populations that are screened at each of the stages vary in terms of a number of important respects and the criteria utilized in according sanctions may derive from this rather than from preconceived notions concerning what is in the child's best interests. Probably, these are mutually reinforcing dimensions of the same problem.[31]

Clearly, further research which takes into account greater variety of independent variables, the orientation of agents of social control, other possibly relevant social audiences, and a number of communities is called for. Beyond this, however, greater attention must also be given to theoretical formulations with respect to what the societal reaction consists of and how and why it varies. This research has certainly indicated that present theoretical formulations along these lines are far from being adequate.

Discussion

In terms of the theoretical orientation utilized in this research, the development of career deviance concomitant with the adoption of a deviant role is a function of the societal reaction to behavior that has been identified and defined as deviant. Career deviance is thus closely linked to the severity of the reactions that take place in that as the reactions become more severe, the greater is the likelihood that the offender will be accorded a deviant status, and subsequently, develop a deviant role.

The screening process is of crucial significance for discovering the processes by which juveniles come to acquire the legal status of delinquent, i.e., adjudication as a delinquent by the juvenile court.[32] The acquisition of this status has been shown to be dependent upon much more than simply committing a delinquent act or even a delinquent act of considerable severity. A constellation of other factors seem to be operating so as to prevent even the majority of those offenders committing the most serious types of acts from acquiring this status. As we have indicated, these factors include not only the degree of the deviation, but also the amount of deviance engaged in, the situations in which the deviance is committed, the place where the deviance occurs, and the unfavorability of the personal and social biography of the deviant. This leads to the implication that many juveniles who have acquired the legal status of "delinquent" differ from many juveniles who have not acquired this status in terms of a number of characteristics, but *not necessarily* in terms of having engaged in different types of delinquent behavior.

The legal status of delinquent does not seem to be easily attainable, however. While a chief function of primary agencies of social control is to identify, define, and sanction juvenile offenders (i.e., to accord deviant statuses), our evidence indicates that these agencies give the offender ample opportunity to avoid the status. This is indicated by the fact that the number of previous offenses is consistently significant as a criterion in the screening process. It is usually only after failure (and, generally, repeated failure) to discontinue the commission of delinquent acts that juveniles find themselves appearing in the juvenile court for adjudication as a juvenile delinquent.[33] The key

---

[31] See Becker, *Outsiders, supra* note 1 at 161.

[32] See Turk, "Prospects for Theories of Criminal Behavior," 55 *J. Crim. L., C. & P. S.,* 457–458 (1964).

[33] First offenses constitute 38.2% of the offenses occurring at the police level of analysis, but only 7.3% of those at the juvenile court level and 4.0% of the offenses that result in institutionalization. On the other hand, offenses involving offenders who have committed five or more previous offenses constitute 20.4% of the offenses occurring at the police level of analysis, but 58.1% of those at the juvenile court level and 70.4% of the offenses that result in institutionalization.

here does not seem to be "normalization" of the delinquent behavior, but instead the withholding of the more severe sanctions available to each agency of social control until the offender demonstrates by further misbehavior that the use of these sanctions is warranted. While sheer chance might result in the identification of the offender as one who has engaged in delinquent behavior, the acquisition of the status of a delinquent appears to involve considerably more than chance. In general, it involves especially the commission of the more serious types of delinquent acts, persistence in the commission of these acts, and commission by juveniles who are approaching the age of legal responsibility for their actions.

If this is the case, there are interesting theoretical and methodological implications for the study of delinquent behavior. The data available from primary agencies of social control may provide a more adequate indication of career delinquents rather than of delinquent behavior as such. If systematic deviant behavior characterizes the career deviant, then many juveniles who eventually appear in the juvenile court and who are institutionalized must be so classified since they have progressed to these stages in the legal-judicial process by virtue of relatively persistent delinquent behavior. A more adequate understanding of the functioning of the screening process may lead to a more accurate delineation of the processes involved in career deviance as well as a more accurate assessment of the meaning of official statistics on crime and delinquency.

But there are practical implications involved as well. While our research has focused on only some of the many variables that may be relevant in screening, it seems to be a safe conclusion that legalistic variables play a significant role in the process at all of the stages considered. The use of full-time juvenile specialists in police and probation departments has not apparently produced drastic shifts in the bases for handling juvenile offenders. Instead, the seriousness of the offense committed, the offender's previous record, his age, and other variables that may be readily correlated with how control agents are thought to handle adults assume the greatest overall importance of all the variables used in this research. Presumably, they would remain important even if other variables had been introduced.

If the more severe dispositions (referrals supervision, institutionalization, etc.) are designed to prevent further misbehavior on the part of offenders so disposed of, then control agents utilize these dispositions on the basis of criteria which may not necessarily be most appropriate. That is, before counselling services, probation supervision, institutional correctional programs, and other facilities are implemented the offender must generally have committed serious offenses, committed a number of previous offenses, and be relatively old. Offenders who may warrant and, perhaps, profit by these programs and services are generally denied access to them if they do not meet these criteria.

It appears to be necessary, then, to involve control agents in training programs in which they are informed that a variety of characteristics and/or situations other than simple legalistic variables may be used to predict the future behavior of offenders and that the utilization of such might be a more adequate means of selecting dispositions that will eventuate in the prevention of further delinquent behavior. As the situation exists at present, it is apparent that delinquent careers may be fairly well underway before formal rehabilitative measures are implemented.

In May, 1967, the Supreme Court of the United States reversed the adjudication of Gerald Gault, a fifteen-year-old boy from Arizona, who was charged with making lewd phone calls and committed to the State Training

School. In this selection Neigher discusses the implications of the historic *Gault* decision in which the Supreme Court examined the process of adjudication in juvenile courts and considered for the first time the constitutional rights of children in juvenile courts.

To place the *Gault* decision in its proper constitutional perspective, Neigher provides a useful discussion of the "basic protections" provided by the Bill of Rights, as well as the historical bases for these protections. In the *Gault* decision the Supreme Court considered the applicability of six constitutional rights to juvenile court cases: (1) the right to notice of the charge of delinquency, (2) the right to counsel, (3) the privilege against self-incrimination, (4) the right to confront and cross-examine complainants and witnesses, (5) the right to a transcript of the proceedings, and (6) the right to appellate review of the juvenile court's decision. Although the Court did not rule on the last two issues, it did officially introduce the concept of due process into juvenile courts. It ruled that when a petition is filed alleging that a child is delinquent, the child and his parents must be given adequate and timely notice of the hearing and the nature of the charges — an elementary requirement for fairness. In proceedings to determine delinquency in which a juvenile's freedom and parental custody are in jeopardy, as is the case if the hearing may result in commitment of the child to an institution, the child and his parents not only must be given written notice of the hearing and the particulars of the alleged misconduct, but also must be notified of the child's right to be represented by counsel. If the parents cannot afford to retain counsel, a lawyer must be appointed to represent the child. The Court also concluded that the privilege against self-incrimination is applicable in proceedings involving juveniles as it is in criminal cases, and finally, the Court stated that if the child does not make a valid confession, he has the right to confront his accusers at the hearing and to have the alleged act of delinquency proven by sworn testimony of witnesses who are available for cross-examination.

Although these points are extremely important, the scope of *Gault* is limited. The Court did not demand that the juvenile court become a juvenile criminal court; it did not extend all of the constitutional rights and procedures granted to adults in criminal courts to children in juvenile courts. The constitutional issues involved in the introduction of hearsay evidence in a juvenile court remain unanswered, as do the questions regarding unreasonable searches and seizures, grand jury indictment, double jeopardy, a speedy trial, a public trial, excessive bail, excessive fines, and cruel and unusual punishment, to name only a few. Because it deals only with a limited number of constitutional rights of juveniles facing adjudication as delinquents, the *Gault* decision also leaves unanswered many other questions concerning the legal process for juveniles. The opinion does not deal with procedures or constitutional rights in the pre-judicial phase, such as intake procedures or the informal handling of cases by the police, nor does it consider the post-adjudicative stage, that is, the disposition of a case after a finding of delinquency.

Another decision of the Supreme Court deserves mention. Although the Court had considered the question of interrogation of children in 1962 (Rubin [1963]), it examined a specific procedure of the juvenile court for the first time in the case of *Kent.* In 1966 the Court reviewed the case of Kent, a sixteen-year-old from the District of Columbia, who was arrested on a charge of rape. Although confined to the narrow issue of the transfer of a case from the juvenile to the criminal court by means of waiver, the Court's opinion in *Kent,* as Neigher observes in his epilogue, was a prologue to *Gault.* (See an earlier selection entitled "Procedural Justice for the Juvenile" for a further discussion of *Kent.*) Rubin (1967:356) describes the case as follows: "After interrogation by the police and detention at the Receiving Home, the juvenile court judge entered an order reciting that, after 'full investigation,' he waived the jurisdiction of the juvenile court and transferred Kent for criminal trial. In criminal court Kent was convicted and sentenced to a prison term of thirty to ninety years. The juvenile court made no findings and recited no reason for the waiver. The District of Columbia juvenile court law states no criteria or procedure on waiver, merely requiring 'full investigation.' The Supreme Court held that, in addition to the 'investigation provision,' there must be 'procedural regularity sufficient in the particular circumstances to satisfy the basic requirements of due process and fairness,' and it cited a hearing, effective assistance of counsel, and a statement of reasons as elements of such requirements. It implied that, in general, juvenile courts should provide greater protection for the child, not less than that afforded adults in criminal trials." In emphasizing the basic requirements of due process and fairness the Court laid the groundwork for its historic *Gault* decision.

REFERENCES

Sol Rubin, "Developments in Correctional Law," *Crime and Delinquency,* 9 (April 1963), pp. 189–198.
———, "Developments in Correctional Law," *Crime and Delinquency,* 13 (April 1967), pp. 356–366.

ALAN NEIGHER

The Gault *Decision: Due Process and the Juvenile Courts*

On May 15, 1967, the Supreme Court of the United States ruled that juvenile courts must grant to children many of the procedural protections required in adult criminal trials by the Bill of Rights. In this, the *Gault* [1] decision, the Supreme Court for the first time con-

From *Federal Probation,* 31 (December 1967), 8–18. Reprinted by permission.
[1] *In Re Gault,* 387 U.S. 1 (1967).

sidered the constitutional rights of children in juvenile courts.

It is not questioned that *Gault* will have a major impact on the future of juvenile courts in this country, many of which having for years operated under a philosophy that made ordinary procedural safeguards seem evil. It is submitted, however, that the *Gault* decision is neither a panacea for children in trouble nor an onerous burden for juvenile law enforcement officers. The decision will hopefully protect young people from being given indeterminate "correctional" sentences for making allegedly obscene phone calls that no one thinks necessary to verify. The decision may make life a bit more difficult for judges and probation officers. It is clear that at the very least, *Gault* will grant some semblance of consistent legal protection to the child.

But there are some popular misconceptions concerning the scope of *Gault*. As an example, the front page of the May 16, 1967, *New York Times* headlined an otherwise excellent summary of the decision as follows: "High Court Rules Adult Code Holds in Juvenile Trials . . . Finds Children Are Entitled to the Basic Protections Given in Bill of Rights." [2] But the decision does not accord to juveniles all of the protections of the Bill of Rights. All juvenile courts — with the exception of the District of Columbia — are, in fact, state courts. The Bill of Rights has not yet been made applicable in its entirety to state criminal proceedings. Further, the *Gault* decision was limited to but a few Bill of Rights issues. This must be kept in mind, although, as will be later noted, the decision was as significant for what it *suggested* as it was for what it actually held as binding legal precedent.

Thus, before the decision may be discussed in terms of its implications for the juvenile courts, a brief examination is in order as to what the "basic protections" of the Bill of Rights are, and whether these protections have been extended to state (and thereby juvenile) proceedings.

Bill of Rights and the Fourteenth Amendment

The Bill of Rights [3] means the first Ten Amendments to the newly written Federal

[2] *New York Times*, May 16, 1967, p. 1, col. 1 (city ed.).

[3] For excellent summaries of the entire Constitution from which much of the following material on the Bill of Rights is drawn, see Antieau, *Commentaries on the Constitution of the United States (1960)*, and The Younger Lawyers Committee of the Federal Bar Association, *These Unalienable Rights* (1965).

Constitution, proposed to the state legislatures by the First Congress in 1789. The Bill of Rights was intended to be a series of limitations on the three *federal* branches: The Congress, the Executive, and the Judiciary. These proposed limitations were a practical political necessity, to mollify local concern over the sanctity of state autonomy in many areas of the law, and thereby speed ratification by the necessary nine state legislatures.

Of these Ten Amendments, six are not directly related to the criminal process. These are the First, Second, Third, Seventh, Ninth, and Tenth. Left for consideration, therefore, are the Fourth, Fifth, Sixth, and Eighth Amendments. And of these four, the Fourth and Eighth were not at issue in *Gault* and will be treated briefly.

Before these Amendments are discussed, the Fourteenth Amendment must be considered because it is closely related to the concept of federalism and because it affects not only those Amendments related to the criminal process, but also the entire Ten Amendments and their applicability to the states.

The Bill of Rights was expressly intended to be a check on federal power. There was nothing in the original Constitution to prevent the states from formulating their own systems of criminal administration, and indeed, the Tenth Amendment provides that "The powers not delegated to the United States by the Constitution; nor prohibited by it to the States, are reserved to the States respectively, or to the people."

After the Civil War, almost a century after the ratification of the Constitution (which included the Bill of Rights), Amendments Thirteen, Fourteen, and Fifteen were enacted, largely for the benefit of the newly emancipated slaves. Amendment Thirteen abolished slavery; Amendment Fifteen provided that race, color, or previous condition of servitude shall not be a disability for voting.

Amendment Fourteen was written partly to assure fair and equitable treatment on the part of state authorities to the newly emancipated. For our purposes, its most pertinent part is Section 1, which provides: ". . . No State shall make or enforce any law which shall abridge the privileges or immunities of citizens of the United States; nor shall any State deprive any person of life, liberty, or property, *without due process of law;* nor deny to any person within its jurisdiction the equal protection of the laws."

Thus, the "due process" clause of the Fifth Amendment was made applicable to the states. However, the vague and sweeping concept of due process was slow in making its impact felt on the states which had been left virtually autonomous in formulating criminal procedures. But in recent years, on a case-by-case basis, the Supreme Court has made *some* of the Bill of Rights protection binding on the states through the due process clause of the Fourteenth Amendment. Of those protections now applicable to the states included are several under those Amendments not relevant to the criminal process (especially freedom of speech under the First Amendment), and these need not be considered here.

The Fourth Amendment was largely a reaction to the Writs of Assistance issued in the colonies prior to the Revolution, which gave British revenue officers nearly unlimited authority to search private dwellings and to seize goods. Consequently, the Fourth Amendment reflects the Founders' jealous regard of the right to privacy — to be secure against unreasonable invasion of one's person, property, and home. The Fourth Amendment now applies in full to both federal and state authorities.

The Fourth Amendment provides for the security of people "in their persons, houses, papers, and effects against unreasonable searches and seizures." The laws pertaining to warrants — for both search and arrest — are too technical to be set out here. Suffice it to say that, as to searches and seizures of property, unless there is consent, individuals and their possessions or dwellings cannot be searched or seized without a warrant, except when this is justified by the surrounding circumstances and is done in a reasonable manner.

The Fourth Amendment prohibits unwarranted and unreasonable arrests, but it does not require that the police obtain a warrant for every arrest. The police may arrest without a warrant where the arresting officer actu-

ally sees the commission of a misdemeanor or a felony; also, the arresting officer may arrest without a warrant when he has "probable cause" to believe a felony has been committed. Probable cause is difficult to define precisely, but it may generally be stated that it is the existence of such facts and circumstances as would lead a reasonable person to believe that the suspect to be arrested is guilty of the offense.

Where a warrant must be obtained, it must specifically describe the person to be arrested. A general warrant — one that is to be filled in at the arresting officer's convenience — is not valid. An arrest made pursuant to an invalid warrant is unlawful. A warrant for either arrest or search and seizure may be issued only by a magistrate or judge; police officers have no authority to issue warrants.

The Fifth Amendment

The First Congress included a specific provision regarding grand jury indictments as the first clause of the Fifth Amendment. The purpose of the provision is to insure that persons will not be brought to trial arbitrarily when there is no reasonable basis for believing they are guilty of a crime, and that those who are brought to trial will be adequately informed of the charges against them. The Supreme Court has held that the due process clause of the Fourteenth Amendment does not require a state to provide grand jury indictment, so long as the state provides other means of insuring justice to the accused.

The next clause provides that no person "shall . . . be subject for the same offence to be twice put in jeopardy of life or limb." The Founders' sense of fair play led them to include in the Fifth Amendment the concept that the Government should not be able to harass and persecute a man by trying him repeatedly for the same offense. The double jeopardy prohibition has not yet been binding on the states. However, the states are bound by the due process clause of the Fourteenth Amendment; thus, successive trials which flaunt the principles of justice and fair play are not permitted.

The Fifth Amendment next provides that no

person "shall be compelled in any criminal case to be a witness against himself. . . ." The history of inquisition and torture in the Old World gave the Founders ample reason to provide against the idea that a man should be forced to incriminate himself by his own words. The privilege has two aspects: (1) the right to be free from coercion designed to extract a confession; and (2) the right to remain silent without having an inference of guilt drawn from that silence.

Freedom from coerced confessions has long been recognized as basic to due process and neither federal nor state governments may extract a confession by force. Force need not be physical; mental coercion such as threats or interrogation to the point of exhaustion would make a confession coerced, and thereby invalid.

The second aspect of the privilege against self-incrimination is the right to remain silent. This is the right invoked by those who "take the Fifth." This right, too, has recently been extended to apply to the states under the Fourteenth Amendment. A criminal defendant has the right to refuse to testify entirely; his failure to take the stand may not even be commented upon by the prosecution in either the federal or state courts. A witness, on the other hand, must take the stand if called, and must claim the privilege one question at a time. The privilege applies not only to criminal trials, but extends also to those before congressional committees, grand juries, and administrative agencies.[4]

The privilege against self-incrimination was highly relevant to the *Gault* decision.

Following the self-incrimination provision appears the most sweeping concept of American jurisprudence: that no person shall "be deprived of life, liberty or property without due process of law." We have seen that the "due process" concept was later duplicated in the Fourteenth Amendment.

If there exists a legal concept not susceptible

[4] The privilege has one notable exception: A person has no right to remain silent if a statute (federal or state) gives him immunity from prosecution — that is, if the government is prevented from prosecuting him on the basis of his testimony.

of precise definition it is due process. It means justice; it means judicial fair play. It is perhaps the very essence of our constitutional tradition. It is both "substantive" and "procedural" — it prohibits the making of laws that are unfair in themselves, and it prohibits unfair application of the law.

Due process applies to Congress in its lawmaking authority, and forbids laws that are arbitrary or unreasonable. And when the Executive Branch exercises a law-making or rule-making function, it, too, must exercise substantive due process.

Procedural due process requires that the laws, once made, be applied fairly. It means than an individual has the right to be fairly heard before he stands to lose life, liberty, or property. It requires a fair trial in a criminal case and a hearing by an impartial tribunal in a property case.

Procedural due process considerations were at the heart of the *Gault* decision.

The Sixth Amendment

The Sixth Amendment is of particular importance to the *Gault* decision. Of the entire Bill of Rights, it is the one most particularly concerned with the rights of an accused in a Federal criminal trial. The text of the Sixth Amendment follows:

In all criminal prosecutions, the accused shall enjoy the right to a speedy and public trial, by an impartial jury of the State and District wherein the crime shall have been committed, which District shall have been previously ascertained by law, *and to be informed of the nature and cause of the accusations; to be confronted with the witnesses against him;* to have compulsory process for obtaining witnesses in his favor, *and to have the assistance of Counsel for his defense.* [Emphasis added.]

The right to a jury trial in criminal prosecutions was considered so important to the Founders that they included the right in the main body of the Constitution as well as in the Bill of Rights: Article III, Section 2, commands that the "Trials of all Crimes, except in Cases of Impeachment, shall be by Jury. . . ."

The Sixth Amendment establishes the basic requirement that the accused be tried by the traditional jury of 12. On the other hand, the states are *not* required to provide trial by jury, although many do by virtue of their own constitutions. Some states provide for juries of 8 or 10, rather than 12. However, the Fourteenth Amendment mandate that the states provide due process requires that whatever form of trial the states do provide must be fair.

Not "all criminal prosecutions" by the Federal Government require jury trials. Military trials, criminal contempt proceedings, or petty offenses punishable by small fines or short periods of imprisonment may be conducted without juries. When the right to jury trial applies, this right may be waived, and the defendant may be tried by a judge alone, where both the defendant and the Government so agree, with the consent of the trial judge.

The Sixth Amendment further provides that "the accused enjoy . . . a speedy and public trial." The history of the Inquisition and the Court of the Star Chamber was not lost on the Founding Fathers. These Courts were notorious for their practices of detaining accused persons for long periods, and interrogating witnesses in secret. The Sixth Amendment provided against these abuses by insuring that the accused has the right to defend himself while witnesses and evidence are still available. The wisdom of this protection is readily apparent if one considers the anxiety involved in a prolonged criminal prosecution. Thus, if an accused is not afforded a speedy trial, he may not be tried at all. As to what constitutes a "speedy trial" suffice it to say that standards of reasonableness must govern. The right to a speedy trial has not yet been held binding upon the states under the Fourteenth Amendment, although an obvious prolongment would probably violate due process.

The right to a *public* trial is a basic right under due process, and this right does extend to defendants in trials conducted by the states. The presence of the public and representatives of the press acts as a guarantee that the court will proceed appropriately. The Supreme Court has not yet determined whether all trials must be freely open to the public or whether circumstances will permit a limitation on the type of spectators allowed.

The next protection afforded under the Sixth Amendment is the right to an impartial jury. The definition of "impartial" as used here has two aspects. First, there must be an opportunity for a cross section of the community to serve as jurors. Exclusion because of race, religion, national origin, or economic status violates the defendant's Sixth Amendment rights, whether the trial be federal or state. The cross-section concept does *not* require that every jury be composed of all the various racial, religious, ethnic, or economic groups of the community. It does prohibit court officials from *systematically* excluding any of these groups.

Second, the right to an impartial jury also involves the problem of publicity surrounding the trial. The First Amendment guarantees of free speech and freedom of the press must be balanced against the accused's right to be accorded a jury that will consider his case with an open mind. Modern communications techniques have added great complexity to this problem. The Supreme Court held in the case of Dr. Sam Sheppard that due process is violated where widespread newspaper publicity saturates the community so as to make it virtually impossible to find a panel of impartial jurors.

The Sixth Amendment next requires that a person be tried by "an impartial jury of the State and District wherein the crime shall have been committed, which District shall have been previously ascertained by law." This provision insures that a person will be tried only in that area where the crime was committed — where evidence and witnesses should be readily available, unless circumstances dictate that an impartial trial can only be had elsewhere. It is also required that Congress define in advance the boundaries of the Districts in which crimes shall be tried. The Supreme Court has not yet dealt with the issue of whether the due process clause of the Fourteenth Amendment limits the states in determining where trials for state offenses may be held.

Of great relevance to the *Gault* decision is the next phrase of the Sixth Amendment, which provides that the accused shall enjoy the right "to be informed of the nature and cause of the accusation." Thus, the accused must be informed of the charges against him sufficiently in advance of the court proceedings to allow him a reasonable opportunity to prepare a defense. Also, such notice must specify the alleged misconduct with reasonable particularity. Again this guarantee obtains, whether the trial be federal or state.

The second clause of the Sixth Amendment also was critical to the *Gault* decision. It provides that the accused shall enjoy the right "to be confronted with the witnesses against him." The philosophy underlying this clause is that the accused should be met by his accusers face-to-face, and be able to subject the testimony of the witnesses against him to cross-examination. The right to confrontation is a basic due process protection and applies to state, as well as to federal, courts.

The Sixth Amendment next provides that an accused be entitled to have the court compel witnesses to appear and testify if they are unwilling to come voluntarily. A refusal to so compel witnesses to testify on behalf of the accused violates the right to a fair trial, and consequently offends the due process clause. Although the Supreme Court has not dealt directly with the issue, it does not seem likely that such a basic fair trial protection would fail to be held binding on the states under the Fourteenth Amendment.

Finally, the Sixth Amendment provides that the accused shall "have the assistance of counsel for his defense." There was no right to counsel prior to the enactment of the Bill of Rights, and the accused had to rely on the graces of the trial judge to act as his counsel. The inclusion of this right in the Sixth Amendment reflected the belief of the Founders that most defendants are vastly unprepared to protect themselves against the resources of the state's prosecution machinery. The accused today in both federal and state proceedings has the right to counsel in felony cases, and in misdemeanor cases where the accused is in jeopardy of incarceration. In such cases, the recent *Escobedo* and *Miranda* decisions have extended the right to counsel beyond the trial stage; the accused is now entitled to counsel

when the investigation focuses upon him so as to attempt to elicit incriminating statements. The reader should note that it is at this point, also, that the Fifth Amendment's privilege against self-incrimination attaches.

The Eighth Amendment

Statutes prohibiting excessive bail and cruel and unusual punishment had been enacted in precolonial England and in the constitutions of a number of colonies. These prohibitions were reflected in the Eighth Amendment which reads: "Excessive bail shall not be required, nor excessive fines imposed, nor cruel and unusual punishment inflicted."

It has not been definitely settled whether the provisions of the Eighth Amendment are applicable to the states under the Fourteenth Amendment.

Bail is a mechanism designed to insure the appearance of a defendant in court; by posting bail, the defendant undertakes to guarantee his appearance in court or else forfeit a sum of money. The amount of bail required is generally set by the magistrate who commits an arrested person to custody. Not every accused person is entitled to bail — military personnel and those accused of capital crimes are generally denied such release. But where the accused is entitled to bail, the Eighth Amendment requires that it not be "excessive." Such factors as the defendant's criminal history, the seriousness of the crime and ability to pay are relevant to the issue of excessiveness. There is generally no right to bail after conviction pending appeal; requests for such bail are left largely to the discretion of the trial judge.

As to the excessive fine provision, it is generally left to Congress to prescribe the limits of fines and to the trial courts to decide what fine should be imposed in a particular case. The Supreme Court has refused to review fines levied by the lower federal courts.

There are no precise standards as to what constitutes cruel and unusual punishment. The death penalty is not of itself cruel and unusual; what is forbidden by very early tradition of Anglo-American law is the infliction of unnecessary pain in the execution of the death sentence.

It is apparent that the Eighth Amendment, like its companions, leaves many problems unanswered, especially because the Eighth Amendment's prohibitions are not yet binding on the states. The law of bail — especially as it applies to the indigent accused — is in a state of re-evaluation. There are those who have argued, in the wake of the Chessman case, that long delay in execution is cruel and unusual punishment; indeed, there are many who argue that by modern standards, the death penalty is itself cruel and unusual punishment.

It is not pretended that the above summary of certain of the Bill of Rights criminal protections is an authoritative treatise. Indeed, entire volumes have been written on some individual Amendments. It is only hoped that the reader be informed of these protections so that the *Gault* decision might be placed in its proper constitutional perspective.

The Case of the "Lewd and Indecent" Phone Call

Gerald and another boy were taken into custody in the morning of June 8, 1964, by the Sheriff of Gila County, Arizona. The police were acting upon a verbal complaint from a Mrs. Cook, a neighbor of the boys, that she received a lewd and indecent phone call. Both of Gerald's parents were at work that morning and no notice of the police action was left at their home. Gerald's mother learned of his being taken to the Children's Detention House only after Gerald's older brother went to look for him at the home of the other boy. At the Detention Home, the mother and brother were told "why Jerry was there" and that a hearing would be held the next day at 3 o'clock.

A petition praying for a hearing was filed on June 9 by an Officer Flagg which recited that "said minor is under the age of 18 years and in need of protection of this Honorable Court [and that] said minor is a delinquent minor." The petition was not served on the Gaults and they first saw it 2 months later.

On June 9, a hearing was held in the chambers of Juvenile Judge McGhee with Gerald, his mother, his brother and the probation officers being present. No formal or informal record of this hearing was made. Judge McGhee questioned Gerald about the telephone calls without advising him of a right to counsel or a privilege against self-incrimination. There is conflicting testimony as to Gerald's answers. Both Officer Flagg and Judge McGhee stated that Gerald admitted making at least one of the indecent remarks while Mrs. Gault recalled that her son only admitted dialing Mrs. Cook's number.

Gerald was released from the detention home without explanation on either the 11th or the 12th (again the memories of Mrs. Gault and Officer Flagg conflict) pending further hearings; a hearing was held before Judge McGhee on June 15th. Mrs. Gault asked that Mrs. Cook be present but was told by the Judge that "she didn't have to be present." Neither the Gaults nor Officer Flagg remembered any admission by Gerald at this proceeding of making the indecent remarks, though the judge did remember Gerald's admitting some of the less serious statements. At the conclusion of the hearing, Gerald was committed as a juvenile delinquent to the State Industrial School "for the period of his minority [6 years] unless sooner discharged by due process of law."

No appeal is permitted under Arizona law in juvenile cases. Gerald filed a writ of habeas corpus with the Supreme Court of Arizona which was referred to the Superior Court for hearing. Among other matters, Judge McGhee testified that he acted under a section of the Arizona Code which defines a "delinquent child" as one who (in the judge's words) is "habitually involved in immoral matters." The basis for the judge's conclusion seemed to be a referral made 2 years earlier concerning Gerald when the boy allegedly had "stolen" a baseball glove "and lied to the Police Department about it." No petition or hearing apparently resulted from this "referral." The judge testified that Gerald had violated the section of the Arizona Criminal Code which provides that a person who "in the presence of or hearing of any woman or child . . . uses vulgar, abusive or obscene language, is guilty of a misdemeanor. . . ." The penalty for an adult convicted under this section is a fine of $5 to $50, or imprisonment for not more than 2 months.

The Superior Court dismissed the habeas corpus petition, and Gerald sought review in the Arizona Supreme Court on many due process grounds. The Arizona Supreme Court affirmed the dismissal of the petition.

The appellants, in their appeal to the United States Supreme Court, did not raise all of the issues brought before the Supreme Court of Arizona. The appeal was based on the argument that the Juvenile Code of Arizona is invalid because, contrary to the due process clause of the Fourteenth Amendment, the juvenile is taken from the custody of his parents and committed to a state institution pursuant to proceedings where the Juvenile Court has virtually unlimited discretion, and in which the following basic rights are denied: Notice of the charges; right to counsel; right to confrontation and cross-examination; privilege against self-incrimination; right to a transcript of the proceedings; and right to appellate review.

These were the questions before the Supreme Court in the *Gault* decision. The Court explicitly noted that other issues passed upon by the Supreme Court of Arizona, but not presented by the appellants to the Supreme Court of the United States, would not be considered. This is consistent with the Court's strict practice of reviewing — if it chooses to review at all — only those issues actually presented to it.

The Decision

The *Gault* decision was handed down May 15, 1967, a little over 5 months after its oral argument was heard by the Supreme Court. Mr. Justice Fortas wrote the opinion for the majority which was, in effect, 8 to 1. Justice Fortas was joined by Chief Justice Warren and Justices Brennan, Clark, and Douglas. Mr. Justice Black concurred with the result but argued that juveniles in jeopardy of confinement be tried in accordance with all of the Bill of Rights protections made applicable to the states by the Fourteenth Amendment.[5] Mr. Justice White concurred with the majority except for Part V concerning self-incrimination, confrontation, and cross-examination which he

felt need not be reached, since the decision would be reversed on other grounds.[6] Mr. Justice Harlan concurred in part and dissented in part: he concurred with the majority insofar as it held that Gerald was deprived of due process of law by being denied adequate notice, record of the proceedings, and right to counsel; he dissented on the grounds that the other procedural safeguards imposed by the Court might discourage "efforts to find more satisfactory solutions for the problems of juvenile crime, and may thus now hamper enlightened development of juvenile courts." [7]

Only Mr. Justice Stewart dissented in full. Although acknowledging the shortcomings of many of the juvenile and family courts, he maintained that the procedural safeguards imposed by the decision would abolish the flexibility and informality of juvenile courts and would cause children again to be treated as adults.[8]

In summary form, the decision held as follows:

Notice of Charges.[9] — A petition alleging in general terms that the child is "neglected, dependent or delinquent" is sufficient notice under Arizona law.[10] It is not required that the petition be served upon the parents. No facts need be alleged in the initial petition; the Arizona Supreme Court held that such facts need not be alleged until the close of the initial hearing. No petition at all was served upon Gerald or his parents prior to the initial hearing.

The Arizona Supreme Court rejected Gerald's claim that due process had been denied because of failure to provide adequate notice on the following grounds: that "Mrs. Gault knew the exact nature of the charge against Gerald from the day he was taken to the detention home"; that the Gaults had appeared at the two hearings "without objection"; that advance notice of the specific charges or basis for taking the juvenile into custody and for the hearing is not necessary because "the policy of the juvenile law is to hide youthful errors

---

[5] *In Re Gault, supra* note 1, at 59–64.

[6] *Id.* at 64–65.
[7] *Id.* at 65–78.
[8] *Id.* at 78–81.
[9] *Id.* at 31–34.
[10] Ariz. Rev. Stat. Ann. tit. 8, § 222 (1955).

from the full gaze of the public and bury them in the graveyard of the forgotten past."

The Supreme Court rejected these arguments, noting that the "initial hearing" in this case was in fact a hearing on the merits of the case. The Court stated that even if there was validity to the practice of deferring specific notice on the grounds of protecting the child from the public eye, it must yield to the due process requirement of adequate notice. Therefore, a hearing where a youth's freedom and the parent's right to custody are in jeopardy may not be held unless the child and his parents or guardian be first notified in writing of the specific issues that must be met at that hearing. Such notice must be given at the earliest practicable time and sufficiently in advance of the hearing to permit preparation. Mere "knowledge" of the kind Mrs. Gault allegedly had of the charges against Gerald does not constitute a waiver of the right to adequate notice because of its lack of particularity.

Right to Counsel.[11] — The Arizona Supreme Court had held that representation of counsel for a minor is discretionary with the trial judge. The Supreme Court disagreed, noting that neither probation officer nor judge can adequately represent the child. Since a proceeding where a child stands to be found "delinquent" and subject to loss of liberty is comparable in gravity to an adult felony prosecution, the juvenile needs the assistance of counsel for the same reasons underlying the inclusion of the right in the Sixth Amendment: The juvenile — even less than the average adult criminal defendant — is not prepared to cope with the complexities of the law or of building an adequate defense. Thus, the due process clause of the Fourteenth Amendment requires that in state proceedings which may result in commitment the child and his parent must be notified of the child's right to be represented by counsel. If they are unable to afford a lawyer, one must be appointed for them.[12]

[11] *In Re Gault, supra* note 1, at 34–42.
[12] The Court emphasized as "forceful" the Report of the President's Commission on Law Enforcement and Administration of Justice, *The Challenge of Crime in a Free Society*, pp. 86–7 (hereinafter cited as Nat'l Crime Comm'n Report) (1967), which recommended: "Counsel should be appointed as a matter of course wherever

The Court discounted the holding of the Arizona Supreme Court that since Mrs. Gault knew that she could have appeared with counsel, her failure to do so was a waiver of the right. Notification of the right to counsel plus "specific consideration" of whether to waive the right must precede a valid waiver. Without being expressly advised of the right (and Mrs. Gault was not so advised) there can be no "specific consideration" and thus, no waiver.

Self-Incrimination, Confrontation, and Cross-Examination.[13] — It will be recalled that at the June 9 hearing, Judge McGhee questioned Gerald about the telephone calls without advising him of his right to counsel or his right to remain silent. The judge and Officer Flagg stated that Gerald admitted making at least one of the indecent remarks; Mrs. Gault recalled only that her son admitted dialing Mrs. Cook's number. The Arizona Supreme Court rejected Gerald's contention that he had a right to be advised that he need not incriminate himself, saying that the "necessary flexibility for individualized treatment will be enhanced by a rule which does not require the judge to advise the infant of a privilege against self-incrimination."

The Supreme Court rejected this view and held that any admissions that Gerald allegedly made were improperly obtained in violation of the Fifth Amendment's privilege against self-incrimination. The Court traced the history underlying the privilege, and observed: "One of its purposes is to prevent the State, whether by force or by psychological domination, from overcoming the mind and will of the person under investigation and depriving him of the freedom to decide whether to assist the State in securing his conviction." The court implied

coercive action is a possibility without requiring any affirmative choice by child or parent." *In Re Gault, supra* note 1, at 65. Also cited was HEW, *Standards for Juvenile and Family Courts*, Children's Bureau Pub. No. 437–1966, p. 57 (1966) (hereinafter cited as *Standards*) which states: "As a component part of a fair hearing required by due process guaranteed under the 14th Amendment, notice of the right to counsel should be required at all hearings and counsel provided upon request when the family is financially unable to employ counsel." *In Re Gault, supra* note 1, at 39.
[13] *Id.* at 42–57.

that no less than the freedom from coerced confessions is the importance of the reliability of the admission or confession. Such reliability, especially as to alleged admissions or confessions from those of Gerald's age, must undergo careful scrutiny, for, in the Court's words: "It would indeed be surprising if the privilege against self-incrimination were available to hardened criminals but not to children. The language of the Fifth Amendment, applicable to the States by operation of the Fourteenth Amendment, is unequivocal and without exception. And the scope of the privilege is comprehensive." [14]

The State of Arizona argued that the Fifth Amendment provides only that no person "shall be compelled in any *criminal case* to be a witness against himself" and should therefore not apply through the Fourteenth Amendment to state juvenile proceedings. The Supreme Court held that the privilege is not based upon the *type* of proceeding in which it is involved, "but upon the nature of the statement or admission made, the exposure which it invites." Since the privilege may be invoked in a civil or administrative proceeding, the court noted that it would make no difference whether juvenile proceedings are deemed "civil" or "criminal." The court took the opportunity to express its disapproval with these labels, and noted that in over half of the states, juveniles may be placed in adult penal institutions after a finding of delinquency.[15] The Court stated: "For this purpose, at least, commitment is a deprivation of liberty. It is incarceration against one's will, whether it is called 'criminal' or 'civil.' And our Constitution guarantees that no person shall be 'compelled' to be a witness against himself when he is threatened with deprivation of his liberty. . . ."

The Court noted that "special problems may arise with respect to waiver of the privilege by or on behalf of children, and that there may well be some differences in technique — but not in principle — depending upon the age of the child and the presence and competence of parents." And as special care must be taken before the privilege is validly waived, so also must admissions obtained without the presence of counsel be subject to the greatest scrutiny. Here we see the Fifth Amendment's self-incrimination provision to be vitally interwoven with the Sixth Amendment's right to counsel.

The "confession" of Gerald, made without counsel, outside of the presence of his parents, and without advising him of his right to remain silent served as the basis for Judge Mc-Ghee's finding of delinquency. Since this "admission" or "confession" was obtained in violation of those rights noted above, the Supreme Court searched for another basis on which the judgment might rest. There was none to be found. There was no sworn testimony. The complainant, Mrs. Cook, did not appear. The Arizona Supreme Court held that "sworn testimony must be required of all witnesses" including those related to the juvenile court system. The Supreme Court held that this is not sufficient: In the absence of a valid confession adequate to support the determination of the Court, confrontation and sworn testimony by witnesses available for cross-examination were essential for a finding of "delinquency" and a subsequent order depriving Gerald of his liberty.[16] The court made it clear, therefore, that an adjudication of "delinquency" or a commitment to an institution is invalid unless the ju-

[14] The Court cited to this point *Standards, supra* note 12, at 49, for authority that prior to a police interview, the child and his parents should be informed of his right to have legal counsel present and to refuse to answer questions. This provision of the *Standards* also suggests that the parents and child be informed of their right to refuse to be fingerprinted, but the Court refused to express any opinion as to fingerprinting as this issue was not before the Court. *In Re Gault, supra* note 1, at 49.

[15] HEW, *Delinquent Children in Penal Institutions,* Children's Bureau Pub. No. 415-1964, p. 1 (1964).

[16] For this point, the Court again cited *Standards, supra* note 12, at 72–73, which states that all testimony should be under oath and that only competent material and relevant evidence under rules applicable to civil cases should be admitted into evidence. Also cited was, *e.g.,* Note, "Rights and Rehabilitation in Juvenile Courts," 67 *Colum. L. Rev.,* 281, 336 (1967): "Particularly in delinquency cases, where the issue of fact is the commission of a crime, the introduction of hearsay — such as the report of a policeman who did not witness the events — contravenes the purpose underlying the Sixth Amendment right of confrontation." (Footnote omitted.) *In Re Gault, supra* note 1, at 56–57 n. 98.

venile is afforded the same protections respecting sworn testimony that an adult would receive in a criminal trial.

Appellate Review and Transcript of Proceedings.[17] — The Supreme Court did not specifically decide whether there is a right to appellate review in a juvenile case [18] or whether juvenile courts are required to provide a transcript of the hearings for review, because the decision of the Arizona Supreme Court could be reversed on other grounds. Notwithstanding its failure to rule directly on this issue, the Court pointed out the undesirable consequences of the present case, where: no record of the proceedings was kept; no findings or grounds for basing the juvenile court's conclusions were stated; and the reviewing courts were forced to reconstruct a record while Judge McGhee had the "unseemly duty of testifying under cross-examination as to the events that transpired in the hearings before him." [19]

Epilogue

It should be evident to the reader that the legal precedents handed down by the *Gault* decision are neither numerous nor complex. At any proceeding where a child may be committed to a state institution, that child and his parent or guardian must be given notice in writing of the specific charges against the child sufficiently in advance of the proceedings to permit adequate preparation. The child and his parent must be notified of the child's right to be represented by counsel, and if financial considerations so require, counsel must be appointed for them. The child and his parents or guardian must be advised of the child's right to remain silent. Admission or confessions obtained from the child without the presence of counsel must undergo the greatest scrutiny in order to insure reliability. In the absence of a valid confession, no finding of "delinquency" and no order of commitment of the child for any length of time may be upheld unless such finding is supported by confrontation and sworn testimony of witnesses available for cross-examination.

If indeed the *Gault* decision were significant only for the black-letter law, summarized above, the demands made upon our juvenile judges and probation officers would be rather easy to comply with. The few mandates of *Gault* would eventually become implemented (with, of course, varying degrees of enthusiasm). However, the decision cannot be read solely in the light of its few binding precedents.

Some may recall that it was the same Justice Fortas who wrote for the majority in the *Kent* [20] decision, which a year prior to *Gault* considered the requirement for a valid waiver of "exclusive" jurisdiction of the juvenile court of the District of Columbia so that a youth could be tried in the District's adult criminal court. The essence of *Kent* was that the basic requirements of due process and fairness be met in such a proceeding. But although confined to the narrow issue of waiver proceedings, *Kent* was a prologue to *Gault* insofar as it expressed disenchantment with the course of juvenile justice in this country, which was expressed in an often-quoted sentence: "There is evidence . . . that there may be grounds for concern that the child receives the worst of both worlds: that he gets neither the protections accorded to adults nor the solicitous care and regenerative treatment postulated for children." [21]

With this warning, an alert was sounded in

---

[17] *Id.* at 57–59.

[18] The Supreme Court has yet to hold that a state is required to provide any right to appellate review, *Griffin v. Illinois*, 351 U.S. 12, 18 (1956).

[19] The Court cited, *e.g.*, *Standards*, *supra* note 12, at 8, which recommends "written findings of fact, some form or record of the hearing" "and the right to appeal." It recommends verbatim recording of the hearing by stenotypist or mechanical recording. *Id.* at 76. Finally, it urges that the judge make clear to the child and family their right to appeal. *Id.* at 78. Also cited was, *e.g.*, Nat'l Crime Comm'n Report, *supra* note 12, at 86, which states that "records make possible appeals which, even if they do not occur, import by their possibility a healthy atmosphere of accountability." *In Re Gault*, *supra* note 1, at 58–69, n. 102.

[20] *Kent v. United States*, 383 U.S. 541 (1966).

[21] *Id.* at 556, citing Handler, "The Juvenile Courts and the Adversary Systems: Problems of Function and Form," 1965 *Wis. L. Rev.*, 7 (other citations omitted).

Kent for what would become in *Gault* an indictment of the juvenile courts. Despite the limitation of issues actually adjudicated in the decision, *Gault*, taken as a whole, is a comprehensive note of concern over the administration of juvenile justice in this country. Part II of the decision [22] dealing largely with background and history contains 41 footnotes citing materials covering the entire ambit of juvenile justice, from custody to treatment, from probation to psychiatric care, and including numerous books, studies, and articles critical of virtually every aspect of the juvenile process. In Part II the parens patriae doctrine — the concept of the state assuming the role of substitute parent — was challenged on both historical grounds ("its meaning is murky and its historic credentials are of dubious relevance") and on legal grounds ("[T]he constitutional and theoretical basis for this peculiar system is — to say the least — debatable."). The nomenclature attached to "receiving homes" or "industrial schools" did not, in the Court's view, alter the practical reality that these are institutions of confinement where juveniles may for years be deprived of their liberty. The Court was careful to note that the "substitute parents" of the early reformers' ideology have, in fact, become guards, state employees, and fellow juveniles incarcerated for offenses ranging in scope from "waywardness" to rape and murder.

It is therefore apparent to the reader of Part II of the *Gault* decision that the case was not, as the narrow scope of its holding might wrongly suggest, decided in the abstract. Part II was a harsh and critical prelude to the decision. It was tempered with concern for a system of justice that the Court suggests has fallen short of its early hopes and aspirations, and it was laced with documentation of these failings. It is submitted that the marked distaste for the course of juvenile justice in this country, which permeated the decision, was of itself a prologue (as *Kent* was for *Gault*) for further decisions by the Supreme Court extending the due process clause into other aspects of juvenile proceedings. To speculate on the direction of such hypothetical extensions

would be indeed foolish. As noted earlier, the Supreme Court selects only a small fraction of those cases submitted to it for review, and of these, only those issues necessary to dispose of a case are actually adjudicated (the appellate review and transcript issue in *Gault* is an example).

For those who are understandably concerned with the present, the *Gault* decision leaves many questions unanswered. Mr. Justice Fortas wrote in *Gault* that "neither the Fourteenth Amendment nor the Bill of Rights is for adults alone." But if indeed they are not for adults only, the Fourteenth Amendment and the Bill of Rights are not yet for children completely. The *Gault* decision did not cover the procedures or constitutional rights applicable to the pre-judicial or post-adjudicative stages of the juvenile process.[23] Thus, the body of law now pertaining to the rights of the adult criminal suspect when he is first brought into custody does not yet apply to the juvenile suspect. It is yet to be decided whether the Fourth Amendment's prohibitions against unreasonable searches and seizures, protections made fully binding upon the states, will affect the kind of evidentiary matter admissible against the child in an adjudicatory proceeding. The Fifth Amendment's right to a grand jury indictment and the double jeopardy prohibition have not yet been made fully binding upon the states by the Supreme Court, and their relevance to juvenile proceedings are uncertain.

One may ponder whether prolonged confinement in a "receiving home" pending a hearing on the merits would violate the Sixth Amendment's guarantee of a *speedy* trial, if this right is held to be firmly binding upon the states. The Sixth Amendment's guarantee to a *public* trial, which is binding upon the states, may have significant implications for juvenile hearings, which have by statute in a large proportion of the states been closed to the public. The Sixth Amendment's guarantee that the accused be entitled to have the court compel witnesses to appear and testify, a right closely related to the right of confrontation, has potential relevance to juvenile hearings, and can-

---

[22] *In Re Gault, supra* note 1, at 12–31.   [23] *Id.* at 13.

not be ignored (although this right is not yet firmly binding upon the states under the Fourteenth Amendment).

One might further consider the Eighth Amendment and its prohibitions against cruel and unusual punishment, excessive fines, and excessive bail. If any or all of the Eighth Amendment is eventually made binding upon the states, how will the course of juvenile justice be affected? Is it cruel and unusual punishment to deny to a child those safeguards not considered by *Gault* and then subject that child to confinement in an institution of limited treatment facilities? Does unconditional relegation to a "receiving home" pending a hearing infringe on the prohibition against excessive bail?

That these issues may legitimately be framed, in the light of the Supreme Court's refusal in *Gault* to accept the traditional noncriminal label attached to juvenile proceedings is, in the writer's opinion, the greatest significance of the decision. It is not possible to even speculate as to the extent to which the Supreme Court is prepared to go in according to juveniles the procedural safeguards available to adults in criminal proceedings. All that is clear is that the sweeping, intangible concept of due process has at last been officially introduced to our juvenile courts.

Issues in Treatment
and Prevention

Shannon's discussion of the problem of competence to help is based on recognition that there are competing explanations of delinquent behavior, as well as conflicting approaches to treatment. He suggests three positive and two negative criteria of competence whereby decisions can be made regarding which groups or professions are competent to deal with various types of deviant behavior, including delinquent behavior. It is essential to recognize that the criteria Shannon proposes can be used with reference to *any* profession or group claiming competence to help those whom the society defines as in need of help.

The author then discusses a variety of settings in which research may be conducted, and he notes some of the problems associated with each of the potential research settings. Emphasizing the importance of a carefully designed research project, Shannon examines the implications each setting has for research designs, particularly in reference to selection of an adequate sample of the population about which the researcher wants to make inferences.

LYLE W. SHANNON

The Problem of Competence to Help

No more than a generation ago in many, if not most, parts of the United States a person might have engaged in behavior that would have resulted in classification or definition by society as deviant or problem behavior, but unfortunately neither appropriate institutional facilities nor professional assistance might have been available. Even the layman is aware today of the attitudes that prevailed toward certain types of deviant persons only a generation or

so ago. Aside from the grimmest custodial approach, and perhaps a general attitude of condemnation, the community often had little to offer, much less an understanding of the process whereby the person engaging in deviant behavior happened to become that way. This is not entirely untrue today, as witnessed by some explanations of deviant behavior suggested by the layman.[1]

[1] A New York mechanical engineer contends that "juvenile delinquency can be eliminated completely with the aid of corrective shoes and eye

From *Federal Probation*, 25 (March 1961), 32–39. Reprinted by permission.

On the other hand, the present situation is quite different in many respects. In our large metropolitan areas we may find that there are various professional and nonprofessional groups competing for the privilege of helping the less fortunate, those who have been defined as deviants or persons with a problem by the larger society. Not only are they anxious to help, but they no longer condemn the deviant, they may even consider him to be normal rather than abnormal.[2]

But still, these competing groups, so willing to help, have one thing in common with those who did not appear as anxious to help at an earlier period — they remain without an adequate explanation of the process whereby deviants have acquired the patterns of behavior about which everyone is so concerned and how they should be treated.[3]

You may say that the professional who wishes to help does understand the behavior with which he is confronted, otherwise he would be unwilling to assume the responsibility of helping. The fact that there are so many competing explanations and conflicting approaches to treatment for a specific form of deviant behavior is evidence to the contrary and cause for concern.[4] Since there are competing groups of persons claiming competence to help and competing explanations of deviant behavior, the question of determining competence arises; this is a thorny question and not readily settled.

Although the less fortunate persons in our society have some freedom of choice, they are restricted in many ways as soon as they are defined as deviants and thus are relatively powerless to decide to what extent they will be helped and who will help them.[5]

Criteria of Competence

What are the criteria of competence? How may we decide which groups or professions are competent to deal with the various types of deviant behavior with which we are concerned, with the behavioral types whom the larger society defines as in need of help? The following criteria are suggested:

Postive Criteria

1. *The ability to predict human behavior.* Can the group claiming competence predict what people will do under certain circumstances? Can they make "if, then" statements with any high degree of accuracy about the behavior with which they claim themselves competent to deal? [6] If these questions can be

---

glasses." He states, "If the human body is properly balanced, that is, if a person has both mental and physical balance, that person is not apt to be badly behaved or commit a crime." At the same time a Milwaukee pigeon raiser wishes to join the fight against juvenile delinquency. . . . "If we could encourage young men to take an interest in pigeon racing there would be less juvenile delinquency because they wouldn't have as much time to get into trouble."

[2] See Marshall B. Clinard, "Criminal Behavior is Human Behavior," *Federal Probation*, March 1949, pp. 21–27.

[3] See: Francis A. Allen, "The Borderland of the Criminal Laws: Problems 'of Socializing' Criminal Justice," *The Social Service Review*, June 1958, pp. 107–119. On page 114, Allen states, "Ignorance, of itself, is disgraceful only as far as it is avoidable. But when, in our eagerness to find 'better ways' of handling old problems, we rush to measures affecting human liberty and human personality, on the assumption that we have knowledge which, in fact, we do not possess, then the problem of ignorance takes on a more sinister hue. One of the most alarming aspects of the current agitation for reform of criminal justice and related areas is the apparent willingness of some proponents of reform to substitute action for knowledge, action of the sort that often results in the most serious consequences to the affected individuals. Unfortunately, this is a tendency found too frequently among lawyers of the more 'progressive' variety."

[4] No one has portrayed the situation more lucidly than has Percival Bailey in, "The Great Psychiatric Revolution," *The American Journal of Psychiatry*, November 1956, pp. 387–406. This is one of the most authoritative and well documented articles that can be found on this issue.

[5] There is a possibility that eagerness to help may have as its consequence certain types of action without due process. This has been of concern to many persons who are just as interested in effectively dealing with the problem behavior but aware of the desirability of judicious procedures. See Paul W. Tappan, "The Adolescent in Court," *The Journal of Criminal Law and Criminology*, September–October 1946, pp. 216–229 and "Treatment Without Trial," *Social Forces*, March 1946, pp. 306–311.

[6] A vast literature exists on parole prediction in criminology. Several representative articles are

answered in the affirmative, then there is some evidence of competence.[7]

What must we conclude if a group contends that predictions of human behavior cannot be made? What would we say about an engineer who refused to predict whether or not a bridge constructed in a specified fashion could withstand a specified load? What would we say if a medical doctor claimed the competence to treat persons with a certain type of disease and refused to make predictive statements about the likelihood of recovery for persons treated in the manner *specified?* If the chance of recovery is minimal, the doctor states that it is. If the chance of recovery is almost 100 percent, he states that fact.

But is the ability to predict sufficient? It is necessary, but not sufficient.

2. *The ability to modify or control human behavior.* If a particular professional group has the ability to modify the behavior of deviant persons so that they conform to the norms of the society of which they are a part, does that group meet the test of competence? This may be answered with a "perhaps."

It is possible to appear to modify behavior without actually being the change agent. First of all we must be sure that change in the desirable direction has been due to the efforts of the professional persons involved. This is not an easy task and we shall say more about it in another part of this article. Assuming that the desired change is brought about by the therapy of the professional persons involved, is it re-

lated to or derived from the explanation of the deviant behavior accepted by that professional group? That is, is the treatment or therapeutic activity of professional persons consistent with their explanation of the process whereby deviant persons become the way that they are? If not, then why are members of this professional group with this particular explanation of the deviant behavior those whom we entrust with the responsibility of helping? Wouldn't an effective therapy be even more effective if it was derived from an explanation of the behavior in question? It would appear that the success of the therapy employed was probably related to the fact that it contained in some cases or to some extent the elements of a more appropriate therapy that would be derived from a better, in the scientific sense, explanation of the behavior in question.

3. *The existence of a body of scientific research that tends to support the explanation of the professional group in question and with which the therapy in question appears to be consistent.* A scientific discipline in the behavioral sciences has a theory or theories of behavior based on its conception of man. From this theory of human or deviant behavior, or specific types of deviant behavior, is derived a set of interrelated hypotheses. Predictions are made of what will happen under certain circumstances or what will be found under certain circumstances. The test of the hypothesis involves observing, measuring, recording and statistically manipulating the relevant data.[8]

If a body of research exists that is supportive of hypotheses that could be derived from the theory of behavior held by a particular professional group, then we may be inclined to accept that group as competent to work in the field. This is close to the already-suggested criteria, but is not the same. External evidence supportive of the group's explanation is not the same as evidence of the ability of members of the group to make predictions or the same as evidence of ability to modify or control behavior. What is called for here is research that

---

cited as examples of the research that has been conducted on this decision-making problem: Lloyd E. Ohlin and Otis Dudley Duncan, "The Efficiency of Prediction in Criminology," *The American Journal of Sociology*, March 1949, pp. 441–452; Otis Dudley Duncan, Lloyd E. Ohlin, Albert J. Reiss, Jr., and Howard R. Stanton, "Formal Devices for Making Selection Decisions," *The American Journal of Sociology*, May 1953, pp. 573–584; and Daniel Glaser, "The Efficacy of Alternative Approaches to Parole Prediction," *American Sociological Review*, January 1955, pp. 283–287.

[7] The ability to make value judgments, i.e., "ought" statements, must not be confused with scientific generalizations to which we refer as "if, then" statements. Everyone is capable of making value judgments and professional or scientific status gives one no special competence in this respect.

[8] For a discussion of procedures mentioned herein see: Roy G. Francis, "The Relation of Data to Theory," *Rural Sociology*, September 1957, pp. 258–266.

tests hypotheses that could be derived from the theory or theories of human behavior held by a particular professional group.

Negative criteria

1. *Existence of a body of research indicating that a group has not been able to effectively deal with the behavior in question although it may purport to have such ability.* If scientific research shows, for example, that those who have received a given therapy from a given professional group improve no more than those who have not, then there is a question as to the competence of the professional group contending that the approach in question is appropriate.[9]

2. *Existence of a body of evidence that the group is so torn by dissension that it cannot be considered to have a unitary approach to the problem behavior.* There are such a multitude of approaches and explanations within the discipline that no particular approach can be called the ". . . . ." explanation and approach to such and such behavior.[10] That is not to say

that individuals or subcategories of individuals within a particular profession may not have a theory of human behavior from which may be derived hypotheses that have been or are testable by scientific research and which serve as a basis for an effective program of treatment or therapy.

Most important of all the criteria listed is the ability to move from a theory of deviant behavior to verified hypotheses and a program of training, therapy, treatment, or re-education with a tested effectiveness on a large proportion of those to whom it is directed.[11]

The ability to effectively modify human behavior comes from research and experimentation. It is one thing to say, let us try this out and see what happens, but it is quite another thing to be able to say, if we do this, such and such is likely to happen a given percent of the time.

Possible Conclusions

If the choice had to be made today, we could make one by evaluating available studies. This should be done by an independent group not attached to any particular theory of human behavior or program for dealing with the deviants in our society.

Unfortunately, they would probably end up by saying that no one is now competent to claim the ability to deal effectively with vari-

---

[9] There have been a number of pioneering efforts in this regard. Persons who conduct research leading to such conclusions are not often well received by members of their professions following publication of the findings. If the research is conducted by a group defined as competitors, the reaction may be even less favorable. As examples of such studies see: LaMay Adamson and H. Warren Dunham, "Clinical Treatment of Male Delinquents: A Case Study in Effort and Result," *American Sociological Review*, June 1956, pp. 312–320; Edwin Powers and Helen Witmer, *An Experiment in the Prevention of Delinquency,* New York: Columbia University Press, 1951, pp. 337.

[10] For a penetrating criticism of the psychiatric approach see: Michael Hakeem, "A Critique of the Psychiatric Approach to Crime and Correction," *Law and Contemporary Problems*, Autumn 1958, pp. 650–682. This is a most detailed exposition of the conflicts within psychiatry. Professor Hakeem cites the leading psychiatrists of the country chapter and verse in his contention that the profession is torn over basic issues in reference to various forms of deviant behavior. The author has seen no evidence to contradict Professor Hakeem's charges.

In the same journal see: Frank E. Hartung, "A Critique of the Sociological Approach to Crime and Correction," *Law and Contemporary Problems,* Autumn 1958, pp. 703–734. Professor Har-

tung points out that sociology is not a unitary discipline and that "sociologists hardly seem to agree on anything." He goes on to say that, "Criminologists are so free in destroying and rejecting each other's theories and hypotheses that criminology must appear nihilistic to the outsider." Lest it seem that sociology and psychiatry are in the same boat, it should be noted that sociologists are more than reluctant to claim that they are in basic agreement and that sociology as such has the answer to the problem of dealing with the deviants in our society. Some of the important controversies in sociology are described with detailed references to the pertinent sociological literature.

[11] See: Donald R. Cressey, "Application and Verification of the Differential Association Theory," *Journal of Criminal Law, Criminology and Police Science,* May–June 1952, pp. 43–52 and "Contradictory Theories in Correctional Group Programs," *Federal Probation,* June 1954, pp. 20–26.

ous problem areas. The various alternative conclusions might be as follows:

1. Research indicates that a particular professional group has an explanation of either human behavior or some specific deviant behavior that has been verified by research. This group has also developed a program for dealing with the behavior that grows out of their explanation. Research has also shown that the treatment or training is effective. We have already indicated that this will probably not be the conclusion that any independent team of evaluators would reach.

2. Research indicates that there are competing explanations of human behavior or specific deviant behavior and that prevention and control programs based on them have about the same effectiveness. Therefore, each explanation contains an element of the complete explanation of the behavior and each program built on an incomplete explanation has less efficiency than it would have if built upon a fuller explanation of the behavior in question.

Which explanation and which program would we select under such circumstances? From the standpoint of the taxpayer, we should select the program that is least expensive and from the humanitarian viewpoint that which is most readily available, particularly if the short-run view is taken.

If the long-run view is taken, then further research and experimentation would be called for at the same time that some application of existing knowledge was made.

3. Research indicates that no group or profession has demonstrated the ability to effectively deal with deviant behavior; research shows that treatment results in no greater improvement than that which accrues by simply leaving persons with a behavioral problem alone. In this case the cry for more money, for a saturation approach, is indeed uncalled for.[12]

In the case of either of the latter two conclusions, we might wish to carefully examine the training of persons dealing with deviant behavior. It may well be that it is unreasonable to expect them to have much success in developing theories of human behavior or corrective or treatment programs considering the training they have had and the nature of the problem with which they are confronted.

The sociologist, for example, is not trained to administer drugs in the fight against disease. The medical doctor is usually not trained in the structure of social organizations and in the functioning of social systems, and is thus ill-equipped to deal with human behavior.

The Research Setting

This is indeed a thorny question. Where research should be conducted depends pretty much on the kind of behavior with which we are concerned. Actually, there are a variety of settings in which we may conduct it:

1. in the community, in the neighborhood, in the industrial plant, in the office
2. in the settlement house, in the boys' club
3. in the detention center, in jail
4. in the juvenile court, in adult court
5. in the diagnostic center, in the reception center
6. in the guidance clinic, in the out-patient clinic
7. in the training school, in the reformatory, in prison
8. in the school, in the dormitory, in fraternity or sorority
9. in the hospital
10. in the mental hospital

Dedicated people have engaged in research in each of these places in an attempt to enable us to better understand, predict, and control human behavior.

---

[12] Cressey has pointed out that no matter how a program works out, personnel maintaining either theoretical or practical interests in the control of crime and delinquency, for example, develop a vocabulary of motives for justifying what they are doing. This entire article demonstrates an unusual degree of perceptivity on the part of the author. Donald R. Cressey, "The Nature and Effectiveness of Correctional Techniques," *Law and Contemporary Problems*, Autumn 1958, pp. 754–771. The obstacles to and difficulties involved in evaluating programs are discussed at length in this particularly thought-provoking article.

The handicaps present in the research setting have frequently prevented people from stating with scientific assurance that they have found out what they have set out to find out. This is usually no criticism of the researcher as an individual, but largely a reflection of the difficulties involved in setting up an adequate research design or the selection of an adequate sample of the population about which it is desired to make inferences. Another handicap may be lack of training in methods of research.

Most unfortunate of all, however, is the fact that persons active in programs dealing with various types of deviant behavior have failed to realize the inadequacy of their research designs and of the data that they have collected. They often have tended to labor under the impression that since they are working with juveniles or some other problem group they must naturally know more about them than do others. This has been unfortunate and has tended to prevent them from benefiting from the constructive criticism of persons with more specialized research training. We must also decide whether the research being undertaken aims at discovering the process whereby the deviants have acquired patterns of behavior that distinguished them, or whether it attempts to find out what effect a particular program has on a particular type of deviant. A setting in which it is not possible to learn what we wish to know about processes of deviant behavior may still be a setting in which we can learn a considerable amount about how people, that is the specific kind in which we are interested, react to a particular institutional setting or program designed for modifying behavior.[13]

For example, institutional research may enable us to determine the most efficient way of handling various types of institutionalized deviants in order to keep them quiet and less troublesome, or to enable them to return to society in a minimal length of time. The fact that persons may react in an aggressive fashion in the institutional setting gives us some idea of the custodial and training problem faced by the administration and staff of institutions.

Problems Related to the Research Setting

In a short paper it is not possible to go into all of the problems associated with each different research setting. A few examples have been selected for exploration and emphasis.

Research in the Community

From a strictly sociological viewpoint the community is the ideal setting for research. Here we may study the deviant in his natural habitat and from our research derive a program for dealing with the deviant in the environment within which he must ultimately make an adjustment.[14]

There are a variety of obstacles to research in the community, depending on the level at which it takes place. If it is desired to select a sample of delinquents and nondelinquents, we have no way of knowing who belongs in the population of delinquents as contrasted with nondelinquents. The same may be said for other forms of deviant behavior. If we turn to police records of contacts with juveniles, we are dealing with those types of juvenile delinquents whose behavior is of such a nature that it is visible to the police and defined by them as of concern to the community. Certain types of research can be conducted with data obtained from police records, but its limitations must be known. It is possible, for example, to present the ecology of official delinquency from police contact data and to describe delinquents as contrasted to nondelinquents by residence, age, sex, etc. Further,

[13] The effectiveness of a wide variety of programs designed to deal with juvenile delinquency is taken up in considerable detail in Helen L. Witmer and Edith Tufts, *The Effectiveness of Delinquency Prevention Programs*, Washington: U.S. Department of Health, Education, and Welfare, p. 50. The authors conclude that research on the effectiveness of delinquency control programs leaves us with relatively little certain knowledge about how to control delinquency.

[14] The Back of the Yards or Chicago Area Project developed out of research conducted by Professor Clifford R. Shaw and his associates. See: Anthony Sorrentino, "The Chicago Area Project After 25 Years," *Federal Probation*, June 1959, pp. 40–45. The program of the New York City Youth Board is likewise based on research on juvenile delinquency in the community.

it is possible to use police records as a basis for sampling officially delinquent and officially nondelinquent juveniles.

On the other hand, when studying delinquency in the community, one might commence with a sample of juveniles, selected at random.[15] Interviews or questionnaires would then be given in order to classify each juvenile as delinquent or nondelinquent according to an operational definition of delinquency, or to place the juvenile on a delinquency continuum, as more properly might be the procedure.[16] The shortcomings of the interview, no matter how much "depth" is involved, will probably never deter us from its use in social research. We must minimize its shortcomings by maximizing the skill with which it is applied to specific research situations.

Another approach to community research involves either participant or nonparticipant observation. William F. Whyte's classic study, *Street Corner Society*, attempted to describe delinquency in the neighborhood or the social organization of a delinquent neighborhood.[17] Some of the difficulties involved in this approach are that the observer may not see everything that should be seen, that the data

may not be readily quantifiable, and that reporting tends to become impressionistic and colored by the original or newly acquired biases of the observer. Participant or nonparticipant observation is an appropriate beginning and presents us with theory-building data and hypotheses that should be tested by more rigorous research procedures.

It is not feasible to go into community studies further at this point; suffice it to say that the sociologist is interested in research on delinquency or other deviant behavior as it develops in the community.[18] The sociologist's position is that programs for effective control of deviant behavior will ultimately be based on research at the community level.

Research in the Settlement House

A settlement house population consists of a group of boys, some delinquent, and some not, who are usually involved in the settlement house program because of their residential propinquity to it.[19] They are readily accessible and make a handy population for study. Often they are more upwardly mobile than are other juveniles in the same neighborhood. Due to the fact that they are not representative of any particular group of deviants or nondeviants, research based on such a population has had an unfortunate beginning if there is any intention of generalizing to a larger population.[20]

Research in the Detention Center

Another frequently made mistake is the assumption that a detention center population is

[15] See: Robert McGinnis, "Randomization and Inference in Sociological Research," *American Sociological Review*, August 1958, pp. 408–414.

[16] For work on the problem of scaling delinquency see: F. Ivan Nye and James F. Short, Jr., "Scaling Delinquent Behavior," *American Sociological Review*, June 1957, pp. 326–331 and "Reported Behavior as a Criterion of Deviant Behavior," *Social Problems*, Winter 1957–1958, pp. 207–213.

[17] William F. Whyte, *Street Corner Society*, Chicago: The University of Chicago Press, 1943. Also see by Whyte, "A Slum Sex Code," *American Journal of Sociology*, July 1943, pp. 24–32. For an anthropologist's contribution, see: Walter B. Miller, "Lower Class Culture as a Generating Milieu of Gang Delinquency," *The Journal of Social Issues*, 1958, pp. 5–19; "Implications of Lower Class Culture for Social Work," *The Social Service Review*, September 1959, pp. 219–236. Also see: Albert K. Cohen and James F. Short, Jr., "Research in Delinquent Subcultures," *The Journal of Social Issues*, 1958, pp. 20–37. Failure to take the values of the community into consideration in planning treatment is cited as a cause of failure by Jacob Chwast, Carmi Harari, and Irving Weisman, "Why We Fail," *Federal Probation*, March 1958, pp. 36–42.

[18] It should be emphasized that there is no implication that only sociologists and anthropologists are interested in research at the community level. For an example of research that the sociologist considers pertinent see: Margherita MacDonald, Carson McGuire, and Robert J. Havighurst, "Leisure Activities and the Socioeconomic Status of Children," *The American Journal of Sociology*, May 1949, pp. 505–519.

[19] For a study of the possible effects of a boy's club on delinquency see Roscoe C. Brown, Jr., *A Boy's Club and Delinquency*, New York: New York University Press, 1956, p. 28.

[20] A good example of such a study is William H. Sheldon's *Varieties of Delinquent Youth*, New York: Harper and Bros., 1949. Sheldon's method of selecting his "sample" was by no means the only or most crucial shortcoming of the research.

a sample of juvenile delinquents. First of all, it has the characteristics of an official population of juveniles and, secondly, it usually contains dependent and neglected as well as delinquent juveniles. Even if the delinquents are sorted out from the others, they are the juvenile delinquents whose behavior has been viewed as a more serious type by the authorities, who came from a home in which authorities hesitate to leave them, or for some other pertinent reason have been detained rather than released to their parents pending adjudication. They have been singled out from all other juveniles with whom the police have had contact and perhaps for reasons that may involve the personal whim of the detaining authority.

Furthermore, since they have been detained, it is very likely that they are now looking at the world about them in a somewhat different manner than previously. They may now be playing the role of the young hoodlum for the benefit of authorities. They may play the role that they think will be of the greatest benefit to them in terms of their evaluation of the authorities and their conception of what the authorities expect of the juvenile. The detention center delinquent may be frightened and experiencing quite new feelings, particularly if deprived of freedom for the first time. However the detention center juvenile may be looking at society while in detention, it is difficult to determine whether or not this is the juvenile that we would find on the outside.

Any tests that are given to the juvenile within this setting are likely to elicit from him feelings of rejection, of not being loved, or of anxiety. The immediate behavior of the juvenile will be influenced by his new surroundings, physical and human. None are more aware of the hazards involved in attempting to make reliable measures of "personality" than are the psychologists.

Research in the Juvenile Court

This is similar to the detention center, but here the emphasis might be on data obtained from casework reports and the efficacy of one kind of disposition as contrasted with another in preventing recidivism.

The juveniles who reach the stage of either informal or formal disposition of their cases are more likely to be the serious, persistent offenders. Nevertheless, the decision-making process is important at this point as well. The opinions and attitudes of the juvenile court judge and his staff, as well as the behavior of the juveniles, are crucial determinants of who will be here. Valuable studies may be made at this level, but this is not the level at which to attempt to learn the process whereby juveniles become delinquent. It is here that we may attempt to determine something about the factors that influence the decision to define a juvenile as a serious delinquent or the decision to deal with a juvenile in one manner rather than another. How important, for example, is family status as contrasted with economic status in influencing a judge's decision? [21] How does this vary from judge to judge?

Research in the Diagnostic Center

The population of a diagnostic center depends on the attitude of judges toward juvenile delinquency, their conception of the diagnostic center and the intake policy of the diagnostic center. The diagnostic center population, by the very nature of the selection procedures of the community and the center, will be unrepresentative of the juvenile delinquents in our society.

Quite aside from the grossly unrepresentative nature of the delinquents to be found in such an institution, a most abnormal environment has been provided for the study of delinquent behavior. The diagnostic center is far removed physically and in social structure from the natural habitat of the juvenile. The most painstaking researcher or therapist finds himself working in a setting that may greatly influence the social behavior of the juvenile and which cannot be factored out from other stimuli that have influenced the juvenile's previous behavior. This complicates the task of the researcher and therapist. The researcher concludes that the diagnostic center is a poor

[21] See for example: F. Ivan Nye, *Family Relationships and Delinquent Behavior*, New York: John Wiley and Sons, Inc., 1958, pp. 23–33.

place to study the processes whereby juveniles have acquired delinquent patterns of behavior.

One other handicap facing the diagnostic center researcher, or therapist for that matter, is the lack of control groups. The professional staff assumes that the behavior observed in the center is the behavior of a delinquent juvenile, assuming that this has been the basis for referral. How well might it be that a nondelinquent control would behave in the same manner if placed in that particular institutional setting. One way to handle this would be to send samples of controls through the center along with those juveniles referred as a consequence of their problem behavior. This is difficult to do in a relatively free society.

If the professional staff does observe the biased sample of delinquents that is to be found in the typical diagnostic center, anything that is learned cannot be generalized to the vast bulk of juvenile delinquents who are not admitted to such an institution.

These are some of the problems faced by professional persons who spend their lives attempting to understand and help juvenile delinquents and other types of deviants.

Research in the Guidance Clinic

The guidance clinic is very similar to the diagnostic center in one important respect and that is the selectivity of any group of juveniles whom one would be able to study as a consequence of their referral to such an establishment. It is true that increasing numbers of juveniles are being referred to guidance clinics and for reasons that would not lead most of us to believe that there is any mental disorder behind their behavior. Nevertheless, a sample of guidance clinic juveniles or children of any age does not provide a basis for making inferences about the behavior of delinquent juveniles or juveniles in general. This is, of course, a disappointing conclusion for child guidance clinic personnel to accept if they are oriented toward research. In such a situation the best thing that they might do would be to study randomly selected controls from the larger population of juveniles so as to better ascertain the extent to which their clients are representative of other populations about which they may be inclined to make inferences. They may find that the characteristics of their clients which they believed to be discriminating and related to problem behavior are found with the same frequency in a normal population whose behavior has not led to their referral. This does not lead to the conclusion that there is then something abnormal and problematic about the entire juvenile population, as some are inclined to conclude.

Additional studies of the effectiveness of child guidance clinics are also needed.

Research in the Training School

Training school boys and girls are usually made up of boys and girls whose serious delinquent depredations have been persistently brought to the attention of the authorities. Several studies have shown that, quite aside from their official records, anonymous questionnaires reveal that the admitted delinquencies of training school boys and girls are more serious and more persistent than those of a high school population from the same region. It is true that there is some selectivity in institutional populations of this type on a basis other than the depredations committed by the juveniles, but these are the juveniles whom the community and its representatives consider to be of a type that requires most careful attention and deprivation of their freedom during a program of rehabilitation.

In spite of the obstacles that are encountered in such a research setting, some very exciting and significant contributions can be made by the ingenious researcher. The existence of a subculture in the training school may soon result in the delinquent's acquisition of roles that challenge the best efforts of the researcher. The basic problem is to find out what should be done in order to maximize the likelihood of adjustment on the outside in the larger society after a period of training in isolation from that environment. Completely aside from studies of the process whereby the juvenile acquired the pattern of behavior that resulted in his institutionalization, studies may be made of the process of adjustment to the institution, of role playing, of attitudinal change and of success or failure on parole, basing the decision to parole or not on institutional and background data.[22]

Conclusion

This has been a rather brief overview of the problems to be encountered by the researcher in a variety of settings, as well as a statement of the criteria which may be employed in determining who is competent to help the less fortunate people in our society. Although most of the references have been made to research problems in juvenile delinquency, the same

[22] Some idea of what sociologists know about correctional institutions is summarized in: Lloyd E. Ohlin, *Sociology and the Field of Corrections*, New York: Russell Sage Foundation, 1956, 58 pp. For a detailed description of the social system of a correctional institution see: Donald Clemmer, *The Prison Community*, Boston: The Christopher Publishing House, 1940, 341 pp. and a paperback, New York: Rinehart and Co., 1958.

basic problems exist for any other type of deviant behavior in which we may be interested.

The crucial importance of a carefully designed research project cannot be overemphasized. While the researcher is beset with difficulties in this respect, it should be a challenge to his ingenuity. He should not be ready to accept defeat, particularly when attempting to provide for adequate control groups, but should insist on a research design that will enable him to test the hypotheses that he has set out to test.

Instead of a call for more of this or that program for training, rehabilitation or therapy, the cry should be for a research-oriented, experimental approach — so that problem behavior may be better understood, predicted and controlled in the future than it is at present.

In this paper Toby identifies two logically distinct principles, extrapolation and circumstantial vulnerability, on which "early identification and intensive treatment" programs may be based; as examples of each, he analyzes the Cambridge-Somerville Youth Study and the New York City Youth Board's application of the Gluecks' Social Prediction Table. In the preceding selection Shannon describes the importance of a behavioral theory from which accurate predictions can be made. In a similar vein, Toby observes the limitation of predictions which are not based on theory — mechanical predictions do not provide guidance for treatment. In this regard Voss and Elliott (1968:39–40) suggest that "if one's predictions are not derived from theory then one cannot *explain* delinquency. Though an investigator might be able to predict delinquency accurately with a set of disparate factors, the implications of his predictive device for ameliorative efforts would not be clear, i.e., he would not have an explanation of delinquency and might face grave difficulty in attempting to derive a coherent etiological framework incorporating his several factors." Toby questions whether those who are identified as "potential delinquents" will necessarily be helped by intensive treatment; in fact, he suggests the possibility of a boomerang effect from differential or discriminatory treatment of those presumed to be predelinquents.

In Toby's assessment of the Cambridge-Somerville Youth Study, conviction for at least one major crime in a state or federal court serves as the criterion against which the effectiveness of the treatment program is assessed, whereas in the Youth Board's study the criterion of delinquency is adjudication in the juvenile court as a delinquent (Voss [1963]). Consequently, the two studies assessed in this selection are not directly comparable in terms of the outcome criterion employed.

Commenting on this paper, Harris (1968:507) observes that in the Cambridge-Somerville study "the percentage convicted is greater in the treatment than in the control group for good and fair neighborhoods, but it is greater in control than treatment groups in poor and worst neighborhoods." Harris (1968:507) suggests that differential stigmatization may explain the differential effectiveness of the special treatment according to the socioeconomic level of the neighborhood: "First, such special treatment is more conspicuous in good than in poor neighborhoods — there is greater likelihood of stigmatization. Secondly, stigmatization is likely to be more harmful to the individual's self-concept in good neighborhoods, because in these neighborhoods one's evaluation of his self-concept is more likely to coincide with the evaluation of conventional members of the society."

REFERENCES

David B. Harris, "On Differential Stigmatization for Predelinquents," *Social Problems*, 15 (Spring 1968), pp. 507–508.

Harwin L. Voss, "The Predictive Efficiency of the Glueck Social Prediction Table," *Journal of Criminal Law, Criminology and Police Science*, 54 (December 1963), pp. 421–430.

——, and Delbert S. Elliott, "Delinquency, Opportunity and the Prediction of Delinquent Behavior," *Criminologica*, 6 (August 1968), pp. 39–50.

JACKSON TOBY

An Evaluation of Early Identification and Intensive Treatment Programs for Predelinquents

The "early identification and intensive treatment" approach to delinquency control is breathtakingly plausible. A plausible argument is not necessarily correct, as Columbus showed those who believed that the world was flat. "Early identification and intensive treatment," though probably not as erroneous as the flat-world theory, is more a slogan or a rallying cry than a realistic assessment of the difficulties that delinquency control programs must over-

From *Social Problems*, Vol. 13, no. 2 (Fall 1965), pp. 160–175. Reprinted by permission of the Society for the Study of Social Problems.

A preliminary version of this paper was published in *Social Work*, 6 (July 1961), pp. 3–13. The research on which it is based was financed by the Ford Foundation.

come. This paper points out the need for sharper definition of the implicit assumptions of "early identification and intensive treatment" programs and then examines two of the best-known early identification programs in the light of this need.

Early identification programs are based on either of two logically distinct principles: extrapolation or circumstantial vulnerability. The principle of extrapolation assumes that predelinquents are youngsters in the early stages of a delinquent way of life; the principle of circumstantial vulnerability assumes that youngsters who have been exposed to circumstances believed to cause delinquency are likely to become delinquent. The Cambridge-Somerville Youth Study emphasized the extrapolative approach to prediction. "Difficult boys" and "average boys" were nominated by teachers and policemen. The expectation of adolescent delinquency was based primarily on quasi-delinquent behavior during preadolescence. Although the three raters on the Cambridge-Somerville research team made a clinical assessment of each case and made predictions on a variety of family and personal circumstances, the great majority of the predictions were that difficult boys would remain difficult and average boys, average.[1] Early identification meant

in short that anti-social tendencies would persist and develop further — unless checked by outside intervention. This is quite different from identifying potential delinquents by a theory of delinquency which holds that youngsters exposed to certain sociocultural conditions will become delinquent. Yet the latter is also called "early identification." Criminologists Sheldon and Eleanor Glueck claim to be able to predict delinquency on the basis of factors distinct from the child's early behavior: (1) affection of mother for the boy; (2) affection of father for the boy; (3) discipline of boy by father; (4) supervision of boy by mother; and (5) family cohesiveness.[2] The New York City Youth Board has attempted to test this claim by applying the Glueck prediction table to a sample of 223 boys who in 1952 entered the first grade of two New York City schools in high delinquency neighborhoods. Note that the Cambridge-Somerville approach to prediction is less ambitious than the Youth Board-Glueck approach. One can extrapolate without knowing much about causes. One presumably ought to know a great deal about the causes of delinquency if one hopes to make accurate predictions on the basis of the sociocultural circumstances to which the child is exposed.

This distinction between an extrapolative prediction and a circumstantial prediction, though clear in theory, is often obscured in practice. Diagnostic interviews or self-rating scales (like the Minnesota Multiphasic Personality Inventory) combine the youngster's reports about his own antisocial behavior and/or attitudes with his reports about his family and neighborhood environment. Thus, in many attempts at early identification, the basis for the prediction of future delinquency is not clear.[3] Of course, it can be contended that a better

---

[1] Professor Robert Stanfield found in his re-analysis of the Cambridge-Somerville data that 81 to 84 percent of the "difficult" referrals were given a *delinquent* prognosis; 59 to 68 percent of the "average" referrals were given a *nondelinquent* prognosis. (Personal communication, March 24, 1965.) Nevertheless, the extent to which the raters were influenced by the source and nature of the referrals is not clear. The seeming extrapolations might be accounted for by systematic differences in the environmental circumstances of "difficult" and "average" boys. The three raters themselves claimed to give considerable weight to the nature of the neighborhood and the family situation. See Donald W. Taylor, "An Analysis of Predictions of Delinquency Based on Case Studies," *Journal of Abnormal and Social Psychology*, 42 (January 1947), pp. 45–46. Recall, however, that the design of the study was such that the raters started with a bimodal universe: boys identified by teachers and policemen as troublesome and boys identified as law-abiding. Although the ratings ranged from minus 5 (most delinquent) to plus 5 (most nondelinquent), comparatively few borderline ratings (zero) were made. In characterizing the predictions as extrapolative, I am assuming that a troublesome boy was predicted to be more or less delinquent depending on his family and neighborhood situation and a law-abiding boy was predicted to be more or less nondelinquent, but troublesome boys did not usually get into the nondelinquent prediction range nor law-abiding boys into the delinquent range by virtue of their family and neighborhood situations. In Tables 1 and 2, any prediction from minus five to minus one was considered a prediction of delinquency, and any prediction from plus five to plus one was considered a prediction of nondelinquency. Zero predictions were eliminated from the analysis. See also the discussion in Edwin Powers and Helen Witmer, *An Experiment in the Prevention of Delinquency: The Cambridge-Somerville Youth Study*, New York: Columbia University Press, 1951, pp. 29–36.

[2] Sheldon and Eleanor Glueck, *Unraveling Juvenile Delinquency*, New York: Commonwealth Fund, 1950; Sheldon and Eleanor Glueck, *Predicting Delinquency and Crime*, Cambridge, Massachusetts: Harvard University Press, 1959; Eleanor T. Glueck, "Efforts to Identify Delinquents," *Federal Probation*, 24 (June 1960), pp. 49–56.

[3] D. H. Stott, "The Prediction of Delinquency from Non-Delinquent Behavior," *British Journal of Delinquency*, 10 (January 1960), pp. 195–210.

prediction can be made if it is based *both* on the child's early behavior and on his exposure to known deleterious influences. Possibly so. However, such predictions emerge like sausages from a sausage machine but without real insight into *why* they are correct. The drawback of predictions made without theory becomes all too evident when treatment is attempted. Since the prediction is mechanical and does not imply an understanding of the causes of delinquency, it provides no guidance for treatment. "Treatment" becomes an umbrella word meaning all things to all men. A therapeutic program based on family casework is not the same thing as one based on individual psychotherapy, the improvement of reading skills, participation in organized sports, or vocational counseling.

Predictions made without a theory of delinquency causation can be matched with a treatment program that is similarly eclectic. Sometimes it is very difficult indeed to find out what "intensive treatment" consists of. The therapist may contend that each case is unique and that treatment is tailored to the individual case. One might well be suspicious of such vagueness. Vagueness can conceal two kinds of ignorance: ignorance as to what is causing the antisocial behavior and ignorance of the best strategy of intervention. In any case, most "individual treatment" programs and programs claiming to "co-ordinate" community resources are in practice not genuinely eclectic. They implicitly answer the question, "What kind of treatment?" by selecting resources ideologically congenial to the agency. For example, the same predelinquent child may be treated through casework techniques if he comes to the attention of one agency and through group work techniques if he comes to the attention of another. Presumably the type of treatment selected should be governed by the etiological factor involved in the youngster's predelinquency. The type of treatment selected by practitioners of "individual treatment" seems more closely related to the practitioners' preconceptions than to the child's problems. This is said, not to condemn efforts to treat predelinquency, but to point out that in the present state of knowledge the fre-

quently invoked analogy between medical practice and delinquency control is misleading. Whereas medical practice aims at precise diagnosis and specific treatment, early identification and intensive treatment of delinquency usually address themselves to an unknown problem with an unproved technique. Is it any wonder that the few treatment programs that have been rigorously evaluated reveal disappointingly small effects? For instance, the Cambridge-Somerville Youth Study offers little support to proponents of "early identification and intensive treatment" as an approach to delinquency control. Whereas 41 percent of the 253 boys in the treatment group subsequently were convicted of at least one major crime in a state or federal court, 37 percent of the 253 boys in the control group were so convicted. Considering (a) that treatment began by age 10 for 121 boys and by age 13 for the remaining 132, and (b) that treatment lasted for four years or more for 171 boys, *more* criminality in the treatment group is rather surprising. The McCords point out that only 12 of the 253 boys had intensive therapy (according to their quite reasonable criteria of "intensive"), and they suggest that for this reason intensive treatment was not really tested. Perhaps so. On the other hand, hardly a probation or parole system in the United States gives as intense supervision as was given routinely in the course of the Cambridge-Somerville Youth Study. The case loads of Cambridge-Somerville workers were 34 youngsters per counselor at the beginning of the study and even fewer when the boys grew older.[4]

Tacit Assumptions of Early Identification and Intensive Treatment Programs

Presumably the rationale of early identification is to economize treatment efforts. Otherwise, society would expose all youth to whatever resources are available for delinquency control. But in order to achieve economy, the

[4] See Powers and Witmer, *op. cit.*, pp. 85, 88; William and Joan McCord, *Origins of Crime: A New Evaluation of the Cambridge-Somerville Youth Study*, New York: Columbia University Press, 1959, pp. 20, 26, 29, 38–39.

predictions must be accurate. If delinquency occurs in too many cases where nondelinquency was predicted or *fails* to occur in too many cases where it *was* predicted, economy may not be realized. Once the predictions are found to be sufficiently accurate, greater intensity of treatment efforts is possible because youngsters not in danger of becoming delinquent can be ignored.

The conditions under which accurate predictions may be anticipated are therefore important. For the occurrence of adolescent delinquency to be predicted accurately from either preadolescent behavior or preadolescent circumstances, no crucial etiological factors should make their appearance after the original predictions have been made. For instance, in the New York City Youth Board project, the ratings of the family backgrounds of the 223 boys were made when they were 6 years old. If family relations are the major factor in delinquency and if family relations change appreciably in the course of the study, the predictions ought not to be very accurate.[5] Peer group relations are even more prone to change than family relations. Since studies of adolescent street-corner groups reveal that youngsters who join such groups are more likely to commit delinquent acts than youngsters who do not join such groups and since delinquent groups rarely recruit members younger than 10, preadolescent ratings of school misbehavior or family background ought not to predict delinquency during adolescence very accurately. Of course, if we assume that early childhood experiences are so important that they establish a differential vulnerability for all subsequent experiences, early predictions might be ac-

curate despite later changes in family and peer relations. Freudian psychiatrists subscribe to this assumption of the disproportionate importance of early socialization; sociologists, on the other hand, believe that socialization continues throughout life and that the course of a child's life can be radically changed by subsequent experiences.

Correct identification of youngsters who will ultimately become delinquent is the first step of "early identification and intensive treatment" programs. The second step is to upset these initially correct predictions by an effective treatment program. It is usually assumed by the proponents of "early identification and intensive treatment" that treatment is effective merely by being intensive. This is not necessarily so. The focusing of treatment efforts on youngsters most likely to become delinquent necessarily involves special handling for them. It is extremely difficult for a focused treatment program to avoid stigmatizing the recipients of the "benefits" of the program. Early identification does not necessarily imply early stigmatization, but early *discriminatory* treatment seems to. Thus, it is conceivable that a boomerang effect will occur and that greater intensity of exposure to treatment will be *less* effective than less intense but less discriminatory exposure. Suppose, for instance, that a community has an organized recreational program for *all* children up to the age of 16. Someone convinces the city fathers that organized recreation can prevent delinquency, and the program is changed to focus on identified predelinquents. Instead of 1,000 boys using the facilities occasionally, 200 boys use them frequently. Before leaping to the conclusion that these 200 boys are less likely to become delinquent, let us consider what the impact of their segregation is on "predelinquents." We know from experience with ability groupings in the schools that the evaluations of the adult world cannot be concealed from youngsters. Just as the children in the "dumb" classes know that they are not in the "smart" classes, these 200 boys are unlikely to think of themselves as the pride of the community. It is possible that less intensive recreational participation would have been more effective in arresting their delin-

---

[5] Professor Isidor Chein of New York University suggested that the Youth Board rate the family situations of the 223 boys *again* several years after the original ratings were made. How well would the two sets of ratings correlate with one another? If the later ratings were less closely related to outcome than the earlier ratings, this would tend to support the Glueck hypothesis that the early family situation is the major factor in delinquency. If the later ratings were more closely related to outcome than the earlier ratings, this would suggest that the contemporary situation — familial and extrafamilial — is more important in the genesis of delinquency than the Gluecks think.

quent tendencies than the more intensive — and incidentally more stigmatizing — exposure.[6]

The Cambridge-Somerville Youth Study and the New York City Youth Board Prediction Study did not assess the effect of neighborhood, ethnic background, or socio-economic status on the *accuracy* of their predictions. As a result, they missed an opportunity to clarify the conditions under which predisposing personal or family factors eventuate in delinquency. I propose to examine both studies in the light of these omissions in order to demonstrate that explicit consideration of the social context is necessary for further progress in delinquency *prediction* and ultimately control.

The Cambridge-Somerville Youth Study

Table 1 shows a positive relationship between the original predictions of delinquency or nondelinquency made in 1937–38 and the outcomes as of 1956.[7] Insofar as errors of prediction occurred, they were mainly overpredictions of delinquency. That is, of the 305 boys for whom delinquency was predicted, 191 turned into "good" boys (63 percent); but only 18 of the 150 for whom *nondelinquency* was predicted subsequently committed offenses (12 percent). Bear in mind that the Cam-

bridge-Somerville Youth Study assumed that, unless the service program were successful, preadolescent boys who manifested antisocial behavior would continue such behavior in adolescence. In point of fact, the majority of identified predelinquents did *not* persist in their delinquent activities. The obvious question is: Why not?

It might be possible to find out why delinquency was overpredicted and, hopefully, the conditions making for more accurate predictions if the data in Table 1 were partitioned into meaningful subsamples. For example, various ethnic groups are represented in the study population: "Italian," "Other Latin," "Negro," "Eastern European," "Western European," and "Native American."[8] If predictions were more accurate for Italian boys than, say, for native American boys, this might throw light on the relationship between cultural values and delinquency.[9] Similarly, several socioeconomic levels were represented in the study population. If predictions were more accurate for slum-dwelling youngsters than for boys living in better residential neighborhoods, this might throw light on the relationship between social class and delinquency. Table 2 explores the latter question by breaking down the data of Table 1 into subsamples of neighborhoods. What does Table 2 reveal about the effect of the socioeconomic milieu?

Facts

1. Predictions of delinquency were more likely to be made in slum neighborhoods than in better residential neighborhoods. Seventy-five percent of the 290 boys from slum neighborhoods were predicted by the raters to become delinquent as compared with 54 percent of boys from better neighborhoods.

---

[6] Proponents of early identification and intensive treatment might argue that stigmatization occurs but that it is helpful in preventing delinquency (by nipping the deviant tendency in the bud). Law enforcement officials sometimes use this argument, but they usually talk in terms of "punishment" rather than "treatment." Social workers and psychiatrists seem unwilling to face the logical possibility that well-intentioned "treatment" can do more harm than good. For an analysis of the comparative consequences of punishment and treatment, see Jackson Toby, "Is Punishment Necessary?" *Journal of Criminal Law, Criminology and Police Science*, 55 (September 1964), pp. 332–337.

[7] The unpublished tabulations in Tables 1 and 2 were made available to me through the graciousness of Professor William McCord of Stanford University, Professor Gordon W. Allport of Harvard University, Dr. Stanton Wheeler of the Russell Sage Foundation, and Professor Robert Stanfield of the University of Massachusetts. Note that these tabulations include boys from both treatment and control groups. Since the treatment program proved ineffective, the exclusion of treatment cases from the analysis was unnecessary.

[8] The ethnic data relating to the study population do not appear in *Origins of Crime* but are found in a second volume, which explored the causes of alcoholism rather than crime. For information on ethnic groupings, see William and Joan McCord, *Origins of Alcoholism*, Stanford, California: Stanford University Press, 1960, p. 38.

[9] See Jackson Toby, "Hoodlum or Business Man: An American Dilemma," in Marshall Sklare, ed., *The Jews*, Glencoe, Ill.: The Free Press, 1958, pp. 542–550, for a discussion of the relationship between ethnic background and delinquency.

Table 1

Comparison of Original Predictions and Final Outcomes of Boys in the Cambridge-Somerville Youth Study

	Outcomes		
Predictions	*Delinquent*	*Nondelinquent*	*Total*
Delinquent	114	191[a]	305
Nondelinquent	18[a]	132	150
Total	132	323	455

[a] Errors of prediction.

Table 2

Partition of Cambridge-Somerville Youth Study Cases by Neighborhood of Residence

	Outcomes					
	In slum neighborhoods			*In better neighborhoods*		
Predictions	*Delinquent*	*Non-delinquent*	*Total*	*Delinquent*	*Non-delinquent*	*Total*
Delinquent	90	126[a]	216	24	65[a]	89
Nondelinquent	12[a]	62	74	6[a]	70	76
Total	102	188	290	30	135	165

[a] Errors of prediction.

2. Predictions of delinquency were more likely to be correct in slum neighborhoods than in better neighborhoods. Forty-two percent of the 216 boys predicted delinquent from slum neighborhoods actually became so as compared with 27 percent of the 89 boys predicted delinquent in better neighborhoods.

3. Predictions of *nondelinquency* were more likely to be correct in better residential neighborhoods than in slum neighborhoods. Ninety-two percent of the boys predicted nondelinqent from better neighborhoods remained law-abiding as compared with 84 percent of the boys predicted nondelinquent in slum neighborhoods.

4. The differences between the later delinquency rates of troublesome and conforming preadolescents are striking. In slum neighborhoods, 42 percent of the troublesome preadolescents, as contrasted with 16 percent of the conformists, subsequently committed offenses. In the better residential neighborhoods, 27 percent of the troublesome preadolescents, as con-

trasted with 8 percent of the conformists, subsequently committed offenses.

Interpretation

1. Predictions of delinquency could have varied by neighborhood for either one of two reasons (or a combination of both):

a. Because preadolescent misbehavior at school and in the community is more common in slum neighborhoods than in better residential neighborhoods.

b. Because preadolescent misbehavior was likely to be discounted by the Cambridge-Somerville raters on the basis of favorable family situations, and such situations are more frequent in better residential neighborhoods. That is to say, the raters were more likely to predict nondelinquency or to assign an undecided (zero) rating if the troublesome preadolescent came from a "good" neighborhood.

2. The greater tendency of predictions of delinquency to come true and predictions of nondelinquency to be incorrect in slum neigh-

borhoods may be explained by differing neighborhood traditions of delinquency. Precisely how these traditions originate and are sustained is not clear. One relevant factor is a concentration of disorganized families exercising ineffective control over children, especially over adolescent boys.[10] Another is the proliferation of highly visible street-corner groups that are frequently delinquent. Sociologists have suggested that the weakness of family control and the influence of the peer group are different sides of the same coin.[11]

3. The negligible tendency of *conforming* preadolescents to become delinquent in later years — in both slum neighborhoods and in better residential neighborhoods — may mean that boys controlled effectively by their parents in preadolescence continue to be controlled effectively in adolescence and young adulthood. External controls, however, may not be so crucial as the conforming preadolescent develops a nondelinquent self-conception that insulates him from involvement in delinquent peer groups.[12] Thus, the delinquent peer group is likely to have a quite different impact on troublesome and on conforming preadolescents. Not only were the differences between the delinquency records of the troublesome and the conforming preadolescents substantial in later years. The conforming preadolescents from slum neighborhoods had a less delinquent record than the troublesome preadolescents from the better neighborhoods.

4. The reason or reasons for the overprediction of delinquency are not clear. An obvious possibility is that a considerable amount of delinquency goes unrecorded.[13] If this "hidden delinquency" could somehow be put into the record, the predictions might well seem more accurate. Another possibility is that delinquent tendencies were somehow "nipped in the bud." Troublesome preadolescents were salvaged. The difficulty with this interpretation is that the planned program of intervention did not result in a lower delinquency rate in the treatment group as compared with the control group. As a matter of fact, Table 3 suggests more strongly than the overall treatment group-control group comparison that a boomerang effect might have occurred.[14] The difference between the treatment group and the control group in the "good" neighborhoods was greater than the difference in the "worst" neighborhoods. This difference can be explained by sampling peculiarities. On the other hand, it is clear that the program of intervention was not *more* successful in the better residential neighborhoods. Since delinquent peer group influences are relatively weak in better residential neighborhoods, one would expect a program of delinquency prevention to have a *better* chance in such neighborhoods. The planned treatment program of the Cambridge-Somerville Youth Study staff may have been ineffectual; yet there is still the possibility that unplanned circumstances intervened to arrest delinquent tendencies. For example, parents may have moved to more wholesome communities to escape the delinquent influences of the slum. (The neighborhood ratings in the Cambridge-Somerville files date from the start of the study; they do not take into account subsequent moves.) The possible benefits of movement into low-delinquency neighborhoods is, unfortunately, pure speculation.

New York City Youth Board Prediction Study

The New York City Youth Board Prediction Study differed from the Cambridge-

[10] Jackson Toby, "The Differential Impact of Family Disorganization," *American Sociological Review*, 22 (October 1957), pp. 505–512.

[11] Frederic M. Thrasher, *The Gang*, Chicago: University of Chicago Press, 1927; William Foote Whyte, "Social Organization in the Slums," *American Sociological Review*, 8 (February 1943), pp. 34–39.

[12] Walter C. Reckless, Simon Dinitz, and Ellen Murray, "Self-Concept as an Insulator Against Delinquency," *American Sociological Review*, 21 (December 1956), pp. 744–747; Simon Dinitz, Frank R. Scarpitti, and Walter C. Reckless, "Delinquency Vulnerability: A Cross Group and Longitudinal Analysis," *American Sociological Review*, 27 (August 1962), pp. 515–517.

[13] Fred J. Murphy, Mary M. Shirley, and Helen L. Witmer, "The Incidence of Hidden Delinquency," *American Journal of Orthopsychiatry*, 16 (October 1946), pp. 286–296.

[14] William and Joan McCord, *Origins of Crime*, pp. 71, 204.

Table 3

Delinquency Among Treatment Boys and Control Boys in the Cambridge-Somerville Youth Study, by Type of Neighborhood

Type of neighborhood	% of convictions in treatment group (N = 233)	% of convictions in control group (N = 250)
Good	38	26
Fair	37	33
Poor	40	44
Worst	46	49

Somerville Youth Study in important respects. In the first place, all the boys for whom delinquency predictions were made came from two high-delinquency neighborhoods. Second, the predictions were based on home visits by social workers when the youngsters entered the first grade. They gave negligible weight to a factor particularly stressed in the Cambridge-Somerville Youth Study, the boy's own behavior. The critical question, of course, is: By what mechanism do "bad" family situations lead to delinquency in high-delinquency neighborhoods? Consider two quite different mechanisms by which a bad family situation might lead to delinquency:

1. Parental rejection and neglect damage the personality of the developing child. Lack of impulse control results from pathological socialization.[15] The psychopathic or neurotic boy reacts with violence to trivial provocations, sets fires, and steals purposelessly.

2. Parental inadequacy and neglect, by reducing family control, thereby orient the boy toward his agemates in the neighborhood.[16] (The family and the peer group are in a sense competing for the allegiance of boys in high-delinquency neighborhoods.) If the peer group is delinquent, a boy's desire for acceptance by his peers tempts him to participate in delinquent activities.

The Youth Board researchers do not make clear which of these mechanisms they suspect has greater influence. Although both are prob-

ably at work, mutually reinforcing one another to produce delinquency, a delinquency control program cannot do all things at once; hence it would seem desirable to be explicit about suspected etiological mechanisms. In point of fact, the intensive treatment program undertaken by the Youth Board addressed psychiatric problems; a clinic was set up in one of the two schools, and treatment was offered by a team consisting of psychologists, psychiatrists, and social workers to all of the boys predicted delinquent by the original Glueck scale.[17] The boys who were likewise predicted delinquent in the other school were to serve as a control group. Although the experimental program lasted four years, it failed in its objective. As in the Cambridge-Somerville Youth Study, members of the treatment group were no less likely to become delinquent than members of the control group.[18] A possible explanation for the failure is that the treatment program was predicated on the first mechanism whereas the second mechanism may have been more relevant to the delinquency of these

---

[15] Kate Friedlander, *The Psychoanalytic Approach to Juvenile Delinquency*, New York: International Universities Press, 1944.

[16] Thrasher, *op. cit.*

[17] New York City Youth Board, Research Department, *A Study in Variance from Predicted Delinquency: A Study of 20 Negro Boys Who Were Overpredicted*, mimeographed, 1962, ch. 4.

[18] Based on a personal conversation with Mrs. Maude Craig, research director of the Youth Board. To the best of my knowledge the New York City Youth Board has not published a full account of this experiment, apparently on the assumption that something went wrong in the execution of the experiment that did not reflect on its underlying assumptions. This attitude strikes me as dubious, particularly in view of the Youth Board's awareness of the similar results of a project in Washington, D.C., which also used the Glueck scale to identify predelinquents and which also attempted clinical treatment. *Ibid.*, p. 58.

Table 4

A Comparison Among the Youth Board Two- or Three-Factor Table, The Glueck Five-Factor Table, and a Single Factor (Public Assistance) in Predicting Delinquency

	Outcomes, 7 years later		
1952 predictions	Delinquent	Nondelinquent	*Total*
Based on five factors			
Probably delinquent	17	50[a]	67
Probably nondelinquent	4[a]	152	156
Total	21	202	223
Based on two or three factors			
Probably delinquent	13	24[a]	37
Probably nondelinquent	8[a]	178	186
Total	21	202	223
Based on single factor (economic status of family when boy entered school in 1952)			
Public assistance	13	39[a]	52
No public assistance	8[a]	163	171
Total	21	202	223

[a] Errors of prediction.

underprivileged boys. Let us examine the relationship between predictions and outcomes in the light of this hypothesis.

Table 4 reports the relationship between 1952 predictions and 1959 outcomes utilizing three different prediction techniques:

1. the five-factor scale designated by the Youth Board at the beginning of the research as the official prediction device; [19]

2. a two- and three-factor scale developed late in the research to adapt the Glueck scale to the ethnic groups represented in the Youth Board population (especially Negroes); [20]

[19] Sheldon and Eleanor Glueck, *Unraveling Juvenile Delinquency*, New York: Commonwealth Fund, 1950.

[20] Further modifications of the Glueck scales occurred after eight years. Instead of getting rater agreement on total scores, the Youth Board researchers insisted now on rater agreement on each factor going into the score. Second, aware of the fact that the scales were overpredicting delinquency, the Youth Board researchers reviewed some cases and reclassified them from probably delinquent to probably nondelinquent. These

3. a single-item predictive device (based on whether or not the family was receiving welfare assistance in 1952), the purpose of which is to provide a basis for comparing the predictive power of the Youth Board scales with predictions based on a readily available socioeconomic datum.

Note that the original five-factor prediction table made 54 errors, more than the 47 errors made by the table based on the public assistance criterion alone. The two- and three-factor table did considerably better: only 32 errors. But *why* did the two- and three-factor table do better than the five? What factors were eliminated? The revised scale used "mother's

changes were seemingly made for cogent research considerations. Unfortunately though, they were made long after the research began and could no longer be regarded as uncontaminated "prospective predictions." For a history of these changes, see New York City Youth Board, *An Experiment in the Use of the Glueck Social Prediction Table as a Prognosticator of Potential Delinquency*, mimeographed, October 1961.

supervision" and "cohesiveness of the family" supplemented by "father's discipline" in those cases "where a father or father substitute has been in the home a sufficient length of time to have had an influence in the boy's life." [21] From this improvement of prediction resulting from the elimination of "affection of mother for the boy" and of "affection of the father for the boy," it might be inferred that these factors are not important to the etiology of delinquency in this population. (Bear in mind that the universe consists of boys from *high-delinquency* neighborhoods.) Eleanor Glueck assures skeptics that "this is not the case." [22] She explains the greater accuracy of the two- and three-factor table as compared with the original five-factor table as due to inconsistency of ratings of parental affection by social workers of different intellectual persuasions and to the difficulty of making ratings for families where the father has long been out of the home. To me this argument is not convincing. Only 28 of 224 boys lacked fathers (or father substitutes) in the home for a major portion of their lives, and presumably the absence of mothers or mother substitutes was rarer.[23] Why was "affection of the *Mother*" not a useful predictive item? Mrs. Glueck's argument is essentially that parental affection is etiologically important but that the Youth Board researchers were unable to measure parental affection reliably. An alternative interpretation is that parental *affection* is less closely correlated with delinquency in high-delinquency neighborhoods than is parental *control*. The explanation of the greater accuracy of the shorter scale as compared with the five-factor scale may simply be that mother's supervision, family cohesiveness, and father's discipline are more closely related to parental control than are affection of the mother and affection of the father.

Is there any other evidence in favor of the hypothesis that parental control is the crucial

variable affecting the accuracy of the Youth Board predictions? The Youth Board itself provided such evidence in a study of 20 Negro boys who were predicted delinquent by the five-factor Glueck prediction table and failed to become so in the subsequent eight years.[24] In a chapter entitled, "Mother's Supervision Counteracting Peer Group Environment," the author of the Youth Board monograph (Dr. Philip W. Furst) emphasizes the role of the mother or mother-substitute in preventing gang membership or defining it as undesirable (dangerous). "She uses various means: exhortation, reason, rewards, example, tongue-lashing, threats, discipline, manipulation of the environment, coaxing, cajoling. And this process goes on with ever broadening content into the middle teens and beyond." [25] *Seven* of these 20 boys had been rated in 1952 as effectively supervised by the mother — as contrasted with *two* of 14 Negro boys predicted delinquent who confirmed the prediction.[26] Four additional boys "were saved in the school years by mothers' supervision even though the mothers' original supervision ratings were poor. . . ." [27] In another four cases, recognition of the *grandmother's* part in supervision and in the cohesiveness of the family might have led to a more hopeful prediction. For instance, one of the two boys out of the 20 considered to have the *highest* probability of becoming delinquent had little contact with his parents. "What the interviewer did not grasp in 1952 . . . was the fact that the person who really counted in those children's lives was the marvelous grandmother in whose home the family was living." [28] Thus, 15 of the 20 incorrect predictions of delinquency might have been avoided by emphasizing parental control more strongly.

Those mothers and mother-substitutes who were concerned about supervising the activities of their sons may have been distressed at the growing crime problems of their neighborhoods. Although the schools were selected by the Youth Board in 1952 because they lay in

21 *Ibid.*, p. 10.

22 Eleanor T. Glueck, *op. cit.*, pp. 55–56.

23 New York City Youth Board, *op. cit.*, 1961, p. 13. Note that the total of 224 boys includes one Puerto Rican youngster not included in earlier reports I have examined and therefore not included in Tables 4 or 5.

24 New York City Youth Board, *op. cit.*, 1962.

25 *Ibid.*, pp. 28–29.

26 *Ibid.*, p. S6.

27 *Ibid.*, p. S15.

28 *Ibid.*, p. 36. See also pp. 63–68.

high-delinquency neighborhoods, the delinquency rates in the two neighborhoods increased over the ten-year period of the study. Three families moved from the Bronx to rural areas, at least one for the express purpose of providing better child supervision.[29] Bear in mind that choice of neighborhoods was limited for these 20 Negro families. Furthermore, half of them were receiving public assistance at some time during the study, reflecting economic disabilities that must have also reduced their opportunities to relocate. Nevertheless, eight of the twenty families had moved by 1961 to better neighborhoods. Perhaps it is only a coincidence, but four of the seven families where the mother's supervision was rated effective in 1965 had relocated into neighborhoods with lower delinquency rates — as compared with four of the 13 families where the mother's supervision was poor.

Residential mobility was not confined to Negro families; 29 of the 53 white boys in the Youth Board study were Jewish, and other studies have shown that Jewish families move readily to better neighborhoods when their old communities deteriorate.[30] Mobility is not motivated exclusively by a concern for the upbringing of children, important though this is; population flow is to be expected in a large city. The Youth Board researchers have complained about the difficulty of keeping track of 61 boys scattered by 1961 in out-of-town schools in 12 states, Puerto Rico, and Malta.[31] And of course moves occurred within New York City. Regardless of the motivation for residential moves, however, an important consequence is to provide a new environment for children. Of 14 boys predicted *nondelinquent* in 1952 whose families moved to a *better* neighborhood, none became delinquent; of 31 boys with exactly the same prediction score whose families moved to neighborhoods with the *same* or *worse* levels of delinquency, 7 became delinquent.[32] The Youth Board has not yet analyzed the moves of all the families in the study in relation to prediction scores and outcomes. Hence, it is not known whether boys predicted *delinquent* in 1952 were less likely to become so if their families moved to better neighborhoods. It sounds plausible.

If indeed weak family control predisposes a boy living in a high-delinquency neighborhood to become delinquent, it would be helpful to know the ethnic and socioecenomic circumstances that reinforce this tendency. The question is not *whether* the various prediction tables predict delinquency but *how* both successful and unsuccessful predictions provide clues to underlying causes and ultimately to programs of intervention. As an illustration of this approach Table 5 breaks down the relationship between the two- and three-factor prediction table and delinquent outcomes (shown in Table 4) for three ethnic groups and two socioeconomic statuses.[33] What does Table 5 reveal about the reinforcing effect of the social milieu?

Facts

1. Predictions of delinquency were more likely to be made for Negro boys than for Puerto Rican or white boys. Twenty-one percent of the 131 Negro boys were given better than a 50-50 chance of becoming delinquent — as contrasted with 13 percent of the 39 Puerto Rican boys and 8 percent of the 53 white boys. To look at the data in another way, of the 37 boys predicted delinquent, 33 were Negro or Puerto Rican.

2. Although the number of cases in some categories were very small, e.g., only four *white* boys and five *Puerto Ricans* predicted delinquent, predictions of delinquency were more likely to be correct and predictions of nondelinquency to be wrong for Negroes and Puerto Ricans than for whites. Whereas one

[29] *Ibid.*, pp. S7–8.

[30] *Ibid.*, p. 4; Nathan Glazer and Daniel Patrick Moynihan, *Beyond the Melting Pot: The Negroes, Puerto Ricans, Jews, Italians, and Irish of New York City*, Cambridge, Massachusetts: M.I.T. Press, 1963, pp. 53–67, 160–163.

[31] New York City Youth Board, *op. cit.*, 1961, p. 15.

[32] New York City Youth Board, Research Department, *A Study of Mobility and Delinquency in a Sample of Boys in Glueck Project*, mimeographed, February 1963, p. 6.

[33] Mrs. Maude Craig, research director of the Youth Board, graciously provided unpublished data on the economic status and the ethnic backgrounds of the 223 boys in the study.

Table 5

Differential Impact of a "Bad" Family Situation on Economically Dependent and on Self-sufficient White, Negro, and Puerto Rican Families

| | | 1959 outcomes | | | | | |
| | | For 1952 Public assistance families | | | For 1952 self-sufficient families | | |
Ethnic background	1952 predictions two- and three-factor table	Delin-quent	Non-delin-quent	Total	Delin-quent	Non-delin-quent	Total
White	Probably delinquent	1	2[a]	3	0	1[a]	1
	Probably nondelinquent	0[a]	0	0	0[a]	49	49
	Total	1	2	3	0	50	50
Negro	Probably delinquent	4	9[a]	13	4	11[a]	15
	Probably nondelinquent	4[a]	19	23	3[a]	77	80
	Total	8	28	36	7	88	95
Puerto Rican	Probably delinquent	3	1[a]	4	1	0[a]	1
	Probably nondelinquent	1[a]	8	9	0[a]	25	25
	Total	4	9	13	1	25	26
All	Probably delinquent	8	12[a]	20	5	12[a]	17
	Probably nondelinquent	5[a]	27	32	3[a]	151	154
	Total	13	39	52	8	163	171

[a] Errors of prediction.

out of four of the white boys predicted delinquent became so, 36 percent of the Negroes and Puerto Ricans predicted delinquent fulfilled the prediction. None of the 49 white boys predicted nondelinquent became delinquent but 8 percent of the Negro and Puerto Rican boys did within seven years.

3. Predictions of delinquency were more likely to be made for boys from public assistance families than for boys from self-sufficient families. Thirty-eight percent of the 52 public assistance boys were given better than a 50-50 chance of becoming delinquent — as contrasted with 10 percent of the 171 boys from self-sufficient families.

4. Predictions of delinquency were more likely to be correct and predictions of nondelinquency more likely to be wrong for public assistance families than for self-sufficient families. This tendency was characteristic of white, Negro, and Puerto Rican families looked at

separately; the fact of public assistance had an adverse effect on outcomes regardless of ethnicity.

Interpretation

1. Since the predictions of delinquency were based on pathological family situations, the greater tendency for predictions of delinquency to be made in Negro and Puerto Rican families must be due mainly to the greater incidence of family disorganization in these ethnic groups. This disorganization is highly correlated with dependency and, very likely, with employment opportunities. Note, for example, that only 16 percent of the boys from self-sufficient Negro families were predicted delinquent — as contrasted with 36 percent from dependent Negro families.

2. Recall that in the Cambridge-Somerville Youth Study the greater tendency for predictions of delinquency to come true and predic-

tions of nondelinquency to be wrong in slum neighborhoods was interpreted as due to differing neighborhood traditions of delinquency. In the Youth Board study we see again a greater tendency for predictions of delinquency to come true and predictions of nondelinquency to be incorrect in disadvantaged segments of the population, this time among Negroes and Puerto Ricans and among the children of welfare recipients rather than among boys from poorer neighborhoods. Part of the explanation here may be that ethnic traditions of delinquency are analogous to neighborhood traditions of delinquency. Obviously, however, differing ethnic traditions of delinquency cannot explain the fact that boys from public assistance families were more likely to become delinquent within the same ethnic group and the same Glueck prediction category. It is unlikely that public assistance families constitute a community within a community and that the children of such families have a distinct tradition of delinquency. Possibly boys from economically dependent families are more likely to be *recorded* as delinquents than boys from self-sufficient families who are behaving similarly; this assumes that the police know the welfare status of the family and discriminate against the most deprived. This seems to me far-fetched. More likely, economic disadvantage has adverse effects on the school adjustment and (ultimately) on the occupational opportunities of public assistance children.[34] Their greater proneness to delinquency may stem from their lesser hopes for and commitments to legitimate enterprises.[35]

3. Bear in mind that all of the preadolescent boys followed up in the Youth Board Prediction Study came from two high delinquency neighborhoods characterized by considerable gang activity. Yet those members of the Study population *predicted nondelinquent*, i.e., closely supervised by their parents, usually avoided

delinquent associates and bore out the prediction. Exceptions to this generalization are Negro boys from public assistance families predicted nondelinquent; 17 percent of them became delinquent within seven years. Perhaps the double disadvantage of race prejudice and poor economic prospects reduced their stake in conformity.[36]

4. One reason for the overprediction of delinquency is that Table 5 does not include *all* delinquencies committed by the boys in the study from 1952 to 1959; some delinquent acts were undetected or unrecorded. Another reason for the overprediction of delinquency in Table 5 is that some boys became delinquent for the first time *after* 1959. But there remains the possibility that many of the prophecies of delinquency were defeated because deliberate as well as unintentional interventions occurred in the lives of these boys. Families moved to neighborhoods with fewer delinquent gangs; boys joined boys' clubs or the Boy Scouts; social agencies helped the families to solve their problems and thereby improved parental supervision; the schools offered remedial education to slow learners.

Conclusion

The problem of delinquency control has long been the subject of jurisdictional disputes among sociologists, psychologists, social workers and psychiatrists — not to mention lawyers and the police. Recently, "early identification and intensive treatment of predelinquents" has attracted much interest, and it seemed at first that this approach offered a relatively uncontroversial technique of delinquency control.

Careful analysis of two notable experiments in early identification and intensive treatment of predelinquents shows that intellectual confusion lurks beneath the surface plausibility of early identification and intensive treatment. The following issues have not been resolved:

[34] Richard A. Cloward and Lloyd E. Ohlin, *Delinquency and Opportunity*, Glencoe, Ill.: The Free Press, 1960.

[35] Larry Karacki and Jackson Toby, "The Uncommitted Adolescent: Candidate for Gang Socialization," *Sociological Inquiry*, 32 (Spring 1962), pp. 203–215.

[36] Jackson Toby, "Social Disorganization and Stake in Conformity: Complementary Factors in the Predatory Behavior of Young Hoodlums," *Journal of Criminal Law, Criminology and Police Science*, 48 (May–June 1957), pp. 12–17. Arthur L. Stinchcombe, *Rebellion in a High School*, Chicago: Quadrangle Books, 1964, chs. 3 and 4.

1. Does early identification depend on extrapolating antisocial tendencies already observable in the preadolescent boy or girl into adolescence? Or does early identification consist of locating youngsters who have been exposed to family or community experiences known to cause delinquency?

2. Can *early* identification be accurate? The issue of accuracy is essentially a theoretical problem. Accurate early identification is possible only (a) if no crucial etiological factors make their appearance *after* the predictions are made or (b) if early experiences establish a differential vulnerability for all subsequent experiences.

3. What *kind* of intensive treatment should be given? Does the type of treatment have to be individualized according to the problem of the youngster? Or are all types of treatment equally effective with all types of delinquents providing treatment is "intensive"?

4. How intensive must "intensive treatment" be and how early must it start in order to satisfy the early identification and intensive treatment formula? (The McCords have dismissed the negative results of the Cambridge-Somerville Youth Study as irrelevant to the validity of the early identification and intensive treatment approach because the treatment program was not sufficiently intensive.)

5. How can early identification and intensive treatment programs avoid "self-fulfilling prophecies"? If the treatment program concentrates its efforts on youngsters who are especially vulnerable to delinquency, how can it justify its discriminatory policy except by stigmatizing predelinquents? And may not the delinquency-producing effects of the stigmatization equal or exceed the delinquency-preventing benefits of the treatment?

6. Finally, is it likely that an effective approach to delinquency control can emerge without clarification of the underlying intellectual issues in the etiology of delinquency? Although they approached early identification of predelinquents in theoretically distinct ways, both the Cambridge-Somerville Youth Study and the New York City Youth Board Prediction Study show that attention to the social context can improve the accuracy of predictions. The neighborhood of residence in the Cambridge-Somerville Youth Study and the dependency status of the family and its ethnicity in the New York City Youth Board Prediction Study were relevant to later outcomes. However, in neither study is it clear *why* predictions of delinquency were more likely to be correct and predictions of nondelinquency wrong for youngsters of disadvantaged social origins. The relationship among social origin, family functioning, individual self-conception, and peer group influence was ignored. Can a theoretically blind prediction technique provide the basis for effective intervention?

Miller proposes that expressions of public concern about delinquency serve unstated psychological functions for adults as individuals and structural functions for agencies and institutions with explicit responsibility in the area of juvenile delinquency. There is widespread agreement that prevention is preferable to a concentration on treatment of those already involved in delinquent activities. Yet, the existing social arrangements provide a variety of agencies and institutions devoted to handling offenders, but few if any existing institutional structures are geared to delinquency prevention. As a result, delinquency prevention becomes a minor responsibility in agencies with other primary objectives.

That this has an important bearing on the effectiveness of prevention programs is documented in Miller's description of the experience of one large eastern city with a community-based prevention program. To maintain its continued existence, each institution gives greater priority to achievement of its stated objectives than to efforts at delinquency prevention. Inter-institutional conflict, which Miller describes along six dimensions, results in a lack of coordination and mutual blocking of efforts. Whereas prevention requires application of existing knowledge regarding the etiology of delinquency and potentially useful ameliorative techniques, the focus of action efforts must be shifted from the relations between implementing institutions and the juvenile population to the relationships among the intricately inter-related organizations which maintain an interest in the area of delinquency.

WALTER B. MILLER

Inter-Institutional Conflict as a Major Impediment to Delinquency Prevention

Juvenile delinquency is a major area of concern in the United States today. Although there is evidence of some increase in the actual incidence of juvenile crime, it is equally evident that the intensity of public concern over this issue has increased far more rapidly than the demonstrated statistical increase. This paper will focus, not on juvenile crime as such, but on the larger adult community, and, in particular, on that segment of the community which maintains explicit responsibility in this area.

It is the thesis of this paper that the nature of current concern over juvenile delinquency serves important latent functions for substantial segments of the adult community. If this thesis is true, we would expect to find, as in all areas where a significant discrepancy exists between the overt or recognized aspects of a phenomenon and its covert aspects or latent functions: (1) Discrepancies and contradictions between officially stated policy and actual operating procedure; (2) recurrent failure to follow through on plans whose objectives conform to officially stated positions but whose execution would in fact run counter to the latent function; (3) much conflict over goals and methods both between concerned institu-

From *Human Organization*, 17 (Fall 1958), 20–23. Reprinted by permission.

tional systems and between sub-units within these systems. The net result of these forces would be to produce action stalemates both through failure to take action and through mutual blocking of efforts to the end that the latently functional status quo is preserved.

That public concern over juvenile delinquency serves *psychological* functions for adults as individuals has been maintained by several investigators. This paper will attempt to show that the nature of current institutional practice regarding delinquency serves important *structural* functions as well; that is, for the great majority of organized institutions which maintain programs directed at juvenile delinquency, the adoption of operating procedures and philosophies which would be effective in reducing juvenile crime would, in fact, pose severe threats to the viability of the institution. The focus here will be on the area of delinquency *prevention* rather than on methods of dealing with the adjudicated delinquent. Since the area of prevention is far less structured and has developed fewer established operating procedures than the area of treatment or disposition, the dynamics of institutional functioning in this area are revealed in much sharper relief.

It has been established that there is far more law-violating behavior by adolescents than is officially acted on; according to one study, the actual number of potentially arrestable delinquents is three times that of those actually arrested. Once an individual is officially apprehended for the commission of a delinquent act or acts, a whole series of established procedures are set into motion; the individual may be released with a warning, put on probation, or sentenced to undergo a variety of corrective measures ranging from a citizenship course through psychiatric treatment to straight confinement. But in the area of "prevention" things are much less well established. There is growing sentiment to the effect that "prevention" of juvenile crime would be a much sounder procedure than attempting to deal with the individual once he has already committed a crime, and would be much more economical in the long run. But then the question becomes — how does one "prevent"? Once something has happened you can take steps as a consequence of that occurrence, but what steps should you take for something that has not happened yet, but which might? Thus, while there are many well-established institutions — courts, police, correctional institutions, psychiatric agencies — whose operating procedures and philosophies are geared to handling individuals who have committed delinquent acts and been apprehended, there are, with a few exceptions, *no* established institutional structures whose major responsibility is delinquency prevention, and whose institutional values and operating philosophies are geared to that objective. Existing organizations undertake prevention, if at all, as a relatively minor adjunct to major institutional responsibilities which lie elsewhere — a fact which has important bearing on the potential effectiveness of prevention programs.

Following sections will describe very briefly the experience of one large eastern city in attempting to institute and maintain a "preventive" program on the community level. In 1950, rising public apprehension over juvenile delinquency in general, and gang violence in particular, produced demands for action from many quarters. Since gang activity was a focus of concern, and much gang delinquency is undetectable or undetected, traditional approaches based on restriction or treatment were seen as unfeasible, and pressures to institute some sort of community-based preventive program were exerted on the major institutional structures with assumed or assigned responsibility in the area of juvenile crime.

I

The city contained scores of intricately interrelated organizations, both public and private, varying widely in size, scope and method of operations, and in assigned or claimed area of jurisdiction or concern with juvenile crime. Of these, about a dozen public and private organizational groupings maintained major responsibility in the area of juvenile crime. The principal public agencies were the municipal government, the recreation department, the police department, the courts, the public schools, and the state youth corrections division. Major private groupings were medical and psychiatric clinics, social work agencies, churches, universities, and various special cause groups, such as ethnic associations and crime prevention societies.

Initial pressures produced a variety of statements as to the desirability of a preventive program, but no action. A complex set of maneuvers was carried on for about three years, usually involving the appointment of special committees which then appointed a study group which turned in a set of recommendations strongly affirming the desirability of a preventive program, and at the same time explaining why such a program was not the responsibility of that particular organization. This continuing stalemate was finally broken early in 1953, primarily through combined pressures from two ethnic groups, the Jews and the Negroes, after a prominent Jewish clergyman had been murdered, allegedly by a Negro teenage gang. The Jews, acting through their organized representative groupings, inferentially charged the Negroes with anti-semitism; the Negroes, through their organized groupings, intimated that this charge indicated anti-Negro sentiment on the part of the Jews. Two other groups whose interests were being threatened by gang activity — the public schools and the settlement houses — added their pressures to those of the Jews and Negroes, and, in the spring of 1953, a central delinquency committee was created, comprising representatives of over one hundred youth-concerned groupings in the metropolitan area, including the major groups cited above. At the time this committee was formed, many statements were made by all groupings — police, courts, the municipal administration, churches, private agencies — pledging their fullest mutual cooperation in this enterprise aimed at coping with the city gang problem.

Despite the sense of urgency and crisis which attended the organization of the central committee, no concrete action was taken for more than a year. This year was filled with indecision, groping for direction, and constant mutual blocking and conflict, sometimes veiled, sometimes overt, among the agencies represented on the central committee. A great variety of proposals was forwarded and debated, reflecting many divergent conceptions of the causes and proper treatment of juvenile crime, and the group seemed unable to reach any agreement on a positive course of action. After six months, a sociology professor at a local university was persuaded to accept responsibility for formulating a plan of action, and in June of 1954 — four and a half years after the initial moves, and a year and a half after the murder which had broken the stalemate — a special demonstration project in delinquency prevention was set up in one district of the city. By this time, several of the major organizations originally represented on the central committee had terminated active affiliation — principally, the police and the Jewish clergy. The Jews lost interest rapidly when it developed that anti-semitism had played a relatively small role in gang attacks on Jews.

The prevention project, which was to operate for three years, was staffed primarily by social workers, and included three service programs — a program of direct service to selected "delinquogenic" families, a community organization program, and, as a major effort, a program of direct work with delinquent corner gangs. Although it was the creation of the central committee, once project operations actually started, the committee became progressively disenchanted with its offspring. As the project took action in more definite and visible ways, it became clear that many of its methods and the operating philosophies behind them

were in radical conflict with the institutional ideals of the various groups represented on the central committee. This was evidenced in responses ranging from passive non-participation, through withdrawal, to active opposition.

During the three years of the project's existence, the executive board of the central committee became a battleground for its component organizations, with the project and its methods serving as a pawn in these conflicts. After the first meeting, at which a project worker presented a report on his activities, the representative of the Catholic Archdiocese resigned in indignation from the executive board. Following this incident, a watchdog committee was set up to oversee the project; the chairman of this committee was a Protestant clergyman who was strongly opposed to major methods of the project. About a year later the project became involved in direct conflict with the state division of corrections, with enmity reaching sufficient intensity that the corrections division issued an order forbidding its parolees to participate in project activities, and, in fact, jailed one parolee who defied this order. The social agencies initially regarded the program with great suspicion, as did the schools. During the latter part of the program the city recreation department representative on the central committee, incensed by a report issued by the project, demanded that no further reports be issued unless approved by the central committee. During the second year, funds to support the project, which were raised by the central committee, became increasingly difficult to obtain, and about this time the committee's original chairman, who had been active in initiating and supporting the project, was replaced, without his prior knowledge, by another man who was far less assertive.

Shortly after the start of the project's third year, its director resigned, partly because of increasing difficulties in obtaining financing, and no attempt was made to replace him with a person of equivalent status. Before the director left, he formulated a detailed proposal for the establishment of a permanent delinquency prevention agency under state and municipal auspices, using the project's experience as the basis of recommendations. The three-man committee chosen to present this program to the mayor and governor consisted of an amiable but aged chairman and the two most outspoken opponents of the project on the central committee. The recommendations for a state-municipal program presented under these auspices were rejected both by the mayor and governor. Once the program was officially terminated, the central committee appeared eager to forget that it had ever existed. Although federal support for post-project research had been obtained, members of the central committee were most reluctant to permit such continuation and questioned the right of the project to have sought these funds, despite the fact that authorization had been officially voted.

During the period when the project was subject to increasing opposition by its parent organizations on the central committee, these agencies were also engaged in attacking one another both in the arena of central committee meetings and through other media. A judge accused the police of inefficiency in dealing with delinquents and in keeping adequate crime statistics; a police chief accused the social welfare agencies of coddling delinquents; the director of a medical group accused the corrections division of increasing the delinquency of those in their care; a Catholic prelate accused the social work agencies of neglecting religion in their dealings with delinquents; a psychiatric agency head accused the police of harmful advocacy of punitive measures; the Archbishop accused enforcement agencies of politically motivated laxness in prosecuting delinquents; a group of legislators attempted to oust major officials of the youth corrections department over the issue of personnel qualifications. In addition, sub-units within these larger organizations feuded with one another; a judge accused other judges of excessive leniency in dealing with juvenile offenders; a committee of the school department claimed that some teachers were fostering delinquency by being unable or unwilling to cope with school behavior problems; the Police Commissioner castigated and demoted a sizable group of patrolmen, charging them with inefficiency in dealing with juveniles in their area of jurisdiction; a Protestant clergyman claimed that some Protestant sects were failing in the fight against delinquency by remaining too aloof from community involvement.

II

We have, then, a situation which involves these elements: first, a social phenomenon — gang violence — which is universally condemned; a crisis incident which arouses deep feelings and provides a spur to direct action; the mobilization and pledged cooperation of all the major concerned institutional groupings of a major American city; and then — much delay and misdirected energy by these institutions in setting up a project to which they become progressively more hostile; constant inter-institutional conflict over a variety of issues; and finally a virtual stalemate in launching any sort of effective action to cope with the problem. This situation is by no means unique; it is found in many cities faced with similar problems; in particular, conflicts between the police, churches, courts, social agencies, and schools in the New York City gang situation have been widely publicized. This prevalent phenomenon — apparently universal agreement on a basic objective, gang control, coupled with mutual conflict leading to almost complete blocking of action, may be explained by focusing on the *means* proposed to secure the end — means which derive from the operating philosophies of the various concerned organizations. This paper suggests that operating philosophies may be *non*functional for the purpose of reducing juvenile crime, and that a consequence of differences in institutional philosophies is that a significant proportion of energy potentially directable to delinquency reduction is instead expended in conflict between institutions.

The nature of these differences may be illuminated by specifying six dimensions along which conflict takes place: these relate to differences in conceptions of the *etiology* of delinquency; of the *disposition* of the delinquent; of the *approach priority*; of the appropriate *organizational method*; and of the proper *status of personnel*.

Morality-Pathology. A major difference in assumptions as to the etiology of juvenile crime, as well as other forms of behavior, involves fundamental concepts of human nature. According to one school of thought, deviant or criminal behavior must be viewed in terms of morality and immorality; an individual is morally responsible for his own behavior, and failure to conform to norms and standards represents a triumph of evil forces over good in an inner struggle for which the individual is held personally responsible. The opposing school maintains that deviant or criminal behavior should be viewed in terms of sickness and health; that an individual who violates social and legal norms is, in fact, driven by inner forces over which he has relatively little control, and which have their origins in pathological conditions of the organism.

Individual Locus-Social Locus. A second important difference involving etiological concepts relates to the locus of deviant behavior. One school attributes criminal behavior to forces within the *individual* — moral or physical-psychological — which may be dealt with by corrective measures directed at the individual; the other school finds the significant factors in the nature of the *social milieu,* and sees basic alterations in social conditions as the necessary course of action.

Restriction-Rehabilitation. This dimension relates to the proper method of dealing with offenders. The restrictive school of thought advocates the separation or isolation of the individual from normal social intercourse on the assumption, first, that the *protection of society* is the paramount necessity, and second, that punishment both serves as a deterrent to future violation and is merited in consequence of transgression. This dispositional prescription is generally forwarded by those espousing the morality concept of etiology. The treatment or rehabilitative school, basing procedure on the "pathology" conception of etiology, postulates "cure" or directed efforts to modify behavior patterns of the offending individual as of prime importance, with his restoration to normal social interaction a desired objective.

Action-Research. This dimension relates to consideration of priority in approaching the problem. One school maintains that the urgency of the situation, or the intensity of need, demands immediate action, based on the best knowledge currently available; the other maintains that far too little reliable information exists as to the nature of the involved phenomena and methods of treatment, and that the most productive expenditure of energy can be made by undertaking systematic research to gain essential knowledge.

Localization-Centralization. This dimension concerns the issue of the most desirable method for organizing preventive programs; one school believes that programs should be undertaken within and by the local community, on the grounds that only local people are sufficiently familiar with the special conditions of the local situation for adequate understanding, and that local autonomy must be maintained; the centralization school maintains that the nature and magnitude of the problem demand mobilization of resources which local groups, operating independently, could not afford, and that, to be effective, resources must be pooled and efforts coordinated to avoid duplication and overlap.

Lay-Professional. This dimension relates to the qualifications and status of personnel who are to implement preventive programs. One school holds that only those who manifest characteristics similar to those of the subject population — either through similarities in class or locality status — can be effective, and that attributes essential to effectiveness, such as warmth and sympathy, are independent of training; the other school maintains that work in so difficult an area demands that practitioners be exposed to a course of professional training which both imparts knowledge as to specialized procedures and eliminates those whose personality characteristics would be detrimental to this kind of work.

The various institutional structures related to delinquency tend to maintain characteristic syndromes of these etiological and procedural positions. The described positions are seldom maintained in the "pure" form, since they are presented here as polar extremes which define variable dimensions — and "middle positions," such as equal stress on action and research, may be taken, but most institutions involved do maintain definitely identifiable positions of varying intensity along these dimensions. Conflicts along the varying dimensions take place, both *between* and within, concerned institutions, but intra-institutional differences are generally concealed from public notice. The most severe conflict occurs between institutions which take extreme opposing positions on all or most of these dimensions; conflict is less severe when there is disagreement on only one or two. For example, the major juvenile court of the city described above strongly supported the "morality" and "individual locus" concepts of etiology, the restrictive dispositional method, action priority, and localized organization. The major child psychiatry clinic supported the "pathology" etiological concept, rehabilitative treatment method, centralized organization, and use of professional implementary personnel. These positions put the two organizations in direct conflict in four of the six dimensions; in agreement over one — individual etiological locus — and in minor opposition over the action-research issue. Similar comparisons could be made between each set of involved institutions.

Summary

The argument of this paper may be summarized as follows: There is much conflict over the issue of proper procedure among the different groups which maintain varying orders of responsibility for delinquency prevention. This conflict results in a lack of coordination and mutual blocking of efforts leading to a stalemate in reference to a community-supported objective. But these conflicts over method derive from the basic institutional philosophies of the several institutions; although these philosophies may be effective in facilitating achievement of the stated objectives of the institution, their maintenance is vital to the institution's continued existence and this latent objective has greater priority than the achievement of the institution's explicit objectives, and much greater priority than achieving objectives only peripherally related to the institution's primary explicit aims.

This situation would appear to have important implications for delinquency prevention. It would imply that the major impediment to effectiveness in this field relates more to the nature of relations among the various concerned institutions than to a lack of knowledge as to effective procedure. Much is now known about the causes of delinquency and promising ameliorative techniques have been developed. The principal difficulty lies in the *application* of these techniques, and any realistic possibility of such application depends almost entirely on existing institutional structures. This would suggest a shift in emphasis in current research and action efforts, from a primary focus on the relations between implementing institutions and the subject population, to the relationships among the institutions themselves. Both research and action efforts involve severe difficulties since they will touch on areas intimately related to the visibility of the institution — areas all the more charged and sensitive, since they are frequently unconscious or implicit.

Differential treatment of delinquents is based on the premise that a form of treatment which is effective for some types of offenders may be detrimental to other types. In this paper Warren attacks the question, "What kinds of treatment programs conducted by what kinds of workers in what kinds of settings are best for what kinds of juvenile offenders?" In the differential use of program elements, not only offenders but also treatment workers, treatment environments, and treatment methods were classified. This permitted the "matching" of workers, settings, and methods with types of delinquents. The classification of delinquents utilized in the treatment efforts Warren describes is based largely on psychological development. Comparison of these types with those discussed by Rodman and Grams in Section II may be instructive.

Warren concludes that delinquents can be classified reliably in ways relevant to treatment and that many offenders can be treated in the community without prior institutionalization. However, the available evidence suggests that those who identify with a deviant value system may be more effectively handled by means of incarceration. The studies described in this selection have produced other usable findings, though a number of questions regarding differential treatment remain to be explored.

MARGUERITE Q. WARREN

The Case for Differential Treatment of Delinquents

Beginning with the Community Treatment Project (CTP) in 1961, a number of experimental treatment projects for delinquents have developed around a theory of *differential* use of program elements. The question asked in this series of studies has been: What kinds of treatment programs conducted by what kinds of workers in what kinds of settings are best for what kinds of juvenile offenders? In order to approach these investigations, it has been necessary to have a way of classifying offenders, a way of classifying workers, a way of classifying treatment environments, and a way of classifying treatment methods. Assuming that one's goal is an over-all reduction in delinquency, one can — with these various classification schemata — proceed to "match" treaters, environments, and methods with types of delinquents in a manner calculated to bring about the maximum positive impact.

Rationale for Differential Treatment

One of the few agreed-upon "facts" in the field of corrections is that offenders are not all alike; that is, they differ from each other, not only in the form of their offense, but also in the reasons for and the meaning of their crime. Some individuals violate the law because the peer group on which they are dependent for approval prescribed criminal behavior as the price of acceptance, or because the values

From *The Annals of the American Academy of Political and Social Science*, 381 (January 1969), pp. 47–59. Reprinted by permission.

which they have internalized are those of a deviant subculture. Other individuals break laws because of insufficient socialization, which has left them at the mercy of any except the most protected of environments. Still others are delinquently acting out internal conflicts, identity struggles, or family crises. This list is, of course, illustrative, not exhaustive.

If one accepts the notion that offenders are different from each other in the reasons for their law violations, the implication follows that attempts to change the offender into a nonoffender will vary in ways which are relevant to the cause. Ideally, the goals of treatment will relate in some direct manner to the causes of the delinquency, and the treatment methods will relate specifically to the goals for the various offender subgroups.

The case for differential treatment was given support by two studies conducted in California during the 1950's.[1] In both of these studies, specific treatment methods — in one study, individual interview therapy and in the other, three types of group treatment — were found to be differentially effective with different types of offenders. Both studies showed that by lumping together all kinds of offenders, the

[1] J. D. Grant and M. Q. Grant, "A Group Dynamics Approach to the Treatment of Nonconformists in the Navy," *The Annals*, Vol. 322 (March 1959), pp. 126–135; S. A. Adams, *Interaction between Individual Interview Therapy and Treatment Amenability in Older Youth Authority Wards*, Vol. 2, California State Board of Corrections Monograph, 1961, pp. 27–44.

beneficial effects of the treatment program on some individuals, together with the detrimental effects of the same treatment program on other individuals, masked and cancelled out each other. It is likely that, in many treatment studies, this masking effect has occurred because the data have not been viewed in sufficiently complex fashion or because the crucial dimension — the classification of subjects in a treatment-relevant way — was missing.

History of Differential-Treatment Projects

The series of projects to be described have been jointly sponsored by the State of California and the National Institute of Mental Health. They all involve programs developed within the California Youth Authority, the state agency to which county courts commit youthful offenders who are beyond the handling capabilities of county probation departments. The target population of these studies may thus be described as serious or habitual delinquents.

Phase I of the Community Treatment Project has been operating now for more than seven years. This study, being conducted in California's Central Valley, involves a comparison of the impact of institutional and intensive community-based programs on particular subgroups of the delinquent population. The intake cases are first identified as eligible or ineligible for the community-based program. Approximately 90 percent of girls and 70 percent of boys have been declared eligible, with the primary reason for exclusion being assaultive behavior.[2] Eligible cases are then randomly assigned to institutional and community programs. The research design calls for following both those cases assigned to the traditional Youth Authority program (the Controls) and those cases assigned to the community program (the Experimentals) in terms of subsequent behavior in the community and in terms of personal and attitude change as re-

[2] Details about the characteristics of eligible and ineligible cases, as well as comparison of the Experimental and Control populations, are available in the numerous research reports of the project, obtainable from Dr. Ted Palmer, Community Treatment Project, 3610 Fifth Avenue, Sacramento, California.

flected in psychological tests given before and after intensive treatment.

No assumption was made that either community or institutional programs would be preferable across-the-board. Instead, the questions asked were: For what kinds of delinquents is a community alternative to institutionalization feasible and preferable? What kinds of delinquents require or benefit from a period of incarceration? Findings have, in fact, shown a considerable advantage to the community-based program for all delinquent subtypes combined (that is, a comparison of total Experimental versus total Control cases), as indicated both in parole criteria and in test-score changes. However, there have been even more dramatic differences between the two programs when the various delinquent subtypes have been considered separately — several subgroups showing a large difference in favor of the community program, one subgroup showing a difference in favor of the institution program, and several subgroups showing contradictory evidence or minimal differences.

By 1964, the feasibility of treating a large proportion of the juvenile offender population in intensive community programs, rather than in institutions, was a settled issue. In addition, it was clear that the community program offered higher success rates than the traditional Youth Authority program. What was unclear — and what is, perhaps, unclear in all comparisons of one large, complex program with another large, complex program — was which particular program element or combination of elements accounted for the difference in success rates. For example, the differences in favor of the community program might be attributable to the particular treatment model being used, superior staff, differential decisions, specific community attitudes, simple avoidance of the institution, or numerous other factors. In an effort to sort out some of these factors, Phase II of the Community Treatment Project was begun in the San Francisco area. This experiment involves a three-way design in which two types of community programs are being compared with each other and with the traditional institutional program. One of the community units is based on the treatment model developed in Phase I of CTP (the Differential-Treatment Model), and the second community unit is based on a different theory and treatment model (Guided Group Interaction). Consistent with the study of *differential* impact, assessment of the three programs is being made with regard to the various delinquent subtypes, separately.

Study of Differential-Treatment Environments

Beginning in 1965 and 1966, two projects were launched which had as major themes the study of differential *settings* or the attempt to develop treatment *environments* which are specific to the management and to the growth needs of specific subgroups within the delinquent population. The first of these projects was the Preston Typology Study.[3] Using an experimental-control design, delinquent youth of a given subtype were placed randomly in homogeneous living units (that is, only boys of one subtype in the unit) and in the traditional heterogeneous living units. The staff's task in the experimental units was to develop management and treatment techniques specific to the needs of the offenders in their particular living unit. The researchers' task was to describe the environment which developed in each experimental living unit, and to compare the impact of the program on experimental boys of a given subtype with the impact of the regular program on boys of the same subtype placed in the heterogeneous units.

The second study of differential settings involves the use of group homes for cases involved in the Central Valley units of the Community Treatment Project.[4] The development

of intensive community-based programs made apparent the frequent necessity for out-of-home-placement resources. This need relates to the observation that some types of delinquents in some types of settings appear to have little or no alternative to delinquency. For example, a child whose major way of relating to the world is conformity to the power which surrounds him may have little alternative to delinquency in a high-delinquency neighborhood; similarly, a child who is acting out a family problem may have little alternative to delinquency in his own home. These considerations have led to more frequent use of out-of-home placements in CTP than is typical of large case-load field programs. In addition to the size of the problem, differential-treatment thinking suggests that home atmospheres and attitudes which may be helpful to some kinds of delinquent youth may be nonhelpful or even detrimental to other kinds of youth. The goals of the Group Home Project then were to develop five types of group homes (four to six youths in each) — each home representing a range of environments specifically related to the growth and development needs of particular types of delinquent youth.

Study of Differential-Treatment Models

A further attempt to carry out the study of the differential impact of specific treatment methods on various subtypes of delinquents began in 1968 in the Northern California Youth Center Project. This program is being implemented in two institutional settings and is also based on organization of the population into homogeneous living units by subtype. The Karl Holton School is developing its treatment program around behavior-modification (operant conditioning) principles; and the O. H. Close School, around transactional analysis principles.[5] As in CTP, Phase II, the question

[3] C. F. Jesness, "Preston Typology Study: Final Report" (Sacramento, Calif.: Institute for the Study of Crime and Delinquency, in collaboration with California Youth Authority, 1968). (Mimeographed.)

[4] L. W. Look and M. Q. Warren, "Differential-Treatment Environments for Delinquents: Project Proposal" (Sacramento: California Youth Authority and National Institute of Mental Health, 1966). (Mimeographed.); see also J. W. Pearson and T. B. Palmer, *Differential-Treatment Environments for Delinquents*, California Youth Authority and National Institute of Mental Health Research Report No. 1 (Sacramento, 1967).

[5] C. F. Jesness, "Differential Treatment for Delinquents in Institutions: Project Proposal" (Sacramento: California Youth Authority, Institute for the Study of Crime and Delinquency, and National Institute of Mental Health, 1967). (Mimeographed.)

being asked is: Which treatment model shows the greatest payoff for each specific subtype of the offender population? An interesting additional complication in this institutional study relates to the question of what particular forms each theoretical model will take when applied to the various subgroups of the population.

Matching of Clients and Workers

An area of study which runs through all of these projects involves the attempt to "match" clients and workers. There has long been clinical experience — and some research evidence as well — which suggests that few, if any, workers relate equally well with all types of youth or are equally comfortable with the range of treatment styles and stances required by the full variety of offenders. Based on this premise, the Community Treatment Project began in 1961 to hire as workers individuals whose area of sensitivity, talents, and interests appeared to be "right" for given types of youth. An attempt was then made to develop for each worker a case-load made up of delinquents for whom the worker's "natural" style of relating and his areas of belief and concern seemed particularly appropriate. To the extent possible, homogeneous (by delinquent subtype) case-loads were built. Although these efforts at matching were at first based on intuition, interest in tying down the dimensions of worker and client crucial in the matching increased rapidly as the interactions among the treatment strategy, the worker's ability to carry out the treatment plan, and the youth's reaction to worker and plan became known. Research activity in this area increased rapidly.[6]

Matching has become an important program element in all subsequent projects mentioned here (with the exception of the Guided Group Program in CTP II which calls for heterogeneous groups). Although the data indicate the extreme importance of the matching factor in differential-treatment planning, the crucial

experiment has yet to be conducted. Matching has been included in the various projects as one of *several* elements which were varied concurrently; thus, the unique contribution of the matching *per se* has not been studied extensively. A purposeful study of matching and mismatching is now in the proposal stage as one experiment of the Community Treatment Project, Phase III.

Classification of Delinquents

At the heart of all these studies of differential treatment is the classification of the target populations into treatment-revelant categories. The classification system utilized in all of these experiments is based on Interpersonal Maturity Level (I-level) theory.[7] The first application of the theory to the offender population began in the early 1950's in a study of military offenders (see footnote 1 in this article). A major elaboration of the Interpersonal Maturity Classification occurred in 1960–1961 with the beginnings of the Community Treatment Project.

The original theoretical formulation described a sequence of personality (or character) integrations in normal childhood development. This classification system focuses upon the ways in which the individual is able to see himself and the world, especially in terms of emotions and motivations; that is, his ability to understand what is happening between himself and others as well as among others. According to the theory, seven successive stages of interpersonal maturity characterize psychological development. They range from the least mature, which resemble the interpersonal reactions of a newborn infant, to an ideal of social maturity which is seldom or never reached in our present culture. Each of the seven stages, or levels, is defined by a crucial interpersonal problem which must be solved before further progress toward maturity can occur. All persons do not necessarily work their way through each stage, but may become fixed at a particular level. The

[6] T. B. Palmer, *Personality Characteristics and Professional Orientations of Five Groups of Community-Treatment-Project Workers: A Preliminary Report on Differences among Treaters* ("Community-Treatment-Project Report Series," No. 1, 1967).

[7] C. E. Sullivan, M. Q. Grant, and J. D. Grant, "The Development of Interpersonal Maturity: Applications to Delinquency," *Psychiatry*, Vol. 20, 1957, pp. 373–385.

range of maturity levels found in a delinquent population is from Maturity Level 2 (Integration Level 2 or I_2) to Maturity Level 5 (I_5). Level 5 is infrequent enough that, for all practical purposes, use of Levels 2 through 4 describes the juvenile delinquent population. It should be stressed that interpersonal development is viewed as a continuum. The successive steps, or levels, which are described in the theory, are seen as definable points along the continuum.

The elaboration that came with the development of the Community Treatment Project was based on the assumption that although a diagnosis of Integration Level (I-level) identified a group of individuals who held in common a certain level of *perceptual differentiation*, not all individuals in this group responded to this perceptual level in the same way. An attempt was then made to classify within each I-level according to *response set*. There appeared to be two major ways in which the Integration Level 2 (I_2) individual responded in his perceptual frame of reference. Similarly, there appeared to be three typical response sets among delinquent I_3's, and four typical response sets among delinquent I_4's. In this manner, the nine delinquent subtypes were identified. These nine subtypes were originally described — as part of the proposal for CTP, Phase I — by lists of item-definitions which characterize the manner in which the members of each group perceive the world, respond to the world, and are perceived by others. The description of the nine delinquent subtypes, with predicted most-effective intervention or treatment plans, combined to make up the original statement of the Differential Treatment Model.[8] This Model has been revised and expanded over the years of experimentation in CTP. The most recent edition in print was published in 1966.[9]

[8] S. Adams and M. Q. Grant, "An Evaluation of Community-Located Treatment for Delinquents: Proposal for CTP, Phase I," 1961 (Mimeographed).
[9] M. Q. Warren, and the Community Treatment Staff, *Interpersonal-Maturity-Level Classification (Juvenile): Diagnosis and Treatment of Low-, Middle-, and High-Maturity Delinquents* (Sacramento, Calif.: Community Treatment Project, 1966).

Brief descriptions of the three maturity levels (Integration Levels or I-levels), as well as the nine empirical subtypes, found in the juvenile delinquent population are given below:

Maturity Level 2 (I_2): The individual whose interpersonal understanding and behavior are integrated at this level is primarily involved with demands that the world take care of him. He sees others primarily as "givers" or "withholders" and has no conception of interpersonal refinement beyond this. He has poor capacity to explain, understand, or predict the behavior or reactions of others. He is not interested in things outside himself except as a source of supply. He behaves impulsively, unaware of anything except the grossest effects of his behavior on others.

Subtypes: (1) *Asocial, Aggressive* (Aa) responds with active demands and open hostility when frustrated. (2) *Asocial, Passive* (Ap) responds with whining, complaining, and withdrawal when frustrated.

Maturity Level 3 (I_3): The individual who is functioning at this level, although somewhat more differentiated than the I_2, still has social-perceptual deficiencies which lead to an underestimation of the differences among others and between himself and others. More than the I_2, he does understand that his own behavior has something to do with whether or not he gets what he wants. He makes an effort to manipulate his environment to bring about "giving" rather than "denying" response. He does not operate from an internalized value system but rather seeks external structure in terms of rules and formulas for operation. His understanding of formulas is indiscriminate and oversimplified. He perceives the world and his part in it on a power dimension. Although he can learn to play a few stereotyped roles, he cannot understand many of the needs, feelings, and motives of another person who is different from himself. He is unmotivated to achieve in a long-range sense, or to plan for the future. Many of these features contribute to his inability to predict accurately the response of others to him.

Subtypes: (3) *Immature Conformist* (Cfm) responds with immediate compliance to whomever seems to have the power at the moment. (4) *Cultural Conformist* (Cfc) responds with conformity to specific reference group, delinquent peers. (5) *Manipulator* (Mp) operates by attempting to undermine the power of authority figures and/or usurp the power role for himself.

Maturity Level 4 (I$_4$): An individual whose understanding and behavior are integrated at this level has internalized a set of standards by which he judges his and others' behavior. He can perceive a level of interpersonal interaction in which individuals have expectations of each other and can influence each other. He shows some ability to understand reasons for behavior, some ability to relate to people emotionally and on a long-term basis. He is concerned about status and respect and is strongly influenced by people he admires.

Subtypes: (6) *Neurotic, Acting-out* (Na) responds to underlying guilt with attempts to "outrun" or avoid conscious anxiety and condemnation of self. (7) *Neurotic, Anxious* (Nx) responds with symptoms of emotional disturbance to conflict produced by feelings of inadequacy and guilt. (8) *Situational-Emotional Reaction* (Se) responds to immediate family or personal crisis by acting-out. (9) *Cultural Identifier* (Ci) responds to identification with a deviant value system by living out his delinquent beliefs.

The delinquent subtypes, along with their code names and the proportions they represent in the CTP population, may be summarized as in Table 1. It is with respect to these nine delinquent subtypes that the various projects have sought differentially to define treatment goals as well as the various elements — environments, methods, worker styles — of the treatment strategies.

What Has Been Learned So Far

The series of studies on differential treatment of delinquents has produced a number of usable findings and products. These studies have contributed support to several program directions as well.

1. A theory of personality and interpersonal development (I-level) has been elaborated. The theory provides a classification of offenders which can be reliably used and which has relevance to treatment-planning, goal-setting, and program-organization. I-level classi-

Table 1
Delinquent Subtypes: Code Names and Proportion of Population

Code name		Delinquent subtypes	Proportion of population (%)
I$_2$	Aa	Asocial, Aggressive	<1
	Ap	Asocial, Passive	5
I$_3$	Cfm	Conformist, Immature	16
	Cfc	Conformist, Cultural	10
	Mp	Manipulator	14
I$_4$	Na	Neurotic, Acting-out	20
	Nx	Neurotic, Anxious	26
	Se	Situational-Emotional Reaction	3
	Ci	Cultural Identifier	6
			100

fication is now being used for all new intake into the California Youth Authority. A large number of other correctional agencies, both within and outside California, are also organizing parts of their programs around I-level and Differential Treatment concepts. The Center for Training in Differential Treatment has been established, having as one goal the development of training curricula for those agencies. The Training Center itself is a research project, investigating the ways in which training and consultation can support correctional agencies in their efforts to develop more rational and effective treatment programs.

2. The operational feasibility of treating a large proportion of the delinquent population in the community, without prior institutionalization, has been clearly demonstrated. The community-based program appears to have its greatest advantages over the institutional program for the subtypes identified as: Acting-out Neurotic (Na), Cultural Conformist (Cfc), and Manipulator (Mp). The Situational-Emotional Reaction subtype (Se) can be handled very successfully in the community program, although this group also does well following institutionalization. These four subtypes combined represent almost 50 percent of the population eligible for the community program. Evidence to date suggests that the Cultural Identifier subtype (Ci) may be more

effectively handled in a program involving in-carceration, although success of this group in the community program continues to increase each year while the success rate for Controls does not change. This subtype includes 6 per-cent of the population. For the three remain-ing subtypes,[10] the data do not, at this time, point to a clear advantage for either program. If recidivism rate alone is considered the most important of the criteria, then two of these three subtypes — Anxious Neurotic (Nx) and Asocial, Passive (Ap) — would have an ad-vantage in the community program.

3. The feasibility of developing a range of treatment atmospheres in group home settings has been shown. Four of the five theoretically defined group home environments have been located and/or developed with some degree of success. . . .

4. Not enough follow-up data are yet in on CTP, Phase II, to indicate which subtypes have greater success in the Differential Treat-ment unit compared with the Guided Group Interaction unit. However, over-all (for all subtypes combined) parole outcomes in the Differential Treatment unit in San Francisco are generally similar to those in the Central Valley units, suggesting that the success of the community program in Phase I was not simply the function of a particular location, commu-nity, or population. Early, but inconclusive, data do suggest that community treatment in a large metropolitan area may offer a greater op-portunity structure than a smaller community — which is important for some subtypes — but may also represent a greater hazard in terms of peer pressure for delinquency — which is im-portant for other subtypes.

5. There is little support for the view that sheer avoidance of institutionalization *per se* explains the lower failure rates of CTP Ex-perimentals. A direct test of random assign-ment of comparable cases to the institutional programs and to the regular parole programs has not been conducted. However, within the Control group, there are a number of cases who were returned directly from the Recep-

tion Center to their community without first having been sent to an institutional program. These cases, for whom institutionalization was simply avoided, have a somewhat higher pa-role-failure rate (57 percent at fifteen-month follow-up) than the Control cases who went through the institutional programs (48 percent failure).

6. A product of the differential-treatment studies is a set of increasingly elaborate tech-niques and strategies for working with a de-linquent population. Collectively, this set of techniques and strategies for each of the delin-quent subtypes being treated in the community setting is referred to as the Differential Treat-ment Model, 1966 edition.

7. As a result of the success of the Commu-nity Treatment Project, the California Youth Authority is now operating five in-lieu-of-institutionalization community units in addi-tion to the four CTP units. In addition, the favorable experiences in CTP made a major contribution to the development of the Proba-tion Subsidy Law, passed in the California legislature in 1965. It was apparent that, if in-tensive treatment conducted in the youth's home community could be successful when or-ganized through a state agency, the same re-sults might well be accomplished by the county probation departments without com-mitment of the youth to the state. The legisla-tion calls for a maximum payment of $4,000 to a county for every criminal adult or young de-linquent *not* committed to a state correctional institution but whose incarceration was ex-pected on the basis of past performance. Quotas for individual counties have been established on the basis of past commitment rates, adjusted for anticipated county popula-tion growth. An important aspect of the Sub-sidy Law is that, in order to qualify for the funds, a county must not only reduce commit-ments but must also *define* a treatment pro-gram which has reduced commitments as a goal. Thus, for example, a county may not qualify by simply reducing probation case-loads; some further plan must be in evidence.

Forty-one of California's fifty-eight counties are now participating in the subsidy plan. Sub-sidy units in twenty probation departments

---

[10] Too few youths identified as Asocial, Aggres-sive have been declared eligible for the community program to make study possible.

have so far received training in differential treatment from the Training Center. During 1967–1968, the county earnings exceeded $9½ million. There are now a substantial number of empty beds in Youth Authority institutions for the first time in its history.

8. Among the most clear-cut of the findings from the Preston Typology Study is that homogeneity (by delinquent subtype) in the living units of a training school consistently decreased unit-management problems. Significantly fewer serious rule-infractions and peer problems were reported in the experimental units. Transfers out of the living units for closer confinement were also fewer in the homogeneous units. Sufficient follow-up parole data are not yet available to indicate clearly the more long-range treatment impact of the experimental program. Some treatment-impact clues, however, are to be found in psychometrics and behavior ratings from early and late in the institutional stay. These measures show the greatest advantages of the Experimental over the Control program to be for the subtypes Manipulator (Mp), Cultural Conformist (Cfc), and Acting-out Neurotic (Na).

The impact of these findings on the agency is a general movement toward homogeneous living units in many of the institutional programs. Even though the final treatment-evaluation data are not in, apparently the management advantages are convincing. Many questions should still be raised in this area. Although, with present data, it is difficult to make a case for random heterogeneity, it may well be that *planned* combinations of the subtypes would have even more advantages than homogeneous units.

9. The differential-treatment studies have given support to the view that treatment can usefully be conceptualized as a product of at least four major, coexisting interactions — interactions between type of program, type of treatment environment, type of client, and type of worker. The analyses of CTP data show the serious distortions introduced when viewing the target population as though it were a homogeneous collection of individuals. For example, in comparing the total Experi-

mental group with the total Control group, one misses the information that, although the former has a higher success rate than the latter, the Cultural Identifier group does better following incarceration. Additionally, a distorting factor is introduced by not taking type of worker into account. Thus, for example, Experimental cases who — on *a priori* grounds — were well-matched with their workers in CTP had a parole failure rate of 19 percent on a fifteen-month follow-up, while another group of Experimental cases who were not well-matched had a failure rate of 43 percent.

10. Data from these studies indicate, not only that the treatment process with offenders must be viewed with a realistic degree of complexity, but also that the measurement of change must be viewed with the same complexity. Since the Differential Treatment Model specifies goals for each of the subtypes, it is necessary to develop methods of measuring progress toward these specific goals, rather than to assume that certain changes always have a positive or negative meaning. Two examples may be given. Although increased conformity may be a goal generally hoped for in an offender group, increased compliance is a very negative sign in the subtypes identified as I_3 Conformist. Although one typically anticipates that increased self-acceptance will occur with improvement in treatment, there are several subtypes whose self-acceptance is already exceptionally high in comparison with other dimensions such as self-control, responsibility, and socialization. In this instance, hoped-for change could be defined as a better balance between self-acceptance and these other factors, perhaps even involving a decrease in self-acceptance.

11. Program-assessment is complicated by still another factor which involves differential decision-making. In action-research programs such as those described here, it is impossible to conceal from decision-makers information regarding the Experimental or Control status of a particular case. The data suggest that this information does make a difference in actual decisions made by the Youth Authority Board. For example, Experimental cases in CTP tend more often to be restored to parole following

an offense than do Control cases. Experimental workers more often than regular parole agents request a restoration of the youth to parole when some growth has been shown or when the worker believes that a change in treatment plan may make a major difference. The intensive work with the Experimental cases also makes more visible to the decision-makers the improvement in a youth (for example, school and job performance and attitudes toward authority figures) even when the change has not been sufficient to eliminate all delinquent behavior. Differences in restoration practice undoubtedly account for some of the success-rate differences. Complicating the picture still further, but to some extent equalizing the advantages for Experimental and Control groups, evidence is available that — because of the high surveillance rate on the Experimental caseloads — "hidden delinquency" (that is, unknown to the parole agent) is more frequent among Control cases.

Issues Remaining

Many areas of the differential-treatment theme remain to be explored and further tested. Already mentioned is a purer test of the impact on treatment of matching and mismatching workers and clients. Beyond the exploratory studies, crucial tests of well-defined differential environments need to be run. Questions still need to be asked with respect to the kinds of youth for which treatment should preferably be started in the protection of a residential program. For example, there is a sizable proportion of various subtypes which do not succeed in present programs, either in or out of institutions. What kinds of treatment programs — in or out — can be developed for them?

Continued efforts to study this question are proposed as part of CTP, Phase III. CTP experience to date has suggested that the likelihood of achieving specified treatment objectives with certain offenders would be considerably increased if treatment were to begin, not within the community proper, but within a differential-treatment-oriented *residential* setting. The percentage for which the "treatment of choice" would begin in a residential pro-

gram is estimated at from only 5 percent (for subtypes Cfm, Ap, and Se) to perhaps as much as 50 percent (for subtype Ci). In a complex Experimental-Control design, the Phase III proposal calls for utilizing a Differential Treatment Model within a community program and within both short-term and longer-term institutional programs to bring into sharper focus a number of issues: Which of the early goals in treatment with the various subtypes can be better achieved in a residential program and which in a direct community program? Which treatment goals for the various subtypes *must* be achieved in a residential setting in order to protect society and the youth as well? What varying periods of time in an institutional setting are necessary in order to achieve particular goals?

Many of these issues reflect the general "irrationality" of present correctional programs. Frequently, the decision regarding incarceration or not, as well as the decision regarding *length* of incarceration, are made solely on the nature of the offense or on the basis of offense history. The decisions are made prior to (or even without) assessing the nature of the problem involved in a particular youth's delinquency, and without establishing the treatment goals on which later "rational" decisions regarding release should depend.

An example which illustrates the questionable "rationality" of present correctional systems is found in decision-making regarding which youths are eligible for direct release to community-based programs. The delinquents judged ineligible for CTP have been followed in terms of parole-success criteria on release from Youth Authority institutions. Compared with the Control cases, who also went through the institutional programs, the ineligible group has a much lower parole-violation rate (only 30 percent failure at fifteen-month follow-up compared with 48 percent for Controls). Although this information is not surprising, since other studies have shown assaultive offenders to represent a low-violation-rate group, the conclusion that the ineligibles represent a better-risk group for community programs than the eligible group seems apparent.

By and large, the ineligibility decision represents a response to perceived community objection to release of assaultive individuals. In questioning the rationality of this response, an assumption is being made regarding the hierarchy of goals for the correctional process. It is only if one assumes the primacy of the rehabilitative goal (that is, changing the offender into a life-long nonoffender or life-long noncost to society), that the decision to incarcerate the "good risk" offender appears "irrational." If, instead, one accepts the legitimacy of such goals as deterrence of others, punishment, or retribution, then this decision to incarcerate may seem more logical. Present-day public concern with "safe streets" adds to the pressure on decision-makers to incarcerate when in doubt. The differential-treatment programs have attempted to maintain a clear focus on the goal of rehabilitation with the consequent emphasis on moving as far as possible toward rational decision-making with that end in view.

Contributions of the Studies

The series of studies in differential treatment have been rather successful in teasing out some of the many complexities which interact in the correctional treatment process. A beginning has been made in sorting out the differential contributions to success, or lack of it, made by offender characteristics, worker character-

istics, treatment atmospheres, and treatment methods. Evidence that it is *only* a beginning comes from the ratio of questions answered to questions raised. Some information which is immediately usable in programming has been found. Some general program-direction has received support.

The model of action research which has been followed calls for two major strategies — a tied-down experimental-control design whenever possible so that some hard data are available *and* process-oriented exploratory research which permits the detailed viewing of the complexities and interactions among the treatment elements. A unifying theoretical orientation guides the exploratory research in the direction of systematic hypothesis development. In this manner, the second experiment grows logically out of the leads of the first, and the third out of the leads of the second.

To the extent that differential-treatment research has a claim to fame, it is, perhaps, best placed in the area of trying to pin down more precisely the ways in which specific elements of the correctional process are *aimed* at intervening in specific aspects of the delinquency and its meaning. From a program point of view, this theme takes the form of attempting to insert a greater degree of rationality in the effort to change offenders into nonoffenders.

Community Programs
and Prospects

Many citizens believe that imprisonment is the appropriate way to respond to criminals and delinquents. Recognizing that there is no feasible alternative to institutionalization for the handling of offenders who are a serious threat to society, sociologists observe that most offenders do not constitute such a threat and that institutional treatment has limited possibilities. It is difficult to change attitudes in an institutional setting, and the stigma attached to those who have received institutional treatment limits the possibility of rehabilitation and reintegration in conventional society. Further, in large institutions the informal organization or inmate subculture may block treatment efforts. However, at Highfields (McCorkle, Elias, and Bixby [1958]; Weeks [1958]), a small residential treatment center for twenty delinquent boys, impressive efforts were made to establish an atmosphere of rehabilitation among the boys that would counteract their delinquent attitudes and behavior.

The Provo Program, described in this selection, is similar to that of Highfields, except that it is a community-based program in which the boys reside in their own homes. The Provo Experiment offers an example of the application of sociological theory to the treatment of delinquents. Delinquency is viewed as a group phenomenon, and the rehabilitation program is not designed to treat the delinquent boy as an individual offender, but according to his membership in and identification with the delinquent system.

The treatment program consists of two phases, intensive treatment and community adjustment. In the first phase, the absence of formal structure is designed to make peer-group interaction the principal rehabilitative tool and also permits the participants to examine the role and legitimacy of authorities in the treatment system and, hence, perceptions of other authorities. The rehabilitation system also provides the boys opportunities to examine the utility of conventional and delinquent alternatives. In describing the second phase of the program, Empey and Rabow indicate how the peer group can be used to perpetuate the norms of the treatment system. For example, status is granted for law-abiding behavior and for willingness to confront other boys.

Although the Provo Experiment offers valuable lessons for those interested in treating delinquents, the use of deviants in the treatment of deviants remains controversial. It is, therefore, important to recognize that such therapeutic efforts are consistent with sociological theory. Cressey (1965: 55) uses differential association and more general symbolic interactionist theory to discuss the social psychological foundations for the use of criminals in the rehabilitation of criminals; he writes that "group therapy for criminals ought to be effective to the degree that the criminal-as-an-agent-of-change prevents criminals from using the 'techniques of neutralization' — the verbalizations — which he, himself, used in perpetuating offenses, and to the degree that new anticriminal verbalizations are substituted." The fundamental idea is that "as a person tries to change others, he necessarily must use the verbalizations appropriate to the behavior he is trying to create in those others" (Cressey [1965:56]); thus, the same mechanisms which produce criminality or delinquency can be used to change offenders into nonoffenders. A pitfall in such efforts must be avoided. This is the problem of avoiding the presentation of verbalizations in the treatment process that make delinquents worse. That is to say, antidelinquent views must be upheld so that the outcome of treatment is not a different and possibly more serious delinquent.

Raising the classic question of means and ends, Gordon (1962:256) comments on the similarities of the techniques used at Pinehills to those employed by the Communists on American prisoners of war in Korea: "One sees the leverage of the group being applied to the individual by way of public confessions, the demand for candor, the infinite patience and inscrutability of authority. There appears the 'carrot and stick' technique along with the utilization of role disruption and social anxiety as motivating forces. Beyond that, one is reminded how systematically and thoroughly the integrity of psychological privacy is undermined." In response, Erickson and Empey (1962:258) say that to "break" a person under intolerable stress is one thing, but to use stress to modify perceptions and to permit examination of alternatives and opportunities is quite different: "In contrast to the religious revival or Communist techniques which leave a person in a condition of high suggestibility, but without adequate means for understanding, our approach concentrates upon means by which a delinquent group can expand its understanding."

REFERENCES

Donald R. Cressey, "Social Psychological Foundations for Using Criminals in the Rehabilitation of Criminals," *The Journal of Research in Crime and Delinquency*, 2 (July 1965), pp. 49–59.

LaMar T. Empey and Jerome Rabow, "Reply to Whitney H. Gordon," *American Sociological Review*, 27 (April 1962), pp. 256–258.

Whitney H. Gordon, "Communist Rectification Programs and Delinquency Rehabilitation Programs: A Parallel?" *American Sociological Review*, 27 (April 1962), p. 256.

Lloyd W. McCorkle, Albert Elias, and F. Lovell Bixby, *The Highfields Story* (New York: Henry Holt and Co., 1958).

H. Ashley Weeks, *Youthful Offenders at Highfields* (Ann Arbor: University of Michigan Press, 1958).

LA MAR T. EMPEY

JEROME RABOW

The Provo Experiment in Delinquency Rehabilitation

Despite the importance of sociological contributions to the understanding of delinquent behavior, relatively few of these contributions have been systematically utilized for purposes of rehabilitation.[1] The reason is at least partially inherent in the sociological tradition which views sociology primarily as a research discipline. As a consequence, the rehabilitation of delinquents has been left, by default, to people who have been relatively unaware of sociological theory and its implications for treatment.

This situation has produced or perpetuated problems along two dimensions. On one dimension are the problems engendered in reformatories where authorities find themselves bound, not only by the norms of their own official system, but by the inmate system as well. They are unable to work out an effective program: (1) because the goals of the two systems are incompatible; and (2) because no one knows much about the structure and function of the inmate system and how it might be dealt with for purposes of rehabilitation.[2]

Furthermore, the crux of any treatment program has ultimately to do with the decision-making process utilized by delinquents in the community, *not* in the reformatory. Yet, the decisions which lead to success in "doing time" in the reformatory are not of the same type needed for successful community adjustment. Existing conditions may actually be more effective in cementing ties to the delinquent system than in destroying them.[3]

The second dimension of the problem has to do with the traditional emphasis upon "individualized treatment."[4] This emphasis stems from two sources: (1) a humanistic concern for the importance of human dignity and the need for sympathetic understanding;[5] and (2) a widespread belief that delinquency is a psychological disease and the offender a *"sick"*

From *American Sociological Review*, October 1961, pp. 679–695. Reprinted by permission of the American Sociological Association.

The inception and continuation of this experiment were made possible through the co-operation of the Judge (Monroe Paxman) and staff of the Third District Juvenile Court, a voluntary group known as the Citizens' Advisory Council, and Utah County Officials. Evaluation is supported by the Ford Foundation. Grateful acknowledgment is made to all involved.

[1] Donald R. Cressey, "Changing Criminals: The Application of the Theory of Differential Association," *American Journal of Sociology*, 61 (July 1955), p. 116.

[2] Daniel Glaser maintains that the prison social system has not received the study it merits. Most writing about prisons, he says, is "impressionistic," "moralistic," "superficial," and "biased," rather than "systematic" and "objective." "The Sociological Approach to Crime and Correction," *Law and Contemporary Problems*, 23 (Autumn 1958), p.

697; see also Gresham M. Sykes and Sheldon Messinger, "The Inmate Social System," in *Theoretical Studies in Social Organization of the Prison*, Social Science Research Council, March 1960, pp. 5–19; and Lloyd W. McCorkle and Richard Korn, "Resocialization Within Walls," *The Annals of the American Academy of Political and Social Science*, 293 (May 1954), pp. 88–98.

[3] Sykes and Messinger, *op. cit.*, pp. 12–13; Richard McCleery, "Policy Change in Prison Management," *Michigan State University Political Research Studies*, No. 5, 1957; Richard A. Cloward, "Social Control in the Prison," in *Theoretical Studies in Social Organization of the Prison*, *op. cit.*, pp. 20–48; and Stanton Wheeler, "Socialization in Correctional Communities," *American Sociological Review*, 26 (October 1961), pp. 697–712.

[4] Cressey, *op. cit.*, p. 116.

[5] For example, see John G. Milner, "Report on an Evaluated Study of the Citizenship Training Program, Island of Hawaii," Los Angeles: University of Southern California School of Social Work, 1959, p. IV. Irving E. Cohen implies that anything which interferes with the establishment of "confidence, sympathy and understanding" between adult and offender interferes with the effectiveness of the individualized approach. See "Twilight Zones in Probation," *Journal of Criminal Law and Criminology*, 37, No. 4, p. 291.

person.[6] If, however, sociologists are even partially correct regarding the causes for delinquency, these two points of view overlook the possibility that most persistent delinquents do have the support of a meaningful reference group and are not, therefore, without the emotional support and normative orientation which such a group can provide. In fact, a complete dedication to an individualistic approach poses an impasse: How can an individual who acquired delinquency from a group with which he identifies strongly be treated individually without regard to the persons or norms of the system from which he acquired it? [7]

A successful treatment program for such a person would require techniques not normally included in the individualized approach. It should no more be expected that dedicated delinquents can be converted to conventionality by such means than that devout Pentecostals can be converted to Catholicism by the same means. Instead, different techniques are required for dealing with the normative orientation of the delinquent's system, replacing it with new values, beliefs, and rationalizations and developing means by which he can realize conventional satisfactions, especially with respect to successful employment.

This does not suggest, of course, that such traditional means as probation for dealing with the first offender or psychotherapy for dealing with the disturbed offender can be discarded. But it does suggest the need for experimental programs more consistent with sociological theory, and more consistent with the sociological premise that most *persistent* and *habitual*

offenders are active members of a delinquent social system.[8]

This paper presents the outlines of a program — the Provo Experiment in Delinquency Rehabilitation — which is derived from sociological theory and which seeks to apply sociological principles to rehabilitation. Because of its theoretical ties, the concern of the Experiment is as much with a systematic evaluation and reformulation of treatment consistent with findings as with the administration of treatment itself. For that reason, research and evaluation are an integral part of the program. Its theoretical orientation, major assumptions, treatment system, and research design are outlined below.

Theoretical Orientation

With regard to causation, the Provo Experiment turned to a growing body of evidence which suggests two important conclusions: (1) that the greater part of delinquent behavior is not that of individuals engaging in highly secretive deviations, but is a group phenomenon — a shared deviation which is the product of differential group experience in a particular subculture,[9] and (2) that because most delin-

---

[6] Michael Hakeem, "A Critique of the Psychiatric Approach to Juvenile Delinquency," in *Juvenile Delinquency*, edited by Joseph S. Roucek, New York: Philosophical Library, 1958. Hakeem provides a large bibliography to which attention can be directed if further information is desired. See also Daniel Glaser, "Criminality Theories and Behavioral Images," *American Journal of Sociology*, 61 (1956), p. 435.

[7] Cressey, *op. cit.*, p. 117. LaMay Adamson and H. Warren Dunham even imply that the clinical approach cannot work successfully with habitual offenders. See "Clinical Treatment of Male Delinquents: A Case Study in Effort and Result," *American Sociological Review*, 21 (June 1956), p. 320.

[8] One program consistent with this premise is the Highfields Residential Group Center in New Jersey. Modern penology is indebted to it for the development of many unique and important aspects. See Lloyd W. McCorkle, Albert Elias, and F. Lovell Bixby, *The Highfields Story: A Unique Experiment in the Treatment of Juvenile Delinquency*, New York: Henry Holt & Co., 1958; H. Ashley Weeks, *Youthful Offenders at Highfields*, Ann Arbor: University of Michigan Press, 1958; and Albert Elias and Jerome Rabow, "Post-Release Adjustment of Highfields Boys, 1955–57," *The Welfare Reporter*, January 1960, pp. 7–11.

[9] Richard A. Cloward and Lloyd E. Ohlin, *Delinquency and Opportunity: A Theory of Delinquent Gangs*, Glencoe, Ill.: The Free Press, 1960; Albert K. Cohen, *Delinquent Boys: The Culture of the Gang*, Glencoe: The Free Press, 1955; Albert K. Cohen and James F. Short, Jr., "Research in Delinquent Subcultures," *The Journal of Social Issues*, 14 (1958), pp. 20–37; Solomon Kobrin, "The Conflict of Values in Delinquency Areas," *American Sociological Review*, 16 (October 1951), pp. 653–661; Robert K. Merton, *Social Theory and Social Structure*, Glencoe: The Free Press, 1957, Chapters IV–V; Walter B. Miller, "Lower Class Culture as a Generating Milieu of Gang Delinquency," *The Journal of Social Issues*,

quents tend to be concentrated in slums or to be the children of lower class parents, their lives are characterized by learning situations which limit their access to success goals.[10]

Attention to these two conclusions does not mean that emotional problems,[11] or "bad" homes,[12] can be ignored. But only occasionally do these variables lead by themselves to delinquency. In most cases where older delinquents are involved other intervening variables must operate, the most important of which is the presence of a delinquent system — one which supplies status and recognition not normally obtainable elsewhere. Whether they are members of a tight knit gang or of the amorphous structure of the "parent" delinquent subculture,[13] habitual delinquents tend to look affectively both to their peers and to the norms of their system for meaning and orientation. Thus, although a "bad" home may have been

instrumental at some early phase in the genesis of a boy's delinquency, it must be recognized that it is now other delinquent boys, not his parents, who are current sources of support and identification. Any attempts to change him, therefore, would have to view him as more than an unstable isolate without a meaningful reference group. And, instead of concentrating on changing his parental relationships, they would have to recognize the intrinsic nature of his membership in the delinquent system and direct treatment to him as a part of that system.

There is another theoretical problem. An emphasis on the importance of the delinquent system raises some question regarding the extent to which delinquents are without any positive feeling for conventional standards. Vold says that one approach to explaining delinquency ". . . operates from the basic, implicit assumption that in a delinquency area, delinquency is the normal response of the normal individual — that the non-delinquent is really the 'problem case,' the nonconformist whose behavior needs to be accounted for." [14] This is a deterministic point of view suggesting the possibility that delinquents view conventional people as "foreigners" and conventional norms and beliefs as anathema. It implies that delinquents have been socialized entirely in a criminal system and have never internalized or encountered the blandishments of conventional society.[15]

---

[14] (1958), pp. 5–19; Clifford R. Shaw, *Delinquency Areas,* Chicago: University of Chicago Press, 1942; Clifford R. Shaw, Henry D. McKay, *et al., Juvenile Delinquency and Urban Areas,* Chicago: University of Chicago Press, 1942; Edwin H. Sutherland, *Principles of Criminology,* 4th ed., Philadelphia: Lippincott, 1947; Frank Tannenbaum, *Crime and the Community,* Boston: Ginn and Co., 1938; F. M. Thrasher, *The Gang,* 2d rev. ed., Chicago: University of Chicago Press, 1936; William F. Whyte, *Street Corner Society,* Chicago: University of Chicago Press, 1943.

[10] Richard A. Cloward, "Illegitimate Means, Anomie, and Deviant Behavior," *American Sociological Review,* 24 (April 1959), pp. 164–176; Cloward and Ohlin, *op. cit.;* Robert K. Merton, "Social Conformity, Deviation, and Opportunity-Structures: A Comment on the Contributions of Dubin and Cloward," *American Sociological Review,* 24 (April 1959), pp. 177–189; Robert K. Merton, "The Social-Cultural Environment and Anomie," *New Perspectives for Research on Juvenile Delinquency,* edited by Helen Kotinsky, U.S. Department of Health, Education, and Welfare, 1955, pp. 24–50; Merton, *Social Theory and Social Structure, op. cit.*

[11] Erik H. Erikson, "Ego Identity and the Psycho-Social Moratorium," *New Perspectives for Research on Juvenile Delinquency, op. cit.* pp. 1–23.

[12] Jackson Toby, "The Differential Impact of Family Disorganization," *American Sociological Review,* 22 (October 1957), pp. 505–511; and F. Ivan Nye, *Family Relationships and Delinquent Behavior,* New York: John Wiley and Sons, 1958.

[13] Cohen and Short, *op. cit.,* p. 24.

[14] George B. Vold, "Discussion of Guided Group Interaction and Correctional Work," by F. Lovell Bixby and Lloyd W. McCorkle, *American Sociological Review,* 16 (August 1951), p. 460.

[15] As Glaser points out, sociologists have tended to be deterministic and to ally themselves with psychiatrists in the struggle against classical legalists and religious leaders over the free will versus determinism issue. He labels this struggle as a "phony war," involving polemics more than reality. However, he says the war is losing its intensity because of a declining interest in metaphysical issues and a recognition of the importance of voluntaristic rather than reflexive conceptions of human behavior. Contrary to their protestations, the determinists, for example, recognize that humans are aware of alternative possible courses of behavior and make deliberate choices between them. See "The Sociological Approach to Crime and Correction," *op. cit.,* pp. 686–687.

Actually, sociological literature suggests otherwise. It emphasizes, in general, that the sub-parts of complex society are intimately tied up with the whole,[16] and, specifically, that delinquents are very much aware of conventional standards; that they have been socialized in an environment dominated by middle-class morality;[17] that they have internalized the American success ideal to such a degree that they turn to illegitimate means in an effort to be successful[18] (or, failing in that, engage in malicious, or retreatist activities);[19] that they are profoundly ambivalent about their delinquent behavior;[20] and that in order to cope with the claims of respectable norms upon them, they maintain a whole series of intricate rationalizations by which to "neutralize" their delinquent behavior.[21]

This suggests that delinquents are aware of conventional structure and its expectations. In many conventional settings they can, and usually do, behave conventionally. But it also suggests that, like other people, they are motivated by the normative expectations of their own subsystem. Consequently, when in the company of other delinquent boys, they may not only feel that they have to live up to minimal delinquent expectations but to appear more delinquent than they actually are, just as people in church often feel that they have to appear more holy than they actually are.

If this is the case, the problem of rehabilitation is probably not akin to converting delinquents to ways of behavior and points of view about which they are unaware and which they have never seriously considered as realistic alternatives. Instead, the feeling of ambivalence on their parts might be an element which could be used in rehabilitation.

An important sociological hypothesis based on this assumption would be that the ambivalence of most habitual delinquents is not primarily the result of personality conflicts developed in such social *microcosms* as the family but is inherent in the structure of the societal *macrocosm*. A delinquent subsystem simply represents an alternative means for acquiring, or attempting to acquire, social and economic goals idealized by the societal system which are acquired by other people through conventional means.

If this hypothesis is accurate, delinquent ambivalence might actually be used in effecting change. A rehabilitation program might seek: (1) to make conventional and delinquent alternatives clear; (2) to lead delinquents to question the ultimate utility of delinquent alternatives; and (3) to help conventional alternatives assume some positive valence for them. It might then reduce the affective identification which they feel for the delinquent subsystem and tip the scales in the opposite direction.

Major Assumptions for Treatment

In order to relate such theoretical premises to the specific needs of treatment, the Provo Experiment adopted a series of major assumptions. They are as follows:

1. Delinquent behavior is primarily a group product and demands an approach to treatment far different from that which sees it as characteristic of a "sick," or "well-meaning" but "misguided," person.

2. An effective program must recognize the

---

[16] Sutherland, it will be recalled, maintained that "While criminal behavior is an expression of general needs and values, it is not explained by those general needs and values since non-criminal behavior is an expression of the *same needs and values*." *Op. cit.*, pp. 6–7, italics ours. The accuracy of the statement would hinge on the definition of "needs" and "values." See also David J. Bordua, *Sociological Theories and Their Implications for Juvenile Delinquency*, U.S. Department of Health, Education, and Welfare, 1960, p. 8, and Robin M. Williams, Jr., *American Society*, New York: Alfred A. Knopf, 1955, Chapter 11.

[17] Cohen, *op. cit.*, p. 133.

[18] Merton, *Social Theory and Social Structure*, *op. cit.*

[19] Cloward, *op. cit.*, and Cloward and Ohlin, *op. cit.* See also Robert Dubin, "Deviant Behavior and Social Structure: Continuities in Social Theory," *American Sociological Review*, 24 (April 1959), pp. 147–164.

[20] Cohen, *Delinquent Boys, op. cit.*, p. 133; Cohen and Short, *op. cit.*, p. 21. See also John I. Kitsuse and David C. Dietrick, "Delinquent Boys: A Critique," *American Sociological Review*, 24 (April 1959), p. 211.

[21] Gresham M. Sykes and David Matza, "Techniques of Neutralization: A Theory of Delinquency," *American Sociological Review*, 22 (December 1957), pp. 664–670.

intrinsic nature of a delinquent's membership in a delinquent system and, therefore, must direct treatment to him as a part of that system.

3. Most habitual delinquents are affectively and ideologically dedicated to the delinquent system. Before they can be made amenable to change, they must be made anxious about the ultimate utility of that system for them.

4. Delinquents must be forced to deal with the conflicts which the demands of conventional and delinquent systems place upon them. The resolution of such conflicts, either for or against further law violations, must ultimately involve a community decision. For that reason, a treatment program, in order to force realistic decision-making, can be most effective if it permits continued participation in the community as well as in the treatment process.

5. Delinquent ambivalence for purposes of rehabilitation can only be utilized in a setting conducive to the free expression of feelings — both delinquent and conventional. This means that the protection and rewards provided by the treatment system for *candor* must exceed those provided either by delinquents for adherence to delinquent roles or by officials for adherence to custodial demands for "good behavior." Only in this way can delinquent individuals become aware of the extent to which other delinquents share conventional as well as delinquent aspirations and, only in this way, can they be encouraged to examine the ultimate utility of each.

6. An effective program must develop a unified and cohesive social system in which delinquents and authorities alike are devoted to one task — overcoming lawbreaking. In order to accomplish this the program must avoid two pitfalls: (a) it must avoid establishing authorities as "rejectors" and making inevitable the creation of two social systems within the program; and (b) it must avoid the institutionalization of means by which skilled offenders can evade norms and escape sanctions.[22] The occasional imposition of negative sanctions is as necessary in this system as in any other system.

[22] McCorkle and Korn, *op. cit.*, pp. 88–91.

7. A treatment system will be most effective if the delinquent peer group is used as the means of perpetuating the norms and imposing the sanctions of the system. The peer group should be seen by delinquents as the primary source of help and support. The traditional psychotherapeutic emphasis upon transference relationships is not viewed as the most vital factor in effecting change.

8. A program based on sociological theory may tend to exclude lectures, sermons, films, individual counseling, analytic psychotherapy, organized athletics, academic education, and vocational training as primary treatment techniques. It will have to concentrate, instead, on matters of another variety: changing reference group and normative orientations, utilizing ambivalent feelings resulting from the conflict of conventional and delinquent standards, and providing opportunities for recognition and achievement in conventional pursuits.

9. An effective treatment system must include rewards which are realistically meaningful to delinquents. They would include such things as peer acceptance for law-abiding behavior or the opportunity for gainful employment rather than badges, movies or furlough privileges which are designed primarily to facilitate institutional control. Rewards, therefore, must only be given for realistic and lasting changes, not for conformance to norms which concentrate upon effective custody as an end in itself.

10. Finally, in summary, a successful program must be viewed by delinquents as possessing four important characteristics: (a) a social climate in which delinquents are given the opportunity to examine and experience alternatives related to a realistic choice between delinquent or non-delinquent behavior; (b) the opportunity to declare publicly to peers and authorities a belief or disbelief that they can benefit from a change in values; (c) a type of social structure which will permit them to examine the role and legitimacy (for their purposes) of authorities in the treatment system; and (d) a type of treatment interaction which, because it places major responsibilities upon peer-group decision-making, grants status and recognition to individuals,

not only for their own successful participation in the treatment interaction, but for their willingness to involve others.

The Treatment System [23]

The Provo Program, consistent with these basic assumptions, resides in the community and does not involve permanent incarceration. Boys live at home and spend only a part of each day at Pinehills (the program center). Otherwise they are free in the community.[24]

History and Locale. The Provo Program was begun in 1956 as an "in-between" program designed specifically to help those habitual delinquents whose persistence made them candidates, in most cases, for a reformatory. It was instigated by a volunteer group of professional and lay people known as the *Citizens' Advisory Council to the Juvenile Court.* It has never had formal ties to government except through the Juvenile Court. This lack of ties has permitted considerable experimentation. Techniques have been modified to such a degree that the present program bears little resemblance to the original one. Legally, program officials are deputy probation officers appointed by the Juvenile Judge.

The cost of treatment is financed by county funds budgeted through the Juvenile Court. So near as we can estimate the cost per boy is approximately one-tenth of what it would cost if he were incarcerated in a reformatory. Research operations are financed by the Ford Foundation. Concentrated evaluation of the program is now in its second year of a six-year

operation. Because both the theoretical orientation and treatment techniques of the program were in developmental process until its outlines were given final form for research purposes, it is difficult to make an objective evaluation of the over-all program based on recidivism rates for previous years, especially in the absence of adequate control groups. Such an evaluation, however, is an integral part of the present research and is described below.

Relations with welfare agencies and the community, *per se*, are informal but extremely co-operative. This is due to three things: the extreme good will and guiding influence of the Juvenile Court Judge, Monroe J. Paxman,[25] the unceasing efforts of the Citizens' Advisory Council to involve the entire county as a community, and the willingness of city and county officials, not only to overcome traditional fears regarding habitual offenders in the community, but to lend strong support to an experimental program of this type.

Community co-operation is probably enhanced by strong Mormon traditions. However, Utah County is in a period of rapid transition which began in the early days of World War II with the introduction of a large steel plant, allied industries, and an influx of non-Mormons. This trend, both in industry and population, has continued to the present time. The treatment program is located in the city of Provo but draws boys from all major communities in the county — from a string of small cities, many of which border on each other, ranging in size from four to forty thousand. The total population from which it draws its assignees is about 110,000.

Despite the fact that Utah County is not a highly urbanized area, when compared to large metropolitan centers, the concept of a "parent" delinquent subculture has real meaning for it. While there are no clear-cut gangs, *per se*, it is surprising to observe the extent to which delinquent boys from the entire county,

---

[23] Except for the community aspects, the above assumptions and the treatment system are similar to those pioneered at Highfields. See McCorkle, Elias, and Bixby, *op. cit.* The Provo Program is especially indebted to Albert Elias, the present director of Highfields, not only for his knowledge about treatment techniques, but for his criticisms of the Provo Experiment.

[24] The idea of a community program is not new. The Boston Citizenship Training Group, Inc., a non-residential program, was begun in 1934–36. However, it is for younger boys and utilizes a different approach. A similar program, initiated by Professor Ray R. Canning, in Provo, was a forerunner to this experiment. See "A New Treatment Program for Juvenile Delinquents," *Journal of Criminal Law and Criminology*, 31 (March–April 1941), pp. 712–719.

[25] Judge Paxman is a member of the Advisory Council of Judges to the National Council On Crime and Delinquency and of the symposium that prepared M. K. Rosenheim (ed.), *Justice for the Child: The Juvenile Courts in Transition* (New York: Free Press, 1962).

who have never met, know each other by reputation, go with the same girls, use the same language, or can seek each other out when they change high schools. About half of them are permanently out of school, do not participate in any regular institutional activities, and are reliant almost entirely upon the delinquent system for social acceptance and participation.

Assignees. Only habitual offenders, 15–17 years, are assigned to the program. In the absence of public facilities, they are transported to and from home each day in automobiles driven by university students. Their offenses run the usual gamut: vandalism, trouble in school, shoplifting, car theft, burglary, forgery, and so forth. Highly disturbed and psychotic boys are not assigned. The pre-sentence investigation is used to exclude these people. They constitute an extremely small minority.

Number in Attendance. No more than twenty boys are assigned to the program at any one time. A large number would make difficult any attempts to establish and maintain a unified, cohesive system. This group of twenty is broken into two smaller groups, each of which operates as a separate discussion unit. When an older boy is released from one of these units, a new boy is added. This is an important feature because it serves as the means by which the culture of the system is perpetuated.

Length of Attendance. No length of stay is specified. It is intimately tied to the group and its processes because a boy's release depends not only upon his own behavior, but upon the maturation processes through which his group goes. Release usually comes somewhere between four and seven months.

Nature of Program. The program does not utilize any testing, gathering of case histories, or clinical diagnosis. One of its key tools, peer group interaction, is believed to provide a considerably richer source of information about boys and delinquency than do clinical methods.

The program, *per se,* is divided into two phases. Phase I is an intensive group program, utilizing work and the delinquent peer group as the principal instruments for change. During the winter, boys attend this phase three

hours a day, five days a week, and all day on Saturdays. Activities include daily group discussions, hard work, and some unstructured activities in which boys are left entirely on their own. During the summer they attend an all-day program which involves work and group discussions. However, there are no practices without exceptions. For example, if a boy has a full-time job, he may be allowed to continue the job in lieu of working in the program. Other innovations occur repeatedly.

Phase II is designed to aid a boy after release from intensive treatment in Phase I. It involves two things: (1) an attempt to maintain some reference group support for a boy; and (2) community action to help him find employment. Both phases are described below.

Phase I: Intensive Treatment

Every attempt is made in Phase I to create a social system in which social structure, peer members, and authorities are oriented to the one task of instituting change. The more relevant to this task the system is, the greater will be its influence.

Social Structure. There is little formal structure in the Provo Program. Patterns are abhorred which might make boys think that their release depends upon *refraining* from swearing, engaging in open quarrels or doing such *"positive"* things as saying, "yes sir," or "no sir." Such criteria as these play into their hands. They learn to manipulate them in developing techniques for beating a system. Consequently, other than requiring boys to appear each day, and working hard on the job, there are no formal demands. The only other daily activities are the group discussions at which attendance is optional.

The absence of formal structure helps to do more than avoid artificial criteria for release. It has the positive effect of making boys more amenable to treatment. In the absence of formal structure they are uneasy and they are not quite sure of themselves. Thus, the lack of clear-cut definitions for behavior helps to accomplish three important things: (1) It produces anxiety and turns boys towards the group as a method of resolving their anxiety; (2) It leaves boys free to define situations for themselves: leaders begin to lead, followers begin to follow, and manipulators begin to manipulate. It is these types of behavior which must be seen and analyzed if change is to take place; (3) It binds neither authorities nor the peer group to prescribed courses of action. Each is free to do whatever is needed to suit the needs of particular boys, groups, or situations.

On the other hand, the absence of formal structure obviously does not mean that there is no structure. But, that which does exist is informal and emphasizes ways of thinking and behaving which are not traditional. Perhaps the greatest difference lies in the fact that a considerable amount of power is vested in the delinquent peer group. It is the instrument by which norms are perpetuated and through which many important decisions are made. It is the primary source of pressure for change.

The Peer Group. Attempts to involve a boy with the peer group begin the moment he arrives. Instead of meeting with and receiving an orientation lecture from authorities, he receives no formal instructions. He is always full of such questions as, "What do I have to do to get out of this place?" or "How long do I have to stay?", but such questions as these are never answered. They are turned aside with, "I don't know," or "Why don't you find out?" Adults will not orient him in the ways that he has grown to expect, nor will they answer any of his questions. He is forced to turn to his peers. Usually, he knows someone in the program, either personally or by reputation. As he begins to associate with other boys he discovers that important informal norms do exist, the most important of which makes *inconsistency* rather than *consistency* the rule. That which is appropriate for one situation, boy, or group may not be appropriate for another. Each merits a decision as it arises.

Other norms center most heavily about the daily group discussion sessions. These sessions are patterned after the technique of "Guided Group Interaction" which was developed at Fort Knox during World War II and at Highfields.[26] Guided Group Interaction emphasizes

[26] See F. Lovell Bixby and Lloyd W. McCorkle, "Guided Group Interaction and Correctional

the idea that only through a group and its processes can a boy work out his problems. From a peer point of view it has three main goals: (1) to question the utility of a life devoted to delinquency; (2) to suggest alternative ways for behavior; and (3) to provide recognition for a boy's personal reformation and his willingness to reform others.[27]

Guided Group Interaction grants to the peer group a great deal of power, including that of helping to decide when each boy is ready to be released. This involves "retroflexive reformation."[28] If a delinquent is serious in his attempts to reform others he must automatically accept the common purpose of the reformation process, identify himself closely with others engaged in it, and grant prestige to those who succeed in it. In so doing, he becomes a genuine member of the reformation group and in the process may be alienated from his previous pro-delinquent groups.[29] Such is an ideal and long-term goal. Before it can be realized for any individual he must become heavily involved with the treatment system. Such involvement does not come easy and the system must include techniques which will impel him to involvement. Efforts to

Work," *American Sociological Review*, 16 (August 1951), pp. 455–459; McCorkle, Elias, and Bixby, *The Highfields Story, op. cit.*; and Joseph Abrahams and Lloyd W. McCorkle, "Group Psychotherapy on Military Offenders," *American Journal of Sociology*, 51 (March 1946), pp. 455–464. These sources present a very limited account of techniques employed. An intimate knowledge would require attendance at group sessions.

[27] Other goals relating to the emphasis upon group development, the role of the group therapist, and the nature of the therapeutic situations have been described briefly elsewhere. See *The Highfields Story, op. cit.*, pp. 72–80.

[28] Cressey, *op. cit.*, p. 119.

[29] Vold maintains that guided group interaction assumes that there is something wrong inside the individual and attempts to correct that. He is right in the sense that it emphasizes that an individual must accept responsibility for his own delinquencies and that no one can keep him out of prison unless he himself is ready to stay out. Vold, in our opinion, is incorrect if his remarks are taken to mean that the group does not discuss groups and group processes, what peers mean to a boy or how the orientations of delinquent groups differ from that of conventional society. *Op. cit.*, p. 360.

avoid the development of formal structure have already been described as one technique. Group processes constitute a second technique.

Before a group will help a boy "solve his problems" it demands that he review his total delinquent history. This produces anxiety because, while he is still relatively free, it is almost inevitable that he has much more to reveal than is already known by the police or the court. In an effort to avoid such involvement he may try subterfuge. But any reluctance on his part to be honest will not be taken lightly. Norms dictate that no one in the group can be released until everyone is honest and until every boy helps to solve problems. A refusal to come clean shows a lack of trust in the group and slows down the problem-solving process. Therefore, any recalcitrant boy is faced with a real dilemma. He can either choose involvement or relentless attack by his peers. Once a boy does involve himself, however, he learns that some of his fears were unwarranted. What goes on in the group meeting is sacred and is not revealed elsewhere.

A second process for involvement lies in the use of the peer group to perpetuate the norms of the treatment system. One of the most important norms suggests that most boys in the program are candidates for a reformatory. This is shocking because even habitual delinquents do not ordinarily see themselves as serious offenders.[30] Yet, the tradition is clear; most failures at Pinehills are sent to the Utah State Industrial School. Therefore, each boy has a major decision to make: either he makes serious attempts to change or he gets sent away.

The third process of involvement could only occur in a community program. Each boy has the tremendous problem of choosing between the demands of his delinquent peers outside the program and the demands of those within it. The usual reaction is to test the situation by continuing to identify with the former. Efforts to do this, however, and to keep out of serious

trouble are usually unsuccessful. The group is a collective board on delinquency; it usually includes a member who knows the individual personally or by reputation; and it can rely on the meeting to discover many things. Thus, the group is able to use actual behavior in the community to judge the extent to which a boy is involved with the program and to judge his readiness for release. The crucial criterion for any treatment program is not what an individual does while in it, but what he does while he is *not* in it.

The fourth process involves a number of important sanctions which the group can impose if a boy refuses to become involved. It can employ familiar techniques such as ostracism or derision or it can deny him the status and recognition which come with change. Furthermore, it can use sanctions arising out of the treatment system. For example, while authorities may impose restrictions on boys in the form of extra work or incarceration in jail, the group is often permitted, and encouraged, to explore reasons for the action and to help decide what future actions should be taken. For example, a boy may be placed in jail over the week-end and told that he will be returned there each week-end thereafter until his group decides to release him. It is not uncommon for the group, after thorough discussion, to return him one or more week-ends despite his protestations. Such an occurrence would be less likely in an ordinary reformatory because of the need for inmates to maintain solidarity against the official system. However, in this setting it is possible because boys are granted the power to make important decisions affecting their entire lives. Rather than having other people do things to them, they are doing things to themselves.

The ultimate sanction possessed by the group is refusal to release a boy from the program. Such a sanction has great power because it is normative to expect that no individual will be tolerated in the program indefinitely. Pinehills is not a place where boys "do time."

Authorities. The third source of pressure towards change rests in the hands of authorities. The role of an authority in a treatment system of this type is a difficult one. On one

---

[30] Delinquents are like other people: The worst can never happen to them. See also Mark R. Moran, "Inmate Concept of Self in a Reformatory Society," unpublished Ph.D. Dissertation, Ohio State University, 1953.

hand, he cannot be seen as a person whom skillful delinquents or groups can manipulate. But, on the other hand, he cannot be perceived permanently as a "rejector." Everything possible, therefore, must be done by him to create an adult image which is new and different.

Initially, authorities are probably seen as "rejectors." It will be recalled that they do not go out of their way to engage in regular social amenities, to put boys at ease, or to establish one-to-one relationships with boys. Adult behavior of this type is consistent with the treatment philosophy. It attempts to have boys focus upon the peer group, not adults, as the vehicle by which questions and problems are resolved.

Second, boys learn that authorities will strongly uphold the norm which says that Pinehills is not a place for boys to "do time." If, therefore, a boy does not become involved and the group is unwilling or unable to take action, authorities will. Such action varies. It might involve requiring him to work all day without pay, placing him in jail, or putting him in a situation in which he has no role whatsoever. In the latter case he is free to wander around the Center all day but he is neither allowed to work nor given the satisfaction of answers to his questions regarding his future status.

Boys are seldom told why they are in trouble or, if they are told, solutions are not suggested. To do so would be to provide them structure by which to rationalize their behavior, hide other things they have been doing, and escape the need to change. Consequently, they are left on their own to figure out why authorities are doing what they are doing and what they must do to get out of trouble.

Situations of this type precipitate crises. Sometimes boys run away. But, whatever happens, the boy's status remains amorphous until he can come up with a solution to his dilemma. This dilemma, however, is not easily resolved.

There is no individual counseling since this would reflect heavily upon the integrity of the peer group. Consequently, he cannot resolve his problems by counseling with or pleasing adults. His only recourse is to the group. But since the group waits for him to bring up his troubles, he must involve himself with it or he cannot resolve them. Once he does, he must reveal why he is in trouble, what he has been doing to get into trouble or how he has been abusing the program. If he refuses to become involved he may be returned to court by authorities. This latter alternative occurs rarely, since adults have more time than boys. While they can afford to wait, boys find it very difficult to "sweat out" a situation. They feel the need to resolve it.

As a result of such experiences, boys are often confused and hostile. But where such feelings might be cause for alarm elsewhere, they are welcomed at Pinehills. They are taken as a sign that a boy is not in command of the situation and is therefore amenable to change. Nevertheless, the treatment system does not leave him without an outlet for his feelings. The meeting is a place where his anger and hostility can be vented — not only against the program but against the adults who run it. But, in venting his confusion and hostility, it becomes possible for the group to analyze, not only his own behavior, but that of adults, and to determine to what end the behavior of all is leading. Initial perceptions of adults which were confusing and provoking can now be seen in a new way. The treatment system places responsibility upon a boy and his peers for changing delinquent behavior, not upon adults. Thus, adult behavior which was initially seen as rejecting can now be seen as consistent with this expectation. Boys have to look to their own resources for solutions of problems. In this way they are denied social-psychological support for "rejecting the rejectors," or for rejecting decisions demanded by the group. Furthermore, as a result of the new adult image which is pressed upon them, boys are led to examine their perceptions regarding other authorities. Boys may learn to see authorities with whom they had difficulties previously in a new, non-stereotyped fashion.

Work and Other Activities

Any use of athletics, handicrafts, or remedial schooling involves a definition of rehabilitation goals. Are these activities actually important in changing delinquents? In the Provo Experiment they are not viewed as having an inherent value in developing non-delinquent behavior. In fact, they are viewed as detrimental because participation in them often becomes criteria for release. On the other hand, work habits are viewed as vitally important. Previous research suggests that employment is one of the most important means of changing reference from delinquent to law-abiding groups.[31] But, such findings simply pose the important question: How can boys be best prepared to find and hold employment?

Sociologists have noted the lack of opportunity structure for delinquents, but attention to a modification of the structure (assuming that it can be modified) as the sole approach to rehabilitation overlooks the need to prepare delinquents to utilize employment possibilities. One alternative for doing this is an education program with all its complications. The other is an immediate attack on delinquent values and work habits. The Provo Experiment chose the latter alternative. It hypothesized that an immediate attack on delinquent values, previous careers, and nocturnal habits would be more effective than an educational program. Sophisticated delinquents, who are otherwise very skillful in convincing peers and authorities of their good intentions, are often unable to work consistently. They have too long believed that only suckers work. Thus concentration is upon work habits. Boys are employed by the city and county in parks, streets, and recreation areas. Their work habits are one focus of group discussion and an important criterion for change. After release, they are encouraged to attend academic and vocational schools should they desire.

The Starter Mechanism: Putting the System in Motion

There are both theoretical and practical considerations relative to the purposeful creation of the social structure at Pinehills and the process by which it was developed. The foregoing discussion described some of the structural elements involved and, by inference, suggested the means by which they were introduced. However, the following is presented as a means of further clarification.

The first consideration involved the necessity of establishing structure which could pose realistically and clearly the alternatives open to habitually delinquent boys. What are these alternatives? Since in most cases delinquents are lower-class individuals who not only lack many of the social skills but who have been school failures as well, the alternatives are not great. Some may become professional criminals but this is a small minority. Therefore, most of them have two principal choices: (1) they can continue to be delinquent and expect, in most cases, to end up in prison; or (2) they can learn to live a rather marginal life in which they will be able to operate sufficiently within the law to avoid being locked up. Acceptance of the second alternative by delinquents would not mean that they would have to change their entire style of living, but it does mean that most would have to find employment and be willing to disregard delinquent behavior in favor of the drudgery of everyday living.

Until these alternatives are posed for them, and posed in a meaningful way, delinquents will not be able to make the necessary decisions regarding them. The need, therefore, was for the type of structure at Pinehills which could pose these alternatives initially without equivocation and thus force boys to consider involvement in the rehabilitative process as a realistic alternative for them.

By the time delinquents reach Pinehills they have been cajoled, threatened, lectured, and exhorted — all by a variety of people in a variety of settings: by parents, teachers, police, religious leaders, and court officials. As a consequence, most have developed a set of manipulative techniques which enable them to "neutralize" verbal admonitions by appearing to comply with them, yet refraining all the while from any real adherence. For that reason, it was concluded that *deeds*, not *words*, would be required as the chief means for posing clearly the structural alternatives open to them.

Upon arrival the first delinquents assigned to Pinehills had every reason to believe that this was another community agency for which they possessed the necessary "techniques of

[31] Glaser, "A Sociological Approach to Crime and Correction," *op. cit.*, pp. 690–691.

neutralization." It was housed in an ordinary two-story home, and authorities spent little time giving instructions or posing threats. It must have seemed, therefore, that Pinehills would not constitute a serious obstacle for which they could not find some means to avoid involvement.

The following are examples of happenings which helped to establish norms contrary to this view. After attending only one day, a rather sophisticated boy was not at home to be picked up for his second day. Instead, he left a note on his front door saying he was at the hospital visting a sick sister. Official reaction was immediate and almost entirely opposite to what he expected. No one made any efforts to contact him. Instead, a detention order was issued by the court to the police who arrested the boy later that evening and placed him in jail. He was left there for several days without the benefit of visits from anyone and then returned to Pinehills. Even then, no one said anything to him about his absence. No one had to; he did not miss again. Furthermore, he had been instrumental in initiating the norm which says that the principal alternative to Pinehills is incarceration.

A second occurrence established this norm even more clearly. After having been at Pinehills for two months and refusing to yield to the pressures of his group, a boy asked for a rehearing in court, apparently feeling that he could manipulate the judge more successfully than he could the people at Pinehills. His request was acted upon immediately. He was taken to jail that afternoon and a hearing arranged for the following morning. The judge committed him to the State Reformatory.[32] Since that time there has never been another request for a rehearing. In a similar way, especially during the first year, boys who con-

tinued to get in serious trouble while at Pinehills were recalled by the court for another hearing and assigned to the reformatory. These cases became legendary examples to later boys. However, adults have never had to call attention to them; they are passed on in the peer socialization process.

Once such traditions were established, they could yet be used in another way. They became devices by which to produce the type of uncertainty characteristic of social settings in which negative sanctions should be forthcoming but do not appear. The individual is left wondering why. For example, not all boys who miss a day or two at Pinehills now are sent to jail. In some cases, nothing is said to the individual in question. He is left, instead, to wonder when, and if, he will be sent. Likewise, other boys who have been in serious trouble in the community are not always sent to the State Reformatory but may be subjected to the same kind of waiting and uncertainty. Efforts are made, however, to make it impossible for boys to predict in advance what will happen in any particular case. Even adults cannot predict this, relying on the circumstances inherent in each case. Thus, both rigidity and inconsistency are present in the system at the same time.

The same sort of structural alternatives were posed regarding work. Boys who did not work consistently on their city jobs, where they were being paid, were returned to Pinehills to work for nothing. At Pinehills, they were usually alone and had to perform such onerous tasks as scrubbing the floor, washing windows, mowing the lawn or cutting weeds. They might be left on this job for hours or weeks. The problem of being returned to work with the other boys for pay was left to them for their own resolution, usually in the group. So long as they said nothing, nothing was said to them except to assign them more work.

This type of structure posed stark but, in our opinion, realistic alternatives. It was stark and realistic because boys were still living in the community, but for the first time could sense the omnipresence of permanent incarceration. However, another type of structure less stringent was needed by which boys could re-

---

[32] Co-operation of this type between the Juvenile Courts and rehabilitative agencies is not always forthcoming. Yet, it also reflects two things: (1) the fact that Judge Paxman sentences only those boys to Pinehills who are habitual offenders; and (2) the fact that it is his conviction that rehabilitation must inevitably involve the Court's participation, both in posing alternatives for boys and in determining the effectiveness of various approaches.

alistically resolve problems and make choices. Since, as has been mentioned, peer-group decision-making was chosen as the means for problem-resolution, attention was focussed upon the daily group meetings as the primary source of information. It became the focal point of the whole treatment system.

The first group, not having any standards to guide it (except those which suggested resistance to official pressures), spent great portions of entire meetings without speaking. However, consistent with the idea that deeds, not words, count, and that a group has to resolve its own problems, the group leader refused to break the silence except at the very end of each meeting. At that time, he began standardizing one common meeting practice: he summarized what had been accomplished. Of silent meetings he simply said that nothing had been accomplished. He did point out, however, that he would be back the next day — that, in fact, he would be there a year from that day. Where would they be, still there? The problem was theirs.

When some boys could stand the silence no longer, they asked the group leader what they might talk about. Rather than making it easy for them he suggested something that could only involve them further: he suggested that someone might recite all the things he had done to get in trouble. Not completely without resources, however, boys responded by reciting only those things they had been caught for. In his summary, the leader noted this fact and suggested that whoever spoke the next time might desire to be more honest by telling all. Boys were reluctant to do this but, partly because it was an opportunity to enhance reputations and partly because they did not know what else to do, some gave honest recitations. When no official action was taken against them, two new and important norms were introduced: (1) the idea that what is said in the meeting is sacred to the meeting; and (2) that boys can afford to be candid — that, in fact, candor pays.

The subsequent recitals of delinquent activities ultimately led to a growing awareness of the ambivalence which many delinquents feel regarding their activities. In the social climate provided by the meeting some boys began to express feelings and receive support for behavior which the delinquent system with its emphasis on ideal-typical role behavior could not permit.

Eventually, the meeting reached a stage where it began to discuss the plethora of happenings which occurred daily, both at Pinehills and elsewhere in the community. These happenings, rather than impersonal, easily speculated-about material, were urged as the most productive subject matter. For example, many boys had reached the stage of trying devious rather than direct methods of missing sessions at Pinehills. They came with requests to be excused for normally laudatory activities: school functions, family outings, and even religious services. But, again adults refused to take the traditional course of assuming responsibility and making decisions for boys. Boys were directed to the meeting instead. This not only shifted the responsibility to them, but provided the opportunity to develop five important norms: (1) those having to do with absences; (2) the idea that the place for problem-solving is in the meeting; (3) that everyone, not just adults, should be involved in the process; (4) that if a boy wants the meeting to talk about his problems, he has to justify them as being more important than someone else's; and (5) that any request or point of view has to be substantiated both by evidence and some relevance to the solution of delinquent problems.

It became obvious that even simple requests could be complicated. Boys found themselves using their own rationalizations on each other, often providing both humorous and eye-opening experiences. The climate became increasingly resistant to superficial requests and more conducive to the examination of pressing problems. Boys who chose to fight the system found themselves fighting peers. A stubborn boy could be a thorn in the side of the whole group.

The daily meeting summaries took on increased importance as the leader helped the group: (1) to examine what had happened each day; (2) to examine to what ends various efforts were leading — that is, to examine what various boys were doing, or not doing, and what relevance this had for themselves and the group; (3) to suggest areas of discussion which had been neglected, ignored, or purposely hidden by group members; and (4) to describe the goals of the treatment system in such a way that boys could come to recognize the meaning of group discussions as a realistic source of problem-resolution.

The structural lines associated with the meeting eventually began to define not only the type of subject matter most relevant to change, but the general means for dealing with this subject matter. However, such structure was extremely flexible, permitting a wide latitude of behavior. Great care was taken to avoid the institutionalization of clear-cut steps by which boys could escape Pinehills. Problem solving was, and still is, viewed as a process — a process not easily understood in advance, but something which develops uniquely for each new boy and each new group.

Finally, in summary, the Pinehills system, like many social systems, has some rigid prerequisites for continued membership. The broad structural outlines carefully define the limits beyond which members should not go. However, unlike most extreme authoritarian systems, there is an inner structure, associated with the meeting, which does not demand rigid conformity and which instead permits those deviations which are an honest expression of feelings.

The admission of deviations within the structural confines of the meeting helps to lower the barriers which prevent a realistic examination of their implications for the broader authoritarian structure, either at Pinehills or in society at large. Boys are able to make more realistic decisions as to which roles, conventional or delinquent, would seem to have the most utility for them.

This brief attempt to describe a complex system may have been misleading. The complexities involved are multivariate and profound. However, one important aspect of the experiment has to do with the theoretical development of, and research on, the nature of the treatment system. Each discussion session is recorded and efforts are made to determine

means by which treatment techniques might be improved, and ways in which group processes can be articulated. All would be very useful in testing theory which suggests that experience in a cohesive group is an important variable in directing or changing behavior.

Phase II: Community Adjustment

Phase II involves an effort to maintain reference group support and employment for a boy after intensive treatment in Phase I. After his release from Phase I he continues to meet periodically for discussions with his old group. The goal is to utilize this group in accomplishing three things: (1) acting as a check on a boy's current behavior; (2) serving as a law-abiding reference group; and (3) aiding in the solution of new problems. It seeks to continue treatment in a different and perhaps more intensive way than such traditional practices as probation or parole.

Efforts to find employment for boys are made by the Citizens' Advisory Council. If employment is found, a boy is simply informed that an employer needs someone. No efforts are taken by some well-meaning but pretentious adult to manipulate the boy's life.

These steps, along with the idea that delinquents should be permitted to make important decisions during the rehabilitative process, are consistent with structural-functional analysis which suggests that in order to eliminate existing structure, or identification with it, one must provide the necessary functional alternatives.[33]

Appropriateness of Techniques

Many persons express disfavor with what they consider a harsh and punitive system at Pinehills. If, however, alternatives are not great for habitual delinquents, a program which suggests otherwise is not being honest with them. Delinquents are aware that society seldom provides honors for *not* being delinquent; that, in fact, conventional alternatives for them have not always promised significantly more than

[33] Edwin M. Schur, "Sociological Analysis in Confidence Swindling," *Journal of Criminal Law, Criminology and Police Science*, 48 (September–October 1957), p. 304.

delinquent alternatives.[34] Therefore, expectations associated with the adaptation of conventional alternatives should not be unrealistic.

On the other hand it should be remembered that, in terms familiar to delinquents, every effort is made at Pinehills to include as many positive experiences as possible. The following are some which seem to function:

1. Peers examine problems which are common to all.

2. There is a recurring opportunity for each individual to be the focal point of attention among peers in which his behavior and problems become the most important concern of the moment.

3. Delinquent peers articulate in front of conventional adults without constraint with regard to topic, language, or feeling.

4. Delinquents have the opportunity, for the first time in an institutional setting, to make crucial decisions about their own lives. This in itself is a change in the opportunity structure and is a means of obligating them to the treatment system. In a reformatory a boy cannot help but see the official system as doing things to him in which he has no say: locking him up, testing him, feeding him, making his decisions. Why should he feel obligated? But when some important decision-making is turned over to him, he no longer has so many grounds for rejecting the system. Rejection in a reformatory might be functional in relating him to his peers, but in this system it is not so functional.

5. Delinquents participate in a treatment system that grants status in three ways: (a) for age and experience in the treatment process — old boys have the responsibility of teaching new boys the norms of the system; (b) for the exhibition of law-abiding behavior, not only in a minimal sense, but for actual qualitative changes in specific role behavior at Pinehills, at home or with friends; and (c) for the willingness to confront other boys, in a group

setting, with their delinquent behavior. (In a reformatory where he has to contend with the inmate system a boy can gain little and lose much for his willingness to be candid in front of adults about peers, but at Pinehills it is a primary source of prestige.) The ability to confront others often reflects more about the *confronter* than it does about the *confronted*. It is an indication of the extent to which he has accepted the reformation process and identified himself with it.[35]

6. Boys can find encouragement in a program which poses the possibility of relatively short restriction and the avoidance of incarceration.

7. The peer group is a potential source of reference group support for law-abiding behavior. Boys commonly refer to the fact that their group knows more about them than any other persons: parents or friends.

Research Design

An integral part of the Provo Experiment is an evaluation of treatment extending over a five-year period. It includes means by which offenders who receive treatment are compared to two control groups: (1) a similar group of offenders who at time of sentence are placed on probation and left in the community; and (2) a similar group who at time of sentence are incarcerated in the Utah State Industrial School. Since it is virtually impossible to match all three groups, random selection is used to minimize the effect of sample bias. All three groups are drawn from a population of habitual delinquents who reside in Utah County, Utah, and who come before the Juvenile Court. Actual selection is as follows:

The Judge of the Court has in his possession two series of numbered envelopes — one series for selecting individuals to be placed in the *probation* treatment and control groups and one series for selecting the *reformatory* treatment and control groups. These series of

---

[34] Gwynn Nettler has raised a question as to who perceives reality most accurately, deviants or "good" people. See "Good Men, Bad Men and the Perception of Reality," Paper delivered at the meetings of the American Sociological Association, Chicago: September 1959.

[35] Support for this idea can be found in a recently developed matrix designed to measure the impact of group interaction. See William and Ida Hill, *Interaction Matrix for Group Psychotherapy*, mimeographed manuscript, Utah State Mental Hospital, Provo, Utah, 1960. This matrix has been many years in development.

Figure 1
Selection of Treatment and Control Groups

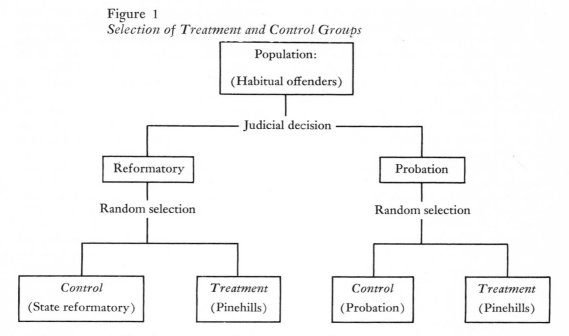

envelopes are supplied by the research team and contain randomly selected slips of paper on which are written either *Control Group* or *Treatment Group*.

In making an assignment to one of these groups the Judge takes the following steps: (1) After hearing a case he decides whether he would ordinarily place the offender on probation or in the reformatory. He makes this decision as though Pinehills did not exist. Then, (2) he brings the practice of random placement into play. He does so by opening an envelope from one of the two series supplied him (See Figure 1). For example, if he decides initially that he would ordinarily send the boy to the reformatory, he would select an envelope from the *reformatory* series and depend upon the designation therein as to whether the boy would actually go to the reformatory, and become a member of the *control* group, or be sent to Pinehills as a member of the *treatment* group.

This technique does not interfere with the judicial decision regarding the alternatives previously available to the Judge, but it does intercede, after the decision, by posing another alternative. The Judge is willing to permit the use of this alternative on the premise that, in the long run, his contributions to research will enable judicial decisions to be based ultimately on a more realistic evaluation of treatment programs available.

In order to make the comparison of treatment and control groups more meaningful, additional research is being conducted on the treatment process. Efforts are made to examine the problems involved in relating causation theory to intervention strategy, the role of the therapist in Guided Group Interaction, and the types of group interaction that seem most beneficial. Finally, a detailed examination is being made of the ways in which boys handle "critical incidents" [36] after release from treatment as compared to the way they handled them prior to treatment.

Summary and Implications

This paper describes an attempt to apply sociological theory to the treatment of delinquents. It concentrates not only upon treatment techniques, *per se*, but the type of social

[36] John C. Flanagan, "The Critical Incident Technique," *Psychological Bulletin*, 51 (July 1954), pp. 327–358.

system in which these techniques must operate. The over-all treatment system it describes is like all other social systems in the sense that it specifies generalized requirements for continued membership in the system. At the same time, however, it also legitimizes the existence of a subsystem within it — the meeting — which permits the discussion and evaluation of happenings and feelings which *may* or *may not* support the over-all normative structure of the larger system.

The purposeful creation of this subsystem simply recognized what seemed to be two obvious facts: (1) that the existence of contrary normative expectations among delinquent and official members of the over-all system would ultimately result in the creation of such a subsystem anyway; and (2) that such a system, not officially recognized, would pose a greater threat, and would inhibit to a greater degree, the realization of the over-all rehabilitative goals of the major system than would its use as a rehabilitative tool.

This subsystem receives not only official sanction but grants considerable power and freedom to delinquent members. By permitting open expressions of anger, frustration, and opposition, it removes social-psychological support for complete resistance to a realistic examination of the ultimate utility of delinquent versus conventional norms. At the same time, however, the freedom it grants is relative. So long as opposition to the demands of the larger system is contained in the meeting subsystem,

such opposition is respected. But continued deviancy outside the meeting cannot be tolerated indefinitely. It must be seen as dysfunctional because the requirements of the over-all treatment system are identified with those of the total society and these requirements will ultimately predominate.

At the same time, the over-all treatment system includes elements designed to encourage and support the adoption of conventional roles. The roles it encourages and the rewards it grants, however, are peer-group oriented and concentrate mainly upon the normative expectations of the social strata from which most delinquents come: working- rather than middle-class strata. This is done on the premise that a rehabilitation program is more realistic if it attempts to change normative orientations towards lawbreaking rather than attempting (or hoping) to change an individual's entire way of life. It suggests, for example, that a change in attitudes and values toward work *per se* is more important than attempting to create an interest in the educational, occupational, and recreational goals of the middle class.

The differences posed by this treatment system, as contrasted to many existing approaches to rehabilitation, are great. Means should be sought, therefore, in addition to this project by which its techniques and orientation can be treated as hypotheses and verified, modified, or rejected.

Arnold describes the situation in the Merecaido family as a vivid illustration of the task faced by a program, such as Mobilization for Youth, designed to curb delinquency. Mobilization for Youth was a government-sponsored project based on the theoretical position of Cloward and Ohlin (see Section IV). Now defunct, Mobilization for Youth in effect offered a "supermarket of social services." The project was designed to expand the opportunities of youth in slums; its three-pronged attack stressed work, education, and community organization. Arnold views Mobilization for Youth, which involved an expenditure of more than fourteen million dollars, as a failure.

One implication of Arnold's commentary is that, as in many efforts directed toward helping the poor and unemployed, this project may have alleviated middle-class unemployment, because many social workers and other "middle-class types," including sociologists, were employed with adequate salaries. The greatest value of this selection, however, lies in the author's placement of delinquency and solution of the problem of delinquency in the larger social context of poverty, unemployment, and discrimination in the United States. Unemployment is high among ghetto youths and is directly related to school dropout, which in turn Arnold attributes to the second-class education — or miseducation — offered slum residents. (A similar position is adopted regarding the school and employment by the President's Commission [1967:41–56].) According to Arnold, make-work programs, even fourteen million dollar ones, are not the answer; real job opportunities are. In taking this stance Arnold agrees with the idea underlying Mobilization for Youth; he is critical of the program because it did not provide viable job opportunities.

Similarly, Arnold is not opposed to efforts at community organization, as long as all groups in the community, including the poor, are included. Nor is he opposed to the project's efforts to develop new techniques to educate children reared in slums. His point is that such "patchwork" efforts cannot serve as a substitute for revision of the priorities of the society. Over the years it has become common for sociologists to indicate that delinquency is rooted in the social organization; in this selection the meaning of that statement is brought "down to earth" in terms of the poor who live in substandard housing, receive an inadequate education, and face economic exploitation, and if they are members of minority groups, also meet barriers of discrimination. Arnold suggests that as long as society places its highest priorities on meeting the needs of the military-industrial complex and continually increasing the consumption of material goods in order to maximize profits, the needs of many children will go unmet — and the problem of delinquency in our affluent nation will not be solved.

REFERENCE

The President's Commission on Law Enforcement and Administration of Justice, *Juvenile Delinquency and Youth Crime* (Washington, D.C.: U.S. Government Printing Office, 1967).

ROBERT ARNOLD

Mobilization for Youth: Patchwork or Solution?

There are two signs on Manhattan's E. 2nd St. One in neat blue letters announces the headquarters of Mobilization for Youth. The

From *Dissent*, 11 (Summer 1964), 347–354. Reprinted by permission.

other in scrawled yellow paint stakes out 2nd St. as "Dragon's Territory"; beneath it the same hand has painted its biography, "I Was a Teenage Junkie."

Between these signs stands an investment of

over fourteen million dollars on the part of federal, state and local agencies and the research of a team of social workers, psychologists, and community planners in the largest effort mounted thus far to attack delinquency in a slum neighborhood.

Angel Merecaido is seventeen, the oldest son of a family of six. Together with his parents and younger brothers and sisters he shares a three-room apartment on E. 11th St. His father works in a factory producing electric hot plates (take home pay, after taxes and dues for a "sweetheart" union that guarantees him the minimum wage, is $44.63); his mother works off-the-books part-time in a non-union dress shop. The family receives supplementary assistance from the city's welfare department.

The major responsibility for the care of the Merecaido children belongs to Ivette, Angel's 12-year-old sister. At an age when other youngsters are leaving their dolls to enter into the mysteries of adolescence, Ivette is "in fact" the mother of two children. She must see to it that they are fed and washed, and that the household is cared for.

Angel dropped out of school last year, at the minimum age of sixteen. He did not complete the ninth grade. Since that time he has worked 87 days as a delivery boy for a local laundry (pay 75 cents per hour). Every other Wednesday he must report to a probation officer; he was arrested six months ago for breaking into a school. The officer has threatened to have his probation revoked if he does not find a steady job.

Angel's situation is typical of the plight of hundreds of thousands of youngsters growing up in the depressed metropolitan areas of the United States. Poverty, violence, over-crowded living, and fragmented family life form the backdrop against which these slum children must attempt to act out the drama of growing up.

Nearly 50 percent of all youth in the lower-income bracket drop out of school before high school graduation (an estimated 30 percent of youth entering the U.S. labor force in the 1960's will not have finished high school). Twenty-five percent of them are three or more years behind in reading, as well as all other academic areas, by the time they reach junior high school. Of the 71,854 sixth graders in New York City in 1962, 36.8 percent were one or more grades behind in reading, and 10,778 were on the third-grade level or below. The bulk of this retardation occurs among the non-white group; better than 20 percent of all non-white youth are functionally illiterate.

A Pocket of Permanent Poverty

Disease has not failed to take its toll of the slum child either. Close to 50 percent of slum youth are in grave need of psychological, as well as academic, help by the time they leave high school. Among families with incomes ranging from $2,000 to $3,999 in 1958, 8 percent of all persons were either disabled or limited in their activities by chronic ill health. The majority of this ill health was to be found among three groups, Negroes, the very old, and the very young — the three groups in the population least able to protect themselves. Among Negroes the fetal death rate is almost twice as high, the infant mortality rate twice as high, and the maternal death rate nearly four times as high as that for whites.

The world of Dick and Jane, the middle-class children of the first grade reader, could not be more remote from the experience of the slum child if he lived on the moon. Instead of white picket fences, private houses, and Big Dan, the friendly policeman who says, "Hello little Jane," the slum child is daily confronted with hunger, violence, and disease.

He does not expect to see father walking up the steps, briefcase in hand. Many of these children have never seen father, or maybe they've seen two or three fathers, but never with a briefcase in hand. In his world the cop may be nice until you get big and then he is afraid of you. You are a "nigger" or a "spic" and he is "The Man." He arrests you and shoots the friends you grew up with, and you drop garbage or bricks on his head for turning off the hydrant on a steaming summer night.

No one has to tell the slum child that Negro teenagers have the highest unemployment rate of any group in the labor force. The facts are sitting on his stoop.

Against this background Mobilization for Youth came to work on the Lower East Side. Two years of planning and research financed by the National Institute of Mental Health, the Department of Health, Education and Welfare, the New York School of Social Work, and the Ford Foundation preceded it. The results are expected to set the pattern for the development of similar government-sponsored programs in urban communities throughout the nation.

Manhattan's Lower East Side, the area designated by the project, is one of the oldest slums in the United States. Its history is that of successive waves of migration, each generation bringing a fresh group of immigrants to seek the promise of a new life in America.

Today, as in the past, it is this "melting pot" character that marks the Lower East Side. However, the new migrants are no longer strangers. They are citizens born in the United States, part of the more than a million and a half Negroes and Puerto Ricans who have come to New York and other northern cities in the past decade.

Like the generations of immigrants who preceded them, the Negroes and Puerto Ricans have come to the city in search of jobs and a better way of life. They have turned to New York's unskilled labor pools as their one source of escape.

Instead of jobs and security, however, they have found the tragedy of life in "El Barrio," Harlem, and the Lower East Side: rows of dirty, graying tenements facing each other across streets scarred with refuse, the cries of numberless infants, the six-story climbs through rat-infested, urine-stinking hallways.

The facts of prejudice and an economy that tends to drive its poorest members into a gray land of hopelessness have created among the newest migrants to the Lower East Side a pocket of more or less permanent poverty. At any one time it can be safely estimated that between 10 and 20 percent of the population is dependent on some form of public assistance.

II

Mobilization for Youth came to the East Side with a theoretical framework which stressed the social causation of delinquency. In its view "much delinquency can be understood as representing illegitimate ways of achieving success-goals. The 'fighting gang' seeks to achieve prestige ('rep') through violence; the criminal gang seeks to achieve money ('scores') through theft; the 'consumption gangs' (drug and alcohol-using) have retreated from the struggle and accepted defeat." Unless such young people can be provided with expanding opportunities, the problem of juvenile delinquency cannot be dealt with.

Mobilization for Youth proposed a three-pronged attack in the following areas: work, education, and community organization.

First, to stress the importance of creative work as an alternative to delinquency, Mobilization proposed the creation of an "Urban Youth Service Corps" and "Youth Jobs Center." The corps would provide paid employment on projects of social utility for several hundred unemployed out-of-school youngsters, while the job center would attempt to reach the "hard-to-place" youngster with specialized vocational guidance.

Second, the program proposed to create experimental projects in education to overcome the barriers facing "the slum child in the slum school." It was planned to create a laboratory school to demonstrate methods of teaching lower-income youngsters and a "Homework Helper" program whereby low-income but talented high school students would be hired to tutor low-income elementary school students who are failing academically.

Finally, Mobilization proposed to develop in the residents of the community the necessary skills to cope with their own problems. One way would be to strengthen the Lower East Side Neighborhoods Association. The other, through direct effort on the part of Mobilization for Youth, would be to help the isolated community residents organize themselves to solve their problems.

Mobilization for Youth set itself a difficult task. Delinquency does not lend itself to simple panaceas. Confronted by the hard realities of slum life, the best theory as to the causation and cure of delinquency may run aground.

The question then is: how successful has Mobilization for Youth been in confronting these realities in its more than two years on the Lower East Side?

The answer: it has largely been a failure. In terms of achievement and impact on the community, Mobilization has little to show. A couple of coffee shops have been opened, a service station has been leased from an oil company to provide work experience for a few dozen youths, slightly over 150 youngsters have been placed in subsidized work projects, and some 100 high school juniors and seniors have been employed as tutors to about 300 elementary school pupils. However, the chief impression one receives from a close examination of the program is that it has been a costly failure employing more social workers than youngsters.

In the Negro and Puerto Rican community, the majority distrust the motives of Mobilization and its chief ally, the Lower East Side [1] Neighborhoods Association, and feel that these groups are more interested in securing publicity than in improving conditions. The attitude of the independent organizations working in the area has been similar. As George Von Hilsheimer, a member of Mobilization's Board of Directors, stated, Mobilization has been "wasting money" on contacts with the Board of Education and established settlement houses, while rarely giving money to experimental and independent groups.

Where money has been given, as in the case of the March on Washington and the recent School Boycott, the general impression has been that Mobilization was covering its bets to insure a fail-safe operation.

Many of the youngsters in the area feel that Mobilization has placed a premium on gang membership in terms of its employment program and other services. One junior high school boy, who took part in a picket line protesting Mobilization's employment policies,

---

[1] LENA is a loose federation of established settlement houses and predominantly middle-class community organizations active on the Lower East Side. It is divided into several neighborhood councils. The majority of its active membership and leadership comes from the cooperative housing projects below Delancey St. (ILGWU Houses, etc., and the middle-class area around Cooper Square). It has very little contact or influence within the Negro and Puerto Rican community.

declared, "I don't want to kill somebody to get a job."

Coupled to this charge is the complaint that the uniforms worn by the young people employed by the project cost $5–$6, while Mobilization only pays 75 cents to $1 per hour to those who get jobs. The boys feel that the social workers "get their money easy, we have to work hard. They just sit there writing with a pencil." It is interesting that Mobilization's salaries for beginning social workers are among the highest in the New York area.

Basic Problems Remain

None of the above observations, however, answer the question of why Mobilization has failed.

Why has Mobilization failed?

There is no simple answer. The failure involves much more than the usual problems of shortage of funds and inadequate staff. More money and staff would simply mean frosting the cake. What I would suggest is that the failure involves a much larger failure on the part of the government to solve the basic problems of poverty, unemployment, and discrimination in this country.

Some 26 million young people will be entering the labor force in the current decade. This means there will be better than 2.5 million new job seekers every year. To meet this demand the American economy would have to create at least 25,000 new jobs every week for the next 10 years. However, as the official "Manpower Report of the President" recently noted, the annual economic growth rate dropped from 3.8 percent in the years 1947–1957 to 2.9 percent for the years 1957–1962 and the average annual increase in nonfarm jobs has fallen from 700,000 to 175,000.

Among young people unemployment has reached crisis proportions. During the school months of 1962, an average of 700,000 youths between the ages of 16 and 21 were out-of-school and out-of-work. In New York City, 76,800 youths between the ages of 14 and 24 were out-of-school and out-of-work. Of that number 32,700 young men were neither in school nor in the labor force: they had given up hope of finding jobs.

For school drop-outs, unemployment rates

are three to four times as high as those of the adult labor force. In a recent job survey of an area in a large city, 90 percent of out-of-school youth were found to be jobless. For Negro and Puerto Rican youth the figures are even higher; the national average unemployment rate for Negro and other non-white youth is roughly double that for white youth. In one predominantly Negro slum area of 125,000 people, approximately 70 percent of boys and girls between 16 and 21 were both out-of-school and out-of-work. In New York City the unemployment rate for 14- to 19-year-olds was 17.8 percent for non-whites as opposed to 8.4 percent for whites, while for Puerto Ricans the rate was more than 20 percent.

The prospects for these youngsters are dim. Of the million and a half unattached individuals who did not finish high school in the United States, 55 percent live in poverty; of the over 8 million heads of families who did not finish high school, 33 percent live in poverty. These figures become more telling when we remember that the bulk of this educational deprivation is in the non-white group — 60.6 percent of all non-white families live in poverty; 66.4 percent of all non-white individuals live in poverty.

Confronted by the out-of-school and out-of-work youngster and the over-all problems of permanent unemployment and poverty in the United States, the government has chosen to respond with inadequate and antedated crash programs. The basic fallacy of such thinking becomes apparent when we examine Mobilization for Youth's employment program. Their proposals do not seriously attempt to cope with the problem of unemployment and job training; rather, they substitute a program of make-work for viable opportunities for these youngsters.

Make-work programs, their social utility aside, are no substitute for real work. Even if programs like Mobilization's could provide employment for significant numbers of presently unemployed and unemployable youth, which they cannot, they would be no alternative to real job opportunities. Rather than providing the training and status afforded by

meaningful work, these programs amount to a tacit admission by government that there is no place in society for these young people.

As currently proposed, the government's program to help unemployed youth is totally inadequate. The Youth Conservation Corps and other local projects similar to Mobilization for Youth would at most provide employment for only a little over 60,000 young people. The total expenditure by the federal government, as first outlined by President Kennedy, would not be more than $100 million the first year, about the cost of a single atomic submarine.

Clearly more than make-work is necessary if we are to meet the demands of these young people for jobs. An all-out effort must be made to increase our rate of economic growth, control the forces of automation, and train these youngsters before unemployment begins to reach the recession levels of 7 percent.

In addition, the government must outlaw discrimination in hiring through the passage of an enforceable Fair Employment Practices Act. At present, although Negroes account for over 10 percent of the population, they represent less than 1 percent of the apprentices in such skilled trades as carpentry and toolmaking. It makes little sense to train young people in these trades, as Mobilization has done, if there are no opportunities for jobs.

Education and the Slum

Nor can the problem of the slum child in the slum school be solved merely through adding experimental schools and specially trained teachers — although these are necessary. Nor can they be solved through reading clinics and incentive programs. To believe they can, is to ignore the basic facts of the slum child's existence.

The slum child in the slum school receives a second rate education by virtue of the fact that he lives in a slum. When the total environment of the child is inadequate, how can his education do anything but conform to the pattern?

As Henry Salzman, Secretary of the Ford Foundation's Great Cities Gray Area Program, pointed out recently, "The magnitude of the problem has made it clear that the problem cannot be solved through reading specialists. There will never be enough of them. . . ."

Conant and other semi-official spokesmen have admirably stated the difference between slum education and that of the middle class school. However, they have failed to clearly face the issue. In a society which assumes that the priorities to be imposed on the educational situation are those of the war-economy and the Organized System — i.e., more technicians to feed the military-industrial complex, ever-increasing consumption, maximum profits — it is impossible to meet the real needs of children.

No amount of patchwork can solve the problem of the slum school apart from the total context of slum life. As long as families are herded together in pigsties called apartments; as long as parents are separated from their children all day working in sweatshops; as long as human beings are robbed of their sense of worth in the interest of maximum profits, hundreds of thousands of youngsters are destined to be intellectually mutilated.

Finally, Mobilization for Youth's proposals fail to take into account the realities of power within the community. The Negro and Puerto Rican living on the Lower East Side today is almost totally cut off from any effective political control of his community. He is literally trapped between the forces of dislocation which seek to exploit him and the bureaucratic structure of a government over which he has no control. Without effective political power, he cannot muster enough strength to fight exploitation.

By aligning itself with the Lower East Side Neighborhoods Association, rather than seeking to place control in the hands of Negroes and Puerto Ricans, Mobilization has tended to strengthen the position of the middle class forces in the community, rather than that of its weakest members. It is difficult to see where such an alignment will benefit the Negroes and Puerto Ricans — particularly in the area of housing, where they are already hard pressed by the recent development of the Lower East Side as a speculative housing market.

If there is a lesson to be learned from this failure, it is that no effort at changing the pattern of slum life can hope to succeed without attempting to destroy the context of poverty and deprivation in which Negroes, Puerto Ricans, and other minorities are forced to live. Until the barriers of discrimination, substandard housing, inadequate education, and economic exploitation are finally removed, there can be no true progress toward changing the face of the Lower East Side or any other slum neighborhood.

According to Toby's analysis, those interested in delinquency are not likely to run out of work for a long time. Such a view may seem to be highly pessimistic, but unless appropriate ameliorative action is taken, the effects of three major social trends will be high rates of delinquency. The first of these is the ever widening generation gap. In an agrarian society, boys learn the requirements of the adult role from their fathers, and, similarly, girls learn the skills of a woman from their mothers. However, in an industrial society children do not work with their parents; family and centers of employment are separated. Youth are expected to obtain an education and their free time is spent in the company of other youth. Toby also mentions the importance of relative deprivation — to be poor in an affluent society produces greater resentment than it does in a poor society. Finally, an important consequence of industrialization is urbanization; Toby suggests that the traditional agents of socialization and social control may be less effective in an urban setting.

It is evident that limited patchwork efforts will not suffice, but the most promising strategy to reduce the delinquency rate is not immediately apparent. Toby emphasizes that research and experimentation are essential; and he perceives the provision of educational and occupational opportunities for youth to be of critical importance, as is reduction of the autonomy of youth and adequate preparation for the assumption of adult roles. An important implication of Toby's analysis is that it is not necessary to take a pessimistic view regarding delinquency rates if industrial societies like the United States are willing to invest the funds required to meet the needs of youth in the age of space exploration. If, however, the provisions for youth are geared to a horse-and-buggy era, then high rates of delinquency are to be expected in industrial societies.

JACKSON TOBY

The Prospects for Reducing Delinquency Rates in Industrial Societies

Distant parts of the contemporary world — Japan, Sweden, Australia, Yugoslavia — report an upsurge in adolescent delinquency.[1] We cannot be certain whether these increases reflect an upward trend in adolescent rebelliousness, temporary dislocations caused by World War II, or greater efficiency in the collection of delinquency data. Even in the absence of statistical and journalistic reports, however, an examination of the impact of urban-industrial societies on young people suggests — to me at any rate — that delinquency will be a massive problem for a long time to come.

Trends Contributing to Delinquent Behavior

Specifically, I perceive three social trends contributing to youthful misbehavior.

1. *The sociocultural gulf between adolescents and adults is widening.* Parent-youth conflict is no new phenomenon.[2] But in contemporary society the world of the adolescent and the world of the adult are becoming more and more differentiated. An important reason for this is technological: Industrial societies have increasing need for skilled and responsible workers and decreasing use for unskilled labor. This changed industrial requirement is reflected in the later entry into the labor force of 20th century adolescents as compared with youngsters in previous centuries.[3] It is re-

From *Federal Probation*, 27 (December 1963), 23–25. Reprinted by permission.

[1] Second United Nations Congress on the Prevention of Crime and the Treatment of Offenders, *New Forms of Juvenile Delinquency: Their Origin, Prevention and Treatment* (Report prepared by the Secretariat), New York: United Nations, Department of Economic and Social Affairs, 1960, pp. 24, 26, 32. Although increases in delinquency are reported throughout the world, some baffling exceptions were noted. For example, Belgium reported a *decrease*. Similarly, there is evidence that Denmark, unlike the rest of the Scandinavian countries, showed a persistent decrease in delinquency. European Committee on Crime Problems, *Juvenile Delinquency in Post-War Europe*, Strasbourg: Council of Europe, 1960.

[2] Kingsley Davis, "The Sociology of Parent-Youth Conflict," *American Sociological Review*, 5, August 1940, pp. 523–535.

[3] John D. Durand, *The Labor Force in the United States, 1890–1960*, New York: Social Science Research Council, 1948.

flected also in the increased utilization of the system of formal education in all the industrial countries. Not only is formal education a necessary preparation for professional, technical, and executive employment, but the purely custodial function of the school as well should not be underestimated; parents find it useful to have a safe place to send their children for a portion of the day.

The fact that adolescents mostly go to school and adults mostly go to work helps to explain the phenomenon of "teenage culture." [4] It is not the whole explanation. The affluence of industrial societies creates the material basis for cultural differentiation. That is to say, industrial societies allocate to adolescents substantial discretionary purchasing power, and this enables adolescents to demand (and obtain) distinctive clothing, motion pictures, phonograph records, recreational facilities, and eating and drinking establishments. [5] From the viewpoint of understanding delinquency, however, the extension of formal education is probably more important than the development of the adolescent market. The reason for this is that mass formal education has created an adolescent limbo for children with educational disabilities. For academically successful children, school is a bridge between the world of childhood and the world of adulthood. For children unwilling or unable to learn, school is a place where the battle against society is likely to begin. [6] I suspect that none of the industrial societies has solved this problem, that none has a successful program for inte-

grating the least educable tenth of the population into adult society.

2. *The sting of socioeconomic deprivation is increasing.* Poverty is nothing new. On the contrary, it is affluence that is new. But the relationship between subjective dissatisfaction and objective deprivation is more complicated than was at first thought. [7] Poverty cannot cause crime but resentment of poverty can, and, curiously enough, resentment of poverty is more likely to develop among the relatively deprived of a rich society than among the objectively deprived in a poor society. This is partly because affluent industrial societies are also secular societies; the distribution of goods and services here and now is a more important preoccupation than transcendental concerns, e.g., eternal salvation. [8] It is also because the mass media — to which television has been a recent but important addition — stimulate the desire for a luxurious style of life among all segments of the population. These considerations explain why the sting of socioeconomic deprivation can be greater for the poor in rich societies than for the poor in poor societies. They also throw light on the higher crime rates of affluent societies as compared with poorer ones and on the increase of adolescent delinquency rates in times of prosperity as compared with times of depression. [9] Bear in mind that, relative to adults, adolescents are a poverty-stricken and powerless minority. Perhaps they resent their disadvantaged status less when they observe adults almost as badly off as they.

I infer from the increasing affluence of industrial societies and from the principle of relative deprivation that resentment of socioeconomic deprivation is growing. This resent-

[4] See Vol. 338 of *The Annals of the American Academy of Political and Social Science* devoted to *Teen-Age Culture* (November 1961); the Winter 1962 issue of *Daedalus* devoted to *Youths: Change and Challenge;* and James S. Coleman, *The Adolescent Society,* Glencoe, Illinois: The Free Press, 1961.

[5] Dwight Macdonald, "Profile," *New Yorker,* November 22, 1957; Mark Abrams, *The Teenage Consumer,* London: London Press Exchange, 1960; T. R. Fyvel, *Troublemakers: Rebellious Youth in an Affluent Society,* New York: Schocken Books, 1962.

[6] Jackson Toby, "Orientation to Education as a Factor in the School Maladjustment of Lower-Class Children," *Social Forces,* 35, March 1957, pp. 259–266.

[7] Samuel A. Stouffer, *et al., The American Soldier,* Vol. 1, Princeton: Princeton University Press, 1949, pp. 124–130; 172–173; 178–182; 208–211; 250–254; 279–280; 525–527; 542–543; 562–564.

[8] Harry C. Bredemeier and Jackson Toby, *Social Problems in America,* New York: John Wiley & Sons, 1960, pp. 60–62.

[9] Edwin H. Sutherland and Donald R. Cressey, *Principles of Criminology,* 5th ed. New York: J. B. Lippincott, 1955, p. 193; Daniel Glaser and Kent Rice, "Crime, Age, and Employment," *American Sociological Review,* 24 (October 1959), pp. 679–686.

ment contributes to adult crime as well as to delinquency.

3. *The effectiveness of traditional agencies of socialization and social control is decreasing.* Cases of inadequate socialization and inadequate social control exist in every society. It is easy to exaggerate the pathological aspects of industrial society generally and city life in particular.[10] It is also easy to confuse transitional problems arising from large-scale immigration or from internal migration from rural to urban areas with fundamental problems of socialization and social control.[11] Nevertheless, when these exaggerations and confusions are discounted, there still remain characteristics of industrial society which pose obstacles to effective control over the young. Most obviously, the anonymity of the large city reduces the coercive power of adults over children. Even a well-integrated family in a stable neighborhood does not exercise the kind of supervision that is possible in isolated rural areas.[12] But the complexities of city life — the fluctuations of the labor market, the innovations in technology, the flow of population, the conflict of values — make some considerable amount of family and neighborhood disorganization a chronic problem.[13] Formal agencies of control — the police, the courts, the reformatories — attempt to compensate for these weaknesses of the informal control system, but urban industrial conditions are not conducive to high levels of efficiency on the part of these formal agencies.[14]

[10] C. Wright Mills, "The Professional Ideology of Social Pathologists," *American Journal of Sociology*, 49, September 1943, pp. 165–180.
[11] For a discussion of "the transitional aspects of urbanism," see Ronald Freedman, *et al.*, *Principles of Sociology*, rev. ed. New York: Henry Holt, 1956, pp. 446–448.
[12] Jackson Toby, "The Differential Impact of Family Disorganization," *American Sociological Review*, 22, October 1957, pp. 505–512.
[13] Henry D. McKay, "Basic Considerations in Delinquency Prevention," Testimony in *Hearings before the Subcommittee to Investigate Juvenile Delinquency of the Committee on the Judiciary*, United States Senate, May 28 and 29, 1959, pp. 164–173.
[14] Jackson Toby, "Criminal Motivation: Sociocultural Analysis," *British Journal of Criminology*, 12, April 1962, pp. 317–336.

Cleavages in adult society reinforce the three delinquency-producing forces we have just discussed. For example, it is no accident that Negro delinquency rates far exceed white delinquent rates in the United States. The disadvantaged position of Negro adults in American society has implications for the behavior of Negro children. The difficulties of Negro men in the labor market contribute to the instability of family life and thus to inadequate socialization and weak social control. The double pressure of poverty and prejudice compels most Negro families to live in crowded slum housing, thus dramatizing to youngsters their deprivation relative to the white community and feeding their feelings of resentment. Partly as a result of these factors in the adult community, partly as a result of educational and commercial developments in industrial society generally, Negro youth culture has a great vitality and autonomy, and these qualities make Negro adolescent gangs even more difficult to "tame" than white gangs.[15] Needless to say, *ethnic* cleavages are not the only exacerbating circumstances. Insofar as social stratification generates quasi-independent *class* cultures, which are sharpened by ecological concentrations of multiproblem families within the city, delinquent subcultures are perpetually being reinforced.

Are We Willing To Pay the Price?

The foregoing analysis implies that delinquency reduction in industrial societies is a tremendous task. The forces contributing to delinquency are powerful; to neutralize them requires a major commitment of resources. Many of those who are on the side of the angels now — when they think that the "solution" to delinquency lies in a few more settlement houses or somewhat larger allocations to juvenile aid bureaus — will lose interest in delinquency control when they realize that it does not come cheap. Even if industrial so-

[15] Rigorous studies of the comparative difficulty of redirecting Negro and white gangs do not seem to exist. My opinion is based on my contact with street worker programs in New York, Chicago, Cleveland, Los Angeles, and San Francisco, and my interpretation of the extensive literature on subcultural delinquency.

cieties grow sufficiently concerned about the waste of youth that delinquency represents to be willing to pay the price, the most promising strategy of intervention is not immediately apparent. It will take considerable research and experimentation before answers to questions like the following are discovered:

1. *Can industrial societies provide educational and occupational opportunities for all youth — those from the lower classes as well as those with meager intellectual endowment?*

This issue is far more complex in the United States than it is in Sweden because ethnic discrimination puts additional obstacles in the way of equality of opportunity. But the problem is broader than ethnic discrimination. As long as a high standard of living is a universal goal and as long as the educational and occupational systems are the basic income-allocating mechanisms, youngsters who are marginal students and later marginal workers will be potential recruits for delinquent gangs. The question is: Are nonacademic curriculums and sheltered employment programs in the eyes of disadvantaged youth good enough substitutes for the schooling and jobs they cannot win in open competition? [16]

2. *Can industrial societies reduce the autonomy of "youth cultures"?*

Not all autonomous youth groups are delinquent. Probably the majority of street-corner cliques, hot-rod enthusiasts, and rock-and-roll fans are only mildly unconventional. But as long as these groups are insulated from adult influences, they are *potentially* delinquent. On the other hand, church groups, 4-H clubs, Scouting, the Y.M.C.A., boys' clubs, and settlement houses are to varying degrees under the control of conventional adults; hence their antisocial potentialities are negligible. From this point of view, delinquent gangs are simply a portion of the large number of autonomous youth groups in an industrial society.

The problem of bringing autonomous youth groups under adult influence is complicated by the increasing differentiation of the adolescent from the adult world. The school performs the bridging task well, but only for the intellectually superior half of the population. Street workers — or, as they were first called by the New York City Youth Board, "detached workers" — attempt to bridge the gap for "bopping" gangs in underprivileged neighborhoods. New organizational forms must be developed for channeling the interests of adolescents who are not necessarily delinquent but who are committed neither to school nor to work. In this connection, it seems to me that education for marriage could contribute greatly to adolescent integration into adult society. In most industrial countries, youngsters drift into marriage with little or no preparation for the responsibilities involved. Perhaps the tacit assumption is that parents provide the necessary guidance, but the existence of autonomous youth cultures suggests that even well-integrated families have limited influence over their adolescent children. Prepared or not, youngsters marry. Interest in "going steady" and, ultimately in marriage, is strong enough to break up delinquent gangs and to reintegrate alienated boys into conventional adult society.[17] That is to say, marriage serves to bridge the gap from irresponsible adolescence to responsible adulthood for those adolescents, including delinquent gang members, capable of making marriage work. For some, however, marriage is a personal failure and also a misfortune for the children resulting from it. Can industrial societies "reach out" aggressively to adolescents — and especially to those no longer in school — with educational programs to provide better understanding of the requirements of marriage in complex urban communities? This we do not know.

Conclusion

Adolescent delinquency may be part of the price industrial societies pay for their afflu-

[16] The effects of current efforts to increase educational and occupational opportunities for deprived adolescents on the Lower East Side of Manhattan will clarify this issue. See *A Proposal for the Prevention and Control of Delinquency by Expanding Opportunities*, New York: Mobilization for Youth, Inc., December 9, 1961.

[17] Larry Karacki and Jackson Toby, "The Uncommitted Adolescent: Candidate for Gang Socialization," *Sociological Inquiry*, 32, Spring 1962, pp. 203–215.

ence, their freedom from oppressive social controls, and their willingness to give young people a relatively long period of preparation for adult responsibilities. This does not mean that high rates of delinquency are inevitable, but it suggests that panaceas are unlikely. The lowering of delinquency rates will come about only if the fuller participation of youth in major institutions becomes a priority value — important enough to justify large expenditures not only for the education and job-training of intellectually marginal youth but also for the development of the civic, marital, and aesthetic potentialities of all adolescents.